Causality and Neo-Stages in Development

Gerald Young

Causality and Neo-Stages in Development

Toward Unifying Psychology

Springer

Gerald Young
Glendon College
York University
North York, ON, Canada

ISBN 978-3-030-82539-3 ISBN 978-3-030-82540-9 (eBook)
https://doi.org/10.1007/978-3-030-82540-9

This Springer imprint is published by the registered company Springer Nature Switzerland AG
The registered company address is: Gewerbestrasse 11, 6330 Cham, Switzerland

Preface

Causality

Why do humans behave the way we do? What causes behavior in nonhuman species and in humans? How can we explain human development and its causation? What are the mechanisms in the causation of behavior that help explain it? Does the pattern of human development give some insight into the pattern of hominid evolution? Does contemporary culture reflect patterns in human development and our evolutionary past? What is the relationship between individual development and population-level descriptions?

These questions are among the many posed by the book, and the preface documents many others. At times, I provide the basic contours of my responses to the questions raised, but at other times I will let the reader delve into the book for the answers. The three major themes of the book are on causality, development, and unifying psychology. My approach for all three can be considered contentious, for example, should causality be given the emphasis it has in the book, and indeed in the book series which I have authored on the topic (Young 2011, 2016, 2019)? Can causality be a focus for unifying psychology and is that even a possible mission? Do stages exist in the developmental process, or is that argument a return to global theorization that no longer is relevant today?

With respect to causality, the strong argument of the book, and the preceding ones in the book series, is that humans should be characterized as *Homo Causa*. Not only do we seek the causes of behavior, and our causality thinking develops, but also it is part of our human distinctiveness and is the epitome of our sapiens traits. So the book is about causality in the psychological sciences, but also it is about causality in the human mind and enterprise.

Stages

Are there stages in human development? Can the standing conception of stages be revised to fit contemporary understanding of development? Will this type of improvement in the concept influence those who do not support stage conceptions of human development? Can cognitive developmental stage theories be integrated? Are socio-affective stage theories related to them, or could they be mapped onto them? Is there a general stage scaffold that shows the parallel course in the unfolding of both stage processes? Can stage models of development be constructed to cover the full lifespan, from the prenatal phase to the end point of life phase? Would better conceptualization of cognitive developmental stage theories lead to better research on the networking of the individual's developing cognitive structure and how its concepts interrelate? Would better socio-affective stage theories lead to better understanding of patients who display problematic developmental courses and give better insight into how to help them?

The approach taken in this book, and in the three others (Young 2011, 2016, 2019) that preceded it on the topic of causality, development, and unification in psychology, is that stage models that build on pre-existing ones can be constructed and integrate across different domains. The concept of stages had to be modified in order to accomplish the task and make them more than formal descriptions of the phases in development without realistic, applicable descriptions of the contents of the stages and how they arise and differentiate individually in people. Stages are not maturational ladders that impose on development but are co-actionally constructed wholes that integrate the behaviors and underlying cognitive and related schemes that underpin them. Stages do not exist as reflections of origin theories in psychology. Rather, they need contemporary revisions, including of the stage concept itself, as the author has done with the concept of neo-stages. Moreover, they exist at multiple levels that interact bottom-up and top-down in dynamic transitions as micro-development and macro-development proceed.

Do stages have substages in development? Are the patterns of substages recyclic over stages, and reflect common underlying change processes? Are there fractalization patterns evident in this regard? Are stages of change models consistent with substage models of development? Are there common change processes at work here and elsewhere? What are the substage names that would allow for a common change process language?

The present approach is that there are 5 stages in development over the lifespan and that each has 5 cyclically recurring substages (25 steps in development). The author constructed the present stage model by examining prior Piagetian-type models (and Eriksonian ones). In this preface, I do not get into details of the stage names and the substage names. Suffice it to say, they are lifespan and integrate the Piagetian and Eriksonian, the first time that has been attempted in so much detail, especially when substages are considered.

The value of the present approach to stage modeling is that it has been applied to multiple areas of development, including of social self-working schemata on the

Piagetian side of the model and problems that develop in people according to the Eriksonian side of the model. But the modeling has been applied much more broadly, such as to causal cognition and to the development and the evolution of culture.

Can stages (or substages) co-exist? Does the development of a particular stage over the lifespan mean that prior stages are totally integrated, or can they exist simultaneously? Can an individualized subset of behaviors and concepts associated with a particular (sub)stage be used to meet the online adaptive requirements of the task or situation at hand? Can multiple subsets over (sub)stages be deployed simultaneously? In short, is there this type of yoking in development within neo-stage modeling of stages and substages? Do they help explain cognitive task performance from a Piagetian point of view? Can the yoking carry over to the integration of cognitive and socio-affective schemas associated with the Eriksonian side of development?

Causality Again

Does systems theory help understand the change process, for example, in the evolution of attractor landscapes and complex adaptive systems? Are changes in systems linear or nonlinear? What mechanisms facilitate the change from one organizational regime in a system to the next? Is that process self-organized? Does it include emergence? Does circular causality play in the process? Do systems have multiple levels? If so, do top-down ones and bottom-up ones interact? Can intermediate ones function both ways? Can networks qualify intra-level organization in systems? Do network concepts such as nodes and edges, along with centrality, hubs, and small worlds, help explain system organization? Could a hybrid model of systems and networks overcome the criticisms and limitations of each?

Returning to the question of causality and mechanisms, can one underlying concept be used that cuts across neurons, brain, and behavior? Do all three domains share a common mechanistic process? If genes are the ultimate distal factors in phenotypic expression, what are the most salient proximate factors? Could their actions be described in terms of the same overriding process, or at least the intermediate levels between them? Are the different levels of the systems that develop in the person from a systems point of view amenable to re-description in terms of this common process in the causation within the levels of a system, and also in how they interact? Could inhibition be a common factor in these regards? Activation? How can these two terms be combined into one concept? Can it help explain empirical data?

The particular concept that I developed related to an underlying common function cutting across neuron, brain, and behavior is activation-inhibition coordination. This refers to more than a balance but a genuine coordination, as in the infant reaching and then grasping, while controlling interfering movements. The infant's right hand does this better, and one could ask if the left hemisphere is specialized for activation-inhibition coordination relative to the right hemisphere. The neuronal architecture of the left hemisphere in terms of networks supports this conceptualization. The right hemisphere, then, would be specialized for less complex behavior, such as outright inhibition.

The biopsychosocial model is critical to some areas of behavioral explanation, such as in rehabilitation and therapy, but is acknowledged to have limitations. Can it be revised to overcome these limitations, such as better specifying the mechanisms intrinsic to it? Should the term be revised for psychology, for example, why should a term in psychology include the psychological portion in only one part of the term? If different models of causality are proposed, are they compatible? Can a systems, network, and biopsychosocial understanding of the causality of behavior lead to deeper understanding of the causes of behavior by their synergistic interaction? Can extant concepts in psychology be considered from the framework of the biopsychosocial model, or its variants? For example, the present work examines executive function from this framework.

Traditionally, the causes of development are taken to reside in Nature, Nurture, or both in their interaction. But these are passive concepts. The psychology of the individual counts; therefore, the concept of the biopsychosocial makes sense. People are agents in their own development, e.g., in having a belief in free will, in coping, and in resilience. Moreover, Nature and Nurture are monolithic ways of understanding the bio and the social aspects of behavioral causation. For nature, for example, genes means polygenes for complex human behavior. Epigenetics influences genetics by "silencing" genes, e.g., even in maternal stress fetally. The brain is a complex system now considered in terms of the connectome and interregional connectivity more than static lobe function. That said, the brain is not responsible for behavior—we are. The brain facilitates; we dictate, at least when we are able to choose. On the environmental side, there are layers to the environment and they interact, as per ecological approaches. Parents are crucial in this regard, for example, creating infant neonatal inter-synchronicity (inter-subjectivity). But parents vary in care giving skill and development can go awry. Does the present Neo-Eriksonian model assist in helping to understand patients? Is the model liable to testing, such as developing a questionnaire based on it?

Other questions come to mind about our agency in behavior. What are the mediating mechanisms? Are the environmental units impinging on the person (stimuli, situation, stressor) passively received and acted upon without their psychological transformation? Or, are they selected for saliency, subjective needs, etc., based on past history, experiences, and priors? How is meaning formulated in this regard? Are there mediating filters at the perceptual and cognitive levels? How much do they condition responses? When do they begin to develop in the human? Are sensorimotor schemas that Piaget had described pertinent to the question? If so can they be expanded to include socio-affective aspects? Are cognition and socio-affective schemas and structure really separate? Can combined structures in this regard help explicate processes such as the development of attachment-based internal working models? What happens when development goes awry? Could a concept such as the cognitive (mis)perception of the other help in the mediation process from reception to cognition and action?

Further, what is the relationship between energy and causation? Does the concept of free energy help in understanding behavior? Can it be extended into psychological energetics? How does a concept such as this one relate to other causality ones in the book? Another one is psychological co-regulation. Self-control resides in relations, not in the individual. Indeed, the whole concept of interaction needs reconceptualization; given the constant transactional flow in social interaction, perhaps it is best to refer to it as intra-action, given the ongoing reciprocal reworkings of the social units of an interaction as the interaction proceeds.

The latter concept is esoteric, but it makes a point. It verges on the philosophical more than the psychological. The book broaches philosophy to some extent, for example referring to the concept of neo-reductioconstructivism. As with the concept of intra-action, the overriding epistemic understanding of the person appears to reside in relationism as a world view, but one tempered by positivistic components. The book is replete with new terms that have been developed to communicate better the ideas expressed therein, as with these examples. The book even ends with a new one, that of transemic.

Broad Scope

The book increasingly expands its scope as it proceeds. Two chapters near the end deal with whole new areas not previously included in the prior books in the series, nor up to this point in the book. They stem from the goal of including defense mechanisms within its theoretical orbit, given the Neo-Eriksonian focus in the prior books and this one. However, it proved impossible to relate defense mechanisms to the Neo-Eriksonian model. This led to trying to place defense mechanisms within the wider adaptation, stress, and coping field. That also proved difficult. So I had to examine more closely that field. It led to the concepts of defensivity and offensivity, among others, and a matrix model of 48 ways we try to adapt to stress, based on the fight-flight-freeze model. The book is replete with other extensions that bring it beyond its original focus. Another one is its venture into couple work in much greater detail than in the prior books. Finally, the book extends into trans-disciplinary ideas, such as considering causality as a unifying factor in other disciplines and also placing psychology in the vanguard in this regard, as through the present book series.

Unification

How endemic is causality as a concept in psychology and other disciplines? It appears central to every sub-discipline in psychology, but is causality acknowledged as such? Indeed, causality represents a potential thread of commonality over the sub-disciplines of psychology, and findings in one sub-discipline seamlessly speak to others. It seems the one common factor in psychology sub-disciplines, but is that enough to suggest that it can serve as an axis in integrating psychology, giving it a unitary basis? How extensive should the integration of psychology be? The science of psychology seeks to describe behavior and infer its origins at multiple levels, but can causality be an apex concept in determining the integration and indeed unification of psychology? Perhaps that is a premature task to undertake and perhaps realizing it is impossible because of the origins of psychology, its definition, and its sub-disciplines that are often siloed. If the goal is to find the unifying constructs in psychology, can the task ever be completed or must it remain a project in continual process, much like human development itself?

Theories

Do the stalwart global theories of psychology still have a role to play in it? Darwin initiated modern understanding of evolution through the concept of natural selection in publications over 150 years ago, and his work is still seminal and cited. But his theory has evolved over the past 175 years. Freud developed psychoanalytic theory beginning about 125 years ago, and it is still a subject in contemporary publications. His concepts of the unconscious, defense mechanisms, stages in psychosexual development, and so on are still germane to modern psychiatry and psychology. But his theory has evolved, for example, in the work of Erikson. There are Neo-Eriksonians now, but note they have not revised his eight stages to any degree, focusing instead on the psychosocial and mutualistic interactions in development rather than the psychosexual nature of the stages. Piaget developed his concepts of stages in cognitive development and also he described processes involved in change of the schemas and operations involved, for example, through accommodation and assimilation. But Neo-Piagetians developed different stage models, both in terms of the stages and the substages, and they investigated more proximate mechanisms involved in cognitive development, such as working memory. Contemporary Neo-Piagetian research has not focused on the stages in Piaget's and the Neo-Piagetian models, but is that an oversight that hinders understanding development? Maslow is the most data-mined name in psychology, but his work does not have influence currently, although his concept of self-actualization is still widespread. Can his model be revised? Can it be placed in a common stage model with a Neo-Piagetian and Neo-Eriksonian one? Does the model have import beyond psychology, as per the ethics modeling with it undertaken by the author?

Is self-actualization still the apex concept that can characterize mature development? Where does Erikson's concept of generativity fit into the picture? Are other concepts equally valid, such as the one based on Lèvinas's concept of responsibility, which is reworked into the one of Re-responsibilities in the present work? Does this latter concept have value? What about inner peace as presently defined; does it help understand the course and direction of lifespan development? What about consciousness? Here, I am not referring to consciousness as per having remnants in the neurovegetative state of catastrophic brain injury. Nor am I referring to basic awareness that children might have. I am not referring to mediation by microtubules and the like. Rather, I am referring to broad awareness through the human ability for abstract thinking. The adult might develop a supra-consciousness and the like relative to the initiating consciousness of the teenager. This is consistent with the Neo-Piagetian notion of a postformal stage after the abstract one of the teenager. Should consciousness in these senses constitute our penultimate defining attribute?

Exceptionalism

This leads to the question of human exceptionalism, uniqueness, or distinctiveness. Relative to our forebears and contemporary nonhuman primates such as chimpanzees, what makes us unique? Tomassello's recent book provides a coherent answer about cognitions unique to us in the first 6 years of life (and about social behavior that is unique to humans, as well). Chapter 12 in the book examines the question, acknowledging Tomassello's contribution to the question, but it adds that the abstract thought that develops in teenagers is an exceptional human acquisition. The chapter proposes a 30-step model of the evolution and development of culture that reinforces this conclusion. It examines the history of proto-hominins in this regard, as well, integrating prior models. The cultural model that is developed refers to hyper culture, which applies to contemporary humans. Other places in the book refer to the formal educational structures that we create for our children as part of human uniqueness. Perhaps there are evolutionary forces beyond natural selection that are at play here.

Innovation

The book is replete with innovations. The concept of the book itself is innovative. There is little prior work on unifying psychology, for example, that has taken hold in the field. The idea of causality as central to unifying psychology is innovative, as well as the notion that humans are *Homo Causa* due to our penchant for seeking causes and learning causes. The 25-step lifespan developmental model is unique even if based on prior models. The generic five-step change model that underlies it is innovative. The combination of systems theory, network theory, the biopsychosocial model, and the concept of activation-inhibition coordination as a unifying causal model of causality is innovative. The addition of transemics and transemification to that theoretical complex represents a truly unique idea, because it is novel to the psychological literature generally. There are new models for executive function, stress dysregulation, inner peace, adaptation and coping, exceptionalism, and cultural evolution and development. The latter points to the innovations that extend beyond psychology to other disciplines, as do the concepts of transemics and transemification.

Research

Generally, empirical data are critical to psychology and any science. The data address hypotheses formulated by researchers. Generally, hypotheses, or the investigative questions for a study, stem from theories and models, which are often mini and targeted. Or, they might stem from an analysis of a literature review in terms of gaps evident in the review. Theories and models try to fit data to its parameters. The process might be forced or conjectural, and other theories and models might better fit the data. In this book, I have tried to show when that is the case? But this still leaves open the question of the validity of the theorizing undertaken. Often, in this regard, I refer to the nomological network of theories. Theories have to be integrated themselves and speak to each other. Have my efforts in this regard been successful? Does Occam's razor suggest simpler theories? But are simpler theories too mini? Is there value in global theories that mini-theories cannot provide? Does the present approach to theorizing depend too much on global theories? Or, have they been sufficiently updated and revised so that they constitute valid theories that can suggest pertinent targeted theories and hypotheses that are testable?

Do they help with psychology's replication crisis? Perhaps the latter exist because of narrow hypotheses and theoretical formulations that led to the questioned research in the first place. It is argued that better and broader theorizing might mitigate the replication crisis. Perhaps going up to the top-down level in these regards is more pertinent than focusing on bottom-level replications in the scientific process. The book refers to the science formula, and that could speak to the matter.

The book does not hesitate to define its terms, allowing for operationalization and falsification. It includes suggestions for questionnaires in this regard, as well. It even attempts new definitions of terms in psychology and farther afield. It even attempts to redefine psychology. As well, it redefines culture.

Practice

Psychology is marked by an experimental and practice divide. Does the present approach bridge that divide? Are the models offered applicable to both aspects? Are these models testable in both aspects? Causation in the psychiatric arena refers to etiology. Does the current modeling apply to etiological conceptions? The book examines disorders such as PTSD and suggests improvements and additions, for example, with stress dysregulation disorder. Does this type of approach have clinical utility? Should the DSM generally be revised according to the suggestions made in the book?

Literature Reviews

Where required, the book reviews the literature to the topics that apply to it. It does so comprehensively. There are two chapters just on literature reviews that deal with the major topics of the book. Whenever required, other chapters present detailed literature reviews. When new concepts are developed, I search data mining engines in psychology and elsewhere to determine the originality of the terms and cite articles that might be relevant. I learn a lot from prior literature and hope the same applies to you as you read this book. Or, at least you query some basic concepts and assumptions in the field.

Overall

The present book, and the series generally on causality, development, and unification in psychology, are complex ones that are quite theoretical and require reflective thinking. But they are grounded and challenging, as this preface indicates. The books might lead to new openings in psychology, science, and practice, so the challenge might be informative and rewarding. It was written from that perspective and with the reader in mind.

North York
ON, Canada

Gerald Young

References

Young, G.: Development and Causality: Neo-Piagetian Perspectives. Springer Science + Business Media, New York (2011)

Young, G.: Unifying Causality and Psychology: Being, Brain and Behavior. Springer International Publishing, Cham (2016)

Young, G.: Revising the American Psychological Association Ethics Code. Springer International Publishing, Cham (2017)

Young, G.: Causality and Development: Neo-Eriksonian Perspectives. Springer International Publishing, Cham (2019)

Acknowledgments

This book would not have been written without the unstinting support of the Springer Nature book publishing team, and especially the editor Sharon Panulla. I owe many thanks to Joyce Chan for her intelligence and application in typing, proofing, and shepherding the book toward production. The production team at Springer Nature always work under duress and accomplished their tasks for this book with accuracy and useful suggestions. As for my professional context, Glendon College at York University gave me a half-course leave to speed up the process. My colleagues, students, and patients provide an additional source of inspiration and deserve my thanks. My family, from extended ones, to spouse and children, down to our grandchildren, are the ultimate sources of support, and I thank you all.

Contents

About the Author

Gerald Young is a Full Professor in Psychology at Glendon College, York University, Toronto, Canada. He is a Fellow of the Association for Psychological Science (APS) and the American Psychological Association (APA). He has received awards from the American Psychological Association and the Canadian Psychological Association (CPA), including for lifetime achievement. Young is Editor-in-Chief of the journal *Psychological Injury and Law*, which he founded, and his work in that area has led to invited speaker addresses at scientific conferences. His most recent books are *Revising the APA Ethics Code* (Springer, 2017) and *Causality and Development: Neo-Eriksonian Perspectives* (Springer, 2019). He has appeared as an expert witness for a case involving the Supreme Court of Canada. His practice covers rehabilitation and couples/families.

Chapter 1
Introduction

This book is about the integration of psychology at multiple levels, including toward its unification. It deals with the integration or unification of psychology in terms of causality, development, science and practice, and cross-disciplinarity.

(a) Causality can constitute a unifying theme in psychology, and indeed in the sciences generally. It is involved in everything undertaken in science, either implicitly or explicitly. This book proposes unique causality mechanisms that can cut across neuron, brain, and behavior and their organization/networking within and between levels (activation-inhibition-coordination). This book takes an integrated biopsychosocial perspective to brain, behavior, and their organization. It asserts that humans constitute *Homo Causa*, with causality seeking and understanding characterizing the species and affording its adaptation, fitness, or survival and reproduction. Therefore, in all these guides, causality represents a unifying aspect of the present work on psychology and related disciplines and of human behavior itself.

(b) Development can constitute a unifying theme in psychology in that all human faculties develop and do not appear de novo in the species. Even puberty is conditioned by downstream biological, psychological, and social factors; the adult is an extension of the developmental trajectory of the child and adolescent. There are stage and nonstage theories about development; this book attempts an integration such that its developmental component also can be viewed as a step toward the unification project in psychology. The developmental stage component itself is an integration in that it presents a unified substage-stage theory of 25 steps over the lifespan that cuts across Neo-Piagetian and Neo-Eriksonian theories developed by the author. The model is couched in the concept of neo-stage, which allows for both normative and individual trajectories in development.

(c) Psychology has experimental and practice components, and this book attempts to bridge in its own way this chasm by indicating better approaches to psychiatric

G. Young, *Causality and Neo-Stages in Development*,
https://doi.org/10.1007/978-3-030-82540-9_1

classification and by applying the integrated neo-stage model therapeutically to patient needs. Also, it includes two chapters related to defense mechanisms in this regard. Psychology is a science both empirical-wise and practice-wise, and these aspects of the professional stand in a reciprocal relationship. Research participants and patients both constitute individuals in normative research findings and in assessment and therapeutic practices.

(d) Psychology can be integrated with associated disciplines, such as evolution and anthropology in their common endeavors. The last substantive chapter of this book considers the development of culture using the present developmental model as an analogue starting point. It leads to a 30-point model of the evolution and development of culture. The two chapters before that one consider defense mechanisms, but from a broader perspective that includes the general field of adaptation, coping, and stress. Considering other disciplines in relation to psychology enriches its study, for example, with respect to causality.

(e) The developmental approach of this book has formed the basis for ethical models, including psychological, psychiatric, medical, and health work ethics codes, in general. In this sense, this book extends its unification project into new areas beyond the original scope. The author's work in the area integrating psychological injury and law can be viewed from the same perspective.

(f) This book is highly theoretical, referring to worldview, meta-theory, theory, and mini-theory. This book refers to the author's work in this regard in terms of modeling. For causality, it also refers to explanation, mechanism, causation, causes, etiology, etc. This book is not only consistent with contemporary theorizing in these regards, but aims to be empirical and testable, as with proposed questionnaires, network models of stages, etc. The theoretical nature of this book might prove difficult to approach for some readers, but the concepts, theories, and models are meant to be well-explained and defended, allowing for science to build on them.

In the end, unification in any science must be considered an ongoing project with an infinite trajectory of better ongoing integration. Moreover, the project calls constantly for elaboration and innovation, and some of the themes in this regard in the present work include revising the understanding of the scientific process and even of the definition of psychology itself. This book is a start toward an integrative process in psychology and in science based on its premises and products. As indicated, it reflects the human condition as reflecting the species as *Homo Causa*. Therefore, this book reflects back on the human causality imperative by advocating for its imperative in psychology and in science generally. Causality constitutes a fertile ground for the unification project in psychology and in science and this book is dedicated to that proposition.

This first chapter in this book gives an overview of this book and then chapter summaries. It prepares the way for an in-depth presentation of the current unification project in psychology and its prolific contents.

Note that the voice of the present work at times to the personal "I" after using the third person approach to introducing a chapter. The APA style manual suggests that the author's voice should be clear in writing, but readers might want a more impersonal approach, so at times I gravitate between the styles, depending on the chapter.

Note that the following summary of this book presents its main ideas in several ways, for example, as overviews, chapter summaries, commentaries, and in a figure. This redundancy assures that its main points are made well and in different frameworks that are complementary. It would be very easy to dismiss the book even before reading it in depth, given its major themes—(a) stages exist in development; (b) causality is critical to psychology and to the human psyche; (c) unifying psychology is possible; and (d) theorizing is important to psychology, and the extensive theorizing in the book will help the field move forward. However, this book justifies the value of these themes and presents them in new ways, such as in the concept of neo-stages and an integrated Neo-Piagetian/Neo-Eriksonian model.

Overview

This book represents a broad integration of several major themes in psychology toward its unification. It is based on three books by the author in 2011, 2016, and 2019, which are described in the first part of this new book, and new material since those books were written. That constitutes its second part, and it included an extensive literature review supportive of the work and the new expansions and innovations extending from it. Unifying psychology is an ongoing project that has no end-point, but the present work suggests several major axes toward that end. First, causality is the only theme that cuts across all areas of psychology, so it represents the prime axis in the present psychology unification project. The importance of unifying psychology lies in its fragmented, disparate nature that leaves it in silos prone to self-isolation and lack of interdisciplinary learning and expansion. Causality provides a common bridge across the diverse areas of psychology, and also related disciplines in that regard, including genetics, neuroscience, evolution, philosophy, and psychiatry. Second, the present work champions activation-inhibition coordination as a prime mechanism cutting across causality in brain, neuron, connectivity, and behavior relations. Neuronal activity is based in excitation and inhibition and that function can be translated into the concept of activation-inhibition coordination. The author developed the concept of activation-inhibition coordination in his work on early infant reaching, in which the right hand exhibited smoother integration of components of reaching and contact, reflective of inhibitory control of interfering movement while behavioral activations were being sequenced toward goal success. This led to the postulate that the left hemisphere is the seat of activation-inhibition coordination, while the right hemisphere is specialized for less refined inhibitory skills, such as outright inhibition. Contemporary neuroscience is providing different language that reflects an activation-inhibition coordination in the left hemisphere through concepts such as the left hemisphere having a tighter small-world structural organization relative to the right. The author has proposed how concepts in systems theory and network modeling can be combined together with the one of activation-inhibition coordination to build a plausible model of how networks are organized and differentiate.

On the development side of the model building, the author has constructed an integrated lifespan stage model of development across the Piagetian cognitive and the Eriksonian socio-affective domains. The model is based on the concept of neo-stages, which mitigates standard criticisms of developmental stage models. First, the modeling involved allows for individual differences in cognitive development and the stages are not considered universal ones deriving from an imposed maturational or biological programming or unfolding. Second, the stages involved are Neo-Piagetian, with a different trajectory compared to Piaget's, although heavily based on them. For example, the five-stage sequence includes a preliminary reflexive stage before the infant sensorimotor one, the pre-operational and concrete operational stages are combined into a peri-operational period, and the adolescent formal abstract stage is followed by an adult postformal stage referred to as collective or superordinate abstract intelligence. Each stage includes 5 substages of coordination, hierarchization, systematization, multiplication, and integration, leading to a 25-step lifespan model in development consisting of 5 stages × 5 substages. As for the Neo-Eriksonian modeling, the eight stages in Erikson's original eight-stage model of development were aligned with the Neo-Piagetian (sub)stage model and 17 new ones were added to complete the series. These socio-affective steps do not develop exactly in concert with the cognitive ones because each represents a developmental challenge or crisis that can go awry without proper environmental support and the like, as Erikson had argued for his stage series. Moreover, difficulties in traversing the challenges carry forward and affect successful navigation of further challenges that materialize from one socio-affective step to the next.

The new work in the second portion of this book extends the primary work in the first portion, both in terms of causality and in terms of development. The second portion includes about twice as many chapters as the first portion. This includes new ways of conceiving causality and applying it to laterality development, and further work on clinical applications of the stage model. Also, the area of couple work is examined from the stage perspective. New concepts related to the main themes are represented, including the science formula, executive function, stress dysregulation disorder, inner peace, and ethics, as well as topics related to defense mechanisms and the topic of human uniqueness, all toward showing the present modeling's rich potential. The last chapters of the book have added work on adaptation, coping, stress, defense mechanisms, the evolution and development of culture and the development of causal cognition, and transemics a novel term of psychology. The present work is potentially important for the replication crisis in psychology because it provides a broad theoretical framework that can be used to place empirical work and predict outcomes in research. There is no reason why psychology cannot be at the forefront in unifying diverse science and scholarly fields under the causality umbrella and why humans should not be considered *Home Causa*.

The literature review is extensive concerning the book's major themes, including on unification, causality, and development. The new concepts in the book can help formulate testable hypotheses in psychology, and indeed science generally, and that should be its fundamental contribution. The book marries origin theories in the field, once they are modified, not only amongst themselves but also with the causality portion of the present work and its new elaborations and extensions. In this sense, its reach reflects the activation-inhibition coordination process that inspired it in the infant, reaching coordination that the author had witnessed early in his career.

Chapter Summaries

Chapter 1. The first chapter introduces the central concepts of the book and the book contents for each chapter. It begins with a book description, which has two major parts. In the first part, after the book introduction, four chapters outline the integrated model in Young's (2011, 2016, 2019) books, and the chapter summaries describe how that is accomplished. The second part of this book has eight new chapters that expand the themes of the first three Young books that had been reviewed in Chaps. 2–5. They present more details on the new expansions and innovations made by the author to his work on unifying psychology, causality, and development, aside from conducting literature reviews. The concluding chapter explores different areas in the author's scholarship unrelated to the core themes in the book. The first chapter follows the book's chapter surveys with a brief philosophical section highlighting an integrated (neo)empiricist, positivistic, reductionistic and constructivist model. It examines the worldview approach of the book, which integrates relationism. It concludes on the replication crisis in psychology and how the book can mitigate the crisis by affording a broad view of psychology that argues against its siloed approach. There is more than a replication crisis in psychology—it has become especially empirically driven and in need of better global conceptualization beyond the resultant local hypothesis-driven empirical research.

Chapter 2. This chapter explains in-depth the present neo-stage model of development and its origins. It examines competing Neo-Piagetian models and how the author integrated them into his model while adding to them. It shows how the new model incorporates data supportive of the other models, explains inconsistencies in them, and finds that data supportive of other models actually support the new model even better than the originals. It also shows how the Neo-Eriksonian model was constructed by inserting Erikson's 8 stages into the new 25-step Neo-Piagetian model and creating 17 additional steps. This is done by considering both the characteristics of the Neo-Piagetian step associated with each one and the Eriksonian steps both before and after each one. The chapter shows the extension of the model into self-development, needs development in terms of a Neo-Maslovian model that integrates Eriksonian developmental stages, in particular, and emotional development. According to their evolution based on the Piagetian substages in infancy, the infant is seen to express tens of emotions. This chapter also explores the origins of the cardinal causality concept underpinning the book on activation-inhibition coordination.

Chapter 3. The third chapter of the book provides an in-depth analysis of critical concepts on causality, offering a broad spectrum of work that the author integrated into his unified account of causality. This chapter focuses on the biopsychosocial model, systems theory, networks, and activation-inhibition coordination. It discusses genetics, epigenetics, the brain and its lateralization, free will, etc. It arrives at an integrated causal model of behavior, referred to as the biopersonalsocial model. The biopsychosocial model is a misnomer as applied to psychology. The replacement of the "psycho" component by the "personal" term allows for the influence on behavior outcome of motivation, belief in free will, personality, coping resources, etc. The social component of the model includes contextual, ecological, environmental influences on behavior broadly conceived. This chapter explores the evolutionary roots of behavior as well. Neuroscience is critical in psychology, but should not lead to a reductionist model of behavior.

Chapter 4. This chapter in the book elaborates mainly on the work of Young's Neo-Piagetian/Neo-Eriksonian 25-step lifespan developmental model along with causality. Specifically, this chapter presents the concept of neo-stage, which integrates concepts such as microdevelopment/macrodevelopment coordination to present a modified, workable (sub)stage development model and stage transition concept. Further, this chapter shows how areas such as the development of the theory of mind and responsibility might develop according to the model's steps. As for expanding the Neo-Eriksonian portion of Young's model, this chapter shows how each of the 25 steps of the model can describe differently patient problems in ways consistent with the characteristics of each of the steps. The model indicates that, as the 25 steps in the model develop in the person, they are not lost in development but can exist simultaneously and can be yoked together, in part and individual ways specific to the task at hand, in order to deal with cognitive or socio-affective issues that arise in development.

Chapter 5. This chapter completes a review of the three books written by the author on causality, development, and unifying psychology (Young 2011, 2016, 2019). First, it begins with a more detailed description of networks and indicates how networks can evolve systemically to higher-order levels, including by way of activation-inhibition coordination. Then, it looks at the stages of change model (from contemplation to resolution) and how it reflects Young's five generic steps or substages of change (from coordination to integration). Next, it examines these two change processes in terms of possible underlying attractor dynamics. Steps in co-regulation appear related to the five steps, such as ways of working with patients (e.g., stories they tell; case formulation). Next, the steps involved are related to knowledge construction processes and scientific exploration. In an elaborate table, the steps are related to the development of theory and meta-theory/meta-modeling. Next, figures relate the steps in further developing the S-O(BAMP)-R model that the author had created. The last application of the five-step change model applies it to the development of free will.

Note. The next seven chapters of the book expand the summary of the Young (2011, 2016, 2019) books that had been undertaken in Chaps. 2–5. The first of the chapters begins by delving into recent literature that supports the work of Young in his 2011, 2016, and 2019 books. A later chapter (Chap. 8) covers the literature in 2020. One chapter expands the conceptual range of the book by applying the causal modeling in the prior chapters to the disparate topics of couples and laterality (Chap. 7). Another chapter explores extensions into six topics not covered previously, such as executive function (Chap. 9). Then, four chapters (Chaps. 10–13) extend beyond typical psychology topics, exploring (a) general adaptation, coping, and stress, (b) defense mechanisms, and (c) the development and evolution of culture. The concluding Chap. 14 after these eight ones that have been summarized explores the author's other integrative efforts in psychology, especially in ethics.

Chapter 6. The author undertook a literature review of material published in 2019 in the broad array of areas covered in Young's three initial books. The literature is massive in amount of relevant publications; thus, it necessitates a yearly review, resulting in a second literature review chapter for 2020 literature. Generally, the literature supports the present integration or can be interpreted as supportive. In this particular chapter (6), the topics covered include philosophy, causality, unification, developmental causality, handedness, brain lateralization, networks, cognitive networks, activation-inhibition coordination, the DSM, Piaget/Neo-Piagetians, and Erikson/Neo-Eriksonians. Generally, the literature supports Young's conceptualizations and adds different insights for some of them. As well, this chapter carefully examines some of the literature that is not consistent with his views.

Chapter 7. This chapter explores innovations that show the range of applicability of Young's modeling, as well as new ideas related to them. In particular, this chapter examines an applied area, that of couple work. It demonstrates how couple compatibility/incompatibility can be examined from the lens of networks, systems, activation-inhibition coordination, stages, etc. Young develops an integrated network/systems/activation-inhibition coordination model in this regard, a model that is also applied to other areas, such as laterality. This chapter considers stage transitions through the concept of cognitive generalization. It presents a within-substage five-substep model to complement Young's 5 stage × 5 substage 25-step model in development, which underscores the fractalization that appears to take place in development. This chapter concludes with a new causality model of psychological energetics.

Chapter 8. The literature related to the major themes of the book continues to burgeon. The literature reviewed in this chapter is organized around the following themes: unification and causality, beginning with subtopics of unification and of mechanism. Here, the work of Gaj (2016) and Henriques (Henriques 2011; Henriques and Michalski 2019) are reviewed, in particular. Henriques has written the primary competing model to the present psychology integration effort. There are similarities that this chapter points out, but differences too, including in the respective definitions of psychology. Generally, the present author suggests the Integration Continuum toward unifying these differences. The next part of the literature review in this chapter being described is on publications in integration in psychology. This chapter moves into recent literature on philosophy, causality mechanisms, systems, networks, combined modeling, activation-inhibition coordination, and unifications fields. Then, it considers recent developmental publications—on Piagetian research, Eriksonian research, causal learning, developmental dynamics, executive function, and developmental lateralization.

Note. The yearly literature reviews undertaken in Chaps. 6 and 8 are important for the book because they provide conceptual and empirical support for the central ideas of the book. The modeling in the book offers a framework with which the current literature is analyzed and the literature never disappoints in offering work supportive of the present enterprise. That literature points to complementary ideas, as well.

Chapter 9. This chapter describes six further innovative concepts on disparate topics related to the themes of the overall work. First, it explains the science formula, which is a reworking of the rigorous scientific conceptualization, observation methods, and, where possible, empirical testing of the concepts. This chapter advocates that placing causality at the forefront in the science formula and science activity and psychology will help move science and psychology toward integration. Second, this chapter presents an extension of the 25-step neo-stage model by indicating how, at each stage, a romantic couple in turmoil might split the relationship, or how they might stay in it and why. Third, this chapter presents a new model of executive function (EF) that builds on the concept of activation-inhibition coordination and the view that EF is deployed in adaptation and problem-solving generally. Fourth, this chapter proposed a new addition to the DSM-5.1 (or DSM-6), called Stress Dysregulation Disorder. In particular, it has been proposed as a better way of integrating the DSM-5's PTSD category of trauma reaction and the ICD-11's category of complex PTSD. Next, the author presents a revised concept of inner peace as constituting the penultimate human psychological attribute we strive for and act from. Finally, based on the current five-substage developmental model, this chapter presents a speculative model of development in larger entities beyond the domain of development (e.g., societal, evolution).

Note. The two chapters in the present book with elaborations and innovations (Chaps. 7 and 9) are important for the book because based on the conceptualizations presented in Chaps. 2–5 on the original work developed in Young's (2011, 2016, 2019) books. They configure in the nomological network of concepts that can extend from that work and from the work of others on which the latter is based. There are some ideas that appear unrelated at first glance, but they broaden the overall network of ideas in the overall project, and effort is made to show their place in that project.

Chapter 10. People attempt to protect their psychological integrity in numerous ways, in terms of dealing with both internal conflicts and perceived external stressors. This chapter develops a model of adaptation and coping based on the concept of defensivity/offensivity. It includes 48 categories or types of adaptivity/coping in a matrix model. The model is built on the fight-fight-flee response model of reactions to stress, and adds 45 other categories to the matrix. The dimensions of the model include direction and degree of overtness/covertness, in particular. The model adds to the dimensions two types of categories related to dominance-submission and the self. The matrix builds on work on appraisal and schema filtering of incoming stimuli and stress, such as in models related to the Bayesian brain. The matrix is not built directly with work on defense mechanisms, but addresses them and provides a scaffold on which defense mechanism theory and type construction can be expanded. This chapter relates the author's 25-step Neo-Eriksonian model to the concept of defensivity/offensivity. It proposes both hypo and hyper difficulties in navigating emerging challenges and crises at each developmental step in the Neo-Eriksonian model, while viewing them as defensivity and related themes.

Chapter 11. This chapter presents a comprehensive literature review related to its major themes, especially focusing on adaptation and coping and on defense mechanisms. The former section reviews the contemporary literature on adaptation and coping, in support of the current approach of attempting to place the area of defense mechanisms in a broader scope. The latter section of the literature review underscores strides in the field and, at the same time, provides commentary on how the field can move forward. The areas covered in the first portion of the literature review include: (a) the Bayesian brain, predictive processing; (b) stress, coping, adaptation; (c) the fight-flight-freeze system; and (d) alexithymia and suppression. The second portion focuses on defense mechanisms, with sections on (a) general considerations; (b) developmental considerations; and (c) adult considerations. This chapter discusses an integrated model on adaptivity, proactivity/protectivity, defensivity/offensivity, and defense mechanisms. Next, this chapter proposes the terms of defense mentalism and defense modality to accompany the term of defense mechanism. Next, it proposes a 15-point stress mitigation/magnification scale (SMMACS). It places defense mechanism in a seven-tiered model with defense function at the top. Finally, it introduces the concept of activation-inhibition coordination relational coregulation.

Note. Chaps. 11 and 12 are important for the book because they expand the reach of the book outside of its major themes and they cover disciplines beyond psychology. In this vein, Chap. 10 presents a matrix model of adaptation, coping, and stress, which is an interdisciplinary field. Chapter 11 continues to relate defense mechanisms to that interdisciplinary field. On the one hand, defense mechanisms stem from psychiatry, and on the other hand, the classic defense mechanisms are reviewed for what they are but their conceptualization includes complementary ideas.

Chapter 12. This chapter presents a 30-step model of cultural evolution extrapolated from the present Neo-Piagetian/Neo-Eriksonian developmental model. Each developmental step in the model was analyzed for its implications culturally. The cultural model refers to preculture and then moves up to first-order hyper culture, and consequently second- and third-order hyper culture based on it. The latter phases of the model are based on the abstract stages of development in the Neo-Piagetian model. They refer to abstract thought in the adolescent, collective intelligence, or superordinate abstract thought in the adult and, finally, for the time that there will be human–machine interfacing, communal collective intelligences. These abstract thought stages condition the higher-order stages in cultural formation and expression. These abstract stages in cultural evolution also speak to the question of human exceptionalism or uniqueness. Human exceptionalism needs to be viewed from the perspective of a qualitatively distinct underpinning in an abstract thought-based culture, as per the present model. The distinctiveness of humans relative to other extant species and proto-hominins is not just a question of degree but of kind. Contemporary nonhuman primates do not think abstractly. At one point our evolutionary ancestors acquired these skills, but not at the same level of quality as in contemporary humans. Humans engage in causal cognition, co-constructed with the other. Advanced causal cognition is another way of conceiving human uniqueness. Modern culture reflects these higher-order abstract cognitive skills, making the degree of complexity in our culture another distinguishing feature of humans. As the latter continue to evolve in human–technological and even interspecies interfacing, human cultures will grow exponentially in complexity, but the complexification in this regard has initiated through inter-culture fusion.

Note. Chapter 12 is important for the general themes of the book because it emphasizes that causal cognition is essential to human evolution. It examines research having that perspective, thus complementing the present emphasis on causal cognition in humans, and their development. In effect, it affords a different pathway supporting the notion that humans are *Homo Causa*.

Chapter 13. This chapter applies the concept of transemics to the major themes in the Young books and emerges with new innovations for that project. Transemics refers to the change process involved in globality-particularity and whole-part dynamics. It relates to the terms etic and emic, but transemic is more than etic due its transactional and transformational nature. This chapter illustrates transemics in action because it shows how the concept can be applied. Specifically, Young's five-step change model involves attractors, and complex adaptive systems, and they are reworked according to the global/whole-particularity/part distinction in the transemic process. Next, this part of this chapter offers hypothetical examples in terms of the five-step change process and how examining them transemically helps in their elaboration. The examples refer to the teen engaging with peer groups and a minority culture seeking its rights. Next, this chapter presents an integrated model of learning and education of humanization and dealing with dehumanization according to the five-step change model. This modeling is based on an integration of the previously presented five-step models for learning and education. A humanization program like this can help in the decolonialization process, and sensitization to indigenous psychologies, for example. This chapter continues with examining the major themes of the present book in terms of transemics. The last section of this chapter presents a literature review and discussion of transemitization and its narrativization.

Note. Chapter 13 is important for the general themes of the book because it extends the concepts of the book into the humanities and social sciences through the concept of transemic, which is a general change process that is applicable across a broad range of disciplines. This chapter gives a detained explanation of the concept and shows how it applies to the major themes of the book, giving them even more substance and validity.

Chapter 14. This chapter presents the most recent publications by the author, which illustrates his integrative and unifying bent in other areas of psychology. First, he has attempted integration of various ethics codes into a universal ethics code for all health workers, including in medicine, psychiatry, psychology, and other disciplines. He began with an analysis of the APA and CPA ethics codes in a 2017 book (Young 2017), and continued with articles (e.g., Young 2020). Another ethics focus concerned a chapter written by the author on patient and related rights according to the author's integrated model of five core ethical principles, which are based on his developmental model, that is, a Neo-Maslovian model integrated into the Neo-Piagetian/Neo-Eriksonian one. Similarly, the concluding chapter of the present book includes a section on children and youth rights that includes on the five core principles in the ethical model. Next, this chapter explores the author's integrative efforts across the field of psychological injury and law, a field that he boosted with the first books in the area (e.g., Young 2014), the first dedicated journal, and recent articles. These contributions to the field illustrate the value of integration in psychology, besides the present author's potential work toward an integration at multiple levels.

Note. Chapter 14 that ends the book adds work from the author's other scholarship that reveals its extent and integrative efforts. The foundational assumptions of the book that integration and unification are necessary in psychology require careful theoretical work. Workers will reject some of the basic premises of the book, such as (a) stages occurring in development through the integrative Neo-Piagetian/Neo-Eriksonian model presented, and (b) causality cohering all sub-disciplines in psychology to the point it can be its unifying theme. However, the reader should at least consider the arguments and their nuances in these regards, the new ways they are broached, and so on, without rejecting their possibility at the outset. For example, they offer theoretical, research, and practice implications heretofore not in the psychological and related literature.

Mapping the Book's Chapters. Figure 1.1 maps the 14 chapters in the book according to their degree of separation from the kernel theme of the book. This demonstrates its far-reaching approach, yet one built on a few central components (unification, causality, development, including neo-stages). Also, it shows which chapters are more directly related to the kernel topic and which ones cast further afield.

The kernel core of the book concerns the unification project in psychology, the central role causality could play in the project, and the primary role that development could play in that regard, including through the concept of neo-stages. Relatedly, the four books in the present series on the topic, including this one, all build on the author's Neo-Piagetian/Neo-Eriksonian model.

The core chapters in the book that present the core themes of the book, as elucidated in the prior three books in the series (Young 2011, 2016, 2019), are indicated in the next two concentric rings of the figure. The two basic chapters on the book's core themes are placed in the first inner circle. The second layer to this inner concentric circle model lists the two chapters that add depth to the basic ones.

Next, the concentric circles list the two chapters on comprehensive literature reviews that support current conceptualization. All the major core themes of the book are covered in the reviews, and some others that presage the elaborations and extensions to come in succeeding chapters.

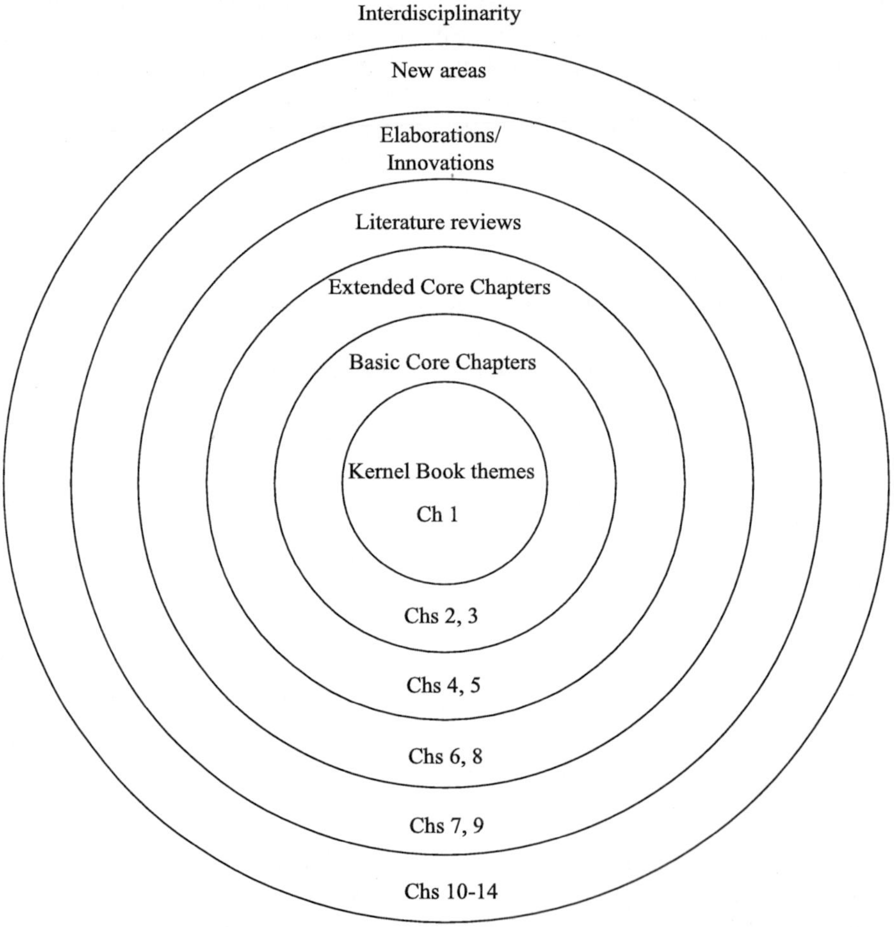

Fig. 1.1 The degrees of separation relating the chapters of the book to the book's kernel themes
The figure indicates the organizational structure of the book chapters. They indicate the organic growth of the chapters from its kernel themes to new areas not considered in the prior books of the four-book series

The next concentric circle in the figure indicates the two chapters with extensions and elaborations related to the core themes of the book. However, some of them cast the net further afield, or include topics that are much broader.

Next, an outer concentric circle indicates the later chapters in the book that cover totally new areas not covered previously in the book. It illustrates that the book is organic and grew in scope as the writing proceeded.

Finally, in the sixth degree of separation from the kernel book topic, one could add the interdisciplinary reach of the book. For example, other disciplines could profit from unification, considering causality at the forefront in these regards, and placing the progress made though this book (and others in the series) on the matter as one starting point in this ongoing endeavor.

Philosophy and Science

The book reviews the author's approach to the philosophy underlying it. The same type of integration bent that he had brought to psychology applies to its philosophy. That is, the present author created a philosophical model of Neo-reductioconstructivism. It builds on other models and allows that reality is both positivistic and amenable to empirical investigation, yet socially constructed, as well. Moreover, the two philosophical stances can be combined into one superordinate philosophical position. The person, as well, has an empirical yet constructivist stance in her/his knowledge acquisition. Piaget considered himself a constructivist because the stages that he described reflect the active, exploratory constructivist mind of the child more than the outcome of direct teaching in the educational environment. He considered himself a genetic epistemologist rather than a developmental psychologist because he was interested in how knowledge acquisition proceeds in the child both through cognitive adaptative mechanisms and through the stages over the lifespan. Research reveals how causal learning is critical to child development, and this work has characterized the human as *Homo Causa* in this regard. In this sense, we are all genetic epistemologists!

Relationism is a primary worldview (Overton 2015), one that I share and elaborate on in my work. It is consistent with Piagetian constructivism but embeds human uniqueness in the relational context. We do not exist outside the social; our brains are social, etc. But I add that, philosophically, the penultimate human characteristic is re-responsibility, which follows from Levinas's concept of responsibility. In our mature phase, should we get there, we should be constantly dedicating ourselves to all our responsibilities, from those to the self, to family and friends, to community and all others, and the planet and all its faun and fauna.

The present book has constructed an inclusive model of behavior, and the discipline of psychology. It proposes that causality can form an axis in the unification project of psychology and that neo-stages, as they develop, can form the axis that binds developmental description into a common format. By its broad theoretical scope, the present work can give an anchor to help in the empirical investigation in psychology and reduce the siloes that prevent more intra-domain interaction in psychology. This might serve to break the retraction watch cycle in psychology; with a broader theoretical understanding of behavior, it might be easier to design experiments that deal with the complex array of factors that govern causality and the complex developmental process that characterizes it.

Conclusions

Book Summary

The present book reviews the three books on development and causality by Young (2011, 2016, 2019) and extends, elaborates, and adds innovations. The three major topics of the three books at the base of the present book are: (a) a Neo-Piagetian model consisting of 25 steps in cognitive development over the lifespan; (b) a corresponding 25-step Neo-Eriksonian model; and (c) the causality underpinnings to development, in general. The developmental model relates Neo-Piagetian and Neo-Eriksonian steps, or (sub)stages, in development. Similarly, in the 2019 book, I presented the concept of neo-stage because of doubts and criticisms of the stage concept. In this regard, in the present work, I refer to the developmental model that I have constructed as the Neo-Piagetian/Neo-Eriksonian neo-stage model.

There are 12 core chapters in the present review and elaboration of the 3 Young (2011, 2016, 2019) books that accompany the introductory and concluding chapters. The 12 chapters are divided into 6 parts, with 2 chapters each. The first two chapters give the fundamentals of the books and the integrated models therein, using some tables and figures. The next two chapters elaborate with more tables and figures the three major topics. These four chapters summarize the Young work well, while the eight chapters after that provide extensions, elaborations, and innovations. The first two chapters in this second part of the book consist of new work on the three topics in the three original books in the Young book series, including more tables and figures. The next two chapters give a recent literature review, as well as application to couple work and psychological energetics. These two chapters conclude with conceptualization related to fractals as a central unifying aspect of both psychology and causality, which is applied to a substep model in substages (for identity development). It ends with a supplement that further elaborates the application of new concepts in the present work to the areas of lateralization and couples. The next two chapters of the present book provide new material for the causality, development, and unification project by Young. They continue elaborating the present Young model, the literature review, and the innovations that mark the book generally. For example, they deal with literature into 2020 that support or reflect the Young work. They present new concepts on the models, such as in couple work in relation to the Neo-Eriksonian model. And they present conceptualizations related to science generally, executive function, stress disorder, and inner peace as the penultimate human exceptionalism. The next two of the core chapters of the book are on the topic of defense mechanisms. They present a matrix model of 48 adaptation and coping styles, elaborating the fight-flight-freeze stress response model. They include the concepts of defensivity and offensivity, and relate them to the author's 25-step Neo-Eriksonian model. They call for relating the term defense mechanism with others. The second to last chapter of the book considers the evolution and development of culture in the context of human exceptionalism. It presents a 25-step model in these regards, while adding 5 steps to the contemporary and future scenes in that evolution/development. It considers causal cognition a glue to the process, while presenting a 25-step model of its evolution and development. The last substantive chapter of the book continues in considering areas beyond psychology, this time by proposing a concept that applies not only to psychology but also equally to other disciplines in the social sciences and humanities. The concept is that of transemics, which is another generic change process concept.

Although the first four core chapters of the book (Chaps. 2–5) review the content of the three Young books on development and causality, the text in this first portion of the core chapters in the book is all new: it is not duplicated or paraphrased in any way from the three books but is totally novel. A good portion of the tables and figures in these chapters are novel as well. However, most of them are reduplicated with permission from the publisher, this being needed because they present the material succinctly and well. Even for that aspect, though, the author tried to present some of these tables and figures in novel ways. Overall, the book is constituted by 14 chapters; 10 of which are entirely new and 4 of which have new text and some new tables and figures, but with many tables and figures from material already published (and acknowledged as such).

Market

The book on the topic of causality, development, stages, and the unification of psychology is a vast one that spreads to many areas of psychology. It will be read by theorists in psychology across a broad scope of the discipline. Those seeking more specific mechanisms to help explain their work will find my approach to the general mechanism of activation-inhibition coordination a fruitful one to consider. Those seeking a more general causal framework will find my biopersonalsocial model a useful one. Advanced workers will refer to and elaborate my combined systems/network/activation-inhibition coordination model. Laterality, handedness, and hemispheric specialization researchers will especially find the latter model useful and empirically valid. The book will be read by researchers in neuroscience, brain-behavior relationships, etc. It will be useful in the clinical context, too, given its Neo-Eriksonian aspect and how I have applied it to the therapeutic context. Workers trying to change the DSM-5 nosology will find my suggestions useful. I can continue but the point is made—the book has a broad scope in topics that extend beyond psychology and it not just theoretical but has potential applications and uses.

Other Books

On Unification. Attempted unification in psychology has been a spotty endeavor, but there is one book that comports with the present one in its approach. There are older classic books on the topic, as per Gaj (2016), but the one by Gregg Henriques is the most recent and the best. Henriques (2011) entitled his book *A new unified theory of psychology*. It covers a wide range, like the present book. It builds on the concept of the tree of knowledge, in particular, and attributes to the human the exceptional skill of justification, which is somewhat like the present focus on collective abstract intelligence. His major concept is the tree of knowledge, which might be too general relative to the present concepts. He does not delve deeply into causality or mechanisms, unlike myself. He does refer to levels, which are somewhat like stages. He does refer to higher-order thought processes through justifications. He describes four levels in behavior, which is similar to the five levels (stages) in development in the present model. That said, Henriques does not deal with the types of elaborations and innovations found in the present work. The latter approach ends up being quite different from that of Henriques, and it adds significant concepts to the field that are quite different from those in his approach. It is noted that the present modeling toward the unification of psychology involved four books written over a decade rather than just one book, and these books are quite long. The present approach to integrating psychology respects the vastness of the field, covers a lot of it, and reflects the perceived requirement that works integrating psychology should cover much of it.

On Development. Demetriou and Spanoudis (2018) have written the major competing work developmentally to the present work. Their book is entitled *Growing minds: A developmental theory of intelligence, brain, and education.* They refer especially to the cognitive psychological mechanism or cognizance process, which involves cognitive consciousness to an extent. They have also developed a Neo-Piagetian stage model of cognitive development much like that of Piaget and of the Neo-Piagetian Case (1985), with four stages compared to the five in the present model. The other major Neo-Piagetian theorist, Fischer (1980), has written on cognitive developmental processes rather than his own Neo-Piagetian stage model. In short, competing books and publications to the present approach on Neo-Piagetian stages are few, and they do not have the same extent of (sub)stages compared to the present approach. Furthermore, the present model is the only one that integrates a Neo-Eriksonian socio-affective approach to the cognitive Neo-Piagetian model construction undertaken. Erikson's original eight-stage sequence has remained intact since its origin. For example, Newman and Newman (2017) examined the developmental life cycle from the perspective of Erikson's stages in lifespan development. To conclude, Erikson's model has been rarely changed in the literature. Publications related to it still hew to his eight-stage model, unlike the present work, with its 25 steps (as mentioned, it has added 17 steps to Erikson's eight-step sequence, in order to have parallel Neo-Piagetian/Neo-Eriksonian (sub)stages).

On Causality. There are very few books with causality in the title, although that situation is improving. Uller and Laland (2019) published one on evolution, and Shrout et al. (2011) have a good epidemiological one. In statistics, Pearl (2009) is a leader in the field. His approach is quite compatible with Woodward's (2003) interventionist philosophical approach to causality. In the three Young books on which the current book is based, they had listed the few causality titles in the field and had examined their contents. But almost none are psychological in nature, especially recently, or they are very specific to the specialty of the book (e.g., Corrigan 2014). Further, a book search on books in causality in search engines finds mostly the books of the present author listed. The author of this present book considers himself a leader in that field, and the present book will add to that "cause." All that said, if cognate terms are used such as genetics, brain, and evolution, the number of books on the topic of causality (or causation) is endless. However, the present approach is to have a common way of integrating these different approaches to causality, for example, in a biopsychosocial approach. That term has several excellent recent books (Melchert 2015).

Review. Overall, the present book extends the ones by Young (2011, 2016, 2019), and together, the four books stand as a unique contribution to the field of psychology. Reading the first part of the present book will give the details of the three original books by Young; reading the second part will give elaborations and extensions in this fertile endeavor to give a basis for the project toward unifying psychology. See Table 1.1 for a summary of the book's major contributions.

Apologia and Appreciation. The reader might find typos despite best efforts from myself, assistants, and production. These are inevitable, but do not detract from the conceptualizations in the book. I admit they can cause confusions, and do write me if anything is striking at gyoung@yorku.ca. In Young (2011) I recall a table note that was misplaced. In Young (2016) the book was 2500 Word doc pages long, and I recall one section with several paragraphs in the wrong order, but it was still understandable. In Young (2019), there is a table with some columns having their contents in reverse order, although the correct order becomes clear on inspection and, moreover, but the same table is presented in this book corrected. Overall, the number of words over the four books in the project well exceeds one million so that the few typos should not detract from its overall quality, at least, I hope.

As for that quality, it took four books and those millions of words to elaborate the models and their support, which would have been impossible in a series of articles, so I am grateful to Sharon Panulla and Springer Nature for affording the opportunity. Relative to other books or theorists, collectively, these books offer a new vision for psychology in several respects. Sometimes in them, older work is revised and resurrected, such as the Piagetian, and sometimes totally novel views are offered, for example, the steps in the development of causal cognition based on the current Neo-Piagetian model and the steps in the development of culture. I performed a last-minute check of the literature to see if anything like my model of contemporary cultural development comes close to the number of steps that I propose, and nothing

Table 1.1 Major contribution and innovations in the present book on causality, development, and unification

Contribution	Explanation
Development	The book presents an integrated Neo-Piagetian/Neo-Eriksonian 25-step lifespan model of development. The model consists of five stages × five substages that cyclically re-occur. The Neo-Piagetian series sets the stage for the corresponding Neo-Eriksonian development. However, transitions here depend on the environment, mutuality, etc., so that crises might arise, as per Erikson, given the opposition in the poles (positive, negative) of the model. Overall, there is an integration in the Neo-Piagetian model constructed over the works of Fischer and Case, in particular, there is an integration in creating corresponding steps in the Neo-Eriksonian model, especially given its original eight-step sequence and that 17 other steps had to be added, and there is an integration of classical stage theory that describes universal stages and the approach that allows for broad individual differences in cognitive development, including in (sub)stage development. The latter issue led to the development of the concept of neo-stages, which includes microdevelopment/macrodevelopment coordination.
Causality	The present book advocates for causality as a unifying denominator in psychology, but only as an ongoing project that continues. The causality approach of the book integrates multiple perspectives in causality, including the biopsychosocial, nonlinear dynamical systems theory, network modeling, hierarchical modeling based on the prior two approaches, and activation-inhibition coordination over cell, neuron, brain regions, the brain in toto, and behavior and its organization. It presents this model in the case of diverse areas, such as laterality, hemispheric specialization, transitioning from one (sub)step in development to another, couple work, and so on. The concept of activation-inhibition coordination was derived from the author's work on the development of early reaching and the better efficacy of the right hand in this regard. It led to the concept that the left hemisphere is specialized for refined activation-inhibition coordination from early on. Given the primacy of effort to understand causality by the human, the book refers to humans as *Homo Causa*.
Unification	The book argues for the extension of causality as a unifying theme across the sciences. In this sense, adoption of the present approach to unifying psychology would place psychology at the forefront in the sciences and efforts to unify it. The book describes the scientific process in novel terms that can cut across all sciences.
Innovation	The book is replete with multiple innovations, starting out with its approach to the major issues of development, causality, and the unification project for psychology. Other innovations include integration of Maslow's five-step hierarchical needs model into the five-stage model that had been developed, in a Neo-Maslovian model. The book has applied applications, for example, in the Neo-Eriksonian model. Also, it suggests ways to revise the DSM nosological system, and adds Stress Dysregulation Disorder as a generic disorder, for example, to cover PTSD and complex PTSD. It presents a model of societal evolution. It presents a 48-category matrix of adaptation, coping, and defensivity/offensivity. It presents a model of cultural evolution and development based on its developmental model. It offers a model of the development of causal co-cognition. It presents the generic change process of model transemics.
Adjunct Areas	The book describes the author's other areas of research in ethics and in psychological injury and law. It shows how contributions in these two areas relate to and borrow from the author's other work, e.g., in creating a five-principle model toward constructing a unified health work ethics code and in applying the causality model in the book toward understanding the sequelae of mild traumatic brain injury.

appears close to that. Therefore, there is much room for empirical work based on the model, as well as that of the development of causal cognition, which is what good theory is about, opening new avenues of research. Finally, the last chapter's work on children's rights and on ethics is not only based on the stage model of the present work, giving coherence to seemingly unrelated topics to the main themes of the book, but also, it suggests avenues for practice and ethics codes, bringing the theoretical work of the book to the ground of what we cherish most—our children, their protection, and their future.

References

Case, R.: Intellectual Development: Birth to Adulthood. Academic Press, Cambridge (1985)

Corrigan, P.W.: The Stigma of Disease and Disability: Understanding Causes and Overcoming Injustices. American Psychological Association, Washington, DC (2014)

Demetriou, A., Spanoudis, G.: Growing Minds: A Developmental Theory of Intelligence, Brain, and Education. Routledge, London (2018)

Fischer, K.W.: A theory of cognitive development: the control and construction of hierarchies of skills. Psychol. Rev. **87**, 477–531 (1980). https://doi.org/10.1037/0033-295X.87.6.477

Gaj, N.: Unity and Fragmentation in Psychology: The Philosophical and Methodological Roots of the Discipline. Routledge, London (2016)

Henriques, G.: A New Unified Theory of Psychology. Springer, New York (2011)

Henriques, G., Michalski, J.: Defining behavior and its relationship to the science of psychology. Integr. Psychol. Behav. Sci. **54**(2), 328–353 (2019). https://doi.org/10.1007/s12124-019-09504-4

Melchert, T.P.: Biopsychosocial Practice: A Science-Based Framework for Behavioral Health Care. American Psychological Association, Washington, DC (2015)

Newman, B.M., Newman, P.R.: Development Through Life: A Psychosocial Approach, 13th edn. Cengage Learning, Boston (2017)

Overton, W.F.: Relational developmental systems and developmental science. In: Lerner, R.M., Overton, W.F., Molenaar, P.C. (eds.) Handbook of Child Psychology and Developmental Science: Vol. 1. Theory and Method, 7th edn, pp. 9–62. Wiley, Hoboken (2015)

Pearl, J.: Causality: Models, Reasoning, and Inference, 2nd edn. Cambridge University Press, Cambridge (2009)

Shrout, P. E., Keyes, K. M, & Ornstein K. (Eds.). (2011). Causality and Psychopathology: Finding the Determinants of Disorders and Their Cures. Oxford: Oxford University Press

Uller, T., Laland, K.N. (eds.): Evolutionary Causation: Biological and Philosophical Reflections. MIT Press, Cambridge (2019)

Woodward, J.: Making Things Happen: A Theory of Causal Explanation. Oxford University Press, Oxford (2003)

Young, G.: Development and Causality: Neo-Piagetian Perspectives. Springer Science + Business Media, New York (2011)

Young, G.: Malingering, Feigning, and Response Bias in Psychiatric/Psychological Injury—Implications for Practice and Court. Springer Science + Business Media, New York (2014)

Young, G.: Unifying Causality and Psychology: Being, Brain and Behavior. Springer International Publishing, Cham (2016)

Young, G.: Revising the American Psychological Association Ethics Code. Springer International Publishing, Cham (2017)

Young, G.: Causality and Development: Neo-Eriksonian Perspectives. Springer International Publishing, Cham (2019)

Young, G.: Toward a unified health work ethics code. Ethics, Medicine, and Public Health. **15**, 100590 (2020). https://doi.org/10.1016/j.jemep.2020.100590

Chapter 2
Development, Stages, and Causality

The present work constitutes a summary of the three-book series by Young (2011, 2016, 2019) that takes place in the first portion of the book, with much new material in the second portion of the book, including two chapters on current literature and other chapters on extensions, elaborations, and innovations. In the series of three sourcebooks for the present one written by the author, he constructed a lifespan developmental model based on the stage models of Piaget and Erikson, while integrating approaches to causality in psychology toward unifying psychology. The work had innovated in developing a revised concept of stage, called neo-stage. It had created a 25-step Neo-Piagetian lifespan model consisting of 5 stages, each with 5 substages that cyclically re-occur. Also, it included a corresponding Neo-Eriksonian model of 25 steps.

Although all three Young books present the core areas of cognitive development, socio-affective development, and the topic of causality, the first book in the series especially delved into Neo-Piagetian models, comparing and contrasting them. The second book in the series focused on causality and includes a section on the DSM and its relation to the RDoC. The third book in the series applied the Neo-Eriksonian model to psychotherapy.

The present three-book summary reviews all these areas and applies the work to couple therapy. It adds extensions, elaborations, and innovations, such as for the concepts of psychological energetics, executive function, stress disorder, and inner peace.

The causality portion of Young's books is the focus of the book's unifying project for psychology. The major area in this regard concerns laterality; the prior Young books and the present book cover the developmental literature on lateralization, focusing on the concept of activation-inhibition coordination (think infant reaching in these regards). In addition, throughout the work, the book explores network and systems theories in terms of behavioral causality, showing how they can be combined and can inform neo-stage theory.

G. Young, *Causality and Neo-Stages in Development*, https://doi.org/10.1007/978-3-030-82540-9_2

The project undertaken does not articulate a complete model but only a beginning. For example, the study of developmental stages has petered out for the most part, and any attempts to revise and expand stage conceptions require further elaborations beyond those that have been broached. Moreover, the topic of causality in psychology is so broad that attempts to integrate it fully are premature and risk being considered solely a compendium of causal influences. Therefore, in the trilogy of books on the topic, Young has written a comprehensive account of: (a) how the concept of stages in development can be reworked as neo-stages; (b) how stages and their transitions can be explained in terms of specific causal mechanisms according to contemporary approaches to causality; (c) how an integrated 25-step model of 5 Neo-Piagetian cognitive stages and 5 recursive substages within each stage can accommodate prior Neo-Piagetian models; (d) how there are parallel Neo-Eriksonian stages and substages that could develop in correspondence to the Neo-Piagetian (sub)stages; and (e) how the combined Neo-Piagetian/Neo-Eriksonian lifespan developmental model provides a unifying scaffold for understanding other developmental acquisitions, while not trying to argue that all development is stage-like or that stages develop uniformly in all humans.

To clarify what the three causality and development books by Young (2011, 2016, 2019) are *not* about: (a) They do not try to endorse original developmental stage conceptions nor original developmental stage models (Piaget, Erikson). Rather, they present a novel integrated lifespan stage model across cognitive and socio-affective development. (b) They do not simply list the disparate presumed influences and mechanisms on causality in psychology without an effort to integrate them. Rather, they focus on novel mechanisms of development and of change generally. (c) They do not ignore the most recent research on causality nor on development in order to preserve outdated positions on these topics. Rather, the literature review is recent and comprehensive; it consistently reveals evidence and arguments in support of the present approach. (d) They do not pretend to have a final approach toward unifying causality, unifying psychology, and unifying causality with psychology. Rather, this project is considered ongoing and in need of constant renewal, much like development itself. (e) They do not present untestable models. Rather, the models presented are verifiable, constituting valid approaches to theorizing. (f) They do not ignore the empirical support for other competing models. Rather, in the prior Young books, the author Young took great pains to show how competing models, at times, include conceptualization and empirical testing that are more consistent with his approach to development and causality than the competing models. (g) The models are not reductionist to programmed maturation of stages and substages nor to brain and body mediated causal mechanisms of behavior and its change. Rather, the approach to development and causality taken in the three books is that influences on development are multifactorial and range from the brain and biology to the environment (e.g., adversity, parenting, schooling), and then to a role for the developing person her/himself (e.g., in coping, in believing in free will). (h) The three prior books do not ignore other major contemporary theorists who are deemed to have made significant contributions to the field (e.g., Maslow 1943, historically and attachment theorists contemporaneously). Rather, these books attempted to update and integrate all relevant models into the work. (i) The three prior Young books are not simply academic exercises without practical import. Rather, they deal with the therapeutic implications of the proposed model, especially in its Neo-Eriksonian portion. Also, they consider revisions to the diagnostic manuals in the field and even propose new entries, aside from redefining mental disorder itself. (j) Finally, the prior Young books are not just about psychology. They venture into cognate disciplines, from philosophy and ethics to neuroscience and evolution, in order to present a broad vision that can help unify psychology, causality, and their intersection.

The origins of the developmental model that Young has formulated lie in the author's early work on (a) Piaget (Young 1977), (b) on facial expressions in infants from a Darwinian perspective (Young and Gouin Décarie 1977), and (c) on the study of infant laterality (Young et al. 1983a, b, c). The early Piagetian research pointed to individual differences in Piagetian cognitive development, which is an enduring theme throughout the three books under discussion. The study on infant facial expressions underscored the evolutionary influences on development. The infant laterality research emphasized the biological bases for development. Specifically, for the latter, the author studied handedness development and formulated the concept of activation-inhibition coordination as he watched babies reaching, which is a concept that is central to the present work. For this topic, Young continued with two chapters in 1990 in which he also presented his Neo-Piagetian model and related it to Neo-Eriksonian development (Young 1990a, b). He further developed the model and its implications in a 1997 book (Young 1997). As Young branched out from development into rehabilitation and forensics in his clinical practice, this led to research on malingering and a 2014 book (Young 2014), in which causality is a critical topic (also Young et al. 2006, 2007). The 2017 book (Young 2017) written on ethics used a Neo-Maslovian model as a theoretical basis (the Maslow model was revised based on the Neo-Piagetian/Neo-Eriksonian one). As Young further developed his modeling, he published articles on topics related to causality and development (e.g., Young 2012, 2015).

Finally, the author's most current publications continue to elaborate on adjunct areas in his integrative efforts, particularly, in ethics (Young 2020a, b), and psychological injury and law (Young 2020c; Young et al. 2020).

It is impossible to summarize and expand fully in a new book, three books that involved over 5000 Word document pages, or well over one million words. In this present work, this book has given the basics of the concepts and literature on the three major topics in the three books, but it has been impossible to reference all this work. Therefore, the reader is referred to the references in the three original books for the ample reference base cited in the books. Next, the book presents in-depth its major models. Then, it turns to some innovations in applying it. I turn to use the personal voice "I" in the next section of the book.

The Neo-Piagetian/Neo-Eriksonian Model

Piaget

In this present work on the three Young books that present an integrated developmental-causal model (Young 2011, 2016, 2019), Piaget's work stands at the forefront. I have revised the model so that it covers the full lifespan. The accompanying table describes in-depth this Neo-Piagetian model (see Table 2.1). It consists of five stages with five cyclically recurring substages. This section of the present work also describes the model's logical underpinnings, the cross-model comparisons that had been undertaken in leading to it, and its empirical base (often derived from the other models). The following gives the core outline of the model with some commentary.

Piaget developed a cognitive developmental model that includes stages and mechanisms for their development. He described early infant development as sensorimotor (not representation-based). In the various versions of his stage model, the sensorimotor stage seemed a constant (Droz and Rahmy 1974; as presented in Table 3.2 in Young 2011). The third and fourth stages in his stage model (concrete operational stage, formal operational stage) were also present throughout various presentations of the model.

Piaget varied a lot in how he presented the second stage of his model, the preoperational stage. At times, he referred to it as intuitive, or he considered it a substage of the concrete period. Piaget did not describe stages before the sensorimotor one (e.g., applicable prenatally), nor did he describe an adult stage post-formally. At times, he included substages involving two steps in each stage, except in the sensorimotor stage, for which he described six substages.

Neo-Piagetians. Other Neo-Piagetians attempted to alter Piaget's stage model and the substages included in the stages. In particular, Fischer (1980) and Case (1985) each developed a three-step substage model of cognitive development, with the substages cyclically repeating within each stage (see Table 2.2). Fischer referred to his three-step substage model of cognitive development as involving sets, maps, and systems; alternatively, Case referred to them as unifocal, bifocal, and elaborated coordinations.

Despite the superficial similarity between Fischer's and Case's models of substages that recur within stages in cognitive development, Table 2.2 reveals important differences in the models. First, the typical ages associated with the sequence of substages over the lifespan in Case and Fischer do not always match. Although their developmental models generally correspond in the substages for the preoperational and abstract stages, the ages are quite different. Moreover, the sensorimotor and concrete operational stages have poor correspondence across the two models. This illustrates the gaps in Fischer's model, especially in his sequence of substages from infancy to adulthood. Young (2011) showed that Fischer appears to have skipped age periods (e.g., at 1 1/2–2 years, and 9 years relative to Case's and my own model)

Table 2.1 A model of 25 steps in Neo-Piagetian cognitive development and Neo-Eriksonian social-affective development

Level	Neo-Piagetian stage	Neo-Piagetian substage	Age range	Neo-Eriksonian stage	Neo-Eriksonian substage
1	Reflexive	Coordination	Earlier fetal life	Nonparticipatory reflexive socio-emotions	Distance acts vs. no acts
2		Hierarchization	Quite premature		Nursing vs. rootless acts
3		Systematization	Somewhat premature		Outcome vs. outcast acts
4		Multiplication	Full-term newborn		Care giving vs. careless giving acts
5		Integration	0–1 month		Emotional vs. malemotional acts
6	Sensori-motor	Coordination	1–4 months	Pre-participatory socio-affects	Dyadic vs. dysdyadic acts
7		Hierarchization	4–8 months		Trust vs. mistrust acts
8		Systematization	8–12 months		Sociability vs. unsociability acts
9		Multiplication	12–18 months		Autonomy vs. doubt acts
10		Integration	18–24 months		Interdigitational vs. dedigitational acts
11	Peri-operational	Coordination	2–3.5 years	Peri-participatory social cognitions	Superordinate vs. discoordinate acts (quasi-participatory)
12		Hierarchization	3.5–5 years		Initiative vs. guilt acts
13		Systematization	5–7 years		Identification vs. problematic identification acts
14		Multiplication	7–9 years		Industry vs. inferiority acts (participatory)
15		Integration	9–11 years		Role vs. role confusion acts

(continued)

Table 2.1 (continued)

Level	Neo-Piagetian stage	Neo-Piagetian substage	Age range	Neo-Eriksonian stage	Neo-Eriksonian substage
16	Abstract	Coordination	11–13 years	Hyper-participatory social mutuality	Conscious vs. contraconscious acts
17		Hierarchization	13–16 years		Identity vs. identity diffusion acts
18		Systematization	16–19 years		Nurturing vs. misnurturing acts
19		Multiplication	19–22 years		Intimacy vs. isolation acts
20		Integration	22–25 years		Universal vs. self-singular acts
21	Collective intelligence	Coordination	25–28 years	Superordinate participatory collective sociality	Metacollecting vs. disillusionment acts
22		Hierarchization	28–39 years		Generativity vs. self-absorption acts
23		Systematization	39–50 years		Catalytic vs. midlife crisis acts
24		Multiplication	50–61 years		Ego integrity vs. despair acts
25		Integration	61– years		Cathartic vs. abandonment acts

Adapted from Young (1997, 2011, 2012); mostly Table P.1 in Young (1997)

in constructing his model. That said, Fischer made important contributions; for example, Case kept the four-stage model of Piaget, albeit changing the labels, while Fischer innovated by creating a Reflex stage and an adult period (system of systems). Also, he collapsed the preoperational and concrete operational periods into a representational stage, which is consistent with Piaget's variations on his stage model, as well as my own approach. (Case later added an orienting stage to precede the sensorimotor one.) Table 2.2 also shows Mounoud's (1986) model of the substages in cognitive development. It consists of a five-step recursion over three stages (the conceptual stage is like Fischer's collapsed Representational one). In developing my own model of the recursive steps in cognitive substage development, I considered all three prior models and ended up with a five-stage × five substage model, as per Table 2.1.

The critical factor in creating my five-stage × five-substage model of Neo-Piagetian development lay in the quality of Piaget's observations of his own children when they were infants. These careful observations helped lead to Piaget's six-step substage model in the sensorimotor period. Unlike in the models of Case and Fischer, which were formulated based on their research with older children, in my modeling, I did not dismantle Piaget's original six-step substage model in infancy. Both Case and Fischer ended up rendering Piaget's original six-substage

Table 2.2 Some contemporary Neo-Piagetian models of cognitive development

Fischer (1980 on)			Case (1985 on)			Mounoud (e.g., 1986)		
Stage	Substage	Age	Stage	Substage	Age	Stage	Substage	Age
Reflex	Set	1 mo-						
	Map	2-						
	System	3-						
Sensorimotor	Set	4-	Sensori-motor	Precoord (a)	0 mo	Perceptual	Global (b)	0 mo-
	Map	8-		Unifocal	4-		Applic	1-
	System	12-		Bifocal	8-		Related	4-
				Elabor	12-		Analysis	8-
							Synthesis	12-
Representational	Set	2 yr-	Inter-relation-al	Unifocal	18-	Conceptual	Global (b)	18-
	Map	5-		Bifocal	2 yr-		Applic	3 yr-
	System	7-		Elabor	3.5-		Related	5-
							Analysis	7-
							Synthesis	9-
			Dimensional	Unifocal	5-			
				Bifocal	7-			
				Elabor	9-			
Abstract	Set	12-	Abstract	Unifocal	11-	Semiotic	Global	10-
Formal	Map	16-		Bifocal	13-		Applic	11-
Operational	System	20-		Elabor	16–19		Related	13-
	System of Systems	26+					Analysis	15-
							Synthesis	16–18

Note. (a) Precoord = Precoordination; Elabor = Elaboration. (b) Global = Global code; Applic = Code applied; Related = Codes related

Adapted from Young (1990a)

In Young (1990a), I presented this table that served as the basis for the present model's formulation. By juxtaposing the three main Neo-Piagetian theorists at that time (Fischer, Case, Mounoud), the comparative advantages of each became evident, as well as their differences, gaps, and inconsistencies

At that time, Case had not added his orienting period before the sensorimotor one, so Fischer's innovation in having an initial reflexive period stood out. His idea of referring to the combined preoperational and concrete operational periods as representational seemed acceptable because Piaget had done the same thing. He had added a postformal period but had yet to refer to it to acquiring principles

Case had kept the traditional four-step Piagetian sequence of sensorimotor, preoperational, concrete operational, and formal operational intelligence, but he modified the labels. Many theorists refer to the formal stage as abstract, as he did. Also, his use of the terms of interrelations, dimensions, and vectors for the last three of Piaget's stages, respectively, is consistent with Piaget's conceptions. However, I refrained from using these labels, partly because of their ambiguities and limitations. For example, the concept of interrelations is too general and can apply socially at any age as well as cognitively. For the concrete operational period, although there is an increase in

(continued)

Table 2.2 (continued)

dimensional thought, the child is acquiring reversibility in thought, particularly, at this age, according to Piaget. Moreover, dimensional thought is just one of the four major types of logical justifications on conservation tasks that Piaget described for this period. Piaget termed this type of thought as compensatory. The others concerned reversibility (negation) and identity, in particular; see Young (1977)
As for Mounoud, I did not use his description of the child's combined preoperational and concrete operational stages, which he referred to as "conceptual," given that infants could be understood to be forming concepts, too. Similarly, he described the formal period as a semiotic one, but the semiotic function is used differently in other fields, such as linguistics
As for comments on the substage cycles presented in the various theories, briefly, Fischer and Case each have a three-step cyclic recursion of substages within stages, Mounoud's model has five, and my model has five, as well. I had wanted to respect the integrity of Piaget's original sensorimotor substage series and built a five-step cyclic recursion of substages based on them by removing the first one and referring to it as a separate stage (reflexive)
As for each period's age, I started with the age period that Piaget had identified for the sensorimotor period (up to 2 years). Also, in prior and subsequent cycles of the substages, I respected the age ranges provided by Piaget and added to them, as necessary, for example, by splitting them where needed. Therefore, I did not abandon critical age transitions that Piaget had described for any one age period
Case had adopted a similar approach to fit his cyclic recursion of substages; he either used the age points offered in Piaget, or split them. However, Fischer did not follow the same approach. For example, in the literature available to me at that time, Fischer left a gap in his substage sequence at the 18-month period relative to Piaget, Case, and myself. That is, whereas we three described a new substage emerging in the 18–24-month period, although to some extent we disagreed on its label and contents, Fischer had bypassed this age period as a distinct one in constructing his model. Note that in later publications, the gap switched to the second year to the 3½ year period, which is also problematic

sensorimotor sequence in infancy into three-step ones. To the contrary, I kept intact Piaget's six-step substage sequence, but did implement one change. That is, I considered the first substage of Reflex Exercise as part of a stage of Reflexes that precedes the sensorimotor one, leaving a five-step substage sequence for the sensorimotor stage itself, with these five steps standing for consideration for the cyclic recursion model of substages over stages that I was in the middle of formulating. Note that Mounoud's five-step substage model was fitted to each stage in his model, like in my approach. He appeared to have used the first five of the six Piagetian sensorimotor substages (but gave them labels that differed from Piaget). In his cyclic recursion of substages, he considered the first substage of the ensuing preoperational period (labeled conceptual) as starting at 18 months, like Fischer did, and unlike myself and Piaget. Although Piaget considered the sixth sensorimotor stages as mental (invention of new means), he still considered it action-based, too (e.g., a toddler opens her mouth before opening a drawer). Note that one can conjecture that Mounoud had chosen not to dismantle the six-step sensorimotor substages of Piaget, because, like myself, he had undertaken his Piagetian research on the infancy period.

To summarize, it appears that my own model takes the best of the others while building on Piaget's original model without dismantling or sacrificing it. I examined closely Piaget's original six-step substage model in the sensorimotor stage, trying to decipher the nature of the underlying cognitive acquisition described. Piaget used terms for them such as primary circular reactions and coordination of secondary schemes, which are difficult to generalize to other stages and the proposal that all stages have equivalent cyclically recurring substages. By going back and forth between the sensorimotor stage and the stages both before and after it in the Neo-Piagetian model that was being developed, I arrived at a five-step substage model of development that fit both the preceding reflexive period and the ensuing cognitive stages right into adulthood. The five substages are called: coordination, hierarchization, systematization, multiplication, and integration.

Then, I elaborated the five stages involved in the model, and indicated that it started with a Reflexive period that covered the prenatal period into the birth period, and ended with a postformal period right into the end phases of life, called Collective Intelligence. That is, as adults, relative to adolescents and their abstract, formal thought, as adults, we create superordinate collective abstract structures, we brainstorm collectively together better, in a group intelligence, and we cohere better together cognition and emotion. As for the preoperational and concrete operational stages of Piaget, I combined them, but with a new term, "perioperations," as in the perioperational stage.

In further modeling, (a) I referred to the first two substages in any one five-substage sequence as primary and the last three as secondary (see Table 1.9, p. 17; in Young 2011). In my model, Piaget's original preoperational stage is considered the primary peri-operational phase and the concrete operational age is considered the secondary perioperational phase. (b) It worked out that the ages for the substages in my model fit very well Case's model, at least for the substage sequence that he had elaborated. Case had used Piaget's age ranges for his substages or split them, such that it appeared to be that there were no missing age periods in his sequence of age periods, unlike the case for Fischer.

Erikson

The next major task in developing the combined Neo-Piagetian/Neo-Eriksonian model involved extrapolating from the Neo-Piagetian cognitive developmental series (5 stages × 5 substages) over the lifespan to a possible corresponding Neo-Eriksonian series. The original Eriksonian stage model consists of 8 stages, so I had to interpolate 17 others to arrive at 25 parallel steps in Neo-Piagetian and Neo-Eriksonian development. It did not make sense to put any of the original Eriksonian stages in correspondence with the Reflex stage. This left the dilemma of how to place the eight Eriksonian stages in parallel with the other four Neo-Piagetian stages and their five substages each. It turned out that the best match was to fit two Eriksonian stages in each of the four Neo-Piagetian stages, and moreover, in correspondence with the second and fourth substages, in particular. As I had done in seeking the nature of the substages across the recursions over stages in the proposed Neo-Piagetian model, I had to seek the nature of the interpolated substages in the Neo-Eriksonian model. I undertook this task by considering both the nature of the

Neo-Piagetian substages with which I was working for any interpolated Neo-Eriksonian substage and the nature of the preceding and following steps in the series.

As for the labels of the Neo-Eriksonian stages, these were constructed in Young (2012). They moved through a nonparticipatory (reflexive) to pre-participatory sequence (sensorimotor), and then to a peri-participatory (perioperational), hyper-participatory (abstract), and superordinate participatory (collective intelligence) sequence (see column 5 of Table 2.1). The particular Neo-Eriksonian substage sequence, which includes the eight original Eriksonian stages, is offered in column 6 of the table. The substages are referred to as involving acts to indicate their (preparatory) participatory nature. Note that Neo-Eriksonian substages do not necessarily develop at the same ages as their equivalent Neo-Piagetian substages. There might be fixations, regressions, and other complications that delay them, compromise them, and so on.

Self

One of the clearest examples of how empirical data modeling approaches fit the present model compared to other Neo-Piagetian ones concerns self-development. Young (1997) showed that Sroufe's (1990, 1996) six-step model of self-development in infancy is consistent with the Piaget's substages in the sensorimotor period in infancy and, consequently, also is consistent with Young's Neo-Piagetian model for the infancy period. Selman's (1980) five-step model of self-development in the preschool to early adolescent period fits those models, as well. Finally, Loevinger's model of ego development from the age periods corresponding to the peri-operational multiplication to the collective coordination substages of Young's Neo-Piagetian model maps quite well conceptually with the present model (e.g., Loevinger 1976). A similar parallel exists with the work of Kohlberg (e.g., Kohlberg and Ryncarz 1990). This parallel between Young's model of Neo-Piagetian development and other models of self-development gives support to the model and helped me to develop a 25-step sequence of self-development based on it. At the same time, in Young (2011) I showed how Harter's (1999) model of self-development has been mapped onto Fischer's Neo-Piagetian model, but with its inconsistencies inevitably included (see Young 2011, pp. 172–173).

Further, continuing with the theme of self-development, I showed how Blatt's (2008) distinction between the self-definitional and relatedness self-components of the self can evolve through the 25 steps of the present model. I accomplished this by synchronizing Blatt's distinction with a Neo-Maslovian model of hierarchical and developmental needs that I had developed based on the current Neo-Piagetian/Neo-Eriksonian model. The Neo-Maslovian model was also used in the elaboration of five ethical principles suggested to revise the APA ethics code (see Fig. 2.1 and Table 2.3).

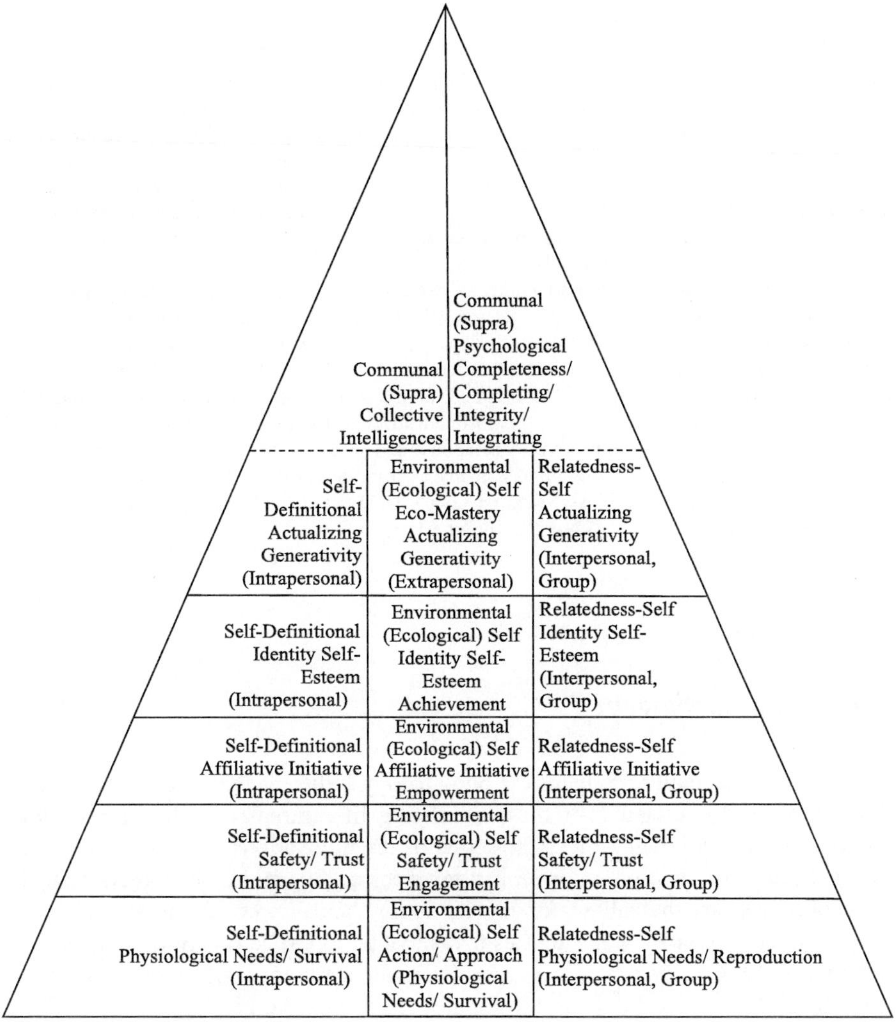

Fig. 2.1 Neo-Maslovian hierarchy of self-definitional, relatedness self, and environmental self needs

The figure gives simplified terms for each of the revised motivational needs in the combined model of Maslow (1943, 1970), Erikson (1980), and Blatt (2008). The major revision entertained of Maslow concerns dividing his different levels of needs into two components, depending on what part of the self is involved. The left-hand column refers to the needs related to the personal self, while the right-hand column refers to the needs of the self in relationship. Blatt referred to polarities of experience in terms of self-definition and relatedness, and I borrowed these terms for this aspect of the model

In addition, for this version of the Neo-Maslovian model in the present work relative to the original revision in Young (2011), I added a middle column related to a third component of the person, or the mastery/competence, instrumental/environmental aspect of behavior. In particular, this aspect of the model is derived from Forbes (2011), Deci and Ryan (1995), Haidt (2012), and Janoff-Bulman and colleagues (e.g., Janoff-Bulman 2009)

(continued on page 32)

Fig. 2.1 (continued) As for Erikson's model of eight stages in lifespan development, there appear to be two stages in his model that correspond to each of the four more advanced needs of Maslow's model. Therefore, in deriving the labels for the present combined model, I referred to the first of the two Erikson's stages involved in each case. As for the most basic physiological level of needs, I referred to the Darwinian concept of survival and reproduction, using the latter for the personal component and the former for the relatedness component. Note that the terms used to describe the needs also refer to attachment theory for the safety level and affiliation instead of love for the middle level (after Kenrick et al. 2010)
The Piagetian component of the model adds an extra level at the peak to account for changes in cognition and behavior that would derive as the person transitions from the formal to the postformal period, which I refer to as the stage of collective intelligence (Young 2011). Another change made to the original Maslovian revision of the hierarchy of needs model is that I included a superordinate level to the one of self-actualization and related psychological development, such as generativity. This new partial level of the penultimate level in the model concerns "psychological completeness," which is partially akin to Erikson's ego integrity and which corresponds to the stage of collective intelligence cognitively in my own model. (Adapted in part with permission from Springer Science + Business Media. Young (2011); with kind permission from Springer Science + Business Media B.V. [Figure 19.3, Page 452])

Innovations

Stages and Substages

The nature of the major model of the book trilogy indicates that it was created both through a solid knowledge of the pre-existing literature, as well as innovations based on it. The following gives the scope of the innovations over the three books under discussion. (a) Some concern more precise definitions. (b) Others concern conceptualizations that allow for understanding and empirical investigation. (c) Others concern broader mini-theories that serve an umbrella function in integrating other work. (d) Finally, others are expansive models, theories, and meta-models that shed insight on the workings of development and of causality.

With respect to definitions, for example, the books consider the difference between causality and causation. Young (2011; p. 662) indicated that causality especially concerns process, which is the reason why it is the term chosen for use in the three books, aside from it being used generically more than the term causation.

Diverse

In Young (2011), aside from presenting my own work, in particular, on cognitive development through five stages, I ventured beyond the model. For example, I referred to a possible next stage in cognitive development as Communal Collective Intelligences, which involves co-opting other intelligences into our own, including those of other species and in artificial intelligence/computers.

Table 2.3 Five reworked/novel principles in the APA Ethics Code in relation to Maslow's hierarchical model of needs

Maslow level	Ethical principle	Brief description
1. Immediate physiological needs	1. Life preservation	Psychologists protect the physical integrity of all others, for example, as it applies to suicide and homicide. Psychologists protect children from the dangers of abuse and negligence. Psychologists act to preserve the sanctity of life, its survival. Psychologists respect the principle that torture is not permissible nor ethical
2. Safety	2. Caring beneficence/nonmaleficence	Psychologists achieve the competence needed to benefit the people they work with, especially the vulnerable; they safeguard their welfare. Psychologists aim to do no harm, or minimize it
3. Love (affection, belongingness)	3. Relational integrity	Psychologists build relationships, and behave with openness, honesty, fairness, trust facilitation, rapport encouragement, a genuine presence, and mutual respect in a two-way interaction or dialogue. They emphasize the humanity of the other
4. Esteem (respect)	4. Respect for the dignity and rights of persons and peoples	Psychologists respect the inherent self-worth of every individual and all groupings of people. Psychologists respect the fundamental individual and collective rights of all peoples related to their dignity and sense of self-worth. Psychologists respect rights to voluntary informed consent, privacy, confidentiality, anonymity, etc. Psychologists deeply respect the autonomy and self-determination of all individuals or groupings and rights of individuals and peoples to: nondiscrimination, fairness, equity, justice in this regard, and personal and collective (e.g., cultural minority status) identity
5. Self-actualization	5. Promoting and acting from justice in society	Psychologists ensure that the parties dealing with their patients/clients do so in an equitable and just manner

Note. APA = American Psychological Association
Adapted from Young (2017) [Third Column of this Table taken from Table 3.1, pg. 64]

Also, in Young (2011), I indicated that cognitive skills that exist in relation to the stages and substages do not get integrated in higher-order skills as the latter appear, and so are lost to the developing person for use. Rather, as a new (sub)stage emerges in development, skills that are associated with the prior (sub)stage are not integrated into the newly appearing one. Therefore, cognitive skills associated with different stages can co-exist in development. This allows them to be used in conjunction by the individual in problem-solving. So, the skills associated with (sub)stages can exist in parallel and their skills deployed in combination in attempts to resolve a problem at hand. This concept was referred to as yoking, and when the cognitive skills associated with multiple (sub)stages are activated (and work) together in yoking, the associated skills of the (sub)stages involved can be viewed as multiple (cognitive) intelligences. What of the models of Gardner and Sternberg? The traditional multiple intelligences referred to in these latter models would seem to provide names for the domains to which the present model of multiple intelligences applies.

Table 2.4 The cognitive (mis)perception of the other and individual/group response at each cognitive stage

Stage	Cognitive misperception of the other	Individual/group response
1. Reflexive	Negate (abuse/reject/deny)	Obliteration vs. Nihilism
2. Sensorimotor	Subjugate (repress, oppose/compete, impose, manipulate)	Sterilization vs. Revolution
3. Peri-operational	Pacify/tantalize	Assimilation vs. Resistance
– Preoperational	First-order	First-order
– Concrete operational	Second-order	Second-order
4. Abstract	Limit, partially liberate	Involution vs. Evolution
5. Collective intelligence	Humanize	Equalization vs. Emancipation

The model of the cognitive (mis)perception of the other indicates that, at the lowest levels of (mis) perception of the other, we treat the person as an infant or young child (levels 1 and 2) of the model. Because of these levels' devaluing nature, the person is considered as not having much equal rights, which thereby justifies any abuse or suppression undertaken. (3) As for perceiving the other only in terms of the person being akin to an older child, at best, the person engaging in the misperception treats the other as someone who could be canalized or manipulated easily due to their perceived lack of cognitive sophistication. In the last stages of the model (4 and 5), the person perceives the other as functioning as a teenager or adult, or in the model's more mature levels

The table also indicates how individuals or groups might respond to the perceiver, misattributing maximum cognitive capacity and engaging in mistreatment as a result. Individuals might be children or partners; the group might be minorities as perceived by majorities. When the misperception is equivalent to the reflexive level, the other will be overpowered and feel obliterated. If there is an effort to avoid obliteration, the only option might be a nihilistic, chaotic behavior, because all other options might not be possible. For the perception of being like a sensorimotor entity, the perceived might feel neutralized or sterilized at best. If there is any fight possible, it will be more overt than nihilistic, and it might be an overtly revolutionary one. If the person is perceived equivalent to child-like with some cognitive skills at best, it will foster a more subtle aggressive counter-response, should it take place, which we call resistance. The first-order level at this level will be more intuitive/automatic than logical/reflective, consistent with the preoperational stage associated with it. If the stage is the concrete operational one, the second-order level of resistance will have logical/reflective elements but limited to the physical, tangible environment and options rather than abstract, intangible ones. The latter type will be found in the evolutionary/emancipation responses of the individual group's later responses

The table has presented a model of the cognitive (mis)perception of the other or how individuals perceive the other according to their own predominant developmental socioemotional level. Most likely, each individual simultaneously functions at all five levels of the model (in terms of actual, desired or most mature behavior, etc.). Also, the relative proportion of the five levels in any one person should vary according to the situation, issue, person being related to, their own history, and so on. The same applies to the development in couples and societies; they might also have one major way of (mis)perceiving the other, but do vary

Adopted with permission of Springer Science+Business Media. Young, G. (1997). *Adult development,* therapy, *and culture: A postmodern synthesis*. New York: Plenum; with kind permission from Springer Science+Business Media B. V. [Table 7.1, Page 156; slightly modified]

The Young (2011) book also examined other Neo-Piagetians beyond the ones mentioned so far. Of course, Pascual-Leone was the first Neo-Piagetian (e.g., Pascual-Leone et al. 2010), but he did not change the stage formulation presented by Piaget. Commons (2008) developed a lifespan model of cognitive stages in development. It is based on his postformal model for the adult, with Fischer's (1980) model added to it to make it lifespan. However, Young (2011) showed that in Commons' model: (a) the postformal stages appear to be missing a stage between the first and second one; (b) Fischer's prior stages were not adopted quite as presented; (c) the model is not divided into stages and their substages, unlike the case for Fischer, Case, myself, and others; (d) just as Fischer's model appears to be missing steps, for example, at 2 years and 7 years, so does Commons' adaptation; (e) some of the examples provided by Commons do not fit the stage mentioned for them but reflect the stages that are missing in his model; (f) some of the labels for the stages do not make the best of sense, for example, "calculatory" for the first (reflexive) one, sensory or motor for the second one, which is sensorimotor; (g) the sequence of stages was not rationally derived in full, sometimes being a pastiche; and (h) nor was it first derived from an empirical analysis of children or adolescent cognitive performance. Overall, then, compared to my own model of 25 steps in lifespan cognitive development (5 stages × 5 substages), Commons' model is missing 10 steps, and some of the ones described reflect inconsistencies and concerns.

Young (2011) included two chapters on language development, which is one area that Neo-Piagetians investigate. The chapters presented a literature review on linguistic cohesion and coherence in textual discourse and narratives. Moreover, they presented scales of discourse complexity that are tied to the Neo-Piagetian model. Cognitive development affords one basis for language development, and language development recursively influences cognitive development. Humans are storytelling beings, and the study of the relationship between cognitive development and linguistic and language development can profit from a Neo-Piagetian framework.

Finally, the 2011 Young book examined philosophical questions related to epistemology. It adopted a synthetic approach to positivistic and constructivist approaches, referring to a co-existential epistemology. The 2016 Young book examined the issue further and adopted a "neo-reductioconstructivist" viewpoint of epistemology. It is consistent with the present stage modeling approach to development, which is constructivist (the child is an active participant in her/his own cognitive development, for example). It is also consistent with a realist and reductionist viewpoint to basic biological processes, while admitting emergence of higher-order levels in self-organization, so that top-down and bottom-up processes intercoordinate in development.

Social-Emotional

In terms of concepts and theories, the underlying basis of the present work is that cognitive and socioemotional development is indissociable. Cognitive and affective structures do not exist apart, and they are separated in the literature only for heuristic purposes. Socioemotional development takes place within the space allowed for by cognitive development. As espoused in my model, cognitive and socio-affective development are integrated with fundamental cognitive-socioemotional schemas or structures. Further, they manifest parallel substages in cognitive and socioemotional development (per the present 5 stage × 5 substage Neo-Piagetian/Neo-Eriksonian model, and the multiple socio-affective structures that develop through the stages and substages). Some of the latter include the concepts of the cognitive (mis)perception of the other, which relates to how we perceive others (our developmental charges/children; our romantic partners; minorities) in relation to the development of basic underlying Neo-Piagetian substages within the proposed sequence of stages (and fixations and regressions therein) (see Table 2.4). Essentially, the model indicates that, to varying degrees, with improper perception of the other cognitively, corresponding abuse or improperly dealing with the other is facilitated socioemotionally. Another integrated cognitive/socio-affective concept that has been constructed in the present framework concerns the theory of mind or taking the perspective of the other. The present approach considers it a socio-affective as much as a cognitive acquisition (reading more than just the mind of the other), and so is conceived as the "construction of the cognitive-emotional-body of the other" (which also develops substage by substage according to the present model).

As for the basic emotions themselves, the predominant view is that there is a small subset of emotions that constitute a primary evolutionary set. However, in Young (2011), I indicate how at least four emotions emerge with each new substage in the model in the last Reflexive and the five sensorimotor substages (i.e., according to Piaget's original six-substage sensorimotor model) (see Table 2.5). The table shows that the model of basic emotions that I developed includes 6 types × 2 activity levels × 2 goal compatibility (and consequent hedonic tone classes), with at least 2 examples in each of the 24 resultant grids in the model. Therefore, the model goes well beyond the traditional category models that are biological/evolutionary-based (e.g., Ekman et al. 1969). Furthermore, contemporary emotion research is consistent with my approach. Cowen and Keltner (2020) found at least 28 categories of emotions in the everyday life of adults, and they were linked to gradients of meaning, much like in my cognitive Piagetian approach to their categorization in infancy.

A major integration accomplished by the present work indicates how attachment theory is compatible with it. In particular, the present model expands the concept of internal working models or representational structures (IRMs), that cohere attachment experiences into schemes (such as "I am lovable"; "the environment (caregiver) loves me" in the case of secure attachment) into social-self working schemata, in order to indicate their social affective and experiential nature. Also, the present

Table 2.5 Levels of emotional development in the first 2 years of life

Type (age in months)	Activity	Goal compatibility/Hedonic tone: Compatible (positive)	Not (negative)
Arriving (0–1)	Reactive	Relief, contentment	Distress, discontentment
	Active	Engagement, quiescence	Disengagement, disgust, fussiness
Possessing (1–4)	Reactive	Joy, delight	Wariness, aversion
	Active	Pleasure, interest, acceptance	Unpleasure, boredom, disappointment, rage
Approaching (4–8)	Reactive	Elation, surprise, exhilaration	Fear, sadness, distrust
	Active	Wonder, fascination	Anger, crankiness
Giving (8–12)	Reactive	Comfort, containment (sense of)	Anxious, worry, displacement escape
	Active	Affection, liking, warmth	Petulance, dislike, aggressive displacement
Desiring (12–18)	Reactive	Coyness, shyness, avidity	Defiance, alarm, jealousy
	Active	Eagerness, satisfaction	Greed, envy, retribution anger
Evaluating (18–24)	Reactive	Pride, selfness (sense of), approval	Shame, embarrassment, prejudice
	Active	Appreciation, love, empathy	Contempt, hate, guilt

The present model of basic emotions in infancy surpasses others in the number of emotions considered as basic. It suggests that there are at least 24 families of emotions that develop in the first 2 years. The model posits that families of emotions develop four at a time in the first 2 years, with each set emerging in concert with a corresponding substage of Piaget's six-substage sensorimotor series. Aside from the model's cognitive dimension, there are two others, which are related to the dimensions of valence/goal compatibility and activation. The cognitive one is akin to a figure-ground dimension because the emotion types that emerge in concert with its substages vary in this regard (e.g., approach-withdrawal). The model integrates the major approaches to the study of emotions, for example, categorical (basic), dimensional, cognitive, functional, and dynamic

Note. The 24 basic emotional categories over the three dimensions in the table can be split into 48 ones by adding of a fourth dimension, that is, one concerning direct (e.g., arrives positively) vs. indirect (e.g., gets other to arrive positively) emotions. For each of the table's cells, the last example refers to indirect emotions, and the other(s) refer to direct ones (except for disappointment and sadness)

Adopted with permission of Elsevier. Reprinted from *Developmental psychology: Cognitive, perceptuo-motor, and neuropsychological perspectives* (C. A. Hauert, Ed.), G. Young (Chapter Author), Early neuropsychological development: Lateralization of functions - hemispheric specialization, Pages No. 113–181, Copyright (1990b), with permission from Elsevier. [Table 7, Page 162]

model shows how socio/self/working schemas can develop through its 25 steps (5 stages × 5 substages) (see Table 2.6).

Continuing with the theme of integrated cognitive socio-affective structures in development, one manner of referring to them in an overarching way that Young (2011) described involved the cognitive/socio-affective complex. Similarly, the latter is involved in self-regulation, which I refer to as self- (cognitive-emotional) regulation in order to highlight its integrated socio-affective nature. Also, I posit

Table 2.6 Social self-schemata in the 25-step Neo-Piagetian (sub)stage model

Stage	Substage	Schema
Reflexive	1	No schemata other than reflex pairings.
	2	Reflex pairs coordinate and react to stimuli.
	3	Primitive schemata form in visual, auditory, haptic, olfactory, gustatory, and kinesthetic activity/exploration; with intermodal system coordinations.
	4	Consistencies in care giving lead to the formation of bodily components-of-context associations. Patterned schemata fire mechanically.
	5	Independent schemata that are not reflex controlled allow contextually adjusted, patterned behavior with emotional integrations.
Sensorimotor	6	Working schemata become increasingly coordinative of the socializing self and the other, but only in the sense of partial components of both (e.g., the baby is contented and experiences pleasure).
	7	As the infant develops a sense of trust, context-activated goals are added to developing schemata, which take on a hierarchical structure (e.g., components of self are interested and delighted in other).
	8	Working schemata include self-defined goals, primitive representations such as images of the caregiver, and the desire for intersubjectivity and proximity and contact. The emotional side of the developing cognitive-affective structure includes feelings of affection and comfort.
	9	The 1-year-old infant acts increasingly autonomous through planned exploratory behavior eagerly implemented, although this does not happen with explicit plans at the behavior's outset (it is "accidental"). The social other is integral to the working schemata being formed, but as an object of sensorimotoric-emotional activity rather than a preconceived representational goal. The primary caregiver who has been sensitive in the first year so that the infant feels "loved" is sought actively in reunion after a brief separation.
	10	Infants at 18 months of age enact symbolically guided, planned activity, but always with a sensorimotoric and affective base. They experience appreciation and pride. Others are understood in terms of the plans, and with consistent participation in them. The infant varies plans involving them on purpose to see the effect.
Peri-operational	11	In symbol plan coordinations, the child's plans are more focused on self-egocentrically, and the other, while schematized more holistically, needs to adjust. A sense of the other as a loving one grows.
	12	The child's symbol plans are more differentiated, with an initiative subordinating the other, who is still responded to with an overriding love, however.
	13	The "I" can take primary perspectives of the self/other through symbol plan systems and Eriksonian "industry," guided by others.
	14	This ability grows and others are seen to evaluate the self.
	15	The child's working schemata include testing of different roles, with others seen as modelers and accepting of this dynamic.

(continued)

Table 2.6 (continued)

Stage	Substage	Schema
Abstract	16	Conscious "I" weighs abstractly.
	17	Identity "I" tests and seeks identity.
	18	Conscientious "I" undertakes adult-(like) functions.
	19	Relativistic "I" delves and debates.
	20	Universal "I" harmonizes.
Collective Intelligence	21	The self is collective, fused, and coordinative.
	22	The self knows priorities, is multiply complex, and can give multiply, and not for taking.
	23	At midlife, the self can create and work to transform personal, social, work, and community systems.
	24	The elder self-reviews the multiplicity of life and lives.
	25	An integrated "I" is really an integrated "We" at life's end.

Note. The table indicates how internal working models might evolve through the 25 steps of the present Neo-Piagetian model, thereby giving them a coherent structure to help explain how they might grow cognitively. Also, I incorporate into these developing working schemata the present developmental model of Neo-Eriksonian steps in socio-affective development. The table presents the positive or secure components to the schemata, in particular. In addition, I add to the schemata the manner in which basic emotions are fundamental to them in the infancy period

(a) The first substages are on the reflex stage. It indicates that working schemata in the first month include basic emotional components and that the caregiver could already be manifesting sensitive care

(b) The next part of the table on the sensorimotor stage presents the critical period in the first 2 years of life when working schemata develop their secure or insecure characteristics. For the self, the schemata evolve in this stage from ones concerned with social coordination to those involved in active attachment and feeling loved, to those that are more symbolic, even if still sensorimotor. For the other, the schemata move from working models of initial social interactions, trust, and caregivers being security-promoting to genuine interactions and constancy as object

(c) In the peri-operational stage, working schemata of the self-start with egocentric conceptions. They move to a better perspective-taking of the other and to testing different roles. The other evolves from being conceived as being adjustable to having rules and modulating growth, to being capable of evaluating and of modeling roles

(d) In the abstract stage, the working model of the self develops from a conscious being to a conscientious and universalizing one. Symmetrically, the other acts to raise consciousness, conscientiousness, and universal empathy

(e) In the collective stage, the self-moves toward generativity, midlife, and end of life concerns. The other is conceived in a mirror way

Adopted excerpts with permission of Springer Science+Business Media. Young, G. (2011). *Development and* causality*:* Neo-Piagetian *perspectives*. New York: Springer Science + Business Media; with kind permission from Springer Science + Business Media B.V. [Middle columns of Table 24.2 to 24.6; Table note of Table 24.2]

how these acquisitions evolve through the 25 steps of the current model. Young (2011) indicated other ways that his stage model could apply to development, such as in how romantic partnerships might evolve positively through stages or how management styles might evolve toward higher-order qualities.

But there are several provisos and limitations to consider in the enterprise undertaken. First, the presentation so far of the integrated model of stages (and substage) has been about the steps involved and not the mechanisms or causes that propel or drive them. Second, the multiple parallels that seem evident both within and across cognitive and socio-affective development do not proceed in a step lock fashion, in unison with simultaneous major transitions from one (sub)stage to the next. Rather, much individual variation manifests and the global and specific intermingle and interact in a complex developmental process that needs detailed explanation. Later, I present the concept of neo-stage to help explain this type of individualized transitioning. Of course, keep in mind that much development does not involve stages, substages, qualitative acquisitions, transitions, etc.

Conclusion

The second chapter of the book is the first substantive one after the book's introduction. It presents the book's core model, particularly on (sub)stages in development from a combined Neo-Piagetian/Neo-Eriksonian point of view. The next chapter elaborates the model and more. The chapter summary for the next chapter gives a fulsome overview of the contributions of Chaps. 2 and 3 to the book, including developmentally, causally, and other innovations.

References

Blatt, S.J.: Polarities of Experience: Relatedness and Self-Definition in Personality Development, Psychopathology, and the Therapeutic Process. American Psychological Association, Washington, DC (2008)
Case, R.: Intellectual Development: Birth to Adulthood. Academic Press, New York (1985)
Commons, M.L.: Introduction to the model of hierarchical complexity and its relationship to postformal action. World Futures. **64**(5–7), 305–320 (2008). https://doi.org/10.1080/02604020802301104
Cowen, A.S., Keltner, D.: What the face displays: mapping 28 emotions conveyed by naturalistic expression. Am. Psychol. **75**(5), 349–364 (2020). https://doi.org/10.1037/amp0000488
Deci, E.L., Ryan, R.M.: Human autonomy: the basis for true self-esteem. In: Kernis, M.H. (ed.) Plenum Series in Social/Clinical Psychology. Efficacy, Agency, and Self-Esteem, pp. 31–49. Plenum, New York (1995)
Droz, R., Rahmy, M.: Reading Piaget, 2nd edn. International Universities Press, New York (1974)
Ekman, P., Sorenson, E.R., Friesen, W.V.: Pan-cultural elements in facial displays of emotion. Science. **164**(3875), 86–88 (1969). https://doi.org/10.1126/science.164.3875.86
Erikson, E.H.: Identity and the Life Cycle. Norton, New York (1980)
Fischer, K.W.: A theory of cognitive development: the control and construction of hierarchies of skills. Psychol. Rev. **87**, 477–531 (1980). https://doi.org/10.1037/0033-295X.87.6.477
Forbes, D.L.: Toward a unified model of human motivation. Rev. Gen. Psychol. **15**(2), 85–98 (2011). https://doi.org/10.1037/a0023483
Haidt, J.: The Righteous Mind: Why Good People Are Divided by Politics and Religion. Pantheon, New York (2012)
Harter, S.: The Construction of the Self: A Developmental Perspective. Guilford Press, New York (1999)

Janoff-Bulman, R.: To provide or protect: motivational bases of political liberalism and conservatism. Psychol. Inq. **20**(2–3), 120–128 (2009). https://doi.org/10.1080/10478400903028581
Kenrick, D.T., Griskevicius, V., Neuberg, S.L., Schaller, M.: Renovating the pyramid of needs: contemporary extensions built upon ancient foundations. Perspect. Psychol. Sci. **5**(3), 292–314 (2010). https://doi.org/10.1177/1745691610369469
Kohlberg, L., Ryncarz, R.A.: Beyond justice reasoning: moral development and consideration of a seventh stage. In: Alexander, C.N., Langer, E.J. (eds.) Higher Stages of Human Development: Perspectives on Adult Growth, pp. 191–207. Oxford University Press, New York (1990)
Loevinger, J.: Ego Development: Conceptions and Theories. Jossey-Bass, San Francisco (1976)
Maslow, A.H.: A theory of human motivation. Psychol. Rev. **50**(4), 370–396 (1943). https://doi.org/10.1037/h0054346
Maslow, A.H.: Motivation and Personality, 2nd edn. Harper and Row, New York (1970)
Mounoud, P.: Similarities between developmental sequences at different age periods. In: Levin, I. (ed.) Stage and Structure: Reopening the Debate, pp. 40–58. Ablex, Norwood (1986)
Pascual-Leone, J., Johnson, J., Agostino, A.: Mental attention, multiplicative structures, and the causal problems of cognitive development. In: Ferrari, M., Vuletic, L. (eds.) The Developmental Relations Between Mind, Brain and Education, pp. 49–82. Springer, New York (2010)
Selman, R.L.: The Growth of Interpersonal Understanding: Developmental and Clinical Analyses. Academic Press, New York (1980)
Sroufe, L.A.: An organizational perspective on the self. In: Cicchetti, D., Beeghly, M. (eds.) The Self in Transition: Infancy to Childhood, pp. 281–207. University of Chicago Press, Chicago (1990)
Sroufe, L.A.: Emotional Development: The Organization of Emotional Life in the Early Years. Cambridge University Press, Cambridge (1996)
Young, G.: Use of negation to justify correct judgments of conservation in boys. Percept. Mot. Skills. **44**, 287–292 (1977). https://doi.org/10.2466/pms.1977.44.1.287
Young, G.: The development of hemispheric and manual specialization. In: Hammond, G. (ed.) The Cerebral Control of Speech and Limb Movements, pp. 79–139. North Holland, Amsterdam (1990a)
Young, G.: Early neuropsychological development: lateralization of functions—hemispheric specialization. In: Hauert, C.A. (ed.) Developmental Psychology: Cognitive, Perceptuo-Motor and Neuropsychological Perspectives, pp. 113–181. North Holland, Amsterdam (1990b)
Young, G.: Adult Development, Therapy, and Culture: A Postmodern Synthesis. Plenum, New York (1997)
Young, G.: Development and Causality: Neo-Piagetian Perspectives. Springer Science + Business Media, New York (2011)
Young, G.: A unitary Neo-Piagetian/Neo-Eriksonian model of development: fundamental assumptions and meta-issues. New Ideas Psychol. **30**(2), 241–249 (2012). https://doi.org/10.1016/j.newideapsych.2011.11.002
Young, G.: Malingering, Feigning, and Response Bias in Psychiatric/Psychological Injury—Implications for Practice and Court. Springer Science + Business Media, New York (2014)
Young, G.: Causality in psychiatry: a hybrid symptom network construct model. Front. Psych. **6**, 164 (2015). https://doi.org/10.3389/fpsyt.2015.00164
Young, G.: Unifying Causality and Psychology: Being, Brain and Behavior. Springer International Publishing, Cham (2016)
Young, G.: Revising the American Psychological Association Ethics Code. Springer International Publishing, Cham (2017)
Young, G.: Causality and Development: Neo-Eriksonian Perspectives. Springer International Publishing, Cham (2019)
Young, G.: Toward a unified health work ethics code. Ethics Med. Public Health. **15**, 100590 (2020a). https://doi.org/10.1016/j.jemep.2020.100590
Young, G.: Psychology, law, ethics, telehealth, and the global pandemic. In: Rezaei, N., Hanaei, S., Saghazadeh, A. (eds.) Integrated Science of Global Epidemics, vol. 9. Springer Nature Switzerland AG, Cham (2020b, in press)

Young, G.: Thirty complexities and controversies in mild traumatic brain injury and persistent postconcussion syndrome: a roadmap for research and practice. Psychol. Inj. Law. **13**(4), 427–451 (2020c). https://doi.org/10.1007/s12207-020-09395-6

Young, G., Gouin Décarie, T.: An ethology-based catalogue of facial/vocal behavior in infancy. Anim. Behav. **25**, 95–107 (1977). https://doi.org/10.1016/0003-3472(77)90071-9

Young, G., Bowman, J.G., Methot, C., Finlayson, M., Quintal, J., Boissonneault, P.: Hemispheric specialization development: what (inhibition) and how (parents). In: Young, G., Segalowitz, S.J., Carter, C.M., Trehub, S.E. (eds.) Manual Specialization and the Developing Brain, pp. 119–140. Academic Press, New York (1983a)

Young, G., Segalowitz, S., Corter, C., Trehub, S. (eds.): Manual Specialization and the Developing Brain. Academic Press, New York (1983b)

Young, G., Segalowitz, S., Misek, P., Alp, I., Boulet, R.: Is early reaching left-handed? Review of manual specialization research. In: Young, G., Segalowitz, S.J., Carter, C.M., Trehub, S.E. (eds.) Manual Specialization and the Developing Brain, pp. 13–32. Academic Press, New York (1983c)

Young, G., Kane, A.W., Nicholson, K. (eds.): Psychological Knowledge in Court: PTSD, Pain, and TBI. Springer Science + Business Media, New York (2006)

Young, G., Kane, A.W., Nicholson, K. (eds.): Causality of Psychological Injury: Presenting Evidence in Court. Springer Science + Business Media, New York (2007)

Young, G., Foote, W.E., Kerig, P.K., Mailis, A., Brovko, J., Kohutis, E.A., McCall, S., Hapidou, E.A., Fokas, K.D.: Introducing psychological injury and law. Psychol. Inj. Law. **13**(4), 452–463 (2020). https://doi.org/10.1007/s12207-020-09396-5

Chapter 3
Development, Brain, and Causality

The chapter begins by elaborating on the author's view of causality. It continues to complete the presentation of the core ideas of the book's modeling.

Causality

Development is about product (what) and process (why, causality). Young (2011) supported a comprehensive model of causality in psychology that is both broad (e.g., biopsychosocial or biopersonalsocial) and specific as to mechanism (e.g., activation-inhibition coordination). It focuses on an array of influences on development, from the biological (e.g., brain workings/networks, evolution) to the psychological/personal (e.g., belief in free will, coping/resilience) to the social/environmental/ecological (e.g., family, education). In the Young books, I innovated the approach to causality in psychology at both the broad and specific mechanism levels. For the former, as indicated, I changed the usual label for the biopsychosocial model to the biopersonalsocial model. This was done because, with respect to psychological causality, it makes no sense to refer to the psychological portion as distinct from the biological and social ones. Moreover, the term biopsychosocial does not capture the dynamic, active, constructive nature of the person contributing to her/his own development, while the term biopersonalsocial allows for that active approach to development. The examples provided in my books indicate the active contribution that the person could make to her/his own development (e.g., there are major positive consequences for people who believe in free will, Baumeister 2008).

G. Young, *Causality and Neo-Stages in Development*,
https://doi.org/10.1007/978-3-030-82540-9_3

Systems

As for innovations at the level of mechanisms in behavioral expression, the concept of activation-inhibition coordination is very specific and can apply across a broad spectrum of different levels of behavior and brain relationships. For example, neuronal function works through activation, inhibition, and their coordination, and the same would apply to neural network formation, cross brain-region organization, etc. Simultaneously, the simplest to the most complex behaviors can be viewed as expressing this basic organizing function. For example, I developed the concept of activation-inhibition coordination in researching reaching and grasping in 1-month olds (Young et al. 1983). In the behavior of the reaching in the 1-month olds, the left hand flailed more while the right hand reached for and contacted the target more, in keeping with a model that the hemispheres are organized from early in life akin to later developmental patterns (e.g., the right hemisphere is spatial; the left is more fine motor). The right hand also opened in more coordination at the target, consistent with an activation-inhibition coordination explanation. The 2011 Young book devotes two chapters that examined the development of lateralization. The 2016 book continues to explore the topic; indeed, the first of portion 2019 book spends nine chapters on the topic, which constitutes the most comprehensive examination of the development of human laterality and its origins in the literature to date.

Activation-Inhibition Coordination.

Returning to the broad view of psychological causality, in the three books under review, I have attempted to formulate an integrated, unified, synthetic model that focuses on cross-level communalities in mechanism. One way that I attempted to build such a model throughout the three books under review is through nonlinear dynamical systems theory (NLDST). The major sticking point to any stage theory is to specify how a more qualitatively advanced step can arise developmentally from previous ones. Does a maturational program facilitate the transition? Can experience boost development to new upper bounds? Even with factors such as these working developmentally, the abrupt shift to a new level of functioning even for one cognitive scheme/representation/operation cannot take place in a linear, additive way, with effects collecting cumulatively. Gradual change would be the norm in development, including cognitively, with changes to the scheme/representation/operation taking place horizontally or in widening of breadth, not vertically or abruptly. For stage concepts to have any validity, they must include a mechanism of change developmentally that acts vertically in the cognitive system at issue. In this regard, NLDST provides a potential mechanism that allows for (sub)stage transitions of the cognitive skills contained therein to higher cognitive functioning levels. In NLDST, system elements exist in a state that strains for equilibrium, even at state configurations that are far from equilibrium. However, when they hover at the edge of change, they can abruptly shift to a new state. The new elemental configuration does not attain an adaptive equilibrium due to some pre-programmed master plan or template but does so spontaneously according to internal component configuration dynamics in context. The system reconfigures by this self-organization process. Moreover, for cognitive development, if the new state attains a higher-order, more complex, or new level of organization hierarchically that is distinct from prior level(s), depending on the contents/domains/tasks involved, the new state could be a new (sub)stage. Or, at least contain one advanced element at that level that could bootstrap other elements to that point, spreading its new skill to other reconfigured elements.

The process just described in system reorganization refers to emergence. The pattern of system elements reaches a new configuration that is not predictable from knowing the system parts. Colloquially, the whole is bigger than the sum of the parts. An example would be the galloping horse that achieves a new gait once a critical speed is achieved. The system is perturbed by changing dynamics to the point that critical elements in the system that function as control parameter variables reach thresholds of change that lead to far-from-equilibrium state change and consequent more graceful/economical organization, or more orderly (less "chaotic," more entropic) organization, at least in the short term.

Another way of characterizing system states concerns attractors, which are system trajectories that consistently gravitate to the same basins, or values defining spaces in the system's range of possible states, even though there might be ongoing perturbations, and drastic ones at that. Moreover, there might be patterns in a system's evolution toward increasing complexity. The following gives a map of five successive changes in system configuration in this regard. (a, b) When perturbations override ongoing attractor state dynamics at the cusp of change, the system might bifurcate into new attractor states, such as with periodic or cyclic attractors, leaving the stable point attractor configuration that had characterized system function and then alternate between them. (c) At another system state period in time, the system might express discontinuous emergence to a chaotic regime, which (despite its name) is really more orderly and encompassing of system dynamics than not. (d) If systems include multiple attractors, they could arrange into complex adaptive systems, as in living systems. (e) Moreover, they might evolve into patterns that are more higher-order, indicative of superordinate complex adaptive systems. In effect, systems might express attractor pattern change from point to periodic to chaotic to complex to superordinate complex types. This might be the underlying system dynamic manifold of five change points that correspond to the five hypothesized iterative substages of the present Neo-Piagetian/Neo-Eriksonian model.

Aside from referring to well-known aspects of NLDST to help explain possible (sub)stage transitions, I developed the concept of circular emergence. Systems arrange hierarchically as they adapt and adjust, and new levels in the system can be created. Just as systems constitute wholes greater than the sum of the constituent parts, so do emergent levels in a system. Higher-order levels can function top-down and influence lower-order levels, and vice versa, in a process of circular causality. In doing so, the levels involved are subject to change, and the potential for new levels emerging in the process heightens. For example, psychologically, cognitive structures might exist to help perceive and filter the external world, and these influence goals, actions, predictions, etc. Nevertheless, a layer of appraisals might mediate the cognitive-behavior link and causally act on both the cognitions higher up and the behaviors lower down in the system. Or, instead of this type of vertical (new level) emergence in a system due to circular causality, an anchored component or axis in the system of elements involved within a level. For example, a child's suite of concepts within a domain, such as numbers, might circularly interact with other components within the domain (necessarily within the level) and disperse its skill-set over the domain and even related ones.

The question of possible differentially functioning and complex levels in a system speaks to the question of reductionism of one upper level of a system to another lower one. Piagetians would argue that cognitive structures have functional impacts and are not just logico-mathematical creations to explain thinking and behavior. Similarly, higher-order cognitions can differentially characterize thinking and have causal impact on thought and behavior. The mental cannot be reduced to the molecule, the neurochemical, the neural structure and its workings, and so on. The patient's mind is as relevant to understanding psychiatric disorder as any aberrant neurophysiology or brain function.

Networks

As much as NLDST offers a plausible mechanistic process of how (sub)stages might arise in development, the risk is that it is not specific enough in terms of how components of a system express tension that lead to tendencies toward change. Systems normally are conservative and resist change perturbations. Systems are adaptive in because they accommodate system dynamics, fit context, adjust, and maintain equilibrium gravitating to what has worked (assimilate rather than changing full-scale in wholesale accommodation). When systems change to perturbation in the sense of adopting new states, they adapt as much as is the case when they resist such change. In both cases, adaptation is online and highly responsive (as the label dynamic would imply). But the concept of adaptation in this sense is missing what might be the drivers of the fit involved. What are the key control parameters of system change? How did their thresholds evolve to current criteria, what is their exact relation to other system components? Are they internal like having a fever or external like the environment being too hot? What is the nature of their coupling to other components of the system and how do other components of the system couple? In component coupling, which is the driver of any pair? When coupling gets complex and multiple, as in networks, the ambiguity in the answers offered for these types of questions would magnify.

To answer these types of questions, network modeling (Borsboom 2008) might offer solutions. Network concepts could work well to help explain how system elements configure and reconfigure in system states and their adaptive evolution.

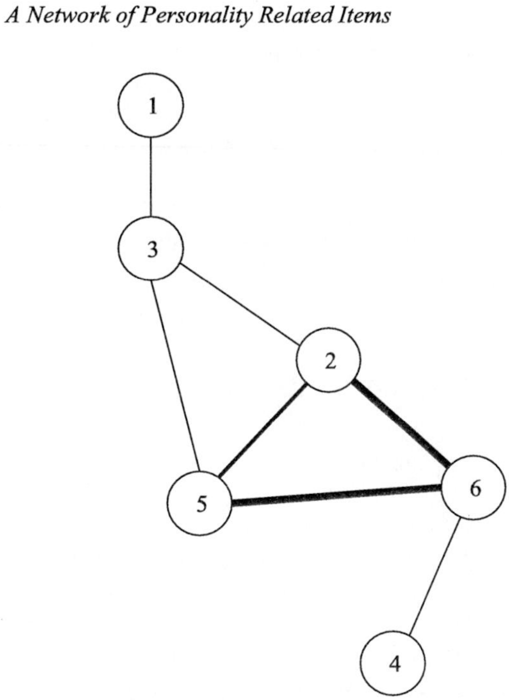

Fig. 3.1 A network of personality-related items The network approach to behavior specifies critical behaviors within sets of behavior, referred to as nodes, and critical relationships across behaviors, referred to as edges Nodes represent behaviors: Edges represent the empirical correlations between behaviors. Numbers in nodes refer to specific behaviors. A stronger correlation is represented by a thicker and darker edge. (Adapted from Schmittmann et al. (2013) based on Epskamp et al. (2011), slightly modified; Adapted from Young (2016) [Figure 7.9, pp. 172])

Figure 3.1 gives a hypothetical example of a network of behaviors/symptoms related to personality traits. The personality trait could be a positive one, like assiduousness. Or, it could be a negative one, like neuroticism (an absence of stability), with individual nodes representing symptoms rather than behaviors. Correlations indicate the links in the network of behaviors (edges). It is understood the correlations are positive, which is a limitation in network analysis. There should be room for inhibitory links aside from activatory-related ones over behaviors/symptoms. The driver nodes are considered activatory or with feedback functions, but that is not depicted in the figure. For example, psychiatrically, poor sleep is a driver of other symptoms, as in PTSD. Later on in the work, I give the example of how cognitive structures can be represented as networks.

To repeat, networks include concepts such as nodes and hubs of elements as well as their linkages (edges). Moreover, empirical research can establish which couplings are primary and which elements are drivers. Network terms include ones that help specify the "centrality" of system elements. A network node or edge can express more centrality or less of it. That is, a node or edge in a network can vary in-betweenness, closeness, or degree in the system, depending on the connectivity involved. Also, nodes or edges can vary in core strength, or resistance to perturbation or change, in a concept akin to the equivalent one in systems theory. A network can express emergence due to causal interactions of nodes. Once more, the language of network modelling overlaps with the language used to describe systems.

But can networks provide the modeling necessary to show how system elements can interact to the point of organizing to a new hierarchic level in a system at issue, such as might obtain in the cognitive architecture of a child? Once more, further theoretical specification is needed, along with more precise mechanisms. How do elemental coupling and multiple component (re)configurations take place other than indicating that they fire sequentially or simultaneously as in neuronal networks? Is there a more general language that specifies how coupling can take place in a system (and decoupling)?

Activation-Inhibition Coordination

As previously described, Young's concept of activation-inhibition coordination provides an inroad to solving the riddle of how system elements might (de)couple as they coordinate in patterns that define states in state space maneuvers. As a generalized explanatory and causal mechanism, activation-inhibition coordination indicates the most basic processes involved in organismic/living entity function. Although I developed the concept from observing the reaching of neonates, it applies to how any behavior might organize and any subservient substrate, such as underlying neuronal activity, might organize. The concept of activation-inhibition coordination (or its lack or dysfunction) can help explain any level of behavior and its organization. Moreover, the concept also explains any level of brain and its organization, the neurobiological linkages and orchestration between them. In this sense, it is an ideal concept to help describe the linkages in networks and how they function.

As for applying the concept of activation-inhibition coordination to network modeling concepts, nodes are considered activation points for the most part, but they need to be conceptually reconceived and empirically tested as activation-inhibition coordination foci. Certainly, hubs and larger modules also should reflect this characteristic. Similarly, edges (links) between nodes, as well as higher-order linkages related to centrality, small worlds, rich clubs, and so on, can be informed and reworked by the activation-inhibition coordination concept. The concept also applies to larger social networks, such as mother-child, family-children, children-school/neighborhood, adult-partner, person-friend, cultural group-society, and so on. Activation-inhibition coordination can be viewed as a skill that can be developed, implemented, monitored, revised, and so on, at multiple levels of the person both within and without, both interior and exterior, etc.

Biopsychosocial

Unifying causality requires viewing it from multiple perspectives and multiple levels. Moreover, it is a project that can never arrive at a finite end because the conceptual and empirical knowledge base keeps expanding and revising. Even in this present work, I have expanded the causality concepts involved, as described in the last paragraph of the prior section. I have tried to find the most basic cross-cutting concepts in these regards as applied to psychology, such as the biopersonalsocial model, nonlinear dynamical systems theory, network modeling, and the mechanism of activation-inhibition coordination. The default option might be the first one of the biopsychosocial model; it is more general and uses a less technical language.

A good portion of the three Young books (2011, 2016, 2019) on development and causality deal with the range of biological, psychological (personal), and social (environmental, ecological) influences on development. They, too, can be viewed as coupling and decoupling according to activation-inhibition coordination mechanisms. In the end, no matter the source, causal factors or influences on behavior and its development do not act in isolation. Influences exert dynamic effects in concert with each other. Different levels within any biological, psychological (personal), and social and related spheres of behavioral influence can also be viewed from a (de)coupling and activation-inhibition coordination perspective. The biopsychosocial concept has been criticized because it is too vague. However, in rehabilitation, it refers to dealing with each of the components rather than just one or the other in isolation when treating people. Causally, it reminds us that dealing with only one aspect of component influences on behavior will not give a full picture of the phenomenon at issue, as with the case for patients who require a whole-person therapeutic perspective.

Moreover, traditional areas or topics within each of the three spheres in the biopsychosocial model can be analyzed in-depth. Establishing exhaustive compendia of factors within each of the biopsychosocial spheres serves well the study of causality because their reciprocal and interactive effects need to be elucidated. In the absence of more rigorous methods, such as with randomized control trials (RCTs) and other experimental procedures. These procedures are often ethically contraindicated, causal study in psychology focuses on graphing these multiple biopsychosocial influences on behavior by using arrows joining boxes, and with strength of multiple regression findings indicated, as well. Rather than criticizing the lack of more precise modeling processes, the causal graphing of behavior and its effects is an important focus, perhaps the best in the circumstances. But such graphing without being comprehensive in examining multiple cross-domain influences and interactions on behavior will be limited in validity. For example, at the biological level, it makes no sense to consider psychological/psychiatric causation without considering the brain/neuroscience, evolution (evo-devo-eco), genetics, epigenetics, and so on. At the psychological level, the mediation of behavioral output by personal factors such as personality, intelligence, coping skills, and proclivities toward vulnerability (susceptibility) vs. resilience requires careful consideration and investigation.

Generally, contemporary understanding of causality in psychology leads to a multifactorial approach to causal agents on behavior. It's not that biology and environment, brain and experience, N × N, and so on are in separate causal slots and meet in co-action. Rather, the co-action is intrinsic to their relationship and their reciprocal relations guide and lead behavioral causation. Moreover, the role of the person her/himself in psychological causality illustrates the personal contribution of the self to an active construction of the psychology of the self. Piaget described cognitive development as an active construction, and he leaned toward dynamical explanations of cognitive development as he learned more about it. In this sense, he presaged major themes considered predominant in the present unifying psychological causality project.

Evolution

Evolution is a biological process that refers to adaptation and change through survival, reproduction, and fit to the environment (ecological niche). It occurs when an extant phenotype of the individual organism involved produces more offspring than competitor conspecifics due to adaptive characteristics for the niche at hand, underwritten by its genotype. The result is that the individual organism involved passes on its adaptive genes concerning the ecological niche that "helped" select them. This process leads to the proliferation of the genotype in the species involved, to the point that the changes that had evolved might propagate novel speciation.

Evolution is not teleological; it does not necessarily lead to more complex phenotypic expression or to new species in speciation. It is flexible to environmental contingencies, and adaptation to ecological niche drives the evolutionary process.

Genes predispose; the environment disposes, and hearkening back to the active self in phenotypic construction, the person "composes." So, evolution is not a passive, laborious process waiting for adaptive rather than deleterious mutations to drive a stagnant genotype and its phenotypic outcome. As much as the biopersonal-social model makes sense in understanding behavioral causation, the same model applies to the evolutionary causation that factors into the formula.

Despite these types of accommodations to understanding evolution, it is still driven by natural selection, which functions to increase the survival and reproduction of the individual organism with an adaptive trait; it is not a group selection process for the most part. For example, co-operation might benefit another social party, but normally self-interest describes the ultimate nature of the benefit involved. Altruism might help a person not related genetically to the helper, but tabs are kept, and altruism becomes reciprocal to the benefit of the initiating altruist.

I have developed a five-step model of the evolution of evolution that considers these evolutionary forces, including kin selection. In the model, I consider each different force as a reflection of natural or organismic selection favoring the individual involved for the phenotypic trait promoted evolutionarily except in the case of group selection. The model refers to the evolution of evolutionary forces a process of an increasing gene co-opting to complement individual-level natural selection. Moreover, in the model, group behavior might not involve only group selection because social (group) behaviors can ultimately reflect self-interest. So, for one of the five evolutionary forces in the model, I coined the term "group-for-individual" selection to distinguish it from "individual-for-group" selection. The latter refers to classic group selection, but the former term is novel. It refers to when the group acts for individuals, such as in teaching, educating, and creating formal schooling, which is a recent historical development. In hunter-gatherer societies, in nonhuman primate groupings, and so on, group structure facilitates individual learning. In my understanding, the group will behave this way, not especially for the group's evolutionary benefit but because the individuals in the group, through having their offspring participate in the education offered derive added survival (and reproductive) advantage.

Evolution itself evolves, and that process can be referred to as dynamic evolution. Species might be more prone to evolution than others, as in evolvability. Darwin's ideas evolved in his lifetime and continue to evolve to the present, in a process of dynamic Darwinism.

Human Exceptionalism

This brings us to the question of human exceptionalism, and multiple hypotheses have been offered. In my own work, in this regard, I have emphasized the teaching/education function of humans. I also have emphasized the concrete operational and abstract/postformal Piagetian (sub)stage acquisitions that humans express. Many animals, especially nonhuman primates, exhibit tool use, language, and other behaviors that have been considered human exceptionalism markers. However, the limited range of teaching/formal education in this regard speaks better to what makes humans human. Indeed, the present book and the research and books on which it is based illustrate that not only that we might be *Homo Causa* but, in addition, we are *Homo Educator*; further, our offspring might be equally conditioned evolutionally to partake in this relatively advanced learning process reciprocally.

Epigenesis

Genetics has been complemented by epigenetics in how genes might change within a lifetime and be transmitted to progeny. In epigenetic processes, the promoter regions of genes are silenced, often through DNA methylation. In the epigenetic mechanism, genes are silenced through effects of the environment, for example, because of maternal stress prenatally. Often, the regions susceptible to methylation effects in DNA are involved in transcription and protein production related to the brain and neurotransmitters, including aspects crucial to mental health. The effect of the environment on genes, in the right circumstances (and with epigenetically modifiable alleles involved), illustrates flexibility in gene translation into phenotype including behaviorally/mentally.

Gene Interactions

Genes do not produce their protein production transcriptions, through RNA messaging from DNA, directly without environmental contextual influences. First, genes are not expressed in isolation (being co-genes). Genes are regulated by how they lead to phenotypic characteristics that interact with the environment, and the effect of other genes in their function is recognized. Second, other ways that genes do not express transposition into behavior linearly, and with little variation in the throughput processes involved, concern—(a) gene-environment correlation of the active type (r G × E); (b) Gene × Environment interactions (G × E); and (c) differential allelic sensitivity to the environment (Belsky and Pluess 2009).

In active gene-environment correlation (r G × E), the proclivities of the growing child act on the caregivers involved, who respond to the child by tailoring the environment to the child. For example, in a piano-playing family, to the parents' surprise, one sibling might differ from the others and request vocal lessons instead of piano lessons, which she has said is boring. This type of gene-environment correlation illustrates that the child has a role to play in her/his own development, and development does not just reflect Nature and Nurture (N × N). As argued previously, a broad model that might capture this active contribution of the self to one's own development could be called the biopersonalsocial model.

G × E interaction does not refer to the vague formula that potential genetic and environmental effects on behavior each accumulate and influence behavior. That type of statement is a given, something like N × N interact in development.

Rather, G × E interactions refer to how specific alleles will affect behavior (or morphology) only when specific environments are also present. If an allele of a gene confers susceptibility to antisocial behavior, for example, the allele will exert its influence only if environmental maltreatment or the like is also present, for example.

Instead of this most general and incorrect interpretation of G × E, the actual interpretation of G × E is that both types of influence on behavior (both the G and E factors) must be present for the interaction to have an effect. That is, in G × E, a particular allele (or set of alleles) must be present and also act in concert with a particular environmental (e.g., parental) mediator, such as early adversity or early maltreatment. If the indicated allele (or allele set) is present without the concomitant early abuse, the outcome for the child and adult will not differ compared to members of the relevant control group. Similarly, if early maltreatment is present but without the presence of the at risk allele or allele set, the child develops normally, when compared to controls. This type of genetic effect illustrates that G × E functions in a combinational rather than additive, cumulative way.

In differential sensitivity, the G × E effect is qualified by findings indicating that, in supportive environments, the at-risk allele (and the susceptibility that it promotes) does not lead to just outcomes equivalent to those in the relevant control group but also to superior positive outcomes. That is, in susceptible individuals, a positive environment promotes superior development beyond the normative outcome. This type of finding has led researchers to qualify vulnerability models involving these types of alleles as susceptibility models. The index allele begets more positive outcomes in favorable early environments or more negative outcomes (e.g., antisocial behavior, delinquency, criminality) in unfavorable early environments. This type of modeling process has been labeled the dandelion-orchid hypothesis. However, the term does not capture the effect of negative environments on "orchid" alleles, so I referred to the label in the differential susceptibility model as the dandelion-(wilting) orchid model.

To sum up, genes exist in multiple interactions with each other. The classic gene by environment interaction (G × E) often involves G × G × E interactions (as well as G × E × E ones, further complicating matters). Moreover, illustrating the exquisite complexity involved in gene action, G × E also could involve differential allelic sensitivity to the environment such that the direction of the effect of the environment could be positive and not only negative when the environment acts positively. This has been called the dandelion-orchid hypothesis. When the susceptible allele is not present, the positive or negative effects of the environment do not occur (most of us are so-called dandelions and not susceptible orchids).

Environment

Aside from hard-core biological/medical model/brain-neuronal networking enthusiasts who adhere to reductionist, exclusionary, eliminative positions, most workers in the field are moderately aware of the environmental/social effects as much as the biological in behavioral determination.

Socially, the role of parents, family, schools, neighborhood, socioeconomic status (SES), racism, poverty, work, political environment, culture, and so on, all require reflection and study for causality. Moreover, the social is always affected by personal perceptions; for example, one's sense of social aloneness varies with personal qualitative evaluation more than quantitative social contacts. According to Young (2011), we live in relational meaning worlds and do not exist in social vacuums; we grow through co-appropriation. The world acts as a social buffer and creates with us co-schemes/co-representations and co-operations. Our needs are co-needs or mutually derived and satisfied. Society produces co-memes. The I is never alone but is a "We." The Me is an "Us." In this sense, each of us is a IWEMEUS. Our existence is a co-existence. Our meaning is relational. Our growth is by and through the other for the other as much as the self. Our responsibilities are never-ending and co-relational. In this sense, they are co-responsibilities.

One more area in which the role of the environment in development appears crucial is when it "gets under the skin." This refers to social genomics. The social world can regulate gene expression, such as through perceived loneliness, which is a health risk factor. Therefore, humans are "meta-organisms." Note that social genomics does not refer to G × E phenomena, gene silencing in epigenesis, and so on. Rather, it concerns the effects on the stress response, immune system, etc., as regulated by gene expression.

Activation-Inhibition Coordination Again

This causality project being described in the present work has supported the mechanistic working of activation-inhibition coordination as a causal mechanism in behavior expression. Inhibition is ubiquitous in behavioral control and expression, and behavioral activation needs the balance of inhibition. When behavior is sensitized to activate without proper inhibitory balance, it could be impulsive, uncontrolled, off-target, spontaneous and interfering, and so on. When behavior is too inhibited, it could be tentative, slow, withdrawn, or even absent when called for. The activation-inhibition coordination mechanism being proposed is a generalized mechanism applicable to behavior, brain, neuron, and so on. Indeed, the brain has been described as integrating behavioral activation systems and behavioral inhibition systems. Moreover, one can conceive personality tendencies, traits, and disorders in terms of different activation, inhibition, and activation-inhibition coordination patterns. A major way of conceiving personality relates to the dichotomy between exteriorization and interiorization, and a similar major way of conceiving psychopathology also involves externalization and internalization. Animal behavior boils down to approach and withdrawal (as well as freezing). All these examples implicate activation-inhibition coordination mechanisms. The frontal lobes are considered a seat of inhibitory function, and aberrant inhibitory function in this regard has been related to attention deficit hyperactivity disorder (ADHD). New additions to the Diagnostic and Statistical Manual of Mental Disorders, fifth edition (DSM-5; American Psychiatric Association 2013), include intermittent explosive disorder, which must express an inhibitory deficit. However, the coordination of inhibition with activation appears the seat of the primary deficit in these regards.

Aside from these telling examples of how the activation-inhibition coordination mechanism can help explain (developing) behavior (and its difficulties/abnormalities), one should consider the micro-moment to micro-moment flow of behavior in context as reflecting a constant interplay of activation, inhibition, and their intercoordination. The major example that I have provided so far, and it served as the basis for formulation of the hypothesis that activation-inhibition coordination is a central mechanism across the different layers of brain, behavior, and their relations, has concerned the directed reaching and ensuing grasping of the neonate. That behavior reflects an exquisite activation-inhibition coordination for the behavior plan involved to be put into effect successfully. The coordination involved in this behavior seems an ongoing dynamic, adjustable, and so on.

Also, activation-inhibition coordination processes seem to take place in concert with and are linked through contextual and social relationships. For example, the social (intersubjective) dance of mother and baby requires the exquisite, refined, quick, and subtle activation-inhibition coordination dynamic that characterizes the baby's fine motor skill behavior. Also, the older infant expressing inter-coordinated synchrony with the caregiver in attachment-related secure contact seeking, acquisition, and maintenance (think of reaching up to a cuddle on the shoulder) seems to evidence the same advanced activation-inhibition coordination socially.

Activation-inhibition coordination as a binding mechanism can also apply to linkages in cognitive development. For example, cognitively, the child is developing constructions in multiple domains. Both within and across them, activation-inhibition coordination coupling can relate them, integrate them, distance one from the other, and so on. The child uses executive functions, including working memory in goal setting and problem resolution in these domains; and, once more, the skills involved are amenable to analysis by activation-inhibition coordination. In this regard, inhibitory control is a classic executive function. Additionally, working memory is essential for executive deployment and problem resolution. Working memory would seem to be honed by adaptive activation-inhibition coordination (think keeping the question at hand in the background while foreground problem-resolution attempts are underway).

Young has developed the strong hypothesis that the left hemisphere is specialized for activation-inhibition coordination no matter the area of cognitive application. It underwrites rapid, advanced, and ongoing activation-inhibition coordination in behavior, such as in infant right-handed reaching/grasping. The right hemisphere's inhibitory functions are less complex, such as in outright inhibition, or less complex or prolonged activation-inhibition coordination, and so on. The activation-inhibition coordination model of left hemisphere function is consistent with other left hemisphere models specialization in the field, such as the left hemisphere being better at analysis, fine motor and language skills, approach, or positive emotions, and so on. Also, the skills attributed to the right hemisphere, such as spatial and holistic integration ones, are consistent with the left hemisphere activation-inhibition coordination model. These skills would appear to require less of that type of coordination than the ones being associated with left hemisphere function. Moreover, the left hemisphere would appear to specialize in activation-inhibition coordination of the right hemisphere and its functioning, thereby being the overall hemisphere integration organizer.

Laterality

Introduction

The posited model of left hemisphere activation-inhibition coordination has been illustrated with early right-hand reaching-grasping behavior. This is consistent with models of laterality development that the hemispheres are specialized in a way equivalent to the adult beginning right from birth, if not before (Vannasing et al. 2016). The data show that, even prenatally, both brain and behavior evidence asymmetries that are consistent with the invariant model of lateralization and not the contrasting one of early equipotential lateralization. That said, the brain keeps developing its neuronal interconnectivities, although these, too, might be more efficiently achieved in the left hemisphere, as per its specialization needs. These findings have led me to develop a left hemisphere specialization model that I refer to as an integrative invariant progressive lateralization model of early laterality. Box 3.1 (which includes Table 3.1) provides a review of the differential left and right hemisphere skills according to the activation-inhibition coordination hypothesis. The left hemisphere is more specialized for this function, according to the model.

Box 3.1 Activation-Inhibition Coordination

Young has applied the activation-inhibition coordination mechanism to help explain left and right hemisphere functional differences (see Table 3.1). Specifically, the left hemisphere is specialized for any behavior or function, including in information processing, which demands immediate, ongoing, and millisecond-by-millisecond integration of the activation and inhibitory processes that govern the behavior/function and its workings. It does not engage in simpler activation and inhibition coordinations, nor does it engage in outright inhibition without activation for the most part. These alternate activation and inhibition functions are specialized in the right hemisphere. The hemispheres work together, but with the left hemisphere governing that control through its cross-hemisphere inhibitory skills.

Table 3.1 Different types of activation-inhibition functions in the left and right cerebral hemisphere

Hemisphere	Type	Description
Left	Longer term synchrony	Complex, sophisticated, interweaving (see next)
	Sophisticated synchrony	Sophisticated, subtle interweaving of activation and inhibitory skills, with appropriate activations taking place because of the suppression of interference due to inappropriate alternative behavior, both when selecting adaptive goal-directed activity and during its (movement) transitions. Both subtle competing movements and gross interfering ones are countered and controlled
	Altering synchrony	Majorly modifying/disrupting sequential activation-inhibition coordinations
Right	Adjusting synchrony	Minorly adapting/refining sequential activation-inhibition coordinations [could be left hemisphere based, depending on context]
	Long damping	Full suppression/damping activity over time
	Short synchrony	Activation-inhibition synchrony instantaneously or for a short time period. In spatial processes, some information as figure highlighted and some as ground moderated

The left hemisphere specializes in a sophisticated interweaving of activation and inhibitory skills. Activation-inhibition coordination especially involves the suppression of interference due to inappropriate alternative behavior, both when selecting adaptive goal-directed activity and during its (movement) transitions (e.g., in language and in fine motor activities)
Adapted from Young (1990a, b, 2011, 2016)

The 2019 Young book presented a comprehensive literature review on early lateralization that supports the activation-inhibition model of left hemisphere specialization development. Also, it examined other relevant models. Briefly, a selection from the literature review indicates the following.

Development

Even at 18 weeks of gestational age, the right hand moves faster toward the eye/mouth regions (Parma et al. 2017). Young and Gagnon (1990) found that 2-day olds differentially turn their heads to low-intensity speech and music sounds (matched) coming from behind them. The speech compared to the music sounds elicited more rightward, turning already at this age, consistent with an early left hemisphere language-related specialization. Fagard et al. (2016) reviewed studies on early reflexes being stronger on the right for the hand and arm. Nagy et al. (2014) found that 2-day olds imitated finger movements (a spatial task) better with the left hand.

Morange-Majoux et al. (2013) found that in 20-week olds, grasping latency was shorter with the right hand. Six-month olds used the right hand more in object acquisition and manipulation (e.g., Michel et al. 2014). Similarly, at 12 months, Potier et al. (2012) found that the right hand excelled in grasping, removing, and transferring objects. For 1- and 2-year olds, the right hand appears specialized for eating type behaviors (e.g., Gonzalez et al. 2015).

As for hemisphere specialization for emotions, positive ones appear specialized in the left hemisphere right from an early age (for 4-month olds, Hane et al. 2008; for 8-month olds, Missana and Grossmann 2014). These findings are consistent with an approach or valence model of hemispheric specialization for emotions, and they are consistent with an activation-inhibition coordination underpinning that specialization.

If the left hemisphere allows for better activation-inhibition coordination along the lines described, the question arises whether its neuronal architecture relative to the right hemisphere, even early in life, supports this skill. In this regard, Ratnarajah et al. (2013) studied asymmetry in the structural connectivity of the neonate brain. They used diffuse tensor imaging (DTI) scan methodology, examining white matter axonal pathways. Findings revealed more efficient left hemisphere structural connectivity, such as better left hemisphere intra-regional integration and "between centrality" connectivity. The authors stated that the left hemisphere appears to possess more efficient circuitry allowing quicker information transfer and flow. These results comport with an early left hemisphere specialization for activation-inhibition coordination.

The left hemisphere specialization for language develops early, and the more manual laterality is right-sided, the more there are associations with language measures, even longitudinally. Mumford and Kita (2016) found that, in 1-year olds, right-hand pointing was related to a larger receptive vocabulary. Nelson et al. (2017) found a relationship between right-hand role differentiated bimanual manipulation at 2 years of age and language scores (expressive) 1 year later. Nelson et al. (2017) referred to Michel's (2012) cascade model of lateralization involving transfer of laterality in one behavior at one age to other behaviors at other ages (e.g., early head turning side predicts later handedness side). In Young (2019), I argued that the cascade model of lateralization could apply both within and across domains.

Causality

Causality needs to be examined at multiple levels. This approach need not imply a reductionist model involving lower-order levels, such as genetics and biophysiological mechanisms, explaining in full any higher-order level. Rather, each causal system's level contribute to the full causal picture, interact accordingly, and stand intrinsically as part of the causal determinants of behavior. Higher-order levels contribute uniquely to the causation of behavior beyond contributions in this regard from lower-order levels.

I have presented comprehensive causal models, such as the biopsychosocial (biopersonalsocial) one, and very specific causal mechanisms, even if generalized, such as activation-inhibition coordination. The broader the model, the more room for criticism that it lacks specifics, is vague, and so on. But a full exploration of causal factors in behavioral determination needs both types of causal modeling. This integrative approach to causal modeling of behavior applies to the premiere example of a causal study in the three Young books (2011, 2016, 2019)—that of the development and evolution of laterality. In particular, Young (2019) analyzed the causal influences suggested for laterality development and showed that the area of study could use a broader perspective.

Most humans are right-handed, but the proportion varies across cultures (Porac 2016). For example, in Japan, parents strongly encourage right-hand use in their children (Schmitz et al. 2017). Michel (2018) described parental shaping of their infants' handedness. The experience that affects handedness could be intrinsic, as when early sensorimotor experiences reinforce right-side use tendencies (Ocklenburg and Güntürkün 2017). Or, the experiences could be extrinsic, even prenatally. Reissland et al. (2014) found that prenatal maternal stress related to left-hand touching in fetuses. Postnatally, mothers prefer to hold their babies on the left side of their bodies (Ocklenburg et al. 2018).

Postnatally, both chronic and acute stress are related to right hemisphere function or shifting to its function (Ocklenburg et al. 2016). Rozin et al. (2016) found a right hemisphere bias for face processing in Asian groups. Generally, hemispheric specialization appears subject to experiential influence, although perhaps not as drastically as handedness.

Genetically, simple Mendelian models of handedness no longer hold currency (e.g., the right-shift model of Annett 1985). Moreover, heritability estimates for handedness are not elevated (Schmitz et al. 2017). Candidate genes explain minimal variance, and research supporting any one of them is not necessarily replicated.

Genetic handedness models currently are more polygenetic, as found in GWAS research (genome-wide association studies; Armour et al. 2014).

In seeking causal models involving genetic influences on handedness, the environment's complementary role needs to be considered beyond factors such as culture and parenting. Specifically, the environment can silence genes through the process of epigenesis, for example, by DNA methylation in the promoter region of genes (see Leach et al. 2014; Schmitz et al. 2018).

Evolution

Introduction. The evolution of lateralization appears not to have one pathway without interruption involving either an early lateralization that did not change over evolutionary time or multiple changes that revealed clear linkages. Rather, different lateralizations (manual, cerebral) might have had different evolutionary courses; the lateralization involved might have taken place through differential sweeps. This notion is consistent with findings in humans that handedness, lateralized manual skills (manual specialization), hemispheric specialization, and other bodily lateralities, including embryonically, are not consistently related to each other.

The right-side bias in animals is evolutionarily old. Babcock and Robison (1989) found that fossilized trilobite remains evidenced by a ratio of 3:1 for right:left dorsal bite marks. These ancient creatures swam in rivers, were attacked from behind, and appear to have swerved to the right to avoid predators. Alternately, their predators might have tended to bite on the right side; the fossils with this right-bias pattern date to 500 million years ago in the Cambrian period.

Multiple contemporary animal species exhibit a lateral bias. For example, European toads use the right forepaw to swipe. Nevertheless, most findings on animal brains support a right hemisphere dominance, for example, honey bees have better olfactory memories on the right side of the brain (Bisazza et al. 1997; Rogers and Vallortigara 2008; respectively). The right side of the brain's spatial skills could be responsible for these types of findings (large-scale information processing and navigation skills; Vallortigara and Versace 2017).

The earliest humans (hominins) appear to have manifested right-handedness (Frayer 2016). Our immediate ancestors (including Neanderthals) also appeared to express right-hand dominance in complex bimanual manipulations, as do contemporary hunter-gatherers in tool-based tasks (Steele and Uomini 2009; Cavanagh et al. 2016, respectively).

As for contemporary nonhuman primates, chimpanzees generally are right-handed for behaviors such as throwing and gesturing (Corballis 2014). The youngest chimpanzees in the Bakoun forest of Guinea used the right hand in tool use activity (to get algae in water). Hopkins (2006) noted that neonatal chimpanzees show right-sided grasping (Fagot and Bard 1995). Generally, nonhuman primates exhibit a right-side preference for unimanual inanimate, object-directed behavior, and gesturing (Forrester 2017; Vallortigara and Versace 2017, respectively). Meguerditchian et al. (2015) emphasized general nonhuman primate right-hand skills for precision grasping with the thumb and index finger and also for complex coordinated bimanual behavior (in the tube task).

Models. Evolutionary models of lateralization vary in terms of the locus of the phenotypic variation that could help account for lateralization differences within and across extinct and extant species. Some models emphasize manual behavior as the driver; others put stress on manual gestures, language, or more general skills. These hypotheses reach the core issue of what exactly differentiates left and right hemispheric skill and specialization in humans.

Forrester (2017) speculated that the left hemisphere's function in great ape nonhuman primates relates to undertaking supra-modal hierarchical processing, which facilitates efficiency in sequential organization. The latter applies to efficient motor and speech behavior, so it is a generalized skill. In an earlier work, Forrester et al. (2015) referred to the left hemisphere being specialized for executive, top-down control of routine behavioral sequences (e.g., in approach, in feeding; i.e., foraging, prey capture, and manipulating nutrient sources). In contrast, the right hemisphere is specialized for processing novel or urgent stimuli (such as in predator avoidance). Other models are less behavior-oriented and more top-down, allowing attainment of goal state (Forrester et al. 2013); intentionality (Cochet and Byrne 2013); predictivity (Sainburg 2014); social target differentiation or cognitive differentiation (Vallortigara and Versace 2017), and attentional (perceptual) differentiation (Rogers et al. 2013). For Rogers et al. (2013), the left hemisphere is specialized for attending to the features (local, similarities, invariances) of stimuli in order to establish category/class membership established by learned rule-based strategies. These properties are accompanied by more specific memory recall and sustained response. To accomplish its ends, the left hemisphere controls distraction, arousal, and right hemisphere activity. In contrast, the right hemisphere attends to variable, novel stimuli features, even if minuscule, allowing for more distraction and global memory, as in spatial functioning and rapid response and arousal to emergencies.

Sainburg's predictivity model is like the attentional model of differential hemispheric functioning (Sainburg 2014). It focuses on left hemisphere predictive skill in motor behavior in terms of body/environment dynamics so that motor trajectories are more precise and coordinated. In contrast, the right hemisphere specializes in error control. Recent neuroscientific research supports the view that the left hemisphere is better at prediction (Avenanti et al. 2017) and efficiency (denser regions of information processing, information segregation; Agcaoglu et al. 2015; Avena-Koenigsberger et al. 2016; respectively).

Sweeps. Evolution of lateralization of function might have proceeded in evolutionary sweeps, with different selective pressures at different evolutionary epochs effecting different lateralizations (Laland 2008). Moreover, culture appears to be involved as a co-director of lateralization evolution. A gene-culture co-evolution in dextralization appears to have been the interactive selective driver involved. The co-evolutionary (gene-culture) model of lateralization (dextralization) speaks to causal models, generally, such as the biopsychosocial one. That is even evolutionarily; culture represents a parallel interactive influence. It would be interesting to determine whether great ape cultural transmission (to offspring), such as in use of tools to capture termites, involves (right-side) manual lateralization and/or (left-side) hemisphere lateralization.

In this sense, early arboreal prosimians might have been right hand (the left hemisphere) dominant for postural support, but later in evolution, the postural support function became left-handed (MacNeilage 2014). There are multiple ways of explaining the shift, for example, postural support in arboreal prosimians species is more demanding manually than the food acquisition it permits for the nonsupportive hand, and so the right hand was preferred for this function. Later on, postural support proved less demanding than the fine motor manipulation involved in the nonsupportive hand, and so was undertaken by the right instead of the left hemisphere. A complementary interpretation is that the arboreal foraging by early prosimians was a spatial function more than an end-process manipulative one and so tapped the spatial skills of the right hemisphere. Later, the manipulation in the food-seeking became paramount relative to the spatial function, and so the switch evolutionarily took place as described.

Common Factors. Of course, these two explanations could overlap and not be opposites. Both could be explained by a more general third aspect, which is what the present model underlines. The left hemisphere is specialized for activation-inhibition coordination, which was the case throughout evolution. The right hemisphere handles skills that are less complex, making it conducive to executing the spatial function compared to the fine motor manipulative one. Thus, when arboreal support is more complex in terms of activation-inhibition coordination than foraging/manipulating, the left hemisphere is involved. The reverse obtains when it is less complex in this regard (whether evolutionarily or developmentally).

A major debate in the evolution of lateralization in hominids relates to whether tools, gestural communication, language, or other drivers promoted the evolution. This begs the question of whether common factors can explain each of these proposed drivers and that the evolution of lateralization preceded these hominid functions and involved something more general and different. For example, Corballis (2014) maintained that the common precursor involved in the prosimian case is left hemisphere specialization for "action dynamics," which applies to grammar-like communication. Other models prefer to emphasize gestures as the overriding evolutionary driver in dextralization (Cochet and Byrne 2013). For example, great apes use the right upper limb to gesture intentions. Another model in this regard supports the evolutionary pressure of bimanual coordination in tool use as driving dextralization. For example, chimpanzees and gorillas demonstrate right-hand action toward inanimate objects (Forrester et al. 2011, 2012). Häberling et al. (2016) postulated that initial left hemisphere specialization in early hominids involved an action-based function that bifurcated into a language-related one and a manual one that included observation and execution of manual actions (involving the mirror neuron system). In all these cases, the argument could be made that activation-inhibition coordination underwrites them.

Brain

Developmental research on brain function and inhibition generally also supports the view that the right hemisphere is specialized for outright inhibition (when it is taking place without activation coordination) (e.g., Collette et al. 2005), while the left hemisphere is specialized for inhibition when it takes place in conjunction with activation coordination (e.g., Gilsbach et al. 2012; in the left frontal gyrus). Similar findings of right hemisphere inhibitory function were presented by Bartoli et al. (2017), Rubin et al. (2017), van Campen et al. (2018). Swick et al. (2008) considered that the left hemisphere plays a more critical inhibitory role than the right hemisphere as task complexity increases. Cerruti (2013) found that stimulating the left prefrontal cortex by anodal stimulation improved performance on a demanding verbal memory task, with similar results in the right homotopic region for cathodal stimulation. The authors referred to hemispheric neural connectivity involving facilitatory and inhibitory links. Grimshaw and Carmel (2014) have a somewhat analogous model of hemispheric specialization to Young's activation-inhibition coordination model (which is considered a left hemisphere function). For them, the left frontal cortex inhibits negative distractions and the right hemisphere positive ones (e.g., in addiction).

See Table 3.1 in Box 3.1 for the ways that Young (2019) posited that the left and right hemispheres differ in terms of inhibitory/activatory coordination skills. The model is consistent and with the activation-inhibition coordination model.

Modeling

In Young (2019), I presented other models that could help understand lateralization and related them to the activation-inhibition coordination model. For example, the latter process could be how neural and brain region network connectivity becomes more complex and integrated over developmental or evolutionary time. Also, attractors might help explain left-right hemisphere functional differences and consequent manual ones, including in any shifting involved, and this might help explain developmental and evolutionary lateralization changes. (Cox and Smitsman (2018) also proposed a dynamical view of "handedness strength.") Nevertheless, attractors themselves might express activation-inhibition coordination mechanisms at work. Embodiment models have been applied developmentally; for example, representations are tied to actions. This type of modeling has not been applied to lateralization, although it could have currency in this regard. For example, activation-inhibition coordination links over manual behavior, gesture/symbolic activity, and so on could reflect nodes of embodied foci that interlink through action.

Generally, the study of causality in development emphasizes the multifactorial nature of causality. Similarly, causal modeling must be multifactorial and borrow from all relevant models in an integrated, unifying project in which new concepts and empirical findings are continually integrated. Laterality research needs to be open to the novel models presented in my work on causality and development. Several innovations have been presented in this regard (or emphases on good models not yet applied (much) to the question, e.g., on attractors) such that the study of laterality, its development, and its evolution can expand in its causal modeling and research.

Free Will

The 2016 Young book, the second in the three-book series on the theme of Causality and Development, especially concentrated on the topic of causality. The book considered integrating causality in psychology from multiple perspectives toward integrating them, yet focused on several major themes. Aside from an underlying generic change mechanism of activation-inhibition coordination, and the systems, network, and embodiment approaches to causality, in particular, as well, it focused on the question of free will in behavior.

Most people believe that they have free will, and that belief has positive benefits psychologically (Baumeister 2008). In Young (2016), I proposed the concept of Freedom in Being, which is like the concept of Dasein (Han-Pile 2013). Figures 3.2 and 3.3 present the concept and its relation to causality. Ultimately, freedom in being concerns not only free will belief but also having a sense of free will. Both develop in the multiplicities of reciprocal engagement with the world as part of agentic (self) co-participation in the world, leading to some element of personal control (over, freedom in) the world. Generally, free will and its belief and sense are part of the multifactorial behavioral causality array that I refer to as biopsycho(personal)social causality.

Examining free will belief and having a sense of free will from a biological, psychological, and environmental perspective leads to related ways of treating them. In this sense, a cross-factor generic approach to treating behavioral causality involves the model of embodiment. Behavior is never divorced from its context nor its enactive (including sensorimotor) components. Therefore, even having a belief in free will and a sense of free will should be considered as linked to embodied factors. In this regard, in Young (2016), I referred to an embodied free will belief and an embodied sense of having free will. This speaks to the broader concepts of embodied free will and embodied free being or embodied freedom in being.

In Young (2016), I presented the concept of free will working models, which I related to the concept of working memory. They are cognitive/socio-affective modes or mindsets related to the growth of belief in free will and having a sense of free will

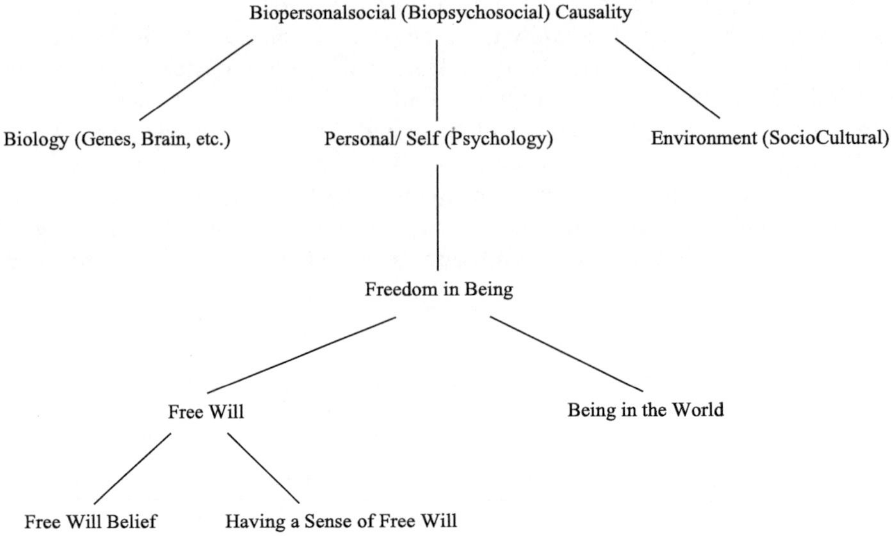

Fig. 3.2 Freedom in being as central to the causality of psychology
Free will is constituted by a cognitive component and by an affective component (free will belief, sense of free will, respectively). Freedom of being is a superordinate concept that includes free will and being in the world. Freedom in being stands at the apex of the suite of concepts on free will. Free will is an essential component of the personal, self-determined psychological forces in the causality of behavior, which are part of the multifactorial biopsychosocial (biopersonalsocial) influences on behavior. (Adopted with permission of Springer International Publishing. Young, G. (2016). *Unifying* causality *and psychology: Being, brain and behavior*. Cham, Switzerland: Springer International Publishing; with kind permission from Springer International Publishing. [Figure 3.5, pp. 60])

(feeling free). When deployed appropriately, they are part of growth toward psychological maturity or completeness (in a process of psychological completing). The concept can be used psychotherapeutically, as might the concept of belief in free will generally. In this regard, Young (2016) presented multiple tables that translate findings on belief in free will into therapeutic questions for patients. One example is that free will belief questions posed to patients might help in eliciting better meaning-making skills and more positive meanings as an outcome (see Table 3.2).

Some questionnaires address belief in free will, and the one of Paulhus and Carey (2011) is widely used. However, I found it too short and not covering the facets of belief in free will that I considered appropriate. Depending on research needs, investigators might want to use the questionnaire that I created on free will belief, or its final version once empirically researched (see Table 3.3). It consists of 35 items in 5 categories (cognitive, social-emotional, self, mental construction, action). The questionnaire illustrates how models that I propose in my work can be empirically investigated. Further, this diversified questionnaire on free will could help elucidate the role of free will belief in behavioral causation.

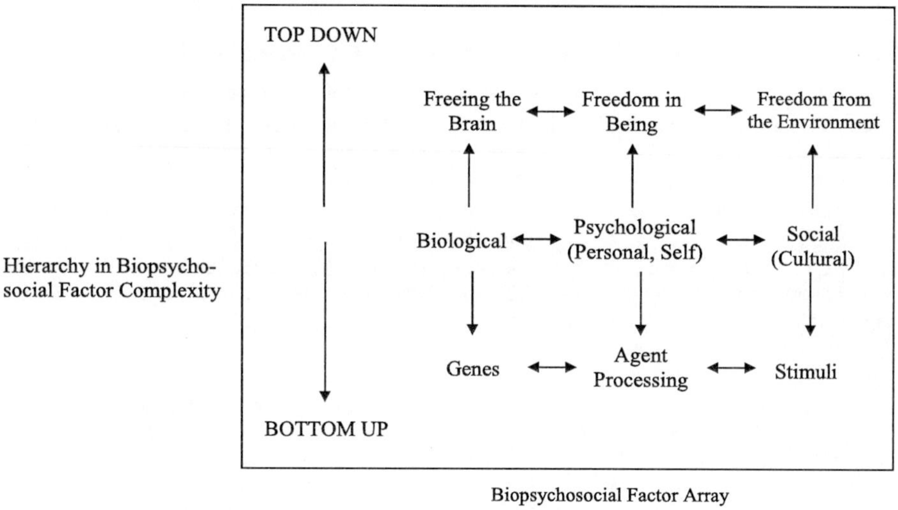

Fig. 3.3 Biopsychosocial causality: a broad vertical/horizontal systems model
The figure models causality in behavior to vary (a) horizontally in terms of its multifactorial (biopsychosocial, biopersonalsocial) influences and (b) vertically in terms of the hierarchical arrangement of its different levels of complexity. At the apex of all three major causal influences on behavior stand constructs related to free will and freedom. Behavioral causality is much more than reaction to lower-order levels in the various interactive causal forces on behavior, such as genes and stimuli producing passive response. Rather, behavior is actively emergent in a system, with self-forces involved psychologically as causal factors. (Adopted with permission of Springer International Publishing. Young, G. (2016). *Unifying* causality *and psychology: Being, brain and behavior*. Cham, Switzerland: Springer International Publishing; with kind permission from Springer International Publishing. [Figure 3.6, pp. 61])

To illustrate further the conceptual innovations that I fashioned in the Young (2016) book, consider the concept of free will environment correlations. Gene-environment correlations refer to the active role a person's individualized phenotypic profile (presumably underwritten by her/his individualized genotypic profile) leads to responses from the environment that are concordant with or fit it, tailoring the response to the proclivities (e.g., talents) involved. Similarly, we choose more constructively when we believe in free will and the environment might mold itself to our choices when they stem from those origins, at least in part.

The Causality Pinnacle

In Young (2016), I presented a range of innovative concepts related to behavioral causality, summarizing them in Table 29.2. Generally, the suite of new concepts related to behavioral causality serves to underscore its potential role as a constant

Table 3.2 Facilitating free will in psychotherapy by promoting better meaning making

Strategy	How can you use this knowledge to help yourself?
Free will is not an illusion; it exists as a belief.	Whenever you think that free will does not exist for you, how can you bring it back as a part of you?
Free will exists on a continuum, rather than being all-or-none.	Sometimes we have a sense that we have less free will than more of it. How can you increase that you have more free will?
There is room for free will in our lives because the world in our future is probable rather than definite (it is not determined without choice involved).	Because things and events in the future are only probable, how can you guide them to where you want them to go?
Our mind also can think differently and generate choices because it can think of options; it is good that there is some leeway for alternatives.	We do not always think the same way every time; how can we take advantage of that and choose better alternatives?
Free will comes from higher levels of our mind in the self and its organization.	Sometimes we are too tired, stressed, and so on, to function at our highest levels. What could we do to make this better so that we can feel we have more free will?
The meanings that we create about the world are ours; that is a sign of free will.	How can we improve the meaning that we give to things so we choose better in what we think, feel, and do? Sometimes we let other people tell us what a situation means; how can we decide this for ourselves, especially if the other person is off-base?
Because we explain and communicate our choices, this is another sign of free will.	How can we improve our explanation and communication better about our choices? This would help improve our sense of free will.
The meanings that we choose guide our behavior; our behavior is not just caused by the outside.	How can we guide our behavior better from the inside? This will help improve our sense of free will too.
Being free means capitalizing on options (opportunities) out there.	How can we guide our behavior better using things from the outside?
The more we regulate ourselves (and our behavior), the more we behave with free will.	How can we be in control better of our thinking, feeling, and doing, and improve our sense of free will?

Note. The left side of this table is adapted from Baumeister (2014). His work describes the role of free will in meaning making. On the right side of the table, I indicate how free will might be promoted on the basis of the understanding of free will in meaning making
Adapted from Baumeister (2014)

(and modifying) unifying force in psychology. This integrative potential of causality in psychology led me to refer to this section as the Causality Pinnacle. Indeed, causality could stand at the apex of what psychology studies and strives to unify. Perhaps the most complex of the new ideas toward integrating causality concerns integrated cross-networks. However, I prepare the terrain to describe the concept by presenting more general and less complex terms.

Aside from the metaphor of causality as a pinnacle, one could also conceive it as a vast causal landscape in which there are multiple concepts and critical axes. The

Table 3.3 The positive free will belief and related belief questionnaire in five major categories (seven examples each)

Category	Examples
Cognitive	I freely see problems as they are.
	I freely choose to find all the options before continuing.
	I can justify in detail why I do anything.
	I freely choose my way in everything I do.
	I always have the choice to make my decisions my way.
	I know what is right for me.
	I always choose to think for myself.
Social-Emotional	I freely choose to help people.
	I freely choose to do what's right for other people.
	Knowing I am free in everything I do lets me take my responsibilities easier.
	I believe that people should pay for the harm they cause others.
	I choose to be moral on my terms and not in the way others tell me.
	The more I believe in freedom in choosing, the more I understand how other people might have problems believing in it.
	The more I believe in freedom in choosing, the more I empathize with people.
Self	I am strong and determined, willful.
	My power lies in me and not in others.
	I can overcome obstacles.
	I am assertive without being offensive.
	I can change myself if I want to or have to.
	I can change things that are not going well.
	When I feel I am being me, people get the best from me.
Mental construction	I make sense of the world my way.
	I explain things and events my way.
	I interpret what happens my way.
	The messages I get from things and events that happen are up to me to make.
	The meanings in things and events come from how I see them.
	Things and events are as important as I let them be.
	What is useful in a situation is for me to decide.
Action	I freely choose to act the way I want.
	I freely choose to live the way I want.
	I can freely choose to act differently than I am acting now.
	I control the series of actions made by me.
	I control the series of actions made by others.
	I keep on track.
	I stop wrong actions.

Note. These questions can be rephrased to construct a general rather than personal free will belief questionnaire. They can stay in the present format, or some items might need to be reversed. The answers can be provided on a 7-point Likert scale (strongly disagree to strongly agree). Factor analytic studies should be constructed to determine their dimensional structure. As per Nadelhoffer et al. (2014), the studies addressing the final organization of the questionnaire should use explanatory factor analysis (principle components, eigenvalues >1, oblique rotations factor loadings >0.400) and then confirmatory factor analysis (checking model fit using the Goodness of Fit index, the Comparative Fit Index, and Adjusted Goodness of Fit index, the Root Mean Square Error of Approximation, and, to a lesser degree, the Chi Square test)

Adopted with permission of Springer International Publishing. Young, G. (2016). *Unifying* causality *and psychology: Being, brain and behavior*. Cham, Switzerland: Springer International Publishing; with kind permission from Springer International Publishing. [Table 19.3, pp. 496] critical ones should emphasize behavioral causation mechanisms, and these should be considered multifactorial and multileveled hierarchically. In particular, in this regard, to date, I have emphasized the concept of activation-inhibition coordination as a generic behavioral causation mechanism linked to multiple mind, body, and brain levels. Further, I coined the term "causalization" to capture the ubiquity of causality in nature. Causality appears to characterize the nature of reality more than actions in context and their effects. At the level of the inanimate universe, there may be a garden of subatomic particles, dark energy, dark matter, and so on. However, there may be a superposition of causality particles (dubbed "causicles") that inhabit the universe (or probabilistic causality particles/waves). Further, I speculated that systems are causality machines that systematize causality, even if there are as yet unknown dark or weird causality corners. The universe might be a causality engine (and ourselves and our behavioral vista) that populate causal fields.

The search for causality understanding might spearhead human cognition, and dynamic causal thinking might typify and maximize it (toward achieving a global causal understanding). We might be *Homo Causa* with causal selves (e.g., being causal; seeking its understanding) as our most primordial and primary attribute. My concept of causal embodiment describes well the causal beings that we are: "Causality is the context in which behavior lives and is defined. We are active agents of causality search, participation, understanding, and use" (Young 2016, p. 724).

Intraaction

Part of the difficulty in grasping psychological causality is that behavior is not isolated in the individual but is co-created in the environment or context. Essentially, behavior is a relational activity; moreover, causality cannot be broached conceptually or empirically without considering the shaping and transformative role of context. For example, depression is not a neurobiological expression within the person but a relational expression over person and context.

Further, behavioral causality cannot be understood without decomposing the concept of relations between person and context. Normally, people are considered to interact with each other or with context. The notion of interaction is ubiquitous in psychology and daily human discourse, as well. It connotes that the interacting parties remain intact and separate as the interaction proceeds. However, in the transactional process between social parties, for example, each reciprocal exchange modifies each of the parties, transforming them beyond their state in a context that had existed prior to the moment. The context and exchange get under the skin and the individual at time T_1 is not the identical person at time T_2, and so on. We are not shelled organisms impervious to the participatory exchanges in which we partake but, rather, open ones, at least to a degree, if any so-called interaction occurs at all.

In this sense, the concept of interactions is insufficient to capture the nature of exchange among participants in social dialogue, for example. Therefore, I created the concept of "intraaction" (or intraactive interaction) to represent the participatory, transformative nature of social exchange. The concept of intraactivism can be coupled with the one of causality because causality inheres in intraactions and is extended by them. These terms (and the one of intraacting interactors) co-exist, and they give shape to a cohesive co-existential causal intraactionism.

Integrated Cross-networks

Another concept that I developed was one that covers diverse network models such as the Connectome and symptom networks. In this regard, I referred to Integrated Cross-Networks (Models). Networks involve collections of relational data and their representations. They might be localized (small world) or dispersed and distributed. Specifically, integrated cross-networks denote multiple network interconnections within and over multiple levels of brain–behavior connections. The networks can be transduced into terms for NLDST, which help explain the change processes involved in their reconfiguration within any one level (e.g., neuronal) or between them (e.g., to the social). The networks could be about within-person connectivities (the intrapersonal connectome) and social ones (the interpersonal connectome). There also could be interfaced interconnections (e.g., technological). When networks involve ongoing dynamics, they are considered "immediate" rather than proximal or distal. The Connectome underlying behavior is proximate to behavior. More distal networks might involve pre-existing family dynamics, for example. These types of networks are all bottom-up types or not involving the higher-order integration in top-down cross-networking linkages. The latter might concern emerging causal forces, such as belief in free will.

Another example of an integrated cross-network is the construct of the neurome, which is a term I created to denote the nervous system, neurons, and neurotransmitters. Other ways of describing the neurome include neuromal network, or a neuroendophenotype. The neurome helps relate the context (stimuli) to the organism and its response in a systemic manner, such that integrated hierarchical levels can be found for each component (and they reciprocally interact). The neurome includes the proposed integrated cross-network both within and across its different networked levels. The neuromal network is quintessentially developmental and so includes the possibility of underwriting qualitative shifts in behavior, such as in (sub)stages. [Aside from the neurome, other collective concepts that I have articulated that cut across behavior and its expression include the phenome and the "loveome"; the full range of affective expression in the latter surely feeds vitality in the expression of the former.]

The ultimate causal network englobes all pertinent factors related to nature, nurture, and ourselves as a third contributing active force in causality. In Young (2016), I referred to this type of causal modeling as GEODS (genes; environment; organism; development; systems). We are continuously developing beings, and development is the one area of psychology that inevitably is involved in all others, either directly or indirectly.

System Networks

The hierarchical levels that might exist within a system, network, or a network organized in systems might include intermediate levels that are highly cognitive, evaluative, attitudinal, and individualized. For example, cognitive filters might have a hostility attribution bias, a paranoid bias, and so on. These intermediate levels in a network/system might have both top-down and bottom-up functions, for example, conditioning interpretation of system input lower down and influencing mood, personality, coping/resilience, and so on, higher up. Finally, the top-down levels in a system, such as in the examples provided, are constantly emerging de novo both in development and ongoing adaptation; also changing once emerged. But this happens with resistance to perturbation and change taking place, as well, until the system reaches a point on the cusp of change in which change can no longer be resisted.

I have referred to networks as characterized by systems organization. Aside from issues such as networks adopting ongoing patterns in node and edge relations that are self-organized, economical and graceful (while resisting perturbation even if far-from-equilibrium until breaking points are reached, e.g., at bifurcation points). A system understanding of networks also includes that they can be characterized as attractors. For example, an attitudinal conflict could be characterized as the system network gravitating from one "point attractor" (positive) to another (negative). I have already mentioned handedness in this regard (e.g., attractors for each hand in use). Another example would be the use of lower-order (e.g., unconscious automatic, System 1) and higher-order (e.g., conscious logical, System 2) thought (and perhaps the developmental (sub)stages that those types of thought imply).

My own work on network modeling consists of a hybrid network model that includes bottom-up and top-down influences. Moreover, these hybrid network models allow for mapping behaviors/systems in individual ways. Networks not only can be described in systems terms, but also they can coalesce into system dynamics that produce higher-order emergent levels in hierarchical organization, such as demonstrated in the top part of Fig. 3.4. In the figure, the Behavior/Symptom networks are represented by four related symptoms, which can be seen as constituting a cluster. Or, the figure can be used to represent four clusters that are associated with a disordered network. For example, in the DSM-5, PTSD has four major symptom clusters, and the figure could be used to represent each cluster or their relations. The traumatic psychiatric reaction that might emerge in patients will not be the one as described in the DSM-5 because each person expressing PTSD does so individually (Young et al. 2014). The symptom networks of people who suffer trauma and reach psychiatric thresholds are extremely heterogeneous. The course of a traumatic reaction that sets in as it entrenches will vary greatly across individuals. The trauma reaction generalizes in individual ways in its effect. It feeds back differentially into the symptom clusters, for example, sensitizing flashbacks, avoidance behaviors, nightmares, rumination, poor sleep, panic attacks/startling, and so on. A reciprocal positive feedback loop is established individually to accentuate both the symptoms and the traumatic reaction. Similarly, the symptoms themselves establish linkages in individual ways, and in which some are causal drivers of the others, magnifying or even initiating them. For example, getting poor sleep magnifies in individual ways the symptoms of PTSD, driving other symptoms associated with the disorder (and in individual ways for each patient). Therefore, PTSD might be a category in the DSM that represents a presumed disorder that develops after trauma; however, the trauma reaction that develops in people does not do so uniformly. Instead, each individual develops trauma reactions in ways that might be unique to them. Similarly, for depression, a patient does not express Major Depression as in the DSM-5 but as a small "d" depression, that is, individualized and contextualized in the patient's life.

The bottom part of Fig. 3.4 presents a causal map of the components of the biopsychosocial (biopersonalsocial) influences on behavior/symptoms. Activation-inhibition coordination constitutes the proposed mechanism that integrates the components in causality. Thus, causality exists at least at two levels in the hierarchies of top-down (e.g., category of PTSD, depression) and bottom-up (e.g., behavior, symptom networks) reciprocal influences on behavior, with other levels (such as appraisals, cognitive filters) also possible in causal mapping.

Behavioral causality involves a dynamic changing aspect, as described in the hybrid model. That is, as networks and levels (higher-order and lower-order) reconfigure as their equilibrium is stretched/perturbed past the cusp of change (or threshold or transition point), the self-organizing emergence that takes place could involve completely new patterns that are unpredictable from prior ones or even from the magnitude of any perturbation (the butterfly effect).

Although a combined network-symptom (hybrid) approach to causality has been emphasized in my work in the three books under review, this hybrid model is only one part of the broad causal nexus that I have integrated. Another interesting way of looking at causality turns around the typical sequence. That is, it prioritizes the person rather than the stimulus before responses, as discussed next. This view is consistent with the emphasis that I have placed on appraisals and cognitive filters in hybrid hierarchies.

S-O(BAMP)-R

One view of reductionism is that stimuli produce commensurate responses without mediation by the organism. Woodworth (1918) developed the Stimulus-Organism-Response (S-O-R) model to counter this behaviorist agenda. Thurstone (1923) advanced the S-O-R perspective by indicating that the mind does not mediate S-R connections; rather, the "causal sequence" begins with the perceiving person. In this regard, Gibson (1966) developed an affordance model of the environment (or stimuli). Information in the environment invites response, just as stairs invite climbing. The perceiver is still the agent; stimuli are not causal in and of themselves.

Clark (2013) presented a generative model similar to the S-O-R-one. Perception is constructed and inferred in order to predict from the base of probabilistic information. The organism tries to match lower-order incoming information to

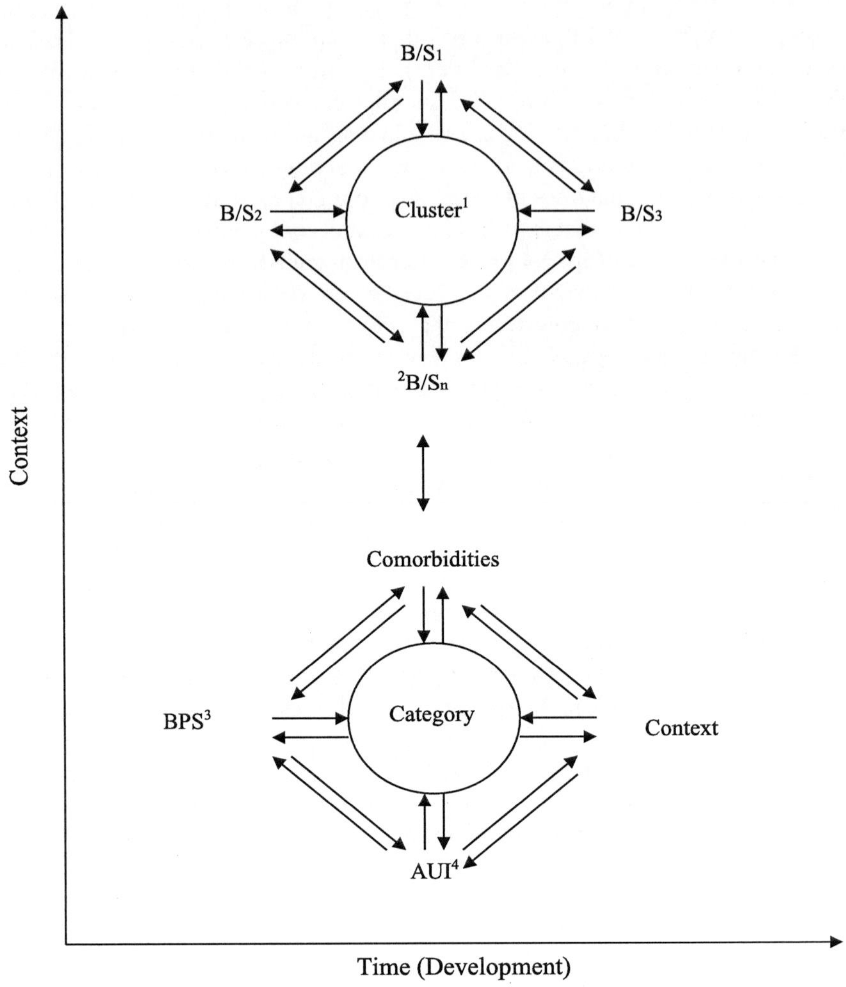

1. Cluster or Clusters

2. Behavior/ Symptom (Others)

3. Biopsychosocial Influences

4. Activation-Inhibition Coordination

Fig. 3.4 An integrative (bottom-up, top-down) behavior/symptom and cause network/construct model higher-order predictions and expectations in order to reduce prediction error; the brain functions as a prediction machine. This model illustrates the fuzziness in each component of the classic S-O-R model; they are not neatly divided as external (S), internal (O), and from internal to external (R).

Figure 3.5 presents the details of my own S-O-R model. It emphasizes the fuzziness of each of the S, O, and R. It adds a Brain-Agent-Mind-Person (BAMP) module. The S-O(BAMP)-R model of stimulus-organism-response relations places behavioral causality in those relations. The person mediates and moderates, impacts and influences in exchange with the environment while considering context and development. The environment invites (does not direct). The response outcome feeds back into the system to predispose it toward facilitating adaptive environmental change, thus, easing environmental hardship. Free will belief is part of the person's causal matrix, freeing her/him from deterministic outcomes. We construct the environment toward shaping it to our needs, we alter our adaptive response to our needs, and we grow in skill base as we do so, even perhaps to emergent higher-order levels of sophistication or complexity both cognitively and socio-affectively.

The S-O(BAMP) model comports with the present focus of the summary of the books by Young (2011, 2016, 2019) that causality is central to psychology and imbues each moment of our environmental sensing, constructive perception and cognition, and action that results. Also, the S-O(BAMP) model is consistent with systems theory, which is central to the present integrative causal model of behavior, but also with network theory, which has yet to be integrated into the S-O(BAMP) model. In this regard, network concepts can clarify the nature of environmental affordances (nodes, hubs, links, small worlds, etc.), the nature of mediating/moderating perception and cognition, and the nature of response actions, I have argued throughout that systems and network modeling are complementary.

Etiology

The causality of behavior refers to both normal and abnormal behavior. In the psychiatric area, causality is referred to as etiology. The medical model focuses on finding a single cause, such as a pathogen, injury, disease vector, or genetic mutation or disruption, for any unique disease, illness, disorder or syndrome, thus

Fig. 3.4 (continued) The figure illustrates how behaviors/symptoms (B/S), their clusters, and their causes might interact. The behaviors/symptoms might have one or more clusters or even patterns that reflect categorical disorders; and the causes include activation-inhibition coordinations. The behaviors/symptoms form networked connectivities that might have causal drivers among them (e.g., poor sleep) and the networks might relate to coordinations in neural circuitry. The networked connectivities are liable to emergence at higher levels of organization, for example, in bootstrapping development of depression. Or, the behavior/symptom complexes involved might be temporary, for example, to solve a problem at hand. That is, the behaviors might concern different cognitive strategies that network together toward problem resolution in context. Overall, then, networks might reflect immediate, online adaptive organizations or more ingrained patterns. Also, they could involve (sub)stage configurations cognitively. (Adapted from Young (2019) [Figure 8.2, pp. 166])

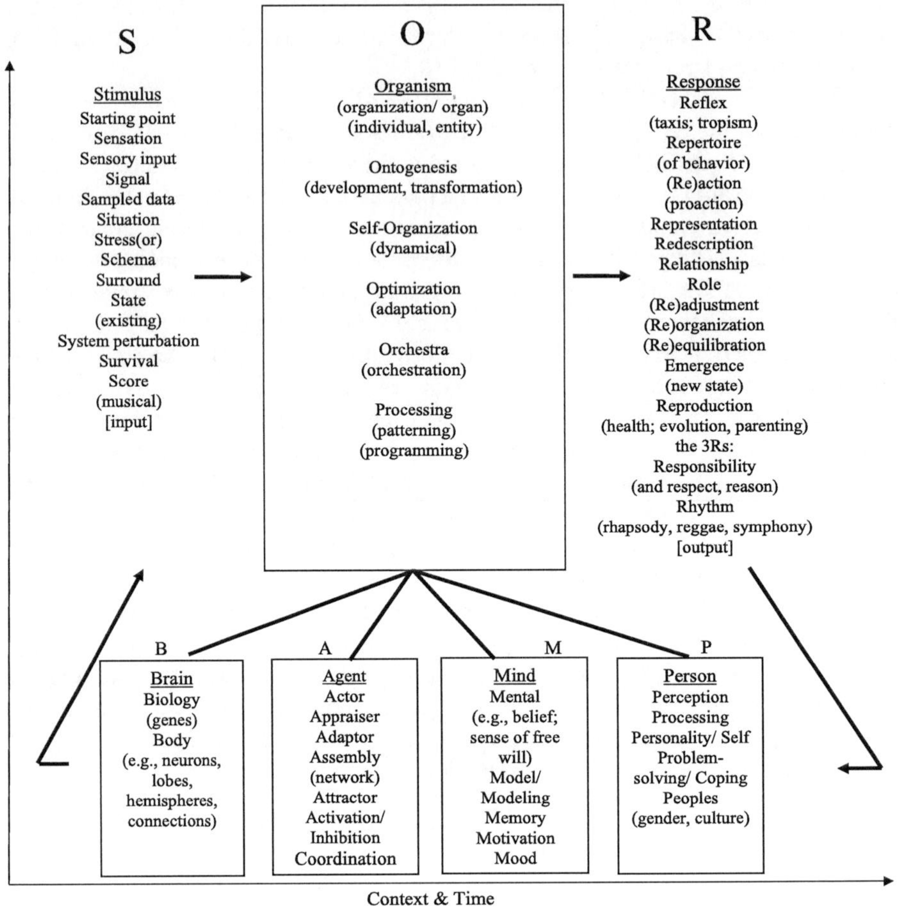

Fig. 3.5 The S-O(BAMP)-R causal psychological model: from stimulus and schema to response and representation
See Fig. 11.1 in Chap. 11 for the caption that applies to a more elaborate version of this figure. Essentially, stimuli are not passively processed leading to a response. Rather, intervening factors, such as subjective stimuli selection, schema mediation, and feed forward mechanisms into behavioral repertoire activation condition the S-R connection. The O (organism) is actively involved through its BAMP (brain, agency, mind, personal factors). (Adopted with permission of Springer International Publishing. Young, G. (2016). Unifying causality and psychology: Being, brain and behavior. Cham, Switzerland: Springer International Publishing; with kind permission from Springer International Publishing. [Figure 28.1, pp. 705–707]; Partly adapted from Young (2011) [Fig. 2.11, p. 43])

facilitating application of a specific medical cure, medication, intervention, or treatment. This type of modeling is difficult to apply in psychiatry and psychology because (a) the typical psychiatric/psychological disorders are not so clearly defined, or carved at the joints, (b) nor are their causes generally known, and (c) nor can specific interventions/treatments be precisely and effectively targeted at them.

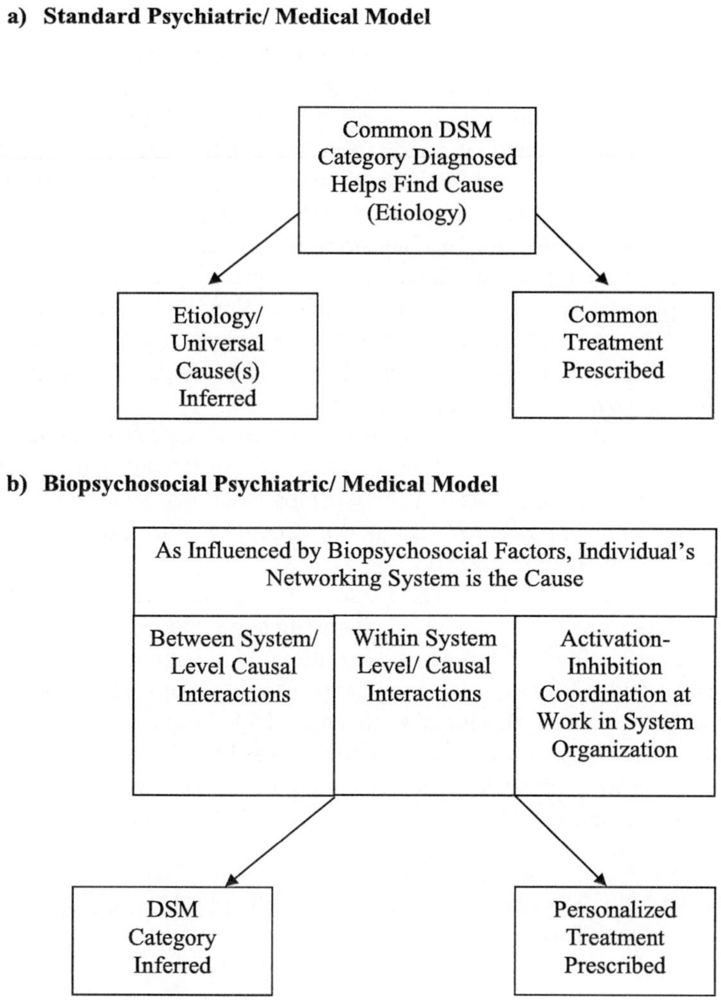

Fig. 3.6 Revised model of causation (etiology) in psychiatry
Instead of inferring cause from the diagnosis, representing the constellation of symptoms, the latter are analyzed for networks, which themselves are causal. This process allows for personalized treatment and consideration of diagnosis as secondary in importance. (Adapted from Young (2016) [Figure 25.9, pp. 643])

Endophenotypes attempt to trace markers of a disease to the lowest levels of its pathway, from genetics to physiology to brain, etc. The medical model predominates in the search, which speaks to specify a particular etiology for each specific disease (disorder) to facilitate a precise treatment (or cure). The etiology would apply equally to all instances of the disease (disorder) (being common to them). In Young (2016), I elaborated a broader endophenotypic model that considered that disease/disorder reflects biopsycho(personal)social contributions, so that markers could involve more than biological markers (see Table 3.4). Conceivably, behaviors themselves might be appropriate markers in this regard (or even their manifestations in tests/questionnaires). Networks cut across brain and behavior, as does the activation-inhibition coordination mechanism so that these too might help in elucidating endophenotypes for disease/disorder.

Figure 3.6 presents another way of examining etiology from a networked perspective. It contrasts the traditional medical model in psychiatry with a biopsychosocial approach that emphasizes the individual patient and her/his symptoms in understanding causation, disorder, and treatment.

Psychology, in particular, has reinforced a dimensional approach to understanding abnormal behavior. This discipline uses tests to understand behavior, which involves percentages, rankings, normal curve comparisons, cut-scores, and so on, so does not consider psychiatric disorders as categorical or all-or-none. Etiology is always multifactorial and probabilistic.

In Young (2016), I suggested a revised assessment approach to psychiatric disorder that considers major axes: communication/language; mood; thought; activity/energy; and function. Table 3.5 presents an outline of my approach, which could help in revising the DSM (to have a complete overview of the resent approach, the reader should check all the relevant tables in Chap. 25 in Young 2016).

Generally, the present approach needs work before clinical use. But it does point the way toward better understanding patients, their networked symptoms, their disorders, and possible individualized treatment options that can help them.

Conclusion (for Chaps. 2 and 3)

This concludes the two chapters of the present book that present the heart of Young's causal and developmental model. Chapters 2 and 3 on Young's (2011, 2016, 2019) Causality and Development book series provide the foundations to the work, especially in terms of the Neo-Piagetian/Neo-Eriksonian 25-step lifespan developmental model and the notion that causality can provide a unifying axis for psychology, albeit as an ongoing project.

Specifically, the chapters have presented Young's lifespan model of Neo-Piagetian/Neo-Eriksonian steps in development (five stages × five substages). The Neo-Piagetian model builds on Piaget's four-stage model and his six substage sequence in the infancy period to elaborate a five-stage × five substage model across the lifespan. This model also builds on the Neo-Piagetian models of Case and Fischer. In addition, Young developed a Neo-Eriksonian 25-step model by showing how Erikson's 8 stages can be placed in parallel to the Neo-Piagetian sequence, leading to 17 new Eriksonian steps to complete the theory construction. Specific topics covered in these chapters related to the 25 steps of the model include

Table 3.4 Candidate endophenotypes: biological and biopsychosocial approaches

	Level	
Area	Vertical	Horizontal
Biological		
Genome	Transcriptome	Protein
	Epigenome	Marks
Neurome (neuroendophenotype)	Nervous system	Peripheral/central
	Neurons	Dendrites/synapses
	Neurotransmitters	Dopamine/serotonin
Brain	Neurons	Network nodes/hubs and edges/links
	Astrocytes	Network centrality/modules (small worlds, rich clubs)
	Region	Network hierarchies/levels
	Lobe	Network systems (self-organization, far-from equilibrium, emergence)
Biopsychosocial		
Function	Control	Executive, reflective/automatic, habitual
	Activation/inhibition	Coordination/discoordination
Behavior	Single	Symptom
	Set	Syndrome/disorder
Assessment	Test	Above cut score
	Battery	Multiple results
Environment	Pre-existing	Adversity, chronic abuse
	Differential susceptibility	Perceptual, allelic
	Trauma	Exposure, horrific
Development	Age	Younger, older
	Learning	Coping/resilience, catastrophize
Therapy	Pharmacological	Multiple, e.g., antidepressants
	Psychological	Multiple, e.g., exposure therapy, CBT; interpersonal

Adapted from Young (2016) [Table 25.2, pp. 640]

self-development, social-emotional development, and the cognitive (mis)perception of the other. With respect to further elaborating on the original Neo-Piagetian/Neo-Eriksonian model, this part of the book has related the five levels of hierarchical needs in Maslow's model to the five stages of his model. The book also refers to the

Table 3.5 Proposed psychiatric assessment dimensions

Grouping	Dimensions
Major	Communication/language
	Mood
	Thought
	Activity/energy
	Function
Secondary	Environment/context
	Relations (e.g., family, partner)
	Social skills
	Coping
	Self/personality
Auxiliary	Age (stage, development)
	Gender
	Culture/minority
	Socioeconomic status
	Medical/physical/neurovegetative
"Dimensional"	Spectrum location
	Frequency
	Duration
	Temporal
	Intensity/severity
Complicating	Self-control
	Substance (ab)use
	Self-deception
	Other-deception
	Aberrant/inappropriate
Rating	0
	(1/2)
	1
	(1½)
	2
	NA/TBA

Adopted with permission of Springer International Publishing. Young, G. (2016). *Unifying* causality *and psychology: Being, brain and behavior*. Cham, Switzerland: Springer International Publishing; with kind permission from Springer International Publishing. [Table 25.5, pp. 644]

self as being constituted by a self-definitional self and a relatedness self, in particular, further differentiating the Neo-Maslovian model.

Second, this portion of the book has examined multifactional behavioral causality, including how it could underpin the development through the (sub)stages described. In particular, the two present chapters have emphasized the areas of systems, networks, and Young's concept of activation-inhibition coordination. The causality approach is multifactorial or biopsychosocial, which Young referred to as biopersonalsocial. Young used the area of laterality as an axis to present causality concepts. Other causality topics considered include evolution, genetics, epigenesis, free will belief, and etiology.

Throughout these two chapters of this book, the work has emphasized innovations, including novel concepts describing humans as *Homo Causa*, interactions as intraactions, the S-O-R model as a S-O(BAMP)-R model, and the philosophical concept of neo-constructivism as neo-reductioconstructivism. The book also innovates in other ways, for example, on laterality (e.g., the nature of specialization in the left hemisphere); how behavior is mediated by the cognitive (mis)perception of the other; how there are different evolutionary forces; and ways of improving psychiatric nosology. Ultimately, the book's broadest innovations refer to the model on Neo-Piagetian/Neo-Eriksonian (sub)stages over the lifespan and the idea that causality can be an integrating nexus in psychology, with that project requiring continued elaboration.

References

Agcaoglu, O., Miller, R., Mayer, A.R., Hugdahl, K., Calhoun, V.D.: Increased spatial granularity of left brain activation and unique age/gender signatures: a 4D frequency domain approach to cerebral lateralization at rest. Brain Imaging Behav. **10**(4), 1004–1014 (2015). https://doi.org/10.1007/s11682-015-9463-8

American Psychiatric Association: Diagnostic and Statistical Manual of Mental Disorders: DSM-5, 5th edn. Author, Washington, DC (2013)

Annett, M.: Left, Right, Hand and Brain: The Right Shift Theory. Erlbaum, London (1985)

Armour, J.A.L., Davison, A., McManus, I.C.: Genome-wide association study of handedness excludes simple genetic models. Heredity. **112**(3), 221–225 (2014). https://doi.org/10.1038/hdy.2013.93

Avena-Koenigsberger, A., Mišić, B., Hawkins, R.X.D., Griffa, A., Hagmann, P., Goñi, J., Sporns, O.: Path ensembles and a tradeoff between communication efficiency and resilience in the human connectome. Brain Struct. Funct. **222**(1), 603–618 (2016). https://doi.org/10.1007/s00429-016-1238-5

Avenanti, A., Paracampo, R., Annella, L., Tidoni, E., Aglioti, S.M.: Boosting and decreasing action prediction abilities through excitatory and inhibitory tDCS of inferior frontal cortex. Cereb. Cortex. **28**(4), 1282–1296 (2017). https://doi.org/10.1093/cercor/bhx041

Babcock, L.E., Robison, R.A.: Preferences of Paleozoic predators. Nature. **337**, 695–696 (1989)

Bartoli, E., Aron, A.R., Tandon, N.: Topography and timing of activity in right inferior frontal cortex and anterior insula for stopping movement. Hum. Brain Map. **39**(1), 189–203 (2017). https://doi.org/10.1002/hbm.23835

Baumeister, R.F.: Free will in scientific psychology. Perspect. Psychol. Sci. **3**(1), 14–19 (2008). https://doi.org/10.1111/j.1745-6916.2008.00057.x

Baumeister, R.F.: Constructing a scientific theory of free will. In: Sinnott-Armstrong, W. (ed.) Moral Psychology: Free Will and Moral Responsibility, vol. 4, pp. 235–255. MIT Press, Cambridge (2014)

Belsky, J., Pluess, M.: Beyond diathesis stress: differential susceptibility to environmental influences. Psychol. Bull. **135**(6), 885–908 (2009). https://doi.org/10.1037/a0017376

Bisazza, A., Cantalupo, C., Robins, A., Rogers, L.J., Vallortigara, G.: Pawedness and motor asymmetries in toads. Laterality. **2**(1), 49–64 (1997). https://doi.org/10.1080/713754252

Borsboom, D.: Psychometric perspectives on diagnostic systems. J. Clin. Psychol. **64**(9), 1089–1108 (2008). https://doi.org/10.1002/jclp.20503

Cavanagh, T., Berbesque, J.C., Wood, B., Marlowe, F.: Hadza handedness: lateralized behaviors in a contemporary hunter–gatherer population. Evol. Hum. Behav. **37**(3), 202–209 (2016). https://doi.org/10.1016/j.evolhumbehav.2015.11.002

Cerruti, C.: Building a functional multiple intelligences theory to advance educational neuroscience. Front. Psychol. **4**, 950 (2013). https://doi.org/10.3389/fpsyg.2013.00950

Clark, A.: Whatever next? Predictive brains, situated agents, and the future of cognitive science. Behav. Brain Sci. **36**(3), 181–204 (2013). https://doi.org/10.1017/s0140525x12000477

Cochet, H., Byrne, R.W.: Evolutionary origins of human handedness: evaluating contrasting hypotheses. Anim. Cogn. **16**(4), 531–542 (2013). https://doi.org/10.1007/s10071-013-0626-y

Collette, F., Van der Linden, M., Laureys, S., Delfiore, G., Degueldre, C., Luxen, A., Salmon, E.: Exploring the unity and diversity of the neural substrates of executive functioning. Hum. Brain Map. **25**(4), 409–423 (2005). https://doi.org/10.1002/hbm.20118

Corballis, M.C.: Left brain, right brain: facts and fantasies. PLoS Biol. **12**(1), e1001767 (2014). https://doi.org/10.1371/journal.pbio.1001767

Cox, R.F.A., Smitsman, A.W.: Action-selection perseveration in young children: advances of a dynamic model. Dev. Psychobiol. **61**(1), 43–55 (2018). https://doi.org/10.1002/dev.21776

Epskamp, S., Cramer, A.O.J., Waldorp, L.J., Schmittmann, V.D., Borsboom, D.: Qgraph: network representations of relationships in data. R package version 0.4.10. http://cran.r-project.org/package=qgraph (2011)

Fagard, J., Margules, S., Lopez, C., Granjon, L., Huet, V.: How should we test infant handedness? Laterality. **22**(3), 294–312 (2016). https://doi.org/10.1080/1357650x.2016.1192186

Fagot, J., Bard, K.A.: Asymmetric grasping response in neonate chimpanzees (pan troglodytes). Infant Behav. Dev. **18**(2), 253–255 (1995). https://doi.org/10.1016/0163-6383(95)90054-3

Forrester, G.H.: Hand, limb, and other motor preferences. In: Rogers, L.J., Vallortigara, G. (eds.) Lateralized Brain Functions: Methods in Human and Non-human Species, pp. 121–152. Springer SBM, New York (2017)

Forrester, G.S., Leavens, D.A., Quaresmini, C., Vallortigara, G.: Target animacy influences gorilla handedness. Anim. Cogn. **14**(6), 903–907 (2011). https://doi.org/10.1007/s10071-011-0413-6

Forrester, G.S., Quaresmini, C., Leavens, D.A., Spiezio, C., Vallortigara, G.: Target animacy influences chimpanzee handedness. Anim. Cogn. **15**(6), 1121–1127 (2012). https://doi.org/10.1007/s10071-012-0536-4

Forrester, G.S., Quaresmini, C., Leavens, D.A., Mareschal, D., Thomas, M.S.C.: Human handedness: an inherited evolutionary trait. Behav. Brain Res. **237**, 200–206 (2013). https://doi.org/10.1016/j.bbr.2012.09.037

Forrester, G.S., Rawlings, B., Davila-Ross, M.: An analysis of bimanual actions in natural feeding of semi-wild chimpanzees. Am. J. Phys. Anthropol. **159**(1), 85–92 (2015). https://doi.org/10.1002/ajpa.22845

Frayer, D.W.: OH-65: the earliest evidence for right-handedness in the fossil record. J. Hum. Evol. **100**, 65–72 (2016). https://doi.org/10.1016/j.jhevol.2016.07.002

Gibson, J.J.: The Senses Considered as Perceptual Systems. Houghton Mifflin, Boston (1966)

Gilsbach, S., Neufang, S., Scherag, S., Vloet, T.D., Fink, G.R., Herpertz-Dahlmann, B., Konrad, K.: Effects of the DRD4 genotype on neural networks associated with executive functions in children and adolescents. Dev. Cogn. Neurosci. **2**(4), 417–427 (2012). https://doi.org/10.1016/j.dcn.2012.05.001

Gonzalez, C.L.R., Flindall, J.W., Stone, K.D.: Hand preference across the lifespan: effects of end-goal, task nature, and object location. Front. Psychol. **5**, 1579 (2015). https://doi.org/10.3389/fpsyg.2014.01579

Grimshaw, G.M., Carmel, D.: An asymmetric inhibition model of hemispheric differences in emotional processing. Front. Psychol. **5**, 489 (2014). https://doi.org/10.3389/fpsyg.2014.00489

Häberling, I.S., Corballis, P.M., Corballis, M.C.: Language, gesture, and handedness: evidence for independent lateralized networks. Cortex. **82**, 72–85 (2016). https://doi.org/10.1016/j.cortex.2016.06.003

Hane, A.A., Fox, N.A., Henderson, H.A., Marshall, P.J.: Behavioral reactivity and approach-withdrawal bias in infancy. Dev. Psychol. **44**(5), 1491–1496 (2008). https://doi.org/10.1037/a0012855

Han-Pile, B.: Freedom and the "choice to choose oneself" in being and time. In: Wrathall, M.A. (ed.) The Cambridge Companion to Heidegger's Being and Time, pp. 291–319. Cambridge University Press, New York (2013)

Hopkins, W.D.: Comparative and familial analysis of handedness in great apes. Psychol. Bull. **132**(4), 538–559 (2006). https://doi.org/10.1037/0033-2909.132.4.538

Laland, K.N.: Exploring gene–culture interactions: insights from handedness, sexual selection and niche-construction case studies. Philos. Trans. R. Soc. B Biol. Sci. **363**(1509), 3577–3589 (2008). https://doi.org/10.1098/rstb.2008.0132

Leach, E.L., Prefontaine, G., Hurd, P.L., Crespi, B.J.: The imprinted gene LRRTM1 mediates schizotypy and handedness in a nonclinical population. J. Hum. Genet. **59**(6), 332–336 (2014). https://doi.org/10.1038/jhg.2014.30

MacNeilage, P.F.: Evolution of the strongest vertebrate rightward action asymmetries: marine mammal sidedness and human handedness. Psychol. Bull. **140**(2), 587–609 (2014). https://doi.org/10.1037/a0034298

Meguerditchian, A., Phillips, K.A., Chapelain, A., Mahovetz, L.M., Milne, S., Stoinski, T., Bania, A., Lonsdorf, E., Schaeffer, J., Russell, J., Hopkins, W.D.: Handedness for unimanual grasping in 564 great apes: the effect on grip morphology and a comparison with hand use for a bimanual coordinated task. Front. Psychol. **6**, 1794 (2015). https://doi.org/10.3389/fpsyg.2015.01794

Michel, G.F.: The concept of homology in the development of handedness. Dev. Psychobiol. **55**(1), 84–91 (2012). https://doi.org/10.1002/dev.21038

Michel, G.F.: How might the relation of the development of hand preferences to the development of cognitive functions be examined during infancy: a sketch? Front. Neurosci. **11**, 739 (2018). https://doi.org/10.3389/fnins.2017.00739

Michel, G.F., Babik, I., Sheu, C.-F., Campbell, J.M.: Latent classes in the developmental trajectories of infant handedness. Dev. Psychol. **50**(2), 349–359 (2014). https://doi.org/10.1037/a0033312

Missana, M., Grossmann, T.: Infants' emerging sensitivity to emotional body expressions: insights from asymmetrical frontal brain activity. Dev. Psychol. **51**, 151–160 (2014)

Morange-Majoux, F., Lemoine, C., Dellatolas, G.: Early manifestations of manual specialisation in infants: a longitudinal study from 20 to 30 weeks. Laterality. **18**(2), 231–250 (2013). https://doi.org/10.1080/1357650x.2012.660163

Mumford, K.H., Kita, S.: At 10-12 months, pointing gesture handedness predicts the size of receptive vocabularies. Infancy. **21**(6), 751–765 (2016). https://doi.org/10.1111/infa.12138

Nadelhoffer, T., Shepard, J., Nahmias, E., Sripada, C., Thomson Ross, L.: The free will inventory: measuring beliefs about agency and responsibility. Conscious. Cogn. **25**, 27–41 (2014). https://doi.org/10.1016/j.concog.2014.01.006

Nagy, E., Pal, A., Orvos, H.: Learning to imitate individual finger movements by the human neonate. Dev. Sci. **17**(6), 841–857 (2014). https://doi.org/10.1111/desc.12163

Nelson, E.L., Gonzalez, S.L., Coxe, S., Campbell, J.M., Marcinowski, E.C., Michel, G.F.: Toddler hand preference trajectories predict 3-year language outcome. Dev. Psychobiol. **59**(7), 876–887 (2017). https://doi.org/10.1002/dev.21560

Ocklenburg, S., Güntürkün, O.: The Lateralized Brain: The Neuroscience and Evolution of Hemispheric Asymmetries. Elsevier, Cambridge (2017)

Ocklenburg, S., Korte, S.M., Peterburs, J., Wolf, O.T., Güntürkün, O.: Stress and laterality—the comparative perspective. Physiol. Behav. **164**, 321–329 (2016). https://doi.org/10.1016/j.physbeh.2016.06.020

Ocklenburg, S., Packheiser, J., Schmitz, J., Rook, N., Güntürkün, O., Peterburs, J., Grimshaw, G.M.: Hugs and kisses—the role of motor preferences and emotional lateralization for hemispheric asymmetries in human social touch. Neurosci. Biobehav. Rev. **95**, 353–360 (2018). https://doi.org/10.1016/j.neubiorev.2018.10.007

Parma, V., Brasselet, R., Zoia, S., Bulgheroni, M., Castiello, U.: The origin of human handedness and its role in pre-birth motor control. Sci. Rep. **7**, 16804 (2017). https://doi.org/10.1038/s41598-017-16827-y

Paulhus, D.L., Carey, J.M.: The FAD-Plus: measuring lay beliefs regarding free will and related constructs. J. Pers. Assess. **93**(1), 96–104 (2011). https://doi.org/10.1080/00223891.2010.528483

Porac, C.: Laterality: Exploring the Enigma of Left-Handedness. Elsevier, London (2016)

Potier, C., Meguerditchian, A., Fagard, J.: Handedness for bimanual coordinated actions in infants as a function of grip morphology. Laterality. **18**(5), 576–593 (2012). https://doi.org/10.1080/1357650X.2012.732077

Ratnarajah, N., Rifkin-Graboi, A., Fortier, M.V., Chong, Y.S., Kwek, K., Saw, S.M., Godfrey, K.M., Gluckman, P.D., Meaney, M.J., Qiu, A.: Structural connectivity asymmetry in the neonatal brain. NeuroImage. **75**, 187–194 (2013). https://doi.org/10.1016/j.neuroimage.2013.02.052

Reissland, N., Aydin, E., Francis, B., Exley, K.: Laterality of fetal self-touch in relation to maternal stress. Laterality. **20**(1), 82–94 (2014). https://doi.org/10.1080/1357650X.2014.920339

Rogers, L.J., Vallortigara, G.: From antenna to antenna: lateral shift of olfactory memory recall by honey bees. PLoS One. **3**(6), e2340 (2008). https://doi.org/10.1371/journal.pone.0002340

Rogers, L.J., Vallortigara, G., Andrew, R.J.: Divided Brains: The Biology and Behaviour of Brain Asymmetries. Cambridge University Press, Cambridge (2013)

Rozin, P., Moscovitch, M., Imada, S.: Right: left: east: west. Evidence that individuals from East Asian and South Asian cultures emphasize right hemisphere functions in comparison to Euro-American cultures. Neuropsychologia. **90**, 3–11 (2016). https://doi.org/10.1016/j.neuropsychologia.2016.06.027

Rubin, T.N., Koyejo, O., Gorgolewski, K.J., Jones, M.N., Poldrack, R.A., Yarkoni, T.: Decoding brain activity using a large-scale probabilistic functional-anatomical atlas of human cognition. PLoS Comput. Biol. **13**(10), e1005649 (2017). https://doi.org/10.1371/journal.pcbi.1005649

Sainburg, R.L.: Convergent models of handedness and brain lateralization. Front. Psychol. **5**, 1092 (2014). https://doi.org/10.3389/fpsyg.2014.01092

Schmittmann, V.D., Cramer, A.O.J., Waldorp, L.J., Epskamp, S., Kievit, R.A., Borsboom, D.: Deconstructing the construct: a network perspective on psychological phenomena. New Ideas Psychol. **31**(1), 43–53 (2013). https://doi.org/10.1016/j.newideapsych.2011.02.007

Schmitz, J., Metz, G.A.S., Güntürkün, O., Ocklenburg, S.: Beyond the genome—towards an epigenetic understanding of handedness ontogenesis. Prog. Neurobiol. **159**, 69–89 (2017). https://doi.org/10.1016/j.pneurobio.2017.10.005

Schmitz, J., Kumsta, R., Moser, D., Güntürkün, O., Ocklenburg, S.: DNA methylation in candidate genes for handedness predicts handedness direction. Laterality. **23**(4), 441–461 (2018). https://doi.org/10.1080/1357650X.2017.1377726

Steele, J., Uomini, N.: Can the archaeology of manual specialization tell us anything about language evolution? A survey of the state of play. Camb. Archaeol. J. **19**(1), 97–110 (2009). https://doi.org/10.1017/s0959774309000067

Swick, D., Ashley, V., Turken, A.U.: Left inferior frontal gyrus is critical for response inhibition. BMC Neurosci. **9**, 102 (2008). https://doi.org/10.1186/1471-2202-9-102

Thurstone, L.L.: The stimulus-response fallacy in psychology. Psychol. Rev. **30**(5), 354–369 (1923). https://doi.org/10.1037/h0074251

Vallortigara, G., Versace, E.: Laterality at the neural, cognitive, and behavioral levels. In: Call, J., Burghardt, G.M., Pepperberg, I.M., Snowdon, C.T., Zentall, T. (eds.) APA Handbook of Comparative Psychology: Basic Concepts, Methods, Neural Substrate, and Behavior, vol. 1, pp. 557–577. American Psychological Association, Washington, DC (2017)

van Campen, A.D., Kunert, R., van den Wildenberg, W.P.M., Ridderinkhof, K.R.: Repetitive transcranial magnetic stimulation over inferior frontal cortex impairs the suppression (but not expression) of action impulses during action conflict. Psychophysiology. **55**(3) (2018). https://doi.org/10.1111/psyp.13003

Vannasing, P., Florea, O., González-Frankenberger, B., Tremblay, J., Paquette, N., Safi, D., Wallois, F., Lepore, F., Béland, R., Lassonde, M., Gallagher, A.: Distinct hemi-

spheric specializations for native and non-native languages in one-day-old newborns identified by fNIRS. Neuropsychologia. **84**, 63–69 (2016). https://doi.org/10.1016/j.neuropsychologia.2016.01.038
Woodworth, R.S.: Dynamic Psychology. Columbia University Press, New York (1918)
Young, G.: Early neuropsychological development: lateralization of functions—hemispheric specialization. In: Hauert, C.A. (ed.) Developmental Psychology: Cognitive, Perceptuomotor and Neuropsychological Perspectives, pp. 113–181. North Holland, Amsterdam (1990a)
Young, G.: The development of hemispheric and manual specialization. In: Hammond, G.E. (ed.) Cerebral Control of Speech and Limb Movements, pp. 79–139. North Holland, Amsterdam (1990b)
Young, G.: Development and Causality: Neo-Piagetian Perspectives. Springer Science + Business Media, New York (2011)
Young, G.: Unifying Causality and Psychology: Being, Brain and Behavior. Springer International Publishing, Cham (2016)
Young, G.: Causality and Development: Neo-Eriksonian Perspectives. Springer International Publishing, Cham (2019)
Young, G., Gagnon, M.: Neonatal laterality, birth stress, familial sinistrality, and left brain inhibition. Dev. Neuropsychol. **6**(2), 127–150 (1990). https://doi.org/10.1080/87565649009540455
Young, G., Bowman, J.G., Methot, C., Finlayson, M., Quintal, J., Boissonneault, P.: Hemispheric specialization development: what (inhibition) and how (parents). In: Young, G., Segalowitz, S.J., Carter, C.M., Trehub, S.E. (eds.) Manual Specialization and the Developing Brain, pp. 119–140. Academic Press, New York (1983)
Young, G., Lareau, C., Pierre, B.: One quintillion ways to have PTSD comorbidity: recommendations for the disordered DSM-5. Psycholo. Inj. Law. **7**(1), 61–74 (2014). https://doi.org/10.1007/s12207-014-9186-y

Chapter 4
Elaborating the Integrated (Sub)stage Model

The chapter begins by presenting in-depth the concept of neo-stage. Then, it moves on to complete the presentation of the major ideas in the three Young books under review.

I developed the concept of neo-stage to provide a revamped model of stage so that it reflects contemporary developments in behavioral organization (e.g., networks, systems) and includes an approach that is more soft than hard. Box 4.1 and Table 4.1 on the concept are taken from Young (2019), with an addition from Young (2016) that had not been applied to the concept of neo-stage in Young (2019), but it fits the concept very well. The box is organized to define the concept of neo-stage, give the concept of microdevelopment/macrodevelopment coordination that it includes, and refer to topics that serve to flesh it out. In this regard, the box discusses, in turn, neo-stages cognitively and socio-affectively, yoking, stage transitioning, multiple modeling, and networking and systems. Note that microdevelopment and macrodevelopment might appear quite different because of their scale differences. However, toward the end of the present work, I indicate how microdevelopment and macrodevelopment might reflect the same generic change processes, occurring in five phases in both cases. That is, the concept of neo-stages appears to entwine intimately micro- and macrodevelopment in a fractalization process.

G. Young, *Causality and Neo-Stages in Development*,
https://doi.org/10.1007/978-3-030-82540-9_4

Box 4.1 Neo-Stage

The concept of stages should be revamped so that it considers the individualized variability in cognitive development while respecting the generalized trajectory in that development that appears to indicate universal stages. In order that this notion is accepted, I propose that it be given the rubric of "neo-stage."

Microdevelopment/Macrodevelopment Coordination

Table 4.1 presents the concept of microdevelopment/macrodevelopment coordination that further elaborates the concept of neo-stage and, as with the neo-stage concept itself, it is new to the field. The following clarifies the content and meaning of each of the terms involved in the concept, and its value for understanding development, generally, and the concept of neo-stage, specifically.

Table 4.1 Microdevelopment/macrodevelopment coordination

Concept	Factors
Microdevelopment	Local, online, immediately adaptive changes in behavior (and including in any underlying schemes, operations, skills, strategies, etc.), for example, in problem-solving, dealing with a task, confronting a stressor, in a crisis.
	Can take place life-long; development is lifespan.
Macrodevelopment	Global, reorganization of the system involved; neither abrupt nor immediate for the most part; can be to a qualitatively different level, concept (e.g., first abstract thought); but that does not imply a new stage, per se.
	Refers to ontogenesis, generally, in contrast to microdevelopment, which refers to learning, adjusting in an ongoing context.
Coordination	Both microdevelopment and macrodevelopment have been described in the literature, but not their coordination as a central mechanism in development.
	Coordination refers to the extent to which microdevelopments lead to macrodevelopments and the balance between the two tracks.
	Effective microdevelopment/macro-development coordination requires: flexibility; stability yet plasticity; experience-dependent responsivity yet resistance to perturbation; inhabiting the cusp of change yet maintaining equilibrium; and possible self-organizing to higher developmental levels through bootstrapping, emergence, circular causality, and so on, at least if all the components needed for the change are available and amenable to it, including biologically, neuronally, cognitively, emotionally, and socially.
	Microdevelopment/macrodevelopment coordination can become dysregulated, too rigid/tight or too disturbed, psychopathological, chaotic/loose, and so on, leading to psychiatric/psychological maladaptive behavior difficulty, dysfunctionality, problems, disorders, and mental disorder diagnoses, as well as impediments to normative, healthy, or otherwise nonproblematic development.
	The concept of microdevelopment/macrodevelopment coordination should not be taken to inform how stages develop, either cognitively or socioaffectively; but the concept does inform the deep processes that lead to stages and their growth.

(continued)

Box 4.1 (continued)

Defined

Cognitive. The concept of neo-stages refers to individualized collections of developing schemes (and operations for the older child) that are microgenetically recruited for dealing with problems and tasks in a domain or subdomain and related cognitive challenges at hand.

Cognitively, the adaptive recruitment of extant schemes or operations is local, ongoing, continuous, and rapid. Unproductive ones are dropped. New ones might be added to the repertoire used, as required. Generally, ones in the repertoire are subject to change to fit the parameters of the problem/task/challenge confronted.

Socio-affectivity. Socio-affectively, the schemes/operations and problem-solving strategies in the Neo-Piagetian stage(s) associated with a Neo-Eriksonian stage(s) at issue also would be similarly recruited microgenetically, but with impediments (e.g., fixation, regression) likely if abuse/neglect or any serious disturbance in mutuality had been experienced. Or, new schemes/operations and problem-solving strategies specific to the socio-affective issue at hand could be created.

In this sense, it is best to conceive of Eriksonian stages in the same way as the cognitive stages in this regard—there are strategies for socio-affective problem-solving that could be elicited, and this happens in individual ways in context microgenetically, which might lead to habitual patterns that are consistent with the labels given to the stages (e.g., trust vs. mistrust).

Yoking. Further, skills associated with different stages can be yoked together in combination if this procedure would be adaptive in the microgenetic online problem-solving in which the developing person is engaged. That is, skills for problem-solving that are associated with one stage or the other never disappear through the mechanism of being integrated, transformed, or otherwise altered by (the skills of) new stages that come along. Rather, they are available throughout the lifespan in problem-solving.

Stage Transitioning. The qualitative emergence of a new distinct skill first happens in one of the schemes/operations involved. The process takes place through the self-organization of the community of schemes/operations, perhaps through circular processes that bootstrap extant schemes/operations. As the new acquisition is applied, it generalizes and forms a higher-order level distinct from extant ones that feedback and create a hierarchical organization of schemes/operations. This process facilitates ground-up or bottom-up microgenetic applications in interaction with top-down or superordinate regulation by the more integrated, generalized, and more advanced skills.

Multiple Modeling. The individualized yoking of schemes and operations that takes place in problem-solving strategies, with different skills recruited

(continued)

Box 4.1 (continued)

from the repertoire in different stages, suggests a model of multiple cognitive intelligences. Moreover, the same type of modeling can be used to create a model of *multiple* emotional intelligences in the socio-affective track.

Networking (and Systems). Network theory has been applied to neurocircuitry but can be applied to the concept of stages to help further elucidate their topography. For example, system models that refer to self-assembly in a spontaneous self-organization of a system once it reaches a critical state of perturbation either due to internal forces, external ones, or both lack concepts of how individual elements of the system relate to each other. Mostly, systems theory concerns macrochanges, such as new attractor basins or their coupling. In contrast, the concept of network circuits, with their nodes and edges, and the central properties that they might express, such as centrality, connectivity, hub organization, small worlds, efficiency, and locality/globality (e.g., van den Heuvel and Sporns 2013), add a new perspective for understanding the organization of the contents of each level of a system and the hierarchical levels of a system.

Fractalization. Microdevelopment might take place through the same generic change processes as has been described for macrodevelopment. As Young (2016) described, Dodge et al. (2013) presented an information processing model in five steps. (a) First, individuals encode situational cues. (b) Next, they interpret the encoded cues. (c) Third, they adopt a goal for the situation. (d) Fourth, they generate possible responses to the encoded cues. (e) Fifth, they engage in decision-making and enact a response.

In the following, I transpose the terms used for the microdevelopmental social information processing five-phase model into the terms used for the macrodevelopmental cognitive development five-substage model: (a) The first step in Dodge et al.'s (2013) social information processing model is analogous to a coordination process response to the situation in that accurate coding is contrasted with possible inaccurate perceptions or hypervigilance to threat cues, which is involved in aggressive behavior (the subject of the Dodge et al. model). (b) Next, the interpretation involved could subsume inappropriate hostile attributions under accurate perceptions, or vice versa, depending on whether there is an aggression-linked bias. This is consistent with the hierarchization process described in the Neo-Piagetian model. (c) Next, the adoption of a goal in the Dodge et al. model is consistent with the Young systematization process model. Goal adaptation appears as a central axis on which adaptation proceeds. (d) Fourth, generating possible behavioral responses in the former model is akin to the multiplication process in the latter model. As goals lead to possible responses, a multiplication seems evident. (e) Finally, decision-making/enacting in social information processing in Dodge et al. reflects the integration process in Young's cognitive developmental model. Enacting the chosen option is consistent with an integrated interpretation of the last step in social information processing.

(continued)

Box 4.1 (continued)

Adopted with permission of Springer International Publishing. Young, G. (2019). Causality *and development:* Neo-Eriksonian *perspectives.* Cham, Switzerland: Springer International Publishing; with kind permission from Springer International Publishing, with some modification [Text Excerpt of 688 words from Chapter 11, p. 247–254; Table 11.8, p. 252].

Adopted with permission of Springer International Publishing. Young, G. (2016). *Unifying* causality *and psychology: Being, brain and behavior.* Cham, Switzerland: Springer International Publishing; with kind permission from Springer International Publishing, with some modification [with the fractalization section at the end adopted from Young (2016), Text Excerpt of 200 words from Chapter 33, p. 811].

Aside from its utility in accommodating to difficulties with classic stage conceptualization, the concept of neo-stage gives a firm basis for how might the present Neo-Piagetian/Neo-Eriksonian stage model validly characterize development. In its understanding of stages, the concept is broad, flexible, and constructed to accommodate the vast array of individual and group (e.g., culture) differences in development that take place cognitively and socio-affectively. Even if universal sequence seems evident on the surface in the steps, they still can function as explanatory scaffolds on which individual differences can map.

The neo-stage concept prepares the way for the presentation in-depth of the Neo-Eriksonian portion of the present model. The latter deals with socio-affective development and is exquisitely individual because of (a) the differences in environmental impacts that impact people, (b) how problematic aspects in development arise because of them, and (c) the individualized train of problematic problems that mark each person as they navigate the 25 steps in the Neo-Eriksonian sequence over the lifetime.

Neo-Piagetian Development

The present work began with the creation of a Neo-Piagetian model of cognitive development consisting of five stages × five substages. However, stage models are not without their critics. Stage models are criticized as both developmentally invalid and empirically untestable. That said, the classic hard stage concept has evolved, and a soft view now predominates (see Fig. 4.1). Moreover, I have supplemented the typical way researchers tackle the empirical study of the stage conception with a network approach, as already described, and add a neo-stage conception of stage that integrates the soft and network views, as presented later on (Box 4.2).

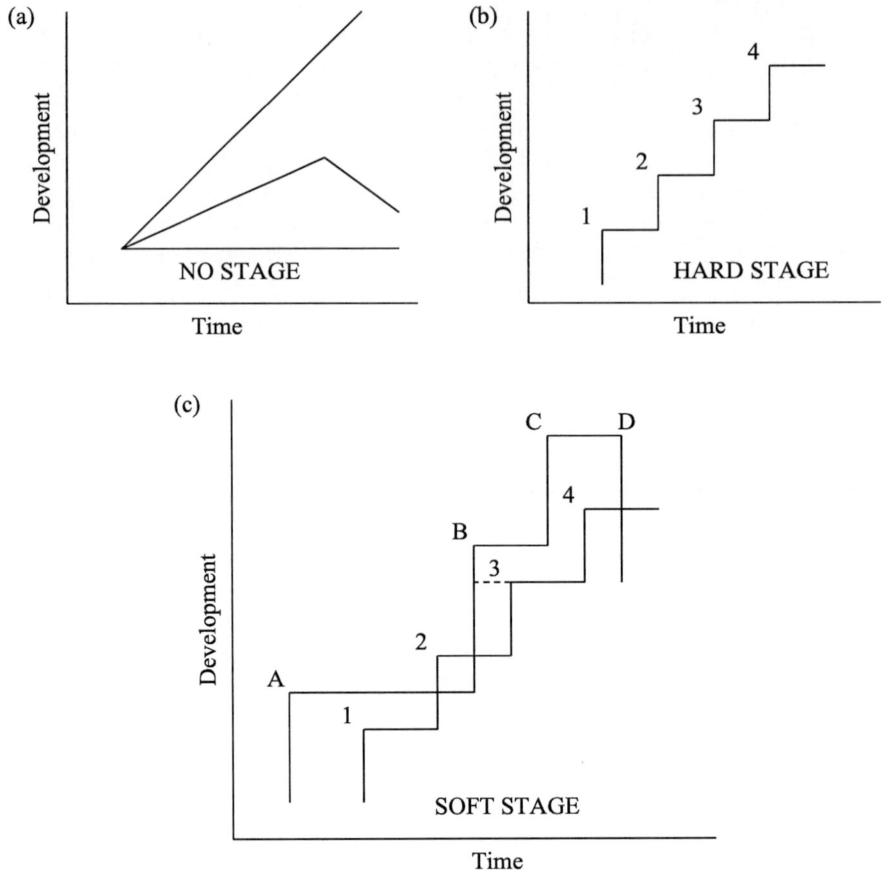

Fig. 4.1 Stage conceptions
The figure illustrates the differences across the development trajectories for nonstage models of development, "hard" stage models, and soft stage models. (a) Nonstage models do not describe universal abrupt shifts in development to qualitatively distinct levels that must develop in an invariant order without skipping a stage. Development can proceed only linearly in an upward trajectory, downward one, be flat, go up then down, down then up, reflect an inverted U curve, and so on, and is individually determined in context for its course in these regards. (b) Hard stage models have the opposite characteristics; universal, invariant, increasingly integrative, organized, and without overlap except in transitions. (c) The concept of soft stages allows for universal type patterns (e.g., as in the trajectory 1234) and individualized ones (as in ABCD). Different patterns can coexist over domains in a family of trajectories. If found, the universal patterns are due to multiple individuals arriving at the same adaptive solutions developmentally in their contexts; it has nothing to do with maturation, preprogramming, etc. The individualized trajectories can include regressions (e.g., point D), fixations, and stopping to develop. The pattern over different trajectories might seem to imply that a stage can be skipped (e.g., compare the placement of points B and 3), assume in this case that they reflect development in two different domains, but this is only due to differential rate of development in different domains/trajectories. The present model is consistent with the soft stage perspective but surpasses it in its neo-stages concept (see text)

Box 4.2 Comparing Fischer's and Young's Neo-Piagetian Models

In Young (2011), I showed that Fischer's model appears to be missing substages at 2, 7, and 9 years, in particular, as well as prenatally and in the adult period, unlike in my own 5-stage × 5-substage lifelong developmental model. Also, I showed how the examples provided by Fischer and colleagues for the development of emotions better fit my model than theirs. For example, in reference to the substage at 18–24 months, the examples provided were as much sensorimotor in nature as purely representational, counter to the Fischerian model that claims that representation emerges at this age. Also, in reference to the missing substage at 2 years, Fischer provided for the first (and only) time in his lifetime body of work a substage, which, in contrast, is generally called for in my model. That is, Mascolo and Fischer (2015) had included a substage at this age period that is representational in nature, which is consistent with each of the work of Piaget, Case, and myself. Specifically, the missing substage at 2 years had been referred to as "compounded representations/internalized standards" (Mascolo and Fischer 2007). Moreover, the single representation substage at 18–24 months had been qualified as "evoked and supported," which, to me, indicates its less than pure representational status.

Inexplicably, in Mascolo and Fischer (2015), the new substage used to help explain the development of socio-affective acquisitions in their prior work on emotional development (Mascolo and Fischer 2007) was not applied to their new work on a related developmental topic, that of moral action in the three domains considered. They referred to the substage in question in terms of Fischer's general model, in which a substage at 2 years of age is excluded. Therefore, and contrary to what I had expected, they did not refer to the 18- to 24-month age period, at least at this point, as being "evoked and supported."

Next, I examine the specific examples provided for moral development in Mascolo and Fischer (2015), which permits me to show their lacunae relative to my own model. In Mascolo and Fischer (2015), the moral action domain of autonomy/rights develops from the substage of a single representation of possession ("mine") at the 18- to 24-month age period to that of reciprocity (give me the toy, return it) at 3.5–4.5 years. As mentioned, but worthy of repetition, in their description of this developmental passage, as per the general critique I had presented in Young (2011) of the Fischerian model, there is no substage between the two substages presented that is applicable to 2 years of age. In this regard, I would add to their substage sequence something like their substage found in Mascolo and Fischer (2007), that is, their substage of "compounded representations/internalized standards." In other words, at this age, there should be the substage of representations/internalized standards or an equivalent. Using their examples, it would be captured by the child returning to the scene, after a child has transgressed someone's rights (e.g., inappropriately saying "mine"), in order to say, "Sorry" (as opposed to simply saying "Sorry" without a return component). Of course, another option would be to

(continued)

Box 4.2 (continued)

use my own model in this regard, which refers to coordinated representations at this age (indeed, the example provided fits this terminology, too).

The clearest example of the need to differentiate a 2-year-old level of representation from ones for 18–24 months and for 3.5–4.5 years in the work of Mascolo and Fischer (2015) concerns the domain that they presented of developing concern for others. In the examples that they provided for an 18-month-old, a child accidentally hurts the mother and says, "kiss, kiss" before kissing the mother. The action component to the representation is evident, which I highlight as the reason for considering this age at one still involving sensorimotor actions, as Piaget had maintained (and unlike what they maintained). For an older child (30 months), in the example provided, the concern for others is expressed verbally only ("poor Donna crying"), which, moreover, appears to be a compounded or coordinated representation ("poor" + "crying"), to use their language (or a coordinated representation, to use my language). Clearly, the example reflects a representation without an action component. However, in Mascolo and Fischer (2015), despite the differences that they reflect about representation for the two ages involved, the two examples they give are both referred to as representational (at the substage of single representations).

To summarize, Fischer's Neo-Piagetian model has fewer substages over the lifespan than my own, and there are striking lacunae in substages that should be present, including at 2 years of age. Moreover, for the same age periods, the description that I give of the substages that make sense is not the same as those in Fischer, e.g., at 18 months of age.

Adopted with permission of Springer International Publishing. Young, G. (2016). *Unifying* causality *and psychology: Being, brain and behavior.* Cham, Switzerland: Springer International Publishing; with kind permission from Springer International Publishing. [Text Excerpt of 904 words from Chapter 37, pp. 902–903].

In the box entitled: Comparing Fischer's and Young's Neo-Piagetian models, excerpted from Young (2016), I show how recent work on the Fischerian model includes major lacunae in the proposed steps in development. Moreover, in the box, I indicate how the examples provided for steps in the age range of concern better fit my 25-step (5 stage × 5 substage) Neo-Piagetian model than the Fischerian one. This type of criticism of other models serves to validate my own. The 2011 Young book examines the lacunae extensively in the Fischerian model and that of Case, further supporting my own.

The next two tables indicate how the five-stage Neo-Piagetian model can be applied to understand a range of developmental acquisitions. The table indicates how consciousness and theory of mind (perspective taking, mind-reading; which I

Table 4.2 Consciousness, self/other moral responsibility

Stage	Consciousness[a]	Cognition-emotion-body of the other	Self-definitional Neo-Maslovian needs	Relatedness self Neo-Maslovian needs	Foundational moral motives[b] (Positive[c])	Responsibility[d]
Reflexive	Nonconsciousness	Nascent intersubjectivity	Immediate physiological needs [e.g., nursing]/survival	Immediate physiological needs [e.g., sex]/reproduction	Life preservation	Responsive
Sensorimotor	Preconsciousness	Embodied mentalization/ intentionality	Safety/trust/security/care	Safety/trust/security/care	Care/linking	Response-able
Peri-operational	Unconsciousness – Lack of consciousness – Repression into unconscious	Representational theory of mind First-order (false belief) Second-order (eyes tasks)	Initiative-education, love (affection) affiliation	Initiative-education, love (belonging) affiliation	Reciprocity/ Respect	Responsibility
Abstract	Conscious	Third-order theory of mind (abstract)	Self-esteem identity (Me-identity) [individualism]	Self-esteem we-identity (Us-identity) [collectivism]	Conscious Identification/ Application	Re-responsibility
Collective Intelligence	Supraconscious	Postformal theory of mind (collective intelligence)	Generativity self-actualization (meaning) [family, work education-instruction, community, culture, collective, planet]	Generativity self-actualization (meaning) [family, work education-instruction, community, culture, collective, planet]	Sanctity/ humanizing	Re-responsibilities

[a](a) In terms of degree of consciousness, the fetal period should be considered one of non-consciousness
(b) One can place the preconscious in the infancy period
(c) The childhood period is one famously marked by the development of the unconscious, as per Freud's psychodynamic model
(d) One classic hallmark of the adolescent period is that it is the beginning of consciousness
(e) Finally, just as the adult could develop a collective intelligence that seems one step above the teenage stage of abstract thought, so the adult could develop a supra-consciousness that is one step above the stage of the opening of consciousness

[b]Haidt (e.g., Graham and Haidt 2012; see Young 2016, p. 838) had elaborated five foundational moral motives, which are: harm/nurturance; fairness/justice; in group/loyalty; authority/respect; and chastity/atheism. Young (2016) had organized them according to his revised Neo-Maslovian model, which has five levels like the original Maslow model. Also, Young's model has two core aspects at each level, concerning self-definition and relatedness (following Blatt 2008). Young (2016) differentiated Haidt's original list of five moral motives by organizing them according to the self-definitional and relatedness component of his Neo-Maslovian model. The present table provides integrated terminology for the dual foundational moral motives at each of the five levels of Young's revised Neo-Maslovian model. The terms selected respect both Young's (2016) reworking of Haidt's terminology for the five foundational moral motives and Young's terminology for the five levels in his Neo-Maslovian model. Thus, they stretch from life preservation and care/linking to

(continued)

Table 4.2 (continued)

conscious identification/application and sanctity/humanizing, with the middle level involving reciprocity/respect. As with Maslow's original model, the present Neo-Maslovian and Neo-Haidtian ones constitute developmental progressions as much as needs/motives complexities

The particular higher-order aspects of the person's developing cognition and socio-affectivity relate to consciousness, the nature of the self, foundational morality, and a sense of responsibility, which together indicate apex psychological completeness or maturity. However, inevitably, the prenatal fetus has a lack at these levels (nonconscious, are not responsible, no self, no concept of any aspect of other, no morals, no meaning or sense of value, etc.). Glimmers along these lines will develop slowly, with the preliminary phases involving reflex growth and nothing more. However, at this first juncture, even basic physiological needs and survival are threatened by a host of possible insults

The person forced to live at this level because of extreme abuse, torture, locking up, or otherwise experiencing life threatening or murderous intentions will not be able to reach beyond the experience except perhaps through hope. Of course, these growth parameters (consciousness, sense of self, sense of other, responsibility, morality) could develop full-fledged before catastrophic events obliterate them, and so hope can be the vanguard of other developmental acquisitions that could reinvigorate and rehabilitate them once the extremely abusive regime is destroyed or otherwise lifted

The person might be partially able to move out of the suicidality ideation/intention orbit, and the therapist should construct this as a first step in the slow walk toward further growth

[c]Negative pole in each case = lack, behaving oppositely, disrupting (purposely)

[d](a) In terms of the five principal stages of the present model, the reflexive period is considered one where the fetus is responsive but not initiatory

(b) In the sensorimotor stage, the infant is more active and agentic, as well as voluntary and selective to some degree. The infant can be considered "response-able"

(c) As for the child, Piagetian logic develops and the child is capable of undertaking responsibility, but is limited in how much can be handled

(d) The adolescent is capable of dedicating the self to a cause in a fanatical way and could commit to one over and over, in a process of constant rededication to the responsibility (although parents would be happy with a rededication to the simpler tasks of life at home and at school). In this regard, I refer to the process as involving re-responsibility

(e) Finally, the adult who arrives at the level of advanced psychological maturity that might accompany the stage of collective intelligence can have the sense of re-responsibility flourish and become multiple and varied, in a process which I term one of re-responsibilities

Note. For each stage, five substages apply (coordination, hierarchization, systematization, multiplication, integration)

Adopted with permission of Springer Science+Business Media. Young, G. (2011). Development and causality: Neo-Piagetian perspectives. New York: Springer Science + Business Media B. V.; with kind permission from Springer Science + Business Media. [Second and Seventh column from Table 35.2, Page 813, its third and fifth column; Third column: Table 15.1, Page 350, its second column; Fourth and Fifth column: Figure 19.4, Page 454; Text Excerpt of 285 words, Page 813–814]

Adopted with permission of Springer International Publishing. Young, G. (2016). *Unifying* causality *and psychology: Being, brain and behavior*. Cham, Switzerland: Springer International Publishing; with kind permission from Springer International Publishing. [Sixth column from Table 34.5, Page 844, its fourth column]

Adopted with permission of Springer International Publishing. Young, G. (2019). Causality *and development:* Neo-Eriksonian *perspectives*. Cham, Switzerland: Springer International Publishing; with kind permission from Springer International Publishing. [Table 13.1, pp. 297–298]

refer to as cognition-emotion body of the other) might develop over the lifespan, according to the five Neo-Piagetian stages (see Table 4.2). The present Neo-Maslovian model, in terms of its suggested developmental trajectory, can be reworked to fit the model, as indicated in columns 4 and 5. I present this Neo-Maslovian model again (see prior Fig. 2.1) because the columns prepare the way for understanding the development of foundational moral motives in the column after that. The last column in the table indicates the pathway in the development of responsibility. Overall, the table indicates how our most advanced social, emotional, and moral acquisitions develop over the lifespan according to the present Neo-Piagetian model.

The present five-stage Neo-Piagetian model has a broad range of ways it can be applied developmentally. My first efforts in these regards included how adult functions, such as relating romantically and managing at work, can reflect the five-stage developmental cycle. For romantic relations, a couple can proceed through the five steps rather quickly compared to the lifetime developmental process indicated by the stages. For the management styles, the worker could adapt any of the five levels involved and not necessarily evolve in the sequence indicated. However, the five levels reflect underlying ways of (mis)perceiving the other cognitively, according to the five stages in the model (see Table 4.3).

As for examples of how the present five-stage Neo-Piagetian developmental models apply over the lifespan, the second and third columns of the table indicate the broad focus that makes sense to highlight at each stage in terms of predominant developmental acquisition and also a very specific development acquisition involving self-esteem. Generally, these extensions of the present five-stage developmental model can be elaborated to include substages. To conclude, in the last paragraphs, I have shown that the five-step substage progression within the Neo-Piagetian model can help understand change processes and that the five-stage model that englobes it has further applications.

To this point, I have shown that the present Neo-Piagetian model appears valid, can explain extant data in the field, can explain data gathered for other Neo-Piagetian models. Moreover, it can predict how other areas of development (e.g., self-esteem) might evolve developmentally. The next section further expounds on the Neo-Eriksonian aspect of the present model.

Neo-Eriksonian Development

Table 4.4 gives the penultimate aspect of the present work; in that it presents details of the 25-step Neo-Eriksonian model that perhaps is its most complex and innovative aspect. The model's steps are considered parallel ones to the equivalent steps in the Neo-Piagetian model on which it is based. The latter is a five-stage × five substage model, but my work on the Neo-Eriksonian model generally foregoes its stage and substage component and generally refers to 25 steps in development.

Table 4.3 Examples of application of the present five-stage model

Stage	Major focus (Young 2016)	Self-esteem (Young 2019)	Marital steps (Young 1997)	Management style (work, home) (Young 1997)
Reflexive	Physical	Roots of self-esteem in the self-efficacy and sense of omnipotence of being able to elicit effectively responsivity in the environment	Attraction	Negate
Sensorimotor	Emotional	Developing a sense of security due to the security promotion of the environment	Attachment	Dominate
Perioperational	Cognitive	Sense of competence and confidence as each social and task-based skill develops, through appropriate support from the environment, leading to a generalized poise and sense of self-esteem	Commitment	Relegate
Abstract (formal)	Conscious	As part of positive identity development, a sense of self-efficacy is further cemented by an appropriate environmental response. A sense of assurance develops in the adolescent's self-esteem. We end up with an adolescent who is self-assured	Growth	Delegate
Collective intelligence	Spiritual	The adult's self-esteem develops positively as the adult engages in the environment, and finds environmental support, as well. The self-esteem is communal, because the person values the state of others and their self-esteem. As their generativity is actualized in their collective actions, adults feel integrated and confident in their communal actions (communal confidence)	Mutuality	Integrate

Note. The table gives examples of how the present five-step model can be applied developmentally (columns 2 and 3) and also to adult spheres that can move through growth steps (columns 4 and 5). The first two examples concern foci in the development of self-esteem. The second two examples indicate correspondences with the five stages involved as applied to relationships with romantic partners and relationships with workers in management

Adopted with permission of Springer International Publishing. Young, G. (2019). Causality *and development:* Neo-Eriksonian *perspectives*. Cham, Switzerland: Springer International Publishing. [First, Fourth, and Fifth Column from Table 11.6, pp. 245]

Adopted with permission of Springer International Publishing. Young, G. (2016). *Unifying* causality *and psychology: Being, brain and behavior*. Cham, Switzerland: Springer International Publishing; with kind permission from Springer International Publishing. [Second column from Young (2016), Table 32.2, pp. 787; Third column from Table 16.1, pp. 444–445]

The Neo-Piagetian model conditions the development that can take place in Neo-Eriksonian terms. However, being at one particular Neo-Piagetian level does not necessarily translate into being at the equivalent Neo-Eriksonian level. This developmental dećalage takes place because, often, people's optimal socio-affective development is compromised by developmental delay, conflicts, adversities, and so on, leading to difficulty navigating well Neo-Eriksonian challenges associated with any one step.

The 25 steps in the Neo-Eriksonian model are described in terms of positive and negative poles, as in Erikson's original model (e.g., Trust vs. Mistrust in infancy; Erikson's famous Identity stage in adolescence). However, I referred to the poles involved as Acts. This emphasizes their active participatory aspect and mutuality in their development through the acts undertaken.

Aside from the goal of having parallel Neo-Piagetian and Neo-Eriksonian lifespan steps in development, the present approach to socio-affective modeling of the Neo-Eriksonian steps in development focused on the therapeutic implications of the model. When patients have experienced an environmental regime that considers them, at best, functioning at one particular developmental level or another, the consequences could be quite detrimental psychologically, especially if they were treated merely like infants (such as to abuse) or children (to control). Most of the description of the 25 steps in the development of the present Neo-Eriksonian model reflects on its therapeutic implications in these regards while including other relevant perspectives (e.g., attachment theory).

It might seem that a Neo-Eriksonian step in development does not resemble much in structure its corresponding Neo-Piagetian stage. The latter concerns schemes and operations that coordinate to help solve cognitive problems; the former concerns positive or negative polarities that tend to manifest in socio-affective behavior. However, cognition and socio-affectivity cannot be so easily separated and what develops are not purely cognitive schemes and operations but cognitive-socioemotional ones that integrate across distinctions in these regards. Cognition is not compartmentalized from emotions, socio-affectivity, etc.

Also, the positive and negative poles in a particular step in the Neo-Eriksonian sequence are not simply about the central opposition involved (e.g., Trust vs. Mistrust) because each step involves the range of cognitive/socio-affective structures (in schemes, operations) that have developed. The cognitive skills used to help solve cognitive skills are applied to the social/emotional arena, as well. In this sense, the present Neo-Piagetian model serves not only to help in understanding its parallel Neo-Eriksonian series but also the nature of its cognitive architecture helps explain how socio-affective problems are confronted toward possible resolution.

I have qualified the cognitive architecture in the Neo-Piagetian series as reflecting network modeling, systems theory, and so on to flesh out how cognitive schemas/structures relate to each other. The same language could be applied to how the negative and positive poles and their components in the Neo-Eriksonian series interrelate. Also, socio-affective developments in the Neo-Eriksonian series will impact cognitive development in the Neo-Piagetian one. The two domains are never really separate, and they mutually influence each other (e.g., in the development of negative cognitive filters in (mis)perceiving the world).

Yoking

Young (2011) developed the concept of Neo-Piagetian multiple cognitive intelligences. I considered the classic multiple intelligences as specifying the domains of activity for the Neo-Piagetian multiple intelligences. In Young's model, each of the 5 Neo-Piagetian cognitive stages (and the full 25 steps when substages are considered) constitutes the basis for a multiple intelligence. Moreover, the cognitive skills characterizing each (sub)stage for a particular individual are not integrated or overridden as each new (sub)stage develops, but they remain and can yoke with other (sub)stages cognitively to better help in cognitive problem solving (e.g., sensorimotor skills helping in abstract mechanical/engineering construction of tools).

The parallels in cognitive and socio-affective development that lay at the heart of the present Neo-Piagetian/Neo-Eriksonian model suggest that, just as there are multiple cognitive intelligences, there are multiple emotional intelligences. In Young (2016), I referred to the latter as multiple socio-affective intelligences.

In keeping with the argument of the indissociability of cognitive and socio-affective function, I argued that the types of cognitive skills that develop in the Neo-Piagetian series could be used in socio-affective crises and challenges. For example, mental schemes and structure become the repository of the issues involved and are used as the person navigates them, even if poorly. Consider a patient who has initiative and generativity problems. The therapist will call on aspects of both areas in which he is doing okay to help bootstrap other areas. The therapist will also seek psychological resources related to other developmental stages, such as possible skills in nurturance. The individual will learn to better yoke extant socio-affective resources and strengths in a network of coping and resilience skills to counter and deal with difficulties in navigating the identity and generativity issues. The hard-working attitudes that had been fostered in the latency period could be applied to this type of multiple emotional (socio-affective) intelligences, as well. In short, we constantly yoke and de-yoke socio-affective skills from various levels of our development to help us navigate ongoing stresses, developmental challenges, and the quest for personal and relational growth. This process goes much deeper than the

Table 4.4 25 steps in growth according to the present Neo-Eriksonian model

Step	Explanation
1. Distance acts vs. No (lifeless) acts (early fetal life)	Even from very early on, people could be rejected a lot, and even severely abused. Their life is at risk (any torture fits here). If this happened to you, you could react by wanting to kill yourself and behaving to hurt yourself. In general, your behavior is very reflexive, not directed well, or on target toward its goal. It is disorganized in its movement, even with wrong distances to targets. Perhaps you feel it is hard to move and feel lifeless.
2. Nursing acts vs. Rootless acts (fairly premature)	As you grew, starting in the early nursing period, you experienced major abuse and yourself was denied or not allowed to grow. You grew feeling that you had no anchor, or were missing roots. You felt helpless and hopeless. Also, you did not feel like caring for yourself. This might have led you to not care for anybody. You felt the same way even when you became a parent (or will feel that way when you have children one day).
3. Outcome acts vs. Outcast acts (that excluded you) (somewhat premature)	From early in life, you developed simple goals and tried to reach them. They got you what you wanted. But maybe the environment (parent) did not even support this basic activity and you were disregarded and not allowed to have any goals. You were treated like an outcast, or not belonging to anything, and were not allowed to speak or be what you wanted. Maybe you became the same way, and greatly ignored people and ignore yourself.
4. Care-giving acts vs. Careless giving acts (full term newborn)	Normally, right from birth, newborns develop a beginning self based on the body and actions, like grasping a finger. But the environment (parent) might not treat the baby well, being negligent and even abusive sometimes. Perhaps the environment (your parent) was uncaring or gave you poor care because of this. So, as you grew, you began to not care for yourself. Or, maybe you went the other way by constantly trying to seek care, but without knowing how.
5. Emotional acts vs. Mal-emotional or negative emotional acts (0–1 month)	Early in life, babies often are emotionally content. But from early on, you were very emotional, frustrated, unhappy, and even were in rage, fear, or both. The environment (parent) was not supportive and did not deal well with your emotions, leading you to have further emotional turmoil or trouble. As you grew, you continued to express a lot of negative emotions, or perhaps you went in the opposite direction, showing no emotions and feeling detached.
6. Dyadic acts vs. Dys-dyadic or poor interaction acts (1–4 months)	Normally, the growing infant is learning how to interact the right way with people. But even then, you experienced a nonsupportive environment (parent). It involved too much control, domination, and manipulation. The result was that, as you grew, you did not learn to interact with people the right way. You were not warm or sensitive. Instead, you were clumsy and confused socially and could withdraw in silence. Or, perhaps you were angry and rejected people.

(continued)

Table 4.4 (continued)

Step	Explanation
7. Trust acts vs. Mistrust acts (4–8 months)	In the first year of life, normally the infant develops a sense of trust or confidence in people. But if the environment (parent) is not supportive, the person might not be able to trust people and create any close relationships. If this happened to you, also you might feel down and without purpose, and be passive or suspicious. Perhaps you became angry inside, too. Or, instead, perhaps you trusted blindly anybody else (and were taken advantage of by them).
8. Sociability acts vs. Un-sociability or poor sociability acts (8–12 months)	Normally, the growing person develops social behavior that helps create positive relationships. This starts in infancy, including in positive attachment to the parent. However, without good parental/ caregiver support, a person could develop insecure attachments and not be good socially even after. Social behavior becomes avoidant, fearful, rejecting, or ambivalent. If this happened to you, perhaps you attached to anybody without being careful about it. Or, perhaps you totally avoided any relations, being super wary and isolated.
9. Autonomy (independence) acts vs. Doubt (dependence) acts (12–18 months)	Normally, like the toddler, we become eager and act for ourselves, feel confident in exploration, and feel satisfied in social behavior. But perhaps your environment (parent) did not give you good support for your independent activity, and you ended up feeling dependent and not confident. You found it hard to take initiative and explore. You become inward and dissatisfied. You even felt dominated. Or, you went the other way; and you became defiant, argumentative, and not cooperative.
10. Interdigitational (give and take) acts vs. De-digitational (give or take) acts (18– 24 months)	As we grow, we learn to interact with give and take (not just giving or taking). But if you did not receive environmental support (parenting) for this, you might have difficulty in sharing, being concerned for others, and feeling fondness and even love. Instead, you might hate people. As for sense of yourself, you might not feel self-pride and even hate yourself. Maybe you seek too much power, or avoid confrontation, so people manipulate you easily.
11. Superordinate (well-coordinated) acts vs. Dis-coordinate (uncoordinated) acts (2–3.5 years)	Normally, we feel "together" (the parts of myself are super coordinated) and do not think that we are "in pieces" (not coordinated). But if your environment (parent) was not supportive this way (was controlling, for example), you did not develop to feel together and felt "in pieces." So you put your personal needs in the middle of everything (being "egocentric," self-centered). Perhaps you were somewhat resistant, too. Or, perhaps you always accepted whatever other people wanted.
12. Initiative acts vs. Guilt acts (3.5–5 years)	The growing person balances being forward (in initiative) and being inward and withdrawing. The person could feel guilty when being too forward. For example, preschoolers might have sexual feelings for the parent (of the opposite sex) that are too forward and do not go away, even without knowing it. If the environment (your parent) does not handle this well, you could develop unconscious (unaware) sexual problems that continue into adolescence onwards, or general problems in initiative (having too much or too little).

(continued)

Table 4.4 (continued)

Step	Explanation
13. Identification and gender acts vs. Problematic identification and gender acts (5–7 years)	In growing, we identify with or want to be like people who are around, especially parents. This helps you learn about and act like the gender that you prefer. But your environment (parent) might not be supportive about this. This could create problems for you, including not wanting to be like the parent or becoming opposite to how is the parent. Or, perhaps you do not identify with anyone and have become narcissistic, uncontrollable, etc.
14. Industry (putting in good effort) acts vs. Inferiority acts (7–9 years)	In growing, normally we enjoy learning, including at school, feel motivated, and develop peer friendships. However, your environment (parent) could have shown little interest in your learning, manipulated you, created harsh rules, etc. This could have led you to lose interest in school and learning, lose self-confidence, have the wrong friends, feel inferior, and even rebel. Or, perhaps you went the other way, and felt too superior, while you became insensitive and lied as needed.
15. Role/personality tryout acts vs. Role/ personality confusion acts (9–11 years)	The growing person tries out different roles, friends, attitudes, and personalities, both for the challenge and having fun. If you had problems in the environment supporting tryouts such as these, maybe you had a hard time exploring them or explored them too much but on the surface only. So you became confused in your tryouts and stopped them. Or, you tried out negative (e.g., antisocial) tryouts in roles/personalities (and you felt different moods, including brooding).
16. Consciousness (being aware) acts vs. Contraconscious (not being aware) acts (11–13 years)	Once the thinking of people becomes logical and abstract, such as in the teen years, they can develop an awareness of the self, other people, the environment, society, and their place in the world. If your environment (parent) was not supportive of this type of thinking and opening, you had difficulties in being aware like this. Perhaps you were less conscious and more conforming than normal, or you were conscious but in fanatical or superficial ways.
17. Identity acts (positive ones) vs. Identity diffusion (or negative identity) acts (13–16 years)	The growing person explores different identities, selves, or questions of "Who I am." Your environment (parent) could interfere in creating a positive identity that you like. This could lead you to: (a) confusion in identity; (b) putting off the search for identity; (c) simply adopting identities of other people without thinking about it; (d) adopting negative identities, such as in teenage gangs/delinquency; or (e) adopting many identities, but all surface, false, or fake ones.
18. Nurturing acts vs. Mis-nurturing (not nurturing) acts (16–19 years)	The growing person engages in caring behavior of other people, to give them support and bring out the best in them. The environment (parent) might not support nurturing, and the person will not nurture or care for people. If this happened to you, this will affect your social relationships. Perhaps you will ignore people, not like them, and so on. Or, perhaps you will nurture people a lot, but only on the surface and without real caring.
19. Intimacy acts (with partner) vs. (Social) isolation acts (19–22 years)	The growing person gives positive effort, including at work or in school, and with any romantic partner and any children. The person feels a deep, long-lasting love for the partner, if any is present, and feels deeply involved in everything done. Without environmental (parental) support (or with past problems), you could reject romance and feel lonely and empty. Or, you could go through the motions and be fake in any relationship with a partner, even behaving roughly.

(continued)

Table 4.4 (continued)

Step	Explanation
20. Universal (general concern for all people) acts vs. Self-singular (self-focused) acts (22–25 years)	The growing adult is concerned for all people and desires to care for or help anybody in need. This is especially true for family but could apply to anyone, too. There is a basic helping moral value felt about everybody. Without getting good support this way, you could become a person who rejects helping others, family and all people included, or only helps them without feeling (or just to get praise).
21. Meta-collecting (seeing the big picture) acts vs. Disillusionment acts (25–28 years)	The young adult could see the big picture of the world and all its interconnections at many joined levels. You could develop concern for the growth of all groups of peoples, wanting them capable of helping other peoples. If things go wrong this way, you could ignore or even act against other peoples, detesting them, and feel disillusioned/down. Or, you could help peoples only because you have been taught to, and you do it only superficially.
22. Generativity (generating) acts vs. Self-absorption (no responsibility) acts (28–39 years)	Growing adults give their best to their responsibilities, from family and relationships, to work and study, to society. The conscious, identity, relating and helping attitudes of the prior steps in life become real in all activities. If problems come up for whatever reason, you could let go of your responsibilities, feel empty, focus only on yourself, and not grow. Or, you might try hard to take your responsibilities, but just on the surface or because of your training.
23. Catalytic (growing others) acts vs. Midlife crisis acts (39–50 years)	Growing adults carry through with all their responsibilities so that everything around them grows or gets better. But problems could develop for you and cause you to let go of all your responsibilities even though you had taken them all on well up to this point in time. You change and act just for the self. You reject loved ones, work, and all your responsibilities. Or, you could keep them and just go through the motions, feeling sad.
24. Ego integrity (feeling good about the self and life) acts vs. Despair acts (50–61 years)	As the years go on, family and relationships grow, work or study continues, and perhaps you help people and society, depending on your situation. You feel comfortable about how life has gone. But if problems happen about this, you could feel very low, depressed, or disappointed. You regret not having given your best in life, not being fully present in everything done, etc. Also, perhaps you get angry, cannot do anything, etc.
25. Cathartic (purifying) acts vs. Abandonment acts (61 years and after)	No matter the age, the person facing death looks back fondly and faces it without fear. You have a broad, wise view of life, how your life was lived, and what death means. You prepare for death with some form of inner peace and spirituality. But if there are problems this way, you will feel alone and abandoned by life at its last moments, and struggle with inner peace, spirituality, and death itself. You might seek last-minute help.

Adopted with permission of Springer International Publishing. Young, G. (2019). Causality *and development:* Neo-Eriksonian *perspectives*. Cham, Switzerland: Springer International Publishing; with kind permission from Springer International Publishing. [Text Excerpt of 2262 words from Chapter 18, pp. 536–540] example provided because the constant online yoking/deyoking takes place over several to many applicable steps from the 25-step series involved. Table 4.4 gives these 25-steps; the combinations and permutations of how they can combine are essentially infinite. Thus, the model underlying them is approaching the complexity of life.

Patients

In Young (2019), I presented an elaborate description of each of the 25 steps in the Neo-Eriksonian model in terms of how it can help patients who are experiencing difficulties in navigating any one of the steps. Patients might have experienced the worst abuses and so have difficulties with the earliest stages of life. Or, they might have had sequential adversities and have multiple developmental issues. I examined each of the stages in terms of 12 topics organized into 3 sections. First, for each step in the Neo-Eriksonian model as applied to patient difficulties, I presented topics in self and relational development, beginning with an interim summary. Then, I shifted to topics on attachment, development, and therapeutic implications. Finally, I considered therapeutic strategies. The specific topics for self and relational development concerned: interim summary; self-response to the cognitive (mis)perception of the other; the positive pole in Eriksonian development; and negative social-self working schemata. For attachment, development and implications, the topics included: patient presentation; behavior/symptom mental scanning; therapy implications; and stress/trauma resilience/coping. For the topic of therapeutic strategies, the specific topics were: relational coregulation; behavior/symptom network/connectivity change (horizontal); behavior/symptom growth, deep change (vertical)/constructing a more positive life story; and consciousness, theory of mind, selves, and responsibility.

It is beyond the scope of the summary in this book of Young's three core books (Young, 2011, 2016, 2019) to give much detail of the contents of these 12 topics for the 25 steps in the Neo-Eriksonian model. However, Table 4.5 provides the difficulties that patients might face with respect to each step. The excerpts for the table were taken from the topic of cognitive (mis)perception, which is one of the cardinal innovations in Young's oeuvre. The excerpts relate to how a patient would present if she/he had experienced a regime like the one for the particular step being described (as per Table 4.4).

To conclude the discussion of the 25 steps in the Neo-Eriksonian model, the descriptions of each stage offered in Table 4.4 function as prototypical examples, and there is much individual variation that would qualify them for any individual person or patient. One way of testing that variability over the lifespan would be to use the 25 descriptions of the steps involved in empirical research by constructing

Table 4.5 The cognitive (mis)perception of the other according to the 25-step Neo-Eriksonian model

Neo-Eriksonian substage	Cognitive (mis)perception (excerpt)
Distance acts vs. No acts (1)	The individual living a regime of being treated reflexively, and fully so, such that any other way of being treated is dismissed, rejected, undermined, or not even acknowledged as possible, is obliterated into silence, or annihilated in psychological, cultural, or even personal (bodily) murder. Dehumanizing genocide and torture are classic examples. [p. 287]
Nursing vs. Rootless acts (2)	The individual who is subject to a degree of cognitive (mis)perception of the other that is inherently abusive, potentially murderous, etc., but with at least some other more positive perceptions contemplated or possible, is essentially suppressed, and even has her/his life in danger. But relative to the extreme abuse associated with the prior substage, the possibility of experiencing a different regime opens some sense of reacting more than in disorganized silence and self-annihilation. [p. 300]
Outcome vs. Outcast acts (3)	The person risks expressing corresponding negative reactions in consequence, focusing on behaviors that are self-destructive and reflect a lack of self-growth, including self-obliteration. The nascent corporal protoself will be undercut and disintegrate in such circumstances. Indeed, the risk for suicidality, addictions, etc., remains as constant possibilities. These risks might arise through the psychiatric/psychological dynamics in this particular substage despite the more primitive and earlier-developed fixated reflexive substages with which these autodestructive behaviors are associated. [p. 306]
Caregiving vs. Careless giving acts (4)	Normally, people are open to receiving caregiving, care, and giving, but this capacity could be compromised and even annulled if one is forced to live in this regime. If the person is not overtly rejecting already, vicious circles in lack of responsiveness, ignoring and rejecting could develop, leading the person to create distance, reject, and refuse receiving/giving care, as the case may be. The other who might be involved with the person and be exposed to her/his behavior (not as the original abuser) could respond similarly to the person. [p. 311]
Emotional vs. Malemotional acts (5)	The person forced to live in an emotional cauldron because of the inconsistent/negative dismissing/negligent, and even abusive/rejecting regime she/he might be exposed to, at least partially, for example, when the social environment is not listening/communicating, will lead to negative (e.g., frustrative) reactions. The self will express primary negative emotions overtly and haphazardly, but perhaps somewhat directed to the source of frustration in the environment. [pp. 316–317]
Dyadic vs. Dysdyadic acts (6)	Due to the undercutting in the growth of the self (referred to as the incipient interactive, intercoordinative, and social self in the case of the very young infant), the self of the maltreated person at this level responds with trying to absorb the discoordinate, controlling messages in the environment, but the person cannot do much more and wilts in any attempt to do so. The externalizing pole in this reaction will involve a self-saturated in anger and revolution to the degree possible in the circumstances. [p. 326]

(continued)

Table 4.5 (continued)

Neo-Eriksonian substage	Cognitive (mis)perception (excerpt)
Trust vs. Mistrust acts (7)	The person who has lived a lack of support akin to what the mid-year infant lives in negative contexts will develop deep inabilities to relate to others with trust/confidence, will interact with personal agendas, and so on. Distrust/mistrust/no trust will predominate. The self will have a core that lacks in initiative, lacks in purpose, expresses goals that are not mutually regulative/reciprocal, and that are without joy/delight/faith. The person will be prone to engage in the type of behavior received—manipulative control, undermining of the self, sabotage/countering/contradiction, and so on—with resultant emotions being either internalizing (sad, dissociated, not trusting) or externalizing (irritable, reactive/revolution). [p. 335]
Sociability vs. Unsociability acts (8)	The adult who lives in a social environment not unlike that of the insecure infant toward the end of the first year of life will develop a sense of self analogous to the one being discussed for the infant, which will be pervaded by a sense of insecurity and which will be underwritten by social behaviors incapable of eliciting security and providing security to the other. The images guiding the behavior will not be positive ones about a securing figure but will be negative ones about insecuring figure(s). Social behavior will be replete with negatives, curt "No's" that cut communication, and falling into communicative disorganization. The emotional reactions could be either internalizing dislike/worry/escape or externalizing aggression. [p. 343]
Autonomy vs. Doubt acts (9)	The adult living an equivalent regime of the infant in this age period will also have issues related to autonomy/exploration, physical independence, and self-confidence. Even if environmental and social initiatives are undertaken, they might not continue to desired ends as self-doubt/dependence creeps in and predominates. The self will be dependent and nonautonomous more than anything else. The concept of the other associated with this self-image also will be limited in undertakings in autonomy; exploratory, independent ways of behaving will not be viewed as inherent in the other. The other will be viewed as manipulative to a degree, absent/nonsupportive psychologically, or both, depending on context. [p. 351]
Interdigitational vs. Dedigitational acts (10)	The adult facing the equivalent regime also will be deficient/aberrant in sensorimotor-mediated symbolic activity in cognitive/social organization. The self will not be organized as a constant permanent psychological entity but as a variable, ephemeral, and changing one, perhaps even at the slightest whim or to the most minor perceived slight.
	Sharing, empathy, give-and-take in relations, affection/nascent love feelings, role exchanges, and social flexibility in detours/reversals will not be evident in the person, with little room for appreciation/pride and vaunting the self in "I" or "Me" statements. The concept of the other similarly will be divorced from these interdigitational and implicative possibilities. The person might experience deep dislike of others/hate and with social skills restricted to not-so-subtle attempts at manipulation. [p. 358]

(continued)

Table 4.5 (continued)

Neo-Eriksonian substage	Cognitive (mis)perception (excerpt)
Superordinate vs. Discoordinate acts (quasi-participatory) (11)	The adult who will have experienced an environment like that of the unsupported 2-year-old will also develop an egocentric self, but one that transforms into an egotistical, selfish, and demeaning one. Criticism of the other will be constant and color social interaction. The goal will be to create confusion/compliance and disrupt/disorganize any planned social organization that considers the desires/wants of the other as relevant. The other will perceive the person as lacking in social skills, fragmented/dispersed, and even hostile/hateful. Indeed, the self-experienced by the person might seem superficially together in its egotistic attitude, but it will be fissured, parcellated, and fragilely knit together, if at all. [p. 369]
Initiative vs. Guilt acts (12)	The adult who has lived in an equivalent regime will be struggling with initiation issues, as well. The self will be initiative-saturated, and uncontrollable or, to the contrary, the self will be initiative-depleted or pacified/too controlled. Guilt will be an overriding emotion experienced. Or, the contrary of feeling guiltless might predominate. Blame will always lie elsewhere, and overt lying about things will be more possible (which would also happen with the guilt-free excessively and uncontrolled initiatory young child). The cognitive apparatus associated with this level of functioning concerns symbol plan hierarchies in the representation involved. [p. 380]
Identification vs. Problematic identification acts (13)	Personality difficulties and disorders are laid. Emotions experienced will parallel the identifications, e.g., oppositional, depressive, or impoverished (flat) ... Psychological vestiges of poor identificatory patterns, including those imposed by the parent, might proliferate and characterize the psychological characteristics of the self. [p. 392]
Industry vs. Inferiority acts (14)	The adult experiencing a similar regime will develop as just described for the child, but even more so. The sense of inferiority/failure might be pervasive, along with a widespread laxity/demotivation. Industry will be absent and idle activity prominent, perhaps with idol worshipping of one sort of another (usually promising quick fixes). Logical rationality will be hidden behind illogic, absent thinking will prevail over thinking through and thought reversal in problem-solving, and seeking help from others will be either maximized or minimized, depending on the style involved. The other will be treated with distance or disrespect, as the case may be, instead of closeness and bonding. [p. 402]
Role vs. Role confusion acts (15)	Whatever deviant direction taken in imagined role/play personality (under- vs. overreacting), the preteen will be restricted/limited, and going through successive imaginations (or their lack) that make any ameliorative efforts more difficult. The same applies to the adult faced with an imagination-constricted environment with respect to role/personality tryouts, except the confusions will be more marked relative to those of the preteen. The person might end up superconservative and conformist and reflect the other's desired roles/personalities and their influences. Or, to the contrary, the person might end up super flaky and anti-conformist and reflect only her/his own influences/suggestions on imagined roles/personalities, or display rejection/behaving oppositely to those of others, or do both. [p. 414]

(continued)

Table 4.5 (continued)

Neo-Eriksonian substage	Cognitive (mis)perception (excerpt)
Conscious vs. Contraconscious acts (16)	Adults will have all these tendencies exacerbated if they had faced an equivalent crisis of consciousness due to an unsupportive environment. Perhaps the most profound effect from having lived in an environment that had been unsupportive of the exploration and freeing of the unconscious into the conscious is the likely development of either hypoconsciousness or hyperconsciousness (but at a pseudo level). The latter type will foment internally yet try to present as placid and peaceful externally. However, leakages and their consequences will be telling and tiring and impede self, cognitive, social, emotional, and socioaffective development. [pp. 429–430]
Identity vs. Identity diffusion acts (17)	The teenager living in an environment that is not supportive of a search for identity might create a hypoidentificatory style or a hyperidentificatory one. The hypoidentificatory teen will cut off identity searching, or not even start the process of searching while adopting identifications molded [by] or foisted on her/him by the environment. The hyperidentificatory teen could be quite superficial/pseudo about the process, and adopt even negative/ anti–/defiant identities.
	The constructed other will be a mirror of these types of identity styles and might be perceived as acting against the teen's identity formation, or perhaps framing ones for the teen, without malevolence (assuming that the identity issues are the first major ones being experienced in development and the environment had been good enough until this time). The patient living an equivalent regime might also be hypo- or hyperidentificatory, and perceive the self and other in these terms. [p. 447]
Nurturing vs. Misnurturing acts (18)	The late teen/adult who has not been well-supported in nurturing, or otherwise has difficulties therein, will not consider the other in the central way as described for the typically developing teen. The other will not be an object of positive nurturing and care. The other might receive misnurturing instead, including in neglect/no nurturing by omission and harming/ misnurturing by commission. Instead of being conscientious toward the other, there might be contraconscientious co-opting of the other for personal needs or conscious harming for whatever reason. Instead of the good person engaging in nurturing, "bad" behavior might be expressed toward the other. Treating the other from the perspective of behaving from adult-like functions will not materialize, and the person might be childish/ petty instead, or even loathing of the other. [pp. 456–457]
Intimacy vs. Isolation acts (19)	The early adult who encounters environmental or other circumstances that are not conducive to establishing intimacy and related adult functions might feel a sense of aloneness and isolation even if there is a romantic partner involved. The relationship might founder in incomplete, insincere, clumsy, or contrary attempts at intimacy. The other might evaluate the person as putting on a façade, either hiding an absent/socialized intimacy or a negative/anti-one, something like passive-aggressive behavior, or superficially expressing intimacy but deeply resenting and rejecting it (as well as the other as the recipient). The other might elicit deep, hateful feelings instead of loving ones. Longing for the other will be replaced by a longing for an end to the relationship or even longing for a second (another) romantic (sexual) partner. [p. 468]

(continued)

Table 4.5 (continued)

Neo-Eriksonian substage	Cognitive (mis)perception (excerpt)
Universal vs. Self-singular acts (20)	The young adult who suspends universal/empathic concern, or who cannot even contemplate feeling and behaving this way, could react with a hypo- or hyper attitude in these regards. The hypo type will reflect a total absence of universal empathy, perhaps to the point of being totally self-indulgent. However, if the person had been socialized to be universally empathic but, nevertheless, not having a deep personal commitment to feel and behave this way, the other will be treated well enough, although only because of the socialization involved (e.g., entrained, imposed). The hyper style will express a pseudo empathy for all others but will be viewed as ersatz/false by careful observers. Hyper types will seek adoration but risk approbation when the veneer of their superficial behavior no longer hides the deep (self-inflating) motivations involved. [pp. 480–481]
Metacollecting vs. Disillusionment acts (21)	The person might be incapable of any generalized altruism to any people and turn uniquely inward toward the self and its needs. The other will be only "another," someone/some people to put on the back burner or even out of awareness completely. In the worst-case scenarios, the other is denigrated, considered beneath the person, who considers herself/himself as the sole person in need of altruism. The world revolves around her/his pedestal, with the columnar statue of the self having empty bulging eyes as much as any origin Greek statue. The person expresses disillusionment with society, but eventually, that could become disillusionment with the self. [p. 496]
Generativity vs. Self-absorption acts (22)	The person might not have the supportive environment to function in this ideal or might otherwise be incapable of it and falter in undertaking it. The person could lapse into stagnation rather than generativity and in self-absorption rather than other-concern. The other could be misperceived as unworthy of a generative attitude and acts or as someone who should do it on her/his own. The other is disempowered, deactivated, and emptied of what is required to succeed. Instead of being a positive role model, the person might become an absent or negative one. Instead of being a mentor, the person might even become a tormentor. Instead of prompting growth and integration, the person might rejoice in regression and disintegration. [p. 507]
Catalytic vs. Midlife crisis acts (23)	The midlife catalysis in generativity that takes place in work/family/society means that the person has become an instrumental support for others. At the same time, the person might be overwhelmed in undertaking these responsibilities and put them on hold/abandon them. The self is doubly invested in as the other is doubly abandoned (doubly in the sense of multiple domains and doubly in the sense of critical junctures for the work/family, others involved). The other becomes not only put on/hold abandoned but also unduly criticized/rejected, leading to confusion (and reflecting the person's confusion). The re-evaluation/redefinition of the self and life trajectory that takes place leads to pining for earlier life periods without the same responsibilities. [pp. 516–517]

(continued)

Table 4.5 (continued)

Neo-Eriksonian substage	Cognitive (mis)perception (excerpt)
Ego integrity vs. Despair acts (24)	The person who despairs of a meaningless life with no ego integrity will be disappointed/depressed, and the mood will extend into the core components of the self/I. It is as if the person is saying—Why did I make those self-centered choices; I lived a life focused on my little pleasures and avoided large stresses instead of seeing the futility of that lifestyle, etc. My life has been joyless and empty instead of satisfying and acceptable? I did not work through troubles but receded into myself and let the troubles take on a permanent life of their own that I assiduously avoided in my self-core. I did not keep my composure, reach out to the other in need, and now feel absolutely alone. I wanted a useful life, but it ended up useless. [p. 521]
Cathartic vs. Abandonment acts (25)	People struggling with end-of-life issues might feel that the world/other/life/universe has abandoned them. They feel turbulence instead of wisdom, fall back instead of looking forward, feel impure rather than purified, feel irrelevant instead of being reverent, feel unintegrated instead of integrated, and feel spiritually alone instead of spiritually transcendent. They are without an overarching vision of the life lived and the fate awaiting them and without any connecting fellowship with any other/humanity, mystery, and infinity. The self feels miserable even fearful. The other is totally discounted, nonexistent. Instead of catharsis in the end-point experience of life, the person feels shut out and shuts out, self-imploding before expiring, and not allowing any other into the last circle. [p. 526]

Adopted with permission of Springer International Publishing. Young, G. (2019). Causality *and development:* Neo-Eriksonian *perspectives*. Cham, Switzerland: Springer International Publishing. [Various Excerpts and pages: Text Excerpt of 359 words from pp. 287–317 in Chapter 13; Text Excerpt of 550 words from pp. 326–358 in Chapter 14; Text Excerpt of 473 words from pp. 369–414 in Chapter 15; Text Excerpt of 636 words from pp. 429–481 in Chapter 16; Text Excerpt of 606 words from pp. 496–526 in Chapter 17]

questionnaires based on them. One value of the present model of Neo-Eriksonian development is that it opens the study of stages or steps in development in the Eriksonian sense beyond Erikson's original eight stages and allows linkages to the Neo-Piagetian (sub)stage sequence underpinning them.

Conclusion

This chapter begins a two-chapter elaboration of the foundational work in the three Young books (2011, 2016, 2019). That elaboration continues in the next chapter. The conclusions to that chapter relate both to it and the present chapter.

References

Blatt, S.J.: Polarities of Experience: Relatedness and Self-Definition in Personality Development, Psychopathology, and the Therapeutic Process. American Psychological Association, Washington, DC (2008)

Dodge, K.A., Godwin, J., The Conduct Problems Prevention Research Group: Social-information-processing patterns mediate the impact of preventive intervention on adolescent antisocial behavior. Psychol. Sci. **24**(4), 456–465 (2013). https://doi.org/10.1177/0956797612457394

Graham, J., Haidt, J.: Sacred values and evil adversaries: a moral foundations approach. In: Mikulincer, M., Shaver, P.R. (eds.) The Social Psychology of Morality: Exploring the Causes of Good and Evil, pp. 11–31. American Psychological Association, Washington, DC (2012)

Mascolo, M.F., Fischer, K.W.: The codevelopment of self and sociomoral emotions during the toddler years. In: Brownell, C.A., Kopp, C.B. (eds.) Socioemotional Development in the Toddler Years: Transitions and Transformation, pp. 66–99. Guilford Press, New York (2007)

Mascolo, M.F., Fischer, K.W.: Dynamic development of thinking, feeling, and acting. In: Overton, W.F., Molenaar, P.C.M. (eds.) Handbook of Child Psychology and Developmental Science. Vol. 1: Theory and Method, 7th edn, pp. 240–317. Wiley, Hoboken (2015)

van den Heuvel, M.P., Sporns, O.: Network hubs in the human brain. Trends Cogn. Sci. **17**(12), 683–696 (2013). https://doi.org/10.1016/j.tics.2013.09.012

Young, G.: Adult Development, Therapy, and Culture: A Postmodern Synthesis. Plenum, New York (1997)

Young, G.: Development and Causality: Neo-Piagetian Perspectives. Springer Science + Business Media, New York (2011)

Young, G.: Unifying Causality and Psychology: Being, Brain and Behavior. Springer International Publishing, Cham (2016)

Young, G.: Causality and Development: Neo-Eriksonian Perspectives. Springer International Publishing, Cham (2019)

Chapter 5
Elaborating Causality in the Unified Model

The chapter begins by presenting work on networks. Then it proceeds to examine causality from other angles.

Networking

Tables 5.1 and 5.2 list network concepts, indices, and definitions for neural networks and social networks, respectively. The former network terms refer to neuroscientific research, such as functional connectivity within and across brain regions, while the latter network terms refer to social relationships among people. A comparison of the two collections of network concepts finds many similarities and some differences. The basic terms of nodes and edges in neuroscience networks are replaced in social ones at times by persons/actors and (social) ties. However, for the individual entity (e.g., neuronal region, person), the major measures of centrality are the same (degree, betweenness, and closeness). Nodes express connectivity (e.g., hubs, paths, and modules), which are functional. They vary in strength (e.g., core, central coherence, and density). Socially, node clusters can express cliques, as well. Networks have dynamical properties, such as reciprocity and feedback. The neuronal networks are described as perhaps having tight organization, such as small-world networking and rich clubs. Generally, these organizations reflect a more condensed and efficient organization. The social network structure includes concepts related to emergence. This approach is quite consistent with my own, as shall be further elaborated below. The causal aspect is consistent with network models of psychiatric symptoms in which critical symptoms are considered drivers of other symptoms (Schmittmann et al. 2013).

G. Young, *Causality and Neo-Stages in Development*,
https://doi.org/10.1007/978-3-030-82540-9_5

Table 5.1 Common social network measures and concepts

Level of analysis	Network measure	Definition
Individual	Degree centrality	Count of an actor's total number of social ties. *Indegree* refers to incoming ties, and *outdegree* refers to outgoing ones
	Betweenness centrality	A node could lie between or connects two nodes that would not otherwise be connected; its extent
	Closeness centrality	A node could be close to all other nodes in the network; its extent
	Structural equivalence	A node could play a similar role within a network; its extent
Group or subgroup	Modularity	A network could divide into modules; its strength. High modularity means a network has dense connections between the nodes within modules but sparse connections between nodes in different modules
	Clique	A *clique* has every individual directly tied to every other individual in a subgroup
	Transitivity	Two nodes could be connected to the same third node and also connected to each other; the extent
Network	Density	The proportion of pairs of nodes that have ties of a given type (existing ties in a network/all possible ties in the network)
	Reciprocity	The proportion of all directional ties that are reciprocated
	Centralization	A network could revolve around one or a few nodes; the extent
	Diameter	Geodesics (paths between two nodes); the longest
	Clustering	A network has clumps (small subgroups within the network with close ties to each other); the extent
Core concepts	Stocks	An accumulation representing a system's memory or state (e.g., in infant behavior)
	Flows	Stocks change because of associated flow dynamics connecting stocks (outflow to inflow, rates)
	Feedback	A structural feature causing cascades in other factors when it affects a stock (positive or negative; could be in balance)
	Systems structure/causal loop diagrams	Illustrate system reinforcing feedbacks, polarities involved, whether vicious or virtuous cycles develop
	Agent-based modeling	Dynamic modeling of system states that includes parameters, rules, environments, emergence, complexity

Adapted from Urban et al. (2014)

Table 5.2 Networks and definitions

Network	Definition
Centrality	A measure on the relative importance that a node or edge occupies within a network architecture (e.g., degree, betweenness, closeness)
Connectivity	The set of node connections
Connector hubs	Function to link nodes over modules
Core	A coherent, highly and mutually interconnected node set or group, facilitating resistance to perturbation
Density	The proportion of pairs of nodes that have ties of a given type (existing ties in a network/all possible ones in the network)
Diameter	Paths between two nodes, and to its longest path
Distance	The shortest topological path in a node pair
Edge	Connections or associations between pairs of nodes; their relationship, interaction, or dependency; refers to categorical existence present or the dimensional strength
Global efficiency	A distance measure
Hub	A node that is influentially important, or central to network interconnectivity; a high-degree network node displaying diverse connectivities over modules
Modules	Communities of strongly or densely interconnected nodes, that is, having a large number of mutual connections with few connections outside these links
Motif	A reduced subset of network nodes and edges, or a subgraph
Network	The links (edges) among nodes in a system, including possible emergent phenomena that arise from the interaction causally of the nodes. The nodes are observed, measurable variables, and each variable is considered as its own entity with the variables explored for their relationships (Bernstein et al. 2017)
Node (vertex)	A fundamental element of a system (e.g., a neuron, a person)
Node degree	Its number of incoming and outgoing edges
Node neighbors	A node's set of connected links
Path	An ordered sequence of unique edges and intermediate nodes; the shortest path between two nodes indicates the minimal number of links for two applicable nodes
Provincial hubs	High-degree network node linking constituent nodes within its module
Random network	Edges between nodes are random
Reciprocity	Concerns the proportion of all directional ties that are reciprocated
Rich club	A set of high-degree nodes with well-connected nodes connecting to each other; the interconnections are greater than expected relative to applicable node degree measures
Small world network	Most nodes in the circuit can be reached from every other node by a reduced number of moves even though they are not direct neighbors

Adapted from Sporns (2011, 2012) and van den Heuvel and Sporns (2013)

Note. Lim et al. (2019) added the distinction between associativity and dissociativity in networks. The concept relates to network robustness. In networks that are isolated, correlations among the features of nodes (e.g., with respect to degree) for nodes connected directly indicate its dissociativity/associativity. The network pattern is associative when high-degree nodes are frequently attached to other ones, with low-degree nodes connected to each other. Hevey (2018) provides a useful review of networks in health research and points out that nodes can be complex in psychology, such as for attitudes. This speaks to the present argument that networks can form hierarchical structures of levels, with ones like attitudes constituting separate levels that stand in reciprocal relations to lower-order behavioral/symptom levels and higher-order ones, like traits

Emergent Circular Causality

Figure 5.1 indicates how different levels in a system can reconfigure and how new higher-order levels can emerge from lower-order ones. Further, it indicates how the different levels in a system reciprocally influence each other and how there are both top-down and bottom-up influences in system function. Causality resides not only in within-level causal driving but also in across-level causation processes. Any network model needs to include not only its system aspect within levels but also its system aspect across levels, including in emergent reciprocal or circular (feedback) causality processes.

As applied to network modeling, the figure shows that lower-order levels in a network can systemically transform to or add de novo emergent higher-order levels, which in turn can influence lower-order levels. For example, as argued in Young (2015), psychiatric system networks can form higher-order psychiatric complexes, such as small-d depression, which can reciprocally influence lower-order levels and their psychiatric symptoms from which they had derived. This does not mean that a universal list of depression symptoms, as per the DSM-5, leads to a sanctioned DSM-5 diagnosis within the individual's symptom repertoire. Rather, generalized feelings of depression magnify in individual ways and add to the person's symptom complex. In this sense, small-d depression develops from psychiatric symptoms before taking on a life of its own and comes to resemble large-D major depression.

Staging

Figure 5.2 illustrates how the evolution of cognitive skills in a domain can develop toward a high-order level. The cognitive skills involved coordinate, creating more refined, adaptive, and inclusive structures that can be (re)created and applied online in context. Ultimately, they possess adaptive properties that are applied successfully enough. However, when contexts no longer allow problem resolution, or when the solutions no longer are deemed adequate, cognitive conflict, reflection, and accommodation take place, thereby allowing increasing coordination with other developing cognitive skills so that a new level of cognitive sophistication emerges. The process of activation-inhibition coordination supplements and solders the developmental shift.

This does not mean that the individual developing to a new, higher-order cognitive (sub)stage develops it in full right away and in a universal manner, nor deploys it in full; indeed, it is as if the higher-order level is a static nonadjustable entity waiting for its full activation. In contrast, cognitive skill deployment is always contextually driven and adaptive-focused to the problem at hand toward arriving at an accommodating bottom-up successful resolution. The bottom-up cognitive contents (e.g., schemas, operations) of a cognitive structure do the work cognitively, not some stored, vast, and unmodifiable entity acting in full and downward.

(a) Emergent Bottom-Up Circular Causality

Superordinate level
(constructed from lower-order levels/ (sub)levels; distinct from them)

↑

Emergent new levels
(constructed from system elements; distinct from them; also, their interactions might create new lower-order levels/ (sub)levels)

↑

System elements
(e.g., symptoms; also, their interaction influences/ creates their elements) [1]

(b) Emergent Top-Down Circular Causality

Superordinate level
(influences/ creates lower (sub)levels/ elements)

↓

Lower-order levels/ (sub)levels
(influence/ create their elements)

↓

System elements in each level/ (sub)level
(as elements change, potential for bottom-up emergent circular causality begins anew) [2]

Note. [1] Configuration/ pattern changes possible, too, within and between (sub)levels.

[2] Bottom-up and top-down causal processes work together reciprocally in system causality

Fig. 5.1 The interaction of top-down and bottom-up emergent circular causality
The figure illustrates the dynamic interaction of bottom-up and top-down processes both within and across levels in a system, including the possibility of the emergence of new system elements, levels, and (sub)levels. It also indicates the change of patterning or configuration possible within and between levels in the system dynamics involved. Briefly, as system elements (e.g., symptoms) or levels/(sub)levels interact, (a) they might influence/create (a) their configuration/patterning, expression, or (b) even de novo emergence. This process may occur through movement from (a) lower to higher levels in the level hierarchy involved (bottom-up), (b) from higher to lower levels (top-down), or (c) reciprocally in both ways. In essence, the figure clarifies that, in system function, bottom-up processes work both within and between levels, as do top-down processes (Adopted with permission of Creative Commons CC-BY. Young, G. (2015). Causality in psychiatry: A hybrid symptom network construct model. *Frontiers in Psychiatry, 6*, 164; with kind permission from Frontiers. [Figure 1, pp. 9])

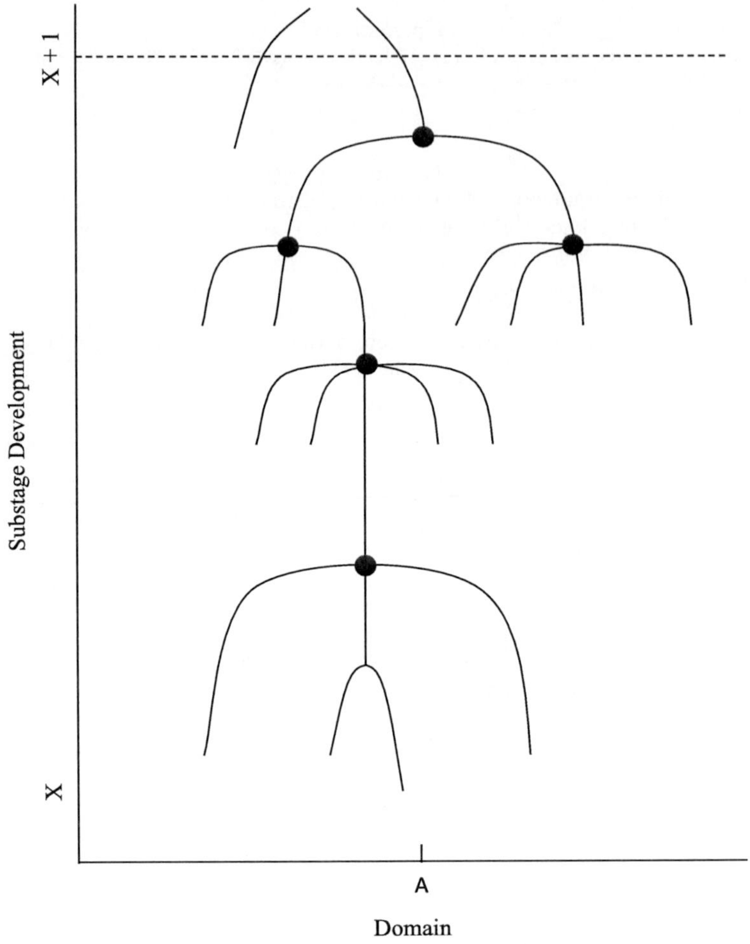

Fig. 5.2 How cognitive structures grow within a substage and into a more complex one following it
The figure illustrates how cognitive structures (e.g., central conceptual structures) grow within a substage and then into a higher-order one, too (in the part of the figure to the left, at the top). Cognitive structures apply to particular domains or subdomains (which are task collections, e.g., quantitative, social, narrative). By following the figure from top to bottom, it shows that they might develop from lower-order schemas into second-order consolidations (or more, depending on the complexity involved). They could end with super-ordinate upper-level integrations, such as mathematical rules, ordered social skillsets, or narrative plot structure knowledge. The figure indicates that domain/task development within a substage can traverse the threshold boundary for the skills involved to those related to the one following it developmentally. The figure can be applied to show how behaviors/symptoms/clusters networking grow within a substage, or perhaps into a higher-order one, too (Adapted from Young (2016). [Figure 37.6, pp. 250])

Mechanism

Figures 5.3 and 5.4 illustrate that activation-inhibition coordination constitutes a critical mechanism to explain behavior, brain, and their relationships. It helps describe behavior and its causal dynamics. It can grow in complexity in both senses. It can allow for the emergence of higher-order levels from lower-order ones. The concept maps well onto models of network function and also nonlinear dynamic system models in these senses. Specifically, in networks, causality is described in terms of network drivers, such as poor sleep affecting other psychiatric symptoms. In systems, coupling is considered an important system element (or level) associative mechanism, as is decoupling/bifurcation. All these processes can be considered to express activation-inhibition coordination mechanisms (and their decoordination). Also, behavior and underlying contributors, such as more proximal brain and neurons factors, and even more distal factors, such as genes and their transcription, all can be considered as coupling–decoupling mechanisms or outputs of activation-inhibition coordination processes. Intralevel linkages to collect and coordinate across node/behavior clustering would require activation-inhibition coordination processes to effect adaptive application. Even the emergence of new levels in a network or system would require activation-inhibition coordination (e.g., control/inhibit intuitive, emotional, or otherwise less rational thought activities in order to activate rational thought activities better or facilitate their emergence).

Change

One of the most telling aspects of the present model is the generality it entails and how it can help explain, accommodate, incorporate, or integrate other models under its rubric. The model's critical components revolve around the 25-step Neo-Piagetian cognitive-developmental stage/(sub)stage lifespan series and the corresponding Neo-Eriksonian socio-affective developmental stage/(sub)stage lifespan series. In both cases, conceptual integration over other models allowed the development of the 25-step (sub)stage model. Furthermore, key acquisitions dictated by the model; such as in self-development, Maslovian hierarchical needs development, social self-working schema development, and narrative skill development; built on the work of precursor modeling contributions.

The third major axis of the present model, beyond the Neo-Piagetian and Neo-Eriksonian ones, that of causality, also involves major innovations based on other models and suggests generalized processes that can help explain other models. For example, the already described concept of activation-inhibition coordination fits this model. That said, the five-step (sub)stage sequence in the present Neo-Piagetian model is consistent with generic change processes in several ways.

First, I had developed the nomenclature for the five-step recursive substage sequence in cognitive development by examining Piaget's six-step substage

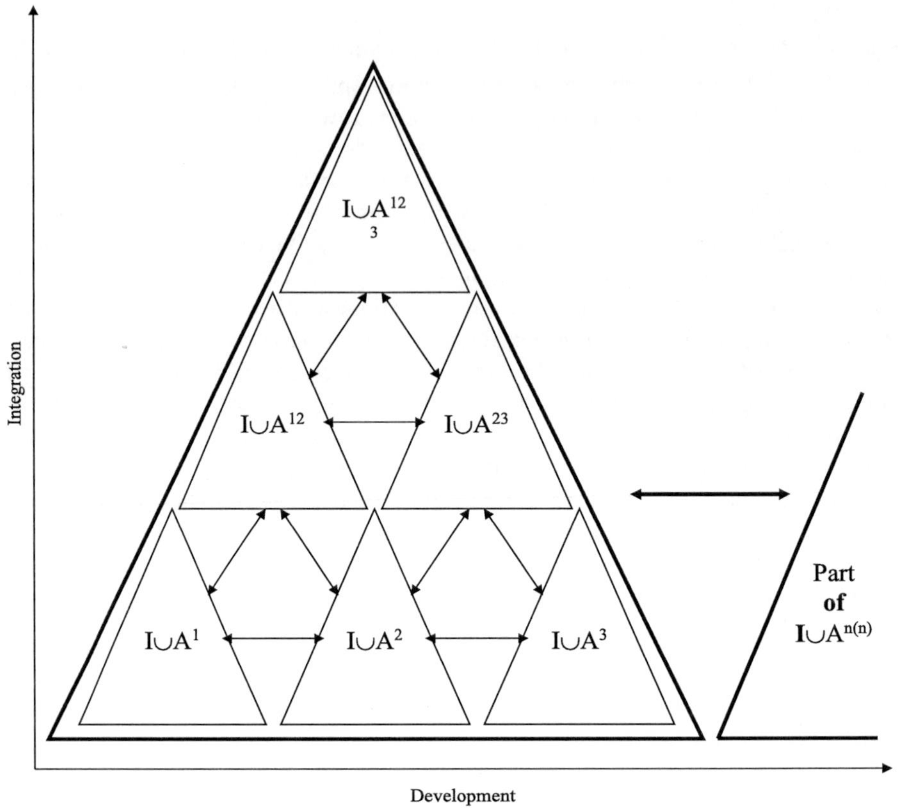

Fig. 5.3 Multilevel, circularly emerging network or system of activation/inhibition coordination network

Note. I inhibition; *A* activation; ∪ coordination (union); *1, 2, 3* first-order network; *12, 23* second-order network; *123* third-order network; n^n – *nth order* n(n); ⤢ reciprocal causality (top-down, bottom-up, including union)

Activation/inhibition coordination (I∪A) can be used both to describe behavior and to qualify the process involved in its unfolding. It applies to all levels of a network. It is a union or compound function, the properties of which are different from those of its components (I, A). As I∪A entities interact and interrelate reciprocally, they form unions themselves, both horizontally within system levels and vertically over levels, including the formation of new, superordinate levels. This process describes how emergence might occur in systems that are neuronal and behavioral in ways analogous to the classic example of how atoms combine to form molecules with properties different from those of the constituents (e.g., wetness in water, H_2O) (Adopted with permission of Springer International Publishing. Young, G. (2016). *Unifying causality and psychology: Being, brain and behavior*. Cham, Switzerland: Springer International Publishing; with kind permission from Springer International Publishing. [Figure 30.1, pp. 747])

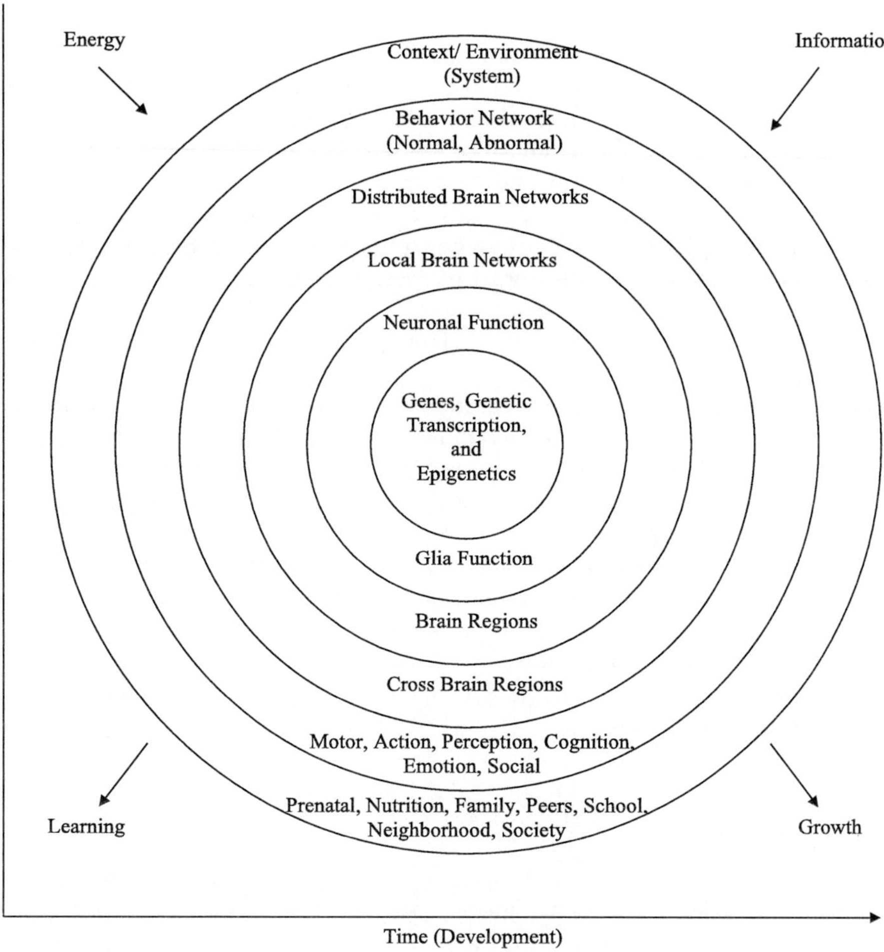

Fig. 5.4 Hierarchical activation-inhibition coordination in brain-behavior network organization The figure indicates the integrated fields of action of activation-inhibition coordination in the brain, behavior, and context. Development starts with genetic transcription and epigenetic modifications therein, right from the prenatal period. These effects mold the developing brain, which is further influenced by the environment in all its variations. The brain is organized in terms of networks, both local and global. Behavior is similarly organized. The figure does not include free will belief as a behavioral component, but it is a factor that can boost a sense of personal agency. The developing person constitutes a system of networks over the brain and behavior that are interlinked hierarchically, and the networks and linkages extend into environmental (social) relationships. The developing person's systems are affected by energy (externally and internally generated) and information (externally and internally generated), which result in system perturbation, and which in turn may result in change (learning, growth (constructive, regressive abnormal)). Activation-inhibition coordination can function as a seamless mechanism binding networks/couplings and their decoupling/change across the multiple, hierarchical levels of the brain behavior-environmental (context, social/developing (and changing)) system. In this sense, activation-inhibition coordination itself constitutes a dynamic system that is hierarchically arranged. It can help explain multiple levels of the causal manifold, from gene and neuronal/brain activity to network causation (critical behaviors/symptoms) as drivers, to environmental/contextual/social causation, etc., as well as explaining problems that might arise in brain or behavior

sequence in the infancy sensorimotor stage (after removing the first reflexive substage in this regard and using it as part of a prior Reflexive stage, this left a five-step sequence to consider). The terms coordination, hierarchization, systematization, multiplication, and integration stem from an analysis of what Piaget's five-step infancy sequence really involved, and if the proposed sequence could help describe development in stages prior and subsequent to the infancy one. Young's three books offer many examples of how the five-step generic change process sequence as described can be applied to other areas of development. Indeed, this qualification applies to other step-like acquisitions, such as in a partner relationship, and even to nonliving systems, evolution in academic inquiry, and so on, that are in the process of change.

Table 5.3 presents a detailed description of the five-step change/substage sequence that is at the core of the present model. The generality of the sequence is illustrated by its ability to describe the classic stages of change model in its terms. For example, in contemplation, existing and possible new behaviors are juxtaposed, as in coordination. In preparation, small behavioral changes are implemented, but the old habits predominate, as in hierarchization. In the third stages of change step of action (see Table 5.4), behavior is undertaken to modify prior behavior one seeks to change, as in systematization (in effect, the hierarchy in hierarchization is reversed and added to). In maintenance, gains are consolidated, as in the present step of multiplication. Finally, in resolution, the issue is resolved, which is like the present step of integration.

Attracting

Another major way that the present five-step generic change/substage model is consistent with more generalized change processes concerns how it might be underscored by, or at least be consistent with, attractor dynamics. Attractors can be organized from the simplest to the most complex. In this sense, they could pass through an evolutionary sequence of point attractors, cyclical attractors, and chaotic attractors, and then move into more complex landscapes with multiple attractors (which I refer to as complex adaptive systems and their superordinate structuring).

Figure 5.5 reviews the parallel developments of stages of change, the five-step change sequence in the present model, and attractor dynamics that might underpin them. For example, precontemplation, or precoordination, implies a point attractor organization. As the system involved gets perturbed beyond the far-from-equilibrium bifurcation point, it cascades into a periodic or oscillatory cyclical attractor, but with the old habit primary. This attractor organization itself might experience impetus to change through dysregulatory system dynamics and nonlinearly evolve into a chaotic attractor regime residing at the cusp of change in the system. At this location in its global state space, even a minor local change could elicit an avalanche of critical change to a chaotic organization (which is a misnomer; the new attractor is more organized). Behaviorally, the new habit involved takes priority. Once a system like

Table 5.3 Substages: details

Substage	Details
Coordination	In the present model, coordination refers to an interrelation of two different cognitive control units (newly emergent and acquired in the previous substage, if applicable). However, the interrelation does not specify which of the units has ascendancy in terms of either a temporal order or a dominant-subordinate relationship. The units exist in a reciprocal balance (pairing, addition, juxtaposition, opposition, etc.) of a back-and-forth nature. If hierarchies are established, they are tentative, tenuous structures
Hierarchization	With the development of the substage of hierarchization, the deficiencies in the just described coordinations are countered. Paired cognitive control units evidence a strengthened dominant-subservient relation and/or a fixed sequence in time
Systematization	Systematization is marked by both an expansion and simplification of hierarchized control units. On the one hand, component units add (recruit) refinements (feedback, extra adaptive behaviors) that permit better on-target adjustment at the onset of the behavior, at its end-point, etc. on the other hand, the new structure meshes into a smoothly operating, more unified whole through a less fixed, hierarchical, and more complementary coordination of the component units
Multiplication	Multiplication refers to the spreading of newly acquired system structures in the prior substage throughout the full system. For example, this takes place by applying the new system to a new domain beyond the one in which the system originated. Or, it refers to the combination of systems (even more than two at a time). This is accomplished both by chaining them over time (either repetitively, but more importantly, by using different ones in each slot), and/or by embedding, in which primary systems are subserved by secondary ones (less elaborate than the primary ones). This produces an element of reversibility in behavior, but not as clearly as in the next substage of integration
Integration	The last substage of integration in the current model of cognitive substage recursion finds multiple cognitive units more precisely differentiated in flexible branching as they are applied. This produces linear sequences or chains composed of strings of component systems different from each other, with some embedded in others. An embedded component system may be just as elaborate as any constituent system of the main string. Moreover, it might unfold in parallel with movements or behaviors of the main string, i.e., it and the main string might unfold simultaneously. In short, the reversibility evident in the organization of this substage is a mature, efficient one. To use Fischer's language, elements of subsets can be paired without compromising the integrity or continuity of the subsets

Adapted from Young (2011) [Text Excerpt on pp. 84–85]

this develops, it can expand and consolidate in the system, as reflected in an attractor dynamic of multiple attractors inhabiting the system landscape, as in complex adaptive systems. The latter becomes integrated as the multiple attractors cohere, which would be expected as a new habit characterizes the widespread behavioral regime exclusively.

Figure 5.6 offers a diagrammatic representation of the attractor sequence just described. Moreover, it gives the example of a mental schema that coordinates with

Table 5.4 Stages of change model

Stage	Explanation
Precontemplation	The person has no intention to change the behavior at issue in the foreseeable future. Most people in this stage are under-aware of their issues
Contemplation	The person is aware that issues exist. She/he thinks seriously about overcoming them, but has not yet committed to taking action. Contemplators struggle with internal conflicts and with the amount of effort, energy, and regression that might be involved in overcoming them
Preparation	The person shortly intends to take action and reports some small behavioral changes ("baby steps"). Although she/he has made some improvement in her/his issues, the person in this stage has not yet reached a threshold allowing for effective action
Action	The individual behaves to modify her/his issues, experiences, and/or context in order to overcome any difficulties. Actions might be undertaken in overt behavior in the timeframe of 1 day to 6 months
Maintenance	The person works to prevent relapse and to consolidate all gains made during the prior stage. This stage extends from 6 months beyond the last one for an indeterminate period. He/she acts to remain free of the issue and/or consistently engages in a new countering behavior for more than 6 months
Resolution	The person resolves the issues that had been confronted but still needs to control the possibility of incompatible behavior that had been controlled manifesting once more

Note. The stages of change model include a last resolution stage that is mentioned rarely in the literature but is nevertheless part of the original conceptualization of the model (e.g., Maddox 1995; Prochaska et al. 1994)
Adapted from Norcross et al. (2011)

another, proceeding to their hierarchization (in terms of conceptual control structures). This leads to a specific rule-based schema forming a system, which can then multiply out and generalize. The text for the figure presents another relevant example related to disorder/dysfunction/disability. Does the behavior involved undermine healthier behavior and then systematize, multiply out, and negatively integrate, leading to impairment and chronicity?

Figure 5.7 amplifies the latter progression, referring to the entrenchment of behavior in the last phase. The figure also gives new terms for the change process, whether progressive or regressive (juxtaposition, dissonance, distancing, propagation, and reflection). However, behavior is about relating to people; in the last column of the figure, the example provided indicates that in relational (psychological) coregulation, self and other knowledge and social structures are juxtaposed/hierarchized, leading to alteration of extant structure in these regards, and then a spreading out and full transformation of the system involved.

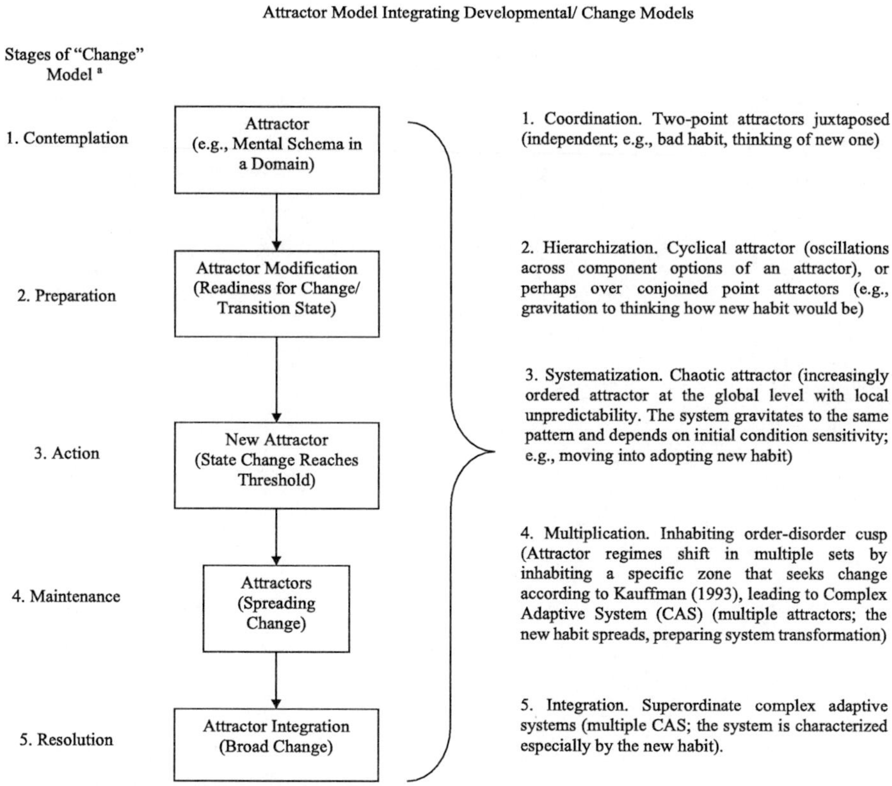

Fig. 5.5 An attractor/complexity developmental model
The figure presents a five-step development model involving the elaboration of attractors and complex adaptive systems (Young 2011, 2016). The five-step change model is a generic one applicable to behavioral change processes (Prochaska et al. 1994). Thus, two independent models of behavioral change, one developmental and one on stages in change, involve five steps
Note. Young (1997) showed the parallel between the Prochaska et al. (1994) stage model of change and the present model of development stages

(a) Specifically, in terms of their stage of contemplating change, the individual can be considered as coordinating the phases involving present condition and future possibility. With respect to attractor modeling, the future better habit is juxtaposed with the existing poorer one

(b) In the next step of preparing/deciding/determining in transitions in therapy, the individual can be considered to hierarchically organize commitment and planning as primary in working toward goals. The new habit begins to take precedence (e.g., its attractor)

(c) In the stage of deliberate action, systematization can be considered to characterize organization, given that deliberate action implies a systemic plan into action. In terms of attractors, this means that a "chaotic" attractor has formed, which is essentially not chaotic at all in its organization

(d) Next, the maintenance phase reflects the spreading out or propagation of gains that have been made into wider regions of the system, resembling what I would call multiplication. In attractor terms, the chaotic attractor morphs into a bifurcating multiple attractor dynamics or complex adaptive system (CAS)

(e) Finally, the step of problem resolution indicates that the system is in dynamic integration. Here, the CAS becomes "superordinate" ([a]Adapted from Prochaska et al. (1994); Maddox (1995)) (Adopted with permission of Springer International Publishing. Young, G. (2019). *Causality and development: Neo-Eriksonian perspectives*. Cham, Switzerland: Springer International Publishing. [Figure 9.1, pp. 186])

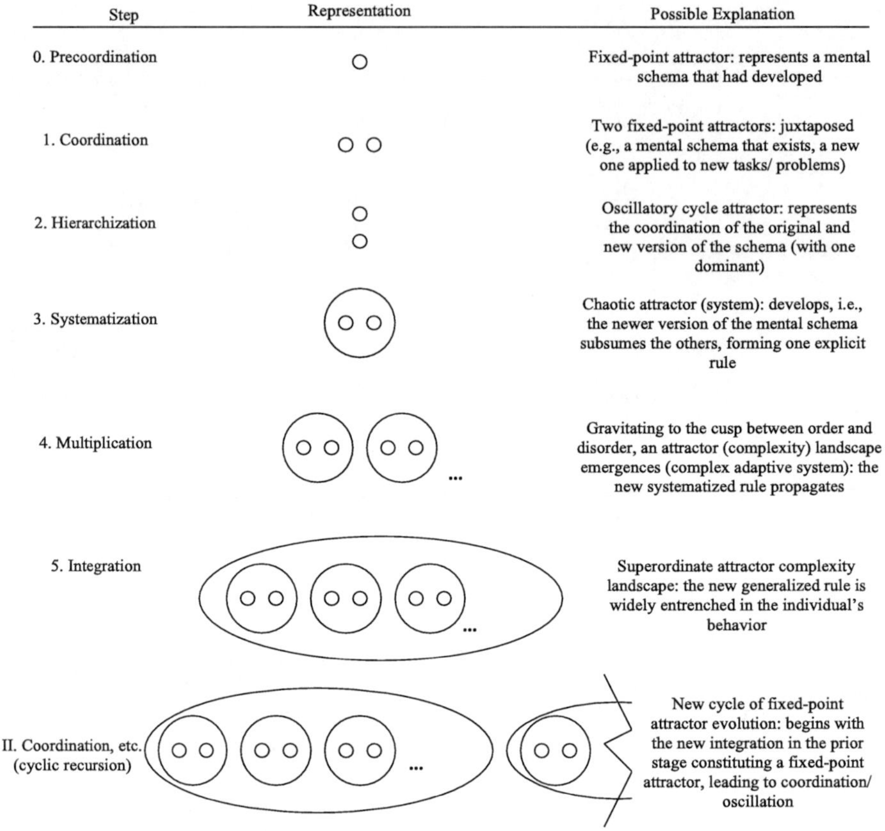

Fig. 5.6 Conceptual control structure development within a domain in terms of attractors/complexity
As mental schemas emerge and spread within a particular domain of a particular stage of cognitive development, they should first be juxtaposed in coordination, then hierarchized with one predominant, and then systematized into a new rule. Next, they should spread out or multiply throughout the system, leading to the integration of a generalized rule that covers all exemplars within the individual's particular cognitive development for the stage at issue
This five-step sequence might correspond to changes in the attractor/complexity organization. That is, attractors might gravitate from fixed point to oscillatory and chaotic ones and then to more complex architecture involving the cusp of change to complex adaptive systems and superordinate complex systems. This model has been applied to substage changes in Young's (2011) Neo-Piagetian cognitive-developmental model. Also, it might apply to both higher (e.g., stage) and lower levels (i.e., domain transitions as they move through the phases of coordination (after precoordination), hierarchization, systematization, multiplication, and integration, with a cyclic recursion potentially taking place after that
In another example, the attractor/complexity model can be applied to disorder/disability or competing health trajectories. The states of health and disorder/dysfunction/disability involved could be seen to pass through five steps of change from simpler coordination to a quite stable integration
Another applied example would be dealing with the challenges/crises presented by each new Eriksonian/Freudian stage that might develop. Do they begin with a challenge/crisis and their solutions, in a

Table 5.5 Working with patients using the five-step generic change model

Step	The stories patients tell	Case formation
Coordination	The patient's narrative is juxtaposed to possibilities presented by the therapist through sensitive guidance	Gather issues, symptoms, "facts" in case (collaboratively)
Hierarchization	The patient begins to place the new story elements in at least one location of her/his narrative as a possible new outlook	Develop initial hypotheses of the primary issue(s) and treatment needs. Revise as new information and responses to implemented therapies/techniques become evident
Systematization	The process takes hold and the new story inhabits the narrative landscape of the patient for that issue	Arrive at a clear understanding of the primary issue(s) and treatment need(s)
Multiplication	The new story propagates throughout the patient's narrative structure	Determine the degree to which they have affected other aspects of the patient's psychology and those of any significant others that might be involved
Integration	It forms an integrated totality of new habits, both in daily living and in understanding past issues, leading to better optics for the future	Proceed to firm up insight in the patient, encourage/monitor techniques that have been effective, and transfer full responsibility for their use (and the person's growth) to the patient.

Adopted with permission of Springer International Publishing. Young, G. (2016). *Unifying causality and psychology: Being, brain and behavior*. Cham, Switzerland: Springer International Publishing; with kind permission from Springer International Publishing. [Second column from Table 33.7, pp. 815; Third column from Table 33.9, pp. 817]

Therapy

As much as the five-step stages of change models are valid, the five-step generic change process underscored can help explain other therapeutic process aspects. Table 5.5 gives two examples in this regard. First, it considers the stories that patients in therapy might tell and how they can change through the present model's five steps. Also, it indicates how patients and therapists can collaborate to create case formulations; for example, what are the major issues at hand and how can they propagate in the system. With appropriate therapy, an integrated perspective on the issues obtains.

Fig. 5.6 (continued) coordination that leads toward resolution and growth, or do they lapse into entrenchment in the crises inherent in the challenges and get worse as development continues, but still toward integration, albeit in a negative mode?
This model of attractor evolution can be applied generically to change in both living and nonliving systems, assuming a consistency for the appropriate conditions of nonlinear dynamical system functioning. It can be applied to different levels of a system because of fractal dynamics, e.g., from one developmental stage to the next, within each of the substages involved, within domains within substages, and so on (Adopted with permission of Springer International Publishing. Young, G. (2016). *Unifying causality and psychology: Being, brain and behavior*. Cham, Switzerland: Springer International Publishing; with kind permission from Springer International Publishing. [Figure 37.3, pp. 913])

Table 5.6 Advanced application of present five-step generic change model

Step	Epistemological construction	Scientific (natural, scholarly) exploration	
		What information; observation; data (product)	Why (process)
Abstract coordination	Two models juxtaposed	Surface search	Tentative explanation
Abstract hierarchization	One hierarchized as predominant	Subsurface probe	Causal mapping
Abstract systematization	New system created subsuming both	Deep microunderstanding	Mechanistic understanding
Abstract multiplication	Other extant models reworked into system	Extension/application	System-wide elaboration
Abstract integration	Integrated model developed	Broad macrounderstanding	Global causality
Superordinate abstract coordination	Cycle repeats, e.g., for positivism or constructivism, depending on which one had been developed first in the above, or perhaps both develop. Ultimately, both streams might be integrated into an overarching epistemological framework	Five-step process repeats in the multiple	

Adopted with permission of Springer International Publishing. Young, G. (2016). *Unifying causality and psychology: Being, brain and behavior*. Cham, Switzerland: Springer International Publishing; with kind permission from Springer International Publishing. [First and Second Column in Table 35.4, pp. 867; Third and Fourth Column from Table 35.2, pp. 864]

Science Modeling

I have applied the five-step generic change process model to the process in the creation of models. Table 5.6 shows how models can be juxtaposed/hierarchized, and then systematized/multiplied out, leading to integration. Also, it shows how deep scientific and related exploration involves search/probing at first, leading to understanding, application, and broad knowledge (integration), or tentative explanations that map, come to include mechanisms, and then elaborate, leading to global understanding (e.g., about causality).

Table 5.7 explores in greater detail the creation of new models according to the present five-step generic change sequence. It applies especially to how new scientific (scholarly) Kuhnian paradigms are created. At the same time, it illustrates the steps in the creation of the present model, which began with the Neo-Piagetian developmental series, extended to the Neo-Eriksonian one, and then integrated both (as in Young 2019 and this present work). The first example in the table shows how knowledge domain learning and then hypothesis testing leads to mini-theory creation, which is construed as a system in present terms. Then, the theory is expanded, leading to broad theory construction. The same procedure applies to metatheory/world view creation. In this case, meta-concepts are gathered and tested, leading to

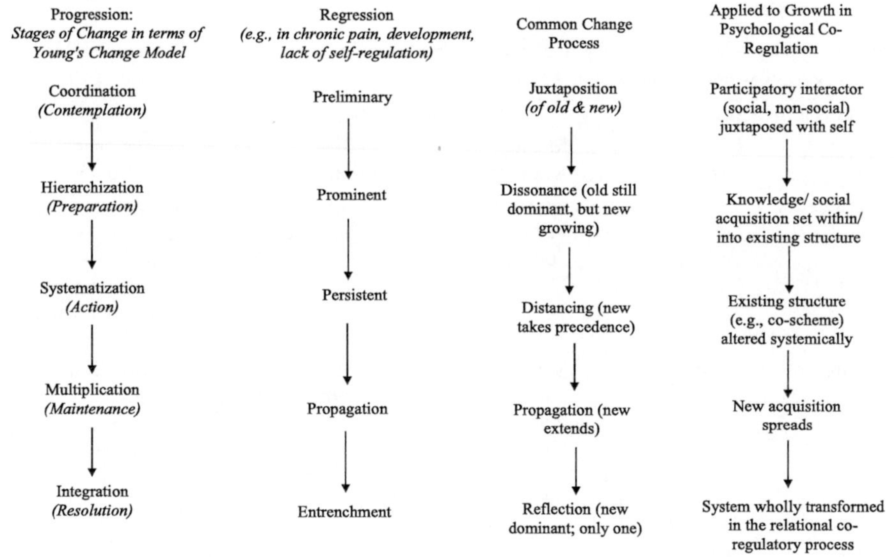

Fig. 5.7 The five-step change process
Self-control needs to be considered in the broader context of relational coregulation. The figure provides a common microchange process that applies to change sequences, whether progressive or regressive. Moreover, it is presented in language that is generic enough to apply to macrochange processes. Thus, the five steps in change that seem to explain generically the five steps involved in the sequence of coordination, hierarchization, systematization, multiplication, and integration that characterize the present model appears to involve: juxtaposition, dissonance, distancing, propagation, and reflection
This type of modeling can be applied to the growth in psychological or relational coregulation. In step a, the self and other one are juxtaposed/coordinated. In step b, the other is viewed as subservient to a dominant self. In step c, the other and self are viewed from a coscheme perspective involving both; distance from the self obtains systematically. In step d, the new acquisition propagates into the person's self architecture and also in coregulatory relations with the other. In step e, the system settles into one of reflection on self and other as coregulated psychological, relational, self-entities (Adapted from Young (2016) [Fig. 33.1, pp. 810]; fourth column adapted from Young (2019) [Table 11.7, pp. 245])

a new mini-metatheory, which is expanded (mid-range) and integrated into a solid meta-theory. For paradigmatic metamodeling, the domain at issue is involved in coordinated data/concept gathering, leading to hierarchization and system mini-metamodel creation. The process continues with multiplying out and integrating metamodeling. In my own approach to the matter, the mechanistic and relational world views need to be integrated rather than seen as oppositional.

The next two figures and the table illustrate how the five-step generic change process can be applied to expand some of my own models, providing a map for doing so. For the S-O(BAMP)-R model, Fig. 5.8 shows both its roots and how it can be expanded and integrated. The factors provided are those in the generic causal

Table 5.7 The relation of theory, metatheory, and paradigmatic metamodel in scholarship, in general, and in science, in particular

Area in construction				
Step	Theory	Metatheory/ worldview	Theory creation example	Paradigmatic metamodel
Coordination	Gathering extant data and concepts in domain of (empirical) inquiry	Gathering extant metaconcepts in domain of reflection	Domain–development	Coordinated gathering of domain components (facts, constructs)
Hierarchization	Subserving acquired knowledge to testable hypotheses and their (empirical) testing; proof of concept	Subserving acquired knowledge to criticism-resistant metaconcepts impervious to falsification; thought experiments	Stage modeling hypotheses	Hierarchical arrangement of knowledge and critical analysis
Systematization	Creating minitheories (leaving the silos), including with further (empirical) inquiry	Creating minimetatheories	Piagetian series (e.g., infant sensorimotor substage for object permanence); Erikson on steps in identity development	Systematizing minimetamodels of the knowledge base
Multiplication	Expanding broader theories (leaving the silos), including further (empirical) inquiry	Expanding broader metatheories (mid-range)	Piagetian stage theory Eriksonian stage theory	Multiplying metamodel scope and application in domain(s)
Integration	Integrating theory in the domain, including with further (empirical) inquiry	Integrating metatheory in the domain	Neo-Piagetian stage theory Neo-Eriksonian stage theory	Integrative metamodeling
Coordination	Five-step process repeats in the multiple		Combined Neo-Piagetian/Neo-Eriksonian stage theory (Young 2011, 2012)	Coordinating over domains

Note. Builds on Overton's (2013, 2015) concept of nested levels of a scientific paradigm for a domain of inquiry: domain; hypotheses to test empirically; theory (e.g., Piaget, Erikson); Mid-range metatheory (e.g., evolution, stage theory); metatheoretical level/world view (e.g., mechanistic, relationism)

Adopted with permission of Springer International Publishing. Young, G. (2016). *Unifying causality and psychology: Being, brain and behavior.* Cham, Switzerland: Springer International Publishing; with kind permission from Springer International Publishing. [Table 35.1, pp. 860]

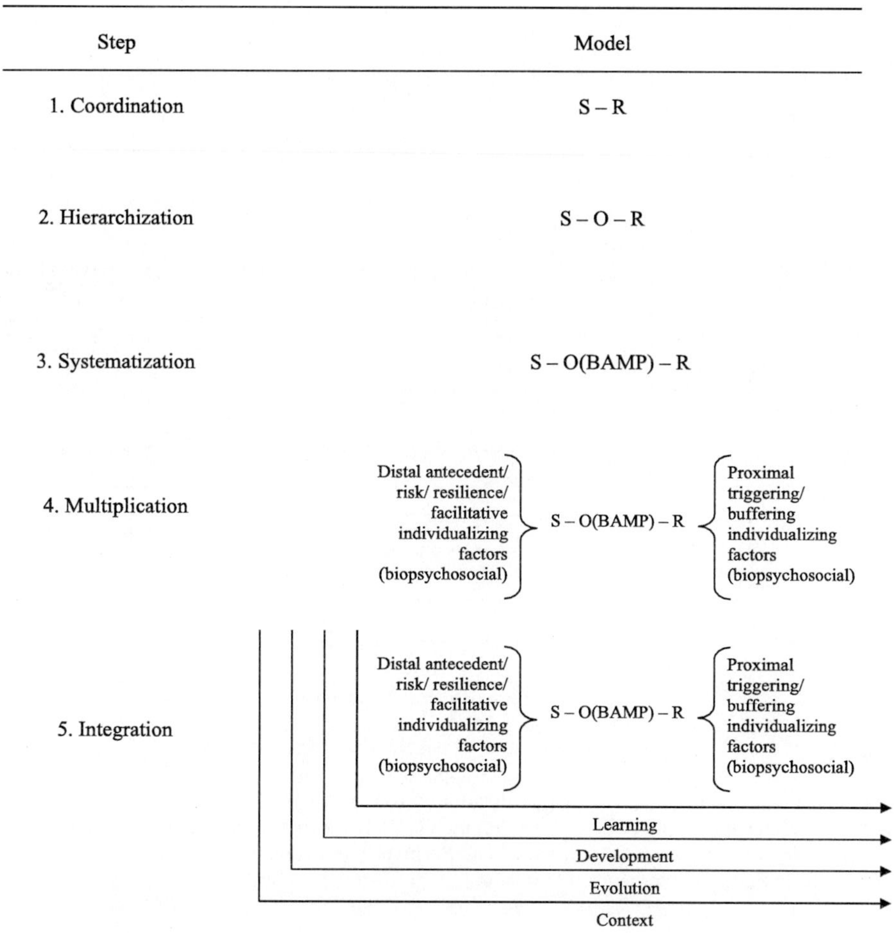

Fig. 5.8 Expanding the S-O-R model according to the five-step generic change model
In this figure, I indicate how the S-R model (and S-O-R) can be elaborated through five steps consistent with the present five-step generic change model to arrive at a more inclusive, integrated one. Specifically, initially, behavior was considered behaviorally as an S-R connection. The S-O-R model added the organism as a mediator in the relation. My new S-O(BAMP)-R model greatly elaborated on the S-O-R model. One could further extend the model by considering the full range of biopsychosocial factors that are involved (multiplying it out). A fully integrated model would add learning/development/evolution considerations and all contextual factors (Adopted with permission of Springer International Publishing. Young, G. (2016). *Unifying causality and psychology: Being, brain and behavior*. Cham, Switzerland: Springer International Publishing; with kind permission from Springer International Publishing. [Figure 33.7, pp. 828])

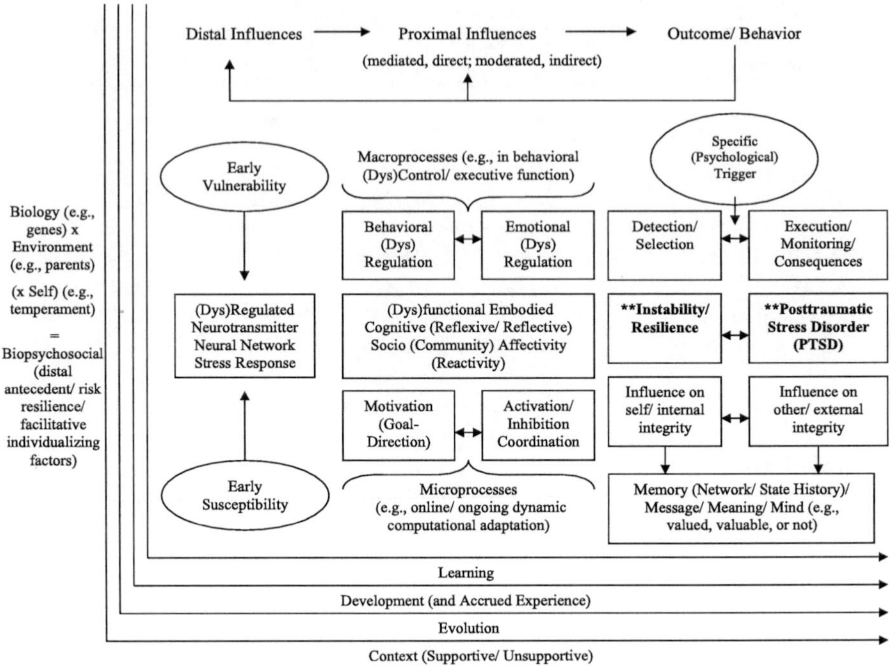

Fig. 5.9 A revised model of the development of posttraumatic stress disorder (PTSD)
The generic behavioral causality model can be applied to most any psychiatric disorder. The figure illustrates that it can help explain the multifactorial causal nature of PTSD (Adopted with permission of Springer International Publishing. Young, G. (2016). *Unifying causality and psychology: Being, brain and behavior*. Cham, Switzerland: Springer International Publishing; with kind permission from Springer International Publishing. [Figure 36.9, pp. 880])

model in Fig. 5.9 for PTSD. That model gives antecedent and simultaneous factors toward the development of resilience or, instead, PTSD, subsequent to trauma. Finally, Table 5.8 shows how the present model of freedom of being can be expanded.

Conclusion (to Chaps. 4 and 5)

The second part of the present work (Chaps. 4 and 5) on Young's three Causality and Development books (2011, 2016, 2019) elaborates upon three major aspects. First, it examines in depth how behavioral change processes might proceed. Second, it examines various acquisitions that appear related to Young's five-stage developmental Neo-Piagetian model (without giving any developments related to the five substages within each stage). Third, it examines the 25 steps in Young's Neo-Eriksonian model that is based on the Neo-Piagetian one.

Table 5.8 Steps in the development of freeing of being/brain

Steps	Model
Coordination	Free will belief, having a sense of free will
Hierarchization	Free will belief × having a sense of free will
Systematization	Freedom in being Free will belief × having a sense of free will = FiB Freeing the brain
Multiplication	FiB1 × FiB2 ×
Integration	FiBi

The table illustrates the manner in which the components in the growth of freedom in being conjoin into a systematized and integrated psychological entity. Freedom in being appears to be a psychological emergence that relates to the most mature psychological acquisition, along with concepts such as wisdom and Eriksonian generativity

(a) In the step of coordination, the two components are juxtaposed (free will belief, having a sense of free will)

(b) Next, the two components begin to cohere

(c) Next, the two components form a system, with an emergent cohering entity of freedom in being that encompasses both (and it includes freeing the brain)

(d) Then, the systematization process in the prior stage expands over contexts/domains

(e) Finally, an integrative freedom in being/brain emerges that is generalized across contexts/domains, and in a constant way in the person

Adopted with permission of Springer International Publishing. Young, G. (2016). *Unifying causality and psychology: Being, brain and behavior*. Cham, Switzerland: Springer International Publishing; with kind permission from Springer International Publishing. [Table 36.3, pp. 882]

This elaboration section uses many tables and figures to present the concepts involved, with some of them new to this present work. Most are taken from Young's three books being summarized, or they are reorganizations of them.

The first major aspect of Young's three-book series on Causality and Development being elaborated in this part of the work concerns change processes in development and otherwise. First, it begins with a more detailed description of networks and indicates how networks can evolve systemically to higher-order levels, including by way of activation-inhibition coordination. Then, it looks at the stages of change model (from contemplation to resolution) and how it reflects Young's five generic steps or substages of change (from coordination to integration). Next, it examines these two change processes in terms of possible underlying attractor dynamics. Steps in coregulation appear related to the five steps, such as through ways of working with patients (e.g., stories they tell; case formulation). Next, the steps involved are related to knowledge construction processes and scientific exploration. In an elaborate table, the steps are related to the development of theory and meta-theory/

meta-modeling. In terms of causality, this part of the book explores the concept of emergent circular causality. The last application of the five-step change model applies it to the development of free will. Also, aspects of the latter model are used in a complex model of PTSD which specifies how triggers might lead to it in the context of a host of biological and environmental causal contributors.

References

Bernstein, E.E., Heeren, A., McNally, R.J.: Unpacking rumination and executive control: a network perspective. Clin. Psychol. Sci. **5**(5), 816–826 (2017). https://doi.org/10.1177/2167702617702717

van den Heuvel, M.P., Sporns, O.: Network hubs in the human brain. Trends Cogn. Sci. **17**(12), 683–696 (2013). https://doi.org/10.1016/j.tics.2013.09.012

Hevey, D.: Network analysis: a brief overview and tutorial. Health Psychol. Behav. Med. **6**(1), 301–328 (2018). https://doi.org/10.1080/21642850.2018.1521283

Kauffman, S.: The Origins of Order: Self-Organization and Selection in Evolution. Oxford University Press, New York (1993)

Lim, S., Radicchi, F., van den Heuvel, M.P., Sporns, O.: Discordant attributes of structural and functional brain connectivity in a two-layer multiplex network. Sci. Rep. **9**, 2885 (2019). https://doi.org/10.1038/s41598-019-39243-w

Maddox, J.E.: Yes, people can change, but can psychotherapists? Contemp. Psychol. **40**(11), 1047–1048 (1995)

Norcross, J.C., Krebs, P.M., Prochaska, J.O.: Stages of change. In: Norcross, J.C. (ed.) Psychotherapy Relationships that Work: Evidence-Based Responsiveness, 2nd edn, pp. 279–300. Oxford University Press, New York (2011)

Overton, W.F.: Relationism and relational developmental systems: a paradigm for developmental science in the post-Cartesian era. In: Lerner, R.M., Benson, J.B. (eds.) Advances in Child Development and Behavior. Embodiment and Epigenesis: Theoretical and Methodological Issues in Understanding the Role of Biology Within the Relational Developmental System. Part A: Philosophical, Theoretical, and Biological Dimensions, vol. 44, pp. 21–64. Elsevier, Oxford (2013)

Overton, W.F.: Taking conceptual analyses seriously. Res. Hum. Dev. **12**(3–4), 163–171 (2015). https://doi.org/10.1080/15427609.2015.1069158

Prochaska, J.O., Norcross, J.C., DiClemente, C.C.: Changing for Good: the Revolutionary Program that Explains the Six Stages of Change and Teaches you how to Free yourself from Bad Habits. Morrow, New York (1994)

Schmittmann, V.D., Cramer, A.O.J., Waldorp, L.J., Epskamp, S., Kievit, R.A., Borsboom, D.: Deconstructing the construct: a network perspective on psychological phenomena. New Ideas Psychol. **31**(1), 43–53 (2013). https://doi.org/10.1016/j.newideapsych.2011.02.007

Sporns, O.: Networks of the Brain. MIT Press, Cambridge (2011)

Sporns, O.: Discovering the Human Connectome. MIT Press, Cambridge (2012)

Urban, J.B., Osgood, N., Okamoto, J., Mabry, P., Lich, K.H.: Developing systems science: extending developmental science with systems science methodologies. In: Molenaar, M., Lerner, R.M., Newell, K.M. (eds.) Handbook of Developmental Systems Theory and Methodology, pp. 95–127. Guildford Press, New York (2014)

Young, G.: Adult Development, Therapy, and Culture: a Postmodern Synthesis. Plenum Press, New York (1997)

Young, G.: Development and Causality: Neo-Piagetian Perspectives. Springer, New York (2011)

Young, G.: A unitary neo-Piagetian/neo- Eriksonian model of development: fundamental assumptions and meta-issues. New Ideas Psychol. **30**(2), 241–249 (2012). https://doi.org/10.1016/j.newideapsych.2011.11.002

Young, G.: Causality in psychiatry: a hybrid symptom network construct model. Front. Psychiatry. **6**, 164 (2015). https://doi.org/10.3389/fpsyt.2015.00164

Young, G.: Unifying Causality and Psychology: Being, Brain and Behavior. Springer, Cham (2016)

Young, G.: Causality and Development: Neo-Eriksonian Perspectives. Springer, Cham (2019)

Chapter 6
Literature Review 2019

The present chapter explores the literature in 2019 that is related to the present work. The topics are varied, consistent with the broad scope of the book.

Philosophy

Gonzalez (2018a) edited a book on Woodward's (2003) causal explanation model of interventionism (causality as intervention). Woodward argued that interventions constitute the sine qua none in establishing causal attribution. Causal reasoning requires both a descriptive, empirical element and a theoretical normative one. Gonzalez (2018b) further articulated that Woodward's approach to causality combines ideals of naturalism with pragmatic applications (doing). Furthermore, causality is pluralistic and not limited to interventionist accounts. Also, scientific explanations are function-oriented. Gonzalez (2018b) added that scientific explanations need to be dynamic, for example, because social life is composed of interconnected complex dynamic systems.

Campaner (2018) examined Woodward's interventionist approach to causality as applied to mental disorder. She referred to different levels of causal influences in mental disorder, from the genetic to the psychological, citing Kendler (2005), among others. She argued that mental processes do have causal efficacy in a mind-to-brain causality. The interventionist approach to causality does not rely on establishing causal mechanisms, but they can supplement it. These mechanisms are fine-grained and exist at the micro- and macrolevels, constituting a biopsychosocial causal pluralism. Experimental interventions (e.g., randomized control trials) have ethical limitations in psychiatry so that the multivariable study of fine-grained causal influences often is the best evidence available to establish causal connections.

G. Young, *Causality and Neo-Stages in Development*,
https://doi.org/10.1007/978-3-030-82540-9_6

Campaner (2018) continued that psychiatry respects general causal models but must seek each patient's unique subjective experiences. General models help frame and also explain the disorder(s) in the particular patient. But understanding the actual causes of a particular disorder for any one patient is critical in treating the person. Mechanistic knowledge is incomplete in psychiatry and stands as mechanistic "sketches." In an evolving neo-mechanist approach to causality, mechanisms exist at different levels, such as the modular neuron and nonmodular thoughts and emotions (Woodward 2013).

Vidunas (2018) explored the dynamics of complex systems from a philosophical point of view. He noted the causal role of critical nonlinear dynamical systems that have gravitated to the edge of chaos, or a region in their state space potentiating change (on the cusp) by their moderate sensitivity to the environment. This region allows for the emergence of higher-order levels with the product explicating downward causation to lower-order levels. This scenario's causality can be described as "delegated" because it is provoked by the causal relationship between a nonlinear dynamical system that is primed for change and an external influence that drives the change. Dubrovsky (2019) also used NLDST to support the notion that free will is an emergent phenomenon in neuronal functioning.

This brief review of causality in philosophy highlights the interventionist (and counterfactual approach of Woodward 2013). Simultaneously, as applied to psychology, the interventionist approach needs to be complemented by a systems one. Woodward himself referred to pragmatics needed for his idealized approach. Behavior results from multifactorial causation, and the latter needs to be ascertained in multiple ways because interventions and manipulations often are limited ethically in psychiatry (and psychology). Moreover, there is little straightforward throughput from cause to mediators to behavior in psychology and psychiatry, and the probabilistic aspect of both cause and effect needs to be recognized. Finally, causation can be studied without detailed knowledge of mechanism through interventionist approaches. However, the mechanisms need to be specified to give causation grounding. This project will bring the study of etiology, consequent mental disturbance, and subsequent treatment toward the precision required.

Causality

Thapar and Rutter (2019) discussed the research designs that could be used in place of interventionist designs toward understanding causality in mental disorders. They considered natural experiments as an option for randomized control trials. For example, in natural experiments, measurements of earlier occurring risks (e.g., exposure) and other variables (e.g., outcomes) are separated by events or situations that occur naturally in the course under investigation.

Cuijpers et al. (2019) specified that research attempting to infer causality (in their case, on the role of common factors in psychotherapy) need to demonstrate the validity of the inference by accounting for possible third variables and be able to explain the timeline (temporality) in the relationship. Good research also needs a good theory to explain it.

Thomas and Sharp (2019) advocated for a science of mechanism in psychopathology research. Their approach focused on an integration of biological, psychological, and environmental perspectives. Causal relations are found internally and also bidirectionally with the environment.

Sharp and Miller (2019) specified that mechanisms in psychology and neuroscience are hierarchically structured. The higher-order levels in mechanistic organization are more general and stable than lower-order ones (e.g., molecular). Regularities can be found at each level, though adopting a reductionist approach in understanding mechanisms over levels does not eliminate higher-order levels because they can provide indispensable information. For example, both psychological and biological findings help in understanding the causality of behavior.

Mascolo and Kallio (2019) also referred to biological and psychological interactions in behavior. For them, psychological processes are higher-order biological ones. Moreover, psychological processes express emergence in properties. The mental can emerge from the biophysical. According to Mascolo and Kallio (2019), the process that describes how psychological processes emerge from biological ones is embodied emergence. Note that Young (2016) described exactly the same process (p. 28), as did Kuniyoshi (2019). Mascolo and Kallio (2019) applied the concept of embodied emergence to the higher-order behaviors of conscious agency and free will.

Important for present purposes, Mascolo and Kallio (2019) reviewed the properties of emergent phenomena. First, the outcome is novel or not predictable from the properties (entities) from which they emerge. Second, they are novel relative to those properties. Third, emergent phenomena are irreducible or not decomposable to the properties from which they emerge and behave differently from them. In strong emergence, it could be that the emerged entity possesses properties that function autonomously relative to its parts. Therefore, they can express downward causation on the lower-order properties. In weak emergence, bottom-up processes dominate from base elements in an upward causation, which is akin to reductionism in some senses. Embodied emergence entails an emergence that includes lower-order (biological) processes so that there is not an abstract, distinct mental emergence. That said, psychological processes involve establishing meaning and significance in context, in a transformative function that is not controlling, as in consciousness.

As for specific research on biological mechanisms in behavior, the research is endless. Three specific examples illustrate different levels of the neurons (central nervous system and associations) as underlying behavioral and psychiatric vulnerabilities, dysfunctions, and disorders. Hammerschlag et al. (2019) found an association of gene sets related to synaptic function (e.g., calcium channel function) across five psychiatric disorders (schizophrenia, bipolar disorder, major depressive disorder, autism spectrum disorder, and ADHD). Areas of the brain involved included the cerebellum and frontal cortex. Kühnel et al. (2019) related alexithymia (present in 10% of the population) to an imbalance in biomarkers of excitation/inhibition in the pregenual anterior angulate cortex (pgACC). The ratio of glutamate (GLU)/GABA proved critical in this regard. Shakiba et al. (2019) studied the effect of adversity in 4- to 6-year-olds and found blunted cortisol response to stress with high experienced adversity.

Also, see Boutwell and White (2019) for an overview of genetics and epigenetics in relationship to health and psychology; Barker et al. (2018) on genome-wide epigenetics; Bueno (2019) on genetics and learning; Mueller and Tronick (2019) on early adversity and effects on the HPA axis; Bolton et al. (2019) on early-life experiences on epigenetics for stress-sensitive neurons; and Folger et al. (2019) on neonatal epigenetics and later social-emotional development up to 18 months.

To summarize the recent study of causality, both systems and mechanisms have been highlighted. The research on psychological causality is endless, and no attempt is made to review it here, except in the area of development (see next section). Systems study brings with it the concept of emergence, including soft and hard emergence. Mechanisms need to be specific and not refer simply to biopsychosocial processes.

Unification

The notion of unification in psychology is still a vibrant one, and it includes hypotheses on lower-order causal processes. In particular, Geary (2019) proposed that the unification of intelligence, health, and aging reflects mitochondrial (energetic organelle) functioning quality. Butler et al. (2019) offered another theory of everything in psychology, referring to the novel hypothesis that the microbiome is influential not only in physical health but also in mental health. Hagerty et al. (2019) and Smith and Wissel (2019) presented a similar point of view. As for the unification of statistical models toward deciphering causality in psychology, refer to Usami et al. (2019). Veissière et al. (2020) integrated the areas of social cognition and the acquisition of culture using the principle of free energy. They referred to the interesting concept of cultural affordances in their "unified" account. Veissière et al. (2020) based their work on the free energy concept in Friston's extensive research program (e.g., Friston 2010). Free energy concerns variational or surprisal energy dynamics that aim to minimize surprise and uncertainty through feedback processes that tune the organism's expectancies to match the environmental contexts in which the organism is functioning. An organism is a predictive machine seeking statistic regularities that constitute the information needed for ongoing adaptation (bounded set of states that can survive as its phenotype).

The latter articles are consistent with the present approach of unifying psychology and of unifying causality. They add new vistas for both projects. These integrative projects did not reach an end-point plateau in my work, despite the aim of my three books on the topics, nor could they. Modeling and research can only further specify the projects and reduce the uncertainty in the endeavor. That said, development is a critical cross-area topic in psychology, and the following examines recent developments in this area in terms of causality. Other developments concerning stage modeling are presented later.

Taking one step back, why the emphasis on integrating/unifying psychology and causality and developing models toward these ends? In Young (2019), I emphasized that psychology is too siloed and that the replication crisis exists partly from a lack of such efforts. Inroads are being made in psychological methods in psychology, but more than methods are required to stem the replication crisis. Moreover, it continues to fester in the field. Tackett et al. (2019) indicated how the replication crisis in psychology has been slower to reach the area of clinical psychopathology research.

Developmental Causality

Data from the decades-long Dunedin study ($N = 918$) illustrate the powerful role of genetic factors in development over the life course (Belsky et al. 2016). The research falls under the purview of socio-genomics and is a genome-wide association study (GWAS). It used a polygenic score involving education-associated alleles or single nucleotide polymorphisms. It examined confounding variables like social class. Outcome variables were spaced lifelong and included early acquisitions, intelligence, and financial planning for retirement. The results supported that genetics contribute even to long-term outcomes related to education and adult success measures, although effect sizes were small. Correlations mediated the associations with the environment and psychological characteristics, including self-control and interpersonal skill (e.g., as observed as early as age 3). These results are considered controversial by some, as are all such results in the Nature-Nurture debate.

Epigenetics is another bioenvironmental process that influences development. Boyce and Kobor (2014) showed that epigenesis stands as a link between early childhood stress and the later health of participants. Goodman et al. (2018) showed that early biobehavioral reactivity predicts epigenetic processes right into emerging adulthood as well as associated consequences (e.g., prodromal mental health developments). The epigenesis examined concerned DNA methylation, and the findings pertained to methylation of DLX5 and IGF2 genes at 15–18 years. The inhibited children group was ascertained using principal component analysis of measures such as stress reactivity protocols to challenges (e.g., social, cognitive) and ANS activity measures. The research included measures of temperament (maternal report, observation, and questionnaire response). The authors concluded that DNA methylation patterns in epigenetic signatures could represent internal biomarkers of behavioral reactivity.

Developmentally, the causality of mental health has been related to fetal origins. When the mother is pregnant, her psychological distress (e.g., perceived stress, life events, internalizing emotions) has long-term consequences for future psychopathology. The research describes the pathways involved and the biological system mechanisms at issue. This type of research highlights that risk factors for psychiatric illness go beyond genes and environment (e.g., parental care).

In this regard, McQuire et al. (2019) presented a multicausal model of psychopathology, in this case, for fetal alcohol syndrome. Factors involved include maternal alcohol use, lifestyle, socioeconomic factors, gestational variables, and genetics. Interestingly, the authors translated their literature review of these predictors (risk) variables into a causal diagram (directed acyclic graph, DAG; Pearl 2009, see their Figs. 1 and 2).

One pathway in psychopathological research has been to study a generalized *p* factor, akin to a generalized cognitive ability factor (*g*). Grotzinger et al. (2019) tested for *p*–*g* correlations (negative) in early childhood, finding that the relationship reflects overlapping genetic and shared environmental factors that are operative in early life, including factors stratified between families.

In another early life modeling paper, Belsky (2019) related early life adversity to later development right into adolescence. However, he advocated for an acceleration effect that is adaptive in context according to evolutionary life-history theory. There are later health risks, but accelerations such as puberty are advantageous evolutionarily. That is development balances trade-offs. Belsky (2019) pointed out that the relative stability for many people in our contemporary environment is only recent historically, and our ancestors did not evolve in such environments.

Porges' (2011) polyvagal theory has evolutionary and developmental implications that Welch (2016) and colleagues (Ludwig and Welch 2019) have elaborated in their models of emotional connection and calming cycles. They studied prematurely born infants to test the models. According to the theories, the fetus/infant's and mother's vagal tone and heart rate are comodulated. Dysregulated autonomic states result from a lack of emotional connection. The latter is evaluated during face-to-face interaction, e.g., in eye contact and cooing, or their absence.

Cole et al. (2019) considered emotional dysregulation as reflecting dynamic, bidirectional processes in context. Their research with preschoolers (Morales et al. 2017) supports a self-other, top-down, and bottom-up model of emotional regulation, which is a skill that improves in the age period studied (2–5 years) for the emotion of fear.

The biology of the child is critical to development and parenting, as well, but the research being described here also refers to other environmental factors, such as perceived maternal distress fetally. A broader view of the environment includes SES and early adversity, as we have seen. But culture often is considered crucial to environmental effects on development. For example, Wente et al. (2017) showed the effects of culture and SES in causal learning in 4- to 5-year-olds. In college students, Sun et al. (2019), showed an effect of culture on willpower and its depletion.

Looking further afield, Moriarity et al. (2019) examined how inflammatory proteins predict depressive symptom change in youth (12–20 years). Williams and Beidas (2018) advised that the study of child psychology/psychiatry needs causal theory and research on mechanisms. To conclude, this section of the literature review, the three Young books on the topic of causality and development had aimed to fulfill this latter need.

Handedness

Three recent reviews/integrations related to handedness and brain specialization have appeared, but they do not deal much with the development of handedness or manual skills. McManus (2019) called for more research on the topic. Króliczak et al. (2019) referred to Michel (2018), who related the development of infant hand preference to basic sensorimotor skills and cognitive abilities. Marcori and Okazaki (2019) related the origins of handedness, especially preterm, to the environment. The latter includes birth stress (e.g., Domellöf et al. 2011), although the authors argued that fetal asymmetric positioning differences contribute to handedness, as well. Right-head turning is found after birth, as well, and facilitates looking at the right hand, which in turn facilitates manual grasping (Michel 2012; Pogetti et al. 2014). As well, the early development of asymmetry in the brain and the hemispheres' neural circuitry also contribute to handedness development.

Research with chimpanzees confirms a right-hand preference for coordinated bimanual behavior on a tube manipulation task and faster right-hand behavior in a termite fishing task using a tool (Bailoo et al. 2019; Hopkins et al. 2019; respectively). Scharoun Benson and Bryden (2019) studied beading and, in some ways, human 3-year-olds behaved manually in terms of hand selection as did adults.

de Kovel et al. (2019) examined factors that influence left-handedness development in a cohort of about 500,000 participants. The early life factors involved included multiple births and breastfeeding. The heritability statistic that was calculated was very weak. Different environmental factors might each contribute very little to left-handedness development but act in concert, for example, prenatally, with the direct effect on handedness reinforcing with further experience as development proceeds. [Note that de Kovel and Francks (2019) queried the replicability of the research on the genetics of handedness.]

Hujoel (2018) examined whether breastfeeding was associated with handedness development in over 60,000 mother-child dyads. Compared to bottle-feeding, breastfeeding was increasingly related to the development of less frequent non-righthandedness in the first year of life. Hujoel concluded that cerebral specialization is established by 9 months, with the environment playing a factor.

Evidence for a biological contribution to handedness development includes research on genetic mechanisms on general morphological and organ asymmetries that develop prenatally in a nodal cascade (Schmitz et al. 2019). The earliest structural brain asymmetry that is known concerns a larger left choroid plexus at gestational age (GA) 11–13 weeks (Abu-Rustum et al. 2013). According to the cited research, leftward occipital lobe and planum temporale asymmetry appear later (20, 31 weeks GA, respectively).

According to Schmitz et al. (2019), 24–26% of phenotypic variance in handedness can be explained by genetic factors. Candidate genes that might be involved include the *PCSK6* gene (proprotein convertase subtilisin/kexin type 6) (e.g., Scerri et al. 2010). This gene is involved in the nodal signaling pathway, which is intrinsic to visceral asymmetry development beginning prenatally. Schmitz et al. examined in depth the epigenetic influences on handedness development, arguing that it is multifactorial in origin.

Berretz et al. (2019) studied the relationship between the *PCSK6* VNTR (variable number tandem repeat) polymorphism and MRI scan findings for the frontal and temporal lobes in a sample of 320 participants. The research follows up on the study by Arning et al. (2013) on the consistency of handedness in relation to the gene. MRI images were analyzed using the Human Connectome project parameters for the brain region ($N = 180$). PCSK6 VNTR groups were: homozygous short (≤ 6 repeats); homozygous long ($\geq$ repeats); and heterozygous short/long (s/l). Asymmetric MRI measures involved cortical thickness and cortical surface. Bonferroni adjustments accounted for the 180 analyses per question. Handedness was evaluated with a standard protocol, the Edinburgh Handedness Inventory (EHI; Oldfield 1971).

As for the results, the investigation found an association between the 33 bp VNTR and gray matter asymmetry in the dorsal anterior superior temporal sulcus (STSda). Specifically, the heterozygous group (s/l allele) demonstrated a stronger rightward STSda asymmetry. The STSda is involved in voice perception. The findings are consistent with a model of lateralization genetically involving genes common at least in part to visceral, manual, and hemispheric functions.

Finally, in a study of data in the UK Biobank, Wiberg et al. (2019) related left-handedness to polygenetic factors, with their GWAS research finding four loci in these regards (rs199512, rs45608532, rs13017199, and rs3094128). The article gives the associations of the genes to their encoding proteins involved in brain development and patterning, as well as microtubule function. Also, the article gives the associations of the loci with brain imaging phenotypes and psychiatric phenotypes. For present purposes, the heritability estimate explained collectively for handedness by the four sites is about 1%. Overall, the genetic variants appear to be involved not only in handedness development but also in brain development and its lateralization.

Recent research generally supports a generalized human and nonhuman primate hand preference, but with task effects. Further, handedness genetics indicate some heritability, but with much influence of the environment and experience in development.

Brain Lateralization

The recent research on the lateralized brain in infancy and childhood is consistent with the research described in Young (2019). The brain appears specialized in ways comparable to the adult right from the early infancy period, and this has long-term ramifications for lateralization development. This pertains to the valence model of hemispheric specialization for emotions, as well. Moreover, early brain lateralization can serve as biomarkers for later developmental problems, such as autism spectrum disorder (ASD) and ADHD. The recent research cited has focused on language areas, the newly discovered frontal aslant tract (FAT), and the frontal and temporal areas generally. The longitudinal aspect of the studies extends into adolescence and adulthood.

Liu et al. (2018) undertook a diffusion tensor imaging (DTI) study with 6-week-old infants, examining dorsal language tracts. They conducted a longitudinal study with language development measures at 18 months and symptoms of ASD at 36 months. The infants (*N* = 34) were divided into low risk (LR) and high risk (HR) for being a person with autism based on whether there was a family history of one or more older siblings with an ASD diagnosis. For language development, the study used the MacArthur-Bates Communicative Development Inventory (CDI; Fenson et al. 2007), in particular. To detect ASD symptoms, the study used the Autism Diagnostic Observation Schedule-2 (ADOS-2; Lord et al. 2012).

The critical white matter tracts in the dorsal language network involve the superior longitudinal fasciculus (SLF). This tract connects the superior temporal gyrus (STG) to the inferior frontal gyrus (IFG) pars opercularis. On DTI scanning, a higher fractional anisotropy (FA) indicates a more robust white matter tract architecture, while a lower FA indicates a more blunted one. The results showed that, in normal developing infants, there appeared to be a more robust structural connectivity in the left hemisphere. These infants showed higher FA in the left SLF. In contrast, HR infants expressed a higher FA in the right SLF. In the SLF, the HR infants expressed more rightward lateralization. Longitudinally, more left white matter integrity in the SLF (and AF, arcuate fasciculus) was associated with higher CDI measure scores for receptive language at 18 months. Finally, more rightward lateralization of the SLF related to more social communication impairments at 36 months. The authors concluded that altered lateralization in the dorsal language tracts connecting the classic Broca and Wernicke language areas when infants are 6-weeks-old predispose infants at risk for autism to its symptoms at 3 years of age.

Diaz et al. (2019) conducted a longitudinal study of infants (*N* = 410) from 5 to 24 months of age on the relationship between maternal insensitivity/intrusiveness, toddler negative affectivity, and hemispheric lateralization for affect in the frontal lobes as measured by baseline EEG. Maternal behavior was scored during a 5-month toy play. Temperament was scored using rating scales and questionnaires (the IBQ-revised; Infant Behavior Questionnaire, Gartstein and Rothbart 2002; the ECBQ Early Childhood Behavior Questionnaire, Putnam et al. 2006). The results indicated complex interactions: maternal sensitivity behavior at infant 5 months of age and also at 24 months of age was associated temperamentally with less affect negativity at the 2-year age mark, but only for infants whose baseline frontal EEG was asymmetric to the left. In contrast, maternal intrusiveness at both ages was associated with later negative affect, but only for 5-month-olds who had shown right frontal EEG asymmetry. The results reflect the valence model of hemispheric specialization for positive and negative emotions (Davidson and Fox 1982; Fox 1994), but add how extrinsic factors (maternal behavior) interact with the intrinsic biological (frontal lobe) characteristics involved.

In a longitudinal study from 5 to 18 years of age (*N* = 70), Garic et al. (2018) studied a newly discovered white matter tract, the frontal aslant tract (FAT), in relation to attention problems and executive dysfunction (as measured by the CBCL; Child Behavior Checklist; Achenbach and Rescorla 2000, 2001, 2003) and the BRIEF (Behavior Rating Inventory of Executive Function; Gioia et al. 2000), respectively. The FAT connects the posterior inferior frontal gyrus (IFG) with the presupplementary and the supplementary motor areas (pre-SMA, SMA, respectively). The study used diffusion-weighted magnetic resonance imaging (DW-MRI). The results supported that reduction in the FAT's right lateralization is related to more executive dysfunction and less attention function. The authors concluded that the study might indicate a potential biomarker for ADHD.

Qi et al. (2019) conducted a cross-sectional study with 5-year-olds, 10-year-olds, and adults in terms of syntactic language abilities (e.g., passive vs. active structure) and relationships to long-range language network structural covariance (in gray matter cortical thickness). They used structural magnetic resonance imaging, especially in preselected language areas (seeds), the left inferior frontal gyrus (IFG), and the left posterior superior temporal gyrus/sulcus (pSTG/STS). Stronger covariance was found in preschoolers who were advanced on the syntactic tasks. The white matter substrate involved, as measured by DWI (diffusion-weighted imaging), also developed according to the age comparisons. This research complements other research on language skills in relation to hemispheric specialization.

Kershner (2019) presented a refined view of networking in cerebral lateralization and applied it to developmental dyslexia. According to Fornito et al. (2016), brain networks involve topologically linked neuronal assemblies, which are activated by relevant events (perceptual/mental) and task demands (attention-modulated). Brain networks configure with small-world properties, i.e., high clustering within networks, high global efficiency, and densely connected hubs (Fulcher and Fornito 2016; Gollo et al. 2018). The hubs allow for changing millisecond connectivity (O'Neill et al. 2016).

Networks are arrangements that serve circuits that are either processing or control in function (e.g., Spagna et al. 2015; Zanto and Gazzaley 2013). Processors function modularly, allowing for specialization. Controllers route the computations that influence the operation of processors. Processors usually function within networks through integrative gray matter function over brain networks. The temporoparietal junction (TPJ) is involved in language, and the left TPJ appears to be a processor (e.g., phonologically) while the right appears to be a controller (in attention).

According to Kershner (2019), another way to examine left-right hemisphere differences is in terms of cortical oscillations. The right hemisphere appears to express a bias for low frequency, e.g., theta range (Giraud and Poeppel 2012), while the left hemisphere appears specialized for high-frequency bias or entraining high, faster frequencies, e.g., the gamma range. The left hemisphere can function with its skills, e.g., gamma sampling of phonetic features, through the right hemisphere first entraining low-frequency signals (e.g., prosody) and transmitting them across hemispheres (Steinmann et al. 2014; Thompson et al. 2016). Kershner (2019) concluded that, in dyslexia, there is an impairment in the right hemisphere attention modulation, especially pertaining to low-frequency encoded information (frontoparietal attention networks).

Kershner (2019) has introduced two new ways of examining hemisphere specialization that were not considered in Young (2019). He articulated that the left hemisphere is more of a processor than a controller and more oriented to sampling high frequencies (e.g., gamma, not theta, sampling of phonetic features), in cortical oscillation. The right hemisphere, then, is specialized in receiving low-frequency signals, e.g., theta oscillations in low frequency (prosodic) signal transmission.

Therefore, in both the modeling cases offered by Kershner (2019), whether in terms of being a processor and sampling high frequencies or the matter of control, the left hemisphere appears to be accomplishing the more complex task, although for both cases, the two hemispheres must work in unison for functional success. Moreover, in both cases, the present model of activation-inhibition coordination of left hemisphere function can provide a more inclusive way of looking at them and a more general function to the models. For example, dealing with phonetic features (and high-frequency cortical oscillations) appears to demand activation-inhibition coordination relative to the skills required for dealing with prosodic information. In contrast, the matter of control is more related to inhibition, per se, which appears more a right hemisphere function by all accounts. For example, dealing with phonetic features (and high-frequency cortical oscillations) appears to demand activation-inhibition coordination relative to the skills required for dealing with prosodic information.

In a study that links this section of the literature review to the next one, Lim et al. (2019) found that, for functional connectivity, compared to the right hemisphere, the left hemisphere is more dissociatively connected. Dissociativity, compared to associativity, allows for networks to resist better perturbation (in this case, to brain injury, epilepsy, etc.).

Networks

Weems (2019) pointed out the network architecture in PTSD. At the symptom level, central symptoms influence other symptoms in the network. At the level of functional brain networks, PTSD generally involves the three main networks—the evidence is that the DMN (default mode network) is weak or hypoactive, the salience network is overactive, and the executive network cannot inhibit the latter.

Borsboom et al. (2018) maintained that network approaches to behavior are not reductionist; that is, that behavior cannot be explained by neurobiological/neurological/neuronal/neurochemical processes. They applied their argument to psychopathology, which for them is not a brain disorder. Rather, analysis of symptom patterns (networks) reveals that they constitute an independent level in psychopathology that is distinct from any brain-associated level. Networks, as their components interact, lead to mental disorders. There is no underlying condition to the symptoms; they have their own reality and their interaction (symptom-symptom relations) drives their expression (e.g., poor sleep as a driver of other symptoms). Biological and psychological factors interact, as well, in mental disorders, for example, in feedback loops. Borsboom et al. (2018) continued that network component interactions can lead to the complex of symptoms in a network to undergo its own activation, such as being trapped in a state of stability in symptom expression. These are examples of global states or patterned fields that emerge out of symptom development.

The concept of networks represents the empirical patterns of covariation in symptom data, organized into clusters (referred to as nodes) and links (referred to as edges). Symptom one could drive symptom two as a "real" pattern independent of any driver from biology or brain state and independent of any causal mental disorder common to the symptoms. Moreover, symptom-symptom connections include those that involve beliefs, desires, emotions, and intentions; for example, craving can drive addictive behavior and feelings of low self-worth can drive depression. Moreover, if our symptoms include negative appraisals of or by the other of ourselves, this can increase symptomatology in the network involved. External contexts and triggers fire symptoms as much as internal perceptions. Whether speaking of network symptoms or externalized drivers, they can be individualized and culturally differentiated. This latter focus on heterogeneity in network structure needs further work. The effect of the environmental context/culture indicates the relational status of symptoms (and networks).

According to Borsboom et al. (2018), this illustrates, among other ways, the holistic nature of symptom network (and modeling). Networks express system properties, with elements unpredictable from lower-level constituents. In this sense, symptom networks are massively multifactorial, e.g., with psychological as much as biological and environmental influences. None of these domains have priority over the others in the causal understanding of symptoms, their clusters (networks), and their expression as psychopathology. Hyland (2019) commented that perhaps we should qualify mechanism networks as much as symptom ones. For a different perspective on the value of symptom analysis, see Ward and Clack (2019).

Cognitive Networks

Figure 6.1 illustrates network modeling with core nodes as drivers of other nodes. For psychiatric symptoms, an example would be poor sleep as a driver of increased depression. This type of modeling has yet to be applied to the development of cognitive skills, as far as is known, even in my own work to date. Therefore, the figure uses the example of critical cognitive skills driving the development of (or enhancing) other cognitive skills. Further, different cognitive skills could be involved. Moreover, in cognitive development, different cognitive acquisition areas might be quite linked, as illustrated in the figure. The expansion of cognitive skills and their consolidation into larger sets would be an individual process conditioned to context and taking place online while leading to stores of skills that can be recalled/

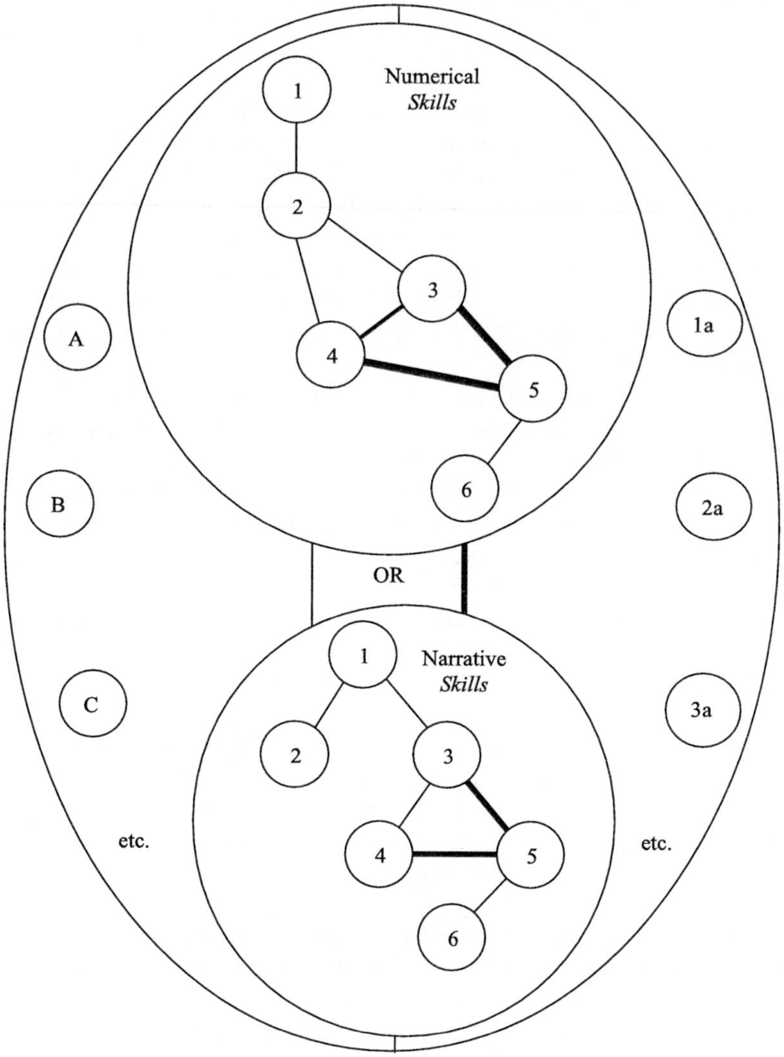

Fig. 6.1 A hypothesized network of cognitive performance skills
Nodes represent skills: Edges represent the relations or links (empirical correlations) between skills. Numbers in nodes refer to specific skills. A thicker and darker edge represents a stronger relation (correlation). The figure gives a hypothesized network of cognitive skills over two domains (for example, numerical and narrative). In both cases, skill number 5 can be seen as a driver of two other skills. Different skill domains might be quite linked or not (e.g., are they both verbal or is one verbal and another spatial?) As indicated in the outer circle to the right (i.e., for the other skills 1a, 2a, etc.), two skill sets might be related enough (e.g., numerical) to create or contribute to more generalized or other skills (e.g., adding, subtracting, and multiplying helping with division). Also, as indicated in the outer circle to the left (i.e., as indicated by skills A, B, etc.), other contributing skills will help develop the skills in the domains (e.g., executive function, memory). Finally, the figure indicates that broader cognitive structures could develop across different domains (e.g., numerical, spatial, narrative), depending on the individual, context, etc., such as in more generalized skills indicative of (sub)stage acquisitions. And those that are expanded across domain networks could reach system thresholds of changes to higher-order (sub)stages, as well. (Adapted from Schmittmann et al. (2013) based on Epskamp et al. (2011), greatly modified)

recreated or otherwise brought into play in cognitive problem-solving. This may lead to more system-wide expansion of the sets into families or related cognitive skills that mutually reinforce their function. The ultimate levels in this regard are (sub)stage-like or (sub)stage conglomerations of cognitive skill sets that can be effectively deployed in cognitive problem solving, and ready to advance to higher-order levels when no longer adequate to the task (in systems language, pushed to the edge of chaos, or the cusp of order-disorder, or changes). This allows the emergence of a qualitatively more advanced sub(stage) to begin to coalesce and coordinate.

In this conceptualization of networks as expressions of nonlinear dynamical system processes, the notion that any particular node could be a hierarchical apex driver of other symptoms is counterbalanced by placing the driver involved within the full system context. Systems are considered to have *collector* variables that express the state of the system and also particular *control* parameter variables that are marked by criteria thresholds of change that lead to system reconfiguration as the system moves beyond them to far-from-equilibrium and "stretches" as an outcome. Therefore, there are similarities in the concept of network driver causal nodes and system control parameter variables that can act on systems and their collector variables. That said, in their contexts, network causal drivers and system control parameter variables act on different levels of the system, the former being quite local and the latter quite global.

This type of contrast illustrates the difficulty in considering relations between network nodes without considering the whole system involved. It would be like isolating local brain region coupling from the full brain and its corollary couplings in trying to understand the local coupling well. Yet, network modeling brings advantages to systems modeling by clarifying better how components within a particular system might interact.

This analysis does not say that network models and systems models are separate and complementary approaches to understanding behavior and/or brain relations. That is, any reading on the Connectome will include an emphasis on its system and nonlinear dynamical system properties. However, the symptom network area of study did not include this type of model collaboration, and in prior publications, I have pointed out this lacuna and the need to accommodate to it (Young 2015).

Activation-Inhibition Coordination

Shine (2019) described integration and segregation of networks in the brain, which appears to be a process akin to activation-inhibition coordination. Segregation is required in the brain and behavior (e.g., processing a particular environmental pattern in order to avoid signal degradation/scrambling). Integration is required, as well (e.g., with context, past experience, internal goals, and prediction). The segregation and integration together necessarily involve the whole brain network. Moreover, two neuromodulatory systems dynamically manage them—the cholinergic basal forebrain one and the noradrenergic locus coeruleus (LC) one.

Functionally segregated brain networks consist of small worlds, or tightly connected modules linked weakly to other networks. In contrast, functionally integrated networks form modules that are not as clear, and these are more interconnected.

Neuromodulatory systems alter neuronal firing by making them less or more likely to fire in receiving incoming glutamatergic signaling from a connecting neuron. Thus, the two systems being discussed are strongly positioned to influence network dynamics. They modulate the "equilibrium between excitation and inhibition in the network" (p. 574).

The LC-related cholinergic system is an ascending noradrenergic system leading to increased arousal—increased acetylcholine to particular cortical locations—thereby increasing network segregation. The basal nucleus-related noradrenergic system leads to an increase in noradrenaline to diffuse cortical locations, thereby facilitating cortical networking integration. [The former system functions through multiplicative gain in neuronal firing, and the latter through response gain.]

The two systems interact not only in cortical network function but also in balancing the sympathetic and parasympathetic systems: the downward projections from the frontal cortex to the LC and to the forebrain function in their balancing. Network dynamics fluidly underwrite function through their segregation and integration. For example, networks segment functionally into units while learning complex motor sequences. Also, effector-specific sensorimotor regions coalesce together, freeing other networks for domain-general processing.

Diagnostic and Statistical Manual of Mental Disorders

All of these topics have import for the debate on the classic approach to psychological classification in the DSM-5, and other approaches, such as the Research Domain Criteria (RDoC; Cuthbert and Insel 2013) and the Hierarchical Taxonomy of Psychopathology (HiTop) (Conway et al. 2019; Kotov et al. 2017; Krueger et al. 2018). Certainly, the network approach is presenting challenges to the discipline of psychiatry and the ways psychopathology is conceived (Persson 2019). My work criticizing the RDoC, and the related topic of how to improve the DSM-5, can be found in Young (2016).

Piaget

The recent literature on Piaget and the Neo-Piagetian approach since the 2019 Young book has been modest, and in this brief review, I added a discussion of some articles that I had not previously cited. There is still doubt whether cognitive stages in development exist (Kamangar et al. 2018), but others value stage models, in general (e.g., Kjellström and Stålne 2017).

Perfors (2016) examined causality in Piaget's writing. For Piaget, causality lies in a system perspective of perturbation and disequilibrium, leading to change and equilibrium. However, unlike what most maintain about Piaget, the perturbation is emotional in nature. A "disturbing" event does not fit the cognitive structure in play. There is a lot of emotional flailing and discord.

Perfors (2016) raised another valuable point—the development of a new stage does not lead to any prior one's disappearance. The new and old stage(s) are intertwined. This concept fits my own yoking model in which the cognitive skills associated with any one step in the present 25-step model can be called into play to solve a particular problem at hand, and multiple skill sets (associated with different steps) can be yoked toward problem resolution.

Perfors (2016) concluded that Piaget's extensive intellectual reach allowed him to create connections and "unify" phenomena that appeared quite different on the surface. This formulation of his oeuvre indicates that he stands as a model for my own unification attempts in psychology.

Lourenço (2001) noted that, for Piaget, child cognition is about performance on tasks. Stages do not exist in the minds of children as living organizations that are causally active. The rules therein are not disembodied but actively constructed. As Piaget and Inhelder (1941) noted, there are so many heterogeneous factors in dealing with a particular task, including the child's individual experience.

As for Neo-Piagetian stage models, Mascolo (2015) reviewed them, listing those of Fischer and Case, in particular (Fischer 1980; Case 1985, respectively). Demetriou's model (Demetriou et al. 2010) builds on Case's. It adds the interesting concept of hypercognitive systems as a mediator in cognitive development. Pascual-Leone's (1970) model adhered to Piaget's four-stage sequence in cognitive development and considered the mental attention function as the appropriate mediator (Pascual-Leone 2018; referred to mental attention as mental energy originally). Note that in his Fig. 1, Mascolo (2015) placed the Fischer and Case models side by side, but he did not comment on their quite notable differences in what steps are found at what ages and the apparent gaps or missing steps in both models (unlike the approach that I took in Young 2011).

Pascual-Leone (2018) reviewed the book by Demetriou and Spanoudis (2018) on their updated Neo-Piagetian model, which includes the concept of cognizance (self-driven, purposeful, conative activity). He also clarified his own mental attention model as a content-free, maturational function that places a limiting ceiling on cognitive stage development through its own mental limitations. Interestingly, the Pascual-Leone model includes an activation and inhibition component that works to keep relevant cognitive activity at the forefront in task problem solving (although a coordination component in these regards is not highlighted, unlike in my own activation-inhibition coordination model).

Lewis (1994) also examined the constraints on cognitive (stage) development. He considered constraints (e.g., culturally, neuronally, maturationally) as soft ones that allow for global emergence of new (discontinuous) cognitive structures, as in self-organizing nonlinear dynamical systems. This does not imply the growth of universal stages, though. Cognitive development is more idiosyncratic and individual than a universal stage model would allow. Indeed, Piaget himself would have it no other way, as shown above.

Shifting from general writing on stages to recent research on particular Piagetian stages, Fioretti and Smorti (2019) examined Piaget's original observations of his children in the infancy period on sensorimotor development (on interesting spectacles). Babik et al. (2018) conducted a study of means-end problem solving, finding inter-task transfer of acquired knowledge at 9 months. Papaleontiou-Louca (2019) found the development of meta-cognitive awareness in the preschool period (earlier than Piaget anticipated). Viarouge et al. (2019) studied number development in 6-year-olds, finding evidence implicating a progressive rather than a discontinuous development in skill in number conservation performance. Also, they argued that skill on the task required inhibition of misleading strategies and of knowledge already acquired. [Also see Bolton and Hattie (2017) and de Ribaupierre and Lecerf (2017) on relations between Piagetian development and executive function, including inhibition.]

Houdé (2019) expanded on his inhibitory model of cognitive development by arguing that the model of System 1 and System 2 thinking can be complemented by adding a third module on inhibition. System 1 is related to unconscious, fast, heuristic, and emotional thinking, while System 2 is related to conscious, slow, logical, and rational reasoning. System 3 is required for this model according to Houdé (2019) because it inhibits the heuristic system, allowing for the activation of the logical one.

My equivalent model to that of Houdé (2019) considers each of the five stages in the Neo-Piagetian model has thinking systems. Moreover, they can be yoked (at least the required skills they possess for the task at hand) in cognitive activity on a varying and individual basis. Finally, this takes place according to the mechanism of activation/inhibition coordination, the efficacy of which correlates with task performance success/resolution.

Commons

Michael Lamport Commons has implemented an extensive active research program based on his Neo-Piagetian cognitive-developmental model (Commons and Richards 1984a, b). He qualifies his model as an "enhancement and simplification" of Piaget's model (Commons and Kjorlien 2016). In Young (2011), in particular, I indicated how his series of stages appear to be missing steps, which is based on the fact that many of his stages before the adult period are taken from Fischer's (1980) model [e.g., I have argued that Fischer's model appears to be missing steps, e.g., at 2 years of age].

Commons and Kjorlien (2016) introduced a new stage to their series, called meta-cross-paradigmatic. Commons and Jiang (2014) had split the sensory or motor stage (a misnomer), by adding an automatic preliminary stage [Note that Common's model does not have a stage and substage structure even though it borrowed from

Fischer, although he has transition steps (Commons and Richards 2002; Ross 2014)]. Giri et al. (2014) considered that stages form integrated wholes. They found that there is only one stage domain over different domains, e.g., social and logic/mathematics/physical sciences. The empirical evidence indicates that stages are not skipped within domains, as per Rasch analysis (e.g., Giri et al. 2014; Li et al. 2014).

Generally, Commons and colleagues develop instruments that fit their sequence of cognitive-development steps that are quite ingenious, such as child care-giving or depression and romantic breakup. Vignettes might be used to elicit responses scored for step level (e.g., Giri et al. 2014; Li et al. 2014). Other work by Commons and colleagues in support of his model are rational literature reviews and integration. For example, Harrigan and Commons (2014) related the stage of development of a species, as established according to Common's model, and the number of neurons estimated for a species. They found an empirical relationship using measures over species, from fruit flies to humans. Harrigan and Commons (2015) argued that Maslow's (1943) needs hierarchy model can be reworked in terms of social perspective-taking skills as determined by Commons' model. The five needs in the model were analyzed for reinforcers in this regard [Note that my own Neo-Maslovian model considered each of the five needs in Maslow's model developmentally and related them to the present Neo-Piagetian/Neo-Eriksonian model].

Commons and Duong (2019) attempted to analyze terrorism from the perspective of the Commons model. More interesting for me, they focused on societal changes that would correspond to the model's steps, from the concrete developmental stage on. Children at this level form cliques. But when applied to social structure, the authors defined the equivalent to social cliques in childhood as: (a) gathering and hunting for subsistence; and (b) human slave and sex-slave traders; or (c) feudal/dictatorial and power-focused [I would think that the parallel suggested here needs revision, and perhaps the next one, as well]. In the next step of abstract thought, for Commons and Duong (2019), loyalty is critical, e.g., to an elite class, and bureaucracies form in governments. Societies functioning at the next formal level will generate true bureaucracies, and democracy can develop. The next stages are associated with a more complex government structure.

Commons et al. (2017) applied the Commons model to symptomatology measures in autism spectrum disorder (ASD). They developed items for each step of the model that might relate to ASD. However, in doing so, some inconsistencies were evident. For example, step 2 was taken to develop at 1–3 months, and one item for this age period (or the equivalent for a child with ASD) involves social referencing (child looks for cues from others about what to do (in ambiguous situations)). Clearly, this skill applies only to the older infant toward 1 year of age. In another example of inconsistency in developing step items applicable to ASD, for step 7, which concerns 3-year-olds, the equivalent school grade given is 1–3, and an example is that the child can write a few sentences. Also, step 11 is missing from the table involved on p. 208 [Note, I have made many typographical errors and minor errors like this one myself, over the three books being summarized, but hopefully not such inconsistent ones].

To conclude the discussion and evaluation of the Neo-Piagetian model proposed by Commons, it is being expanded conceptually and researched empirically, perhaps more than any other. However, it does need more careful work and should be more carefully compared to other Neo-Piagetian models, including my own.

Erikson

Recent research on Erikson's eight-stage lifespan psychosocial (sexual) developmental model has focused on the adolescent identity period and the adult period (Faßbender et al. 2019; Niiyama et al. 2018; Shalka 2019), as well as the older adult period (Dezutter et al. 2019; Filip et al. 2019). None of this research attempts to alter the traditional Eriksonian eight-step developmental model.

Marcia and Josselson (2012) developed a model of how development can go awry in the last four of Erikson's stages in youth and the adult according to extensions of Marcia's (Marcia et al. 1993; Marcia 2002) four identity statuses. Identity achievement and diffusion represent the two poles of the Identity period in Erikson's model. Marcia added the statuses of moratorium and foreclosure. In moratorium, the youth is seeking identity but is stuck. In foreclosure, the youth adopts the identity imposed by the other, e.g., authority figure.

In Marcia and Josselson (2012), for the intimacy, generativity, and integrity stages, the moratorium status was referred to as—preintimate, pseudogenerative, and pseudointegrated, respectively. The foreclosure status was referred to as pseudo-intimate, conventional, and nonexploratory, respectively (see Table 6.1).

For each of the four statuses at each of the four developmental periods discussed, Marcia and Josselson (2012) indicated the specific problems that might arise, as well as the therapeutic approaches to adopt. They noted that Erikson pointed out the

Table 6.1 Four statuses in four psychosocial stages

	Stage/age			
Statuses	Identity/identity diffusion (late adolescence)	Intimacy/isolation (young adulthood)	Generativity/ stagnation (middle age)	Integrity/despair (old age)
1	Identity achievement	Intimate/ preintimate	Generative	Integrated
2	Moratorium	Pseudointimate	Pseudogenerative: agentic, communal	Pseudointegrated
3	Foreclosure	Stereotyped	Conventional	Nonexploratory
4	Identity diffusion	Isolated	Stagnant, self-absorbed	Despairing

Adopted with permission of John Wiley & Sons. Marcia, J., & Josselson, R. (2012). Eriksonian personality research and its implications for psychotherapy. *Journal of Personality, 81*(6), 617–629. [Figure 2, pp. 620]

developmental stages over the lifespan but not their therapeutic implications and practices.

Moratorium is described as a struggling crisis in which the youth becomes stuck. Pseudo-intimate is described as being superficial. Pseudogenerative is depicted as being self-focused, either agentically (for own goals) or communally (with payback expected). Pseudo-integrated is described as putting up a brittle facade.

If the intention had been to define statuses that are equivalent to adolescent identity moratorium in the ensuing three life stages in the Erikson model, these descriptions of those three moratorium-equivalent statuses reveal inconsistencies. None of the pseudo-intimate, pseudo-generative, and pseudo-integrated statuses described are equivalent to an identity struggle or stuckness.

The statuses equivalent to identity foreclosure in the ensuing three stages after adolescence involve stereotyped intimacy, conventional generativity, and nonexploration of integrity. Stereotypical intimacy is characterized as behaving according to the books (lowest common denominator). Conventional generativity concerns giving care to those who adhere to the giver's prescriptions. Nonexploratory integrity means people still live according to others' narratives, as in identity foreclosure. Once more, one finds some inconsistencies in the different foreclosure statuses. The integrity one is specifically a foreclosure, and stereotypical intimacy might be that way, although this is not clear. The conventionally generative carer is more self-absorbed in this schema of Erikson statuses after adolescence than foreclosed in behavior.

Granted, my own work was influenced by Marcia's. However, my approach was quite different in some ways. First, I chose different critical concepts for individuals struggling with moratorium and foreclosure. I referred to hypo and hyper styles for most of each of the crises or issues inherent in the 25 Eriksonian steps of my model (compared to Erikson's 8 stages). The hypo type does not engage in (avoids) the issue at hand, while the hyper type might do so profusely but superficially (like pseudo-moratorium), or like only because she/he was trained (modeled) toward that way (like foreclosed). The hypo and hyper types also include anti typology, such as anti-identities (e.g., delinquency). These terms speak directly to the behavior involved and avoid the two terminologies that are too removed from the behavior (does not represent them well).

Moreover, in describing the four statuses in the four later Erikson stages and then the case studies illustrating them, Marcia and Josselson (2012) referred to carry-over of earlier developmental difficulties in earlier stages as compromising factors in poorly traversing later stages. However, my approach was to indicate potential problems at each of the 25 steps of my Neo-Eriksonian model stemming from difficulties that might arise in the environmental context (e.g., parenting) particular to the stage at issue, with the assumption that nothing untoward had developed previously. This way, the problems at any one step of the 25 steps Neo-Eriksonian as described in my work model are not qualified by earlier problems and can stand alone as specific prototypes of how development can go awry at each step in the lifespan life cycle. In this sense, the cumulative effects of having difficulty navigating earlier steps in development can be much more complex than Erikson envisioned because the present model has 25 steps and associated problems, unlike for his eight-stage sequence. Moreover, the yoking concept is applied to the present model and problems through step combinations can become even more complex through that process.

Conclusion

This chapter conducts a literature review that supports the current conceptualizations on development, causality, and the unification project required in psychology. It reviews multiple areas of causality, including lateralization. It examines research related socio-affective stage modeling to therapy, which the present book greatly elaborates based on its own model. This chapter is reviewed in more depth, along with the next one in the conclusions of the next chapters.

References

Abu-Rustum, R.S., Ziade, M.F., Abu-Rustum, S.E.: Reference values for the right and left fetal choroid plexus at 11 to 13 weeks. J. Ultrasound Med. **32**(9), 1623–1629 (2013). https://doi.org/10.7863/ultra.32.9.1623

Achenbach, T.M., Rescorla, L.: Manual for the ASEBA Preschool Forms & Profiles: An Integrated System of Multi-Informant Assessment. ASEBA, Burlington (2000)

Achenbach, T.M., Rescorla, L.: Manual for the ASEBA School-Age Forms & Profiles: An Integrated System of Multi-Informant Assessment. ASEBA, Burlington (2001)

Achenbach, T.M., Rescorla, L.: Manual for the ASEBA Adult Forms & Profiles: For Ages 18–59: Adult Self-Report, Adult Behavior Checklist. ASEBA, Burlington (2003)

Arning, L., Ocklenburg, S., Schulz, S., Ness, V., Gerding, W.M., Hengstler, J.G., Falkenstein, M., Epplen, J.T., Güntürkün, O., Beste, C.: PCSK6 VNTR polymorphism is associated with degree of handedness but not direction of handedness. PCSK6 VNTR polymorphism is associated with degree of handedness but not direction of handedness. PLoS One. **8**(6), e67251 (2013). https://doi.org/10.1371/journal.pone.0067251

Babik, I., Cunha, A.B., Ross, S.M., Logan, S.W., Galloway, J.C., Lobo, M.A.: Means-end problem solving in infancy: development, emergence of intentionality, and transfer of knowledge. Dev. Psychobiol. **61**(2), 191–202 (2018). https://doi.org/10.1002/dev.21798

Bailoo, J.D., Quinius, B., Schapiro, S.J., Hopkins, W.D., Bennett, A.J.: Freestanding bipedal posture and coordinated bimanual manipulation significantly influence lateralized hand use in rhesus monkeys (Macaca Mulatta) and chimpanzees (Pan Troglodytes). J. Comp. Psychol. **133**(2), 171–182 (2019). https://doi.org/10.1037/com0000137

Barker, E.D., Roberts, S., Walton, E.: Hidden hypotheses in 'hypothesis-free' genome-wide epigenetic associations. Curr. Opin. Psychol. **27**, 13–17 (2018). https://doi.org/10.1016/j.copsyc.2018.07.009

Belsky, J.: Early-life adversity accelerates child and adolescent development. Curr. Dir. Psychol. Sci. **28**(3), 241–246 (2019). https://doi.org/10.1177/0963721419837670

Belsky, D.W., Moffitt, T.E., Corcoran, D.L., Domingue, B., Harrington, H., Hogan, S., Houts, R., Ramrakha, S., Sugden, K., Williams, B.S., Poulton, R., Caspi, A.: The genetics of success: how single-nucleotide polymorphisms associated with educational attainment relate to life-course development. Psychol. Sci. **27**(7), 957–972 (2016). https://doi.org/10.1177/0956797616643070

Berretz, G., Arning, L., Gerding, W.M., Friedrich, P., Fraenz, C., Schlüter, C., Epplen, J.T., Güntürkün, O., Beste, C., Genç, E., Ocklenburg, S.: Structural asymmetry in the frontal and temporal lobes is associated with PCSK6 VNTR polymorphism. Mol. Neurobiol. **56**(11), 7765–7773 (2019). https://doi.org/10.1007/s12035-019-01646-1

Bolton, S., Hattie, J.: Cognitive and brain development: executive function, Piaget, and prefrontal cortex. Arch. Psychol. **1**(3), 1–36 (2017). https://archivesofpsychology.org/index.php/aop/article/view/30

Bolton, J.L., Short, A.K., Simeone, K.A., Daglian, J., Baram, T.Z.: Programming of stress-sensitive neurons and circuits by early-life experiences. Front. Behav. Neurosci. **13**, 30 (2019). https://doi.org/10.3389/fnbeh.2019.00030

Borsboom, D., Cramer, A.O.J., Kalis, A.: Brain disorders? Not really: why network structures block reductionism in psychopathology research. Behav. Brain Sci. **42**, e2 (2018). https://doi.org/10.1017/s0140525x17002266

Boutwell, B.B., White, M.A.: Editorial overview: the confluence of human health, psychology, and genetics: new opportunities to grow our understanding of ourselves. Curr. Opin. Psychol. **27**, 4–7 (2019). https://doi.org/10.1016/j.copsyc.2019.05.001

Boyce, W.T., Kobor, M.S.: Development and the epigenome: the 'synapse' of gene-environment interplay. Dev. Sci. **18**(1), 1–23 (2014). https://doi.org/10.1111/desc.12282

Bueno, D.: Genetics and learning: how the genes influence educational attainment. Front. Psychol. **10**, 1622 (2019). https://doi.org/10.3389/fpsyg.2019.01622

Butler, M.I., Cryan, J.F., Dinan, T.G.: Man and the microbiome: a new theory of everything? Annu. Rev. Clin. Psychol. **15**(1), 371–398 (2019). https://doi.org/10.1146/annurev-clinpsy-050718-095432

Campaner, R.: The interventionist theory and mental disorders. In: Gonzalez, W.J. (ed.) Philosophy of Psychology: Causality and Psychological Subject—Reflections on James Woodward's Contribution, pp. 243–268. De Gruyter, Boston (2018)

Case, R.: Intellectual Development: Birth to Adulthood. Academic Press, New York (1985)

Cole, P.M., Ramsook, K.A., Ram, N.: Emotion dysregulation as a dynamic process. Dev. Psychopathol. **31**(3), 1191–1201 (2019). https://doi.org/10.1017/s0954579419000695

Commons, M.L., Duong, T.Q.: Understanding terrorism: a behavioral developmental approach. Ethics Med. Public Health. **8**, 74–96 (2019). https://doi.org/10.1016/j.jemep.2019.02.003

Commons, M.L., Jiang, T.R.: Introducing a new stage for the model of hierarchical complexity: a new stage for reflex conditioning. Behav. Dev. Bull. **19**(3), 1–8 (2014). https://doi.org/10.1037/h0100582

Commons, M.L., Kjorlien, O.A.: The meta-cross-paradigmatic order and stage 16. Behav. Dev. Bull. **21**(2), 154–164 (2016). https://doi.org/10.1037/bdb0000037

Commons, M.L., Richards, F.A.: A general model of stage theory. In: Commons, M.L., Richards, F.A., Armon, C. (eds.) Beyond Formal Operations : Vol. 1. Late Adolescent and Adult Cognitive Development, pp. 120–140. Praeger, New York (1984a)

Commons, M.L., Richards, F.A.: Applying the general stage model. In: Commons, M.L., Richards, F.A., Armon, C. (eds.) Beyond Formal Operations: Vol. 1. Late Adolescent and Adult Cognitive Development, pp. 141–157. Praeger, New York (1984b)

Commons, M.L., Richards, F.A.: Organizing components into combinations: how stage transition works. J. Adult Dev. **9**(3), 159–177 (2002). https://doi.org/10.1023/a:1016047925527

Commons, M.L., Adhikari, D., Giri, S., Weinberg, M., Baran, J.J., Malik, E.: Measuring developmental outcomes in autism spectrum disorder (ASD). Behav. Dev. Bull. **22**(1), 197–208 (2017). https://doi.org/10.1037/bdb0000065

Conway, C.C., Forbes, M.K., Forbush, K.T., Fried, E.I., Hallquist, M.N., Kotov, R., Mullins-Sweatt, S.N., Shackman, A.J., Skodol, A.E., South, S.C., Sunderland, M., Waszczuk, M.A., Zald, D.H., Afzali, M.H., Bornovalova, M.A., Carragher, N., Docherty, A.R., Jonas, K.G., Krueger, R.F., Patalay, P., Pincus, A.L., Tackett, J.L., Reininghaus, U., Waldman, I.D., Wright, A.G.C., Zimmermann, J., Bach, B., Bagby, R.M., Chmielewski, M., Cicero, D.C., Clark, L.A., Dalgleish, T., DeYoung, C.G., Hopwood, C.J., Ivanova, M.Y., Latzman, R.D., Patrick, C.J.,

Ruggero, C.J., Samuel, D.B., Watson, D., Eaton, N.R.: A hierarchical taxonomy of psychopathology can transform mental health research. Perspect. Psychol. Sci. **14**(3), 419–436 (2019). https://doi.org/10.1177/1745691618810696

Cuijpers, P., Reijnders, M., Huibers, M.J.H.: The role of common factors in psychotherapy outcomes. Annu. Rev. Clin. Psychol. **15**(1), 207–231 (2019). https://doi.org/10.1146/annurev-clinpsy-050718-095424

Cuthbert, B.N., Insel, T.R.: Toward the future of psychiatric diagnosis: the seven pillars of RDoC. BMC Med. **11**, 126 (2013). https://doi.org/10.1186/1741-7015-11-126

Davidson, R., Fox, N.: Asymmetrical brain activity discriminates between positive and negative affective stimuli in human infants. Science. **218**(4578), 1235–1237 (1982). https://doi.org/10.1126/science.7146906

de Kovel, C.G.F., Francks, C.: The molecular genetics of hand preference revisited. Sci. Rep. **9**, 5986 (2019). https://doi.org/10.1038/s41598-019-42515-0

de Kovel, C.G.F., Carrión-Castillo, A., Francks, C.: A large-scale population study of early life factors influencing left-handedness. Sci. Rep. **9**, 584 (2019). https://doi.org/10.1038/s41598-018-37423-8

de Ribaupierre, A., Lecerf, T.: Intelligence and cognitive development: three sides of the same coin. J. Intell. **5**(2), 14 (2017). https://doi.org/10.3390/jintelligence5020014

Demetriou, A., Spanoudis, G.: Growing Minds: A Developmental Theory of Intelligence, Brain, and Education. Routledge, New York (2018)

Demetriou, A., Spanoudis, G., Mouyi, A.: The development of mental processing. In: Overton, W.F., Lerner, R.M. (eds.) The Handbook of Life-Span Development, Cognition, Biology, and Methods, vol. 1, pp. 306–345. Wiley, Hoboken (2010)

Dezutter, J., Toussaint, L., Dewitte, L.: Finding a balance between integrity and despair: a challenging task for older adults in residential care. J. Adult Dev. **27**(2), 147–156 (2019). https://doi.org/10.1007/s10804-019-09332-1

Diaz, A., Swingler, M.M., Tan, L., Smith, C.L., Calkins, S.D., Bell, M.A.: Infant frontal EEG asymmetry moderates the association between maternal behavior and toddler negative affectivity. Infant Behav. Dev. **55**, 88–99 (2019). https://doi.org/10.1016/j.infbeh.2019.03.002

Domellöf, E., Johansson, A.-M., Rönnqvist, L.: Handedness in preterm born children: a systematic review and a meta-analysis. Neuropsychologia. **49**(9), 2299–2310 (2011). https://doi.org/10.1016/j.neuropsychologia.2011.04.033

Dubrovsky, D.I.: The problem of free will and modern neuroscience. Neurosci. Behav. Physiol. **49**(5), 629–639 (2019). https://doi.org/10.1007/s11055-019-00781-5

Epskamp, S., Cramer, A.O.J., Waldorp, L.J., Schmittmann, V.D., Borsboom, D.: Qgraph: network representations of relationships in data. R package version 0.4.10. http://CRAN.R-project.org/package=qgraph (2011)

Faßbender, K., Wiebe, A., Bates, T.C.: Physical and cultural inheritance enhance agency, but what are the origins of this concern to establish a legacy? A nationally-representative twin study of Erikson's concept of generativity. Behav. Genet. **49**(2), 244–257 (2019). https://doi.org/10.1007/s10519-018-9943-x

Fenson, L., Marchman, V.A., Thal, D.J., Dale, P.S., Reznick, J.S., Bates, E.: MacArthur-Bates Communicative Development Inventories: User's Guide and Technical Manual, 2nd edn. Brookes, Baltimore (2007)

Filip, M., Lukavská, K.R., Šolcová, I.P.: Dialogical and integrated self in late adulthood: examining two adaptive ways of growing old. Int. J. Aging Hum. Dev. **90**(4), 337–362 (2019). https://doi.org/10.1177/0091415019831445

Fioretti, C., Smorti, A.: Beyond the anomaly: where Piaget and Bruner meet. Integr. Psychol. Behav. Sci. **53**(4), 694–706 (2019). https://doi.org/10.1007/s12124-019-9477-7

Fischer, K.W.: A theory of cognitive development: the control and construction of hierarchies of skills. Psychol. Rev. **87**(6), 477–531 (1980). https://doi.org/10.1037/0033-295x.87.6.477

Folger, A.T., Ding, L., Ji, H., Yolton, K., Ammerman, R.T., Van Ginkel, J.B., Bowers, K.: Neonatal NR3C1 methylation and social-emotional development at 6 and 18 months of age. Front. Behav. Neurosci. **13**, 14 (2019). https://doi.org/10.3389/fnbeh.2019.00014

Fornito, A., Zalesky, A., Bullmore, E.: Fundamentals of Brain Network Analysis. Academic Press, San Diego (2016)

Fox, N.A.: Dynamic cerebral processes underlying emotion regulation. Monogr. Soc. Res. Child Dev. **59**(2–3), 152–166 (1994). https://doi.org/10.1111/j.1540-5834.1994.tb01282.x

Friston, K.: The free-energy principle: a unified brain theory? Nat. Rev. Neurosci. **11**(2), 127–138 (2010). https://doi.org/10.1038/nrn2787

Fulcher, B.D., Fornito, A.: A transcriptional signature of hub connectivity in the mouse connectome. Proc. Natl. Acad. Sci. **113**(5), 1435–1440 (2016). https://doi.org/10.1073/pnas.1513302113

Garic, D., Broce, I., Graziano, P., Mattfeld, A., Dick, A.S.: Laterality of the frontal aslant tract (FAT) explains externalizing behaviors through its association with executive function. Dev. Sci. **22**(2), e12744 (2018). https://doi.org/10.1111/desc.12744

Gartstein, M.A., Rothbart, M.K.: Studying infant temperament via the Revised Infant Behavior Questionnaire. Infant Behav. Dev. **26**(1), 64–86 (2002). https://doi.org/10.1016/s0163-6383(02)00169-8

Geary, D.C.: The spark of life and the unification of intelligence, health, and aging. Curr. Dir. Psychol. Sci. **28**(3), 223–228 (2019). https://doi.org/10.1177/0963721419829719

Gioia, G.A., Isquith, P.K., Guy, S.C., Kenworthy, L.: Behavior Rating Inventory of Executive Function. Psychological Assessment Resources, Lutz (2000)

Giraud, A.-L., Poeppel, D.: Cortical oscillations and speech processing: emerging computational principles and operations. Nat. Neurosci. **15**(4), 511–517 (2012). https://doi.org/10.1038/nn.3063

Giri, S., Commons, M.L., Harrigan, W.J.: There is only one stage domain. Behav. Dev. Bull. **19**(4), 51–61 (2014). https://doi.org/10.1037/h0101081

Gollo, L.L., Roberts, J.A., Cropley, V.L., Di Biase, M.A., Pantelis, C., Zalesky, A., Breakspear, M.: Fragility and volatility of structural hubs in the human connectome. Nat. Neurosci. **21**(8), 1107–1116 (2018). https://doi.org/10.1038/s41593-018-0188-z

Gonzalez, W.J. (ed.): Philosophy of Psychology: Causality and Psychological Subject—Reflections on James Woodward's Contribution. De Gruyter, Boston (2018a)

Gonzalez, W.J.: Configuration of causality and philosophy of psychology: an analysis of causality as intervention and its repercussion for psychology. In: Gonzalez, W.J. (ed.) Philosophy of Psychology: Causality and Psychological Subject—Reflections on James Woodward's Contribution, pp. 21–70. De Gruyter, Boston (2018b)

Goodman, S.J., Roubinov, D.S., Bush, N.R., Park, M., Farrè, P., Emberly, E., Hertzman, C., Essex, M.J., Kobor, M.S., Boyce, W.T.: Children's biobehavioral reactivity to challenge predicts DNA methylation in adolescence and emerging adulthood. Dev. Sci. **22**(2), e12739 (2018). https://doi.org/10.1111/desc.12739

Grotzinger, A.D., Cheung, A.K., Patterson, M.W., Harden, K.P., Tucker-Drob, E.M.: Genetic and environmental links between general factors of psychopathology and cognitive ability in early childhood. Clin. Psychol. Sci. **7**(3), 430–444 (2019). https://doi.org/10.1177/2167702618820018

Hagerty, S.L., Ellingson, J.M., Helmuth, T.B., Bidwell, L.C., Hutchison, K.E., Bryan, A.D.: An overview and proposed research framework for studying co-occurring mental- and physical-health dysfunction. Perspect. Psychol. Sci. **14**(4), 633–645 (2019). https://doi.org/10.1177/1745691619827010

Hammerschlag, A.R., de Leeuw, C.A., Middeldorp, C.M., Polderman, T.J.C.: Synaptic and brain-expressed gene sets relate to the shared genetic risk across five psychiatric disorders. Psychol. Med. **50**(10), 1695–1705 (2019). https://doi.org/10.1017/s0033291719001776

Harrigan, W.J., Commons, M.L.: The stage of development of a species predicts the number of neurons. Behav. Dev. Bull. **19**(4), 12–21 (2014). https://doi.org/10.1037/h0101077

Harrigan, W.J., Commons, M.L.: Replacing Maslow's needs hierarchy with an account based on stage and value. Behav. Dev. Bull. **20**(1), 24–31 (2015). https://doi.org/10.1037/h0101036

Hopkins, W.D., Mareno, M.C., Schapiro, S.J.: Further evidence of a left hemisphere specialization and genetic basis for tool use skill in chimpanzees (pan troglodytes): reproducibility in two genetically isolated populations of apes. J. Comp. Psychol. **133**(4), 512–519 (2019). https://doi.org/10.1037/com0000183

Houdé, O.: 3-System Theory of the Cognitive Brain: A Post-Piagetian Approach to Cognitive Development. Routledge, New York (2019)

Hujoel, P.P.: Breastfeeding and handedness: a systematic review and meta-analysis of individual participant data. Laterality. **24**(5), 582–599 (2018). https://doi.org/10.1080/1357650x.2018.1555254

Hyland, M.E.: Functional disorders can also be explained through a non-reductionist application of network theory. Behav. Brain Sci. **42**, e12 (2019). https://doi.org/10.1017/s0140525x18001048

Kamangar, S.S.H., Moradimanesh, Z., Mokhtari, S., Bakouie, F.: A dynamical system approach explaining the process of development by introducing different time-scales. Int. J. Neurosci. **128**(12), 1211–1212 (2018). https://doi.org/10.1080/00207454.2018.1486831

Kendler, K.S.: Toward a philosophical structure for psychiatry. Am. J. Psychiatr. **162**(3), 433–440 (2005). https://doi.org/10.1176/appi.ajp.162.3.433

Kershner, J.R.: Neuroscience and education: cerebral lateralization of networks and oscillations in dyslexia. Laterality. **25**(1), 109–125 (2019). https://doi.org/10.1080/1357650x.2019.1606820

Kjellström, S., Stålne, K.: Adult development as a lens: applications of adult development theories in research. Behav. Dev. Bull. **22**(2), 266–278 (2017). https://doi.org/10.1037/bdb0000053

Kotov, R., Krueger, R.F., Watson, D., Achenbach, T.M., Althoff, R.R., Bagby, R.M., Brown, T.A., Carpenter, W.T., Caspi, A., Clark, L.A., Eaton, N.R., Forbes, M.K., Forbush, K.T., Goldberg, D., Hasin, D., Hyman, S.E., Ivanova, M.Y., Lynam, D.R., Markon, K., Miller, J.D., Moffitt, T.E., Morey, L.C., Mullins-Sweatt, S.N., Ormel, J., Patrick, C.J., Regier, D.A., Rescorla, L., Ruggero, C.J., Samuel, D.B., Sellbom, M., Simms, L.J., Skodol, A.E., Slade, T., South, S.C., Tackett, J.L., Waldman, I.D., Waszczuk, M.A., Widiger, T.A., Wright, A.G.C., Zimmerman, M.: The Hierarchical Taxonomy of Psychopathology (HiTOP): a dimensional alternative to traditional nosologies. J. Abnorm. Psychol. **126**(4), 454–477 (2017). https://doi.org/10.1037/abn0000258

Króliczak, G., Gonzalez, C.L.R., Carey, D.P.: Editorial: manual skills, handedness, and the organization of language in the brain. Front. Psychol. **10**, 930 (2019). https://doi.org/10.3389/fpsyg.2019.00930

Krueger, R.F., Kotov, R., Watson, D., Forbes, M.K., Eaton, N.R., Ruggero, C.J., Simms, L.J., Widiger, T.A., Achenbach, T.M., Bach, B., Bagby, R.M., Bornovalova, M.A., Carpenter, W.T., Chmielewski, M., Cicero, D.C., Clark, L.A., Conway, C., DeClercq, B., DeYoung, C.G., Docherty, A.R., Drislane, L.E., First, M.B., Forbush, K.T., Hallquist, M., Haltigan, J.D., Hopwood, C.J., Ivanova, M.Y., Jonas, K.G., Latzman, R.D., Markon, K.E., Miller, J.D., Morey, L.C., Mullins-Sweatt, S.N., Ormel, J., Patalay, P., Patrick, C.J., Pincus, A.L., Regier, D.A., Reininghaus, U., Rescorla, L.A., Samuel, D.B., Sellbom, M., Shackman, A.J., Skodol, A., Slade, T., South, S.C., Sunderland, M., Tackett, J.L., Venables, N.C., Waldman, I.D., Waszczuk, M.A., Waugh, M.H., Wright, A.G.C., Zald, D.H., Zimmermann, J.: Progress in achieving quantitative classification of psychopathology. World Psychiatry. **17**(3), 282–293 (2018). https://doi.org/10.1002/wps.20566

Kühnel, A., Widmann, A., Colic, L., Herrmann, L., Demenescu, L.R., Leutritz, A.L., Li, M., Grimm, S., Nolte, T., Fonagy, P., Walter, M.: Impaired cognitive self-awareness mediates the association between alexithymia and excitation/inhibition balance in the pgACC. Psychol. Med. **50**(10), 1727–1735 (2019). https://doi.org/10.1017/s0033291719001806

Kuniyoshi, Y.: Fusing autonomy and sociality via embodied emergence and development of behaviour and cognition from fetal period. Philos. Trans. R. Soc. B Biol. Sci. **374**(1771), 20180031 (2019). https://doi.org/10.1098/rstb.2018.0031

Lewis, M.D.: Reconciling stage and specificity in Neo-Piagetian theory: self-organizing conceptual structures. Hum. Dev. **37**(3), 143–169 (1994). https://doi.org/10.1159/000278251

Li, E.Y., Commons, M.L., Mille, J.G., Robbinet, T.L., Marchand, H., Ost, C.M., Ross, S.N.: Relationship among measures within the social and moral development domain. Behav. Dev. Bull. **19**(3), 106–113 (2014). https://doi.org/10.1037/h0100595

Lim, S., Radicchi, F., van den Heuvel, M.P., Sporns, O.: Discordant attributes of structural and functional brain connectivity in a two-layer multiplex network. Sci. Rep. **9**, 2885 (2019). https://doi.org/10.1038/s41598-019-39243-w

Liu, J., Tsang, T., Jackson, L., Ponting, C., Jeste, S.S., Bookheimer, S.Y., Dapretto, M.: Altered lateralization of dorsal language tracts in 6-week-old infants at risk for autism. Dev. Sci. **22**(3), e12768 (2018). https://doi.org/10.1111/desc.12768

Lord, C., Rutter, M., DiLavore, P.C., Risi, S., Gotham, K., Bishop, S.: Autism Diagnostic Observation Schedule 2nd Edition Manual. Western Psychological Services, Los Angeles (2012)

Lourenço, O.: What is happening in contemporary psychology to Piaget's developmental processes, stages, and structures? Intellectica Revue de l'Association Pour La Recherche Cognitive. **33**(2), 99–106 (2001). https://doi.org/10.3406/intel.2001.1634

Ludwig, R.J., Welch, M.G.: Darwin's other dilemmas and the theoretical roots of emotional connection. Front. Psychol. **10**, 683 (2019). https://doi.org/10.3389/fpsyg.2019.00683

Marcia, J.E.: Identity and psychosocial development in adulthood. Identity. **2**(1), 7–28 (2002). https://doi.org/10.1207/s1532706xid0201_02

Marcia, J., Josselson, R.: Eriksonian personality research and its implications for psychotherapy. J. Pers. **81**(6), 617–629 (2012). https://doi.org/10.1111/jopy.12014

Marcia, J.E., Waterman, A.S., Matteson, D.R., Archer, S.A., Orlofsky, J.S.: Ego Identity: A Handbook for Psychosocial Research. Springer-Verlag, New York (1993)

Marcori, A.J., Okazaki, V.H.A.: A historical, systematic review of handedness origins. Laterality. **25**(1), 87–108 (2019). https://doi.org/10.1080/1357650x.2019.1614597

Mascolo, M.F.: Neo-Piagetian theories of cognitive development. In: Wright, J. (ed.) International Encyclopedia of the Social and Behavioral Sciences, 2nd edn, pp. 501–510. Elsevier, Amsterdam (2015)

Mascolo, M.F., Kallio, E.: Beyond free will: the embodied emergence of conscious agency. Philos. Psychol. **32**(4), 437–462 (2019). https://doi.org/10.1080/09515089.2019.1587910

Maslow, A.H.: A theory of human motivation. Psychol. Rev. **50**(4), 370–396 (1943). https://doi.org/10.1037/h0054346

McManus, C.: Half a century of handedness research: myths, truths; fictions, facts; backwards, but mostly forwards. Brain Neurosci. Adv. **3**, 2398212818820513 (2019). https://doi.org/10.1177/2398212818820513

McQuire, C., Daniel, R., Hurt, L., Kemp, A., Paranjothy, S.: The causal web of foetal alcohol spectrum disorders: a review and causal diagram. Eur. Child Adolesc. Psychiatry. **29**(5), 575–594 (2019). https://doi.org/10.1007/s00787-018-1264-3

Michel, G.F.: The concept of homology in the development of handedness. Dev. Psychobiol. **55**(1), 84–91 (2012). https://doi.org/10.1002/dev.21038

Michel, G.F.: How might the relation of the development of hand preferences to the development of cognitive functions be examined during infancy: a sketch? Front. Neurosci. **11**, 739 (2018). https://doi.org/10.3389/fnins.2017.00739

Morales, S., Ram, N., Buss, K.A., Cole, P.M., Helm, J.L., Chow, S.-M.: Age-related changes in the dynamics of fear-related regulation in early childhood. Dev. Sci. **21**(5), e12633 (2017). https://doi.org/10.1111/desc.12633

Moriarity, D.P., Mac Giollabhui, N., Ellman, L.M., Klugman, J., Coe, C.L., Abramson, L.Y., Alloy, L.B.: Inflammatory proteins predict change in depressive symptoms in male and female adolescents. Clin. Psychol. Sci. **7**(4), 754–767 (2019). https://doi.org/10.1177/2167702619826586

Mueller, I., Tronick, E.: Early life exposure to violence: developmental consequences on brain and behavior. Front. Behav. Neurosci. **13**, 156 (2019). https://doi.org/10.3389/fnbeh.2019.00156

Niiyama, H., Kontkanen, I., Paavilainen, E., Kamibeppu, K.: A comparison of personality maturity among Japanese youth and Finnish young adult students: a cross-sectional study using Erikson psychosocial stage inventory and sense of coherence scale. Int. J. Adolesc. Youth. **23**(4), 482–495 (2018). https://doi.org/10.1080/02673843.2018.1435418

O'Neill, G.C., Tewarie, P.K., Colclough, G.L., Gascoyne, L.E., Hunt, B.A.E., Morris, P.G., Woolrich, M.W., Brookes, M.J.: Measurement of dynamic task related functional networks using MEG. NeuroImage. **146**, 667–678 (2016). https://doi.org/10.1016/j.neuroimage.2016.08.061

Oldfield, R.C.: The assessment and analysis of handedness: the Edinburgh inventory. Neuropsychologia. **9**(1), 97–113 (1971). https://doi.org/10.1016/0028-3932(71)90067-4

Papaleontiou-Louca, E.: Do children know what they know? Metacognitive awareness in preschool children. New Ideas Psychol. **54**, 56–62 (2019). https://doi.org/10.1016/j.newideapsych.2019.01.005

Pascual-Leone, J.: A mathematical model for the transition rule in Piaget's developmental stages. Acta Psychol. **32**, 301–345 (1970). https://doi.org/10.1016/0001-6918(70)90108-3

Pascual-Leone, J.: Growing minds have a maturing mental attention: a review of Demetriou and Spanoudis (2018). Intelligence. **72**, 59–66 (2018). https://doi.org/10.1016/j.intell.2018.12.001

Pearl, J.: Causality: Models, Reasoning and Inference, 2nd edn. Cambridge University Press, New York (2009)

Perfors, A.: Piaget, probability, causality, and contradiction. Hum. Dev. **59**(1), 26–33 (2016). https://doi.org/10.1159/000447339

Persson, B.N.: Current directions in psychiatric classification: from the DSM to RDoC. In: Garcia, D., Archer, T., Kostrzewa, R.M. (eds.) Personality and Brain Disorders: Associations and Interventions, pp. 253–268. Springer Nature Switzerland AG, Cham (2019)

Piaget, J., Inhelder, B.: Le développement des quantités physiques chez l'enfant. Delachaux & Niestlé, Neuchâtel (1941)

Pogetti, L.S., de Souza, R.M., Tudella, E., Teixeira, L.A.: Moving what is seen: arm visibility modulates infants' manual preference. Dev. Neuropsychol. **39**(5), 331–341 (2014). https://doi.org/10.1080/87565641.2014.932359

Porges, S.W.: The Polyvagal Theory: Neurophysiological Foundations of Emotions, Attachment, Communication, and Self-Regulation. Norton, New York (2011)

Putnam, S.P., Gartstein, M.A., Rothbart, M.K.: Measurement of fine-grained aspects of toddler temperament: the early childhood behavior questionnaire. Infant Behav. Dev. **29**(3), 386–401 (2006). https://doi.org/10.1016/j.infbeh.2006.01.004

Qi, T., Schaadt, G., Cafiero, R., Brauer, J., Skeide, M.A., Friederici, A.D.: The emergence of long-range language network structural covariance and language abilities. NeuroImage. **191**, 36–48 (2019). https://doi.org/10.1016/j.neuroimage.2019.02.014

Ross, S.N.: Fractal model of nonlinear hierarchical complexity: measuring transition dynamics as fractals of themselves. Behav. Dev. Bull. **19**(3), 28–32 (2014). https://doi.org/10.1037/h0100587

Scerri, T.S., Brandler, W.M., Paracchini, S., Morris, A.P., Ring, S.M., Richardson, A.J., Talcott, J.B., Stein, J., Monaco, A.P.: PCSK6 is associated with handedness in individuals with dyslexia. Hum. Mol. Genet. **20**(3), 608–614 (2010). https://doi.org/10.1093/hmg/ddq475

Scharoun Benson, S.M., Bryden, P.J.: Hand selection for role-differentiated bimanual manipulation in a beading task: an assessment of typically developing children. Infant Child Dev. **28**(4), e2136 (2019). https://doi.org/10.1002/icd.2136

Schmittmann, V.D., Cramer, A.O.J., Waldorp, L.J., Epskamp, S., Kievit, R.A., Borsboom, D.: Deconstructing the construct: a network perspective on psychological phenomena. New Ideas Psychol. **31**(1), 43–53 (2013). https://doi.org/10.1016/j.newideapsych.2011.02.007

Schmitz, J., Güntürkün, O., Ocklenburg, S.: Building an asymmetrical brain: the molecular perspective. Front. Psychol. **10**, 982 (2019). https://doi.org/10.3389/fpsyg.2019.00982

Shakiba, N., Ellis, B.J., Bush, N.R., Boyce, W.T.: Biological sensitivity to context: a test of the hypothesized u-shaped relation between early adversity and stress responsivity. Dev. Psychopathol. **32**(2), 641–660 (2019). https://doi.org/10.1017/s0954579419000518

Shalka, T.R.: Trauma and the interpersonal landscape: developmental tasks of the relational self identity site. J. Coll. Stud. Dev. **60**(1), 35–51 (2019). https://doi.org/10.1353/csd.2019.0002
Sharp, P.B., Miller, G.A.: Reduction and autonomy in psychology and neuroscience: a call for pragmatism. J. Theor. Philos. Psychol. **39**(1), 18–31 (2019). https://doi.org/10.1037/teo0000085
Shine, J.M.: Neuromodulatory influences on integration and segregation in the brain. Trends Cogn. Sci. **23**(7), 572–583 (2019). https://doi.org/10.1016/j.tics.2019.04.002
Smith, L.K., Wissel, E.F.: Microbes and the mind: how bacteria shape affect, neurological processes, cognition, social relationships, development, and pathology. Perspect. Psychol. Sci. **14**(3), 397–418 (2019). https://doi.org/10.1177/1745691618809379
Spagna, A., Mackie, M.-A., Fan, J.: Supramodal executive control of attention. Front. Psychol. **6**, 65 (2015). https://doi.org/10.3389/fpsyg.2015.00065
Steinmann, S., Leicht, G., Ertl, M., Andreou, C., Polomac, N., Westerhausen, R., Friederici, A.D., Mulert, C.: Conscious auditory perception related to long-range synchrony of gamma oscillations. NeuroImage. **100**, 435–443 (2014). https://doi.org/10.1016/j.neuroimage.2014.06.012
Sun, X., Cortina, K.S., Miller, K.F., Ning, H.: Willpower as cultural construct: do Chinese students believe less in its depletion? Front. Psychol. **10**, 988 (2019). https://doi.org/10.3389/fpsyg.2019.00988
Tackett, J.L., Brandes, C.M., King, K.M., Markon, K.E.: Psychology's replication crisis and clinical psychological science. Annu. Rev. Clin. Psychol. **15**(1), 579–604 (2019). https://doi.org/10.1146/annurev-clinpsy-050718-095710
Thapar, A., Rutter, M.: Do natural experiments have an important future in the study of mental disorders? Psychol. Med. **49**(7), 1079–1088 (2019). https://doi.org/10.1017/s0033291718003896
Thomas, J.G., Sharp, P.B.: Mechanistic science: a new approach to comprehensive psychopathology research that relates psychological and biological phenomena. Clin. Psychol. Sci. **7**(2), 196–215 (2019). https://doi.org/10.1177/2167702618810223
Thompsȯn, E.C., Carr, K.W., White-Schwoch, T., Tierney, A., Nicol, T., Kraus, N.: Hemispheric asymmetry of endogenous neural oscillations in young children: implications for hearing speech in noise. Sci. Rep. **6**, 19737 (2016). https://doi.org/10.1038/srep19737
Usami, S., Murayama, K., Hamaker, E.L.: A unified framework of longitudinal models to examine reciprocal relations. Psychol. Methods. **24**(5), 637–657 (2019). https://doi.org/10.1037/met0000210
Veissière, S.P.L., Constant, A., Ramstead, M.J.D., Friston, K.J., Kirmayer, L.J.: Thinking through other minds: a variational approach to cognition and culture. Behav. Brain Sci. **43**, e90 (2020). https://doi.org/10.1017/s0140525x19001213
Viarouge, A., Houdé, O., Borst, G.: The progressive 6-year-old conserver: numerical saliency and sensitivity as core mechanisms of numerical abstraction in a Piaget-like estimation task. Cognition. **190**, 137–142 (2019). https://doi.org/10.1016/j.cognition.2019.05.005
Vidunas, R.: Delegated causality of complex systems. Axiomathes. **29**(1), 81–97 (2018). https://doi.org/10.1007/s10516-018-9377-3
Ward, T., Clack, S.: From symptoms of psychopathology to the explanation of clinical phenomena. New Ideas Psychol. **54**, 40–49 (2019). https://doi.org/10.1016/j.newideapsych.2019.01.004
Weems, C.F.: Posttraumatic risk-seeking from a neurodevelopmental network perspective. Clin. Psychol. Sci. Pract. **26**(3), e12295 (2019). https://doi.org/10.1111/cpsp.12295
Welch, M.G.: Calming cycle theory: the role of visceral/autonomic learning in early mother and infant/child behaviour and development. Acta Paediatr. **105**(11), 1266–1274 (2016). https://doi.org/10.1111/apa.13547
Wente, A.O., Kimura, K., Walker, C.M., Banerjee, N., Fernández Flecha, M., MacDonald, B., Lucas, C., Gopnik, A.: Causal learning across culture and socioeconomic status. Child Dev. **90**(3), 859–875 (2017). https://doi.org/10.1111/cdev.12943
Wiberg, A., Ng, M., Al Omran, Y., Alfaro-Almagro, F., McCarthy, P., Marchini, J., Bennett, D.L., Smith, S., Douaud, G., Furniss, D.: Handedness, language areas and neuropsychiatric diseases: insights from brain imaging and genetics. Brain. **142**(10), 2938–2947 (2019). https://doi.org/10.1093/brain/awz257

Williams, N.J., Beidas, R.S.: Annual research review: the state of implementation science in child psychology and psychiatry: a review and suggestions to advance the field. J. Child Psychol. Psychiatry. **60**(4), 430–450 (2018). https://doi.org/10.1111/jcpp.12960

Woodward, J.: Making Things Happen: A Theory of Causal Explanation. Oxford University Press, New York (2003)

Woodward, J.: Mechanistic explanation: its scope and limits. Aristotelian Soc. Suppl. Vol. **87**(1), 39–65 (2013). https://doi.org/10.1111/j.1467-8349.2013.00219.x

Young, G.: Development and Causality: Neo-Piagetian Perspectives. Springer Science + Business Media, New York (2011)

Young, G.: Causality in psychiatry: a hybrid symptom network construct model. Front. Psych. **6**, 164 (2015). https://doi.org/10.3389/fpsyt.2015.00164

Young, G.: Unifying Causality and Psychology: Being, Brain and Behavior. Springer International Publishing, Cham (2016)

Young, G.: Causality and Development: Neo-Eriksonian Perspectives. Springer International Publishing, Cham (2019)

Zanto, T.P., Gazzaley, A.: Fronto-parietal network: flexible hub of cognitive control. Trends Cogn. Sci. **17**(12), 602–603 (2013). https://doi.org/10.1016/j.tics.2013.10.001

Chapter 7
Extensions and Innovations

This chapter begins with applications of the present work to couple work. Then, it extends to other elaborations and innovations, including in psychological energetics. It illustrates the range of the present book, applying to novel areas not yet dealt with by the present modeling, thereby creating new insights into behavior and causality.

A Novel Application to Couples and Couple Therapy

Couple Work

This three-book summary (Young 2011, 2016, 2019) has emphasized the causal nexus of activation-inhibition coordination, systems, and networks. This extension of the present three-book summary (Young 2011, 2016, 2019) includes an innovative application of the approach to causality underscored in the present work to the area of couples and couple therapy. The series of figures presented in this section of the book to conclude it accomplishes this end. The series starts with examining the dimensions underlying couple relations (e.g., passion, compassion) and how they comprise system control parameters (independent variables controlling system order parameters, or dependent variables) in systems. Next, it examines the nature of attractors (positive and negative) in couples. Then, it considers the application of activation/inhibition coordination to therapy. Penultimately, it relates the hierarchical system view of networks and their levels to how stages might work, as in Neo-Eriksonian stages related to couples, e.g., intimacy. This extension of the present modeling into couple work gives a concrete base to the present modeling of behavioral causality. To conclude the present work, the following section includes a free energy model and related "freeing" concepts in terms of psychological energetics. This next section illustrates the continuing innovations that can be made toward the present project of unifying the study of causality and of psychology and their integration.

G. Young, *Causality and Neo-Stages in Development*,
https://doi.org/10.1007/978-3-030-82540-9_7

Activation-Inhibition Coordination

The first figure in the series of eight elaborating the present nexus in behavioral causality to couple work gives an overview of the mechanism of activation-inhibition coordination and related concepts. Network concepts are being married with system concepts (e.g., Borsboom et al. 2018), such as systems configuring as states that are subject to the forces of equilibrium and disequilibrium, for example, at bifurcation points/the cusp of change. However, to my knowledge, the specific manner of how one can integrate networks and systems concepts has not been elucidated in detail. The concept of activation-inhibition coordination might provide a crucial link in these regards.

Figure 7.1 illustrates how networks of behaviors/symptoms can be expressed as activation-inhibition coordination networks in that node linkages can be translated in these terms. Moreover, links between levels in a network and between pairs of networks can be depicted similarly. Systems concepts can help elucidate how networks can develop different levels, with top-down and bottom-up influences, and change dynamically over time as they do so. The example provided concerns the relationship between depression and happiness in an individual, which is akin to the target behavior of compatibility/incompatibility in a couple.

Networks

Figure 7.2 gives a map of a hypothetical couple that expresses either a compatibility mode or an incompatibility mode. The critical behavior (nodes) in each mode is indicated, as well as their links (edges) to other nodes, their strength, etc. Although not indicated, shorter lengths of the linking lines could indicate shorter times to linkages being activated. Also, links could be depicted as activatory or inhibitory, but only activatory ones are indicated. The dyadic linkages between the partners also are indicated. This provides a behavioral network that cuts across the dyad and indicates both their critical drivers to dispute and also pathways to resolution. Recasting a couple's dyadic behavior in terms of networks provides an alternate way of examining both their disputes and what keeps them away from disputes. Note that the compatibility and incompatibility modes have different network organizational structure. The positive one is more tightly integrated, reflecting more centrality, efficient organization, small world structure, and rich clubs. Finally, in both diagrams, each partner has the same primary behaviors in each mode. This depiction is used only for the sake of simplicity. The heterogeneity in couple relations for critical drivers and associated behaviors surely is extensive. Research should take place along these lines both repetitively for individual couples and on average, over them to create empirically derived maps that could help in couple work.

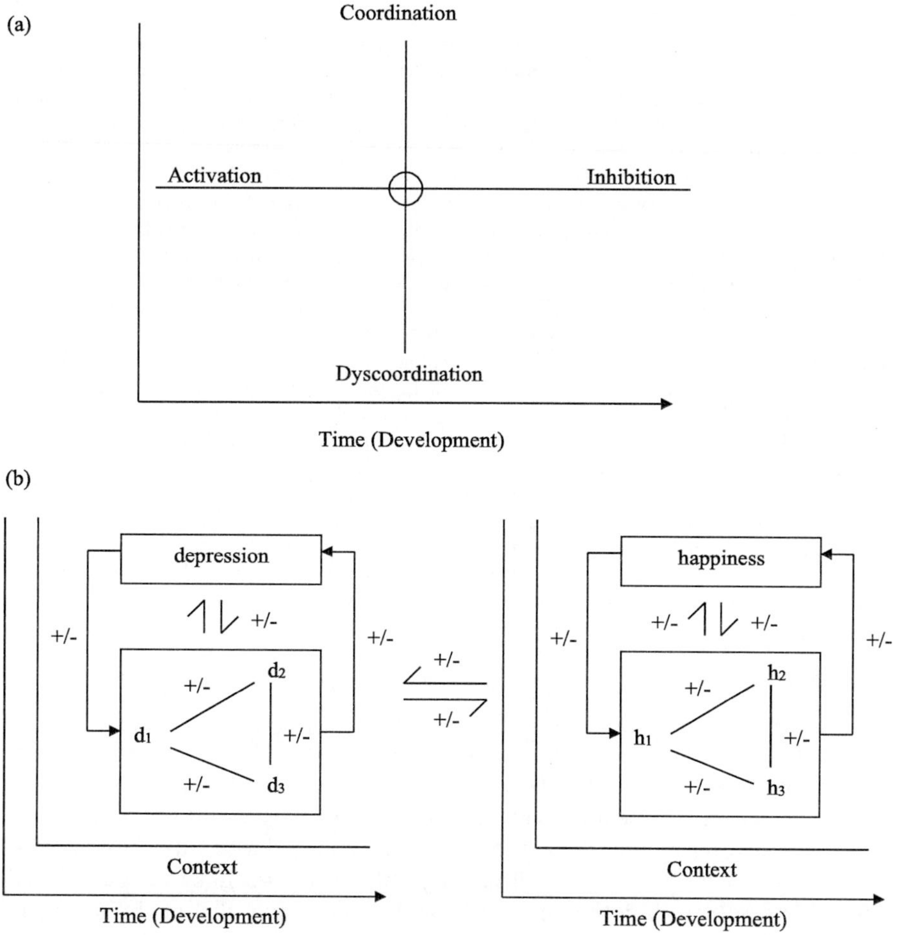

Fig. 7.1 Activation-inhibition coordination: coordination with networks, systems, and stages (**a**) Activation-inhibition coordination consists of separable activation and inhibition components that can coalesce in: positive coordination; or negative dysfunctional coordination (or aberrant, impartial discoordinated attempts at coordination) (dys-coordination). The figure's central point represents an absence along either pole (e.g., no behavior in the horizontal axis, no coordination effort in the vertical axis). Activation-inhibition coordination is a mechanistic concept that applies to all behavior, brain, and behavior-brain expressions. Even the action of biological/physiological/ biomolecular processes that constitute the brain can be expressed in these terms, for example, in patterns of neural firing and networking and the processes underpinning them. The brain is an intricate activation-inhibition coordination machine in its exquisitely complex and fluid, yet messy functioning, and its structural base exhibits the same networks and activation-inhibition coordination function. Finally, behavior exists at multiple levels, from muscular activity patterning; to behavioral adjustment to impinging stimuli, the context, goals, and so on; to complex levels of its integration, such as personality and intelligence. No matter what the level, activation and inhibition coordination can help describe its superordinate patterns, activities, and relations

(continued on page 168)

Fig. 7.1 (continued) (**b**) Activation-inhibition coordination is a general causal mechanism across brain and behavior, and all their levels and connections. As a general causal mechanism, it can be applied to descriptions of behaviors, their networks, their dimensions, and how they arrange into systems and attractors. The second part of the figure depicts graphically how the concepts of activation-inhibition coordination, networks, and systems can be integrated into one causal concept. The example provided concerns depression and its opposition/balance with happiness. The figure indicates how three core depressive symptoms might interrelate in a part of a network of symptoms for a particular individual (with the same network approach applied to happiness). Depression as a small d depression (individualized for the person, depending on which symptoms are core and how they interrelate) might emerge as a separate level in the hierarchical structure of the individual's depression network. The overall system so constructed might express both top-down and bottom-up influences and interactions. Context and time constitute additional variables in the relationship an individual might experience between depression and happiness. All relations in the system [within each network layer (including those not shown, e.g., a different layer for appraisals/cognitive filters); across layers within the individual for either depression or happiness; between depression and happiness; for any links within the person to other than depression or happiness; and ultimately between the person and other people (or activities engaged in)] can be described in terms of positive and negative feedback loops, or activation, inhibition, and their (dys)coordination (as indicated by +/−). Modeling behaviors and symptoms this way allows for the application of systems concepts to alternations in behavior/symptoms, changes in behavior/symptoms, entrenchment in behavior/symptoms, etc., and points the way to how to deal with maladaptation in these regards

Systems

This section of the present work shifts into explaining better the relationship between network concepts and NLDST concepts, such as attractors, through the example of networks of behaviors and their translation into networks in couples (see Fig. 7.2). Networks provide the advantage of indicating behavior-to-behavior links. Systems provide the advantage of discerning patterns over the links and the inferred mechanisms of their evolution to reconfigured patterns, ones that might be wholly unpredictable from the prior patterns.

Attractors express mathematical descriptions of how phenomena characterized in state formats move through their state-space. They respond to variations in indices that govern their state-space trajectories. The movements could be totally random, with no order in state-space position change. However, when the system organization continually gravitates to particular spaces in its state-space, the system could appear to have regions denoting attractors or basins to which they repeatedly gravitate, at least at a global level despite the infinite local variations.

The movement of attractors in the state-space of a system is governed by the system's behavior for the critical indices, dimensions, or variables involved. For couple work, the major dimensions that are related to compatibility-incompatibility (love if you will) would seem to concern (a) passion, (b) compassion, (c) taking care of, and (d) control. In addition, change over time and context need to be considered.

Passion refers to the range of physical, psychological/personal, and spiritual/existential passions. It concerns what inspires us and makes us vital. We bring passion into relationships. Passion could involve uniquely self-focused ends, such as personal hobbies, leisure time pursuits, work, and reinforcer (e.g., alcohol) intake. It could also involve shared foci, such as hiking together, visiting cultural activities

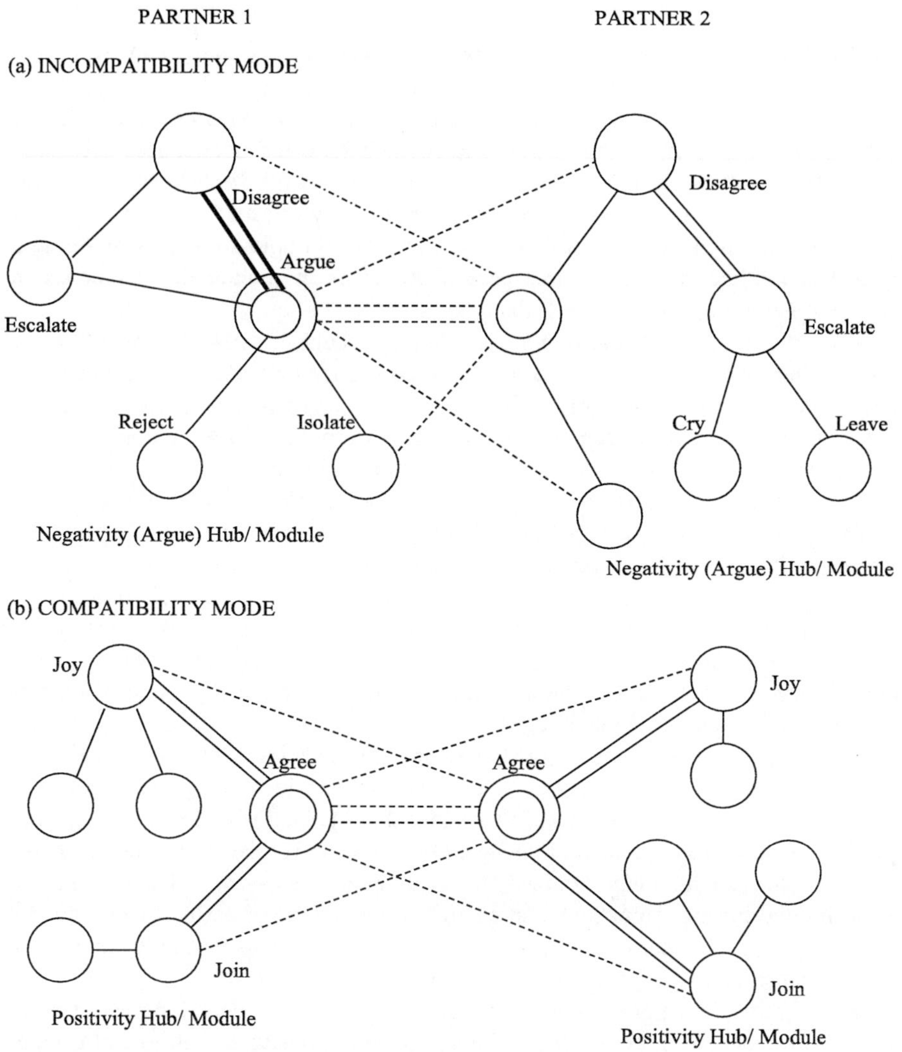

Fig. 7.2 Networks in couple compatibility/incompatibility
(**a**) The figure illustrates a couple functioning in compatibility and incompatibility modes from a behavior network perspective. Figure (**a**) indicates the network of negative behaviors that are linked, with double circles indicating hubs and double lines stronger connections. Nodes are represented by circles. Edges are represented by lines. Dotted lines indicate interactions in the couple (interaction links or edges). Both partners in this hypothetical example express a circuitry of disagreeing, arguing, and escalating, with arguing as the critical driver of more acrimonious behavior. The strength of the links is different in the partners. The outcomes are different, as well, with one partner rejecting/isolating and the other crying/leaving
(**b**) In the compatibility mode each partner expresses a positivity network. They are tightly linked behavioral structures (more central, efficient, small world, rich club, etc.). The couple communicates well – listening, validating, agreeing, and not arguing. The two partners are joyous and join together at all levels – physically, psychologically, and spiritually

and sites together. Extremely, it could involve being concerned only with promoting the partner's passion and subsuming self in the process.

Compassion refers to sensitivity for self and others. It concerns feeling deeply for one's harms and hurts and those of the other. It indicates an openness to sensing those states in the self and in other and committing to fill the lacunae in support involved. It can range from functioning instrumentally to functioning expressively (or both) and cognitively or emotionally (or both). It could simply mean being a good listener, hearing out the other person, and offering good advice. Compassion can be aimed uniquely at the self, the other, or both.

Taking care of, or caring, refers to behaving to help in daily responsibilities or discharging them. It can include activities of personal care and daily living, chores, helping with responsibilities or discharging them, such as at school or work, behaving socially, or generally promoting coping and offering means of coping. A person can focus uniquely on self-care, care for the other, or both.

At one extreme, control refers to having self-control/controlling the self; or it could be about encouraging the same in the other. Power involves seeking imposition of will; one could seek power for oneself, or defer to the other person or otherwise empower the other person. Note that individuals might seek self-control as a defense mechanism, in the sense of not having their equilibrium upset, leading to loss of control/anger when that is not accomplished. Note that context also is about control/power in that its parameters define whether a relationship can initiate, persist, or otherwise maintain its integrity.

These various dimensions of the behavior of couples indicate how the behavior of the partners can vary. Together, the range of behaviors along the dimensions coalesces into control parameters or variables that indicate whether or not the couple system state is at the cusp of change. Once the control parameter meets or surpasses a threshold individualized to a couple, the system has reached a far-from-equilibrium point such that change is potentiated or perhaps facilitated by even a minor further perturbation, as in the butterfly effect. A seemingly compatible couple can shift abruptly into an incompatibility mode.

For example, in the present hypothetical example, one partner expresses a narcissistic pattern according to the dimensions analyzed or lies at the self-end of each of the dimensions. In contrast, the other partner is at the other end of each of the dimensions, which seems self-sacrificial in nature. Perhaps these contrasting dimensional patterns in their relationship permit a co-existence in the compatibility-incompatibility spectrum, but it will have seams that can lead to disruption and violent shifting out of the habitual zone.

Levels

Figure 7.3 helps depict the different networked levels in a couple's system. Systems are constituted by different levels when the self-organization involved allows for emergence of higher-order levels from the organization of the system's elements.

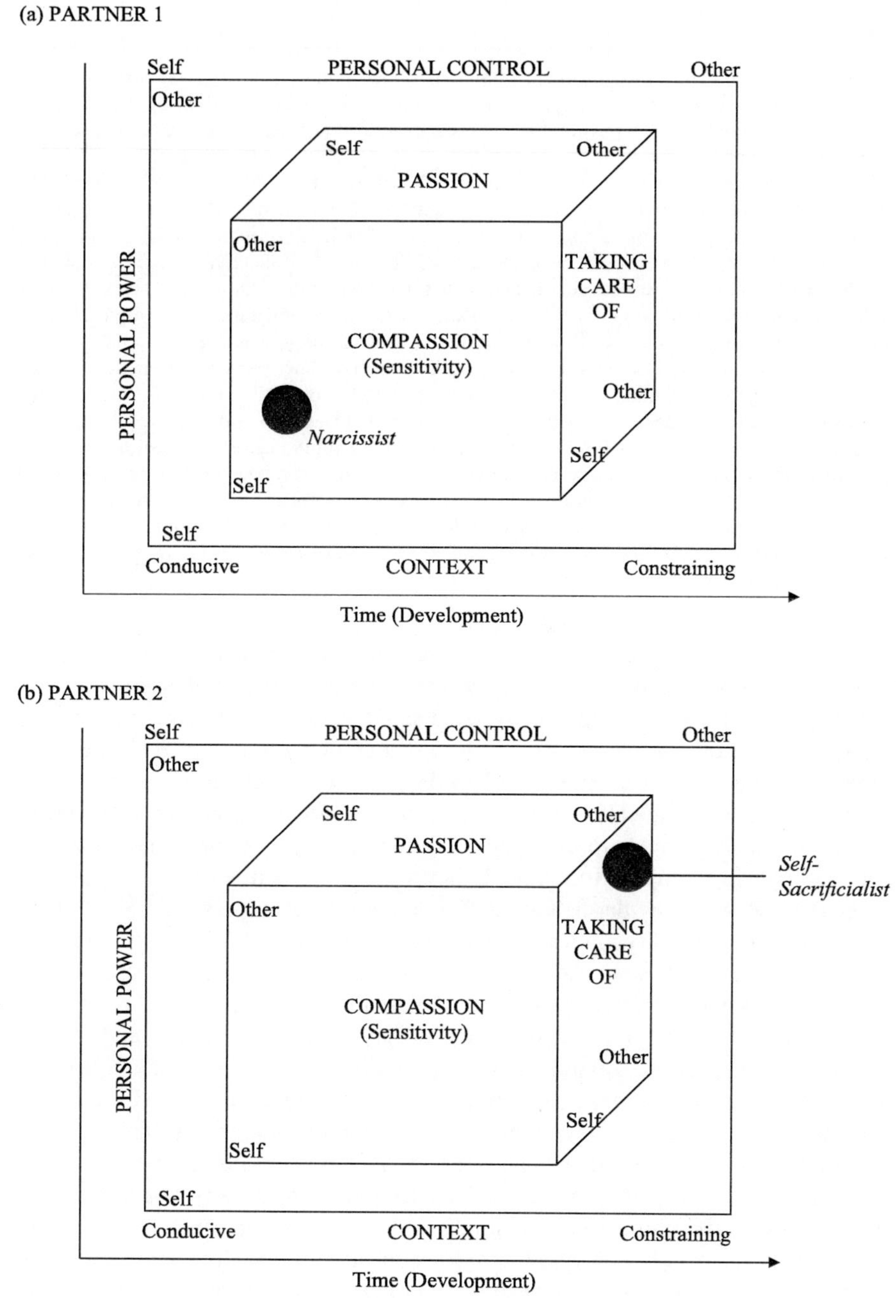

Fig. 7.3 Dimensions in couple compatibility/incompatibility

(continued on page 172)

Fig. 7.3 (continued) The figure illustrates prominent dimensions concerning relationships in couples. Couple behavior varies according to (a) passion, (b) compassion, and (c) caring. For example, a narcissist will be low on compassion for and taking care of the other, and express passion especially sexually (and perhaps without concern for satisfying the partner). The person might have self-reinforcing passions, even addictions, being overly sensitive to her/his own needs, as well. The person might be obsessively fixated on self-care while ignoring the partner this way. The intersection of these dimensions involves control parameters the thresholds of which are highly guarded/protected so as to not reach critical levels of distress. The order or collective parameter is an outcome variable representing the mode affected by the intersecting dimensional attributes and their levels, e.g., incompatibility/self-protection from any attempts to alter the mode. The dimensions of couple interaction especially lead to a superordinate control and power ones, i.e., self or other control and power over self or other (e.g., attempts to control or have power over the other). Lack of the former augments tendencies toward the latter. In couples, other dimensions include context, e.g., does the culture condone or constrain the relationship? Does the family? Are there sufficient jobs/student grants and salaries/funds available to keep the couple viable? The last dimension in the figure refers to the evolution of the couplehood over time, including the effect of developmental change in both parties as time progresses. [The dimensions of control and power are slightly different. For example, control refers to having self-control, or not, and also to encouraging self-control in the other, or not. Power is relational and refers to imposing will. Does one prefer to have power in a couple or cede it to the other?]

Just as systems can express attractors that gravitate to new state configurations at bifurcation points when they reach the cusp-of-change point in equilibrium/stability-disequilibrium/change, so, too, can systems self-organize to bifurcate into distinct levels, with one or more higher-order ones, or one or more lower-level ones. The higher-order one(s) will be capable of having top-down influences on the lower-order one(s), with reciprocal influences the other way, too, as in bottom-up influences.

Network concepts refer to the nodes and links among behaviors and their relationships, but, as originally formulated, they were not described as having distinct levels. Beyond the particular behaviors that couples might express in their compatibility and incompatibility modes, what superordinate levels do we need to consider in order to have a full picture of their systemic interaction? First (as a preliminary comment), it is noted that there are different domains in which couples live beyond the compatibility-incompatibility one, such as their study/work, family, and societal relations. Second, the compatibility-incompatibility modes are already superordinate structures in that they represent principle behavior combinations in the couple's networks that are based on major themes (hubs, modules) in relationships.

Returning to the question at hand, there might be predominant patterns in the modes that govern how they function. For example, compatibility might express a balance between the partners, or one might find a tenuous imbalance that functions like a compatible one, but only within narrow constraints, as in the narcissistic/self-sacrificial example provided. I refer to these predominant relational patterns as fall-back patterns. The couple's system gravitates to them under duress, for example, or they are deeply ingrained, intransigent ones that are tightly bound toward maintaining their stability and resisting any perturbation. Beyond fall-back patterns in couple relationships, there might be openings allowing transitions, facilitating them, etc. These might arise due to provocative system perturbations when the system is stretched to the point of bifurcation (the couple must change, or the couple will separate).

Behaviors derive from overt, open motivations, unconscious motivations, or both. They reflect accurate perceptions of the self and other, inaccurate ones (misperceptions), or both ((mis)perceptions). They stem from adaptive cognitive filters or maladaptive ones (e.g., a hostility bias). Aside from these types of perceptions and filters that guide or constrain dealing with others and how we react to them, behaviors are influenced by higher-order values, principles, morals, etc. These might be high-road ones or otherwise. They might be genuine or, rather, pompous or false incantations. They might be expressed but not followed through in action. They might not be symmetric in a couple, being quite divergent, or they might be comparable and convergent over the partners. Of course, in a couple, primary concerns in these regards relate to honesty, trust, believing in the other, and not creating doubt and jealousy. Is the person trustworthy? Am I acting in a trustworthy manner? Does he/she believe I am (un)trustworthy no matter what I do? Are there personality variables, tendencies, traits, or disorders underlying behaviors and attitudes related to values and filters?

Values and perceptions/filters constitute mental constructions and appraisals that highly influence how partners behave in a couple. They form based on preexisting tendencies and enduring attributes but also concretize through the lived experience in the couple, emerging as primary factors in the couple's behavior and interactions. Therefore, to understand the couple partners and their couplehood, one cannot examine their behaviors only in terms of observable actions. There is an underlying history and underlying socio-affective complex to consider, as well, and they arrange into successively superordinate levels in their system and in individual ways.

Attractors

As represented in Fig. 7.4, the oscillations between compatibility and incompatibility could be represented by an attractor with two cycles that alternate as the system behavior gravitates between the two modes. The bicyclical nature of the attractor specifies transition points at which the system hovers, primed for change. But perturbations might not push the system configuration out of its present regime, and change will be resisted. The consequences for a couple trying to move out of the incompatibility mode could be devastating, and conflicts could continue to spiral out of control. The couple will have to put in effort if this were the case or seek support or professional guidance to break out of habitual vicious circles.

Figure 7.5 indicates how attractor regimes can change form to increasingly more complex levels. The literature gives examples of changes from point to unicyclic to bicyclical attractors and then to chaotic types. In my own work, I added that landscapes of multiple attractors can develop, as in living systems. Couple relations could include multiple attractor compositions over multiple domains, for example, in complex adaptive systems. If the domain attractors themselves cohere into a superordinate system, one could refer to the attractor landscape as constituting a superordinate complex adaptive system. Of course, attractor advancement need not

Level	Type	Representation
IV.	COUPLE [Couplehood/ Couple Modes]	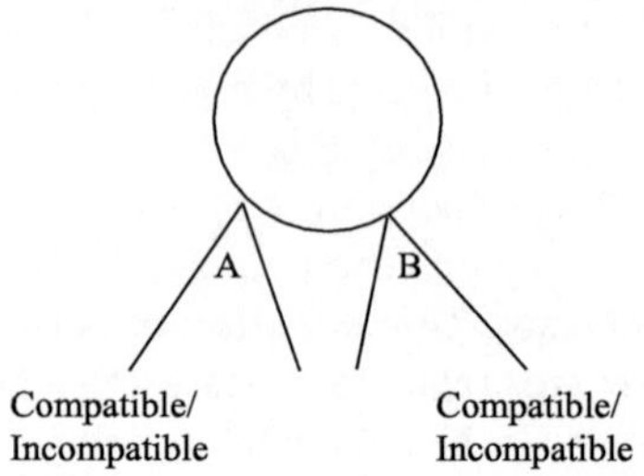
III.	CONSTRUCTIONS/ FILTERS [Values in Each Partner/ Mis(perception) of Self and Other]	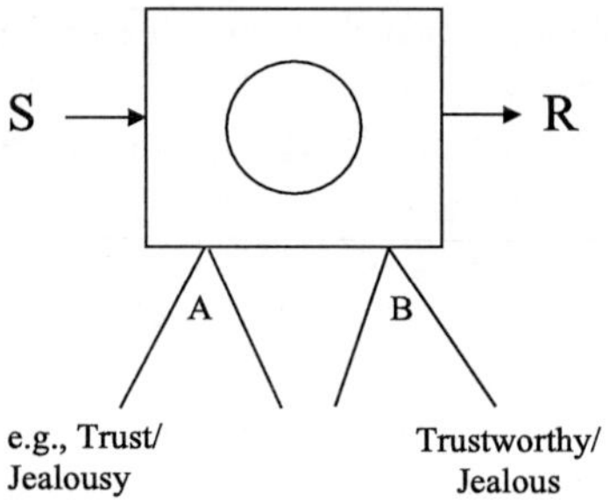
II.	STABILITY AND CHANGE [Fall Back Behavior Patterns/ Transitioning Behavior Patterns]	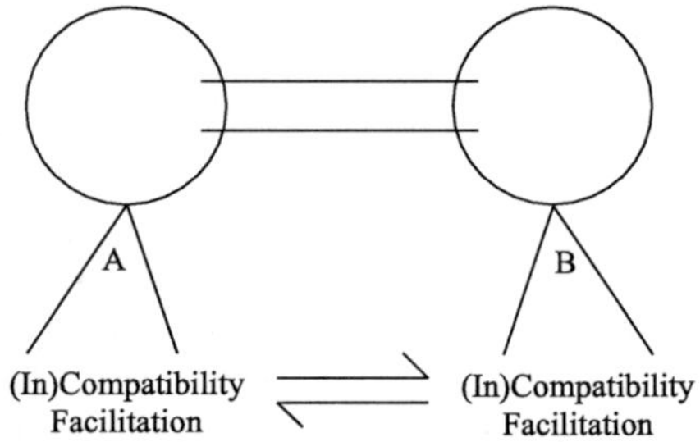
I.	BEHAVIORS AND ORGANIZATION [Behavior Nodes/ Hubs/ Modules // Individual Behaviors]	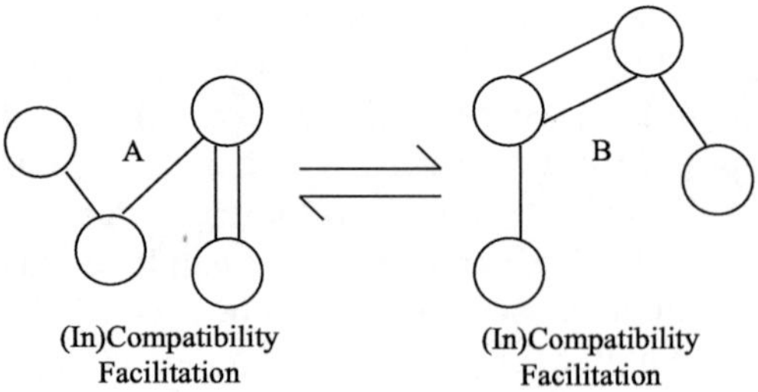

Fig. 7.4 A layered behavior network structure in couples (partners A and B)

be positive. For example, regressions could become equally complex and fill attractor landscapes, as in the development of chronic pain or the prodromal shift to serious mental disorder, expressing maladaptive entrenchment rather than adaptive enhancement. With respect to the example being considered, couples could gravitate to an intransigent incompatibility impervious to any efforts to change it, leading indefinitely to hostile or cold interactions or, ultimately, to separation.

Therapy

The therapist working with couples can face a bewildering presentation of accusations and recriminations. The hostility expressed in the home environment will be transposed into session. When I conduct therapy, I refer to some simple principles no matter the type of patient, at least after rapport is created. For example, it is easier to construct a positive than to suppress a negative. One could always follow a negative with a positive. These kinds of maxims fit with my concept of activation-inhibition coordination and indicate that, just as any behavior or brain-behavior relationship can be analyzed in these terms, so can a couple's behavior and relationship and a therapist's psychotherapy treatment interventions (see Fig. 7.6).

No matter the area examined (actions, emotions, cognition, functionality), behavior can be expressed as activated, inhibited, or coordinated (whether positive or negative). Similarly, there are triggers/themes for each area to consider and transitions possible to new target goals. In both spheres, activation-inhibition coordination provides a framework for understanding the behavior of concern and how to change it.

The extent of change required in a couple's behavior might be minimal touch-ups in that the behavior is synchronized positively, in general. Or, major adjustments will be the focus of sessions, including in suppressing bad habits and replacing them with good ones. I always like to give couples booster ideas like dating, and of course do not engage in blaming as we work constructively on trust-building. In the end, all strategies suggested to the couple are activating positives or inhibiting negatives. These strategies might include inhibiting the inhibitions that inhibit the

Fig. 7.4 (continued) The figure illustrates how a network conception of behavior needs to be complemented by a model in which the network consists of multiple and emerging levels. Behaviors both in individuals and groups (dyads, etc.) form interrelated links, with some of them more in control, being primary, considered drivers, and so on. The first level (I) depicts this basic level in networks. And it depicts this for both partners in a couple and how their networks interact. However, networks can change, and this could be for better or worse in couples. From a systems perspective, the configuration of nodes (behaviors/hub) and edges (behavioral links) in a network resists perturbation and remains stable, or alternately it gravitates (transition toward) change and altered configuration (level II). Level III acknowledges that we need to consider that behaviors reflect underlying perceptions, misperceptions, filters (positive or negative), and overriding values, morals, principles (or their absence). In couples, these often relate to trust(worthiness) and jealousy. Behaviors might not be what they seem. Finally, in Level IV, the characteristics of the couple qua couple emerge as their couplehood matures (positive or negative). Moreover, what stories do they develop together about their couple and are they consistent/inconsistent across the partners?

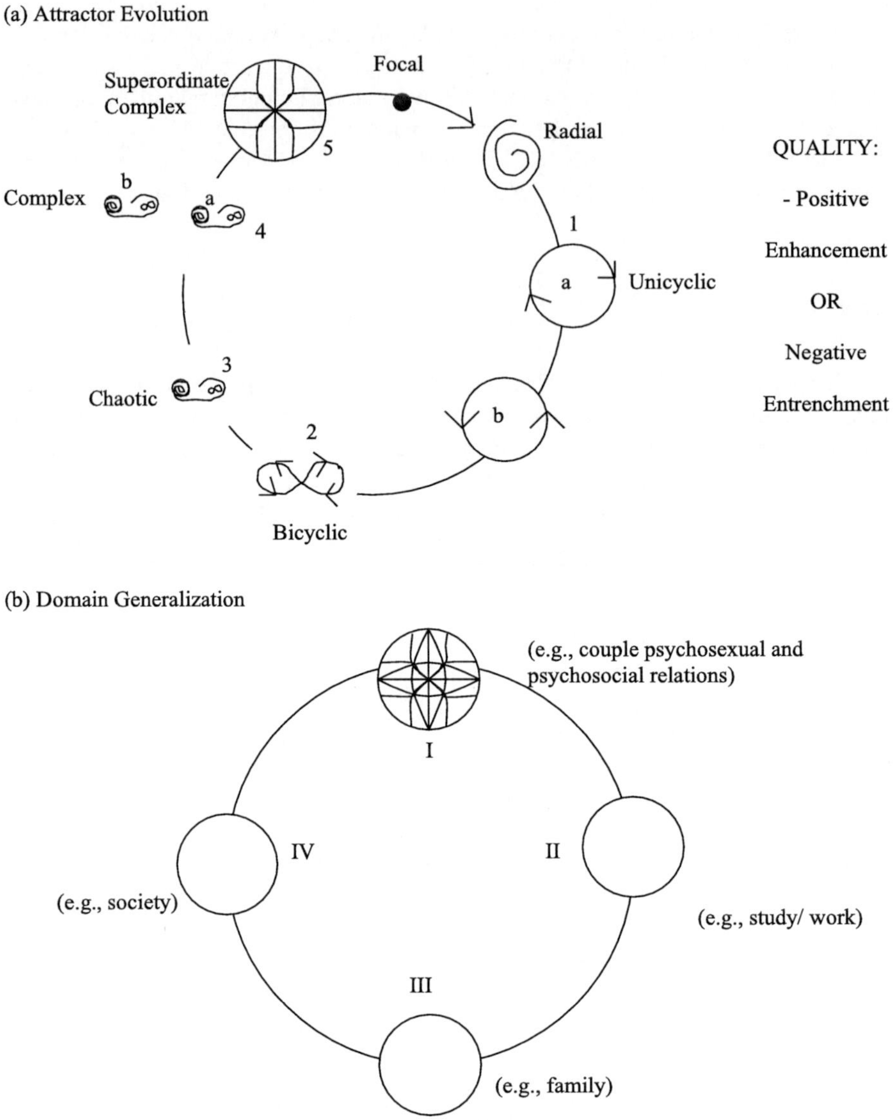

Fig. 7.5 Attractor change in couple compatibility/incompatibility
(**a**) The first part of the figure indicates how attractor configurations in a couple's relationship can evolve from a cyclic attractor (positive or negative), to an alternation of modes, to one that integrates the modes (chaotic attractor), and then to a spreading of attractors to multiple aspects of the relationship. The couple could evolve into a highly organized, integrated partnership for one aspect and then others (with the organization either positive or negative), as in the enhancement of positives and entrenchment of negatives. The latter systems can be referred to as complex adaptive systems and, ultimately, superordinate complex adaptive systems
(**b**) The second part of the figure indicates how integrated systems in a couple in one domain can have repercussions on other domains as systems are developing. For example, the couple establishes their socio-affective (psychosexual/ psychosocial) relations. While developing their study or work life, as the case may be, there are positive or negative impacts on motivation and performance, depending on the nature of their socio-affective coupling. Other areas of impact concern what happens as they begin a family (or what are the effects on their parents, sibs, etc.) and their general relationship to society, culture, etc.

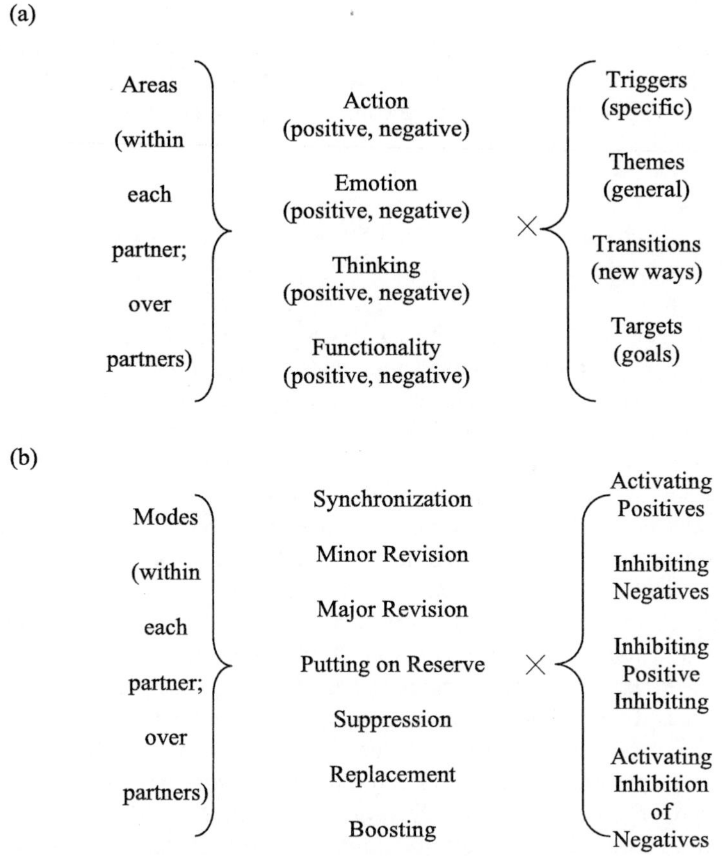

Fig. 7.6 Activation-inhibition coordination couple therapy
(**a**) Therapy is an intersubjective dance, as are all relationships. They take place in fields of parrying and caring back and forth, with strategies implemented toward changing mutual goals. The areas of behavior involved include actions, emotions, cognitions, and functionality (activities). These domains could express positivity or negativity. The couple in therapy could have specific triggers and general themes that mark them, as well as openings to change (new ways), with new target goals possible. This dynamic could be positive or negative. The therapist needs to be fully involved in the moment or aware of all relevant domains in order to help change the domains and their triggers/themes and transitions/targets (goals) toward the positive. This requires an effective analysis of the activation-inhibition coordination dynamics in the domains and analysis of the best procedures/strategies to use therapeutically from the same perspective
(**b**) The dynamic field of interaction in therapy (and in a couple) is moderated by activation-inhibition coordination dynamics. There could an exquisite, refined, long-term synchrony expressed in the relationship in terms of activation/inhibition coordination. Or, minor revision might be needed to ensure optimal functioning. The therapist constantly examines the couple's dynamic using this metric and deploys procedures/strategies to keep it finely honed and get through the presenting problem. However, more than likely, major revisions are needed as aberrant dysfunctionality and incompatibility have set in. Some aspects might need putting them on hold or even being suppressed/stopped and replaced. The therapist (and couple) always seeks ways to boost the couple's relationship (e.g., return to dating, sexual intimacy). In terms of activation/inhibition coordination, all this means activating positives, inhibiting negatives, inhibiting what inhibits positives, and activating inhibition of negatives. The therapist (and couple) should monitor developing positive interactive coordination in these regards

positives and activating required inhibitions of the negatives. Perhaps thinking this way will help the therapist; for example, to boost happiness, one could attempt to augment the happiness or reduce the accompanying low mood, and so on.

Stages

The next step in the current exercise to marry network, systems, and activation-inhibition coordination concepts with stage perspectives on development is the penultimate one, in that the exercise culminates with a figure that indicates the relationship between these various approaches in the context of couple work (see Fig. 7.7). The figure first presents the traditional conception of Eriksonian stages, that is, in terms of oppositional poles, such as Trust vs. Mistrust. It lists the stages most relevant to the question of couple compatibility-incompatibility, that of Intimacy, and related others, including the one of Nurturing that I created in my Neo-Eriksonian series. The figure indicates how Intimacy can be reconceived as a hierarchy of levels in a network, as per systems theory (see Fig. 7.4). The figure caption is extensive and gives the required explanation. The figure excludes mention of the role of activation-inhibition coordination in the suite of behaviors, networking, system levels, and modes in the diagram. However, the figure refers to yoking of behaviors and the different skills, schemes, and operations from different stages in (Neo)Eriksonian sequential development. The means by which behavior/node coupling takes place (and intra-level connections, as well) would involve ongoing dynamic activation-inhibition coordination. For example, briefly, an overarching value in one partner could condition which behaviors/nodes are activated, which others are inhibited, and how the coordination with the partner proceeds.

This concludes an analysis of couple therapy from the perspective of the present modeling process. For a different approach to applying systems theory to dyadic interaction in friendly vs. argumentative conversations, see Paxton and Dale (2017). Future applications of the present work on couplehood could extend the model by examining other relationships, such as citizen (group member) governing body ones from this perspective.

Higher-Order Versus Lower-Order Cognitive Generalization in Stage Transitioning

Sceptics will argue that the mind does not exist, emergence is impossible; a new stage cannot develop discontinuously or relatedly. However, except for extreme behaviorists, the mental is part of the conceptual lexicon in psychology. The task of demonstrating its independence or quasi-independence from biological/brain-related processes is more challenging. The effort in these regards extends into more

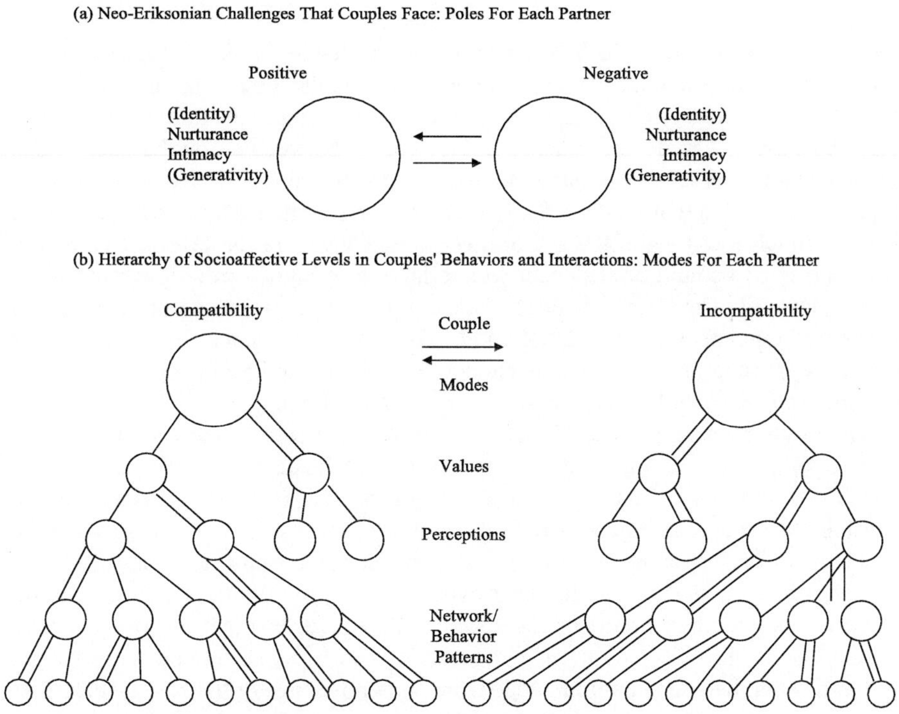

Fig. 7.7 Neo-Eriksonian challenges in couples: poles and modes
(**a**) This part of the figure represents the classical view of an Eriksonian stage crisis or challenge (e.g., Trust vs. Distrust), which I continued to use in my Neo-Eriksonian model, even if I expanded his eight-stage model to 25 steps over the lifespan. The stages/steps most applicable to couples concern intimacy (Erikson) and the preceding stage/step I added (Nurturance). Other relevant ones concern Identity and Generativity (the former might initiate in adolescence but continues lifetime; the latter is about giving to family, study/ work, and society)
(**b**) The tools needed to successfully navigate (Neo)Eriksonian crises involve the same kind of cognitive schemes and operations applicable to cognitive problem-solving (as specified in the (Neo)Piagetian model, for example). These skills organize into networks and patterns in the (Neo)Eriksonian socio-affective realm in the same way they do in the standard cognitive one. They coalesce together for what is needed for the task at hand but also reflect habitual patterns that might override adaptive online construction. Also, personal factors, such as the cognitive (mis)perception of the self and others and values/principles and the like, might affect network/pattern organization and deployment. The skills for successful navigation of new emerging (Neo) Eriksonian crises/challenges need to be flexible, balanced, other-sensitive, and so on, so that the positive pole in the issue predominates
The same applies to the modes that typify the establishment of intimacy in a couple, e.g., compatibility compared to incompatibility. Therefore, we see in the couple, whether analyzed cognitively or socio-affectively, networks of skills and strategies that are yoked together for the situation at hand. The skills might be ones associated with a step in development that is below the actual cognitive level at which one is normally functioning. For example, the young adult in a romantic relationship might use automatic, intuitive, preoperational thought processes to guide socio-affective encounters and function at an equivalent socio-affective stage/step, such as associated with the preschooler. There might be yoking with more rational, emotionally less regressed/ fixated strategies, but secondarily. These developmental disturbances would hamper the use of more mature strategies and complicate the patterns, (mis)perceptions, values, and modes associated with them. The couple will suffer accordingly

esoteric aspects of mind, such as consciousness or having a sense of free will. For present purposes, thoughts, concepts, beliefs, and the like create hierarchical orderings that increasingly remove their components from neurophysiologic and neuronal processes. Moreover, intermediary levels between thought and basic physiochemical processes in the brain and related loci include appraisals, cognitive filters, and the like that mediate the relationship and influence both levels. Overall, there is much top-down influence on lower-order levels in the levels of co-action from biology to cognition. Conceiving a reduction of higher-order levels to lower-order ones will miss elements added to the cognitive process through top-down and reciprocal influences in level interaction. Also, there are factors in the pattern of elements in (cognitive) state that cannot be reduced to the elements involved, whether at a lower-order or higher-order level in a system.

As for emergence, granted, the physical machinery and mental and brain architecture and properties of the organism involved limit the degree of qualitative difference in the outcome of the emergence of any new state in a system relative to the starting base state and its component configuration in context. No matter what the input and effort, spontaneous reorganization cannot create abstract thought in non-human primates, where none has ever existed, due to the limitations in the central nervous system (read brain) of the species. That said, emergence does occur in systems, with new configurations of system elements emerging and with distinct properties that had been unpredictable from any knowledge of the base state and its patterns and properties. In this regard, the human brain's maturational processes afford the development from sensorimotor thought to representational thought to abstract thought, as evident by the research in development.

But, are these acquisitions stage or stage-like, with immediately evidence qualitatively distinct characteristics that emerge from the base state's reconfiguration from which the acquisitions arise? From a conceptual perspective, perhaps a positive answer to this conundrum that bedevils the field of development lies in the present concept of the substages in cognitive development or change processes in cognitive development. Recall that the five-step substage sequence in the present model involves coordination, hierarchization, systematization, multiplication, and integration. The critical step in this sequence for an abrupt stage development or emergence concerns coordination. In coordination, an integrated cognitive unit as established in a prior stage can pair, juxtapose, oppose, or otherwise interrelate with another one of the same type. This implies that the integration achieved in a prior stage generalizes to a new area, domain, or task/topic, by the creation of a superordinate rule, principle, or generic cognitive structure, thereby permitting a second integration to develop that can then be part of the coordination that follows. The cognitive activity in the rule/principle construction represents the qualitatively distinct acquisition that indexes a new stage and the coordination that marks its beginning. [In the first stage, coordination will involve prepared core "knowledges" (Kinzler et al. 2007).]

Note that Charbonneau et al. (1976) had developed the concept of cognitive generalization in the Piagetian context. They had referred to this process to within-stage cognitive acquisitions (in conservation tasks, which Piaget referred to as serial equilibrium). Therefore, it seems that there are different types or levels of generalization applicable to learning and cognition. The most basic type refers to the generalization during basic learning. Then, children can express more cognitive generalizations, such as language learning. Higher-order generalizations will occur cognitively, but these can be differentiated cognitively from simpler to more complex. Abstract generalizations would constitute the most advanced type.

As an example of cognitive generalization in the stage transition context, consider the emergence of representation as defined by Piaget at 2 years of age. This cognitive acquisition does not refer to the simpler skill of representing an object by a word and the like that develops earlier. Rather, it refers to more complex mental and linguistic combinations/coordinations that are invented and symbolically removed or distinct from any physical reality being represented. In 2-year-old representation, there is no sensorimotor association to the representation, as in the last substage of the sensorimotor stage. The complexity of the coordination and combinations involved mentally and linguistically ensure the displacement from the sensorimotor. Think of the child engaging in complex conversations at this age, or complex deferred imitations, or toy play representation scenarios, and so on.

Other Piagetian stage transitions also appear to involve complex combinations/coordinations as they initiate that are reflective of generic cognitive structuring, thereby permitting the coordinations to take place. Abstract (formal) thought initiating in the young teenager appears removed from the concrete logic of the child by the general rule/principles created and their application to coordinated interrelations, as described. Note that the stage transition process being described does not imply that any cognitive generalization leads to a qualitatively distinct cognitive structure indicative of a stage acquisition. The generalization in this case is one step removed or more advanced than in local generalizations (e.g., Truck A, Truck B = Trucks).

Higher-order generalization in the development of qualitatively distinct cognitive stages is just one part of the complex process involved. We need to keep in mind the machinery/architecture that permits it and the underlying genetic/epigenetic processes that underwrite it. Moreover, the networks in the former, e.g., neuronal linkages among nodes, are another critical variable in stage (re)organization beyond system conceptions. [And networks include the social, as in experience-dependent network modification/learning.]

Note that the process of cognitive generalization that has been described can apply to substage transitions as much as stage transitions, although the former is being highlighted.

Revising Neo-Piagetian Mechanism Models

Neo-Piagetians have built new models not only for the stages and substages in cognitive development but also for the mechanisms underlying the changes in the stages. Three of the most active researchers in these latter regards are Pascual-Leone and Demetriou, whom I have already discussed, and Barrouillet. In this section, I examine their work in more depth toward arriving at a more general model that incorporates the best of their modeling. Note that I try to avoid the presentation of their complex terminology as I present their work. It is acknowledged that the area of how cognitive subsystems work in cognitive activity is very complex such that any one model will be incomplete and perhaps contradictory with others. Therefore, the current model should be considered only a heuristic one, albeit with the potential to inform the field.

As an example of the difficulty in constructing an integrated, commonly accepted framework in this field of cognition, consider that Doherty et al. (2019) tested three different models of dual-task costs of working memory, and did not find results that uniquely supported any of them. Working memory refers to the process(es) that facilitate the complex coordination required cognitively for the full range of human thought and related actions. Barrouillet is a leading Neo-Piagetian researcher, and he has studied dual-process theories developmentally (Camos and Barrouillet 2011). For example, Siffredi et al. (2017) found that retrieval in working memory processes activated fronto-parietal regions associated with executive control and attention, unlike the regions found for the distinct processes of encoding and retrieval. Furthermore, there were no age differences in the 8- to 16-year-old sample. This type of research illustrates the detailed, complex research needed to investigate just one aspect of the complex cognitive architecture involved in cognitive development.

Pascual-Leone (e.g., 2019) has taken a much broader view of the study of the cognitive architecture that underlies cognitive acquisition. In his model (e.g., Pascual-Leone (1970), mental attentional capacity (Mc) competes with mental attentional demands (Md) of tasks to determine its effective deployment or not. As M capacity grows, different M levels develop. Arsalidou et al. (2017) gave a fuller account of his model of constructive operators. For present purposes, it is noted that the model refers not only to the executive and to attention but to attentional interrupt (inhibition), affect, motivation, basic learning, logical learning, effortless binding vs. effortful mental attention, and simple and complex function-structure schemes. Interestingly, the authors related left hemisphere function to tasks for which Mc is greater or equal to Md as in problem-solving or logical structural learning, with right hemisphere function for other relationships between Mc and Md, e.g., for more automatic tasks.

For work relating working memory capacity and the Casian notion of central conceptual structures, see Morra et al. (2019). As written previously in this paper, it might be advantageous to translate central conceptual structures in terms of network modeling.

My own work as presented throughout the present work relates left hemisphere function to activation-inhibition coordination. I find the simple-effortful aspect of Pascual-Leone's modeling important, but it needs amplification, perhaps as active vs. passive learning processes and simpler and more advanced learning, as in scheme vs. operational construction.

Demetriou and Spanoudis (2018; see Pascual-Leone 2019) also take a broad view of the cognitive architecture that underlies cognitive development. They considered the primary domain-specific systems in development as: categories; space and time; quantitative; interactions and causes; social; and verbal/language. Central relational mechanisms foster inferences in learning relevant to domains. Consciousness facilitates more complex domain learning. Next, representational capacity works through processes such as working memory. A complex concept added to the modeling involves cognizance, defined as self-driven conative processes, promoting personal and volitional aspects in cognitive growth.

See Kazi et al. (2019) for further work on cognizance in the cognitive development of 4- to 10-year-olds. Specifically, they found that cognizance appears to underlie the awareness of mental state both in the self and the other. The concept encompasses more specific forms of awareness, such as the theory of mind and meta-cognition. Also, among others, it appears bound to executive and reasoning processes.

It would seem to me that this Demetriou-Spanoudis model emphasizes more than the one of Pascual-Leone higher-order cognitive processes, such as inference, consciousness, and cognizance. Moreover, the growing person uses self-driven, or self-activatory processes, in doing so as much as automatic, passive ones, or simpler, imposed ones (e.g., through training), as Piaget himself would have emphasized through his constructionist approach to cognitive development. Previously in this present work, I had referred to generalization as a critical factor in moving from one cognitive (sub)stage to another. Demetriou and Spanoudis (2018) help me clarify that generalization in the case of more advanced cognitive (sub)stage growth involves more complex generalization processes, such as inference.

Together, as per Fig. 7.8, the Pascual-Leone and Demetriou-Spanoudis models of the cognitive architecture underpinning cognitive transitions through (sub)stages lead me to develop an integrative, broad model of the cognitive architecture underlying cognitive (sub)stage transitions that include active, agentic compared to passive learning components at all levels. Also, consistent with the present emphasis on the biopsychosocial model in development (referred to as the biopersonalsocial model), I include in the model all three components of the term, specifying to the degree possible active and passive examples. Finally, the model leads to a hierarchical organization in the cognitive architecture being proposed as relevant to cognitive (sub)stage transitioning, with executive function/cognizance and generalization at the higher levels and mental attention and motivation at lower levels. This illustrates the complementarity of the work of Pascual-Leone and Demetriou-Spanoudis.

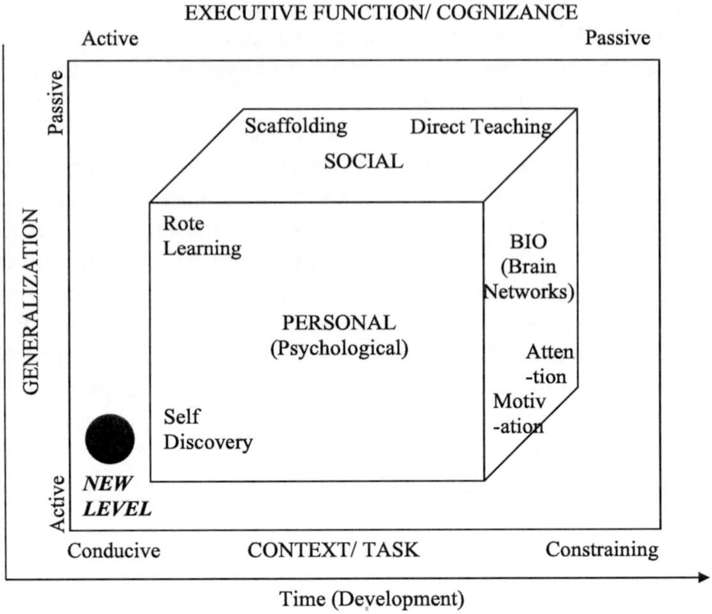

Fig. 7.8 Active and passive transition mechanisms in cognitive (Sub)stage development
The figure presents an integrated, though heuristic (useful, but not fully but mechanistically accurate), portrayal of the factors involved in reaching critical thresholds toward new levels (substages, stages) in cognitive organization in development. The inner cube represents the biopsychosocial factors that are involved. The axes vary, particularly on whether the dimensions are active or passive in influence. In this regard, at the personal level, Piaget emphasized the active cognitive construction of the child, for example, through discovery learning and peer discussions. Although it is not quite the case, rote learning is more of a passive learning. As for the social, represented by teaching, scaffolding would be more active for the child, while direct teaching by an expert would be more passive. For biology, brain networks especially are involved, and they would allow for cognitive (sub)stage advances when critical thresholds are traversed maturationally and organizationally. However, without proper motivation to mentally attend and to learn, these thresholds will not be traversed
The outer cube represents other variables in moving to more advanced levels of cognitive (sub) stage organization. First, the context and task must be facilitative of this growth. Next, the higher-order cognitive processes that mediate cognitive development referred to as executive function, generally must be properly functioning in order to optimize attention and learning. In its broadest sense, executive function includes cognitive processes such as working memory, representation (capacity), problem-solving/seeking, shifting set, inhibition, planning/organizing, monitoring implementation, revising it, and so on. Cognizance refers to self-driven conative processes
Finally, the proximate mediator in the development being described is referred to as generalization. In this context, generalization does not refer to the simpler generalization that takes place in learning because it is a cognitive construction. On the one hand, it could be an active process, such as deploying cognitive activity to make inferences and other higher-order cognitive operations (reflections/ abstractions). On the other hand, it could be a passive process in that change takes place in the cognitive scheme or operation involved simply through the weight of cognitive applications that greatly perturb the existing architecture to the point of activating transition without any inferential or other active generalizing processes

Networks and Systems in Resilience

In the week following my final work on the present modeling, Kalisch et al. (2019) constructed a model of resilience that independently combined network, dynamic systems, and activation and inhibition factors, which is noteworthy, but they accomplished this in a manner that differs somewhat from the present approach (see Fig. 7.9). In particular, they referred to resilience factors (RFs) (e.g., biological, psychological, and social levels) rather than resilience, per se. In the graphics, they constructed network models of bistable mental health vs. mental disorders, using activation of symptoms and their connections. They added RFs as inhibitory mechanisms to the symptom (connection) activations. And they referred to tipping points at energy barriers transitioning from healthy to mentally disordered states.

Therefore, despite the theoretical advances in Kalisch et al. (2019), relative to the present modeling, they (a) excluded a specific activation-inhibition coordination mechanism; (b) did not include activation-inhibition coordination mechanisms within behavior/symptom networks (just referring to activation); and (c) did not elaborate different (and emerging) levels of networks acting in a comprehensive system, with the levels interacting through activation-inhibition coordination mechanisms. In addition, they did not specify that activation-inhibition coordination mechanisms could be active at state-network tipping point transitions, which, in my modeling, I referred to in more classic NLDST terms (e.g., attractors at the cusp of change, the edge of chaos, stretched beyond the point of equilibrium).

Fig. 7.8 (continued) As for the stage transitioning process, the intersection of the variables and factors described might reach an individualized threshold criterion of change for the state of the cognitive system involved, thereby facilitating its shift to a more advanced level. The micro-developmental changes involved could create a system configuration macro-developmentally far-from-equilibrium that leads to a state shift in the cognitive architecture of the person that is consistent with the reconfiguration of, and addition to, the pattern of cognitive skills involved such that a more advanced (sub)stage appears to have developed. The figure depicts that the control parameter for the individual indicated presages a new level of cognitive organization (in the collective variable of the system), and the variables involved uniformly lie toward more the active pole of each of the relevant dimensions

Note that this figure representing the cognitive stage mechanisms for (sub)stages does not include more basic mechanisms that have been described in the present work related to activation-inhibition coordination. In this regard, this type of mechanism would be active in all aspects of the system. For example, working memory would require its active application and effective deployment for facilitating task/problem-solving success. Similarly, the child having been involved in self-discovered learning and more passive learning would express activation-inhibition balancing in her/his cognitive learning and (re)structuring in order to better assure task/problem-solving success

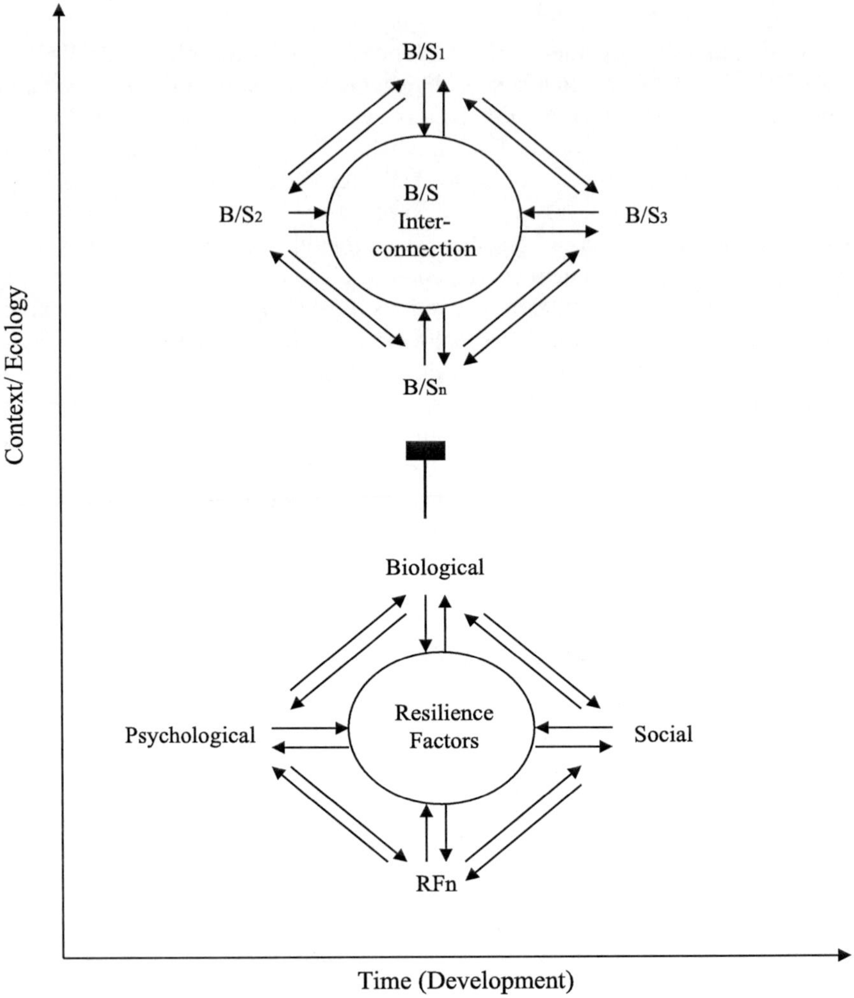

Fig. 7.9 Hybrid network of symptom (S)/behavior (B) inhibitory dampening ([]------) Resilience Factors (RF)

The figure illustrates network interactions for symptoms and how they can be affected by resilience factors (RFs) of a biopsychosocial nature (after Kalisch et al. 2019). The RFs could affect both symptom cluster autoconnections and symptom cluster interconnections. Applying my own work to the model, I would add to the hybrid model depicted that RF factors can be activatory, inhibitory, or work in concert as activation-inhibition coordination. Also, I would add (emergent levels) to the system involved (other network levels). Finally, the input into the system, and not only the quality of the resilience factors, could lead to pushing the system beyond the tipping point to new system states (e.g., from poor mental health to better mental health, or vice versa)

Note. I added behavior to symptom in the figure in order to generalize. I indicated resilience could stiffen better mental health, or, in contrast, lead to its disruption. Potential differing strengths of connections (edges) are not graphed. Also, each B/S could be a cluster with its own autoconnections. Energy input into the network that could alter network dynamics is not shown, nor are hypothetical strengths of the resilience factors (Adopted from Kalisch, R., Cramer, A. O. J., Binder, H., Fritz, J., Leertouwer, I. J., Lunansky, G., Meyer, B., Timmer, J., Veer, I. M., & van Harmelen, A.-L. (2019). Deconstructing and reconstructing resilience: A dynamic network approach. *Perspectives on Psychological Science, 14*(5), 765–777, Copyright © 2019 by SAGE Publications, Inc. Reprinted by Permission of SAGE Publications, Inc. [Figure 7, pp. 772])

Continuing Innovation: Psychological Energetics

To simplify, in the broad integrative psychological model that has been presented in Young (2011, 2016, 2019) and in the present summary of the books and its elaboration in this book, I have developed a 25-step lifespan model and a general mechanism for its development related to activation-inhibition coordination. In my work, free will takes a primary place, as well. Consistent with Piaget, we are active in our own development and believing in free will has a role to play in that. We cannot determine whether free will actually exists, but belief in free will has material consequences (Baumeister 2008). In my work, concepts related to free will belief include freedom in being and having a sense of free will.

Friston (2010) has developed the concept of free energy, which concerns reducing surprisal energy in the fit of the organism to the context in order to optimize adaptation. Similarly, in systems theory, better adaptation is marked by reducing degrees of freedom as systems self-organize to more coordinative structures. However, in systems, when they self-organize to higher-order, emergent levels, they are described as having more degrees of freedom (see Young 2011). Generally, systems optimally gravitate to the cusp of change and resist being only stable, given the inflexibility and poor adaptability of that type of regime. In this sense, one can describe NLD systems as arriving at the space in their dynamic state-space in which they balance losing and gaining degrees of freedom.

In terms of Friston's free energy principle, one could extrapolate this NLD system dynamics and argue that free energy should be construed as hovering in the state-space of organism-contextual interaction such that the interaction is balancing stability-seeking and change-promoting in the bounded survival state of the organism. In effect, the organism not only functions to minimize free energy in many circumstances that require that dynamic, but also in others it acts to increase free energy so that change in its behavioral structure and dynamic can be facilitated if that is the best solution to its adaptive calculation given the statistical (ir)regularities that it is detecting in context.

In this regard, Fig. 7.10 presents a model of free energy, degrees of freedom, and free will that can help understand what organizes and drives human behavior. The model includes the basis for individual differences in this regard, for example, differences in vitality, energy reverberation, and energetics (Young 2016) that influence free energy dynamics. Finally, the free energy energetics variations across individuals and contexts being proposed could be a critical factor in the individual differences that develop in the universal 25-step lifespan model that has been constructed and the activation-inhibition coordination proposed as underlying it. Psychological energetics is a term that could encapsulate the energy dynamic being described. The concept relates psychological activity to material processes, generally, including the brain and enactive embodied processes. At the same time, it allows for emergent properties that increase the steps away from bodily processes and nullify attempts at reduction of psychological activity to them. Plasticity, adaptation, growth, development, learning, and so on, whether in the human case or

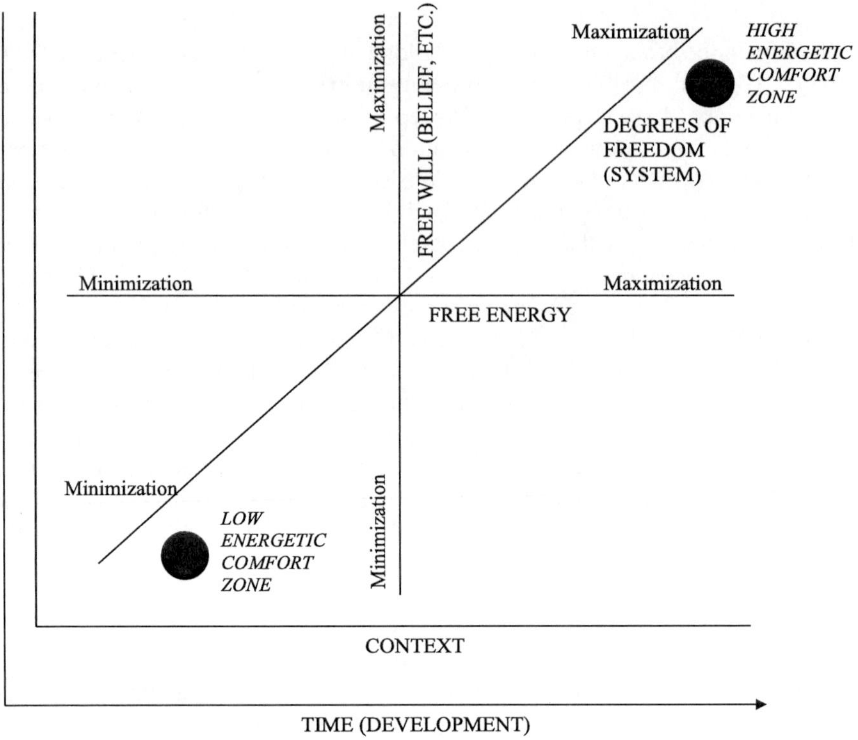

Fig. 7.10 Psychological energetics: variational freedoms in behavior
The figure illustrates different views of freedom/freeing in behavior. (a) First, free energy is not only minimized by organisms in context in order to reduce surprise or dissonance but also possibly maximized, depending on the nature of the context. (b) Also, systems form increasing order, which reduces their degrees of freedom. However, they also act to increase their degrees of freedom in order to increase their adaptability. (c) At the level of human behavior, the belief in free will is adaptive, and it develops with growth but is a variable that can be suppressed or augmented in context, depending. Generally, we optimize adaptation and development by finding the right balance in the context of the distribution of free energy, systemic degrees of freedom, and activation of free will (belief). But individual and contextual differences will arise. For example, someone might have a psychological energetic minimization comfort zone, as depicted by the circle in the lower left of the figure. Or, another person might tend to a maximization strategy, as per the upper right circle. Or, a person might gravitate between these options or try other types of combination. [The same could apply to institutional dynamics]
And context might be a factor, with some more closed and constraining and others more open. Different behaviors could elicit different tendencies, as well, leading to regular deviations from a person's norm. Chunking or automatizing behavior could be construed as freeing up energy, for example, and rigidly engaging in behavior, as minimizing free energy. Reducing cognitive dissonance might be energetically adaptive in most contexts, but people might also seek out cognitive dissonance for different reasons. And different aspects of personality traits could be conceived in terms of psychological energetics, as well as other tendencies, such as creativity. For example, the

others, including institutional, might relate to proper input of, processing of, and output of (psychological) energies. This type of processing could be the lynchpin to higher-order emergence in these regards as well, e.g., new (sub)stages in system growth.

It should be noted that psychological energetics is a term that applies to the human species, in particular, and the reference to the concept of belief in free will in relation to the concept solidifies the use of the term for the human case. However, psychological energetics should be conceived as part of a broader concept of *relational* energetics that could apply equivalently to other species.

Returning to the target behavior of couple work in this section, partners in a couple might express different psychological energetic comfort zones or ones that are more compatible. One partner might seek either low, minimized psychological

Fig. 7.10 (continued) conforming individual could be expressing energetic minimization, while the curious, adventurous, or risk-seeking one could be expressing energetic maximization. Behavioral abnormality might reflect variations along these lines, as well. For example, the depressed person could be construed as minimized energetically and the bipolar person as oscillating in energy

The figure indicates the two extremes of energy minimization and maximization as two opposed points in a three-dimensional space and without differentiation of other patterns. However, from a psychological point of view, minimization or maximization of energy could occur in any combination of the three dimensions and to any degree in each dimension. For people stuck in one way or another in terms of psychological energetics, assuming the model holds any validity, it might matter if one or the other of the dimensions constitutes the primary vector. For example, the person who is rigidly fixated on an addictive habit might have little degree in freedom because of the overly ingrained system organization of the behavior complex involved. Or, a person might have little free energy because her/his psychological characteristics involved would aim to especially minimize surprisal energy, surprise, and unanticipated happenings in the context at hand. Or, the person might have no faith as her or himself as an effective actor or agent in the context at hand, either because of the extreme constraints in the environment (external) or the extreme self-imposed constraints independent of the environment (internal), leading to little expression of free will or its promotion by believing in it

The opposite patterns to these tendencies might arise, for example, the person might have many degrees of freedom to act because the system is integrated effectively and emerging at new levels. This could be an inviting, hospitable context for adaptation, for example, encouraging exploration through niche affordances. Or, the person might experience the chaos of too many degrees of freedom relative to the level of stability required for self-equilibrium and engage in perturbing behavior. Similar oppositions in behavior might be explained by maximized free energy more than degrees of freedom. For example, instead of acting to reduce surprisal and tending toward self-content low-key equilibrium, the person might seek to increase surprisal and, relatedly, high-octane equilibrium, fitting her or his predisposition. However, this process might be pushed beyond the stretching point. Or, otherwise, this zone beyond the stretching point might be sought due to any or all of a multiplicity of factors (due to the genetic or the phenotypic, the molecular or the central (nervous system), or early adversity or continuous environmental stressors). In this risk-disaster zone, free energy is given free rein, and the unexpected might take place in managed proportions (or otherwise with deleterious consequences). As for excess free will and its belief, there might not be enough brakes on behavior, but not necessarily with negative consequences. There could be a heightened sense of seeking and choosing alternative pathways, acting for the common good without thinking of consequences for the self (altruism), and so on. However, having an unfettered sense of free will might rocket into uncontrolled, self-destructive actions that should have been chosen otherwise, unlike positive use of free will energetics or high, maximized energetics, or gravitate between low and high regimes. The other partner might do the same, but either not in synchrony with the other person or with synchrony. Moreover, the crux dimensions in low or high energetic expression might be the same in the partners when they are matched energetically (e.g., related to free energy) or not matched (e.g., one partner is varying on free energy and another on free will belief). This novel approach to understanding couples might help therapists to grasp the constrained nature of each partner in the couple as well as the constraining nature of each partner in the couple.

Fractalization

The concept of fractalization was a central one in Young (2011) and Young (2016) but was barely mentioned in Young (2019). The research on fractalization in psychology is growing exponentially (e.g., Merlone et al. 2019). Fractalization as a process can help understand the similarities in behavior and its organization across different scales. In fractals, structural similarity or equivalent shape is found across different scales of a system, even from the macroscopic to the microscopic (think the equivalent forms of an ocean bay and wavelets lapping at the beach). I have argued that the five-step cyclic recursion of substages in the present Neo-Piagetian model reflects a self-similar fractal pattern relative to the stages that incorporate them. Furthermore, the substeps in the model have been characterized as fractal outcomes. The stages involved refer to: reflexes, sensorimotor schemes, perioperational representations, abstract operations, and collective intelligences. The substages involved refer to: coordination, hierarchization, systematization, multiplication, and integration. In Young (2019), I referred to the substeps as: tentative beginning, clear initiation, improved application, spreading maturation, and systemic synthesis. In order to facilitate application of the concept of fractalization to these three different levels of the cognitive system being described, I add the term consolidation to the middle substep and add the term refinement to the fourth one. This leaves a substep series in the present Neo-Piagetian modeling of stages and substages in cognitive development involving: (a) tentative beginning; (b) clear initiation; (c) consolidation/improved application; (d) spreading maturation/refinement; and (e) systemic synthesis. The 25-step Neo-Eriksonian (sub)stage model should go through the same substeps. The term consolidation in the substep series renders the middle step more like the substage series systematization. The term refinement in the former series serves to help distinguish the term of maturation from the concept of biological maturation with which it is primarily associated.

Another way that fractalization helps in understanding development is by showing how micro-developmental changes are analogous to macro-developmental ones. In Young (2016), I showed how the five steps in the sequence of social information processing presented by Dodge et al. (2013) resembled the development processes in the five substages of the present model. Given the same parallel found with the stages of change model, I have argued that a generic change process applies to multiple developmental levels and, in effect, any behavioral change. Psychology should be construed as the study of behavior, its organization, and its change, and the present modeling seems to provide inroads in the formal understanding of the change process that generally characterized behavior and its organization. Moreover, the generic change model has been shown to apply not only to stage-related changes but also to any changes in behavior and to the similarities in micro and macro changes in behavior and its development. In this sense, I have added to the neo-stage concept presented in Young (2019) that the fractalization process is the intimate connector between the micro-developmental changes that take place online and the macro-developmental processes that characterize stage-like acquisitions [see Box 4.1]. The concept of fractalization adds to the unifying power that the project has attempted both in terms of psychology and of causality, and so should be considered primary.

Substeps. The following illustrates the substep concept's application to the 25-step (sub)stage progression in lifespan development that has been described in the present work by considering the cardinal acquisition of identity achievement in these regards (see Table 7.1). It illustrates that although to date, 25 steps in development over the lifespan have been described in the present work, in the optimal circumstances in which all 25 substages develop for a particular individual, one can find 125 substeps through which the person traverses over the life course.

Note that the concept of substeps within substages complicates the concept of yoking as presently defined and its application to development. It has been proposed that, in yoking, the skills of different substages are available to be combined in individualized ways in context to help deal with a problem at hand, whether cognitive or socio-affective. The addition of substeps to substages in the current conceptualization of development indicates that yoking is influenced by the degree of development of the skills within a substage that might be tapped in the problem-solving at hand, and it constitutes one of the variables that can influence what is yoked generally in dealing with any problem at hand.

Attractor Landscapes as Fractalization Expressions

The substage series of coordination, hierarchization, systematization multiplication, and integration is the middle level in a three-phase fractalization process that includes superordinate stages and subordinate sub-steps, each with five levels. The fractalization is clear in terms of the numbers involved at each level. As for the contents, the underlying attractor landscape evolution that had been ascribed to the five substages (respectively, unicyclic, bicyclic, chaotic, complex adaptive system, superordinate complex adaptive system) would qualify as describing the fractalization similarities at each of the three levels of the system. It is as if different attractor regimes evolve within each of the three levels, and the levels themselves can be described in terms of evolving attractor regimes. In this sense, (a) the reflexive cognitive stage is akin to the unicyclic attractor regime; (b) the sensorimotor one is like the bicyclic one; (c) the perioperational, representation stage is like the chaotic

Table 7.1 Identity achievement in five substeps

Substep	Explanation	Identity
Tentative beginning	The acquisition/skill/schema-operation at issue materializes in the cognitive or socio-affective psychological functioning of the person, but tenuously and in alternation with its absence	The person begins to entertain in one domain a self-defined identity, but it is fragilely present, and alternates with its absence
Clear initiation	The acquisition/skill/schema-operation at issue appears consistently in the psychological functioning of the person	The individual advances to a proclaimed identity in the domain, albeit still with consideration of its absence
Consolidation/ improved application	The acquisition/skill/schema-operation at issue manifests a coherent structure and is applied readily	The identity in the domain concretizes and characterizes the person in the self identity
Spreading maturation/ refinement	The acquisition/skill/schema-operation at issue propagates in the system at issue, for example, replacing less advanced skills, and becomes more adaptively functional	The identity acquisition in the prior step portends development of identity in other domains with the same but adapting characteristics as in the primary domain.
Systemic synthesis	The acquisition/skill/schema-operation at issue characterizes in full the system at issue, with its diverse applications meshed together functionally	The person has the same identity profile develop in several domains that are interlinked coherently in a network of identities over domains

Note 1. Identity domains fall into three major categories: interpersonal, ideological, and existential. The domains were found in a study of the narratives produced by 19-year-olds (McLean et al. 2016). The interpersonal domains include: (1) family, (2) friends, (3) dating, (4) recreation, and (5) sex roles. The ideological domains include: (6) values, (7) religion, (8) occupation/work, and (9) politics. I would add (10) Studying/school roles, and (11) Relating to society. The existential domains include: (12) mortality, (13) mental health, (14) abuse (past), and (15) drugs/ alcohol. I would add a Personal domain category that specifies: (16) Romantic partner, (17) One's children, (18) Caregiving – one's children, (19) Caregiving – other, and (20) Other (miscellaneous – specify) Researchers could investigate the five-step progression in identity development within the first domain and then others that follow while noting the supports and problems that might arise as they develop. This type of research should not focus on problems in identity development, which is a different question. The five-step identity development progression in domains elaborates how identity achievement develops, which is a more differentiated approach than typically encountered, for example, on statuses or narratives. It will be informative to analyze narratives produced this way in order to determine which are predominant as initiated and consolidated, which become coupled as development proceeds, and so on. Also, what personal, contextual, and related variables contribute to individual profiles in these regards? Finally, what might different individual profiles mean for other aspects of development?
Note 2. The example provided in the table on identity can apply readily to any of the 25 steps in the present model, whether cognitively (Neo-Piagetian) or socio-affectively (Neo-Eriksonian)

attractor regime; (d) the abstract stage reflects the complex adaptive system, multi-attractor regime; and (e) the collective intelligence, superordinate abstract stage mirrors the superordinate complex adaptive system regime. As an extension of the fractalization process being described, there could be five levels and not three. For example, bottom-down, change processes might take place at the nanosecond level involving these types of attractor regimes. At the top-up level, stages in human development might reflect larger dynamics, for example, in relation to individual-culture/machine/species interactions. The supplement that follows refers to these types of evolving attractor regimes for couple work.

Supplement

The supplement to the chapter consists of eight figures. It is given next. The captions explain to them, and I do not give expository text. The figures in the supplement modify the ones developed for couples to help in the areas of (a) lateralization and of (b) changing bad habits to good ones. The former set of four figures (see Figs. 7.11, 7.12, 7.13, and 7.14) helps visualize how the concepts of networks, systems, and activation-inhibition coordination triangulate to help visual right- and left-side lateralizations and their interactions. The latter set of four figures (see Figs. 7.15, 7.16, 7.17, and 7.18) helps illustrate how good habits and bad habits are in constant tension and how the shift to good habits can take place (depicted in couples, in particular). The reader can revise these extensions for other research and clinical matters of concern or use them directly. For example, I have already used the latter figures in psychotherapeutic treatment sessions.

Conclusion

Conclusions (to Chaps. 6 and 7)

Chapters 6 and 7 on Young's 2011, 2016, 2019 Causality and Development book series consist of new material on Young's Neo-Piagetian/Neo-Eriksonian 25-step lifespan developmental model and the proposition that cohering causality in an ongoing project constitutes a unifying axis for psychology. Chapter 6 reviews 2019 literature on the major areas of Young's work since his three books were published and surveys the major topics in work (philosophy, causality, developmental causality, handedness, networks, activation-inhibition coordination, the DSM (Diagnostic and Statistical Manual of Mental Disorders), Piaget/Neo-Piagetians, and Erikson/Neo-Eriksonians). Chapter 7 presents novel material on couple work, relating it in an integrated fashion to networks, system attractors, and activation-inhibition coordination. The material includes a generalized mechanistic model of behavioral causality related to free energy, degrees of freedom, and belief in free will, which could also apply to couple work. Also, it considers fractalization as a core mechanistic causal explanatory factor in behavior, its organization, and its change. It offers a substep model of substages in this regard, showing how it might work for identity achievement development. It considers the essential role of higher-order (cognitive)

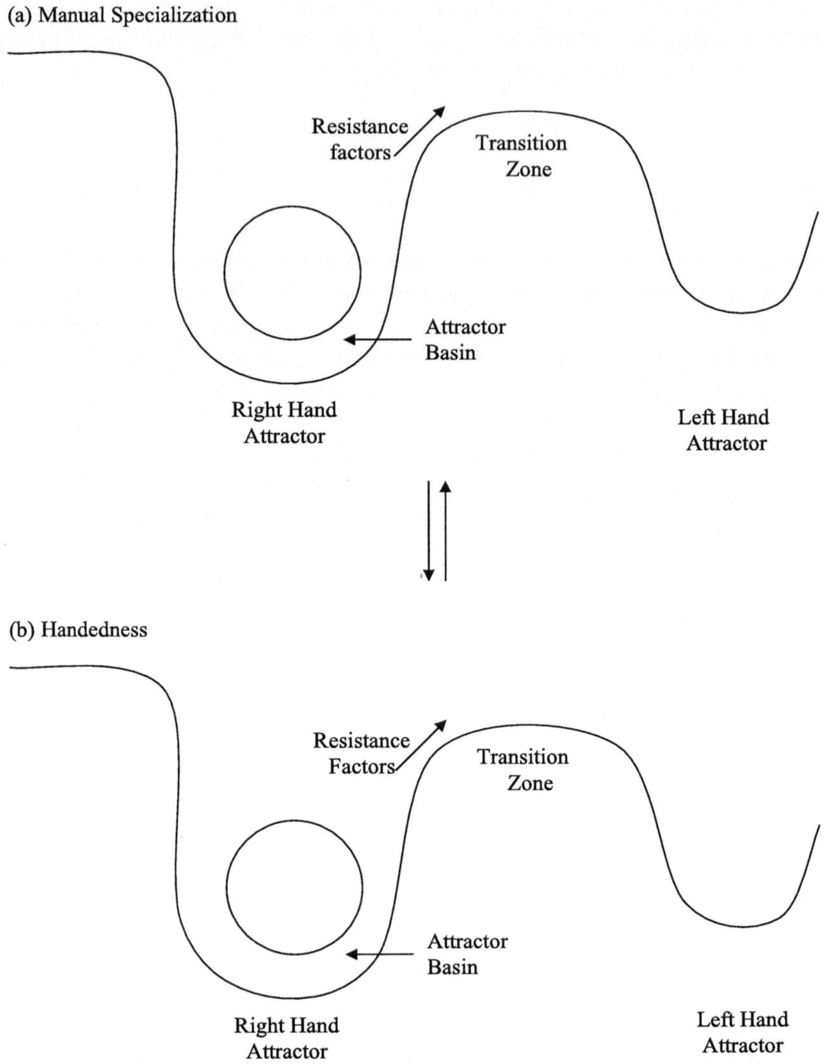

Fig. 7.11 Attractor configuration of manual specialization in relation to handedness (right and left hand for each)
The figure illustrates representation of left and right side manual lateralizations, one for manual specialization and one for handedness, in terms of attractors
Figure (**a**) indicates that while, typically, each hand has its specializations, in this case, the right hand has a stronger affinity for its basin than the left hand, presumably because the right hand is more specialized for the hypothetical behavior being represented, such as would be the case for

generalization in (sub)stage transition. A supplement of figures illustrates how the new concepts in the latter part of the material can be applied to work on left-right differences in lateralization and on depicting good habits compared to bad habits in behavior, both individually and in couples.

Interim Commentary

The present summary and extension of the three books by Young (2011, 2016, 2019) has provided an integrated model that could spur conceptualization and future research in psychology. The modeling involved has included networks, systems, and integrating concepts such as activation-inhibition coordination. The concept of psychological energetics adds a promising causal concept to the general models constructed on Neo-Piagetian/Neo-Eriksonian (sub)stages/steps in development, the causal nexus involved, and the task of unifying these components into a larger ongoing project toward unifying psychology. Future work on the models presented could attempt to relate the concept of activation-inhibition coordination to the systems concepts of repellor attractors and saddle point bottlenecks. Another innovation added to the present three-book summary involves the process of fractalization and how it could be a core unifying theme in psychology and in behavioral causality. Fractal processes could add another focus to research in cognitive or socio-affective stage, substage, and substep development.

Fig. 7.11 (continued) complex fine motor activity. The right-hand specialization in this case would remain in its attractor basin (where the well is deeper) and resist pulls toward disequilibrium even if stretched because of any factors acting toward its destabilization and shift to an alternate attractor (left hand use for the task at hand). Left-hand attractors would be represented by separate manual specializations; such would be the case for manual spatial skills

Figure (**b**) represents the same left–right opposition in manual behavior, but for side preference or handedness. On the one hand, the wells would be shallower for handedness compared to manual specialization because handedness can be influenced by the environment more so than the case for manual specialization, which reflects brain-based differences in specialization. On the other hand, the respective wells in the figure could be represented as deeper for handedness given how handedness entrenches and overrides predilections influenced by the skills of the hemisphere. In these senses, the well on the left for right handedness is represented as deeper than the one for left handedness, which also should be more liable to environmental influence, given its weaker lateralization and greater inconsistency

The arrows showing how the upper and bottom portions of the figure interrelate have been added in order to indicate that manual specialization and handedness are not mirror images of each other. For example, brain-based manual specializations do not directly determine handedness side preference. The arrows indicate a reciprocal influence because, once handedness sets in as deeply entrenched, it can influence the hands used on specialized tasks. Handedness can even lead to overriding skill-based determinations in this regard that are based on lateralized hemispheric manual skills

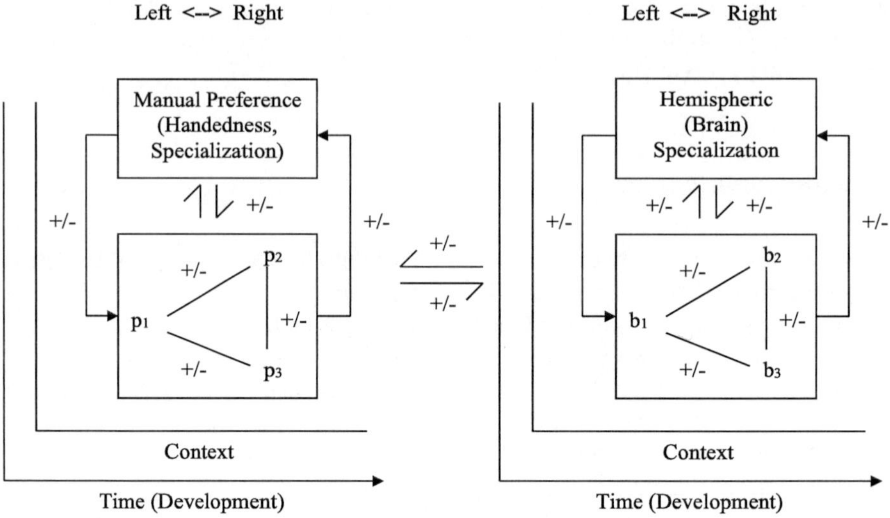

Fig. 7.12 Levels of organization of lateralized manual behavior and lateralized brain function This figure helps explicate further the relationship between manual specialization, handedness, and hemispheric specialization by casting it in terms of networks, multilevel systems, and activation-inhibition coordination (+/−). The networks of manual behaviors and preferences (p) involved in handedness and manual specialization are represented on the left side of the figure, with the dynamic interplay between the left and right side in behavior and preference in these regards also highlighted. On the right side of the figure, the skills of the hemispheres in their specializations are represented in the bottom part of the figure, with the brain-based (b) hemisphere specializations depicted on the top part of the figure, with the dynamic interplay between the left and right side in brain-based specialization in these regards also highlighted. In both the left and right parts of the figure, the top and bottom parts are indicated to have reciprocal interactions. That is, lower-order networks in behaviors/skills not only interact in networks, with some items driving others more than others, but also networks can influence higher-order levels, such as an emerging entrenching handedness in the case of the part of the figure to the left. Similarly, for the right side of the figure, specific hemisphere specialization skills solidify on the left or right of the brain from bottom-up network influences. At the same time, for both the left and right side of the figures, top-down influences can affect lower-order networks. For example, as handedness preferences solidify and entrench, the stability enforces resistance pressures to switch hands in tasks even when the other hand at issue might have a better skill set for the task at hand. Finally, the handedness and specializations of the hand and brain that are occurring in lateralization development are as much the product of systemic, self-organizing emergence as anything else, as systems complexify toward automaticity so as to increase flexibility, adaptability, or both

The present work summarizing Young's (2011, 2016, 2019) Neo-Piagetian/Neo-Eriksonian 25 steps (five stages X five substages) model, and summarizing the causal factors that can help explain development, has argued that the model is a valid and valuable one. It was derived rationally, defends a (neo)stage view of development, and presents causality as a unifying focus in psychology, albeit in an ongoing project of discovery. All of these aspects of the three books and this summary

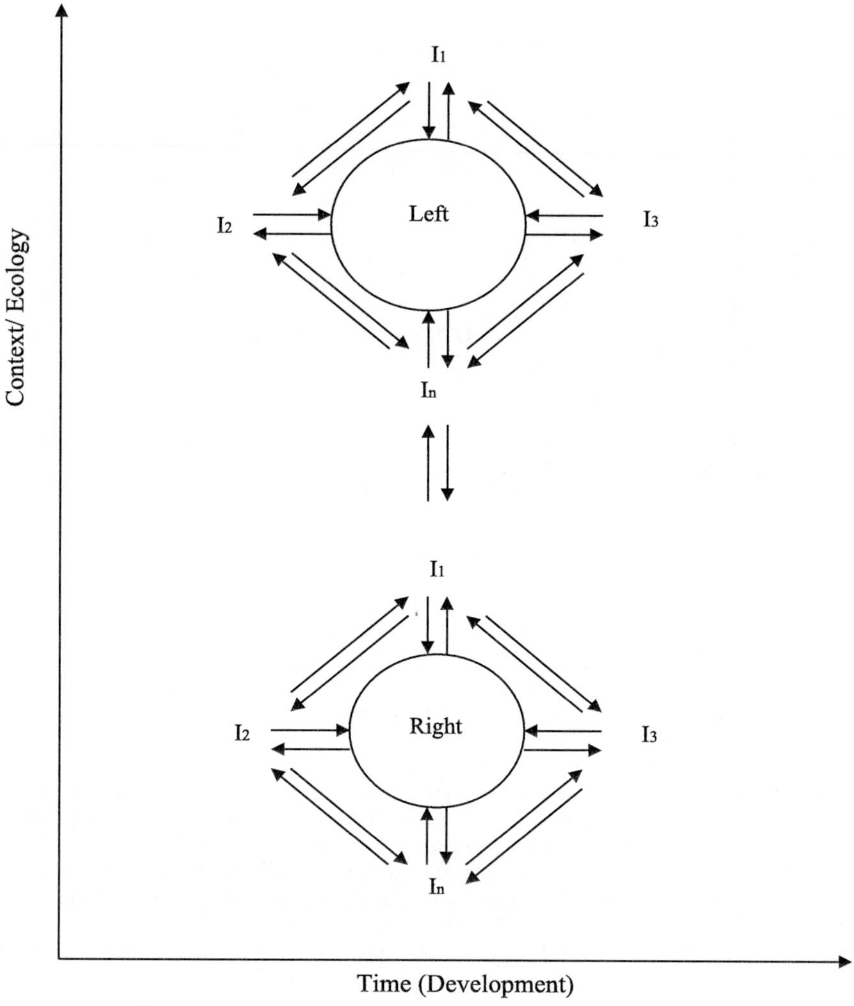

Fig. 7.13 Interactive left- and right-side networks
This figure represents right- and left-side networks in interaction. The lateralization involved could apply to manual preferences, such as in right handedness. It could apply to manual specializations, such as in fine motor right hand skills. It could apply to hemispheric specializations, such as in left hemisphere fine motor skills. The networks indicated are represented by the symbol I, which indicated an item, whether behavioral or brain-based. The figure does not represent different strengths of the linkages (correlations of the links), nor their possible inhibitory as opposed to activatory nature. Moreover, the links are indicated as bidirectional, but that need not be the case, and usually links are unidirectional in network graphing. Particular nodes/behaviors/skills might be drivers of others (think writing for handedness). The figure indicates the left- and right-side tendencies (uses/preferences; skills/specializations, as the case may be) have bottom-up and top-down interactive effects. As top-down tendencies, e.g., in handedness, solidify/entrench, they influence item expression, e.g., in side of manual use, which affects the bottom-up influences by the lower-order networks on upper-level layers of the system involved. The figure does not represent more than two layers in the hierarchical system, but networks themselves might differentiate into more than one layer, as might nay higher-order level, as per separate domains of action having different lateralization tendencies

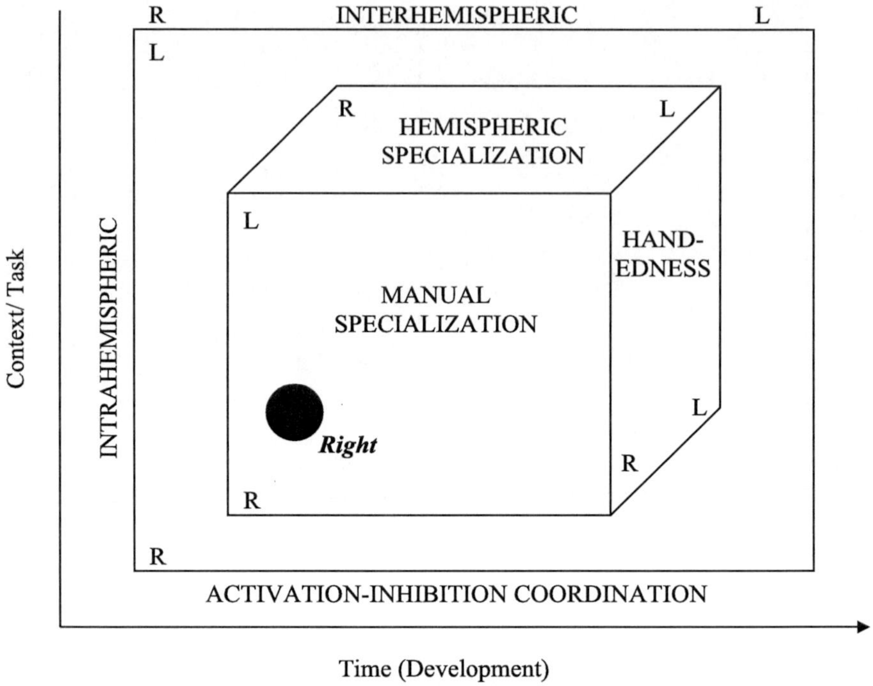

Fig. 7.14 Dimensions in right–left preference/specialization: behavior and brain
The figure indicates the dimensions involved in the control parameter that leads to side tendencies in lateralization. It indicates that the criterial threshold involved in the present case leads to a right-side tendency. This could refer to a behavior on a task or a skill for the task, depending on whether one is addressing handedness/manual specialization or hemispheric specialization. The three lateralizations reciprocally influence each other. Other factors to consider concern interhemispheric and intra-hemispheric interactions, as well as the mechanism of activation-inhibition coordination, which, in the present work, is considered a primary integrative mechanism of brain and behavior

illustrate that my work in the three books constitutes, essentially, a theoretical enterprise, with much integration of other models. At the same time, the present model is based on a comprehensive review of the literature, including in a compare-contrast format of other models. Moreover, there are data that support it through the data of other models that fit with it, and the model is formulated in a way that makes it testable. That said, it would be impossible to test the model in one study, no matter how comprehensive. Testing the present model must be done piecemeal, given its breadth, complexity, and nomological theory network.

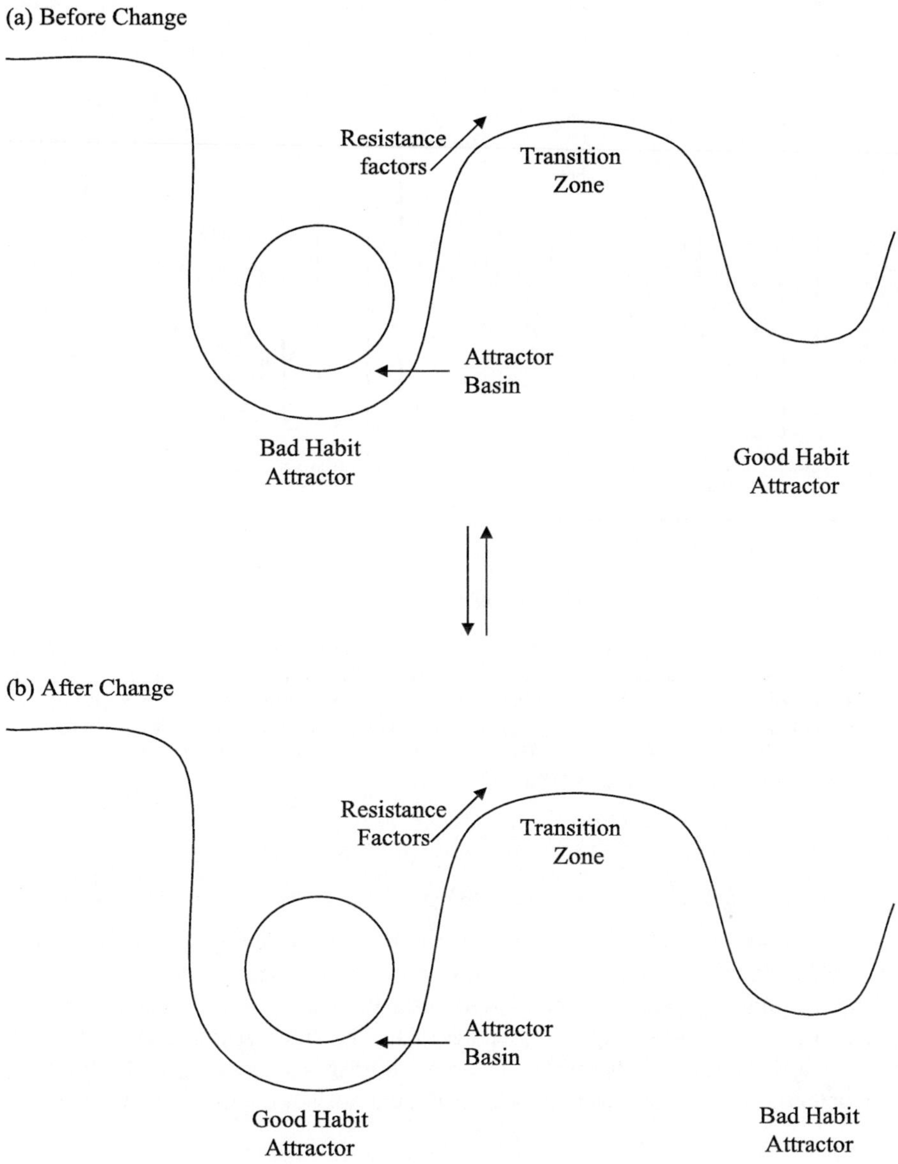

Fig. 7.15 Attractor configuration of good habits and bad habits before and after change
The figure conceives good habits and bad habits as attractors, with one or the other predominating, for example, before and after effort to change or therapy. The attractors are indicated as being in interaction, which is always the case as we develop new ways and they compete with old ways, especially when resistance is lowered, temptations beckon, etc.

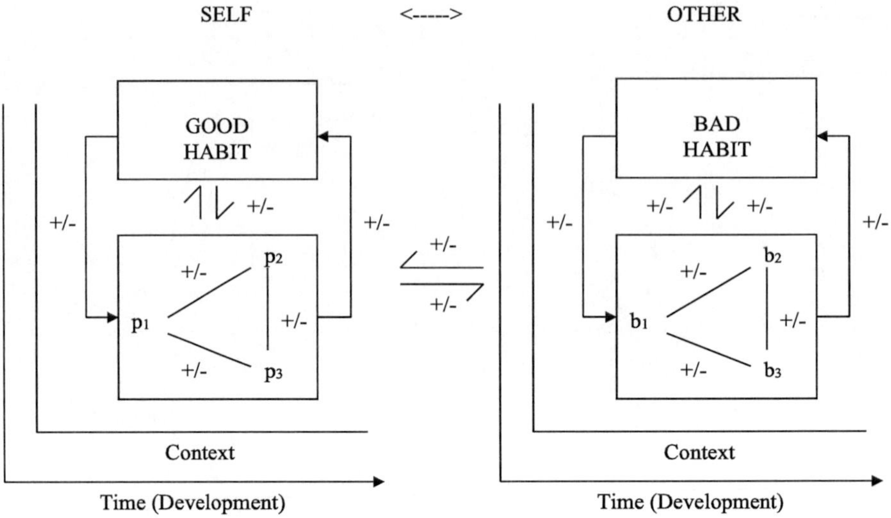

Fig. 7.16 Levels of organization of good habits and bad habits in the self and the other (e.g., couple/family)
The figure indicates the network, system, and activation-inhibition coordination (+/−) dynamics related to the good and bad habits of the person and others. The networks of behaviors comprising the habits are indicated, as well as the higher-order emergent integrations of the behaviors into the habits (think addictions and addiction control). Is the other complicit in or constraining of the bad habit, sharing in it, as well? How can balance be facilitated in good habit–bad habit relations (and in self and other), thereby facilitating control?

Psychology suffers from a replicability crisis, and I have argued that one factor that could explain it is a lack of the type of broad theory being proposed here. The discipline might be too siloed and in need of the kind of theoretical integration proposed here. There is an expanding scope of theory and research taking place in psychology and related disciplines. The present approach to modeling in psychology potentially provides psychology with a viable way of increasing its coherence.

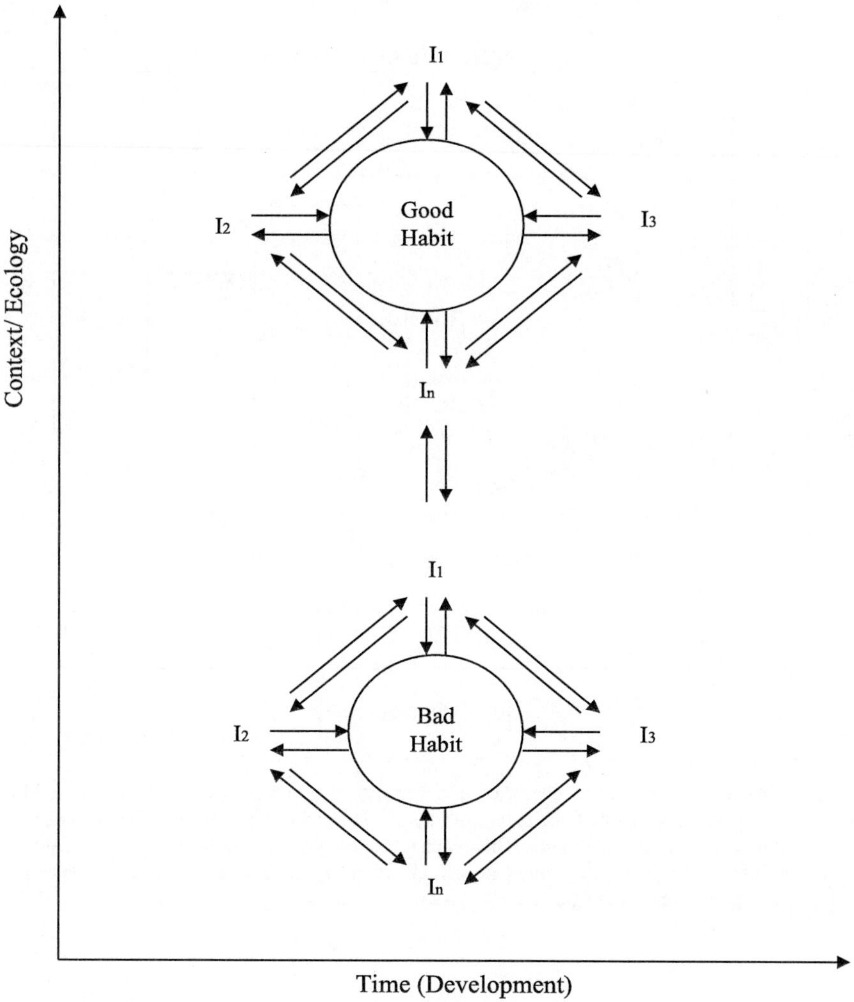

Fig. 7.17 Interactive networks of good habits and bad habits
Good and bad habits are constituted by interactive networks, which themselves interact. They ingrain/entrench and alter network dynamics in doing so, hopefully more on the positive side

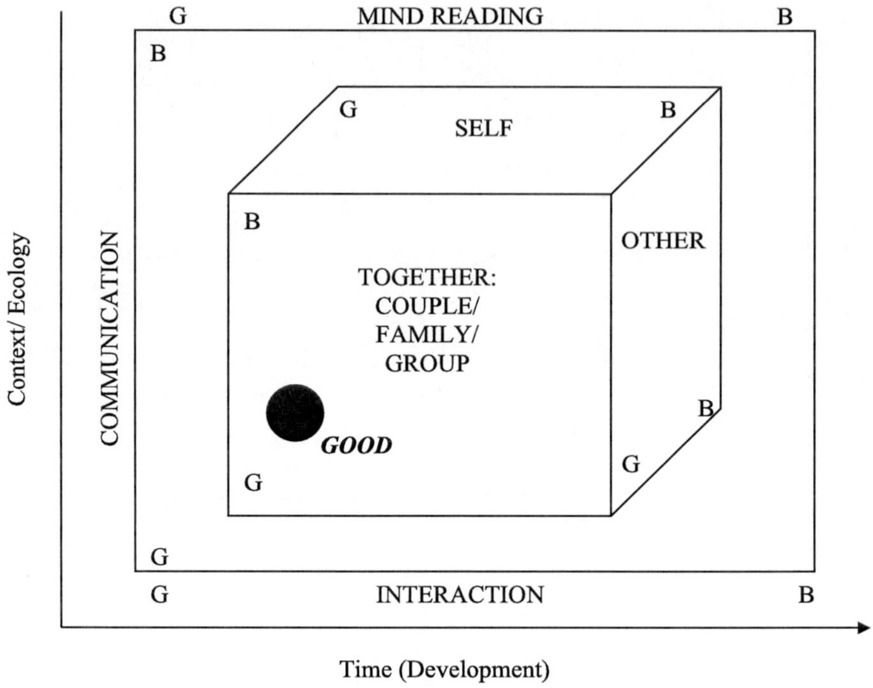

Fig. 7.18 Dimensions in behavior change in good habits and bad habits in self and other
The figure indicates one way to depict couple, family, or group relationships. The individuals involved have good habits or bad habits for communicating and interacting, and also in reading the mind or being aware of self and other. This leads to the couple, family, or group to have good or bad habits. Insight, support, or therapy can help change bad habits at any of these levels to good habits, and help to maintain the gains

References

Arsalidou, M., Pawliw-Levac, M., Sadeghi, M., Pascual-Leone, J.: Brain areas associated with numbers and calculations in children: meta-analyses of fMRI studies. Dev. Cogn. Neurosci. **30**, 239–250 (2017). https://doi.org/10.1016/j.dcn.2017.08.002

Baumeister, R.F.: Free will in scientific psychology. Perspect. Psychol. Sci. **3**(1), 14–19 (2008). https://doi.org/10.1111/j.1745-6916.2008.00057.x

Borsboom, D., Cramer, A.O.J., Kalis, A.: Brain disorders? Not really: why network structures block reductionism in psychopathology research. Behav. Brain Sci. **42**, e2 (2018). https://doi.org/10.1017/s0140525x17002266

Camos, V., Barrouillet, P.: Developmental change in working memory strategies: from passive maintenance to active refreshing. Dev. Psychol. **47**(3), 898–904 (2011). https://doi.org/10.1037/a0023193

Charbonneau, C., Robert, M., Bourassa, G., Gladu-Bissonnette, S.: Observational learning of quantity conservation and Piagetian generalization tasks. Dev. Psychol. **12**(3), 211–217 (1976). https://doi.org/10.1037/0012-1649.12.3.211

Demetriou, A., Spanoudis, G.: Growing Minds: a Developmental Theory of Intelligence, Brain, and Education, 1st edn. Routledge, London (2018)

Dodge, K.A., Godwin, J., The Conduct Problems Prevention Research Group: Social-information-processing patterns mediate the impact of preventive intervention on adolescent antisocial behavior. Psychol. Sci. **24**(4), 456–465 (2013). https://doi.org/10.1177/0956797612457394

Doherty, J.M., Belletier, C., Rhodes, S., Jaroslawska, A., Barrouillet, P., Camos, V., Cowan, N., Naveh-Benjamin, M., Logie, R.H.: Dual-task costs in working memory: an adversarial collaboration. J. Exp. Psychol. Learn. Memory Cogn. **45**(9), 1529–1551 (2019). https://doi.org/10.1037/xlm0000668

Friston, K.: The free-energy principle: a unified brain theory? Nat. Rev. Neurosci. **11**(2), 127–138 (2010). https://doi.org/10.1038/nrn2787

Kalisch, R., Cramer, A.O.J., Binder, H., Fritz, J., Leertouwer, I.J., Lunansky, G., Meyer, B., Timmer, J., Veer, I.M., van Harmelen, A.-L.: Deconstructing and reconstructing resilience: a dynamic network approach. Perspect. Psychol. Sci. **14**(5), 765–777 (2019). https://doi.org/10.1177/1745691619855637

Kazi, S., Kazali, E., Makris, N., Spanoudis, G., Demetriou, A.: Cognizance in cognitive development: a longitudinal study. Cogn. Dev. **52**, 100805 (2019). https://doi.org/10.1016/j.cogdev.2019/100805

Kinzler, K.D., Dupoux, E., Spelke, E.S.: The native language of social cognition. Proc. Natl. Acad. Sci. **104**(30), 12577–12580 (2007). https://doi.org/10.1073/pnas.0705345104

McLean, K.C., Syed, M., Yoder, A., Greenhoot, A.F.: The role of domain content in understanding identity development processes. J. Res. Adolesc. **26**(1), 60–75 (2016). https://doi.org/10.1111/jora.12169

Merlone, U., Panchuk, A., van Geert, P.: Modeling learning and teaching interaction by a map with vanishing denominators: fixed points stability and bifurcations. Chaos Solitons Fractals. **126**, 253–265 (2019). https://doi.org/10.1016/j.chaos.2019.06.008

Morra, S., Bisagno, E., Caviola, S., Delfante, C., Mammarella, I.C.: Working memory capacity and the development of quantitative central conceptual structures. Cogn. Instruct. **37**(4), 483–511 (2019). https://doi.org/10.1080/07370008.2019.1636797

Pascual-Leone, J.: A mathematical model for the transition rule in Piaget's developmental stages. Acta Psychol. **32**, 301–345 (1970). https://doi.org/10.1016/0001-6918(70)90108-3

Pascual-Leone, J.: Growing minds have a maturing mental attention: a review of Demetriou and Spanoudis (2018). Intelligence. **72**, 59–66 (2019). https://doi.org/10.1016/j.intell.2018.12.001

Paxton, A., Dale, R.: Interpersonal movement synchrony responds to high- and low-level conversational constraints. Front. Psychol. **8**, 1135 (2017). https://doi.org/10.3389/fpsyg.2017.01135

Siffredi, V., Barrouillet, P., Spencer-Smith, M., Vaessen, M., Anderson, V., Vuilleumier, P.: Examining distinct working memory processes in children and adolescents using fMRI: results and validation of a modified Brown-Peterson paradigm. PLoS One. **12**(7), e0179959 (2017). https://doi.org/10.1371/journal.pone.0179959

Young, G.: Development and Causality: Neo-Piagetian Perspectives. Springer, New York (2011)

Young, G.: Unifying Causality and Psychology: Being, Brain and Behavior. Springer, Cham (2016)

Young, G.: Causality and Development: Neo-Eriksonian Perspectives. Springer, Cham (2019)

Chapter 8
Literature Review 2020

In Young's first three books in the present series (Young 2011, 2016, 2019), he innovated in multiple ways in relation to the main themes of causality, development, and stages, with causality considered a unifying theme across psychology. Young formulated a 25-step Neo-Piagetian lifespan cognitive model consisting of five stages at the heart of the work, each with five substages that cyclically re-occur. Also, he created a model of corresponding socio-affective Neo-Eriksonian steps. Although all three Young books deal with Young's major themes, the first book in the series especially delved into various Neo-Piagetian models while comparing and contrasting them toward building his own model. The second book in the series focused on causality, for instance, biologically, environmentally, and in terms of psychological contributions, such as one's belief in free will. The concept of activation-inhibition coordination is given prominence for causality and is applied to the area of laterality. In addition, Young explored network and system theories in terms of causality. Young's work includes a section on the DSM (Diagnostic and Statistical Manual of Mental Disorders, 5th ed.; American Psychiatric Association 2013) and its relation to the Research Domain Criteria (RDoC; Insel 2014). The third book in the Young series expanded upon the Neo-Eriksonian model by applying it to psychotherapy, for example, by showing how crises in each of the 25 steps in the model will present to the mental health worker. In this regard, Young especially applies his developmental model to couple therapy.

The next chapter of the present work, the fourth in the book series by Young, renews the call for unifying psychology around causality (and development), as per the supportive literature review on the question. This literature review, completed in December, 2020, was undertaken with peer-reviewed publications since the prior 2019 literature review in Chap. 6 was written. This chapter in the book covers a broad spectrum of articles that reflect the major themes of the work but tries to limit an in-depth presentation of their contents unless otherwise warranted. The first set of articles reviewed in this chapter relates to the integrating theme of unification in

G. Young, *Causality and Neo-Stages in Development*,
https://doi.org/10.1007/978-3-030-82540-9_8

psychology. The second set of articles relates to development. Generally, the articles support the present framework and are interpreted in its terms, while adding to it.

Unification and Causality

Unification and Mechanism

Unification. Gaj (2016) has written a book on unity and fragmentation in psychology, reviewing philosophical and theoretical views on the issue (I missed this book in my literature review in my 2019 book, the third one in the trilogy of books on the unifying psychology project, Young 2011, 2016, 2019). Gaj reviewed five proposals toward unifying psychology, and two are behavioral and older (Kimble 1996; Staats 1996). Two are more contemporary and grounded in central psychological notions—Anderson (2008) on unifying social cognition (and psychology) through a variant of information theory and Sternberg and Grigorenko (Sternberg and Grigorenko 2003; Sternberg et al. 2001) on a unified psychology in the profession as opposed to conceptually. The fifth work on integrating psychology (Henriques 2011) is the only one that has a recent book-length treatment of a general approach to unification in psychology, other than my own work. Except for the latter work by Henriques, I forego summarizing the five psychology unification proposals as well as Gaj's analysis of them.

Henriques' (2011) unifying model includes four main components—on behavioral investment, the influence matrix, the justification hypothesis, and the tree of knowledge, as well as levels in behavior. The behavioral investment theory includes principles of energy economics, evolution, genetics, development, and computational control/information. These levels reflect a biopsychosocial model of behavior, with the added computational/information component as an area of content. The levels of the model include the sensory-motor, operant-experiential, imaginative thought, and linguistic justification. These levels seem developmental and could profit by adding a fifth one related to generalized abstract thought. The influence matrix concerns social motivation and emotion (interpersonal and social relations). Moreover, it represents another content area of psychology, contrasting the perceptual cognitive one with a socioemotional one. The justification aspect of the model represents what makes humans unique and is a higher-order cognitive skill. This aspect of the model is quite consistent with my own, which specifies that Piagetian concrete operational and abstract thought distinguishes humans from other animals cognitively. The tree of knowledge component of the model is too complex to depict here—essentially, it places psychology in the context of other disciplines. It is described by Gaj as somewhat dualistic, but it does include relating justifications to culture. Philosophically, it is interesting to note that Henriques's philosophical stance begins with Morgan's evolutionary emergentism; his approach is embedded in an evolutionary and animal field, even as it seeks human uniqueness. Also,

Henriques attempts to find unifying themes for the science and practice of psychology. These themes are consistent with my own.

Henriques (2011) includes a chapter on the psychology problem, which merits further discussion. First, Henriques reviewed that even the question of the definition of psychology is not resolved. Does it concern behavior in the broadest sense, including consciousness and the like, or is it limited to more specific movements, stimuli, and the like? This issue leads to other ones, such as whether it is one domain of study or disconnected ones, is its study of causality also disconnected, and philosophically and epistemologically, what is its thrust? For the question at hand, can it be unified or is it destined to remain fragmented, and is the unification project even desired or possible? Henriques and Michalski (2019) elaborated on these themes, advocating for psychology being defined as the science of mental behavior. They described a periodic table of behavior, with four dimensions of behavioral complexity—matter, life, mind, and culture. This quite relates to my own integrated biopsychosocial model. The rows of the table concern object-field relations and levels of complexity (part, whole, group). The table relates to Henriques's Tree of Knowledge (Tok) system, which stands as a basis for his unification effort for psychology.

In response to this psychology problem, I recommend that psychology be considered as the scientific *study of behavior and its organization, including toward understanding human behavior, but not exclusively*. Even the study of annelids can reveal principles related to human behavior, for example. Adding the organization component to the definition allows for a broad range of behaviors to be considered as part of psychology, depending on one's predilections, including mind, consciousness, and the unconscious. Further, it allows for systemic thinking, including in terms of nonlinear dynamic systems modeling/chaos and emergent stages and substages in development.

Note that this approach to defining psychology is consistent with the American Psychological Association's (APA) current definition, but it does not include the terminology of "mind," preferring to be more inclusive in wording other than mentioning behavior (VandenBos 2015). Specifically, for the APA, psychology is the study of the mind and behavior, toward their understanding, and it includes broadly "brain to the actions of nations, from child development to care for the aged," and in every possible context.

This present broad and inclusive approach to defining psychology allows for different levels in its study and integration efforts, including toward its unification. For example, at the lower reductionist level, basic descriptions of behavior, acts, stimuli, the environment, and their linkages can be described. Causality can be attributed to specific biological mechanisms, including genetic activity and brain-behavior relations. At the superordinate level, psychology deals with broader themes, such as consciousness/the unconscious, developmental stages, free will belief, and emergence in chaos theory. At the mid-level, the field develops more integrative models or disciplines, such as in social neuroscience, and the causality mechanisms are expanded into epigenetics and the biopsychosocial model. Finally, my own work extends across multiple levels in brain and behavior – for example, I describe the general causality mechanism of activation-inhibition coordination across the brain, neurons, connectivities, and behavior and its organization.

The lower level, intermediate level, and higher-order level in this psychology enterprise that I have described can be referred to as the Integration continuum; all are equally valid in the study and model building of behavior. Clearly, I focus on the top-down level, but all are valuable and should be seen as contributing to the field, with none neglected. In this sense, by prioritizing the unification project in the present work, I am trying to revitalize the validity of the unification project for psychology, especially through the primacy in the study of causality and the specific causality mechanisms being proposed (I have integrated activation-inhibition coordination with the concepts of systems and networks). One could add a fourth superordinate level to the Integration continuum being proposed toward creating a more inclusive approach to psychology. First, at this level, the interrelationship of psychology to other disciplines could be highlighted. Psychology is essential for philosophy, psychiatry, public health, epidemiology, sociology, the humanities and social sciences generally, economics and political science, and so on. Finally, the present emphasis on causality as a focus toward unifying psychology could be a way of unifying these various disciplines under the rubric of all being causality-informed and causality-seeking disciplines. Even the hard sciences could be defined as causality ones (physics, chemistry, etc.). Grosz et al. (2020) maintained that causal inference is a central goal of research in psychology. They advocated for dealing with it directly even when study design does not seem to permit it. Causality is basic to the psychological sciences both empirically and conceptually. Other work reviewed below is highly consistent with these frames.

Trafimow (2020) advocated for more theorizing in psychology, as did Phaf (2020), the article on which he commented. Phaf (2020) maintained that theorizing in psychology should be mandatory, including setting up predictions that test hypotheses strongly, such as by directly pitting them in the process of one against the other, with the hypotheses derived from theorizing. Trafimow added that theories cannot be tested directly; they give directions, and auxiliary assumptions must be added to allow for empirical testing. Trafimow (2020) continued that empirical testing is insufficient for the science of psychology, in that it needs integration and synthesis, on the one hand, and unification, on the other hand. Trafimow (2012) made the distinction between small-scale and large-scale unification; psychology is constructing the latter, but there is no unity on the grander scale. He also distinguished between more immediate mechanisms and grander causality.

Eronen and Bringmann (2021) argued that creating good psychological theory is a difficult process so that the discipline is facing a "theory crisis." Among other points, they advocated for better work on finding causal relationships to prime and to reflect better theory construction. Gervais (2021) argued that better theory can spur the evolution of better science. Needless to say, this book and the prior ones on which it is based support these propositions on the value of theory in psychology, and the search for causality of behavior.

Toomela (2019) did not present a unified psychology model, but he decried the fragmentation in psychology, hearkening back to Vygotsky (1927/1982), who described that unification follows fragmentation. Toomela considers psychology too focused on Aristotle's efficient causation, considering that we should examine all four of his causes (material, formal, final, and well). This is consistent with my own reference to Aristotelian causality in Young (2016). Toomela points out that, for Aristotle, causality includes motion, or change, becoming, or process, which is also consistent with the present dynamic and developmental approach. Finally, Toomela advocates for a structural (e.g., as per Piaget) and systems approach to unifying psychology, both of which are central to my own approach. Toomela (2020) published as part of a special issue edited by Valsiner (2020) on revisioning psychology. It is beyond the scope of the present chapter to review the multiple contributions; however, its major themes are consistent with my own—psychology should be about the individual, experiential person, and study the person evolutionarily, developmentally, and culturally.

About revisioning psychology, Berkman and Wilson (2021) argued for practical theories that can make differences in the real world. This speaks to ecological validity. The present modeling has the applications to psychopathology and psychotherapy advocated for by these authors.

Scheel et al. (2020) advocated for more theory and following its chain in designing research before research is conducted. It called for differential analysis of any one theory with others considered valid. Before testing hypotheses, researchers should establish the conceptual base of the research and establish the causal relationships involved, aside from investigating possible methodological issues. Similarly, van Rooij and Baggio (2021) called for establishing the plausibility of theory before testing it.

Integration. Fittingly, the journal the *Review of General Psychology* published a special section entitled *Re-envisioning General Psychology*. Indeed, one of the articles referred to seeking common ground and point of view in psychology, as well as viewing it from the perspective of big ideas and broad-scale approach (Osbeck 2020). At the same time, Osbeck cautioned that seeking larger frameworks, exploring interconnections and widening the scope of theory and conceptualization does not imply attempts to unify psychology, consistent with the conclusions of Green (2015) and Stam (2004). In my own approach, I have taken a middle ground of indicating that unifying psychology is an ongoing project. However, that common ground can be found in cross-discipline commonalities related to causality and mechanism. Osbeck emphasizes the same in that, for her, the common ground in psychology is its continual self-reflection, ongoing renewal, and refinement of integrative models, including of the discipline's values and inherent philosophical stances.

Osbeck (2020) also noted the tension in psychology between the individual-level variation and systemic level analysis, which is a topic covered in the Young books under discussion. For example, Young (2019) had suggested a neo-stage model of development that describes universal stages. However, the model considers them emergent due to biopsychosocial factors rather than maturational ones only and individually tailored to the person. In a similar vein, Beck and Jackson (2020) described the tension between the idiographic, individual and nomothetic, systemic approaches to personality. Their modeling suggests that people have unique personality structures, but often express developmental consistencies, although environmentally and situationally mutable ones. They call for theoretical work in the area, and the present one offers a partial contribution in these regards.

Frazier (2019) defended the biopsychosocial approach in light if criticisms proffered by Bolton and Gillett (2019). The model has generated enormous research in its support (e.g., see Woods 2019), although it is difficult to study all of its aspects simultaneously in inclusive research. The model is holistic, systemic, multifactorial, and causally targeted, with separate but interrelated levels. For me, the model helps in treating rehabilitation patients because it emphasizes that all three levels of the person's system need to be addressed in their care for therapy to succeed. Also, the model integrates multiple fast-evolving fields in psychology and neuroscience, such as social genomics and psychoneuroimmunology. Finally, it allows for developmental considerations, crucial to the present integrative effort.

Generally, the present work supports a multicausal framework for the study of causality. The psychiatric field also supports a multicausal causal framework, at least empirically. However, the monocausal model still has influence through biological/medical reductionism in psychiatry (Kendler 2019). The reductionist bent in psychiatry is criticized by Eronen (2019). Also, he explicated the levels of approaches to psychopathology. Haslam et al. (2020) criticized the categorical approach to psychopathology, preferring the dimensional approach. The categorical approach lends itself to a biological and reductionist framework. Bakker (2019) developed a taxonomic system to replace that of traditional classification nosologies in psychiatry. This could undermine its reductionist bent. Other workers ask for caution in revising these categorical psychiatric nosologies (Stanton 2020). In short, the psychiatric field is in turmoil, and my own recommendations on how to revise it might contribute quality suggestions to the issue.

Psychology should examine in more detail the heterogeneous nature of causality (Bolger et al. 2019). Bolger et al. (2019) showed how this could be achieved statistically, which means foregoing classic ANOVA designs. In typical between-subject designs, causality is confounded with measurement and treatment errors. In contrast, within-subject/repeated-measure designs avoid this limitation. Individual differences and causal differentiation in subpopulations can be captured better in such designs. For the statistical technique of path modeling, especially structural equation modeling, Brick and Bailey (2020) presented a way of differentiating possible causal models in the statistics in a study. They referred to their process as the matrix of implied causation (MIC). It determines which model of several competing ones fit best the data. It represents the sum of indirect and direct effects (total effects) of each variable in the model to the other variables involved.

Krpan (2020) wrote a provocative piece on how psychology should integrate traditional or connected psychology with out of the box or disconnected psychology. He used the metaphor from information theory that psychological knowledge is constituted by a reduction in uncertainty. The brain may have evolved toward working to reduce uncertainty (Friston 2010). Theory helps in that role by integrating disparate empirical findings, but they might be hodgepodge and eclectic, with inherent limitations rather than having unified principles. Workers such as Henriques (2003, 2011) have attempted to construct unified theories, but "have not come close" in reaching their objectives. A valuable way of increasing psychological knowledge would be to have connected psychology constantly browse co-existing disconnected psychology works in order to integrate it.

I would add that the present work approach is middle of the road: I have built on the shoulders of giants, as in connected psychology, but ones whose luster has been increasingly set aside by connected psychology (e.g., Piaget, Erikson). At the same time, my approach is definitely disconnected, using heuristics and theory from across the scientific board. In essence, a genuine disconnected psychology should "constantly browse theories, methodologies, and approaches" (Krpan 2020, p. 10) developed by connected psychology in order to better inform its work and also to provide novel insights, methods, and data that can inform connected psychology, somewhat like what I have done in my integrative work.

Beller and Bender (2017) reviewed articles published in Frontiers of Psychology in 2015 and found them lacking theoretically, especially in terms of unification attempts. In a hierarchical structure of terms and concepts, they placed those of laws, mechanisms, models, and simulations between the top level of theory and the bottom level of the hypothesis. Laws are verifiable real-world regularities, models are representations, and mechanisms add causality considerations. The authors cited skeptics on unification (Stam 2015), but called for the project. My work fits the call.

Philosophy. At the philosophical level, Kao (2017) promoted the value of aiming for unification in science. She argued that unification should be a guiding strategy for theory construction, even if used only heuristically. This concords with my prior comment. Kling (2019) referred to Whitehead's metaphysics as involving mind-body unity, integration of subjective, objective, and transpersonal experience as a foundation for interpersonal (transpersonal) psychology. This approach is consistent with my model of interactions as intra-actions, which is decidedly thinking disconnectedly and outside the box. Bella (2019) noted that William James had been interested in the topics of causality, emergence, and free will in his work, being antireductionist and authoring a work on a pluralistic universe. He believed that free creativity activity generates novelty rather than factors such as chance in a strictly cause-effect world. Eustice-Corwin (2020) examined the relevance of Nietzsche's concept of Dasein for psychology, similar to my approach of emphasizing a modified concept of being-in-the-world, but he added a developmental emphasis.

Mechanisms. Miłkowski et al. (2019) put forth that mechanisms are the pathway of unity in psychology, which is entirely consistent with the present argument that causality can be a unifying force in the unification project for psychology (and other disciplines, both within them and across to psychology). Mechanisms could be operational elements or ones that are dynamic and non-decomposable. They should not be vacuous terms like triggers, but detailed ones. Their elucidation should start with functional analysis. They should be consistent in their explanation, and parsimonious, offering complete understanding. They should be mapped in their control roles into other mechanisms. They can include contemporary models, such as dynamics and the free energy principle, and I would add network concepts. Miłkowski et al. (2019) have argued that mechanisms are central to understanding behavior and that they can cohere psychology through their common function in behavior. Miłkowski and Nowakowski (2019) added that dynamic systems contain levels, and that one cannot be reduced to the other, with bottom-up ones ultimately the seat of mechanistic constitutiveness. Rather, the levels in a dynamic system interact and do so over multiple time scales, such that the mechanisms at each level in a behavior's hierarchical system require delineation. Nor should explanatory models be singular, for they are explanatorily pluralistic. The Milkowski scheme for the central role of mechanism toward unifying psychology is a proposition that is the same as the present one. It goes on to explicate diverse causal models and mechanisms, such as activation-inhibition coordination, that are cross-cutting mechanisms in behavior, brain, neuronal activity and organization, and their diverse linkages and interactions.

Next in this thread of articles being discussed on mechanism, Gładziejewski (2019) examined Friston's (2010) free energy principle as a unifying factor in cognition and indeed in general brain processes. In the model, living systems act to minimize the free energy in their sensory states, toward avoiding thermodynamic disorder. In order to accomplish this end, they act to minimize predictive error or the difference between expectations of their sensory states and the actual states. Gładziejewski (2019) concluded that the free energy principle is descriptive and heuristic, but agnostic about mechanism. Moreover, that unification in this field will depend on developing precise predictive processing based mechanistic models of cognitive the phenomena involved. Colombo (2017) clarified that this Bayesian approach in the area of cognition will help surpass the antiquated empiricism-nativism debate by reframing it more productively (specifying better the innate implementing structure required to help in functional learning). Geary (2019) proposed the unifying concept of energy dynamics for intelligence, health, and ageing, even referring to mitochondrial energy powerhouses in the cell in this regard. I have referred to energetics to cover these similar concepts, including the free energy principle in these regards (see Chap. 7).

Colombo and Knauff (2020) reviewed a special topic on levels of explanation in cognitive science and pointed out the disparate views and difficulties in integrating levels from molecules to culture. On the one hand, the reductionist camp relates behavior and brain to molecule, yet. Alternatively, culture has a top-down influence on lower levels. Mechanistic accounts need to specify actual mechanisms, and cross-cutting explanations like networks and dynamics have the potential to bridge levels. However, none appear privileged as far as I understand the article. This latter comment illustrates that, for the authors, there is both personal cognition, which might include causal aspects and understanding, and system-wide cognition of common rules and principles in which it is embedded, with multiple causal inputs to it, from the mind, the environment, and the brain. The explanation will likely remain pluralistic rather than unified or disunified.

Systems. Favela (2020) underscored the value of studying complexity in cognitive science because cognition often exhibits complexity characteristics. Although the range of complexity might render it undefinable and inchoate for some, it has major defining attributes that give a definable profile. The most important of the latter are: (a) nonlinearity in its dynamics, or lack of additive, linear relations among the system elements and system outcomes in configuration; (b) possible emergence in its configured states, or novel re-organization unpredictable from an existing configuration or knowledge of system components; (c) self-organization, or lack of a central node or generator in system configuration; and (d) universality, such as common properties across systems, even living and non-living, such as system states at critical phase shift points, at which they are poised to reconfigure at far-from-equilibrium new state configurations (also systems have order and control parameters; respectively, variables that describe the system's macroscopic or collective organization and variables that guide system dynamics). Favela's (2020) description of complexity science is entirely consistent with the present emphasis that it gives a superordinate language to describe the contents and transformative processes in systems, and universally so, such that even developmental and cognitive systems can be described in its terms. The concept of nonlinear, self-organized emergence is exactly the principle developmental mechanism that I had ascribed to the neo-stage concept of how stages and substages develop in my model of Neo-Piagetian/Neo-Eriksonian (sub) stage development over the lifespan (Young 2011). Also, I have described substage/stage relations and even micro and macro relations in development in terms of fractals. It is also a complexity science concept, as described by Favela's (2020) description of fractal structures; or self-similarity at different levels of a macrosystem into the microsystem.

Another important aspect of complexity theory is that of attractors. Reed (2020) mentions them in a big picture article for psychology. Attractors define state configurations in which the field gravitates consistently to pockets in the full geometric state-space available in the system, according to parameter specifications of the variables involved. Among the most well-known are point, bifocal, cyclical, and chaotic attractors (which are actually quite orderly), as well as multiple attractor configurations, as happens in living systems.

Jirsa et al. (2019) presented a novel dynamical model that lies at the basis of a grand unified brain theory. They indicated that their dynamical concept has more currency in this regard than others like the free energy principle. They based their work on low-level motor coordinative dynamical processes, which they consider insufficient to capture higher-order cognition. They referred to a two-tiered fast and slow dynamical system that generally underlies brain and behavior organization. The authors maintained that dynamical models offer more about the process than network models, which are limited to nodes or foci and edges or links. In motor coordination type tasks, nervous system activity generates low-dimensional dynamics, serving to reduce the collection of available neuromuscular degrees of freedom in the sensorimotor system to a reduced number. However, low-dimensional dynamics does not help explain many real-world behaviors. In a higher-order organization that allows for temporal unfolding in more complex behavior, a structured flow on manifolds develop. The model envisages the system is high-dimensional with more degrees of freedom than in low-level dynamics and that it is highly nonlinear. At the lower level dynamics or the creation of behavior in context, the action time scale takes place quickly, in milliseconds, while a slower dynamical regime that is linked to actual task behavior and its changes takes place over seconds, as in cognition and task action behavior. The two dynamics co-exist and influence each other in a rich model; and help explain brain's richness in its adaptation. This model adds detail to the nonlinear dynamical systems model supported in the present work. It supports a multiple level analysis of levels in cognitive behavior. One could add other levels that are more macro in time scale, such as in the development of substages and stages over months and years. We can posit that the degrees of freedom at these higher-order levels have even more degrees of freedom than other levels lower than them in the hierarchical dynamical arrangement of levels in cognition over time.

Networks. As for another causal axis in the present work, that of networks, Robinaugh et al. (2019) reviewed the network approach to psychopathology. Symptoms interact among themselves causally. Rather than reflecting an underlying latent variable, such as depression, the symptoms of depression should be the focus because they drive other symptoms depending on whether their nodes (symptoms) are central and their edges (links) strong. Networks have characteristics, such as connectivity, clustering, and community. Nodes are examined for their centrality or strength. Despite the burgeoning research, modeling of psychiatric symptoms as causal networks need more robust theorizing, as in adding dynamical systems theory and critical evaluation (e.g., Young 2015, cited in this regard).

Bertolero and Bassett (2020) called for cross-level (scale) mechanistic explanations in neuroscience, quite like Young (2015). The brain consists of macro regional networks, micro neuronal networks, and more specific networks between them, such as the visual cortex network. The edges in these networks could be within or between them, and the links within levels influence other levels through intra-level linkages. Similarly, intermediate levels in posttraumatic stress disorder (PTSD) have been found that involve perceptions and appraisals rather than the symptoms themselves (e.g., Frewen et al. 2013). For recent PTSD research from a network perspective, see Cramer et al. (2020), which ends up supporting the DSM nosological approach to PTSD. At the same time, Weems (2020) asked whether the network approach calls into question the reality of PTSD and asks for further theorizing.

Savi et al. (2019) presented a wiring of an intelligence model based on networks. The formalism of the model is complex and beyond the scope of the present chapter. Briefly, intelligence is constituted by evolving, developmental networks in which new knowledge and procedures are wired together in the network's activity of nodes and edges. The model allows for proper study of individual differences in intelligence, yet common properties, too, such as stage development. Network connections can grow through genetics or the environment (education). An individual's network grows into communities and hierarchizes, including into equilibrated states, accounting for generalized abilities. These might bifurcate through growth mechanisms and repair (rewire) mechanisms keep them stable. Learning takes place gradually, one skill at a time, but discontinuous phases might appear when entire clusters grow obtained knowledge (perhaps through generalization, reaching a cusp of change, not specified). Larger clusters are more stable, perhaps meaning they can resist perturbation better, but in systems theory, they would gravitate to the cusp of change and bifurcate when perturbations push the system to the far-from-equilibrium point). To be fair, my parenthetic comments do not account for the mathematical formalisms of the model). Further, Savi et al. (2019) described the wiring intelligence model as a unification one, and one that is quite different from the typical factor analytic model of intelligence, with its "mysterious" latent structures. My only comment here is that a full hierarchical model might have levels in intelligence somewhat equivalent to latent factors and that intermediate levels in the system could be represented by different network structures that influence bottom-up and top-down ones equally in a full system approach. In this sense, new levels in a hierarchical network system can emerge from the interactions in the network. Fesce (2020) also argued that networks allow for emergence, the products of which can influence behavior, such as in the case of subjectivity/consciousness. To conclude, it is acknowledged that the stage development component of the model is not the same as the Piagetian one in cognitive development, but the point is well taken that the network that cognitive skills at any one substage of my Neo-Piagetian model can be represented ideographically by a changing network of nodes and edges.

Lange et al. (2020) elaborated on the network model as it applies to emotions. The latent variable model, for example, is insufficient to explain emotions. Causality does not lie with an underlying latent construct but with the interaction of the components in a network. For example, in an anger network, arousal could be the driver of other emotional components. Networks include nodes and edges, such as just described, but also organizational properties, such as tight linkages with short paths, which make them "small world." According to the authors, networks can create weakly emergent higher-order levels, but they are not strong or have more than weak downward causal effects on the network's microstates or network configurations of the system.

The example of applying network concepts to emotions shows the widespread influence the model is having in psychology. At the same time, I would argue that different levels of a system can develop from bottom level interactions and emerge from them, acting equally on the full system as the original level in the system. Multiple levels can develop this way through emergence and lead to multiple reciprocal interactions among levels in a system. For example, an angry predisposition could develop from lower-order anger networks and trigger quickly lower-order anger reactions. Or, a psychiatric disorder could develop with anger as a central component, such as intermittent explosive disorder, and influence lower-order anger levels and their component network interactions. That is, drivers of the anger-related system could be found both within and between different levels of the individualized systems that develop in people, not to mention the temporal dynamics of change in development that could affect individualized network dynamics and causation.

Hoffart and Johnson (2020) contrasted latent variable approaches to network ones for mental problems, their episodic clusters of temporal structures, and their causal processes. They argued for an extended network approach to better elucidate mechanisms, focusing on episodic clusters in this regard. Any effort to add to network modeling is helpful, but my own approach calls for multilevel hierarchical networks. They would be dynamical, temporal tracking, etc. In a related conceptual article, although not a network one, Zilcha-Mano (2020) argued that mechanisms of change in psychotherapy would be understood better by distinguishing individual traits and state changes.

Combined Modeling. Bayer et al. (2020) combined dynamical and network modeling in their work on social network cognition, referring to activation processes across networks in this regard. Wens et al. (2019) found cross-brain integration of momentary networked (default mode network, DMN) functional connectivities in a dynamic global brain integration, including the default mode network (DMN). Wang et al. (2019b) also linked dynamics and brain networks including the DMN, in their case, to depression. Brette (2018) argued that the brain is dynamic, circular (e.g., coupled to the environment), and distributed in causal structure so that the putative neural (encoding, decoding) code is insufficient to represent its functioning. This is especially true because the causal structure of the neuronal code (e.g., linear) cannot fit the brain's causal structure (e.g., nonlinear). Relations constitute information, not sensory signals, for example. Cell assemblies cannot code or represent relations. By attributing such representations to neural codes, we incorrectly give them the power of causation in the brain, which they do not have. The neuron functions as a dynamic system as much as the brain, and thus there is a coupled dynamic system at two levels (brain, neuron), which themselves are coupled. The metaphor of the neural code does not add substance to this nonlinear modeling of the brain. Behavior itself is considered nonlinear and dynamic throughout my writing. In this view, causality resides in the functioning of the system and not in some extra central generator, supervenient representation, etc., which is consistent with the view of Brette (2018).

Evolution has been the focus of unification attempts across sub-disciplines; with development in Uller et al. (2019) and with ecology in Brady et al. (2019). Uller and Laland (2019a, b) proposed a broad view of causation in evolution. Long dominated by classic Darwinian thought. They argued that evolutionary theory needs to put causality at the forefront. The distinction between ultimate causation (natural variation and selection/evolution/heredity, differential fitness; function/adaptation) and proximal causation (physiology, developmental mechanisms) is a valid one; however, they are complementary without the former being privileged, unlike what classical biology might maintain. In this regard, the causal system in explaining behavior needs to examine the role of the phenotype and not just the genotype as drivers in evolution. For example, in niche construction, the individual acts on the environment to construct favorable adaptive niches for survival and reproduction. Classical genetics is now complemented by epigenetics, cultural evolution or differential collective effects on evolution, the evolution of social learning and developmental plasticity, the transmission of resources by parents to offspring, etc. Causality resides in the whole biological system. According to the authors, the new biology is consistent with the scientific endeavor, generally, which typically attempts to establish causality. Also, see Elimari and Lafargue (2020) for another view of the role network science can play in elucidating evolutionary mechanisms.

Activation-Inhibition Coordination. The activation-inhibition coordination model has been presented as one that can help explain mechanistically different levels of brain-behavior relationships, from the neuronal to the brain network level, and to behavior and its organization. Spencer (2020) theorized that dynamic field theory network modeling of working memory can help explain its development through its underlying neural process. In this regard, Spencer related the sustained attention required in working memory to self-sustained activation of attention-relevant neural populations. During the time that these neurons remain in the active state, the modeling indicates that they excite neighboring neurons locally, while inhibiting surround ones, in a local excitation/surround inhibition function. The surround inhibition creates a barrier to spreading activation. Active sites also inhibit neighbors that are far away in a gradient fashion with respect to the distance involved. This model of neuronal activation and inhibition does not use the term activation-inhibition coordination, but it is consistent with it.

Yang et al. (2019) also combined network and dynamical concepts in their study of emotion systems in adolescence. They considered emotions as dynamically evolving moment-to-moment experiences that build long term patterns, including individually and psycho-pathologically, where applicable. The emotions are synchronized/coordinated and possibly emergent. Emotions reflect activity in the sympathetic and parasympathetic nervous systems, among others, so are activatory and damping/inhibitory. The two systems coordinate or express mutuality in excitatory positive feedback loops and inhibitory feedback loops, which can express dyscoordination and inappropriate escalated equilibrium points. The inhibitory feedback is equivalent to emotional regulation, which should be considered intrinsic to the emotional process. This model contrasts with the more static factor analytic/latent variable approach to emotions. The Yang et al. (2019) work on dynamical emotion expression and development is consistent with the present emphasis that a critical common mechanism in psychology is activation-inhibition coordination, which should be found at all levels from neuron to brain to behavior.

Turner et al. (2020) also developed an activation-inhibition model, and for them it applied to chronic pain. They applied the BAS and BIS systems model to chronic pain, with the acronyms standing for behavioral approach or activation system and behavioral inhibition system, respectively (Gray 1990; Gray and McNaughton 2003). Generally, the inhibition system is associated with the negative consequences in chronic pain, such as a pain being associated with cue for punishment and interference functionally. The present approach to activation-inhibition coordination is somewhat different than the BIS-BAS approach, because it does not regard the systems as independent but as necessarily well-coordinated in adaptive function. The work of Sainburg is consistent with the present approach (e.g., Schaffer and Sainburg 2021), which considers that the hemispheres work in tandem but that the dominant (usually) left hemisphere specializes in predictive rather than reactive control relative to the non-dominant hemisphere, a skill which appears to need a good activation-inhibition coordination (Young 2016, 2019).

I developed the activation-inhibition coordination model of brain and behavior in my work on infant reaching, in which the right hand was found to be better coordinated than the left one (e.g., see Young 2011, 2016). Research on lateralization indicates that the cerebral hemispheres begin differentiating early in life (Vannucci et al. 2019). This does not mean that the environment has no influence, as found in preference shift studies (Marcori et al. 2019). The left hemisphere is posited as the seat of activation-inhibition coordination, with the right hemisphere specializing in less complex inhibition skills, such as outright inhibition. In this context, Tisseyre et al. (2018) found that, in right-handers, mirror movements in the opposite non-active hand were more frequent in left-hand activity compared to right-hand activity. Although not expressed this way by the authors, this finding suggests that in the tasks and measures used, the left hand in non-activity exhibits less mirror movements because of right hemisphere inhibition, which is consistent with the present model. The left hemisphere specializes for the most complex skills, and they can be seen to reflect activation-inhibition coordination (e.g., Strijkers et al. 2019, for language related skills; and Ambrosini et al. 2019, for executive functioning). These skills have evolved (e.g., Prieur et al. 2019) and they are reflected in nonhuman primate chimpanzees (the hemispheres, Hopkins et al. 2019; in social gestures, Roberts et al. 2019).

The literature review to this point has emphasized the unification project that is increasing in psychology and the common mechanisms that might underlie it, including dynamical systems, networks, and activation-inhibition coordination. The present work is the only one in the literature that has attempted to unify the areas of nonlinear dynamical systems theory, networks, and activation-inhibition coordination. The next part of the literature review examines recent integrative efforts in psychology that, in their own way, speak to the unification project more than the dominant specialized silo approach in psychology. However, these articles are simply trying to integrate over areas or ideas and are not seeking more general unifications.

Unification Fields

The following lists a series of recent integrative approaches in psychology, some being at common psychological processes and others being over psychological subdisciplines. Integration partly works against the idea of reductionism, and its typical biological/medical emphasis. An interesting article in this regard is the finding of poor test-retest reliability of common task-related functional fMRI measures (Elliott et al. 2020). This works against using these tasks as biomarkers. Generally, there are not common genetic or environmental influences even in related areas, such as normative personality, abnormal personality traits, and personality disorder symptoms (Kendler et al. 2019). Epigenetic influences moderate the effect so genes, as well (Bierer et al. 2020; Scorza et al. 2020). The mind has components of free will, as evidenced through maplike representations of its comparable internal and external foraging mechanisms (Todd and Hills 2020), adding to the spectrum of causality influences on behavior and further reducing the validity of biological/medical reductionism.

Mele (2018) argued that the scientific criticisms against the notion of free will in behavior are not viable. Genschow et al. (2020) showed that antifree will interventions can alter perception of free will beliefs, but in the case of judges, not their sentencing. Free will belief is therefore an important part of our psychological make-up, and malleable, although most of us do have the belief no matter what is our country or our culture of origin, as per Baumeister. For Baumeister (2018a, b) and Baumeister and Lau (2020) free will is part of the human essence, had evolutionary advantages, and promotes our moral psychology. Baumeister and Lau (2020) argued that causality is multiple, excludes determinism, and allows for multiple possibilities in behavior rather than inevitable outcomes based on deterministic cause and effect. In this argument, belief in free will, and viewing humans as agents in their own behavior, is part of the causal system.

Heyes (2020) referred to evolution (nature) of cognitive mechanisms and the effects of learning in the environment (nurture) on them, but added cultural evolution (social interaction made fit by cultural evolution) to the influences on them. Derex and Mesoudi (2020) referred to a similar concept of cumulative cultural evolution. Armstrong-Carter et al. (2020) referred to the interactive concept of genetic nurture—parent genetics influence rearing environment and consequently offspring outcome. The concept is a social genetic one (Domingue et al. 2018). They studied how the prenatal environment mediates the association between maternal genetics and offspring educational attainment and school readiness development at ages 4–7 years. The results held even when offspring genetics was controlled in seeking the effects of maternal genetics. The maternal genetic effect investigated related to ones known to be associated with maternal education. The prenatal mediators that mediated the investigated relationship concerned maternal SES and secondarily maternal health composite scores. The authors concluded that genes should be considered malleable and the environment is not uniquely exogenous.

Also, in line with this view, Avinun (2019) presented a complex argument that genetics can influence stressful life events and also socioeconomic status; genetics and environment effects become blurred in large-scale genome-wide association studies (GWAS) research, as the results reflect both direct and indirect genetic effects. That said, the environment in terms of early life stresses has been shown to have an independent contribution adolescent major depression, especially early emotional abuse (LeMoult et al. 2020). Similarly, the environment has effects independent of genetics in neurodevelopmental disorders—paternal age, low birth weight, birth defects, perinatal hypoxia, and respiratory distress in the case of autism, for example (Carlsson et al. 2020). [For further research on characterizing the environment, see Evans 2021.]

However, a simple additive effect of the environment in a biopsychosocial model of development is too simplistic. For example, Smith and Pollak (2021) added that the perception of the adversity in the environment in context, more than the objective facts of the early stressor involved, determines the biobehavioral response and whether it is deleterious or not. Mechanism is not mechanical, so to speak, but interactive, in determining neuro-developmental effects of early adversity (e.g., neglect, abuse). [For further research on the interactions of biology and early adversity, see Aafjes-van Doorn et al. 2019, Gunnar 2020, Huang and Starr 2020, Milojevich et al. 2020, Parenteau et al. 2020, Tarullo et al. 2020, Tottenham 2020, and Wade et al. 2020.]. Also, in the Gibsonian view on affordances, or direct perception of the environment without cognitive mediation (Chong and Proctor 2019), it appears that the environment invites perception in and of itself, having an independent status in our psychology.

Another line of research on interactive influences in behavior concerns early social inter-coordinations, even with neonates. Wass et al. (2020) referred to neural entrainment in this regard. The influences are bidirectional, and include concurrent and sequential entrainment in order to engage phase locking, which optimizes infant encoding. Also, interpersonal neural entrainment plays a causal role in early learning in this regard. Similarly, Piazza et al. (2019) referred to time-locked neural coupling. The infants were studied at age 11 months. The neural coupling especially involved their prefrontal cortex (PFC). The authors concluded that the dynamic view of development helps explain the results. Curtindale et al. (2019) examined another kind of synchrony in 4- to 8-month-olds. Video stimuli that were synchronous in social stimuli elicited more sustained attention than asynchronous (visual, auditory) stimuli. And social stimuli showed the effect compared to non-social stimuli. Infants appear selected for rapid social learning in multiple ways, illustrating a multifactorial causality in their early social behavior. That infants learn these types of synchronies illustrates the reciprocal model. Alternatively, Krzeczkowski et al. (2020) showed that, in socially avoidant mothers, the driver in 9-month-old EEG-measured frontal asymmetries (FA) at rest were maternal and not infant resting-state FA in two emotion-eliciting conditions (happy, fear) subsequent to the EEG measurements. [For further interactional synchrony research, see DePasquale 2020 and Novembre and Iannetti 2021.]

Overall, examination of current causality concepts suggests that unifactorial causality as a factor in human behavior is not tenable, either way, in terms of Nature or Nurture. And even simplistic models of causality combining both should be analyzed in depth.

Crespi (2020) explored evolutionary genetics in relation to clinical psychology and psychiatry. He emphasized the dynamical, nonlinear systems view of development and psychopathology. Le and Stein (2019) mapped causal pathways from GWAS research in imaging to neuropsychiatric disorders. They found relations with common genetic variants and disorders such as Major Depression, Attention Hyperactivity Disorder, and Bipolar Disorder, but GWAS typically has limitations in the amount of variation explained in neuropsychiatric outcome. They underscored that brain imaging is not enough to understand causal pathways in these regards, because the pathways indicated need complementary research on cellular and synaptic structure in specific brain regions. They give a rich analysis of endophenotypic and mediational models in the pathway from genetic variation to neuropsychiatric disorder, and the mediating role of the brain, including its structural phenotype. Haynes et al. (2020) proposed a causality model of psychopathology that resembles network approaches. These articles summarize conceptualization and research that are consistent with my own multifactorial causal model of behavior.

In an article on unifying psychoanalysis, Eagle (2020) argued for the centrality of ego psychology. In an article on unifying psychotherapy, Ecker and Bridges (2020) argued that psychiatric symptoms in psychotherapy reflect a common process of emotional learning in semantic memory and memory reconsolidation has a role to play in emotional learning. Strand (2020) attempted to unify biological and learning/cultural accounts of attachment theory in a biobehavioral-cultural bidirectional model. Moriarity et al. (2020) also explored a bidirectional model, in their case for associations between inflammatory biomarkers and depressive symptoms in adolescence. This empirical study found apparent causal associations between dysphoria and an inflammatory phenotype. Inflammation has increasingly been considered a cross-diagnostic mediator in psychopathology. Chahal et al. (2020) related neuroconnectivity biotypes (diffuse, hyper in connection) to adolescent internalizing problems. Harden et al. (2019) examined multiple integrative concepts in their association, including a general factor in psychopathology, transdiagnostic symptoms of psychopathology, and a general executive function. Also, from a causal perspective, they studied genetic associations in these regards. Millgram et al. (2020) related psychopathology to the process of dysfunctional emotional regulation and the dysregulated emotional goals involved. Bresin (2020) wrote an article unifying diverse dysregulated behavior.

Cognitively and in learning, Namkoong and Henderson (2019) argued that abstract thinking serves to reduce causal uncertainty. This fits my own notion that causal thinking is the hallmark of the species, as in the concept of humans as *Homo Causa*. Chater et al. (2020) attempted an integration of Bayesian cognitive science and of judgement/decision making science. They argued that the brain might lie between calculating with probabilities and using representation by approximating probabilistic calculations using sampling methods (Bayesian sampling). Bender (2020) argued that causal cognition is not just statistical but also cultural, taking a broadened view of the activity.

As for learning, Makino (2018) viewed cortical learning in terms of top-down control over unified topics. Bar (2021) developed the concept of the unified mind by integrating top-down and bottom-up processes over multiple domains, from perception, attention, and thought to openness to experience and affect. The mind varies from the broad to the narrow in these regards. These ideas are consistent with those in Chap. 13 on transemics.

The area of the self has seen recent articles devoted to integration. In this regard, Beni (2018) worked on the relational self and Sosa and dos Santos (2018) on impulsivity and self-control. Similarly, Martin (2019) presented a cross-discipline construct of persons and their lives in context, Osborne-Crowley (2020) argued for a unified social cognition and social reality, and Basten and Touyz (2019) referred to the integrating concept of sense of self. Cole et al. (2018) presented a unified model of self-regulation that included executive function and dynamical modeling. Santens et al. (2020) presented a transdiagnostic model on psychopathology related to effortful control. Beauchaine and Cicchetti (2019) used emotion dysregulation in this regard. Relatedly, Sisto et al. (2019) created a transversal definition of psychological resilience. The social area has recent integrative articles at least partially with a dynamic focus (Amazeen 2018; Saxbe et al. 2019). Macpherson et al. (2019) applied the dynamical model to social dynamics in subclinical psychopathology. Lastly, Corr (2019), Petrides (2019), Mullins-Sweatt et al. (2019), and Henriques (2017) have integrative articles on personality. Mullins-Sweatt et al. (2019) focused on disinhibition as a unifying construct in this regard, although I would expand it to activation-inhibition coordination, as we have seen. The Henriques (2017) article is an extension of Henriques' (2011) unified theory of psychology. It referred to five-character-adaptation systems, including justification. Also, its mind-brain system includes four levels—sensory motor, operant experiential, imaginative thought, and linguistic justification. These levels correspond quite well with Piaget's four stages, showing the parallel in his work and mine.

Conclusion

The next section of the literature review treats developmental publications. To review the key themes to date in the literature review, the literature that has appeared in the last year on the major topics included in the present work generally helps make the most critical of the points being made, such as the importance of unifying psychology, causality, and mechanisms, activation-inhibition coordination in this regard, the value of integrated models, dynamical and network models, and practical applications, especially in psychopathology. The next part of the literature review, in particular, is on the developmental topics of Piagetian research, Eriksonian research, causality, dynamics, executive function, and lateralization.

Development

Piagetian Research

Kallio (2020a) provides a benchmark in the transition beyond classis Piagetian thinking to contemporary views of the development of adult thinking. It includes limitations of the Piagetian approach, post-Piagetian developments, and new directions in the field. This review focuses on the Piagetian aspects of the book. In Kallio (2020b), Piagetian developmental cognitive stages are described in terms of the growth toward causal thinking, or cause-effect relations (Inhelder and Piaget 1958; Piaget 1972). We develop toward using scientific hypothetico-deductive thought, as in causal reasoning. The stages are considered universal, with individual differences outside their scope. Causal or logical reasoning evolves continuously within stages and leap into hierarchically arranged superordinate stages at transition points. The adult stage is a formal, abstract one, beginning in adolescence, with no stage developing beyond that one. Other workers applied Piagetian stage theory to the development of moral reasoning (e.g., Kohlberg 1984), which is not reviewed here. Other workers developed different models of stages or their equivalent in development (e.g., King and Kitchener 2002; Perry 1970) and, aside from their description in the Kallio book, they had been described and compared in Young (2011). Theories have been presented with Neo-Piagetian stage and substage sequences or variants (e.g., Commons and Richards 1984; Demetriou and Efklides 1985; Fischer 1980; surprisingly, the model of Case is not mentioned; Case 1991). Many models describing a postformal adult stage have been proposed, as well (e.g., relativistic, dialectic, contextual integrative, Kallio's preferred term, Kallio 2011). As cited by Kallio, see Basseches (2005), Labouvie-Vief (2015), and Sinnott (1998) for postformal Neo-Piagetian theories. Once more, these workers are well-described in Young (2011), aside from presentation in Kallio. My own version of the postformal stage is referred to as Collective Intelligence, and its description attempts to integrate other models (Young 2011). The Kallio book presents a systems view of development, but it uses older literature. Moreover, it argues that Piaget was especially mechanistic and not systemic enough in approach, although Young (2011) had shown that Piaget was integrating systems theory as his work progressed.

The following part of the Piagetian literature review of recently published material is organized according to age period. However, the first article by Ratcliff (2018) underscores that Piaget was more interested in process and the development of competencies than the ages of the acquisitions. Ratcliff (2018) came across previously unpublished notebooks on the observations that he and his wife, Valentine, made together on their first child, Jacqueline, in 1925. His prior work had been on older children. His infancy publications in 1936, 1937, and 1945 were based, in part on these personal observations (Piaget, 1936/1963; 1937/1954; and 1945/1951, respectively). Piaget and his wife included 1200 pages based on 10,000 observations and "experiments," which involved trying to stimulate reactions in Jacqueline through interventions such as trying to elicit imitations. Piaget traced one behavior at a time longitudinally, and showed their relations to other behaviors. Thus, there were multiple, specific, and multi-relational or multi-linked networks of developmental paths that were observed longitudinally.

Piaget formulated infancy "stages" (really substages, Young 2011) to structure his observations, such as for imitation. The body was a focus, as per his qualification of the infant stage as sensorimotor. At the same time, the sensorimotor stage witnesses the growth toward intentionality, representation, but without dismissing embodiment in cognition (Young 2011). According to Ratcliff (2018), the observations made by Piaget and his wife illustrate Piaget's third way stance in the growth of mind and behavior—instead of learning and nativism, that of constructivism. Piaget did not consider himself a developmental psychologist but a genetic epistemologist, in that he was interested in how knowledge acquisition unfolded, the process, the paths, and their linkages, and not just their descriptions. Ratcliff's (2018) conclusion that the infant constructs a growing puzzle (a temporal puzzle) in putting together her personal observations and experiments fits the constructivist stance of Piaget in how the child develops (or grows epistemologically).

Babik et al. (2018) investigated longitudinally means-end problem solving in 6- to 24-month-olds using two tasks to obtain a supported object—pulling a towel and rotating a turntable. The tasks allowed for checking age differences, individual differences, and task transfer in skill. Piaget (1953), of course, had examined means-end problem solving in infancy, and related steps in the acquisition to his six sensorimotor substages. The results confirmed that intentionality was evident earlier on the easier towel pulling task, the infants used diverse exploratory strategies, and they eventually transferred skills between tasks. Not all research supports the Piagetian point of view. For example, Dunn and Bremner (2019) investigated the A-not-B task used in Piagetian object permanence research for the sensorimotor stage. When the experimenter looked at location B, in particular, in the 9-month-olds tested, task success improved, pointing out a heretofore unacknowledged confound in the typical tasks used to investigate the concept.

Rindermann and Ackermann (2020) conducted an interesting study on the relationship, in 4- to 10-year-olds, over three research samples, of intelligence test and Piagetian cognitive task performance. Factor analysis indicated a common intelligence factor, with processing speed more related to the psychometric measure of intelligence and parental education more related to Piagetian task performance. The authors considered that the psychometric tasks used tapped fluid intelligence and the Piagetian ones tapped crystalized intelligence. The Piagetian tasks used in the study varied with age, but the study had common ones over two or more samples (ages), depending, which involved number, classes, invariances, and spatiotemporal relations. The results of the study suggest to this author that the typical assumption in the literature, of Piagetian cognitive development—that, in its nature, it is primarily maturational, universal, and not subject to individual differences and environmental effects—is not tenable. This implication of the research by Rindermann and Ackermann (2020) is consistent with the present neo-stage approach to cognitive development.

Börnert-Ringleb and Wilbert (2018) investigated strategies in concrete operational tasks. The concrete operational stage follows the preoperational stage, which ensues after the sensorimotor stage (Piaget 1947). The children were 7 years old. The tasks were on number conservation, classification, and ball sequencing; all were concrete operational tasks, with number conservation being usually the first to emerge. The study is novel in that it found that children used strategies that Piaget had not considered. For example, according to Piaget, children might reverse operations to establish equality, but this was rarely used as a strategy in this study. The result fits my own observations in Young and Décarie (1977), in which I also identified individual differences in Piagetian conservation behavior. For example, in the reversal operation (negation), unlike what Piaget had considered worth emphasizing.

Morra et al. (2019) studies children from the preschool age to grade 5 in one study and in grades 6 and 7 in a second study. They studied their working memory capacity in relation to quantitative tasks. The tasks chosen were reflective of the concept of central conceptual structures (Case 1991; Case and Okamoto 1996). Central conceptual structures are cognitive ensembles (networks/relations of semantic nodes/schemes) that help integrate domains, such as in narratives and spatial concepts, yet are not like full-scale stages integrating all cognitive concepts within a stage as "structure d'ensemble." The quantitative tests used in the two studies were on number knowledge and rational numbers, respectively. The working memory tests involved a test of backward word span of 2- or 3-syllable words and a test referred to as the Mr. Cucumber test, with a figural intersection test added for the second study, along with forward and listening span tests and a trail making one. The results confirmed the role of working memory in quantitative central conceptual structure development. These results support the Neo-Piagetian search for the mechanisms underlying cognitive development, which is more current in the last decades in Piagetian research than research on (sub)stage sequences.

Kazi et al. (2019) studied longitudinally in 4- to 10-year-olds the novel concept of cognizance in cognitive development. The concept is Neo-Piagetian, and relates to mediators in cognitive development beyond those considered, such as working memory and executive function. Cognizance concerns awareness of cognitive processes, such as awareness of perceptual and inferential origins of knowledge, first-order theory of mind (ToM) and second-order ToM and awareness of procedural characteristics and demands (similarities and differences) between cognitive processes. It is more than meta-cognition, for it is meta-cognition in active cognition, as far as I understand it. The target cognitive task concerned inductive and deductive reasoning. Reflecting is the active component of cognizance, a concept similar to Piaget's reflective abstraction (Piaget 2001).

The Demetriou team (Demetriou and Spanoudis 2018) described four phases, called cycles, in cognitive development that are quite like Piaget's and Case's. They referred to them as episodic representations, realistic mental representations, generic rules organizing representations, and overarching principles. Mastery varies in individuals, over domains. The study used tasks that were keyed to the appropriate phases for the ages of the subjects.

As for the study results, Kazi et al. (2019) found that cognizance takes the lead in the momentum of development within a phase leading toward transformation toward the next one. Also, it stands as a proxy for general change involving reasoning and executive function. The ToM tasks were involved in the results, but so were the other cognizance tasks. They included a perceptual and inference awareness test involving videos in a Raven-like matrix test. Another test involved awareness of cognitive processes, asking which task in paired tasks (reasoning and ToM tasks) easier. Overall, the results give new avenues on the drivers of cognitive development, while supporting a stage-like conception of development akin to Piaget's. My own model of neo-stages is comparable to theirs, as is my neo-stage sequence of reflexive, sensorimotor, perioperational (preoperational and concrete operational), abstract/formal, and postformal collective intelligence stages. Demetriou et al. (2019) conducted another study on children, cognitive development, and cognizance, but this time the latter was the "weak link" in the results. Further research is required on the concept.

Jeon et al. (2019) studied adolescent deductive reasoning stages, arguing that Piaget's (1971) theory applies to this area. They administered a competence profile test of deductive reasoning to 11- to 18-year-olds. They found multiple results that differentiated Piagetian concrete and formal operational stage adolescents.

As for adult development, Girgis et al. (2018) used another Neo-Piagetian theory of adult development in their piece on neuroscience and adult cognitive development (Kegan 1994). They argued that continuous changes in the neural substrate might support discrete developmental stage growth. Specifically, connectionist brain models include dynamic modeling in which relatively small changes in parameters are local and generate qualitative changes leading to stage emergence (e.g., Spencer et al. 2012). Interestingly, Girgis et al. refer to excitatory and inhibitory influences in this regard, e.g., locally excitatory interactions and laterally inhibitory interactions. Reading of Spencer et al. (2012) shows an elaborate model of activation and inhibition interaction in dynamic neural fields, which are modeled fields of layered excitatory neurons and layered inhibitory interneurons. The model does not explicitly mention activation-inhibition coordination nor was their version of the concept applied to behavior itself; or superordinate organization in the brain, unlike myself. Noteworthy, Spencer et al. applied the model to the Piagetian A-not-B task in infancy. As for Kegan's stage model, it has five stages of orders of mind—impulsive, imperial, socialized, self-authoring, and self-transforming. The stages can be seen as akin to my own, but they are more on the socioemotional rather than the cognitive side. In my similar approach, I created parallel Neo-Eriksonian (sub) stages to the Neo-Piagetian (sub)stages, leading to a 5-stage × 5-substage model, or a model of lifespan development with 25 steps.

Akpan et al. (2020) attempted to formalize a nonlinear dynamical mathematical model of stage equilibrium and transition in the context of a computational model for education. They referred to Piagetian equilibrium in this regard, and they also referred to their model as Neo-Piagetian, citing Young (2011). Needleless to say, the mathematics is beyond the scope of the present work, and indeed of my knowledge base to review in depth.

Clinically, Piagetian stage modeling (Piaget 1964) has helped in depression research. Sondermann et al. (2020) found that preoperational thinking was associated with depression severity. They used a scale that measured prelogical and precausal thinking, as per Piaget's model, in this empirical research (e.g., Klein et al. 2018). My own application of Piagetian thought to understanding clinical difficulties has focused on my 25-step Neo-Piagetian/Neo-Eriksonian model (Young 2019).

Eriksonian Research

The recent Eriksonian literature does not include revisions of his classic eight-stage lifespan model. However, several papers have been published on new phases that seem applicable to development in adulthood. Erskine (2019) examined the therapeutic implications of Erikson's (1963) first three stages, which focus on Trust, Autonomy, and Initiative and their polar opposites, respectively, e.g., mistrust. Oron et al. (2020) used Erikson's (1963) theory in their work on early emotional education. Syed et al. (2020) studied personality development from the preschool to the adult years, including in identity development (Erikson 1968). Other adolescent identity research also cites Erikson (1968)—Topolewska-Siedzik et al. (2018) and Verschueren et al. (2019). Lawford et al. (2019) showed the developmental relations between identity development, adult intimacy, and generativity. Three papers present new stages or reconsideration of adult life phases—Athan (2020) on reproductive identity, Mehta et al. (2020) on established adulthood, and Infurna et al. (2020) on the midlife period. Only the last article cites Erikson (1963).

Generally, these articles do not deal with anything applicable to the present Neo-Eriksonian model, aside from indicating that the Eriksonian model still has currency today. The latter three articles on phases in adulthood show that adults confront normative adult tasks and challenges despite perhaps not having passed through in an equilibrated way every step of development as described by the present Neo-Eriksonian model. Difficulty at one level or the other of the adolescent and early adult levels do not stop basic adult development from taking place and responsibilities being taken. But the inner affective life and sociality of the person might be compromised in unique ways at each developmental time point. This is according to the model, depending on the confluence of experience, skill, support, and so on. In this sense, the present model adds to the normative ones by specifying how difficulties at each of the adolescent and adult phases in life can be expounded more clearly by referring to the present model.

Causal Learning

The brain and consequent behavior are considering probability estimate or predictive Bayesian machines, in which priors condition adaptation to the environment by canalizing options to those that limit uncertainty (Brette 2018; Colombo 2017; Gładziejewski 2019). Statistical learning is relevant to causal learning because by seeking out regularities, the causal sequences in perception are apprehended, and the causes of those sequences are understood better, facilitating the adaptive predictions toward reducing uncertainty. Statistical learning is a cross-domain concept, such that it applies to multiple developmental tasks and is not modular. Indeed, it is often accompanied by the argument that behavior is governed by the scale-free cross brain/behavior equilibrium-seeking free-energy principle, in which generalized uncertainty reduction is critical. From an evolutionary point of view, modularism makes sense; we inherit specific skill honed to the ecological niche for reproductive and survival purposes. But more generalized, context-wide skills also foster adaptation and fitness by the plasticity and targeted deployment of the skills to a broader arrange of contexts and required adaptive behaviors. In this sense, the statistical learning perspective is as much a biological and evolutionarily acquired skills as much as one that allows for the environment to affect and condition behavior. Simultaneously, given the current emphasis on the biopsychosocial model and its components, statistical learning allows for ongoing adaptation to the environment and agentic choice to fit the context and future patterns that are predicted. It affords the decision-maker latitude in choices because the predictions are probabilistic and not determined. There is room for individualized motivation, choice preferences, personality, should that apply, and so on, in the decision-making matrix.

Köster et al. (2020) and Saffran (2020) examined infant learning in infancy from the perspective of statistical learning, prediction, and reducing uncertainty, referring to the approach as a unifying one. Köster et al. described the viewpoint of predictive processing (PP) as a mechanism in behavior to reduce predictive errors (Clark 2013). The brain is hierarchically organized, and predictive modeling takes place at every level of the brain system. Learning takes place in the mismatches between prediction and perception, and feedback to higher levels of the system alters the priors for the next required predictions. The infant apperceives statistical regularities in the environment and forms generative models of the environment on which predictive models are based. The brain is Bayesian, constantly computing the probability of environmental events based on incoming sensory information. Saffran (2020) added that infants actively sample the environment to find uncertainty and engage in the world in order to reduce it.

The PP model has been applied to emotions, as well (see Sullivan and Minar 2020). Sullivan and Minar added that emotions are constructed and integrate cognition with it, even in infancy. This is consistent with my own emotional development model, which views the changes in emotions in infancy from a Piagetian substage perspective in the sensorimotor stage. Cowen et al.'s (2019) research supports this view; they described dozens of emotions that must emerge in the dynamics of facial, vocal, and bodily signals of emotions, rendering the classical view of only 6–10 basic emotions antiquated.

The PP framework has been criticized for its nonspecificity about mechanisms and its overgeneralization. Nevertheless, it's a powerful model that I have transported into my own, but with modifications, as per Chap. 11 in the present book and in the model of executive function proposed in the present chapter.

Other research has dealt directly with causal learning. Kuzyk et al. (2019) demonstrated, with 18-month-olds, that causal learning abilities came into play in learning the association between a novel toy and applying a label to it. The infant's sense of uncertainty complicated the process, making unreliable or inaccurate labeling of familiar objects more acceptable when they did not have confidence in their own knowledge. There appears to be an interaction between metacognitive judgements, causal learning and selective trust in the task used. The results show that causal learning has social and self-confidence underpinnings, even in infancy.

The causes of human behavior have led to behavior that attunes to the causes of behavior. Medina and Sobel (2019) found that in 3- and 4-year-olds, mothers who guided children (rather than directed them) to learn a causal system led to more causal learning in the children. The causal system involved was the classic "blicket" detector apparatus, in which "causal" blocks could activate the apparatus to produce a well-known tune (Gopnik and Sobel 2003). Late in the second year, toddlers have learned statistical contingencies about cause-effect, as shown above (e.g., red blocks make the blicket machine play music; Gopnik 2012). Goddu and Gopnik (2020) studied 3- to 5-year-olds in three studies to see whether they can determine causal factors and generalize them. Children develop "over-hypotheses" about causal variables (Goodman et al. 2011). In the Goddu and Gopnik study, it was found that preschoolers use over-hypotheses to test novel situations for cause-effect relations, even based on sparse evidence. They quickly learned the variables that were causally relevant in the card-based causal system created by the experimenters. They determined what might be difference-makers in one causal system and apply their learning to novel ones. The authors referred to the concept of acquires as abstract, but it appears more likely a simpler representation, such as reasoning or interpretation per the following. [Gopnik's group referred to causal learning in different cultures in 4- and 5-year-olds in the same terms; Wente et al. (2017).]

Walker et al. (2020) found that, with supports, even 3-year-olds could reason relationally in a casual apparatus study. This is fitting with the general findings that young children can form and act on causal hypotheses. Tecwyn et al. (2020) investigated Michotte-type collisions in 4- to 10-year-olds, although with the results not as clear for the younger age. They concluded that children could causally order appropriately and respond with a top-down perspective rather than just the perceptual displays when the collisions were manipulated to trick them. That is, they use interpretations to align temporal perception with their causal impressions. Using a novel occupational card procedure, Noyes et al. (2020) found that by 8–9 years of age, with the development beginning at about 6–7 years, children understood the causal role afforded institutions through their actions. This was achieved via recognition of collective aspects of community, social roles, and especially understanding intentions in these regards. Here, the cognitive sophistication in causal reasoning is becoming more advanced developmentally.

Developmental Dynamics

The present work has emphasized nonlinear dynamical systems theory (NLDST) as a critical developmental process model. In the prior section of the present literature review, the value in viewing behavior dynamically was underscored (e.g., Favela 2020). This part of the review considers integrate main themes of a special issue in the journal *Human Development* on the topic (Witherington and Boom 2019a, b) along with an introductory summary of NLDST in Young (2011). In a dynamic system, the current state generates its successive state by a rule or principle of change, producing a trajectory in its state space (van Geert 2019). State spaces have dimensions, and each will have its own state change rule. The dimensions or variables are interconnected in their effects on the whole configuration.

NLDST is not a uniform model and has several conceptual lines (Witherington and Boom 2019a), especially related to whether higher-order levels can emerge from lower-order ones and have an impact on them. However, generally, most would agree that (as per Young 2011): systems can characterize both living and nonliving systems; systems refer to integrated whole, organic structures or state configurations; in systems, the whole is bigger than the sum of the parts; systems organize and re-organize through their intrinsic dynamics; they are not static even if their organization protects its stability in that this process requires constant adaptation in context, too; systems are composed of their components in interaction amongst themselves and with context, including energy and information flow; normally, systems are self-preserving or maintaining/sustaining, seeking stability; systems are open in this regard; systems are self-organizing in that the state configurations that they form reflect the dynamics of the parts in relation to the whole and not some central process; systems do not have internal (prefigured, prescribed) control mechanisms outside of the interaction of the components, or in other terms, causality resides in the component interactions within the system and with context; they struggle to maintain stability or equilibrium arising from their open state and reduce dissipative processes thermodynamically; system configuration reflects its parts and their interaction, therefore, they are marked by variability (individuality) rather than constancy or stability across different exemplars or iterations of the system; the system can have individual trajectories in context, and appear to have an average trajectory that represents a constant process and structure, with variability considered a noise by some approaches; however, in the dynamical view, the variability is not considered noise but the primary information to consider in system dynamics; the system states can change abruptly (nonlinearly) into different configurations or states at critical thresholds that are far from equilibrium, e.g., bifurcating at the cusp of change in their state-space configuration; the states are wholly unpredictable from the constituent parts and can emerge into new forms; the states are dynamic and constantly open to change despite preserving equilibrium to the degree possible; they are dynamic in the sense of having positive and negative feedback processes that serve to amplify or dampen change in cascading effects; systems could reach the transition point of far-from-equilibrium to the point that even a minor perturbation can trigger out-of-proportion change in the system; systems might gravitate to and inhabit the cusp of change bifurcation points to foster contextual adaptation, flexibility, plasticity, and change potential; systems can form emergent levels that have their own properties and form top-down influences on lower-order levels; top-down and bottom-up levels in systems are reciprocally interactive; in all these senses, systems evolve inherently in context, through circular causal processes, in a process of constant adaptive coupling or coordination and decoupling, in a process that I referred to as causal circular emergence.

Advanced mathematics can be used to represent system states and their changes, as successive state system representations gravitates to basins within their state-space phase portraits; the terms used in this regard are "attractors" (think a ball caught in the valley of a landscape and having a harder time escaping the gravity of the well when it is deeper when forces are applied upward to the ball, compared to the case of a less deep well); attractors have cardinal collective or order parameters that serve as dynamical switches or thermostats of the system; control parameters represent the variables that can activate change in the system by acting on order parameters; attractors can dynamically change, even as they resist perturbation; attractors can take simpler forms, such as unipoint or periodic attractors; they can take more complex forms, such as chaotic (really orderly) attractors; living systems have multiple attractor configurations; development might be characterized by evolution through attractor configurations, from simpler to more complex; complexity theory adds nuances to the NLDST model, for example, in Young (2011), attractors in living systems are seen to evolve to higher-order complexity landscapes; fractals, or self-similarity at different levels of a system, help define complex systems, and Young (2011) applied this concept to developmental patterning. Systems do not have an inherent purpose, defined end-states, and so on, because they are constantly evolving *in situ* and individualized ways. They express individualized trajectories in this regard, even in the micro-moments of ongoing adjustment dynamics, let alone long-term development. That said, they show patterns of increasing complexity as they constantly organize and re-organize. This permits increasing ability to adapt to complex contexts, manifest flexibility, or more degrees of freedom (affordances according to van Geert 2019) in their constraints; to move living systems (especially if human), eventually toward self-reflection and positive feedback into the system, in the form of agentic, intentional activity. In the present model, this refers to behaving with the ultimate neo-developmental stage of neo-Piagetian collective intelligence, which does not denote a common collective way of thinking abstractly bur a collection of superordinate abstract ideas and working in groups to get them, too.

Generally, then, system concepts help describe ongoing, immediate micro-time adaptation to context by the configuration of components of the system and also allow for long-term, macro-time adaptive adjustment to the environment, including through active, agentic, feedforward activity through skills, ability, capacities, and potential "powers" (Witherington and Boom 2019a) of the system on the context or environment. There is a debate in the literature whether stages in development exist, and if so, whether dynamical system concepts can help explain them. Moreover, there is debate in the literature about which stage model best fits the empirical data. One way of describing behavior in context and also hierarchical levels interacting with each other relates to nesting (after Witherington and Boom 2019a). Young (2011) devoted his book to describing his novel Neo-Piagetian/Neo-Eriksonian stage-substage model. His model consisted of five stages and five cyclically recurring substages or 25 lifespan steps in development, and applied an evolving attractor-complex system model as underpinnings to the emergence of the steps in the model. Young (2019) developed the neo-stage concept to fit the dynamical conception and obviate some of the criticisms of the traditional stage concept. That said, Witherington and Boom (2019a, b) argued that the stage designation project in structuralism is still a work in process. It needs a conceptual advance and clear definition. It needs a clear description of behavior and function at each level. It needs precision in specifying the hierarchical development through the proposed stages. It needs clarification on how real-time development feeds into stage development. Once more, the current works have attempted to tackle all these issues, and more, including in the extension of the proposed stages in the cognitive realm to parallel stages socio-affectively.

Note that there is a hierarchy from a basic scheme or schema to an abstract idea or even a cognitive stage in the present work, and this is not meant to reify the concepts and argue that any mathematical formula or logical structure that represents them stands for a psychological reality intervening in behavior. At the same time, these structures are constructed individually out of embedded, embodied enactive, contextualized interactive processes, and they form emergent, higher-order levels beyond the molecular, neuronal, and micro-behavioral lower-order levels of the system in which they are involved that have their own separate reciprocal effect on the system through their top-down dynamics.

van Geert (2019) described that causality inheres in a dynamic system through its interactive coupling, self-organization, and emergence properties, in particular, what he refers to as "process causality." Even interventions should be seen through the lens of how successive system states alter the trajectory of states in a system's state space, such that the intervention is co-determinant with the system's ongoing trajectory in the resultant trajectory. New system states could be local, as in ongoing adaptive changes, or global, as in whole stage changes, while there are intermediate forms related to specific domains. A brief review of other articles in the special issue in Human Development under review indicates that a dynamic developmental view is related to ecological psychology (Adolph 2019), is interactivist (Bickhard 2019), systems can be modeled as networks, and these networks can represent change (Di Paolo 2019), which is what I have argued, as well; and people actively Do development (Raeff 2019; I would add actively Do being).

Revising Executive Function

Doebel (2020) proposed a revised executive function (EF) model that was published online after my own model was developed, as described in the next chapter. Her approach is entirely consistent with mine. In my approach, EF relates especially to adaptive problem-solving in any task, and not just those that are higher-order and cognitive or the like. Further, it develops through biopsychosocial factors and is less a neurocognitive acquisition than heretofore presupposed. Third, inhibition is not just one of its components because the overriding concept of activation-inhibition function infuses every component of the EF process. Fourth, there is a generalized activation-inhibition component and then 15 other components in which activation-inhibition coordination is inherent to their proper functioning. Fifth, and pertinent to the Doebel argument, EF involves goal establishment and working toward them. As one would expect in a problem-solving approach to EF, which is consistent with her approach of EF involving specific goal-directed activity/skills in the service of acquiring and maintaining control, in contrast to a general approach to goal setting.

Doebel (2020) criticized the commonly accepted approach that EF involves a set of domain-general components that can be applied to tasks, such as a generalized inhibition skill and self-regulation. The literature has supported a triple component EF concept, with the other two areas being updating working memory and shifting between task sets. These EF component processes orchestrate lower-order cognitive processes in the service of task resolution in goal-directed thought and action. These canonical EF domains were established in neuroscientific research and are thought to reflect endogenous frontal lobe functioning. In children, at first, less than three such functions develop. The empirical research uses factor analytic approaches that seek latent variables, and these three EF functions typically are found. However, Doebel supported the view that individualized knowledge, beliefs, values, preferences, and normative expectations the influence EF. She includes socialization, influence of SES factors, experiential knowledge, interests, motivation, and affect in this context, consistent with my biopsychosocial approach.

The biopsychosocial approach is also supported by other research on EF development. This includes research on early neural substrates (Fiske and Holmboe 2019) and early brain networks (Wang et al. 2019a), prenatal influences (Camerota and Willoughby 2019), parenting influences (Suor et al. 2019), parental EF influences (Korucu et al. 2019), SES influences (Rosen et al. 2019), and attention and learning (Tiego et al. 2019; Blankenship et al. 2019; and Silvers 2020, respectively), with applications to neurodevelopmental disorders (Baez et al. 2019; Vaidya et al. 2020). Troller-Renfree et al. (2020) argued that children develop proactive control processes that replace more passive processing, which fits a biopsychosocial view of EF.

Lateralization in Development

The first part of this literature review has already reviewed research that was not developmental on lateralization. The present section turns to that topic to conclude the recent literature review related to the integrative work being written. Recall that I developed the concept of activation-inhibition coordination in the context of an empirical study of lateralized early reaching. The systematic review of infant handedness by Nelson and Gonzalez (2020) confirms that early reaching is right-handed. Fagard et al. (2020) found similar results with 9- to 15-month-olds, but with inconsistent reliability. Flindall and Gonzalez (2019) reviewed the research on early grasping and found that the grasp to eat action is right-lateralized in skill according to kinematic analysis. They argued that the skill reflects complex motor activity, for which the left hemisphere is specialized. I had argued that the left hemisphere is specialized for such skill due to its superior activation-inhibition coordination dynamic. Hemispheric lateralization is a biological process with genetic underpinnings (Wiberg et al. 2019). But it is also influenced by environmental factors, such as stress (Berretz et al. 2020), environmental input such as music (from 5 to 12 months) Morange-Majoux and Devouche (2018), and maternal education (Younger et al. 2019). Early lateralized manual behavior predicts later language ability in both normally developing and autism (Gonzalez et al. 2020; Dimitrova et al. 2019, respectively). Lateralization patterns are affected in infants at risk developmentally (Cantiani et al. 2019; de Montferrand et al. 2019). The right cerebral hemisphere is specialized for some social skills and activities, which are equally affected by environmental factors (see Watling and Damaskinou 2018; and also Forrester et al. 2018; Malatesta et al. 2019). The hemispheres are specialized differentially for emotions in the frontal lobe. This includes having moderator effects on other psychological aspects, such as negativity (Diaz et al. 2019; Gartstein et al. 2019), and parietal research by Marino et al. 2019).

Conclusions

This chapter in the present work, the book being the fourth in the Young book series on causality, development, and psychology unification, provides an updated literature of the core areas of the work. The review shows that these core concepts in the present work are supported in the recent literature, or at least complement it. The literature reviewed in this chapter is organized around major themes: philosophy, unification in psychology, causality and mechanism, systems, networks, causal modeling, activation-inhibition coordination, and unification fields. Then, it moves to developmental topics on Piaget, Erikson, causal learning, developmental dynamics, executive function, and the development of lateralization. Overall, the most recent literature in the field related to the core themes of the present work illustrates the abundance of auxiliary thought related to the themes, but the specific contents of some of the major innovations of the Young work are found uniquely in his oeuvre. This message is accentuated even more so in the next chapter, in which further elaborations, extensions, and innovations to the present work are presented.

References

Aafjes-van Doorn, K., Kamsteeg, C., Silberschatz, G.: Cognitive mediators of the relationship between adverse childhood experiences and adult psychopathology: a systematic review. Dev. Psychopathol. **32**(3), 1017–1029 (2019). https://doi.org/10.1017/s0954579419001317

Adolph, K.E.: An ecological approach to learning in (not and) development. Hum. Dev. **63**(3–4), 180–201 (2019). https://doi.org/10.1159/000503823

Akpan, T., Joshua, E.E., Uduk, E.I.: Nonlinear dynamics and synchronization of computational cognitive model in educational science. J. Nonlinear Sci. Appl. **14**(1), 15–28 (2020). https://doi.org/10.22436/jnsa.014.01.03

Amazeen, P.G.: From physics to social interactions: scientific unification via dynamics. Cogn. Syst. Res. **52**, 640–657 (2018). https://doi.org/10.1016/j.cogsys.2018.07.033

Ambrosini, E., Arbula, S., Rossato, C., Pacella, V., Vallesi, A.: Neuro-cognitive architecture of executive functions: a latent variable analysis. Cortex. **119**, 441–456 (2019). https://doi.org/10.1016/j.cortex.2019.07.013

American Psychiatric Association: Diagnostic and Statistical Manual of Mental Disorders, DSM-5, 5th edn. Author, Washington, DC (2013)

Anderson, H.N.: Unified social Cognition. Psychology Press, New York (2008)

Armstrong-Carter, E., Trejo, S., Hill, L.J.B., Crossley, K.L., Mason, D., Domingue, B.W.: The earliest origins of genetic nurture: the prenatal environment mediates the association between maternal genetics and child development. Psychol. Sci. **31**(7), 781–791 (2020). https://doi.org/10.1177/0956797620917209

Athan, A.M.: Reproductive identity: an emerging concept. Am. Psychol. **75**(4), 445–456 (2020). https://doi.org/10.1037/amp0000623

Avinun, R.: The E is in the G: gene–environment–trait correlations and findings from genome-wide association studies. Persp. Psychol. Sci. **15**(1), 81–89 (2019). https://doi.org/10.1177/1745691619867107

Babik, I., Cunha, A.B., Ross, S.M., Logan, S.W., Galloway, J.C., Lobo, M.A.: Means-end problem solving in infancy: development, emergence of intentionality, and transfer of knowledge. Dev. Psychobiol. **61**(2), 191–202 (2018). https://doi.org/10.1002/dev.21798

Baez, A.C., Dajani, D.R., Voorhies, W., Parladé, M.V., Alessandri, M., Britton, J.C., Llabre, M.M., Uddin, L.Q.: Parsing heterogeneity of executive function in typically and atypically developing children: a conceptual replication and exploration of social function. J. Autism Dev. Disord. **50**(3), 707–718 (2019). https://doi.org/10.1007/s10803-019-04290-9

Bakker, G.M.: A new conception and subsequent taxonomy of clinical psychological problems. BMC Psychol. **7**(1), 2–33 (2019). https://doi.org/10.1186/s40359-019-0318-8

Bar, M. (2021). From objects to unified minds. Curr. Dir. Psychol. Sci., **30**(2), 129–137. https://doi.org/10.1177/0963721420984403

Basseches, M.: The development of dialectical thinking as an approach to integration. Integral Rev. **1**, 47–63 (2005)

Basten, C., Touyz, S.: Sense of self: its place in personality disturbance, psychopathology, and normal experience. Rev. Gen. Psychol. **24**(2), 159–171 (2019). https://doi.org/10.1177/1089268019880884

Baumeister, R.F.: Free will and the human essence: responsible autonomy, meaning and cultural participation. In: van Zomeren, M., Dovidio, J.F. (eds.) The Oxford Handbooks of the Human Essence, pp. 47–58. Oxford University Press, New York (2018a)

Baumeister, R.F.: Free will and moral psychology. In: Gray, K., Graham, J. (eds.) Atlas of Moral Psychology, pp. 332–337. The Guilford Press, New York (2018b)

Baumeister, R.F., Lau, S.: Why psychological scientists should disdain determinism. Manuscript under review by Perspectives in Psychological Science (2020)

Bayer, J.B., Lewis, N.A., Stahl, J.L.: Who comes to mind? Dynamic construction of social networks. Curr. Dir. Psychol. Sci. **29**(3), 279–285 (2020). https://doi.org/10.1177/0963721420915866

Beauchaine, T.P., Cicchetti, D.: Emotion dysregulation and emerging psychopathology: a transdiagnostic, transdisciplinary perspective. Dev. Psychopathol. **31**(3), 799–804 (2019). https://doi.org/10.1017/s0954579419000671

Beck, E.D., Jackson, J.J.: Idiographic traits: a return to Allportian approaches to personality. Psychol. Sci. **29**(3), 301–308 (2020). https://doi.org/10.1177/0963721420915860

Bella, M.: Novelty and causality in William James's pluralistic universe. Eur. J. Pragmatism Am. Philos. **6**(2), 1–25 (2019). https://doi.org/10.4000/ejpap.1668

Beller, S., Bender, A.: Theory, the final frontier? A corpus-based analysis of the role of theory in psychological articles. Front. Psychol. **8**, 951 (2017). https://doi.org/10.3389/fpsyg.2017.00951

Bender, A.: What is causal cognition? Front. Psychol. **11**, 3 (2020). https://doi.org/10.3389/fpsyg.2020.00003

Beni, M.D.: An outline of a unified theory of the relational self: grounding the self in the manifold of interpersonal relations. Phenomenol. Cogn. Sci. **18**(3), 473–491 (2018). https://doi.org/10.1007/s11097-018-9587-6

Berkman, E.T., Wilson, S.M.: So useful as a good theory? The practicality crisis in (social) psychological theory. Perspect. Psychol. Sci. (2021). https://doi.org/10.1177/1745691620969650

Berretz, G., Wolf, O.T., Güntürkün, O., Ocklenburg, S.: Atypical lateralization in neurodevelopmental and psychiatric disorders: what is the role of stress? Cortex. **125**, 215–232 (2020). https://doi.org/10.1016/j.cortex.2019.12.019

Bertolero, M.A., Bassett, D.S.: On the nature of explanations offered by network science: a perspective from and for practicing neuroscientists. Topics Cogn. Sci. **12**(4), 1272–1293 (2020). https://doi.org/10.1111/tops.12504

Bickhard, M.H.: Dynamics is not enough: an interactivist perspective. Hum. Dev. **63**(Suppl 3–4), 227–244 (2019). https://doi.org/10.1159/000503826

Bierer, L.M., Bader, H.N., Daskalakis, N.P., Lehrner, A., Provençal, N., Wiechmann, T., Klengel, T., Makotkine, I., Binder, E.B., Yehuda, R.: Intergenerational effects of maternal holocaust exposure on FKBP5 methylation. Am. J. Psychiatry. **177**(8), 744–753 (2020). https://doi.org/10.1176/appi.ajp.2019.19060618

Blankenship, T.L., Slough, M.A., Calkins, S.D., Deater-Deckard, K., Kim-Spoon, J., Bell, M.A.: Attention and executive functioning in infancy: links to childhood executive function and reading achievement. Dev. Sci. **22**(6), e12824 (2019). https://doi.org/10.1111/desc.12824

Bolger, N., Zee, K.S., Rossignac-Milon, M., Hassin, R.R.: Causal processes in psychology are heterogeneous. J. Exp. Psychol. Gen. **148**(4), 601–618 (2019). https://doi.org/10.1037/xge0000558

Bolton, D., Gillett, G.: The Biopsychosocial Model of Health and Disease: New Philosophical and Scientific Developments, 1st edn. Palgrave Pivot, Cham (2019)

Börnert-Ringleb, M., Wilbert, J.: The association of strategy use and concrete-operational thinking in primary school. Front. Educ. **3**, 38 (2018). https://doi.org/10.3389/feduc.2018.00038

Brady, S.P., Bolnick, D.I., Barrett, R.D.H., Chapman, L., Crispo, E., Derry, A.M., Eckert, C.G., Fraser, D.J., Fussmann, G.F., Gonzalez, A., Guichard, F., Lamy, T., Lane, J., McAdam, A.G., Newman, A.E.M., Paccard, A., Robertson, B., Rolshausen, G., Schulte, P.M., Simons, A.M., Vellend, M., Hendry, A.: Understanding maladaptation by uniting ecological and evolutionary perspectives. Am. Nat. **194**(4), 495–515 (2019). https://doi.org/10.1086/705020

Bresin, K.: Toward a unifying theory of dysregulated behaviors. Clin. Psychol. Rev. **80**, 101885 (2020). https://doi.org/10.1016/j.cpr.2020.101885

Brette, R.: Is coding a relevant metaphor for the brain? Behav. Brain Sci. **42**, E215 (2018). https://doi.org/10.1017/s0140525x19000049

Brick, T.R., Bailey, D.H.: Rock the MIC: the Matrix of implied causation, a tool for experimental design and model checking. Adv. Methods Pract. Psychol. Sci. **3**(3), 286–299 (2020). https://doi.org/10.1177/2515245920922775

Camerota, M., Willoughby, M.T.: Prenatal risk predicts preschooler executive function: a cascade model. Child Dev. **91**(3), e682–e700 (2019). https://doi.org/10.1111/cdev.13271

Cantiani, C., Ortiz-Mantilla, S., Riva, V., Piazza, C., Bettoni, R., Musacchia, G., Molteni, M., Marino, C., Benasich, A.A.: Reduced left-lateralized pattern of event-related EEG oscillations in infants at familial risk for language and learning impairment. NeuroImage Clin. **22**, 101778 (2019). https://doi.org/10.1016/j.nicl.2019.101778

Carlsson, T., Molander, F., Taylor, M.J., Jonsson, U., Bölte, S.: Early environmental risk factors for neurodevelopmental disorders – a systematic review of twin and sibling studies. Dev. Psychopathol., 1–48 (2020). https://doi.org/10.1017/s0954579420000620

Case, R.: The Mind's Staircase. Exploring the Conceptual Underpinnings of Children's Thought and Knowledge. Lawrence Erlbaum Associates, New Jersey (1991)

Case, R., Okamoto, Y.: The role of central conceptual structures in the development of children's thought. Monogr. Soc. Res. Child Dev. **61**(1–2), v–265 (1996)

Chahal, R., Weissman, D.G., Hallquist, M.N., Robins, R.W., Hastings, P.D., Guyer, A.E.: Neural connectivity biotypes: associations with internalizing problems throughout adolescence. Psychol. Med., 1–11 (2020). https://doi.org/10.1017/s003329172000149x

Chater, N., Zhu, J.-Q., Spicer, J., Sundh, J., León-Villagrá, P., Sanborn, A.: Probabilistic biases meet the Bayesian brain. Curr. Dir. Psychol. Sci. **29**(5), 506–512 (2020). https://doi.org/10.1177/0963721420954801

Chong, I., Proctor, R.W.: On the evolution of a radical concept: affordances according to Gibson and their subsequent use and development. Perspect. Psychol. Sci. **15**(1), 117–132 (2019). https://doi.org/10.1177/1745691619868207

Clark, A.: Whatever next? Predictive brains, situated agents, and the future of cognitive science. Behav. Brain Sci. **36**(3), 181–204 (2013). https://doi.org/10.1017/s0140525x12000477

Cole, P.M., Ram, N., English, M.S.: Toward a unifying model of self-regulation: a developmental approach. Child Dev. Perspect. **13**(2), 91–96 (2018). https://doi.org/10.1111/cdep.12316

Colombo, M.: Bayesian cognitive science, predictive brains, and the nativism debate. Synthese. **195**(11), 4817–4838 (2017). https://doi.org/10.1007/s11229-017-1427-7

Colombo, M., Knauff, M.: Editors' review and introduction: levels of explanation in cognitive science: from molecules to culture. Topics Cogn. Sci. **12**(4), 1224–1240 (2020). https://doi.org/10.1111/tops.12503

Commons, M.L., Richards, F.A.: A general model of stage theory. In: Commons, M.L., Richards, F.A., Armon, C. (eds.) Beyond Formal Operations: Late Adolescent and Adult Cognitive Development, vol. 4, pp. 120–140. Praeger, New York (1984)

Corr, P.J.: A consensual paradigm for personality: introduction to special issue. Personal. Individ. Differ. **152**, 109611 (2019). https://doi.org/10.1016/j.paid.2019.109611

Cowen, A., Sauter, D., Tracy, J.L., Keltner, D.: Mapping the passions: toward a high-dimensional taxonomy of emotional experience and expression. Psychol. Sci. Public Interest. **20**(1), 69–90 (2019). https://doi.org/10.1177/1529100619850176

Cramer, A.O.J., Leertouwer, I.J., Lanius, R., Frewen, P.: A network approach to studying the associations between posttraumatic stress disorder symptoms and dissociative experiences. J. Trauma. Stress. **33**(1), 19–28 (2020). https://doi.org/10.1002/jts.22488

Crespi, B.J.: Evolutionary and genetic insights for clinical psychology. Clin. Psychol. Rev. **78**, 101857 (2020). https://doi.org/10.1016/j.cpr.2020.101857

Curtindale, L.M., Bahrick, L.E., Lickliter, R., Colombo, J.: Effects of multimodal synchrony on infant attention and heart rate during events with social and non-social stimuli. J. Exp. Child Psychol. **178**, 283–294 (2019). https://doi.org/10.1016/j.jecp.2018.10.006

Demetriou, A., Efklides, A.: Structure and sequence of formal and postformal thought: general patterns and individual differences. Child Dev. **56**(4), 1062–1091 (1985). https://doi.org/10.2307/1130117

Demetriou, A., Spanoudis, G.: Growing Minds: A Developmental Theory of Intelligence, Brain, and Education, 1st edn. Routledge, London (2018)

Demetriou, A., Makris, N., Tachmatzidis, D., Kazi, S., Spanoudis, G.: Decomposing the influence of mental processes on academic performance. Intelligence. **77**, 101404 (2019). https://doi.org/10.1016/j.intell.2019.101404

DePasquale, C.E.: A systematic review of caregiver-child physiological synchrony across systems: associations with behavior and child functioning. Dev. Psychopathol. **32**(5), 1754–1777 (2020). https://doi.org/10.1017/S0954579420001236

Derex, M., Mesoudi, A.: Cumulative cultural evolution within evolving population structures. Trends Cogn. Sci. **24**(8), 654–667 (2020). https://doi.org/10.1016/j.tics.2020.04.005

Di Paolo, E.A.: Process and individuation: the development of sensorimotor agency. Hum. Dev. **63**(Suppl 3–4), 202–226 (2019). https://doi.org/10.1159/000503827

Diaz, A., Swingler, M.M., Tan, L., Smith, C.L., Calkins, S.D., Bell, M.A.: Infant frontal EEG asymmetry moderates the association between maternal behavior and toddler negative affectivity. Infant Behav. Dev. **55**, 88–99 (2019). https://doi.org/10.1016/j.infbeh.2019.03.002

Dimitrova, N., Mohr, C., Özçalışkan, Ş., Adamson, L.B.: Early lateralization of gestures in autism: right-handed points predict expressive language. J. Autism Dev. Disord. **50**(4), 1147–1158 (2019). https://doi.org/10.1007/s10803-019-04347-9
Doebel, S.: Rethinking executive function and its development. Perspect. Psychol. Sci. **15**(4), 942–956 (2020). https://doi.org/10.1177/1745691620904771
Domingue, B.W., Belsky, D.W., Fletcher, J.M., Conley, D., Boardman, J.D., Harris, K.M.: The social genome of friends and schoolmates in the National Longitudinal Study of Adolescent to Adult Health. Proc. Natl. Acad. Sci. **115**(4), 702–707 (2018). https://doi.org/10.1073/pnas.1711803115
Dunn, K., Bremner, J.G.: Investigating the social environment of the A-not-B search task. Dev. Sci. **23**(3), e12921 (2019). https://doi.org/10.1111/desc.12921
Eagle, M.N.: Toward an integrated psychoanalytic theory: foundation in a revitalized ego psychology. Clin. Soc. Work J. **48**(3), 257–266 (2020). https://doi.org/10.1007/s10615-020-00768-7
Ecker, B., Bridges, S.K.: How the science of memory reconsolidation advances the effectiveness and unification of psychotherapy. Clin. Soc. Work J. **48**, 287–300 (2020). https://doi.org/10.1007/s10615-020-00754-z
Elimari, N., Lafargue, G.: Network neuroscience and the adapted mind: rethinking the role of network theories in evolutionary psychology. Front. Psychol. **11**, 545632 (2020). https://doi.org/10.3389/fpsyg.2020.545632
Elliott, M.L., Knodt, A.R., Ireland, D., Morris, M.L., Poulton, R., Ramrakha, S., Sison, M.L., Moffitt, T.E., Caspi, A., Hariri, A.R.: What is the test-retest reliability of common task-functional MRI measures? New empirical evidence and a meta-analysis. Psychol. Sci. **31**(7), 792–806 (2020). https://doi.org/10.1177/0956797620916786
Erikson, E.H.: Childhood and Society, 2nd edn. W. W. Norton, New York (1963)
Erikson, E.H.: Identity: Youth and Crisis, 1st edn. W.W. Norton, New York (1968)
Eronen, M.I.: The levels problem in psychopathology. Psychol. Med. (2019). https://doi.org/10.1017/S0033291719002514
Eronen, M.I., Bringmann, L.F.: The theory crisis in psychology: how to move forward. Perspect. Psychol. Sci. (2021). https://doi.org/10.1177/1745691620970586
Erskine, G.R.: Child development in integrative psychotherapy: Erik Erikson's first three stages. Int. J. Integr. Psychother. 10. http://www.integrative-journal.com/index.php/ijip/article/view/145/0 (2019)
Eustice-Corwin, A.C.: Toward a Neo-Nietzschean theory of human development. Hum. Dev. **64**(2), 68–82 (2020). https://doi.org/10.1159/000510971
Evans, G.W.: The physical context of child development. Curr. Dir. Psychol. Sci. (2021). https://doi.org/10.1177/0963721420980719
Fagard, J., Corbetta, D., Somogyi, E., Safar, A., Bernard, C.: Right-handed one day, right-handed the next day? Laterality. **25**(4), 455–468 (2020). https://doi.org/10.1080/1357650x.2020.1729171
Favela, L.H.: Cognitive science as complexity science. Wires Cogn. Sci. **11**(4), e1525 (2020). https://doi.org/10.1002/wcs.1525
Fesce, R.: Subjectivity as an emergent property of information processing by neuronal networks. Front. Neurosci. **14**, 548071 (2020). https://doi.org/10.3389/fnins.2020.548071
Fischer, K.W.: A theory of cognitive development: the control and construction of hierarchies of skills. Psychol. Rev. **87**(6), 477–531 (1980). https://doi.org/10.1037/0033-295X.87.6.477
Fiske, A., Holmboe, K.: Neural substrates of early executive function development. Dev. Rev. **52**, 42–62 (2019). https://doi.org/10.1016/j.dr.2019.100866
Flindall, J., Gonzalez, C.L.R.: On the neurocircuitry of grasping: the influence of action intent on kinematic asymmetries in reach-to-grasp actions. Atten. Percept. Psychophys. **81**(7), 2217–2236 (2019). https://doi.org/10.3758/s13414-019-01805-5
Forrester, G.S., Davis, R., Mareschal, D., Malatesta, G., Todd, B.K.: The left cradling bias: an evolutionary facilitator of social cognition? Cortex. **118**, 116–131 (2018). https://doi.org/10.1016/j.cortex.2018.05.011

Frazier, L.D.: The past, present, and future of the biopsychosocial model: a review of The Biopsychosocial model of health and disease: new philosophical and scientific developments by Derek Bolton and Grant Gillett. New Ideas Psychol. **57**, 100755 (2019). https://doi.org/10.1016/j.newideapsych.2019.100755

Frewen, P.A., Schmittmann, V.D., Bringmann, L.F., Borsboom, D.: Perceived causal relations between anxiety, posttraumatic stress and depression: extension to moderation, mediation, and network analysis. Eur. J. Psychotraumatol. **4**(1), 20656 (2013). https://doi.org/10.3402/ejpt.v4i0.20656

Friston, K.: The free-energy principle: a unified brain theory? Nat. Rev. Neurosci. **11**(2), 127–138 (2010). https://doi.org/10.1038/nrn2787

Gaj, N.: Unity and Fragmentation in Psychology: The Philosophical and Methodological Roots of the Discipline. Routledge, London (2016)

Gartstein, M.A., Hancock, G.R., Potapova, N.V., Calkins, S.D., Bell, M.A.: Modelling development of frontal electroencephalogram (EEG) asymmetry: sex differences and links with temperament. Dev. Sci. **23**(1), e12891 (2019). https://doi.org/10.1111/desc.12891

Geary, D.C.: The spark of life and the unification of intelligence, health, and aging. Curr. Dir. Psychol. Sci. **28**(3), 223–228 (2019). https://doi.org/10.1177/0963721419829719

van Geert, P.L.C.: Dynamic systems, process and development. Hum. Dev. **63**(Suppl 3–4), 153–179 (2019). https://doi.org/10.1159/000503825

Genschow, O., Hawickhorst, H., Rigoni, D., Aschermann, E., Brass, M.: Professional judges' disbelief in free will does not decrease punishment. Soc. Psychol. Pers. Sci. (2020). https://doi.org/10.1177/1948550620915055

Gervais, W.M.: Practical methodological reform needs good theory. Perspect. Psychol. Sci. (2021). https://doi.org/10.1177/1745691620977471

Girgis, F., Lee, D.J., Goodarzi, A., Ditterich, J.: Toward a neuroscience of adult cognitive developmental theory. Front. Neurosci. **12**, 4 (2018). https://doi.org/10.3389/fnins.2018.00004

Gładziejewski, P.: Mechanistic unity of the predictive mind. Theory Psychol. **29**(5), 657–675 (2019). https://doi.org/10.1177/0959354319866258

Goddu, M.K., Gopnik, A.: Learning what to change: young children use "difference-making" to identify causally relevant variables. Dev. Psychol. **56**(2), 275–284 (2020). https://doi.org/10.1037/dev0000872

Gonzalez, S.L., Campbell, J.M., Marcinowski, E.C., Michel, G.F., Coxe, S., Nelson, E.L.: Preschool language ability is predicted by toddler hand preference trajectories. Dev. Psychol. **56**(4), 699–709 (2020). https://doi.org/10.1037/dev0000900

Goodman, N.D., Ullman, T.D., Tenenbaum, J.B.: Learning a theory of causality. Psychol. Rev. **118**(1), 110–119 (2011). https://doi.org/10.1037/a0021336

Gopnik, A.: Scientific thinking in young children: theoretical advances, empirical research, and policy implications. Science. **337**(6102), 1623–1627 (2012). https://doi.org/10.1126/science.1223416

Gopnik, A., Sobel, D.M.: Detecting blickets: how young children use information about novel causal powers in categorization and induction. Child Dev. **71**(5), 1205–1222 (2003). https://doi.org/10.1111/1467-8624.00224

Gray, J.A.: Brain systems that mediate both emotion and cognition. Cognit. Emot. **4**(3), 269–288 (1990). https://doi.org/10.1080/02699939008410799

Gray, J.A., McNaughton, N.: The Neuropsychology of Anxiety: An Enquiry into the Function of the Septo-Hippocampal System. Oxford University Press, Oxford (2003)

Green, C.D.: Why psychology isn't unified, and probably never will be. Rev. Gen. Psychol. **19**(3), 207–214 (2015). https://doi.org/10.1037/gpr0000051

Grosz, M.P., Rohrer, J.M., Thoemmes, F.: The taboo against explicit causal inference in nonexperimental psychology. Perspect. Psychol. Sci. **15**(5), 1243–1255 (2020). https://doi.org/10.1177/1745691620921521

Gunnar, M.R.: Early adversity, stress, and neurobehavioral development. Dev. Psychopathol. **32**(5), 1555–1562 (2020). https://doi.org/10.1017/S0954579420001649

Harden, K.P., Engelhardt, L.E., Mann, F.D., Patterson, M.W., Grotzinger, A.D., Savicki, S.L., Thibodeaux, M.L., Freis, S.M., Tackett, J.L., Church, J.A., Tucker-Drob, E.M.: Genetic associations between executive functions and a general factor of psychopathology. J. Am. Acad. Child Adolesc. Psychiatry. **59**(6), 749–758 (2019). https://doi.org/10.1016/j.jaac.2019.05.006

Haslam, N., McGrath, M.J., Viechtbauer, W., Kuppens, P.: Dimensions over categories: a meta-analysis of taxometric research. Psychol. Med. **50**(9), 1418–1432 (2020). https://doi.org/10.1017/S003329172000183X

Haynes, S.N., O'Brien, W.H., Godoy, A.: A proposed model for the psychometric evaluation of clinical case formulations with quantified causal diagrams. Psychol. Assess. **32**(6), 541–552 (2020). https://doi.org/10.1037/pas0000811

Henriques, G.: The tree of knowledge system and the theoretical unification of psychology. Rev. Gen. Psychol. **7**(2), 150–182 (2003). https://doi.org/10.1037/1089-2680.7.2.150

Henriques, G.: A New Unified Theory of Psychology. Springer, Cham (2011)

Henriques, G.: Character adaptation systems theory: a new big five for personality and psychotherapy. Rev. Gen. Psychol. **21**(1), 9–22 (2017). https://doi.org/10.1037/gpr0000097

Henriques, G., Michalski, J.: Defining psychology and its relationship to the science of psychology. Integr. Psychol. Behav. Sci. **54**, 328–353 (2019). https://doi.org/10.1007/s12124-019-09504-4

Heyes, C.: Psychological mechanisms forged by cultural evolution. Curr. Dir. Psychol. Sci. **29**(4), 399–404 (2020). https://doi.org/10.1177/0963721420917736

Hoffart, A., Johnson, S.U.: Latent trait, latent-trait state, and a network approach to mental problems and their mechanisms of change. Clin. Psychol. Sci. **8**(4), 595–613 (2020). https://doi.org/10.1177/2167702620901744

Hopkins, W.D., Mareno, M.C., Schapiro, S.J.: Further evidence of a left hemisphere specialization and genetic basis for tool use skill in chimpanzees (Pan troglodytes): reproducibility in two genetically isolated populations of apes. J. Comp. Psychol. **133**(4), 512–519 (2019). https://doi.org/10.1037/com0000183

Huang, M., Starr, L.R.: Interpersonal childhood adversity and stress generation in adolescence: moderation by HPA axis multilocus genetic variation. Dev. Psychopathol. **32**(3), 865–878 (2020). https://doi.org/10.1017/s0954579419001123

Infurna, F.J., Gerstorf, D., Lachman, M.E.: Midlife in the 2020s: opportunities and challenges. Am. Psychol. **75**(4), 470–485 (2020). https://doi.org/10.1037/amp0000591

Inhelder, B., Piaget, J.: The Growth of Logical Thinking: From Childhood to Adolescence. Basic Books, New York (1958)

Insel, T.: The NIMH Research Domain Criteria (RDoC) project: precision medicine for psychiatry. Am. J. Psychiatry. **171**(4), 395–397 (2014). https://doi.org/10.1176/appi.ajp.2014.14020138

Jeon, M., Draney, K., Wilson, M., Sun, Y.: Investigation of adolescents' developmental stages in deductive reasoning: an application of a specialized confirmatory mixture IRT approach. Behav. Res. Methods. **52**(1), 224–235 (2019). https://doi.org/10.3758/s13428-019-01221-5

Jirsa, V.K., McIntosh, A.R., Huys, R.: Grand unified theories of the brain need better understanding of behavior: the two-tiered emergence of function. Ecol. Psychol. **31**(3), 152–165 (2019). https://doi.org/10.1080/10407413.2019.1615207

Kallio, E.: Integrative thinking is the key: an evaluation of current research into the development of adult thinking. Theory Psychol. **21**(6), 785–801 (2011). https://doi.org/10.1177/0959354310388344

Kallio, E.K. (ed.): Development of Adult Thinking: Interdisciplinary Perspectives on Cognitive Development and Adult Learning, 1st edn. Routledge, London (2020a)

Kallio, E.K.: From multiperspective to contextual integrative thinking in adulthood. In: Kallio, E.K. (ed.) Development of Adult Thinking: Interdisciplinary Perspectives on Cognitive Development and Adult Learning, 1st edn, pp. 9–32. Routledge, London (2020b)

Kao, M.: Unification beyond justification: a strategy for theory development. Synthese. **196**(8), 3263–3278 (2017). https://doi.org/10.1007/s11229-017-1515-8

Kazi, S., Kazali, E., Makris, N., Spanoudis, G., Demetriou, A.: Cognizance in cognitive development: a longitudinal study. Cogn. Dev. **52**, 100805 (2019). https://doi.org/10.1016/j.cogdev.2019.100805

Kegan, R.: In Over Our Heads: The Mental Demands of Modern Life. Harvard University Press, Cambridge (1994)

Kendler, K.S.: From many to one to many—The search for causes of psychiatric illness. JAMA Psychiat. **76**(10), 1085–1091 (2019). https://doi.org/10.1001/jamapsychiatry.2019.1200

Kendler, K.S., Aggen, S.H., Gillespie, N., Krueger, R.F., Czajkowski, N., Ystrom, E., Reichborn-Kjennerud, T.: The structure of genetic and environmental influences on normative personality, abnormal personality traits, and personality disorder symptoms. Psychol. Med. **49**(8), 1392–1399 (2019). https://doi.org/10.1017/s0033291719000047

Kimble, G.A.: Psychology: The Hope of a Science. The MIT Press, Cambridge (1996)

King, P.M., Kitchener, K.S.: The reflective judgment model: twenty years of research on epistemic cognition. In: Hofer, B.K., Pintrich, P.R. (eds.) Personal Epistemology: The Psychology of Beliefs About Knowledge and Knowing, pp. 37–61. Lawrence Erlbaum Associates, New York (2002)

Klein, J.P., Stahl, J., Hüppe, M., McCullough, J.P., Schramm, E., Ortel, D., Sondermann, S., Schröder, J., Moritz, S., Schweiger, U.: Do interpersonal fears mediate the association between childhood maltreatment and interpersonal skills deficits? A matched cross-sectional analysis. Psychother. Res. **30**(2), 267–278 (2018). https://doi.org/10.1080/10503307.2018.1532125

Kling, S.D.: Whitehead's metaphysics as a cosmological framework for transpersonal psychology. Humanist. Psychol. **47**(2), 181–200 (2019). https://doi.org/10.1037/hum0000124

Kohlberg, L.: The Psychology of Moral Development: The Nature and Validity of Moral Stages (Essays on Moral Development), vol. 2, 1st edn. Harper & Row, Manhattan (1984)

Korucu, I., Litkowski, E., Purpura, D.J., Schmitt, S.A.: Parental executive function as a predictor of parenting practices and children's executive function. Infant Child Dev. **29**(1), e2152 (2019). https://doi.org/10.1002/icd.2152

Köster, M., Kayhan, E., Langeloh, M., Hoehl, S.: Making sense of the world: infant learning from a predictive processing perspective. Perspect. Psychol. Sci. **15**(3), 562–571 (2020). https://doi.org/10.1177/1745691619895071

Krpan, D.: Unburdening the shoulders of giants: a quest for disconnected academic psychology. Perspect. Psychol. Sci. **15**(4), 1042–1053 (2020). https://doi.org/10.1177/1745691620904775

Krzeczkowski, J.E., van Lieshout, R.J., Schmidt, L.A.: Transacting brains: testing an actor–partner model of frontal EEG activity in mother–infant dyads. Dev. Psychopathol., 1–12 (2020). https://doi.org/10.1017/S0954579420001558

Kuzyk, O., Grossman, S., Poulin-Dubois, D.: Knowing who knows: metacognitive and causal learning abilities guide infants' selective social learning. Dev. Sci. **23**(3), e12904 (2019). https://doi.org/10.1111/desc.12904

Labouvie-Vief, G.: Integrating Emotions and Cognition Throughout the Lifespan. Springer, Cham (2015)

Lange, J., Dalege, J., Borsboom, D., van Kleef, G.A., Fischer, A.H.: Toward an integrative psychometric model of emotions. Perspect. Psychol. Sci. **15**(2), 444–468 (2020). https://doi.org/10.1177/1745691619895057

Lawford, H.L., Astrologo, L., Ramey, H.L., Linden-Andersen, S.: Identity, intimacy, and generativity in adolescence and young adulthood: a test of the psychosocial model. Identity. **20**(1), 9–21 (2019). https://doi.org/10.1080/15283488.2019.1697271

Le, B.D., Stein, J.L.: Mapping causal pathways from genetics to neuropsychiatric disorders using genome-wide imaging genetics: current status and future directions. Psychiatry Clin. Neurosci. **73**(7), 357–369 (2019). https://doi.org/10.1111/pcn.12839

LeMoult, J., Humphreys, K.L., Tracy, A., Hoffmeister, J.-A., Ip, E., Gotlib, I.H.: Meta-analysis: exposure to early life stress and risk for depression in childhood and adolescence. J. Am. Acad. Child Adolesc. Psychiatry. **59**(7), 842–855 (2020). https://doi.org/10.1016/j.jaac.2019.10.011

Macpherson, M.C., Marie, D., Schön, S., Miles, L.K.: Evaluating the interplay between subclinical levels of mental health symptoms and coordination dynamics. Br. J. Psychol. **111**(4), 782–804 (2019). https://doi.org/10.1111/bjop.12426

Makino, H.: Top-down control: a unified principle of cortical learning. Neurosci. Res. **141**, 23–28 (2018). https://doi.org/10.1016/j.neures.2018.08.004

Malatesta, G., Marzoli, D., Piccioni, C., Tommasi, L.: The relationship between the left-cradling bias and attachment to parents and partner. Evol. Psychol. **17**(2), 1474704919848117 (2019). https://doi.org/10.1177/1474704919848117

Marcori, A.J., Monteiro, P.H.M., Okazaki, V.H.A.: Changing handedness: what can we learn from preference shift studies? Neurosci. Biobehav. Rev. **107**, 313–319 (2019). https://doi.org/10.1016/j.neubiorev.2019.09.019

Marino, C., Riva, V., Mornati, G., Piazza, C., del Giudice, R., Dionne, G., Molteni, M., Cantiani, C.: Postnatal maternal symptoms of depression and child emotion dysregulation: the mediation role of infant EEG alpha asymmetry. Infant Behav. Dev. **57**, 101321 (2019). https://doi.org/10.1016/j.infbeh.2019.04.003

Martin, R.C.: Including maladaptive anger in psychology courses. Teaching Psychol. **47**(1), 102–107 (2019). https://doi.org/10.1177/0098628319889540

Medina, C., Sobel, D.M.: Caregiver–child interaction influences causal learning and engagement during structured play. J. Exp. Child Psychol. **189**, 104678 (2019). https://doi.org/10.1016/j.jecp.2019.104678

Mehta, C.M., Arnett, J.J., Palmer, C.G., Nelson, L.J.: Established adulthood: a new conception of ages 30 to 45. Am. Psychol. **75**(4), 431–444 (2020). https://doi.org/10.1037/amp0000600

Mele, A.R.: Free will, moral responsibility, and scientific epiphenomenalism. Front. Psychol. **9**, 2536 (2018). https://doi.org/10.3389/fpsyg.2018.02536

Miłkowski, M., Nowakowski, P.: Representational unification in cognitive science: is embodied cognition a unifying perspective? Synthese. (2019). https://doi.org/10.1007/s11229-019-02445-w

Miłkowski, M., Hohol, M., Nowakowski, P.: Mechanisms in psychology: the road towards unity? Theory Psychol. **29**(5), 567–578 (2019). https://doi.org/10.1177/0959354319875218

Millgram, Y., Huppert, J.D., Tamir, M.: Emotion goals in psychopathology: a new perspective on dysfunctional emotion regulation. Curr. Dir. Psychol. Sci. **29**(3), 242–247 (2020). https://doi.org/10.1177/0963721420917713

Milojevich, H.M., Machlin, L., Sheridan, M.A.: Early adversity and children's emotion regulation: differential roles of parent emotion regulation and adversity exposure. Dev. Psychopathol. **32**(5), 1788–1798 (2020). https://doi.org/10.1017/S0954579420001273

de Montferrand, C., Vassel-Hitier, J., Yvon-Chaou, E., Câmara-Costa, H., Dellatolas, G., Chevignard, M.: Language and cognitive outcomes after childhood stroke: theoretical implications for hemispheric specialization. Cortex. **120**, 509–523 (2019). https://doi.org/10.1016/j.cortex.2019.07.020

Morange-Majoux, F., Devouche, E.: Language or music? Environmental influences on infants' handedness from 5 to 12 months. Brain Cogn. **129**, 1–8 (2018). https://doi.org/10.1016/j.bandc.2018.12.003

Moriarity, D.P., Kautz, M.M., Mac Giollabhui, N., Klugman, J., Coe, C.L., Ellman, L.M., Abramson, L.Y., Alloy, L.B.: Bidirectional associations between inflammatory biomarkers and depressive symptoms in adolescents: potential causal relationships. Clin. Psychol. Sci. **8**(4), 690–703 (2020). https://doi.org/10.1177/2167702620917458

Morra, S., Bisagno, E., Caviola, S., Delfante, C., Mammarella, I.C.: Working memory capacity and the development of quantitative central conceptual structures. Cogn. Instruct. **37**(4), 483–511 (2019). https://doi.org/10.1080/07370008.2019.1636797

Mullins-Sweatt, S.N., DeShong, H.L., Lengel, G.J., Helle, A.C., Krueger, R.F.: Disinhibition as a unifying construct in understanding how personality dispositions undergird psychopathology. J. Res. Pers. **80**, 55–61 (2019). https://doi.org/10.1016/j.jrp.2019.04.006

Namkoong, J.-E., Henderson, M.D.: Responding to causal uncertainty through abstract thinking. Curr. Dir. Psychol. Sci. **28**(6), 547–551 (2019). https://doi.org/10.1177/0963721419859346

Nelson, E.L., Gonzalez, S.L.: Measuring infant handedness reliably from reaching: a systematic review. Laterality. **25**(4), 430–454 (2020). https://doi.org/10.1080/1357650x.2020.1726367

Novembre, G., Iannetti, G.D.: Hyperscanning alone cannot prove causality: multibrain stimulation can. Trends Cogn. Sci. **25**(2), 96–99 (2021). https://doi.org/10.1016/j.tics.2020.11.003

Noyes, A., Keil, F.C., Dunham, Y.: Institutional actors: children's emerging beliefs about the causal structure of social roles. Dev. Psychol. **56**(1), 70–80 (2020). https://doi.org/10.1037/dev0000847

Oron, J.V., Navarro-Rubio, S., Luis, E.O.: Emotional education for personal growth in the early years. J. Theor. Philos. Psychol. (2020). https://doi.org/10.1037/teo0000150

Osbeck, L.M.: General psychology as common ground and point of view: enduring and evolving features. Rev. Gen. Psychol. **24**(1), 6–17 (2020). https://doi.org/10.1177/1089268019893974

Osborne-Crowley, K.: Social cognition in the real world: reconnecting the study of social cognition with social reality. Rev. Gen. Psychol. **24**(2), 144–158 (2020). https://doi.org/10.1177/1089268020906483

Parenteau, A.M., Alen, N.V., Deer, L.K., Nissen, A.T., Luck, A.T., Hostinar, C.E.: Parenting matters: parents can reduce or amplify children's anxiety and cortisol responses to acute stress. Dev. Psychopathol. **32**(5), 1799–1809 (2020). https://doi.org/10.1017/S0954579420001285

Perry Jr., W.G.: Forms of Intellectual and Ethical Development in the College Years: A Scheme. Holt, Rinehart and Winston, New York (1970)

Petrides, K.V.: A conceptual application of psychobionomy to the field of personality and individual differences. Personal. Individ. Differ. **147**, 135–143 (2019). https://doi.org/10.1016/j.paid.2019.04.018

Phaf, R.H.: Publish less, read more. Theory Psychol. **30**(2), 263–285 (2020). https://doi.org/10.1177/0959354319898250

Piaget, J.: The Psychology of Intelligence. Routledge, Abingdon (1947)

Piaget, J.: Play, Dreams, and Imitation in Childhood. Routledge, London (1951). (Original work published 1945)

Piaget, J.: The Origin of Intelligence in the Child. Routledge, London (1953)

Piaget, J.: The Construction of Reality in the Child. Basic Books, New York (1954). (Original work published 1937)

Piaget, J.: The Origins of Intelligence in Children. W.W. Norton, New York (1963). (Original work published 1936)

Piaget, J.: Part I: cognitive development in children: Piaget development and learning. J. Res. Sci. Teach. **2**(3), 176–186 (1964). https://doi.org/10.1002/tea.3660020306

Piaget, J.: The theory of stages in cognitive development. In: Green, D.R., Ford, M.P., Flamer, G.B. (eds.) Measurement and Piaget. McGraw-Hill, New York (1971)

Piaget, J.: Intellectual evolution from adolescence to adulthood. Hum. Dev. **15**(1), 1–12 (1972). https://doi.org/10.1159/000271225

Piaget, J.: Studies in Reflecting Abstraction. Psychology Press, London (2001)

Piazza, E.A., Hasenfratz, L., Hasson, U., Lew-Williams, C.: Infant and adult brains are coupled to the dynamics of natural communication. Psychol. Sci. **31**(1), 6–17 (2019). https://doi.org/10.1177/0956797619878698

Prieur, J., Barbu, S., Blois-Heulin, C., Lemasson, A.: The origins of gestures and language: history, current advances and proposed theories. Biol. Rev. **95**(3), 531–554 (2019). https://doi.org/10.1111/brv.12576

Raeff, C.: Distinguishing among varied kinds of developmental processes. Hum. Dev. **63**(Suppl 3–4), 245–254 (2019). https://doi.org/10.1159/000503820

Ratcliff, M.J.: A temporal puzzle: metamorphosis of the body in Piaget's early writings. Constr. Found. **14**(1), 73–81 (2018). http://constructivist.info/14/1/073

Reed, S.K.: Searching for the big pictures. Perspect. Psychol. Sci. **15**(3), 817–830 (2020). https://doi.org/10.1177/1745691619896255

Rindermann, H., Ackermann, A.L.: Piagetian tasks and psychometric intelligence: different or similar constructs? Psychol. Rep. (2020). https://doi.org/10.1177/0033294120965876

Roberts, A.I., Murray, L., Roberts, S.G.B.: Complex sociality of wild chimpanzees can emerge from laterality of manual gestures. Hum. Nat. **30**(3), 299–325 (2019). https://doi.org/10.1007/s12110-019-09347-3

Robinaugh, D.J., Hoekstra, R.H.A., Toner, E.R., Borsboom, D.: The network approach to psychopathology: a review of the literature 2008–2018 and an agenda for future research. Psychol. Med. **50**(3), 353–366 (2019). https://doi.org/10.1017/s0033291719003404

van Rooij, I., Baggio, G.: Theory before the test: how to build high-verisimilitude explanatory theories in psychological science. Perspect. Psychol. Sci. (2021). https://doi.org/10.1177/1745691620970604

Rosen, M.L., Hagen, M.P., Lurie, L.A., Miles, Z.E., Sheridan, M.A., Meltzoff, A.N., McLaughlin, K.A.: Cognitive stimulation as a mechanism linking socioeconomic status with executive function: a longitudinal investigation. Child Dev. **91**(4), 762–779 (2019). https://doi.org/10.1111/cdev.13315

Saffran, J.R.: Statistical language learning in infancy. Child Dev. Perspect. **14**(1), 49–54 (2020). https://doi.org/10.1111/cdep.12355

Santens, E., Claes, L., Dierckx, E., Dom, G.: Effortful control – A transdiagnostic dimension underlying internalizing and externalizing psychopathology. Neuropsychobiology. **79**(4–5), 255–269 (2020). https://doi.org/10.1159/000506134

Savi, A.O., Marsman, M., van der Maas, H.L.J., Maris, G.K.J.: The wiring of intelligence. Perspect. Psychol. Sci. **14**(6), 1034–1061 (2019). https://doi.org/10.1177/1745691619866447

Saxbe, D.E., Beckes, L., Stoycos, S.A., Coan, J.A.: Social allostasis and social allostatic load: a new model for research in social dynamics, stress, and health. Perspect. Psychol. Sci. **15**(2), 469–482 (2019). https://doi.org/10.1177/1745691619876528

Schaffer, J.E., Sainburg, R.L.: Interlimb responses to perturbations of bilateral movements are asymmetric. J. Mot. Behav. **53**(2), 217–233 (2021). https://doi.org/10.1080/00222895.2020.1760196

Scheel, A.M., Tiokhin, L., Isager, P.M., Lakens, D.: Why hypothesis testers should spend less time testing hypotheses. Perspect. Psychol. Sci. (2020). https://doi.org/10.1177/1745691620966795

Scorza, P., Duarte, C.S., Lee, S., Wu, H., Posner, J.E., Baccarelli, A., Monk, C.: Epigenetic intergenerational transmission: mothers' adverse childhood experiences and DNA methylation. J. Am. Acad. Child Adolesc. Psychiatry. **59**(7), 900–901 (2020). https://doi.org/10.1016/j.jaac.2020.03.008

Silvers, J.A.: Extinction learning and cognitive reappraisal: windows into the neurodevelopment of emotion regulation. Child Dev. Perspect. **14**(3), 178–184 (2020). https://doi.org/10.1111/cdep.12372

Sinnott, J.D.: The Development of Logic in Adulthood: Postformal Thought and Its Applications. Springer, New York (1998)

Sisto, A., Vicinanza, F., Campanozzi, L.L., Ricci, G., Tartaglini, D., Tambone, V.: Towards a transversal definition of psychological resilience: a literature review. Medicina. **55**(11), 745 (2019). https://doi.org/10.3390/medicina55110745

Smith, K.E., Pollak, S.D.: Rethinking concepts and categories for understanding the neurodevelopmental effects of childhood adversity. Perspect. Psychol. Sci. **16**(1), 67–93 (2021). https://doi.org/10.1177/1745691620920725

Sondermann, S., Stahl, J., Grave, U., Outzen, J., Moritz, S., Klein, J.P.: Preoperational thinking as a measure of social cognition is associated with long-term course of depressive symptoms. A longitudinal study involving patients with depression and healthy controls. Front. Psychiatry. **11**, 652 (2020). https://doi.org/10.3389/fpsyt.2020.00652

Sosa, R., dos Santos, C.V.: Toward a unifying account of impulsivity and the development of self-control. Perspect. Behav. Sci. **42**(2), 291–322 (2018). https://doi.org/10.1007/s40614-018-0135-z

Spencer, J.P.: The development of working memory. Curr. Dir. Psychol. Sci. **29**(6), 545–553 (2020). https://doi.org/10.1177/0963721420959835

Spencer, J.P., Austin, A., Schutte, A.R.: Contributions of dynamic systems theory to cognitive development. Cogn. Dev. **27**(4), 401–418 (2012). https://doi.org/10.1016/j.cogdev.2012.07.006

Staats, A.W.: Behavior and Personality: Psychological Behaviorism. Springer, New York (1996)

Stam, H.J.: Unifying psychology: epistemological act or disciplinary maneuver? J. Clin. Psychol. **60**(12), 1259–1262 (2004). https://doi.org/10.1002/jclp.20069

Stam, H.J.: The neurosciences and the search for a unified psychology: the science and esthetics of a single framework. Front. Psychol. **6**, 1467 (2015). https://doi.org/10.3389/fpsyg.2015.01467

Stanton, K.: Increasing diagnostic emphasis on negative affective dysfunction: potentially negative consequences for psychiatric classification and diagnosis. Clin. Psychol. Sci. **8**(3), 584–589 (2020). https://doi.org/10.1177/2167702620906147

Sternberg, R.J., Grigorenko, E.L.: Unified psychology. In: Kazdin, A.E. (ed.) Methodological Issues & Strategies in Clinical Research, 3rd edn, pp. 23–47. American Psychological Association, Washington, DC (2003)

Sternberg, R.J., Grigorenko, E.L., Kalmar, D.A.: The role of theory in unified psychology. J. Theor. Philos. Psychol. **21**(2), 99–117 (2001). https://doi.org/10.1037/h0091200

Strand, P.S.: The security-seeking impulse and the unification of attachment and culture. Psychol. Rev. **125**(5), 778–791 (2020). https://doi.org/10.1037/rev0000194

Strijkers, K., Chanoine, V., Munding, D., Dubarry, A.-S., Trébuchon, A., Badier, J.-M., Alario, F.-X.: Grammatical class modulates the (left) inferior frontal gyrus within 100 milliseconds when syntactic context is predictive. Sci. Rep. **9**(1), 4830 (2019). https://doi.org/10.1038/s41598-019-41376-x

Sullivan, M.W., Minar, N.J.: Developmental perspectives on "How emotions are made". Hum. Dev. **64**(2), 47–51 (2020). https://doi.org/10.1159/000506942

Suor, J.H., Sturge-Apple, M.L., Davies, P.T., Jones-Gordils, H.R.: The interplay between parenting and temperament in associations with children's executive function. J. Fam. Psychol. **33**(7), 841–850 (2019). https://doi.org/10.1037/fam0000558

Syed, M., Eriksson, P.L., Frisén, A., Hwang, C.P., Lamb, M.E.: Personality development from age 2 to 33: stability and change in ego resiliency and ego control and associations with adult adaptation. Dev. Psychol. **56**(4), 815–832 (2020). https://doi.org/10.1037/dev0000895

Tarullo, A.R., Tuladhar, C.T., Kao, K., Drury, E.B., Meyer, J.: Cortisol and socioeconomic status in early childhood: a multidimensional assessment. Dev. Psychopathol. **32**(5), 1876–1887 (2020). https://doi.org/10.1017/S0954579420001315

Tecwyn, E.C., Bechlivanidis, C., Lagnado, D.A., Hoerl, C., Lorimer, S., Blakey, E., McCormack, T., Buehner, M.J.: Causality influences children's and adults' experience of temporal order. Dev. Psychol. **56**(4), 739–755 (2020). https://doi.org/10.1037/dev0000889

Tiego, J., Bellgrove, M.A., Whittle, S., Pantelis, C., Testa, R.: Common mechanisms of executive attention underlie executive function and effortful control in children. Dev. Sci. **23**(3), e12918 (2019). https://doi.org/10.1111/desc.12918

Tisseyre, J., Marquet-Doléac, J., Barral, J., Amarantini, D., Tallet, J.: Lateralized inhibition of symmetric contractions is associated with motor, attentional and executive processes. Behav. Brain Res. **361**, 65–73 (2018). https://doi.org/10.1016/j.bbr.2018.12.034

Todd, P.M., Hills, T.T.: Foraging in mind. Curr. Dir. Psychol. Sci. **29**(3), 309–315 (2020). https://doi.org/10.1177/0963721420915861

Toomela, A.: The Psychology of Scientific Inquiry. Springer, Cham (2019)

Toomela, A.: Psychology today: still in denial, still outdated. Integr. Psychol. Behav. Sci. **54**(3), 563–571 (2020). https://doi.org/10.1007/s12124-020-09534-3

Topolewska-Siedzik, E., Cieciuch, J., Strus, W.: Personality underpinnings of identity: the role of metatraits and traits in identity formation modes. Self Identity. **18**(5), 529–549 (2018). https://doi.org/10.1080/15298868.2018.1483964

Tottenham, N.: Neural meaning making, prediction, and prefrontal-subcortical development following early adverse caregiving. Dev. Psychopathol. **32**(5), 1563–1578 (2020). https://doi.org/10.1017/S0954579420001169

Trafimow, D.: The role of auxiliary assumptions for the validity of manipulations and measures. Theory Psychol. **22**(4), 486–498 (2012). https://doi.org/10.1177/0959354311429996

Trafimow, D.: Mandatory theorizing and synthesis: a comment on Phaf (2020). Theory Psychol. **30**(2), 286–291 (2020). https://doi.org/10.1177/0959354319897969

Troller-Renfree, S.V., Buzzell, G.A., Fox, N.A.: Changes in working memory influence the transition from reactive to proactive cognitive control during childhood. Dev. Sci. **23**(6), e12959 (2020). https://doi.org/10.1111/desc.12959

Turner, A.P., Jensen, M.P., Day, M.A., Williams, R.M.: Behavioral activation and behavioral inhibition: an examination of function in chronic pain. Rehabil. Psychol. (2020). https://doi.org/10.1037/rep0000316

Uller, T., Laland, K.N. (eds.): Evolutionary Causation: Biological and Philosophical Reflections. MIT Press, Cambridge (2019a)

Uller, T., Laland, K.N.: Evolutionary causation. In: Uller, T., Laland, K.N. (eds.) Evolutionary Causation: Biological and Philosophical Reflections. MIT Press, Cambridge (2019b). https://doi.org/10.7551/mitpress/11693.003.0002

Uller, T., Feiner, N., Radersma, R., Jackson, I.S.C., Rago, A.: Developmental plasticity and evolutionary explanations. Evol. Dev. **22**(1–2), 47–55 (2019). https://doi.org/10.1111/ede.12314

Vaidya, C.J., You, X., Mostofsky, S., Pereira, F., Berl, M.M., Kenworthy, L.: Data-driven identification of subtypes of executive function across typical development, attention deficit hyperactivity disorder, and autism spectrum disorders. J. Child Psychol. Psychiatry. **61**(1), 51–61 (2020). https://doi.org/10.1111/jcpp.13114

Valsiner, J.: From clay feet to new psychology: starting to move. Integr. Psychol. Behav. Sci. **54**(3), 515–520 (2020). https://doi.org/10.1007/s12124-020-09564-x

VandenBos, G.R.: APA Dictionary of Psychology, 2nd edn. American Psychological Association, Washington, DC (2015)

Vannucci, R.C., Heier, L.A., Vannucci, S.J.: Cerebral asymmetry during development using linear measures from MRI. Early Hum. Dev. **139**, 104853 (2019). https://doi.org/10.1016/j.earlhumdev.2019.104853

Verschueren, M., Claes, L., Gandhi, A., Luyckx, K.: Identity and psychopathology: bridging developmental and clinical research. Emerg. Adulthood. **8**(5), 319–332 (2019). https://doi.org/10.1177/2167696819870021

Vygotsky, L.S.: Istoricheski smysl psikhologicheskogo krizisa. Metodologicheskoje issledovanije. (Historical meaning of the crisis in psychology. A methodological study). In: Luria, A.R., Jaroshevskii, M.G. (eds.) L.S Vygotsky. Sobranije sochinenii., Vaprosy teorii i istorii psikhologii, vol. 1, pp. 291–436. Moscow, Pedagogika (1982). Originally written in 1927; First published in 1982

Wade, M., Sheridan, M.A., Zeanah, C.H., Fox, N.A., Nelson, C.A., McLaughlin, K.A.: Environmental determinants of physiological reactivity to stress: the interacting effects of early life deprivation, caregiving quality, and stressful life events. Dev. Psychopathol. **32**(5), 1732–1742 (2020). https://doi.org/10.1017/S0954579420001327

Walker, C.M., Rett, A., Bonawitz, E.: Design drives discovery in causal learning. Psychol. Sci. **31**(2), 129–138 (2020). https://doi.org/10.1177/0956797619898134

Wang, C., Hu, Y., Weng, J., Chen, F., Liu, H.: Modular segregation of task-dependent brain networks contributes to the development of executive function in children. Neuroimage. **206**, 116334 (2019a). https://doi.org/10.1016/j.neuroimage.2019.116334

Wang, J., Wang, Y., Huang, H., Jia, Y., Zheng, S., Zhong, S., Chen, G., Huang, L., Huang, R.: Abnormal dynamic functional network connectivity in unmedicated bipolar and major depressive disorders based on the triple-network model. Psychol. Med. **50**(3), 465–474 (2019b). https://doi.org/10.1017/s003329171900028x

Wass, S.V., Whitehorn, M., Haresign, I., Phillips, E., Leong, V.: Interpersonal neural entrainment during early social interaction. Trends Cogn. Sci. **24**(4), 329–342 (2020). https://doi.org/10.1016/j.tics.2020.01.006

Watling, D., Damaskinou, N.: Children's facial emotion recognition skills: longitudinal associations with lateralization for emotion processing. Child Dev. **91**(2), 366–381 (2018). https://doi.org/10.1111/cdev.13188

Weems, C.F.: Commentary on the special issue on network analysis: assessment, intervention, theory, and the nature of reality: actualizing the potential of network perspectives on posttraumatic stress disorder. J. Trauma. Stress. **33**(1), 116–125 (2020). https://doi.org/10.1002/jts.22482

Wens, V., Bourguignon, M., Vander Ghinst, M., Mary, A., Marty, B., Coquelet, N., Naeije, G., Peigneux, P., Goldman, S., De Tiège, X.: Synchrony, metastability, dynamic integration, and competition in the spontaneous functional connectivity of the human brain. Neuroimage. **199**, 313–324 (2019). https://doi.org/10.1016/j.neuroimage.2019.05.081

Wente, A.O., Kimura, K., Walker, C.M., Banerjee, N., Fernández Flecha, M., MacDonald, B., Lucas, C., Gopnik, A.: Causal learning across culture and socioeconomic status. Child Dev. **90**(3), 859–875 (2017). https://doi.org/10.1111/cdev.12943

Wiberg, A., Ng, M., Al Omran, Y., Alfaro-Almagro, F., McCarthy, P., Marchini, J., Bennett, D.L., Smith, S., Douaud, G., Furniss, D.: Handedness, language areas and neuropsychiatric diseases: insights from brain imaging and genetics. Brain. **142**(10), 2938–2947 (2019). https://doi.org/10.1093/brain/awz257

Witherington, D.C., Boom, J.: Developmental dynamics: past, present, and future. Hum. Dev. **63**(Suppl 3–4), 264–276 (2019a). https://doi.org/10.1159/000504319

Witherington, D.C., Boom, J.: Conceptualizing the dynamics of development in the 21st century: process, (inter)action, and complexity. Hum. Dev. **63**(Suppl 3–4), 147–152 (2019b). https://doi.org/10.1159/000504097

Woods, S.B.: Biopsychosocial theories. In: Fiese, B.H., Celano, M., Deater-Deckard, K., Jouriles, E.N., Whisman, M.A. (eds.) APA Handbooks in Psychology®. APA Handbook of Contemporary Family Psychology: Foundations, Methods, and Contemporary Issues Across the Lifespan, pp. 75–92. American Psychological Association, Washington, DC (2019)

Yang, X., Ram, N., Lougheed, J.P., Molenaar, P.C.M., Hollenstein, T.: Adolescents' emotion system dynamics: network-based analysis of physiological and emotional experience. Dev. Psychol. **55**(9), 1982–1993 (2019). https://doi.org/10.1037/dev0000690

Young, G.: Development and Causality: Neo-Piagetian Perspectives. Springer, New York (2011)

Young, G.: Causality in psychiatry: a hybrid symptom network construct model. Front. Psych. **6**, 164 (2015). https://doi.org/10.3389/fpsyt.2015.00164

Young, G.: Unifying Causality and Psychology: Being, Brain and Behavior. Springer, Cham (2016)

Young, G.: Causality and Development: Neo-Eriksonian Perspectives. Springer, Cham (2019)

Young, G., Décarie, T.G.: An ethology-based catalogue of facial/vocal behavior in infancy. Anim. Behav. **25**, 95–107 (1977). https://doi.org/10.1016/0003-3472(77)90071-9

Younger, J.W., Lee, K., Demir-Lira, O.E., Booth, J.R.: Brain lateralization of phonological awareness varies by maternal education. Dev. Sci. **22**(6), e12807 (2019). https://doi.org/10.1111/desc.12807

Zilcha-Mano, S.: Toward personalized psychotherapy: the importance of the trait-like/state-like distinction for understanding therapeutic change. Am. Psychol. (2020). https://doi.org/10.1037/amp0000629

Chapter 9
Further Extensions and Innovations

This chapter presents six innovations that extend the innovative stance of the present work and its integrative efforts. First, it tackles science, generally, through the concept of the scientific formula. It elaborates its stage view of development, showing further how couples can be viewed from this perspective. It moves to concepts related to executive function, stress dysregulation disorder, and inner peace. It presents a speculative model of how larger entities, especially societal, might evolve according to the present developmental stage model. Although disparate in contents, the six innovations are consistent with the present unification project for psychology.

The Science Formula: The Nature of Science and Why It Matters

Science is increasingly under attack by polemical actors who do not understand it, choose not to understand, or willfully misrepresent it for non-scientific and even malevolent ends. Science is in the midst of a replicability and retraction crisis, contributing to making it a target to its detractors. Also, science does not have a precise, common definition that works for all its disciplines. For example, the traditional scientific method of experimentation cannot apply to cosmology, and Einstein was famous for his physics thought experiments. One criticism of psychology is that its scientific approach cannot approximate harder disciplines such as physics and chemistry.

As far as we understand it, science can be considered a formula to follow that has both positive (present) and negative (avoidance) attributes. By formula, I mean that science has rigorous attributes that define its thinking process and investigative efforts. Scientists do not deviate from them in their search for verifiable theory and data. An example of the former positive attributes is the rigor that scientists bring to

G. Young, *Causality and Neo-Stages in Development*,
https://doi.org/10.1007/978-3-030-82540-9_9

their theorizing and empirical investigation. An example of the former negative attributes is their abhorrence in supporting unfalsifiable or outlandish claims that lack support; or distort arguments and findings toward supporting their statements.

Scientists follow the scientific formula in order to reduce the uncertainty of their concepts and empirical results. At the theoretical level, they delve into existing ideas, concepts, theories, and models and through critical compare-contrast analysis and synthesis, they emerge with better ideas, ones that can survive critical exploration by others, but often leading to more refined concepts than had been proposed, or even very different ones. At the empirical level, they operationalize their concepts into testable predictions that are exposed to rigorous research methodologies to support or disconfirm them. Then, after they are published, they are subject to critique by others in order to improve their concepts and methods.

The essence of science lies in the rigor both theoretically and empirically that it brings to its effort to understand natural phenomena, physical as well as biological, including humans. There are commonalities across disciplines in the scientific discourse and discovery process, despite disciplinary divergences and differences. At the most basic level, science seeks truth, allowing for the eye of the observer to influence or construct that truth aside from, or in interaction with, the discovered truth directly reflecting nature independently. Science seeks not only description of perceived truth and nature but also understanding of the mechanisms, explanations, or theories that underlie the descriptions. Science is a causality hub that reflects human nature, which I have termed as causal, e.g., in my characterization of our species as *Homo Causa* (Young 2016). Science reflects the epitome of our causal mind and our deep thrust in finding causality.

The present work has argued that causality is the common element in all the subdisciplines in psychology and can serve to integrate or unify it as a common front. Causality cannot be an end-point. In this regard, we will never have the absolute one answer for the causality of human behavior, because of its ongoing revision and verification, as in science generally; psychology as causality is a project or a process, more than a product or a finality. The arguments for the nature of psychology that I am proposing has underscored its causality imperative, a commonality that few would deny yet that no one else has argued as our most fundamental trait. In this sense, recognition of the essence of psychology as being its causality focus would place it at the forefront in science. In the end, science explicitly seeks the same description and causal explanation of natural phenomena as does psychology.

The present work has sought to close the circle of science, psychology, healthy skepticism, seeking truth, theorizing well, rigorously investigating truth claims, and riding the wave of narrowing the gap in the search for uncertainty reduction and eliminating false and fake news in science and narrative about science. Also, psychology is great at understanding the human condition that would lead to these false and fake news that undermine human health and well-being and even its survival. Placing causality at the forefront in the scientific formula and in science activity and psychology unification will do us well in doing science and psychology better, having their disseminated ideas and findings better accepted by the public, and ensuring that it increases in its wave of discovery and respect.

Extension of Couple Work (Couple Therapy) According to the Neo-Eriksonian 25-Step Model

Table 9.1 examines problems in the couple from the perspective of the 25 Neo-Eriksonian steps in development that has been posited. Briefly, it gives 25 ways that romantic partners might react to wrongful behavior by their partners, with which step prominent in this regard depending on the step in the model that might be most salient for their personal development in light of their past history. What might happen at each of the model's steps when the challenges and crises inherent in the steps are the ones being faced by a romantic couple? The reaction of the aggrieved party in the couple might be to stay or leave, depending on the couple dynamic and the individual psychological profiles and context of the parties.

The therapist could use the template of possible reactions according to the model to discern how to approach the aggrieved romantic partner, whether the person leaves or stays, or the couple if both members attend sessions. It might also give insight to the therapist into their patients' past development beyond whatever had been reported to the therapist.

Executive Function as a Critical Causal Mechanism in Behavior

To this point, for the topic of causality in psychology, the present work has not disambiguated the concepts of causality and mechanism. Causality should be central in explaining and modeling behavior. However, the exact mechanisms that specify exactly how causality works in this regard are being elucidated or might not even be known. One needs to adopt a hierarchical approach in understanding causality in relation to the mechanism. Specifying exact mechanisms must remain the goal in causal work in psychology, but the risk always here is reductionism or reducing behavior to specific genetic, physiological, and brain mechanisms. A typical explanatory hierarchy in understanding behavior might have generic modeling at the top of the hierarchy, such as empiricism/positivism or constructivism/relationism, and specific mechanisms might not be included in the modeling. At another level in the hierarchy of behavioral explanation, and globally, one will find particular theories of behavior, such as the behavioral, cognitive, ecological, psychodynamic, or biological/medical. At this level, the models and theories might specify certain mechanisms. Between these two levels lies more integrative models, such as the biopsychosocial, the stress-diathesis, the bioecological, and so on. These levels might include causal mechanisms but should not be criticized when their level of generality cannot provide it. For example, the present work has supported a biopsychosocial framework, but without specifying exactly how the three factors interact in behavior. There are multiple factors in each of the three domains of the model, not to mention developmental and evolutionary aspects. Furthermore, I have argued

Table 9.1 Twenty-five (25) ways to leave or stay with your lover, according to the present 25-step Neo-Eriksonian growth model

Step	Explanation
1. Distance acts vs. no (lifeless) acts	If wronged by a romantic partner and you stay, you keep your distance and feel lifeless, in a continuation of the pattern already present in the relationship. Perhaps you feel that past maltreatment and abuse is repeating itself and there is little you can do, or even want to do. If you leave, perhaps your reaction is even worse. Either way, you could react by wanting to kill yourself and behaving to hurt yourself. In general, your behavior is very reflexive, not directed well or on target toward its goal. It is disorganized in its movement, even with wrong distances to targets
2. Nursing acts vs. rootless acts	If wronged by a romantic partner and you stay, perhaps you do so because you need any anchor for yourself, no matter how terrible the partner behaves. Perhaps you feel that past maltreatment and denial of yourself are repeating and there is little you can do, or even want to do. If you leave, perhaps your reaction is even worse. You feel that you have no anchor, and that you are missing roots. You feel helpless and hopeless, not even taking care of yourself or anybody. If you get a new partner, you might feel even more rootless, or perhaps go the other way, anchoring no matter what
3. Outcome acts vs. outcast acts (that excluded you)	If wronged by a romantic partner and you stay, perhaps you do so because you need to feel included and not an outcast no matter what. Perhaps you feel that you were always excluded, the same thing is happening, and you could never develop your own goals, so staying gives you some direction. If you leave, perhaps your reaction is even worse. You feel without direction, incapable of defining your goals, and furthermore, you feel that you are a person who deserves to be disregarded, not listened to, and not belonging to anything. You greatly ignore people and ignore yourself
4. Care-giving acts vs. careless giving acts	If wronged by a romantic partner and you stay, perhaps you do so because you did not receive good care earlier on at home, and your life schema involves people behaving like this, thereby confirming it. You had received negligent care for the most part, learning that care-giving is without the required care in the behavior, being uncaring or poor in care. If you leave the partner, you continue to not expect good caring, and you continue to give careless care, perhaps even worse than before. Paradoxically, you might seek much care from others, but make too much caring demands
5. Emotional acts vs. mal-emotional or negative emotional acts	If wronged by a romantic partner and you stay, you feel very emotional; and the emotions are negative, intense, and frequent. Perhaps you suppress those emotions in the relationship, being detached but perhaps while seething inside. In either case, you had manifested these patterns, but now they are worse. If you leave and especially if you get another partner, either of those reactions take place, e.g., being frustrated, unhappy, and even in rage, fear, or both, leading you to have further emotional turmoil or trouble. Or, you might show no emotions and feel detached, perhaps seething inside

(continued)

Table 9.1 (continued)

Step	Explanation
6. Dyadic acts vs. dys-dyadic or poor interaction acts	If wronged by a romantic partner and you stay, you express control, domination, and manipulation, accentuating existing patterns in the relationship. If you leave, perhaps your reaction is even worse. You had never learned to interact with people the right way. You were not warm or sensitive socially, but clumsy and confused, withdrawn into silence. Or, perhaps you were angry and rejected people. You repeat these patterns with others, having poor social interaction skills, including with any new partners; and in the latter case, even more so, or you try too hard but clumsily
7. Trust acts vs. mistrust acts	If wronged by a romantic partner and you stay, a sense of mistrust governs all your actions, considering it was not on solid grounds to begin with. You had not had confidence in people already, and your partner magnifies that feeling, hampering your ability to feel close in any relationship. You feel morose and purposeless, and passive and suspicious, which becomes worse if you leave the partner. You might carry a mistrustful anger into the next relationship. Or, instead, perhaps you trust blindly anybody else (and are taken advantage of by them)
8. Sociability acts vs. un-sociability or poor sociability acts	If wronged by a romantic partner and you stay, your sense of insecurity in the relationship grows and your sociability with the partner suffers. To begin with, there were concerns along these lines, which exacerbate. If you leave, perhaps you are quite unsociable or poorly sociable, and cannot establish a secure feeling in relationships. Perhaps you totally avoid any relations, being super wary and isolated. Or, you might attach to anybody without being careful about it. You relate to others in any of the modes of being avoidant, fearful, rejecting, or ambivalent
9. Autonomy (independence) acts vs. doubt (dependence) acts	If wronged by a romantic partner and you stay, your sense of dependence, which had been quite ingrained, is heightened. You become excessively dependent, doubtful, and without motivation to act for yourself, feeling inward, not confident or satisfied socially. You even feel subjugated. Or, you go the other way and leave, but these tendencies magnify, leaving you defiant, argumentative, and not cooperative. Perhaps you seek anyone who can accommodate your dependence, no matter the nature of the person. Or, contrarily, you become super autonomous and avoid any dependence
10. Interdigitational (give and take) acts vs. de-digitational (give or take) acts	If wronged by a romantic partner and you stay, you abandon any reciprocity in giving and taking that you might have had, however minimal. You have an increased difficulty in sharing, being concerned, and feeling fondness and even love. Instead, you might hate your partner. You might not feel self-pride and even hate yourself. If you leave, including in any new relationship, you especially seek to take from others and not give, or you give too much of yourself, denying yourself, in a lack of balance. You could seek power, seek confrontation, and end up manipulating the other easily

(continued)

Table 9.1 (continued)

Step	Explanation
11. Super-ordinate (well-coordinated) acts vs. dis-coordinate ((internally) uncoordinated) acts	If wronged by a romantic partner and you stay, you feel disjointed or "in pieces" (not coordinated). You had not developed to feel together and felt uncoordinated inside, and this feeling propagates more in your psyche. So, as a reaction, you put your personal needs in the middle of everything (being "egocentric," self-centered). Perhaps you become somewhat resistant, too. Or, perhaps you go the opposite way, letting go of your needs as you define them, and always accept whatever other people want, especially your partner if you stay, or a new partner if you do not
12. Initiative acts vs. guilt acts	If wronged by a romantic partner and you stay, you could lose all drive and feel guilty. You could lapse into unconscious patterns of being very inward and withdrawing, or unconscious patterns of desiring sexually a parent, adding to the sense of guilt. You could generally develop unconscious (unaware) sexual problems that seem to come from nowhere, or you could develop general problems in initiative (having too much or too little). If you leave, e.g., for a new partner, you could express even more over-initiating without guilt, or be guilt-ridden and under-initiating, or combinations
13. Identification and gender acts vs. problematic identification and gender acts	If wronged by a romantic partner and you stay, anything admired or identified with in the partner will be compromised or lost. You might query your own identifications, even your gender preferences and sexuality, perhaps not wanting to be like your past self or wanting to become the opposite. Or, perhaps you do not identify with anyone, and become narcissistic, uncontrollable, and so on. If you leave, this turmoil will become more salient. Or, you might accept any new partner, hoping that the person will help you figure out yourself
14. Industry (putting in good effort) acts vs. inferiority acts	If wronged by a romantic partner and you stay, you could feel very inferior, and lose self-esteem. You could lose desire to try in the relationship or in daily chores/activities, or you might even rebel. Also, you could compensate by trying extra hard at work/school. This could lead you to lose interest and you vegetate at home and gravitate to wrong friends. Or, perhaps you go the other way, and feel too superior, while you become insensitive and lie, as needed. If you leave, these trends might worsen, causing a sense of generalized inferiority or, to compensate, workaholism
15. Role/personality tryout acts vs. role/personality confusion acts	If wronged by a romantic partner and you stay, you feel that both your role in the relationship and that your personality have been undercut, and you brood. You had been experimenting unsuccessfully for the most part with different roles, friends, attitudes, and personalities, but that process stops or is jeopardized, taking place either too much or only on the surface. You become more confused in these roles/personality tryouts. Or, you engage in negative (e.g., anti-social) tryouts. If you stay, these possible reactions could be worse, including with any new partners

(continued)

Table 9.1 (continued)

Step	Explanation
16. Consciousness (being aware) acts vs. contra-conscious (not being aware) acts	If wronged by a romantic partner and you stay, you struggle even more with your newly developing awareness and consciousness, e.g., of self, people, environment, society, and the world. But in losing a supportive partner, this type of opening in thinking becomes problematic. Perhaps you become less concerned with becoming conscious and you become more conforming than normal, or you start to seek even more conscious awareness, but in fanatical or superficial ways. If you leave, these changes in conscious opening could multiply. Any new partner will magnify your dilemmas
17. Identity acts (positive ones) vs. identity diffusion (or negative identity) acts	If wronged by a romantic partner and you stay, your pursuit of positive identities, already compromised, will wither, and the pursuit of negative identities will increase. This will lead to more (a) confusion in identity; (b) putting off the search for identity; (c) simply adopting identities of other people without thinking about it; (d) adopting negative identities, such as in teenage gangs/delinquency; or (e) adopting many identities, but all on the surface, false, or fake. If you leave, these diverging acts could diversify, especially should you attempt a new relationship
18. Nurturing acts vs. mis-nurturing (not nurturing) acts	If wronged by a romantic partner and you stay, you become dysregulated and can no longer engage in caring behavior of your partner, to give support and bring out the best in them. This could also apply to other social relationships, with you being depressed. Perhaps you will ignore people, not like them, and so on. Or, perhaps you will nurture people seemingly more than before, but only on the surface and without real caring. Or, you might overly nurture, forgetting about yourself. Your next relationship might be one that struggles with nurturing—To give, receive, or both
19. Intimacy acts (with partner) vs. (social) isolation acts	If wronged by a romantic partner and you stay, you cannot feel positively engaged with your partner, and perhaps you just go through the motions. Or, you might feel this way anywhere in your activities or in relating to people, e.g., at work, in school, and with any other family member, including with any children. You no longer feel any positive feelings for the partner, or perhaps also in everything you do. You could reject further romance and feel lonely and empty. Or, you could try to fake it in a new relationship with a partner, but this risks even behaving roughly in reaction
20. Universal (general concern for all people) acts vs. self-singular (self-focused) acts	If wronged by a romantic partner and you stay, you lose care and concern for people generally. You had been concerned for all people and desired to care for or help your partner or anybody in need. You had a basic helping moral value felt for everybody. Without getting good support this way from your partner, you could become a person who rejects helping others—Family and all people included—Or only help them without feeling (or just to get praise). If you leave, your inward turning could be even worse, and your next relationship especially could become self-concerned

(continued)

Table 9.1 (continued)

Step	Explanation
21. Meta-collecting (seeing the big picture) acts vs. disillusionment acts	If wronged by a romantic partner and you stay, you could become especially disillusioned and down on your life generally. You could lose seeing the big picture of things and their interconnections at many joined levels. You could lose concern for the growth of all groups of peoples, no longer wanting to see them capable of helping other peoples. You could ignore other peoples, act against them, or even detest them. Or, you could help peoples only out of habit, doing it superficially. If you leave, these motivations could increase, and even more so with a new partner
22. Generativity (generating) acts vs. self-absorption (no responsibility) acts	If wronged by a romantic partner and you stay, you could stop giving your best to your responsibilities, not only to the partner but also perhaps to family/relationships, work/study, and society/world. When problems arise, you could have fewer coping resources, let go your responsibilities, feel empty, focus only on yourself, and not grow. Or, you might try hard to take your responsibilities, but just on the surface or because of past habits. If you enter a new relationship, taking responsibilities will be difficult, or you will overextend yourself in compensation
23. Catalytic (growing others) acts vs. midlife crisis acts	If wronged by a romantic partner and you stay, your engagement in your responsibilities and desire to see others grow or get better because of them could be dampened. You could let go all your responsibilities even though you had taken on them well up to this point in time. You could change and act just for yourself. You could reject loved ones, work, and other responsibilities. Or, you could keep them and just go through the motions, feeling sad. If you leave, these possible directions in your life course might accentuate, including with a new partner. This is the classic mid-life crisis
24. Ego integrity (feeling good about the self and life) acts vs. despair acts	If wronged by a romantic partner and you stay, you could develop a generalized despair about yourself and life. You could lose comfort with your life trajectory, family and relationships, work or study, and no longer want to help people and society. Instead, you could feel very low, depressed, or disappointed. You could have regrets in not being capable in giving your best in your life, not being fully present in everything done, etc. also, perhaps you get angry, can't do anything, etc. if you leave, including if there is another relationship, the same would apply, but worse
25. Cathartic (purifying) acts vs. abandonment acts	If wronged by a romantic partner and you stay, you could no longer feel that life had been uplifting, and you could feel alone and abandoned. You are at an age of the person facing death, but could no longer look back fondly and face it without fear. You had had a broad, wise view of life, how you lived it, and what death means. But your sense of an inner peace and spirituality could be disrupted. You could even struggle with death itself. You might seek last-minute help from others, but the risk is that they cannot help with your end-of-life issues or that they magnify in doing so

Note. The table refers to one romantic partner discovering their romantic partner is a wrong choice, for example, being narcissistic, cheating, or even abusive. The wronged partner might choose to stay or leave, partly depending on biological vulnerabilities, if any, and depending on personal, social, and situational dynamics, including difficulties that she or he had encountered in terms of

(continued)

Table 9.1 (continued)

the present Neo-Eriksonian model. The titles of the 25 steps in the model and the oppositional poles for each of them work quite well in describing the ways that an aggrieved romantic partner might react to their poorly behaving romantic partner. I have highlighted the critical term in each of the 25 steps, which gives a snapshot of the 25 ways that one could experience wrongful behavior by a romantic partner. Of course, the wrongful behavior by the partner in a romantic couple might elicit a split in the couple, with no evident psychological difficulties emerging in the leaving party. That said, the difficulties elicited might reflect those in the table
In reaction, the wronged party might decide to stay because, in one way or another, they lack the resources and capacity to react and leave. Or, they might leave but with a resignation and not seeking another partner. Or, they might leave and overreact, e.g., with rapidly seeking another partner and making the same mistake, or another one
The 25 steps in the model are developmental, referring to the lack of support or even abuse at each age associated with the model that might lead to fixations in development, or at least great challenges to navigate the developmental disturbances. However, any one earlier step might become problematic for an individual because of later occurring lack of support or even abuse and not earlier ones. For example, a preteen might suffer from parental abuse only at this age period, which might be repercussions for previously successfully navigated developmental challenges, e.g., a later abuse in a preteen can lead to a lack of Eriksonian trust even though that had developed quite well in infancy. Therefore, the 25 reactions by a wronged romantic partner in the table do not necessarily implicate only earlier developmental problems as per the ages associated with the steps
Finally, although the table illustrates how youth and adults might react to the wrongful behavior of romantic partners in 25 different ways, more than likely various combinations of the 25 patterns might be evident. Moreover, each of the 25 ways represents prototypical patterns that could vary over individuals. Research-wise, the table can be used to create a questionnaire for studies that examine how people might react to a partner eliciting such reactions and the personal factors involved in their differentiation and combination

that the psychological component should be termed personal and include factors such as belief in free will, motivation, personality, and so on. At other levels in this hierarchical description of explanation in psychology, mechanisms become central points. The research on gene X environment interactions provides a critical example in this regard, as do the wide-ranging genomic research seeking poly-genomic influences on behavior. Similarly, the burgeoning network research is specifying behavioral linkages and intercortical linkages and how they relate. Finally, the ecological model is specifying the layers of environmental influence on behavior (Table 9.2).

Then, mechanisms can be specified for their level and complexity: some will be higher-order, such as networks in behavior or brain that predispose behavior in certain directions. Others will be very specific, such as in relation to specific genetic instructions, and physiological and neural patterning. Finally, intermediate levels reside in behavioral organization and brain function, linking higher-order and lower-order mechanistic levels. One such area concerns executive function, and the present chapter articulates a model of EF that includes prior versions but makes it more general, adaptive, ongoing, and linked to goal setting and problem-solving in context, generally.

Executive function (EF) provides a salient mid-level mechanism toward understanding behavioral causality but, in its literature, EF has not been uniformly defined nor uniformly modeled. The concept has neuropsychological, developmental, and behavioral regulation roots, perhaps accounting for the disparate approaches to it.

Table 9.2 An activation-inhibition coordination model of executive function (EF): a hierarchical biopsychosocial-informed model of behavioral/co-relational (psychological) (mis) management processes and products/outcomes

<table>
<tr><td colspan="3">I. Superordinate top-down processes</td></tr>
<tr><td colspan="3">Activation-inhibition (dys)coordination
X (as applied to)
Relational (psychological) co-(dys)regulation
↕</td></tr>
<tr><td colspan="3">II. Midlevel factors/variables</td></tr>
<tr>
<td>Co-relational **X**
(psychological)
Self/other (dys)control
(i.e., self-control)
factors/variables (behavioral, emotional, including physiological, cognitive, including schematic) [including any personal resource Depletion and lifestyle depleting factors, including addictions, poor sleep, poor self-care] and any [biological CNS/ANS factors, e.g., TBI/ physical injuries] and any [vulnerabilities/ susceptibilities/risks, e.g., past traumas/ adversities; other developmental impacts, including abuse; past/pre-existing psychiatric diagnoses/disabilities/impairments; persecution/ poverty/racism; etc. factors/variables]</td>
<td>**Environmental** **X**
Contextual
factors/variables
(situation/location/setting/circumstance, task/problem/stressor, and their components, their demands/constraints, their time limitations, supports/buffers, including social (parents, siblings, family, friends, classmates, co-workers peers), institutional (work, school), or their absence; neighborhood, society/country, ecology) [and *personal context* (demographics/ moderators, e.g.,, age, sex, culture, ethnicity, SES)]</td>
<td>**Personal**
Factors/variables
(mediators)
[motivation/attitude/effort(pace, persistence)]
[tendencies/traits (temperament/personality; including self-esteem/self-confidence; e.g., low)]
[primary skills (resilience/coping skills; cognitive skills communication/language skills social skills) or their lack, errors]
[Efficacy enhancement/
Executive function and secondary skills
A. Inhibition skills
(and their activation in coordination)
[see table 3.1 for inhibition skills]
B. Inhibition-relevant domains
1. Attention/awareness skills (self, context/other)
2. Concentration/focus skills
3. Pattern recognition/ encoding and interpreting/Appraisal skills
4. Goal setting/intentionality skills
5. Problem solving skills (articulating the problem, possible solutions)
6. Working memory (updating) skills
7. Prioritizing/planning/organization (programming, sequencing) skills
8. Statistical learning, causal learning/consequences skills
9. Automaticity/reflexivity; vs. non-reflexivity/ reflectivity skills
10. Flexibility/rerouting, set shifting skills
11. Reward management skills
12. Delay, distract skills
13. Prediction skills
14. Weighing alternatives, decision making skills
15. Action initiation skills
16. Regulating online, monitoring, and revising skills (or their lack/ errors)]</td>
</tr>
<tr><td colspan="3">↕
III. Co-relational/psychological or behavioral (mis)managed products/outcomes
(as expressed through activation-inhibition coordination mechanisms (e.g., in neurons, brain circuits and connectivity, and behavior (action, emotion, communication, cognition) in context</td></tr>
</table>

- Adaptive implemented behavior in context (or their lack, errors)
- Problem solving implementation (attempt) (or their lack, errors)

Note. The table describes a broad model of executive function (EF) that contextualizes it in its biopsychosocial influences. It is meant to apply to any type of organism, and thus is referred to as a model of action efficacy enhancement, which would involve higher-order EFs in mammals. Despite its ubiquity, EF has no one universal definition, but it is generally conceived as the ability for a task at hand to plan and coordinate online a desired adaptive action partly through suppressing interfering activity or alternatives (e.g., Squire 2009). The core EF components have not been specified unequivocally, but the ones that emerge in the literature on a constant basis include inhibitory skills, working memory, attention, flexibility, problem solving, and monitoring. EF has been associated with moderating cortical functions, especially in the frontal lobes/prefrontal cortex, but presently I prefer to take a broad view of problem solving and EF and not limit the model to specific brain-mediated circuitry and only mammalian. This allows for a longer list of skills necessary for successful problem resolution, and the current models lists 15 of them. The title of the table indicates its broad-ranging nature, and that it is informed by a biopsychosocial perspective as well as an expansion of EF in terms of one of its core components of inhibition. Specifically, the current emphasis on activation-inhibition coordination (AIC) as a cross-level causal mechanism over neuron, brain, behavior, and their organization suggests that the inhibition component in EF should be broadened. Moreover, AIC is taken not only to apply as a top-down causal process in behavior and as a core EF component but also as underpinning all the EF core components in one way or another. Thus, inhibition is considered a superordinate EF skill and not merely one of its components, although the efficacy in its deployments affects the 15 components to EF identified in the table. The title of the table also indicates that behavior is considered a co-function of the individual in context and can be managed well or mismanaged depending on a host of factors. The first level of the table indicates that, aside from AIC, a critical aspect of behavioral management is relational or psychological co-regulation (or its dysregulation). As for the mid-level tier of the model, the various biological, environmental, and psychological dimensions to behavior regulation/management are considered, with self-control/coregulation highlighted to the left, and EF to the right. Psychological co-regulation (self-control) is considered broadly in terms of the components of behavior, emotions, cognition, and self. Personal resource depletion affects self-control, and many factors can diminish it, including biological/brain/physical ones as well as past experiences and psychological/psychiatric conditions. The middle column lists the relevant environmental factors involved in behavioral/psychological co-regulation, and for present purposes, the task/problem at hand is critical, as well as its demand characteristics and constraints in context. Personal factors include demographics, but especially concern variables such as motivation/attitude/effort, temperament/personality, self-esteem/confidence, coping skills, and key skills related to socializing, cognition, etc.

As for the 15 core EF components in the present model beyond the inhibition related ones, they are listed tentatively and need further refinement conceptually and empirically. They include classic ones, such as attention, concentration, goal setting, problem solving, working memory, planning, flexibility, and monitoring, but add ones that seem critical to effective adaptation and problem solving. For example, the problem needs to be apperceived well, and so I added core components related to pattern recognition/appraisal as other mediators between stimulus and response. Also, I added the statistical learning and causal learning that even infants seem to engage in these regards. Learning is critical to behavior and has not generally been considered a core component in EF models to date. I added the ability to simplify through chunking/automaticity, or needing to be more deliberative, as in System I and II thought. Of course, there is the impulsivity component that interferes with effective EF, and I referred to the reward system in this regard (seeking immediate gratification, for example). Effective action implementation might require delay and keeping distractions at bay. The brain is now considered Bayesian, which prefers to its predictive capacity, which seems critical to problem solving. Finally, the latter needs quality evaluation of options before decision making, and then making the initiatory step in acting on the matter at hand. As for the inhibitory basis for these 15 proposed core EF components, consider that attention and concentration require control of interference, distraction, etc., in the context of appropriate activation of sustained focus. Deciphering the problem (stimulus, pattern) requires the same type of coordination so figure is distinguished from ground. Goal setting/intentionality determination also requires highlighting the intrinsic importance of the situation at hand through these coordinative processes, and imagining/establishing a viable endpoint to it. Problem solving cannot take place effectively without putting in place a plan that is targeted to the desires end point and keeps under control distractions, mind wandering, etc. Working memory can be verbal, nonverbal, etc., and will work only when the essential elements to the problem and the requisite solution are kept at the forefront, with the rest inhibited. Prioritizing and planning are crucial to problem solving, and clearly would profit from effective AIC. Learning requires effective inhibition of outliers and disrupters to target what is critical, including causally. The navigation between automaticity and deliberation in thought also would seem to be especially tuned to AIC skills. By definition, flexibility/rerouting/set shifting is an apex AIC skill. Reward management requires that impulsivity inhibition, as mentioned as well as the more positive focus that good AIC could allow. Delay/distraction would appear cardinal AIC skills. Prediction, weighing alternatives, and decision making, action initiation, and monitoring all could not unfold well without them

Finally, action/behavior implementation toward desired goals has been described as requiring effective AIC generally as per the present modeling

The present chapter argues that EF function is not just isolated to tasks requiring a higher-order organization construct that intervenes to organize behavior and keep it in track, as the name executive function implies. Rather, it is a common function to help ongoing adaptive behavior to arrive at its ends, especially when problem-solving is involved, as will happen in much of behavior when goals are involved. EF is not an agent within behavioral, regulation, or brain function that stands as an intermediary to input and output, in a homuncular fashion, being the seat of behavior control or being responsible for it. Rather, the brain, behavior, and its organization create a whole system in which no one level is privileged. That said, the integrative, intermediary level in the hierarchical organization of brain, regulation, and brain constituted by EF is a primary node in the network of interrelated functions and their neuropsychological, network, and neurological underpinnings.

The EF model that I have developed is biopsychosocial in scope. It finds at its apex the concept of activation-inhibition coordination as its primary modality, replacing and incorporating the commonly found inhibition function in its modeling. The model is co-relational, fitting with its biopsychosocial modeling. Finally, it includes 15 other modalities that are involved in problem-solving/goal work. This is a broad model but can be simplified to several higher-order factors, such as is typically found, although in the present work, the factors might relate to steps in the goal-setting/problem-solving process.

Template for Stress Dysregulation Disorder

The next contribution of the present work provides a table that can be used in assessments, including for responses to stress, in trauma work, and generally in understanding patient symptomatology in the DSM-5/ICD 11. Table 9.3 presents a list of assessment questions for individuals presenting with complex issues that impact a wide range of psychological/psychiatric behaviors and functions and therefore is consistent with the development of the polythetic criteria for a proposed new addition to the DSM, that of stress dysregulation disorder. The table was constructed from several perspectives. First, it can help individuals confronting and reacting to their presenting problems. It gives the range of core and consequent issues related to immediate or longstanding problems. In terms of helping couples specify their issues, the differential reporting by the partners could help the therapist understand the nature of the reasons for the counseling and the therapeutic directions to take. Second, the table serves as a diagnostic template for common reactions to stress, triggers, and trauma, with the symptoms of PTSD, acute stress disorder, adjustment disorder, major depression, and multiple anxiety and panic disorders quite embedded in it. Third, the organization of the table indicates how long-term complex PTSD might differ from recent-event PTSD. In this regard, although I include in the table the extra complex PTSD symptomatology in the ICD-11 (World Health Organization 2019), which concerns affect dysregulation, negative self-esteem, and social dysregulation, among others. I do not place them as the exclusive primary

Table 9.3 Presenting problem/stressor/trigger/trauma (generalized and individualized) dysregulation: Template for stress dysregulation disorder

Item explanation
(A) Stressor/trigger/trauma/presenting problem
(a) Acute stressor/trigger/trauma. An immediate event such as a motor vehicle accident or natural disaster
(b) Chronic stressor/trigger/trauma. An ongoing trauma or a past one with lingering effects
(c) General presenting problem. Endless possibilities described by the patient(s)
(B) Psychological components dysregulated
(B1) **Core (higher-order, top-down)**
1. Reaction
(i) Immediate/tonic/short term (e.g., peritraumatic)
(a) Hyper-react/greatly emote. For example, fight or flight, scream/rage, catastrophize *(for children, temper tantrums, too)*
(b) Hypo-react/no reaction. For example, freeze, put on a shell, confusion/shock/ in a fog/dazed; dissociate (includes reports of dissociative amnesia, and depersonalization/ derealization) *(for children, stay alone, numb, too)*
(c) Delayed
(ii) Phasic/long term
(a) Constant reaction
(b) Variable, off and on
2. Executive function (EF) For example, problems in inhibition, self-control, reward management, working memory (also called updating), goal orientation/intentionality, motivation/purposefulness, decision making, cognitive flexibility/shifting set, problem-solving, planning/organizing, monitoring
3. Biobehavioral/neurovegetative function For example, problems in sleep, fatigue, eating habits, sexual drive, pain/headaches. (for children, problems in elimination control, too)
(a) Hyper. For example, excessive sleep, nightmares, mania (includes excess energy, inflated self-esteem, hyper goal orientation), overeating, stomach/digestion issues, dizziness, hypersexual, hypersensitivity, muscle tension/pain/headaches/pressure in the head
(b) Hypo. For example, poor sleep, low energy, poor appetite, lost sexual drive, hyposensitivity
4. Experiential/existential (for self/other factors) *(for children, will be manifested less overtly, for example, in (toy) play or its lack)*
(a) OTHER: For example, distrust of others/ world, different in relating to others/ humanity, paranoia
(b) SELF: For example, loss of identity/meaning, don't feel the same person anymore or feel changed on the inside (personality change), negative self-esteem (e.g., worthlessness, helplessness, hopelessness, giving up), lost self-confidence, changed life story/narrative or world view
5. Coping/cry for help For example, unstable, disorganized; poor coping, poor social support; leading to being overwhelmed, complaining/overly seeking help, etc. (for children, associated with whining, brooding, etc.)
(B2) **Consequences (lower-order, bottom-up)**

(continued)

Table 9.3 (continued)

Item explanation
6. Physiological
(a) Hyper. For example, panic, hyper-arousal, exaggerated startling
(b) Hypo. For example, no reaction despite an expected fight or flight response/panic
7. Behavioral
(a) Hyper. For example, argumentative, out of character behavior, motor agitation or restlessness/retardation or slowing, substance abuse/addiction, destructive/risky behavior, distress at reminders and reliving; endless checking/repetitions/preoccupations
(b) Hypo. For example, avoidance, stopping pleasurable activities, social isolation
8. Cognitive
(a) Hyper. For example, mind racing, trying to suppress thoughts and can't, ruminate, reminders are salient, hyper-vigilant, narrowed hyper-focusing/appraising, recurrent thoughts of death or dying
(b) Hypo. For example, can't focus, can't concentrate, mind wandering, distracted, slow/delayed responsivity, can't think rationally anymore; can't decide, avoiding distressing thoughts, memories (and feelings)
9. Emotional/affective
(a) Hyper. For example, a lot of negative affect, especially anxiety, depression, irritability, fear, blame, guilt, shame
(b) Hypo. For example, blunted affect, flat affect
10. Social/relational
(a) Hyper. For example, don't want to be alone, over-dependent, loss of social control, disturbed social behavior
(b) Hypo. For example, withdrawn, detached, distant, abandoning, numb, aloof, estranged
11. Language/communication
(a) Hyper. For example, can't stop talking, interrupting, can't follow/lose track, disputing, very tangential, disordered speech
(b) Hypo. For example, word finding difficulties, short answers, avoiding or little listening, cutting off communication, articulation disruption/slurring
12. Other For example, extreme or quite inappropriate reactions, such as psychotic reactions (hallucinations, delusions, catatonia); suicidal ideation, gestures, and attempts; and/or homicidal or violent ideation, actions
(C) Functional disruption in life roles and tasks For example, dysfunctions in ADLs, work, school, parenting, interpersonal relations
(D) Specify appropriate demographics and context For example, age, sex, life roles, medications, over-medicating

Note. This recommended addition to the DSM-6 or future iterations of the DSM-5 is a broad trauma-related disorder that can encompass PTSD in the DSM-5 and complex PTSD (CPTSD) in the ICD-11, along with other disorders. It can serve as a questionnaire of children, youth, and adults exposed to trauma, abuse, etc. An advantage of the template is that includes both hyper and hypo reactions at multiple points

core symptoms in the table. Rather, they are embedded in the table as fits its scheme, which includes in the core components an initial disruption of biobehavioral/neurovegetative function and experiential/existential issues. Thus, I indicate the core psychological factors that can be dysregulated in psychological/psychiatric matters in assessment. This also includes the consequences symptomatically, with reciprocal feedback possible between these hierarchical levels. The fifth one of these core psychological components concerns coping and a cry for help when the person's coping capacity is overwhelmed (Young 2019a), leading to the consequences mentioned after it. These latter consequences could be of hypo or hyper nature. The table gives a generalized scheme that allows for a wide-ranging of individual differences in the dysregulations that could be evidenced in assessments. It suggests ways that PTSD/complex PTSD could be revised as well as general procedures in understanding psychological/psychiatric disorders in terms of hierarchical levels and how to interview for them in an assessment. Overall, the DSM-5 suffers from liability to overdiagnosis/diagnostic inflation (Fabiano and Haslam 2020), and my work aims for a simplified approach to its organization (Young 2016).

Inner Peace

As traditionally defined, inner peace refers to calmness in face of potential or actual stressors, inner happiness, contentment, or bliss that is an ongoing psychological state, perhaps related to spirituality. In PsychInfo, there are only tens of studies on this topic, with only a handful of relevant ones defining it and providing empirical studies with scales and questionnaires. A perusal of these sources indicates that none offer approaches to inner peace that differs from traditional approaches to defining it.

My own approach to inner peace includes several variations not typically associated with it. First, it is more than a feeling or an outer presentation because it is a way of being. Second, inner peace also involves projecting an outer calmness. Third, it is more than an inner feeling—it is also defined by actions, striving to act. Fourth, it is lived by compassion, empathy, sharing, and helping other people. Fifth, it is not just about a positive, internal calmness and contentment, or even acting with compassion, because it is also about wanting to encourage and activate the same internal feeling that one has about inner peace in other people. That is, therefore, inner peace is about not only feeling internal calmness and acting with compassion but also it is about radiating that calmness and acting in a way that brings peace to other people. Sixth, acting to help people compassionately might not be possible in a particular circumstance, but at least the effort can be made with positive motivation, or the person with inner peace will make an effort to actualize the helping motivating when the timing is right.

Developing inner peace should be a lifelong project because there are always new challenges in undertaking the deep responsibilities that it entails both in self-development and relating to others and the environment. We live to make gains in our personhood and situation partly in order to share those gains, for example, with family or friends or in giving charity, and to become better people willing to share of ourselves at all levels appropriate to the circumstance. The hallmark of inner peace resides in this type of giving and sharing.

Inner peace can be characterized as transformational tranquility. In living from this ethos, we undertake consistent and dynamic growth-generating transactions with our inner self, our social relations, and the world. Throughout the processes of transformational tranquility, we deepen our inner peace and deepen our commitment to help other find inner peace, as currently defined.

Inner peace constitutes the essence of the human essence. It leads us to internal harmony and seeking harmony for others; to internal liberty and seeking liberty for others; to a sense of justice and seeking justice for others; to protecting ourselves, for example, not being taken advantage of and caring for ourselves and protecting others; to internal healing and self-awareness and seeking healing and awareness in others; and to personal growth and promoting personal growth in others (and healthy growth in the planet).

So, in the end, inner peace is partly opposite of how it is traditionally defined. It is not about an inner calmness or spirituality. Rather, it is especially about seeking and creating a feeling of inner peace in other people—that is the best way of getting inner peace for ourselves; the relationship in our growth of inner peace and promoting its growth in others is reciprocal. Inner peace is not about happiness. Rather it is about helping others avoid suffering. It is not about being independent. Rather it is about our total interdependence. It is not about self-confidence or feeling good about the self. Rather, it is about other confidence and how you help other people feel good about themselves and their situation. It is not about being calm no matter the circumstance, because sometimes assertiveness is needed, and it is understood that protecting oneself and loved ones could in some circumstances require actionable assertiveness.

Inner peace defines us, and it characterizes how we should relate to other people and the environment. We cannot have inner peace when we let other people suffer from their stress. We cannot have inner peace when we let the environment/our planet suffer in its stress. Inner peace comes from planetary peace as much as family, friends, and human peace. Inner peace means that we have been given the baton, and we take it gladly, and we carry forth with our heads held high and our hearts wide open to the challenges that life brings. This would include in our growth and defining our place in the universe, helping our planet and helping other people and our planet find and experience peace in the universe.

Given this broad view of inner peace, we can understand that it is a life course and a life mission that is constantly developing, never reaching a plateau and is difficult to attain. At the same time, because it is a trajectory more than an endpoint, each of us in our own ways is developing an inner peace or trying to do so.

There are innumerable ways that we can deviate from inner peace, get sidetracked, and so on. Obvious ways are to reject helping anybody else, living only for yourself, hurting people intentionally, and so on. People could also put on a facade of inner peace where they project an inner calmness, but the facade might mask deep inner disturbance or turmoil. Or, the mask could be self-deception; the person could feel inner calm, but to a degree only. Or, the mask could be totally manipulative to fool other people for personal gain.

When we live for and act from inner peace, we develop internal coherence. When we live from and act from inner peace, we act to create an external coherence. People will express markers of a lack of inner peace through incongruence. There will be a lack of synchrony in the network of their ideas and their logic. There will be a lack of synchrony in their network of feelings and emotions. There will be mismatches in thinking and feeling. What is said will not be what is done. Actions will be incoherent to some degree. There could be false or partial coherence, cognitively, emotionally, or relationally. Excluded ideas, feelings, and others in the networks created will induce disharmonious intrusions to inner peace and its representations and expressions.

People could follow trajectories that are sometimes on the path to genuine inner peace and sometimes not. The conflicts might be evident to self and others, or the conflicts might manifest in indirect ways, such as disputes about daily needs instead of core values and commitments that extend our humanness. The sensitive person or therapist will try to understand the impediments toward the ongoing development of inner peace and its actualization in a sense described. There might be internal psychological conflicts related to ongoing relationships that impede progress in these regards or personal constraints related to job or setting/neighborhood. Or, there might be deep-seated internal psychological conflicts related to past stressors, traumas, or adversities, such as abuse, torture or, persecution.

As presently defined, inner peace is the penultimate human attribute and deserves that we all act to promote it and to prevent it from not developing universally. We all know the idea of being in the moment, inner peace concerns being present in every moment—past, present, and future.

The present modeling process of the human condition has presented 25-steps in development. However, it has not presented a central idea of the human essence, which I hope is now better understood from my perspective as the concept of inner peace. In effect, the 25-step model suggests how inner peace grows throughout the lifespan and gives 25 ways that it can face disturbances in growth. Simultaneously, because the model suggests therapeutic approaches to developmental issues and crises, it also presents ways that the growth toward inner peace that we all seek can be facilitated in therapy. It is beyond the scope of the present work to investigate this idea in depth. However, in following the suggested therapy approach for each of the 25-steps in development that have been described, the therapist is acting to promote the growth of inner peace and all its benefits for the person and the other, including the planet.

The present scholarly exercise on the project unification of the discipline of psychology ends with an essay on the nature of the human essence and, upon reflection, it suggests that the human essence as presently defined in terms of inner (and outer and relational) peace is about the unification of the dynamics of the person in a coherent entity without internal harms or dissonance and without any harming of the other. That is, the unification project of psychology ends with the reflection that the penultimate psychology of the person is about unification of personhood, or at least the lifetime working toward that end. Young (2019b) underscored that personhood includes the uniqueness of the person and how she or he grows relationally; as well as the constancy of the person, in terms of deserving respect, dignity, autonomy, and so on, while undergoing growth toward and into rationality. In non-western cultures, the individual is conceived as being embedded in the collective identity and not as an autonomous, agentic self, a concept which should underscore the present concept of inner peace. When conceived cross-culturally, in its outward orientation, inner peace is not especially about the self or feeding back into the self, but is a genuine inclusive concept involving unification in working toward self, other, and environmental health and well-being.

The concept of inner peace is related to the one of self-transcendence, but differs from it in several ways. The concept of self-transcendence has a rich theoretical and empirical history in psychology. Reed (1991, 2014) gave an elaborate definition that captures its fundamental attributes: it concerns boundaries of the self at the following levels of the person: *intrapersonally* (awareness of philosophies/values/dreams), *interpersonally* (relating to others' and the environment), *temporally* (integrating past and future in a meaningful way for the present), and *transpersonally* (connecting with spiritual/more universal dimensions). It relates to Maslow's concept of self-actualization (Maslow 1943), among others. Erikson and Erikson (1997) considered self-transcendence a ninth stage in the Eriksonian lifespan model.

Relative to the present conception of inner peace, in particular, the concept of self-transcendence lacks the aspect of acting toward/moving into acting as circumstances permit creating an equivalent feeling in the other. Koller et al. (2017) analyzed the Adult Self-Transcendence Inventory, and found it structured around five dimensions, including peace of mind. The latter concerns the person giving value to and acting to maintain a feeling of internal tranquility even when circumstances challenge the feeling, such as those related to personal losses. This concept is quite akin to the internal state associated with the present on of inner peace, but it begs the question of which concept is hierarchically superordinate to the other, inner peace or self-transcendence? It might be best to consider them as reciprocally intertwined and, moreover in this regard, along with other similar concepts such as wisdom, psychological completeness, maturity, and personhood.

Recent research is supportive of an integrated approach to inner peace as presently defined and self-transcendence, and its long-term development. For example, Benish-Weisman et al. (2020) found that self-transcendence related to self-esteem in adolescence in a questionnaire study. Bojanowska and Piotrowski (2019) found that adolescent self-transcendence was related to personal growth and positive relationships, in another questionnaire study. Kim and Park (2020) related self-transcendence to academic self-efficacy and life satisfaction in another adolescent questionnaire study. Tamm et al. (2020) related it to psychological adjustment in adolescents in a questionnaire study. García et al. (2018) related self-transcendence development in adolescence to parenting practices, using questionnaires. Shachnai and Daniel (2020) referred to socialization of self-transcendence in pre-teens, and the consequences in values for that population expressing it more.

For adults, in questionnaire studies, Ponikiewska et al. (2020) found that a sense of communion was related to self-transcendence and Bojanowska and Piotrowski (2018) found that eudaimonic well-being was linked to self-transcendence (also see

Lehman et al. 2019), and Rudnev et al. (2018) found that it related to "conservation." In a narrative study, Reischer et al. (2020) related self-transcendence to humanistic growth themes. In research with questionnaires and fMRI, Kang et al. (2018) and Teed et al. (2020) related self-transcendence, respectively, to the ventromedial prefrontal cortex and medial prefrontal cortex and the anterior cingulate areas. Chen and Mongrain (2020), in a conceptual paper, related self-transcendence to awe and an interconnected (world) self (also see Chirico and Gaggioli 2018, and Li et al. 2019). Diamond et al. (2020) and Crestani Calegaro et al. (2019) related self-transcendence to helping with potential PTSD after disasters/the Holocaust. Wolf et al. (2020) related it to compliance with civic Covid behavior management guidelines. Garland and Fredrickson (2019) argued that mindfulness practices can increase self-transcendence (also see Hanley and Garland 2019; Hanley et al. 2020a, b; McCarthy et al. 2019; Verhaeghen 2019, 2020; Verhaeghen and Aikman 2020; Whitehead et al. 2020).

Evolution of Larger Entities Based on the Five Step Change Model

The present book and prior ones in this four-book series on causality and development is based on a five-stage model that applies over the human lifespan. The model includes five substages for each stage. They help elaborate the change process in development. The present work has applied the model outside of human development, such as to how majorities might (mis)treat minorities, institutions their employees. It has applied it to the steps in the evolution of Darwin's work and the steps in the evolution of the field of developmental psychology. In this section of the chapter, one more innovation continues that application of the present five-substage developmental model for human lifespan development to larger entities, especially societal. This time, the areas of application of the present five-substage model are outside of psychology, per se, although related to it. This section of the book lets the table for these concepts speak for themselves. They concerns political trends and attitudes, religious and spiritual trends and attitudes and, finally, the trends and attitudes that we need to have ourselves and the planet survive (see Table 9.4).

Conclusions

The ongoing project on unifying psychology, causality, and development, and creating elaborations and innovations therein continues with this chapter in the present work. This chapter examines the nature of science, the nature of causality and mechanisms (e.g., on executive function), and the human essence of inner peace as presently redefined. Moreover, it gives two applied considerations related to how

Table 9.4 Extending the present five-substage model of human development to larger entities

Substage	Steps in evolution of political trends in society	Steps in evolution of religion and spirituality	Steps in evolution of the Holocene (will we survive?)
Coordination	Two major political trends have emerged. For simplification: Conservatism and liberalism. They juxtapose, jockey, etc.	Two major religious/ spiritual trends have emerged, and they appear to be reflections of the conservative and liberal split. On the one hand, religious institutions generally gravitate to structure and little freedom from orthodoxy. The liberal equivalent seems to be being spiritual in a broader sense, relating to the whole earth, to internal expression rather than external adherence	Humans have entered the geological phase of the Holocene, in which our activity transforms the earth. The transformative nature of human activity contrasts with ever-present transforming nature of nature itself. Humans have not replaced the latter, merely supplemented it. They juxtapose/jockey in transformative processes of the earth and humanity
Hierarchization	The struggle is to see which one will dominate the other. They might take turns, depending on the society	These opposing views might alternate in which is superordinate in the person, in societies, etc.	Of course, the question is will we behave to the extent that we dominate natural transformative change processes to our own detriment. Right now, much of our activity is heading in that direction
Systematization	Eventually, a broader system develops that integrates the two trends, improves them into a coherent system. It seems we are trying to reach this step	Eventually, systems are created that marries the two perspectives, giving more freedom to orthodoxy in religion and more structure to spirituality to a degree. Young people seem to seek more than older ones this coherent and free-flowing system	Will we be able to develop a coherent life strategy that accommodates biodiversity, respect for the environment, etc.?

(continued)

Table 9.4 (continued)

Substage	Steps in evolution of political trends in society	Steps in evolution of religion and spirituality	Steps in evolution of the Holocene (will we survive?)
Multiplication	Once a wider system develops, it can spread internally in the society, spread to other societies. This multiplication process has characterized other political system formations in the past, albeit less coherent and inclusive than what they could have been	Either locally, or more globally, new religious/spiritual systems will take hold. They could be attractive enough to constitute invitations to join rather than impositions, like in the past	Will that ethic permeate more than one subgroup in a nation state/society, or spread to larger entities?
Integration	Ultimately, the coherent system prevails and characterizes the full societal function for one society. This sets the stage for further evolution across societies as they juxtapose and jockey their systems with this new integrated one	Ultimately, these new religious/spiritual ideas will allow room for all stripes and freedoms of choice for any one, without having in that choice any hint of imposition. This prepares for wider integrations as other ideas are juxtaposed to it	Our survival as a species and the survival of the planet hosting us depends on it

Note. The table gives examples of how the present five-substep model of development can be applied beyond the human case to areas not yet considered in the book

romantic couples might split up (or not) in terms of the crises inherent at each step of the 25 steps of the present 25-step developmental model and related to redefining stress disorder in psychiatric nosology. Finally, it presents a speculative model of how larger entities, including society, might evolve according to the present author's five-stage developmental model. These innovations speak to the fertile ground that the present modeling process provides to psychology, its testable and applied bases, and the ongoing project that it represents. These extensions of the present work on causality, development, and the project of unifying psychology illustrate its reach and the potential for further conceptualizations, research directions, and applications related to it.

The next two chapters continue that innovation project of the present work. The first one concerns adaptation, coping, and stress. It presents a 45-category matrix model that extends the classic fight-flight-freeze response by adding 45 more categories. The second of the two chapters especially focuses on defense mechanisms, and their place in the adaptive, coping, and stress field. The common denominator in the two chapters relates to the proposed concept of defensivity/offensivity.

References

Benish-Weisman, M., Daniel, E., McDonald, K.L.: Values and adolescents' self-esteem: the role of value content and congruence with classmates. Eur. J. Soc. Psychol. **50**(1), 207–223 (2020). https://doi.org/10.1002/ejsp.2602

Bojanowska, A., Piotrowski, K.: Two levels of personality: temperament and values and their effects on hedonic and eudaimonic well-being. Curr. Psychol. (2018). https://doi.org/10.1007/s12144-018-0043-0

Bojanowska, A., Piotrowski, K.: Values and psychological well-being among adolescents – are some values 'healthier' than others? Eur. J. Dev. Psychol. **16**(4), 402–416 (2019). https://doi.org/10.1080/17405629.2018.1438257

Chen, S.K., Mongrain, M.: Awe and the interconnected self. J. Posit. Psychol. (2020). https://doi.org/10.1080/17439760.2020.1818808

Chirico, A., Gaggioli, A.: The continuum of self-transcendence: flow experience and the emotion of awe. Annu. Rev. Cyberther. Telemed. **16**, 67–72 (2018)

Crestani Calegaro, V., Canova Mosele, P.H., Lorenzi Negretto, B., Zatti, C., Miralha de Cunha, A.B., Machado Freitas, L.H.: The role of personality in posttraumatic stress disorder, trait resilience, and quality of life in people exposed to the Kiss nightclub fire. PLoS One. **14**(7), e0220472 (2019). https://doi.org/10.1371/journal.pone.0220472

Diamond, S., Ronel, N., Shrira, A.: From a world of threat to a world at which to wonder: self-transcendent emotions through the creative experience of holocaust survivor artists. Psychol. Trauma Theory Res. Pract. Policy. **12**(6), 609–618 (2020). https://doi.org/10.1037/tra0000590

Erikson, E.H., Erikson, J.M.: The Life Cycle Completed: Extended Version with New Chapters on the Ninth Stage of Development. W. W. Norton, New York (1997)

Fabiano, F., Haslam, N.: Is psychiatry shrinking what's considered normal? New study challenges idea. Real Clear Science. https://www.realclearscience.com/articles/2020/07/17/is_psychiatry_shrinking_whats_considered_normal_new_study_challenges_idea__111467.html (2020)

García, O.F., Serra, E., Zacarés, J.J., García, F.: Parenting styles and short- and long-term socialization outcomes: a study among Spanish adolescents and older adults. Psychosoc. Interv. **27**(3), 153–161 (2018). https://doi.org/10.5093/pi2018a21

Garland, E.L., Fredrickson, B.L.: Positive psychological states in the arc from mindfulness to self-transcendence: extensions of the mindfulness-to-meaning theory and applications to addiction and chronic pain treatment. Curr. Opin. Psychol. **28**, 184–191 (2019). https://doi.org/10.1016/j.copsyc.2019.01.004

Hanley, A.W., Garland, E.L.: Spatial frame of reference as a phenomenological feature of self-transcendence: measurement and manipulation through mindfulness meditation. Psychol. Conscious. Theory Res. Pract. **6**(4), 329–345 (2019). https://doi.org/10.1037/cns0000204

Hanley, A.W., Dambrun, M., Garland, E.L.: Effects of mindfulness meditation on self-transcendent states: perceived body boundaries and spatial frames of reference. Mindfulness. **11**, 1194–1203 (2020a). https://doi.org/10.1007/s12671-020-01330-9

Hanley, A.W., Dorjee, D., Garland, E.L.: Mindfulness training encourages self-transcendent states via decentering. Psychol. Conscious. Theory Res. Pract. (2020b). https://doi.org/10.1037/cns0000262

Kang, Y., Cooper, N., Pandey, P., Scholz, C., O'Donnell, M.B., Lieberman, M.D., Taylor, S.E., Strecher, V.J., Dal Cin, S., Konrath, S., Polk, T.A., Resnicow, K., An, L., Falk, E.B.: Effects of self-transcendence on neural responses to persuasive messages and health behavior change. Proc. Natl. Acad. Sci. U. S. A. **115**(40), 9974–9979 (2018). https://doi.org/10.1073/pnas.1805573115

Kim, M.J., Park, J.H.: Academic self-efficacy and life satisfaction among adolescents: mediating effects of self-transcendence. Child Youth Serv. **31**(4), 387–408 (2020). https://doi.org/10.1080/0145935X.2020.1852920

Koller, I., Levenson, M.R., Glück, J.: What do you think you are measuring? A mixed-methods procedure for assessing the content validity of test items and theory-based scaling. Front. Psychol. **8**, 126 (2017). https://doi.org/10.3389/fpsyg.2017.00126

Lehman, O.V., Kardum, G., Klempe, S.H.: The search for inner silence as a source for eudemonia. Br. J. Guid. Counsell. **47**(2), 180–189 (2019). https://doi.org/10.1080/03069885.2018.1553295

Li, J.-J., Dou, K., Wang, Y.-J., Nie, Y.-G.: Why awe promotes prosocial behaviors? The mediating effects of future time perspective and self-transcendence meaning of life. Front. Psychol. **10**, 1140 (2019). https://doi.org/10.3389/fpsyg.2019.01140

Maslow, A.H.: A theory of human motivation. Psychol. Rev. **50**(4), 370–396 (1943). https://doi.org/10.1037/h0054346

McCarthy, V.L., Bowland, S., Nayar, E., Connelly, J., Woge, A.: Developing a new perspective in late life: the PATH program. J. Adult Dev. **26**, 304–320 (2019). https://doi.org/10.1007/s10804-018-9319-8

Ponikiewska, K., Cieciuch, J., Strus, W.: In search of convergence between the main dimensions of interpersonal and basic human values in the context of personality traits. Pers. Indiv. Diff. **162**, 110003 (2020). https://doi.org/10.1016/j.paid.2020.110003

Reed, P.G.: Toward a nursing theory of self-transcendence: deductive reformulation using developmental theories. Adv. Nurs. Sci. **13**(4), 64–77 (1991). https://doi.org/10.1097/00012272-199106000-00008

Reed, P.G.: Theory of self-transcendence. In: Smith, M.J., Liehr, P.R. (eds.) Middle Range Theory for Nursing, 3rd edn, pp. 109–139. Springer, New York (2014)

Reischer, H.N., Roth, L.J., Villarreal, J.A., McAdams, D.P.: Self-transcendence and life stories of humanistic growth among late-midlife adults. J. Pers. (2020). https://doi.org/10.1111/jopy.12583

Rudnev, M., Magun, V., Schwartz, S.: Relations among higher order values around the world. J. Cross-Cult. Psychol. **49**(8), 1165–1182 (2018). https://doi.org/10.1177/0022022118782644

Shachnai, R., Daniel, E.: Children's concepts of personal values. Infant Child Dev. **29**(6), e2205 (2020). https://doi.org/10.1002/icd.2205

Squire, L.R.: Encyclopedia of Neuroscience. Academic Press, New York (2009)

Tamm, A., Tulviste, T., Tõnissaar, M.: Values of adolescents and values prevailing in the classroom are related to adolescents' psychological adjustment. Eur. J. Dev. Psychol. **18**(1), 56–74 (2020). https://doi.org/10.1080/17405629.2020.1755250

Teed, A.R., Rakic, J., Mark, D.B., Krawcyzk, D.C.: Relative activation patterns associated with self-transcedent and self-enhancement core values: an fMRI study of basic human values theory concepts in males. Soc. Neurosci. **15**(1), 1–14 (2020). https://doi.org/10.1080/17470919.2019.1598893

Verhaeghen, P.: The mindfulness manifold: exploring how self-preoccupation, self-compassion, and self-transcendence translate mindfulness into positive psychological outcomes. Mindfulness. **10**, 131–145 (2019). https://doi.org/10.1007/s12671-018-0959-3

Verhaeghen, P.: The examined life is wise living: the relationship between mindfulness, wisdom, and the moral foundations. J. Adult Dev. **27**, 305–322 (2020). https://doi.org/10.1007/s10804-019-09343-y

Verhaeghen, P., Aikman, S.N.: How the mindfulness manifold relates to the five moral foundations, prejudice, and awareness of privilege. Mindfulness. **11**, 241–254 (2020). https://doi.org/10.1007/s12671-019-01243-2

Whitehead, R., Bates, G., Elphinstone, B.: Growing by letting go: nonattachment and mindfulness as qualities of advanced psychological development. J. Adult Dev. **27**, 12–22 (2020). https://doi.org/10.1007/s10804-018-09326-5

Wolf, L.J., Haddoc, G., Manstead, A.S.R., Maio, G.R.: The importance of (shared) human values for containing the COVID-19 pandemic. Br. J. Soc. Psychol. **59**, 618–627 (2020). https://doi.org/10.1111/bsjo.12401

World Health Organization: International Classification of Diseases, 11th Revision (ICD-11). https://www.who.int/classifications/icd/en/ (2019, October 11)

Young, G.: Unifying Causality and Psychology: Being, Brain and Behavior. Springer, Cham (2016)
Young, G.: The cry for help in psychological injury and law: concepts and review. Psychol. Injury Law. **12**(3–4), 225–237 (2019a). https://doi.org/10.1007/s12207-019-09360-y
Young, G.: Personhood across disciplines: applications to ethical theory and mental health ethics. Ethics Med. Public Health. **10**, 93–101 (2019b). https://doi.org/10.1016/j.jemep.2019.100407

Chapter 10
Adaptation, Coping, Stress, and Development

This chapter is the first of two on defense mechanisms in relation to Young's Neo-Eriksonian model of 25 steps in lifespan development. The first chapter is on modeling and the second is on a literature review and discussion. The first chapter of the two does not discuss defense mechanisms much, in that it creates a framework to embed it in a wider perspective. The second chapter discusses them, but keeps them as presented in the literature, while continuing to broaden the scope to in the area.

This first chapter of the two on defense mechanisms embeds the defense mechanism concept in a wider framework of adaptation and coping. This procedure led to new modeling of the adaptation and coping area of study toward accommodating defense mechanisms. This chapter, then, continues the applications and innovations that mark the present book.

Specifically, this chapter develops the construct of defensivity-offensivity and relates it to both adaptation and coping and to defense mechanisms. As part of this procedure, the chapter creates an expanded fight-flight-flee paradigm of dealing with or coping with stress. In this regard, the chapter presents a 48-category matrix involving both defensivity and offensivity (as well as other dimensions, e.g., related to strategies, distance, and self).

Young's (2011, 2016, 2019a, this book) 25-step Neo-Eriksonian model serves as the basis for another section of the chapter on modeling. It shows how the concept of defensivity/offensivity applies to the lifespan steps in development described in the model. Specifically, 25-step Neo-Eriksonian model of lifespan development can be re-interpreted as providing defensivity and offensivity themes. The Neo-Eriksonian model has been presented extensively in the book to date. But, the table that presents it does so in novel ways, and it feeds back into the section on defensivity-offensivity in the first part of the chapter.

The second chapter in this two-chapter series on defense mechanisms, which follows this one, especially includes a comprehensive literature review that served in the development of the present approach to adaptation, coping, and stress, in particular, and to defense mechanisms, as well. The articles reviewed are recent and

G. Young, *Causality and Neo-Stages in Development*,
https://doi.org/10.1007/978-3-030-82540-9_10

speak to the innovations that the both chapters on defense mechanism in this book have included in their approach to the question.

Model Building

Premises

The theoretical effort undertaken in this chapter and the next on defense mechanisms involves placing defense mechanisms in a broader developmental and psychological perspective. The area of defense mechanisms itself was not altered in this theoretical effort. It has a rich history and reliable and valid measuring instruments.

Any new terminology that was created was to help better situate defense mechanisms in this wider perspective. For example, unconscious defense mechanisms are essential to human psychology, but I referred to them as classic at the end of the next chapter in order to relate them to conscious ways of defending against stress. In this chapter, I refer to the new concept of defensivity, which is not meant to replace defense mechanisms but complement it in the ways described. Also, defensivity is not another way of referring to defensiveness, which is more related to defense mechanisms. Rather, defensivity and its associated term of offensivity stand as intermediate concepts between defense mechanisms and general adaptation, coping, and stress. Therefore, any argument that defensiveness should be used instead of defensivity misses the point.

The other new terms created for the chapter and the next are carefully defined to show their distinctiveness from defense mechanisms. They are not meant to replace the term, and the definitions indicate this. They do not complicate the field with new terminology but allow for the bridging from defense mechanisms to other areas of study. For example, the concept of defense mentalism introduced in the next chapter is not meant to replace the one of defense mechanism but to complement it.

The general adaptation, coping, and stress model created also is not meant to complicate the field, but to show directions in theorizing and research. The original fight-flight-freeze model in this regard is too simplistic, and integrating them into a wider matrix model of terms will help the field.

The 25-step Neo-Eriksonian model also is not meant to complicate the field, but to illuminate the lifespan development in a way that complements the original Eriksonian model. The latter consists of eight stages, and they have been clinically useful. However, the present model of 25 steps has been constructed to fill perceived gaps in the original model. They could help theoretically, in terms of research, and in practice. Indeed, Neo-Eriksonian model speaks sufficiently to the complexity of development and also how it can get disturbed that any biological approach to psychopathology would seem misplaced. For example, the RDoC approach to classification is more biological than it should be, as discussed in Young (2016). The present Neo-Eriksonian model reinforces that conclusion. That said, the biological roots to behavior need clear understanding and careful review, which I have attempted in the literature review of the next chapter in discussing the HPA and SAM neurobiological baes to adaptation, coping, and stress.

The approach and concepts in the chapters are relatively new and therefore do not lend themselves easily to having an extensive literature review in their support. The literature selected spoke to the concepts but did not justify them. It would be confusing to present the literature review first and then the modeling that follows because of the general lack of relationship between the two given the novelty of the conceptualizations made in the chapters.

It was impossible to review in depth the area of defense mechanisms because it is so vast, and there are tens of defense mechanisms listed in the current views on them. Future scholarship can explore better the present understanding of defense mechanisms to the present wider theoretical approach.

The theories modeled in the chapters lend themselves to practical applications and theoretical investigations. For example, the 25-step Neo-Eriksonian model developed by the author is presented in a manner akin to a questionnaire to facilitate further research. Also, it can help therapists explore and analyze patient clinical problems beyond the Neo-Eriksonian model when therapy dictates that the Eriksonian model might be useful. The matrix model of defensivity and offensivity categories in adaptation opens new avenues in adaptation, coping, and stress research beyond the fight-flight-freeze response.

To summarize, this chapter and the next began with the goal of relating defense mechanisms to the present Neo-Eriksonian 25-step stage model, but that task proved difficult. Indeed, I had to take several steps back to make any progress. In this regard, I had to relate the area of defense mechanisms with the area of adaptation, stress, and coping, which is an interdisciplinary one. But that proved difficult, as well. To better accomplish the task, I found that I needed to revise the general approach in that field of adaptation, stress, and coping in order to even attempt relating defense mechanisms to it. In so doing, I found that I had to go quite beyond the classic fight-flight-freeze stress response and create a matrix of 48 categories of adaptation and coping to stress. This included relating that adaptation, coping, and stress field to the concept of defensivity-offensivity, which served as a bridge to the defense mechanism field and to the present 25-step Neo-Eriksonian model. In the next chapter, taking steps back and innovating continue, for example, in creating the new terms mentioned to allow for further bridging of the type described.

In the end, the present chapter is not about defense mechanisms at all, but sets the stage for the next chapter in which that field is discussed and reviewed. The two chapters together accomplish the goal of relating defense mechanisms to the present Neo-Eriksonian model, but the route had been circuitous and the limitations in the project evident and acknowledged. In the process of accomplishing the goal, much new theorizing has been undertaken and should contribute to psychology, psychiatry, and other mental health disciplines.

However, workers seeking more straightforward relationships between extant work in an area, the empirical base, and new concepts and empirical research stemming from that approach will be disappointed. The chapters on defense mechanisms and related areas take a vaster approach and reflect my approach of taking a broad perspective on an area and making new broad theoretical models. Most workers in the field do not take such broad approaches to areas in it. That said, this reticence does not mean that broad efforts such as the present one are premature. Rather, they can inform the field and point to new directions; otherwise, that would be absent from the field.

Moreover, in the present case, the premises behind the efforts have simple roots. The complexity in all my books, including this one, stems from simple questions and reflects simple logical and theoretical modeling processes. For example, the very first question I asked myself had been why are there a different number of stages in the original Piagetian and Freudian models? Can an integrated model be constructed that allows both to be scaffolded on them? This simple question led to the present 25-step developmental model through a rational theoretical construction process; the answer is complex but not the question, but the complex answer involved should not be dismissed because of that complexity.

I have used the same integrative constructive approach in my theorizing throughout my books. Why are there different approaches to the same issue and does taking a few steps back to see the overall area help in finding the core question and whether it has been conceptualized sufficiently? For example, causality is ubiquitous in the sciences, and it can constitute a unifying axis in psychology and beyond, but no worker prior to my books had suggested this. The idea arose by taking a few steps backward and asking myself what is missing.

Similarly, other areas related to causality in my books reflect an integrative stance that had not been contemplated previously. For example, combining network theory and systems theory to better understand causality was quite novel when formulated (Young 2015), especially in terms of how I accomplished the task. Also, the concept of activation-inhibition coordination that applies equally to neurons, brain, and behavior and their interrelations is a novel one, although activation and inhibition are widespread concepts in psychology and related disciplines.

The premises related to this chapter and the next indicate that one needs to read them with the same approach used in constructing them, that is, taking a step backward, or even several, in order to see the whole field. As another note, the same approach should be taken in reading the whole book and the prior ones. If the reader has a reflexive rejection of the concept of stages without reading how my approach is different, the project of the book will be rejected, too. If the reader rejects the way I perceive causality, the books will be set aside. If the idea of unifying psychology under the umbrella of causality is considered invalid, the books will fall by the wayside. If workers in the area of defense mechanisms see the present approach to bridge that area to other ones in psychology and further afield, or misread or misrepresent the chapters, this aspect of my work will be ill-considered, as well.

The same concerns apply to other areas of the innovative, integrative approach that characterizes my thought process. Granted, sometimes depth is sacrificed for breadth, but that can be accommodated in further work. The chapter after this one on the development and evolution of culture will create the same conundrums for the reader. It will take the reader out of the comfort zone with many new ideas and models. Perhaps that is the ultimate contribution of the book, but it comes with attendant risks. Because I point out research and practice directions throughout the book, those risks are somewhat attenuated. I can live with the criticisms related to the risks, as long as they lead to further conceptualization and new directions to psychology and related disciplines based on them.

In a certain sense, the premises in this section of the chapter are a defense of the approach taken to all my books. I considered placing it in Chap. 1, but they were written at this juncture and so belong here. The chapter now turns to the content described in its summary.

Adaptation, Coping, Defensivity/Offensivity

The chapter begins with a figure presenting a model of stimulus-response relations that involves mediation by stimulus selectivity and mental modeling. Next, two figures show the relationship of adaptation/coping, defensivity/offensivity, and defense mechanisms. Next, a figure and two tables present the matrix model of adaptation/coping. Next, and to conclude the first part of the chapter, the section presents a hypothesized network model that integrates adaptation/coping, defensivity/offensivity, and defense mechanisms.

Note that the model building in this work on defense mechanisms in the present book continues after the literature review in the second of the two chapters on the topic. That chapter offers reflections on the overall field of defense mechanisms (even definitionally). It includes a figure that integrates the concepts of adaptivity, proactivity/protectivity, defensivity/offensivity, and defense mechanisms, the latter of which are seen to permeate the full model. Finally, the discussion to end the chapter includes a proposal for a new defense function model in which defense mechanism is embedded and also a new stress mitigation/magnification scale.

Stimulus/Situation/Stressor Schema-Mediation. Figure 10.1 presents an expanded S-O-R model (Stimulus-Organism-Response; Young 2016). Figure 10.1a includes an organism (O) component that mediates between a stimulus (S) component and a response (R) component. Figure 10.1b expands the O component, by considering brain, agent, mind, and person (BAMP). This process yields a model referred to as S-O(BAMP)-R.

The three main portions of the model in Fig. 10.1a can be conceived in terms of the *Defend* function. From a defend process standpoint, stimuli are "defended," or not treated objectively in that they are altered top-down by organismic processes, such as perceptual and cognitive filters. The organism is "defending" itself in the process. In one way or another, the product of the process in behavior can be considered broadly as "defensivity" (or its tangent term of "offensivity"). (Note, the term of defensivity is not being used narrowly and negatively in this context, as in defensiveness.)

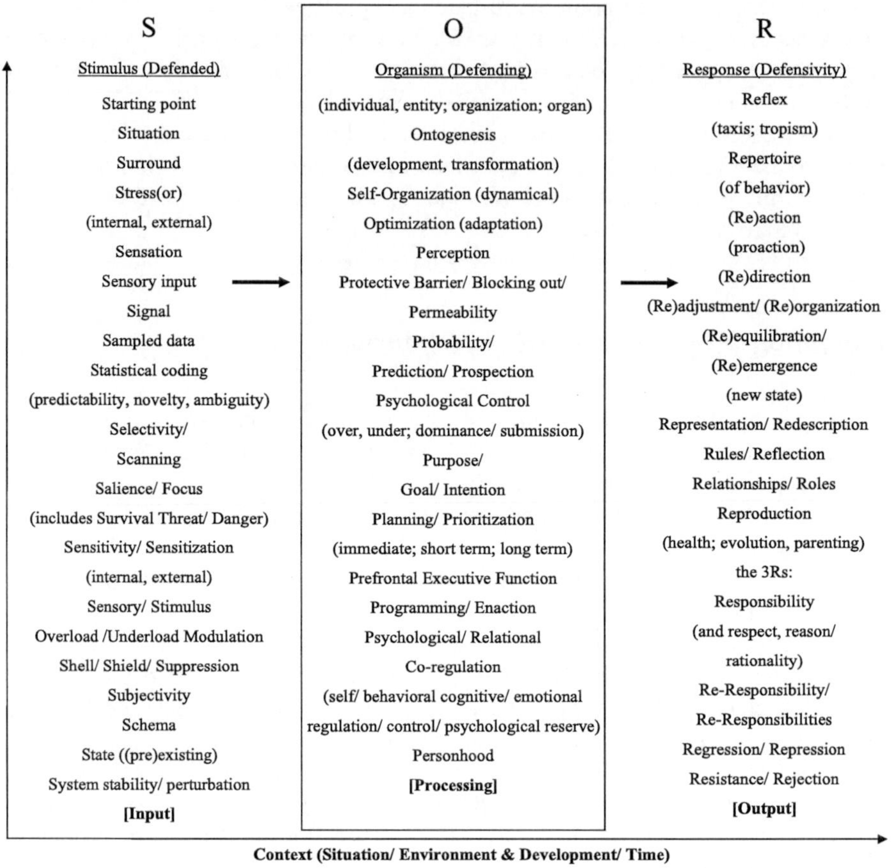

Fig. 10.1 Situating defense mechanisms in a general adaptation, stress, and coping paradigm
The figure presents a model indicating how stimuli/situations/stressors are not passively received and have their effects on the person without the person intervening in the selection/sensitivity/schema mediation involved. Rather, there are feedback and feedforward processes in which the individual actively participates through schema-mediation to alter incoming information toward accommodating to past history, ongoing dynamics, and predictive processing. The model is a revised stimulus-organism response one, with a portion of it referring to BAMP, or brain, agency, mind/mental, and person. The figure also refers to offensivity and defensivity in order to relate it to this theme in the chapter (Partly adapted from Young (2016) [Fig. 28.1, pp. 705])

The S component of the model includes not only stimulus but also situation and stressor. The stimulus is selected by filters, for example, in terms of salience. The filters could lead to selectivity biases toward certain types or classes of behavior, such as in a hostile attribution bias, or perceiving people indiscriminately as hostile. We can scan/select/sensitize either internally or externally (or both). Thus, we can perceive stress as either internal (akin to stress generation), external (an exterior

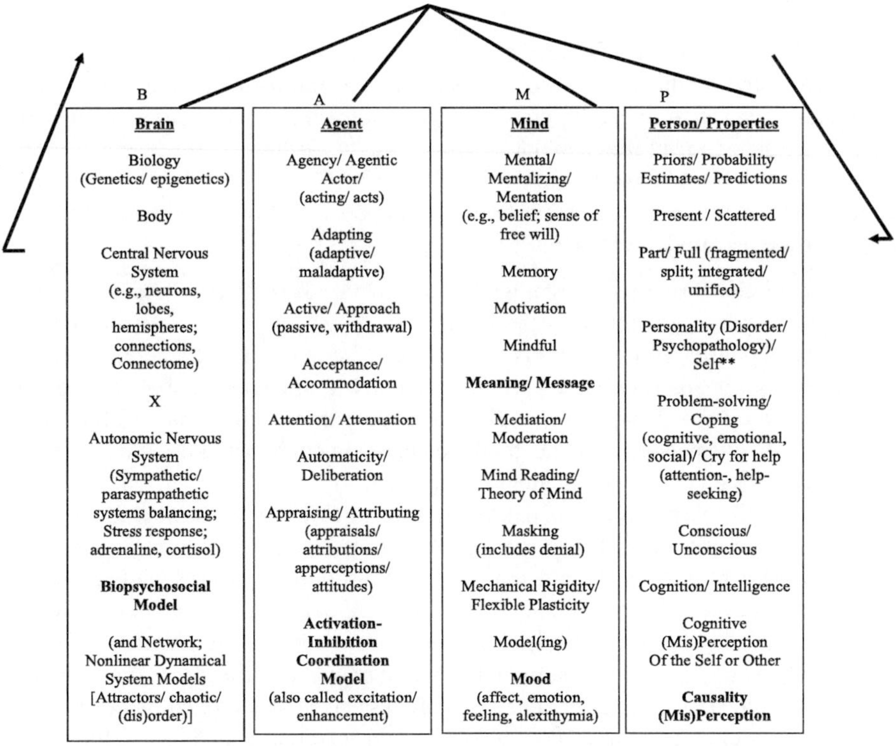

**Self-concept, self-esteem, self-control, self-sabotage/ deception/ blame, self-harm, self-medication, suicidal ideation

Fig. 10.1 (continued)

system-taxing burden) or both. We can react protectively by putting up shells, barriers, masks, and the like. Or, we harden those already in place, which might be adaptive or maladaptive in context. Finally, we might be passive, permeable, and overwhelmed or overloaded.

The O component of the model essentially refers to (a) the developing person in context, and (b) her or his perceptual and cognitive filters that are applied top-down to incoming stimuli, situations, and stressors. The person tries to optimize and adapt, maintain control, keep priorities on track, and so on. However, the person is buffeted by stressors that can derail the ongoing plan, alter priorities, reroute behavior, etc. The person is constituted by a collection of characteristics in whole configurations that could shift pattern and trajectory due to perturbing stressors. The person exists in a reciprocal, mutual relationship with the environment, referred to as relational or psychological co-regulation (Young 2017). Ideally, an integrated sense of personhood develops.

The R portion of the model refers to the standard behavioral reflexes, representations, rules, reflections, roles, and relationships. It refers to the full behavior repertoire instigated by stimuli impacting the organism. The nature of these stimuli depends on the developmental state of the individual (and the nature of the organism involved). However, behavior is not always adaptive, and there could be regression/repression, resistance/rejection, etc. The figure notes the penultimate human attribute of taking responsibilities in the human context (wisdom, maturity, etc.).

The BAMP portion of the model, presented in Fig. 10.1b, elaborates critical components of the organism, from brain to the person's properties. BAMP stands for brain, agent, mind, and person.

(a) For the letter B in the acronym BAMP, these brain-related activities include the stress response governed by the brain. People can react with adaptive phasic stress responses. But, if stress is tonically present in the life of a person, instead of expressing adaptive, short-term flight/fight/withdrawal responses, the person can develop either hyper-cortisolism or hypo-cortisolism. A biopsychological perspective is needed to understand the person in context and the life history of stressors (e.g., abuse, maltreatment) involved.
(b) For A, will the person be active or passive in response to stress, adaptive or maladaptive? What will the organism focus on selectively, and why? What are the apperceptions, appraisals, etc., that filter stimuli, situations, and stressors? Is there acceptance, including of things that cannot change, or avoidance/attack, even if futilely? Are actions deliberative/slower/cool, or automatic/quick/hot?
(c) For M, the mind is the mediator and meaning maker, creating models of impinging stimuli, stress, and situations. This process takes place based on prior histories/experience, contextual contingencies, and developmental phase. Motivation is critical in this process. What perceptual and cognitive models have been constructed, including on the contents of the mind of others, by either intergenerational/parenting mechanisms, the individual her or himself, or other environmental impacts and input? Further, are they mechanically rigid or flexibly plastic? What are the consequences for mood, or even in blocking out feelings and emotions, masking (denials), etc.?
(d) For P, the person might have models governing top-down behavior that allows for full presence in the moment, awareness, sensitivity to the other, and so on. Perception and cognition are linked to action and inference by predictive processing based on priors, probability estimates, and predictions. These are monitored for degree of precision and then revised in a Bayesian brain perspective. Or, there might be a scattered, fragmented, or split presentation, personality, and sense of self. Problem-solving could be maladaptive, more emotional than required, a cry for help, subverted, ineffective, or otherwise problematic. The classic mechanism of repression into the unconscious might apply to stressors, especially those that are internally generated in sequelae from early maltreatment and abuse (or perhaps from unresolved early desires, as per classic psychoanalytic theory). The self and other are misperceived through aberrant filters. The figure suggests that causal perceptions are also the subject of faulty perceptions (think hostile attribution bias, for example).

As for situating defense mechanisms as traditionally defined into this modeling endeavor, it is difficult to place them simply in a general stress and coping paradigm, such as the one offered. The concept of defense mechanisms has a specific origin trajectory in psychodynamic theory and practice. It stems from a specific approach to warding off anxiety/depression. The field operates with different inventories of defenses, usually a few that are emphasized and not more than tens of them. The methodologies to assess and measure them have acceptable psychometric properties. However, it is difficult to place individual defense mechanisms in a general stress-coping paradigm because the latter has a different focus and generally excludes them from consideration. Moreover, the defense mechanisms that have been described have been related to original psychoanalytic and Freudian theory, and rarely to more contemporary approaches, such as Erikson's, let alone the Neo-Eriksonian approach. Young's (2011, 2016, 2019a, this book) Neo-Eriksonian model does not lend itself easily to fitting in the various defense mechanisms and their possible developmental origins. The present work is an initial attempt to bridge the gap across general stress and coping paradigms and Neo-Eriksonian perspectives on the steps in lifespan development. The work acknowledges the limitations in considering each defense mechanism developmentally, and especially in terms of the 25 steps of the Neo-Eriksonian lifespan developmental model.

That said, the Neo-Eriksonian challenges/crises that characterize each step of the 25-step model function as scaffolds on which defense mechanisms could be grafted as part of the person's adaptation and coping responses to the person's current context and developmental phase. That is, referring back to the response component of the present model, and the concept of defensivity, the nature of the defensivity profile of a person, at any one time, is governed by context, developmental history and phase, and so on, and, in this regard, the most adaptive defense mechanisms for the person at the time should be used in the context. The 25 Neo-Eriksonian steps in the present work, then, can be taken to offer defensivity and offensivity themes. Thus, the classic defense mechanisms can be viewed as part of the adaptation and coping protocols used by individuals in their defensivity functioning.

A Model of Adaptation, Coping, and Defensivity/Offensivity. Figures 10.2 and 10.3 present the stimulus filtering/schema construction model in different terms and ways, using the concepts of responsivity, defensivity/offensivity, as well as outcomes. More important, they couch the model in view of the biopsychosocial model and proximal/distal influences in order to emphasize the multiple components that affect behavior (Young 2011, 2016, 2019a, this book). Adaptation/coping reflects a transactional process of organism and its resources and the context, but, as with all behavior, for adaptation and coping behaviors and skills, the organism has biological roots that vary from one member of a species to another, including in biological vulnerabilities. Also, the biopsychosocial lens emphasizes that the full range of influences and impacts on behavior (and its development) are considered in analyzing behavior, which applies to adaptation and coping, too. Finally, the proxi-

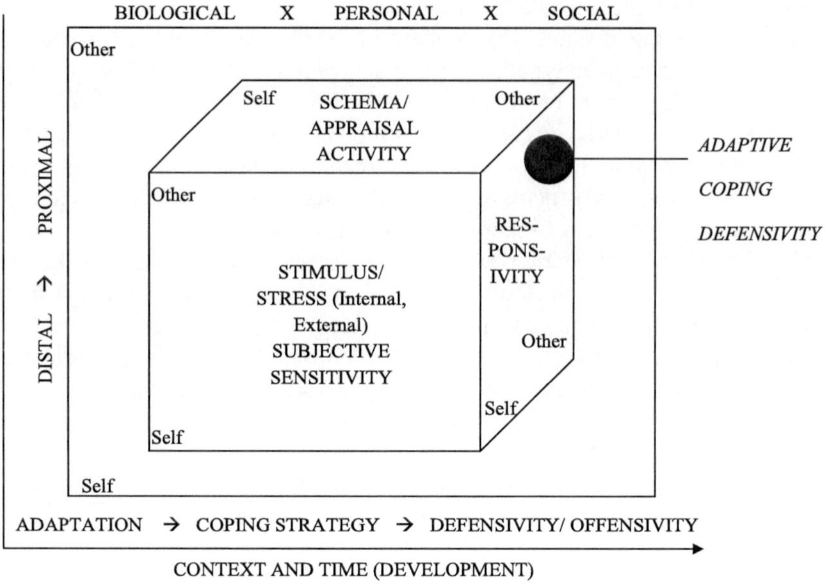

Fig. 10.2 A biopsycho(personal)social, proximodistal, and developmental model of adaptation, coping, and defensivity
The figure illustrates the dynamic process of adapting to stress and deploying defense mechanisms, where required. The three central components of the model are considered dynamic, ongoing, and active. Therefore, all the components are given descriptors that end in -ivity. The same applies to the defense mechanism deployment process—it is referred to as defensivity. Moreover, it is considered in a larger adaptivity process, one in which coping strategies might be employed, and defensivity ones could number amongst them. The stimulus component of the model includes stressors; these can be internally or externally generated. Stimuli/stressors have different degrees of impact on individuals, depending on multiple factors. These factors include sensitivities, the degree of shielding/suppression/discounting, and other personal factors. The latter especially includes the mediational/modeling feedforward mechanisms, e.g., in perceptions, schemas, appraisals, that are evident in processing stimuli/stressors (per Fig. 10.1). Adaptation takes place in context and its parameters change with development. Moreover, the pathways in their expression move from distal factors, e.g., genetics/brain development, to intermediate and proximal factors. These factors could be conducive or constraining factors in moment-to-moment adaptation in context for one coping mechanism/defensivity strategy or another. The influences on the dynamic adaptive process include biological factors, psychological or personal ones, and social/environmental ones, making the gamut of factors collectively biopsychosocial in nature. In the end, adaptation refers to the self and other and their interrelationship, as much as anything else. The figure illustrates a proper balance in all these regards, which leads to adaptive coping and defensivity outcomes

modistal dimension of behavior analysis and its causation also suggests a broad view of behavior. Given the current focus on defensivity/offensivity, and defense mechanisms, this broad view suggests that a narrow psychodynamic view is just the beginning. Figure 10.3 adds the need to consider maladaptive aspect in adjustment and coping (efficacity) and the degree of support that might be found in the environment.

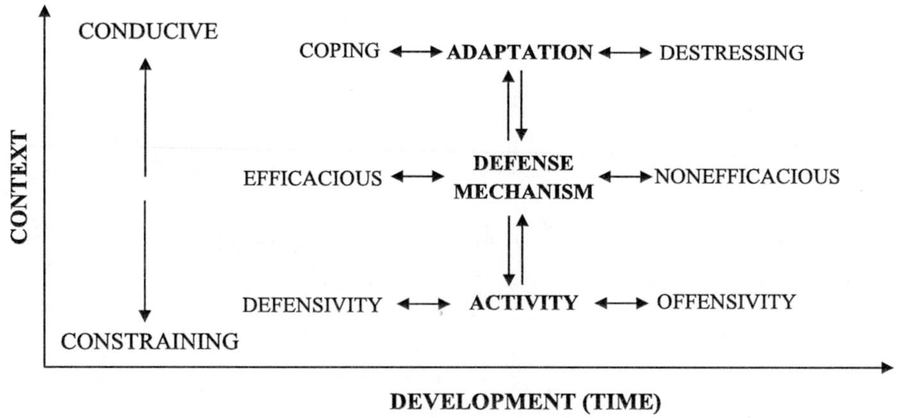

Fig. 10.3 Relationship across adaptation, defensivity/offensivity, and defense mechanisms
The figure illustrates the relationships involving adaptation, activity, and defense mechanisms. Adaptation refers to the ongoing dynamic with the context, and the quality of its integration into its changing circumstance (conducive, constraining). The environment, whether internal or external, might provide challenges, situations, or stressors that overtax or overburden the adaptivity/resilience/resources (internal, external) available to the organism, or apperceived/apprehended as such. This will lead to coping and destressing, as required and as capable
Another way to examine behavior in context is to consider its defensivity and offensivity. The organism needs to survive and reproduce. In this regard, it has inherited, learned, and modified strategies that it can deploy, with constant surveillance, engagement, and disengagement. It can adapt active/proactive stances (e.g., preventative or pre-emptive) or defensive/reactive stances in doing so. Offensivity behavioral patterns are naturally selected, as are defensivity ones. They are general tendencies that can be activated in behavior. They can be deployed, and then modified, as required. The patterns adopted in context depend on the confluence of circumstances, goals, history, individual differences, and so on, that characterize the ongoing dynamic interactions of the organism in context. By themselves, defensivity and offensivity activation patterns do not have a preconceived moral value attached to them. They are part and parcel of the behavior repertoire of the organism and are in constant reciprocal dialogue with the activity imperative of the organism from which they derive and which they constitute
Defense mechanisms are part of the mediators between adaptation and activity in the organism's behavior. They could reflect defensivity, offensivity, and activity, as well as adaptation, coping, and destressing. Some are considered more immature, but they might be elicited by horrific circumstances developmentally, and be adaptive in helping survival in the short term. Others are considered more mature, but that depends on the cognitive complexity of the organism or the developmental level of the person. Once more, the defense mechanism deployed by the organism needs to be considered in context and circumstance without a preconceived notion of its adaptivity and moral standing

Defensivity/Offensivity and Adaptation. Figure 10.4 prepares the central contribution of the chapter by indicating the dimensions in adaptation and coping. The latter take place in a constant dynamic of offensivity and defensivity. When stressors overtax the person's coping and resource capacity, the stress can become detrimental to the person. The quotidian offensivity and defensivity behaviors, actions, and tendencies can go awry, with consequences for defense mechanisms employed.

a) Defensivity

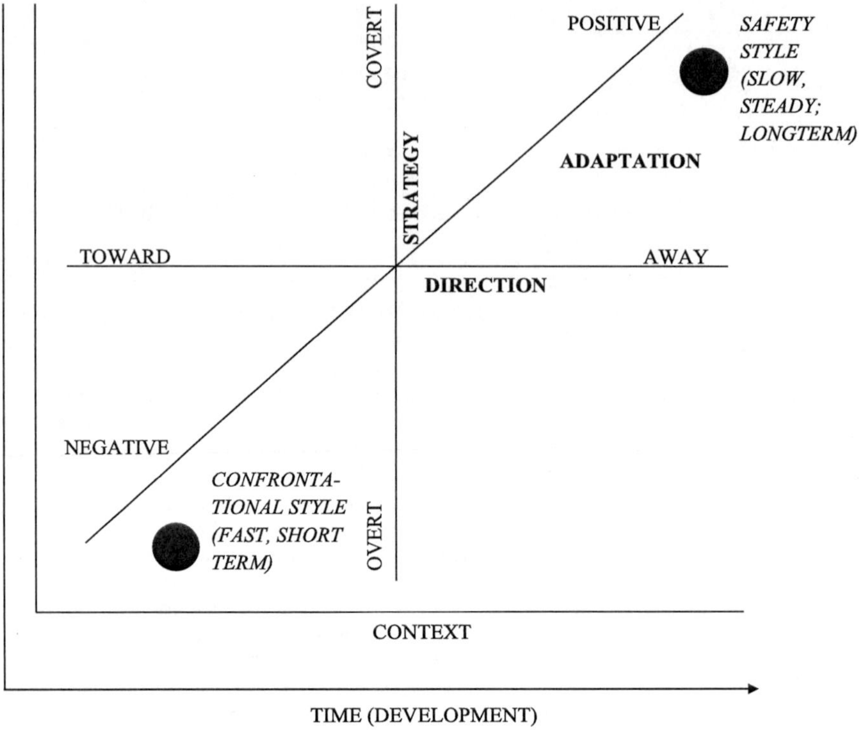

Fig. 10.4 Defensivity/offensivity in adaptation and coping to context and stress
The figure illustrates the dimensions that appear to govern adaptation and maladaptation to stimulus/situation/stressor. The dimensions apply to both defensive and offensive acts and tendencies
The dimensions common to both types of behaviors concern direction (to/way), strategy (overt/covert), and ongoing efficacy/outcome in adaptation/maladaptation (positive/negative). The acts and tendencies that are activated in context depend on multiple factors. These include the dynamic nature of the context, individual differences in the organism (in the human case, e.g., coping skills, social skills, motivation, personality, intelligence, past experiences and their effects), and the nature of the organism (from primitive to human). Individual factors also include the organism's developmental stage/phase, etc. The dimensions of direction and strategy have intermediate loci in their organization. For direction, the tendency is a mixture or half-way in approach. In terms of life history trajectories that have developed from an evolutionary perspective, the slow type is associated with a safe, long-term focus. The fast style is confrontational, short-term focused, risky, etc. (e.g., in the human case, teenage pregnancy could be an outcome). The figure indicates possible trajectories along these lines

b) Offensivity

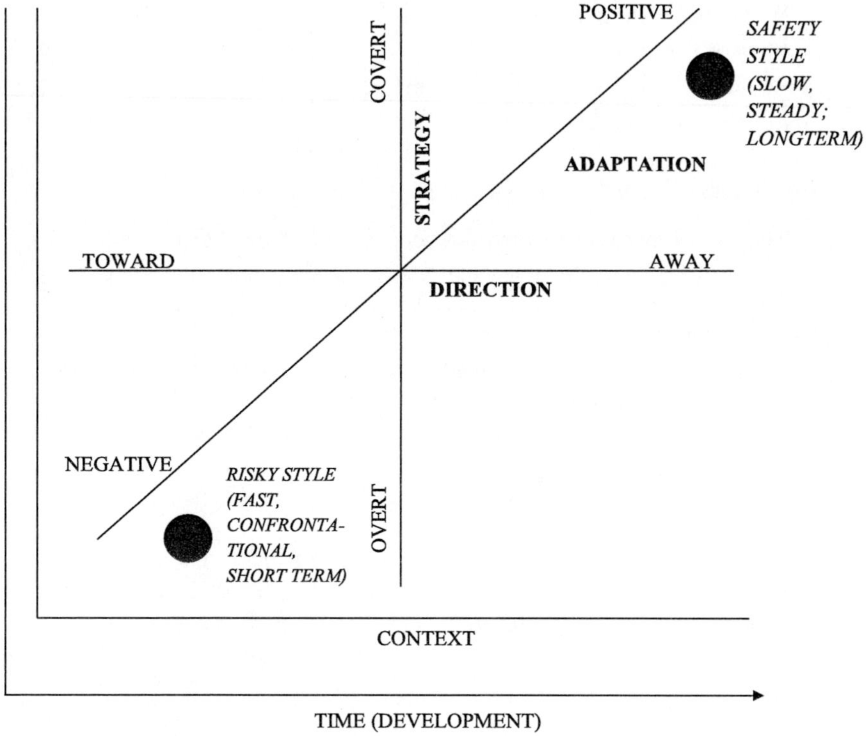

Fig. 10.4 (continued)

Box 10.1. The Strategies and Categories of Adaptation, Coping, Defensivity, and Offensivity

A. Theoretical priors

1. Fight-flight-freeze response (Corr and Cooper 2016)
2. Emotional and problem-focused coping (Lazarus and Folkman 1984)
3. Stress as taxing the multidimensional adaptation and coping system according to the person's appraisal component of the system (Levine et al. 2005)

B. Model building

(continued)

1. What are the dimensions in adaptation and coping?
2. Include strategies/categories that cover all organisms and species, but add those that are especially human, too
3. Include the concept of defensivity/offensivity, which are inclusive stratagems in navigating daily life and its contingencies

C. The dimensions

1. The first dimension to consider relates to direction, to or away; this dimension governs the basic actions and tendencies of all organisms
2. To and away action tendency directions should include intermediate ones
3. As for another relevant dimension, the action tendencies could be overt or covert, with intermediates, as well
4. The intermediate level between overt and covert could be called contending
5. Dominance-submission is a type of action tendency in higher organisms related to the to and away direction
6. Another relevant dimension relates to the self; here, the concerns are filtering incoming stimuli according to mental models, self-construction, crying out for help, and internal conflict

D. Strategy/category building

1. The concept of defensivity is related to the concept of defense mechanism; build the compendium of strategies/categories in adaptation and coping considering defense mechanisms, although not directly but attuned to them
2. The concepts of defensivity and offensivity include behaviors that are biopsychosocial; they reflect inherited tendencies, but are conditioned by personal/psychological factors and skills, and the environment (supportive, not)
3. Developmental models can inform the development of defensivity and offensivity structures and their individual organization in each of us; the present author suggests that the neo-Eriksonian 25-step lifespan model of development, and its associated challenges and crises, depending on the environment, offers a rich ground to investigate defensivity/offensivity actions and tendencies in the developmental course
4. Build the compendium around the strategies/categories of fight-flight-freeze, or add 45 others to the compendium
5. Chart the strategies/categories as a matrix involving: Three levels (overt, contend, covert) × two major dimensions (direction, organism/self-related) × four kinds for each of these dimensions (respectively: Direction: To, intermediate, away, dominance-submission; organism/self: Filter, organism/self-construct, cry for help, internal conflict). This procedure leaves 8 (4 to-away; and similarly, 4 organism/self-

related) strategies/categories in adaptation/coping × 3 levels (overt, contend, covert), or 24 adaptation and coping strategies for each of defensivity and offensivity (48 overall)

6. In charting the strategies/categories for defensivity/offensivity, consider opposite actions/tendencies across the types, as with dominance-submission

E. Comments on the 48 proposed strategies/categories in adaptation and coping

1. See Tables 10.1 and 10.2; the first one is on the directional categories, the second on the organism/self-related ones; otherwise, the matrices are the same in organization
2. Notice the arrows indicating the dynamic adaptation that takes place between offensivity and defensivity in daily adaptation and coping
3. The modeling applies to all organisms, except for certain ones involving self. That said, crying out for help is a ubiquitous natural phenomenon, from plants to birds to humans, as per Young (2019b). Filtering is ubiquitous, as well, but not necessarily through mental modeling. All organisms need to forecast ongoing environmental context and changes in order to survive. Therefore, the chapter refers to this filtering as selectivity/schema formation
4. Even self-construction and internal conflicts could apply to nonhumans; think nonhuman primates growing in groups, learning dominance/submission/deference, etc.
5. Some strategies/coping mechanisms seem direct defense mechanisms in label, but that was not the intent; the labels are general and meant to apply across species and developmental age, but the field of defense mechanisms can use the model to elaborate the relationship between classification of defense mechanisms and the present model of 48 adaptation and coping strategies and categories
6. The defense mechanism field might find that new defense mechanisms could be constructed based on the 48 proposed categories
7. Moreover, it could explore the offensivity and defensivity categories together in these regards

The dimensions along which adaptation and coping vary especially relate to distance and strategy, with quality (adaptation/maladaptation) an added dimension, although not discussed at this point. (Another adaptation/coping dimension relates to the self, as explained later.)

Table 10.1 Categories of distance-related defensivity actions and tendencies

	Strategy		
Direction	Overt	Contend	Covert
A. Defensivity			
To	Fight (physical/ confront; stave off; stand up to)	Fend for (conserve/ preserve) (stay/stay the course)	Fend off (thwart, make deviate)
Power differential (submission)	Cower/flinch	Reframe/cede	Defer to/fawn/comply
Intermediate	Foray (sortie)	Forth and back (back and forth) (includes prepare defense)	Freeze (flex, also flaccid/faint; immobility)
Away	Flight (flee, escape)	Fortify (retreat/regroup) (parcellate/regenerate)	Fence off (withdraw, avoid, hide, detour)
B. Offensivity			
To	Primary aggression (physical, fight, terrorize)	Attrition/chip away	Tertiary aggression (manipulate, deceive)
Power differential (dominance)	Rage to create wariness/ fear (terrorize, victimize, bully)	Threaten/intimidate	Dominance/forceful/ assertive display/ posture
Intermediate	Harass (torment)	Prepare offense	Foment other(s) to aggress the target
Away	Secondary aggression (lure, entrap)	Foment other(s) to aggress the target	Relational aggression[a]

[a]Gillespie (2020) described defensive tactics, but they are really offensive ones in the present context. In the matrix of categories of adaptation and coping, these tactics fit under the umbrella of relational aggression. They include, among others, behaviors that involve: excluding; ignoring; discouraging; denying; distracting, in the sense of detouring around; relativizing, in the sense of minimizing; stereotyping; stigmatizing, distrusting, with the example applicable here being prejudiced against; isolating; rationalizing, in the sense of diminishing; and splitting, with the best example for present purposes being paying lip service only

The table provides examples of defensivity and offensivity actions and tendencies. The first and second portions of the table indicate that the organism gravitates in its adaptivity between offensive and defensive strategies and behaviors, depending on the multiple factors impinging on and guiding the organism. System dynamics govern ongoing adaptivity, but long-term, entrenched styles of adapting have a role to play, too, among other factors

The table uses two of the three dimensions from the model in Fig. 10.4 (related to direction, overt/covert strategy) and considers intermediate levels for the direction dimension. For the strategies dimension, it adds the level of contending between the overt and covert ones. It adds a dimension related to the "to" category, on dominance-submission

The table is the first of two tables that together present the full model of defensivity/offensivity adaptive coping strategies/behaviors. The present table especially relates to the direction (to, away, intermediate, variants). The ensuing table (Table 10.2) relates to organism/self-categories, including internal conflicts. Both a and b in this table involve 12 categories for each of defensivity and offensivity, yielding a total of 24 such categories, which is quite more complex than the alternate paradigms. The next table also includes 24 categories, accounting for the total of 48 categories in the matrix

This present table expands the classic model of the fight-flight response to stress, and its fight-flight-freeze modified version. It creates a 3 × 4 matrix for each of defensivity and offensivity behaviors related to direction, within which the flight, fight, and freeze behaviors are embedded

(continued)

Table 10.1 (continued)

The dimension not considered from the figure on which the table is derived involves adaptation/maladaptation. The particular efficacy of an applied action (tendency) will involve contextual, individual, and related aspects. Therefore, the examples provided do not include their degree of efficacy, appropriateness, quality, or adaptation itself. Moreover, any one action/tendency that is activated in context might be constructive in the circumstances, or not, depending on a host of factors. Organisms adapt and project possibility, but cannot forecast everything or exactly. Organisms select coping mechanisms and defense mechanisms from the repertoires available to them, or what the confluence of influences on the organism (person) call for

The defensivity portion of the table is based on the classic fight/flight distinction, but elaborates it greatly. These two behaviors of fight and flight are overt ones, one in the direction toward and the other in the direction away. For the covert level, we can add equivalents (fend off, e.g., thwart) and fence off (withdraw, avoid, hide), respectively. But even these four options are not enough to cover the various combinations of direction and strategy because there are intermediate levels

The intermediate levels consist of strategies in between toward and away strategies, such as going back and forth and foraying, as required. The crucial one is freezing, which is between a toward and an away defensive response, because the literature now refers to the fight-flight-freeze paradigm in the stress response. Freezing could include responses to the inability to escape, for example, in child maltreatment/abuse (e.g., numb, dissociated, even repress). The covert intermediate type of offensivity is interesting, because it refers to getting others (conspecifics) to engage in aggressive behavior against the targeted individual(s)

Other cells in the table require more elaborate explanation. First, the chapter considers the interaction of the contend intermediate point between overt and covert behavior with the dimension of direction. For the toward direction, this refers to fending for self and to conserving/preserving resources in the situation at hand. For the away direction, this refers to retreating in order to regroup and continue the confrontation. As a physical example, this might involve parcellation/splitting, even literally (think of reptiles losing their tails when attacked), and consequent regeneration (e.g., the skin in the human case). Psychologically, splitting/isolation might be short-term adaptive strategies in this regard

The dominance/submission power differential strategies mirror image each other. The overt to contend to covert ones in offensivity (dominance) refer to, respectively, rage to dominate, threatening/intimidating, and posturing to dominate. The corresponding defensivity (submission) behaviors are, respectively, cower, capitulate/cede, and defer to the other

The four core categories in the revised flight-fight defensivity matrix have been referred to as fending off (e.g., fight), flight, fending for (e.g., stay, stay the course), and fencing off (withdraw, avoid, hide). Respectively, they refer to the interactions of the dimensions of direction and strategy in terms of toward/overt, away/overt, toward/covert, and toward/away. The equivalent offensivity categories that mirror them involve different types of aggression/aggressivity, which are, respectively, primary, secondary, tertiary, and relational aggression, with the respective examples being physically aggressing, entrapping/ensnaring, manipulating, and isolating the other

Of the remaining categories in the matrix, several more require description for offense/offensivity. Strategies not overtly aggressive (contending) include engaging in attrition (to), lying in waiting, e.g., with camouflage (away), and preparing offense (intermediate)

Note that the forth and back/back and forth category includes preparation against offensivity. Organisms waiver between sallying forth, and retreating, and, when required, also, they prepare against incoming offensivity. This could include creating sentineling devices, having receptor systems that serve as early warning signs, communicating with conspecifics (think tree root signaling systems), etc. Also, it could include creating shelters, such as burrows/barricades or buffers. It could refer to hoarding/provisioning survival material/gear. Finally, it could refer to preparing defensive strategies beyond signaling conspecifics (such as engaging in bird mobbing), and priming defense and protective behaviors (and tools, as the case might apply)

Table 10.2 Categories of organism/self-related defensivity and offensivity actions and tendencies

	Strategy		
Type	Overt	Contend	Covert
A. Defensivity			
Organismic/self-filter	Shield/shell	Orientation/attention control	Select/suppress (ignore, deny)
Organismic/ self-construction	Organism/self-builds other's monitoring/ respect	Build resilience	Build competence/ self-confidence/esteem
External Cry for help	Elicit/seek Assistance/aid/help	Elicit seek orientation/ attention	Exhibit hurt/complain (grumble, grouse, grumpy)
Internal disarray/ conflict	Organism/self-bar/ barrier/bury	Organism/self-bend	Organism/self-deflect/ displacement
B. Offensivity			
Alter other's filter	Siege (lay) (sieve, sap)	Distort/confuse	Falsify/reroute Wrongly
Undermine/deflate Other	Block/deter other's self-building/respect	Block/deter Other's resilience	Block/deter other's competence/confidence/ esteem
Block other's Cry for help/getting help	Refuse to help other (deter it)	Refuse to give/deter other orientation/ attention	Refuse to listen/deter shown hurt/complaint
Increase other's internal disarray or conflict	Other bar/barrier/bury	Other bend	Other deflect/ displacement

The table on defensivity/offensivity categories related to the organism/self involves the three strategies of overt behavior, the intermediate one of contending, and covert behavior. The organism/self-categories for defensivity (and offensivity, as well) concern, respectively, filtering (or alter it), build the organism/self (or undermine it), cry for help (or block it; also termed "call for aid"), and internal conflicts (or acting to increase them)

Filtering (perception, schema formation, appraisals, etc.) influences behavioral response. Therefore, it makes sense to add offensivity and defensivity behaviors related to altering filtering and defending against this strategy, respectively. As for the interaction of the filtering tendency with the three strategies of overt, covert, and contending, this refers, respectively, to shielding/putting up a shell, selection/suppression (e.g., ignore, deny information), and control of orientation/attention. Shield and shell constructions are overt, information selectivity is covert, and contending involves control of orientation/attention without selectivity predominating

The cry for help and blocking help types mirror each other. For cry for help in defensivity, this refers, respectively, to seeking help, seeking attention, and complaining, in terms of the overt, contending, and covert levels. The blocking/deterring mirror behaviors are straightforward opposites of these three types

The self-building/deflating types are mirror opposites, as well. For defensivity, we construct a respect by the other for ourselves, resilience, and self-confidence/esteem. These three types relate to the overt, contending, and covert strategies, respectively. In offensivity, the other blocks or deters these acquisitions. The consequences could lead to problems in self-concept, self-esteem, self-control, self-sabotage/deception/blame, self-harm, self-medication, suicidal ideation, resilience, as well as fractionation of the self and how the self presents to and relates to others

The internal types relate to internal conflicts that generate the stress for the individual. They include defensive reactions to the conflicts and offensive reactions. They would allow for place-

(continued)

Table 10.2 (continued)

ment of multiple defense mechanisms into the scheme, such as passive-aggressiveness, projection, other devaluation, and displacement. The defensivity categories for overt, contending, and covert internal conflicts involve, respectively, self-barring/burying, bending, and deflecting/displacement. The equivalent ones for offensivity concern disturbing the same for the other

As for the mirror image offense behavior to the defense one of constructing shields/shells (overt filtering), the category concerns, respectively, laying siege, creating sieves, and sapping the shield/shell involved. The mirror image of selective suppression (defensive covert filtering) stands as falsifying/rerouting wrongly, so as to alter the selectivity processing of the other

Box 10.1 further explains the process in the construction of a model of categories in adaptation and coping in terms of defensivity and offensivity, leading to their presentation in Tables 10.1 and 10.2. The box explains the antecedents that were considered in the model construction (e.g., the fight-flight-freeze model), the specifics of the dimensions of the model, and the form of the matrix presenting the 48 categories involved.

Defensivity/Offensivity Categories. Tables 10.1 and 10.2 present a matrix model of adaptation and coping using the main dimension of defensivity/offensivity. The matric builds on the classic fight-flight-flee stress response, while adding 45 new categories. This portion of the present work appears innovative and potentially has widespread applications in psychology and psychiatry.

We do not behave passively to stimuli, situations, and stressors, but engage in an active field of offensivity and defensivity behaviors, actions, and tendencies. We need to think outside the box that behavior is passive, because there is a constant interactive flow in the organism's context of approach-related outward-acting offensivity and also dynamic protective, reactive defensivity to any offensivity that might be encountered. We engage in offensivity-defensivity transactions and tradeoffs in a manifold of continuous ongoing adjustment to the environment. The pattern of the transactional processes and tradeoffs in offensivity/defensivity could be adaptive or maladaptive. That adaptation could take place in the short term and long term. The adaptation could switch back and forth in terms of efficacious adaptation and ineffective maladaptivity, depending on the context, developmental level, dynamics, and individual differences in the person.

The specific types among the 48 types of offensivity and defensivity categories in this constant flow of behavior that will be selected and effected could become habitual. This process could lead to ingrained behavioral profiles related to categories of adaptation and coping in the person, and thus lead to developing or enduring personality, as the case may be. Ultimately, in this repetitive process of adaptation and coping in terms of the categories of the proposed matrix model, psychological/psychiatric disturbances could develop that are extensive, including development of psychological/psychiatric disorders, impairments, and dysfunctionality.

The matrix model of adaptation and coping being proposed is structured on the concept of offensivity and defensivity. There are 24 categories for each of these two components of the model. The dimensions are the same for both components. The offensivity and defensivity strategies build on a dimension involving strategies (overt, covert, and in between, which is labeled as "contend"). There are two sets of strategies for each of offensivity and defensivity, related to the dimension of direction (to, away) in one case and the dimension of self (related) in the other case. The direction dimension has an intermediate type, as well as an added dominance-submission type. The self-related dimension has an added filtering type, because organisms respond to the environment after filtering the stimuli/situation/stressor according to schemas.

Finalizing these matrix dimensions created a matrix of 48 cells in adaptation and coping, and then the work of filling them began. The procedure followed involved expanding the classic fight-flight-freeze response. In the end, 45 new categories of adaptation and coping were added to the matrix, so that the proposed 48-category matrix is quite original to the field. It constitutes an expanded matrix that frames behavior and their interactions in a comprehensive model of adaptation and coping in behavior, actions, and tendencies.

The dimensions of direction (to, away) and overtness vs. covertness are sensible ones for a model of adaptation and coping, and adding elements such as dominance-submission and self-related aspects augment the comprehensive nature of the matrix. Furthermore, building the matrix on the offensivity-defensivity distinction makes it unique to the field.

Building the matrix model of adaptation and coping on the classic fight-flight-freeze response might seem misplaced because the three types of responses to stressors are associated with cross-species physiological mechanisms. And adding 45 categories to these three types of adaptation and coping might lead to the notion that I have related these 45 new categories to associated physiological mechanisms. However, the nature of the categories in the proposed 48-category matrix does not require associated physiological mechanisms that differentiate them. On the one hand, the matrix applies to all organisms, even one-celled ones, in their offensivity and defensivity flow. Therefore, relating the 45 new categories in the matrix to associated physiological mechanisms, such as is found with the classic fight-flight-freeze stress response, would be inappropriate. (In this regard, the self-related types in the matrix are phrased generically.) On the other hand, the categories in the matrix are not specified for particular behaviors that might affect them, in that more general terminology is given, e.g., fend off. Different behavior profiles in different individuals/organisms as they generate behaviors associated with different categories in the matrix will differ, depending on context, developmental history, etc.

Work in the area of the fight-flight-freeze response has evolved well beyond finding the physiological substrates involved. The major area in the field that has expanded the fight-flight-freeze response relates to reinforcement sensitivity theory. This theory has developed questionnaires that have been statistically analyzed for their structure. It builds on the theory of Gray and McNaughton (2000) that there are Behavioral Activation and Behavioral Inhibition systems that have brain-based correlates. The theory (and resultant questionnaires) has evolved to include a flight-fight-freeze (FFF) system split off from the inhibitory one. This model includes activation and inhibition in an overarching scheme, and although the FFF system has been added to it, the system is not expanded beyond the classic triad, per se (Corr and Cooper 2016; Corr and Krupić 2017).

The present approach also incorporates activation and inhibition in a wider scheme on behavior, but through the concept of their coordination (activation-inhibition coordination). As with the offensivity-defensivity dynamic in transactionally relating to the environment, the flow of activation-inhibition coordination constitutes another level of ongoing transactions with the environment. In the latter case, though, it concerns an underlying causal dynamic that underpins all levels in the behavioral system and their interaction (from neuron to brain to behavior; Young 2011, 2016, 2019a, this book).

Has the exercise of expanding the triad of fight-flight-freeze into a cross-organismic matrix of 48 categories of adaptation and coping been productive, or has it been an empty exercise? Certainly, an answer will be provided to this question by the extent of the use of and research on the matrix. However, examination of some of the exemplars in the adaptation and coping matrix of 48 categories that has been presented here illustrates the value of the present modeling of the behaviors used in the transactional flow of adaptation and coping.

The first group discussed in this regard involves the defensivity terms in the overt and covert strategies of the directional dimension. These terms include the three fight-flight-flee stress response terms as well as others that extend this basic triad with new terms related to them (for consistency, these new terms all use F terms). The second group of terms examined in the matrix in order to illustrate its utility involves offensivity terms in the self-related categories of self-construction (or other destruction for offensivity) and of a cry for help (or blocking that in offensivity). In this optic, consider the following.

For wider terminology for fight-flight-freeze, the matrix in Table 10.1A indicates that the overt to and away directional behavior of fight and flight can be complemented with the term of flinch/cower for dominance-submission (in this case, it is submission). Also, it can be complemented with the term of foray (moving in and out, as required) for the level between to and away (intermediate). The covert terms that correspond to these ones of fight, cower/flinch, foray, and flight, respectively, are fend off, defer to/fawn, freeze, and fence off. Therefore, the matrix of adaptivity and coping that has been created toward expanding the classic fight-flight-freeze triad of stress responses specifically involves two rows that deal with these three terms, with the original fight-flight-freeze response system expanded by creating five new related terms.

For new terminology in offensivity strategies that are related to defensivity strategies involving the self, in this 48-category adaptation and coping matrix, for self-construction/deconstruction, consider the sequence for overt, contend, and covert strategies, which involve, respectively, block/deter the other's self-respect, resilience, and self-confidence/esteem. The block/deters for these categories that are equivalent to them within the type of a cry for help, respectively, consist of: refuse to help or deter the help, refuse to give attention or deter the attention, and refuse to listen to complaints or deter them. Given that offensivity categories that have been

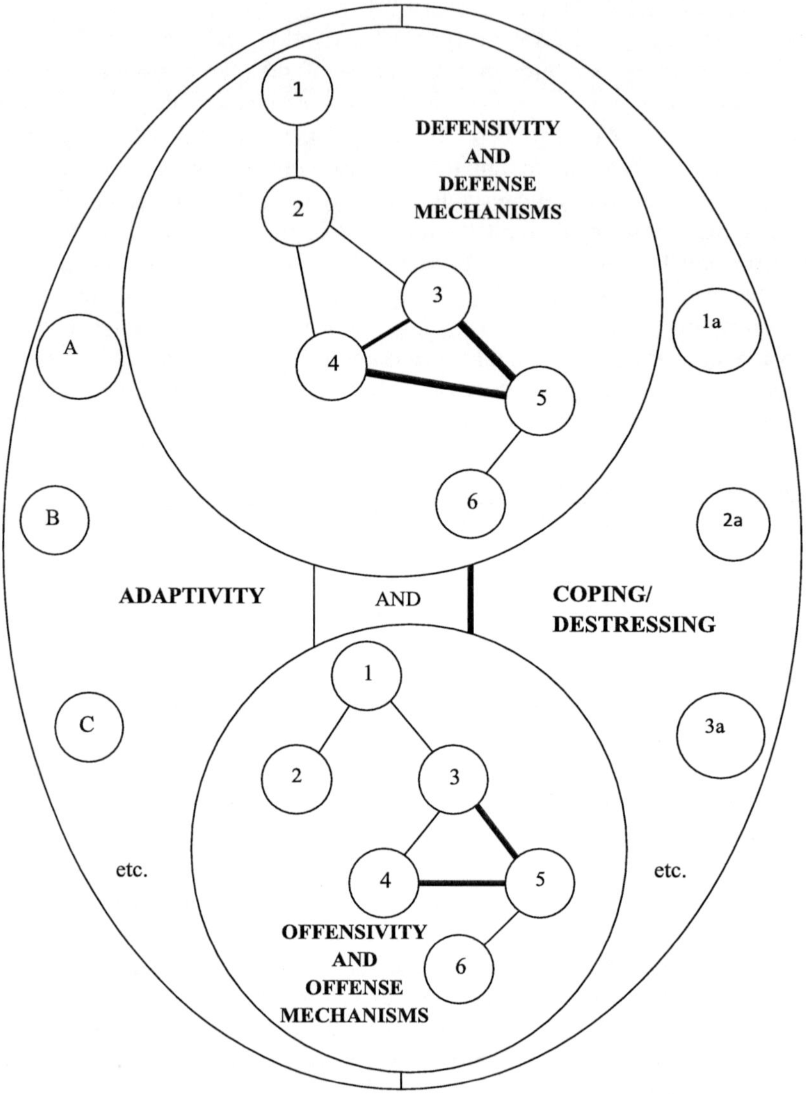

Fig. 10.5 A hypothesized network of deployed defensivity/offensivity and coping/destressing behaviors

The figure illustrates a hypothesized network structure of: (a) adaptation behaviors, (b) coping/destressing components in that behavior complex, and (c) defense mechanisms that might be deployed as part of adaptation and coping. Adaptation generally includes stress management. Activity toward adaptivity includes defensivity and offensivity. They both can be deployed in the ongoing adaptation to context. They both can include defense mechanisms as part of their functioning, depending on context. The nodes of networks are represented as circles, and their links as lines, with the thickness of the lines indicating the strength of the linkages. Nodes and linkages can be linked in tighter, "small worlds," or more diffuse ones. Behavioral networks are assembled online and activated in bottom-up context; they are not deployed by some sort of central, preconfigured, tem-

Fig. 10.5 (continued) plated top-down register. In this model, causality is considered to reside in the network and the strength and direction of the linkages, as well as their patterning. Causality does not reside in some sort of top-down latent variable from which the behaviors stem and coalesce, as represented statistically by factors in factor analysis

In Young's (2011, 2016, 2019a, this book) Neo-Eriksonian lifespan developmental model, 25 developmental challenges/crises are considered to emerge in sequence as the steps in the model develop, depending on the history of the prior developmental steps that had emerged and the problems therein, if any. Each step develops favorably in supportive contexts (or not), as with the Eriksonian infant stage (Trust vs. Mistrust). Young hypothesized that in the ongoing adaptation of the person to context, and considering the adaptive history that predisposes adaptation patterns, the behaviors associated with multiple steps (and not just one step) in the Neo-Eriksonian model can be deployed. The person might gravitate to lower-order behavioral patterns in the developmental progression that had developed because the prior contexts had given them primacy, or they are still adaptive in ongoing context

In present terminology, the person flexibly coalesces co-active behaviors or networks in adaptation, coping, stress management, defensivity, offensivity, and so on, and they can vary in developmental level. Moreover, they can include various defense mechanisms. This will happen if the ongoing adaptation to context should privilege them according to the ongoing, dynamic evaluation of potentially efficacious strategies and behavior in context

In effect, the present modeling indicates that the behavioral networks in adaptation might include defense mechanisms as traditionally defined. The networks do not impose as top-down entities on behavior, though, but they function as part of the bottom-up convergence of ever-changing online adaptation to context. The networks do not manifest as overriding personality tendencies, traits, or even states that factor in particular defense mechanisms into their working. Personality and related variables do not lead the way in adaptation, dictating behavioral networking, including of defense mechanisms. Rather, contextual adaptive contingencies and constraints move the behavioral repertoire in the most adaptive direction, although it is acknowledged that developmental history conditions various preferred strategies. Because they seem preferred, ingrained, or otherwise dominant, they might be construed as top-down influences, such as related to personality, psychopathology, and so on. But even here, the rigidity of the behaviors involved can be analyzed for their behavior networks, components, and intra-network causality rather than superordinate causality related to personality and the like

That said, Young (2015) argued that systems and networks do have top-down influences of superordinate variables, and intermediate ones, such as particular appraisals and perceptions that influence both bottom-up and top-down levels in the system/network. A full causal model of behavior will recognize the bottom-up network level and also the interactions of different levels of the system that are higher order in relation to the bottom-up one. In this sense, co-actional coalescing in the behavioral system takes place among behaviors, among its levels, over developmental steps and their ongoing manifestations in context, over adaptation and activity and their components, in defensivity and offensivity, in the defense mechanisms deployed by self and other, and across self and other in relational co-regulation (which Erikson, e.g., Erikson 1980, referred to as mutuality)

Young's Neo-Eriksonian (sub)stage lifespan model referred to the process of multiple-step deployment in adaptation to context as the process of yoking. Developmental steps do not emerge in sequence and integrate prior steps, but newly emerging ones coexist with prior ones. Multiple steps can be involved in the deployment of their associated behaviors. The behaviors associated with particular steps can be deployed together in pairs or more, as required, for dealing with the context/issue at hand. Granted, earlier developed behavioral manifestations of one particular Neo-Eriksonian step or another evolve themselves as development proceeds, and their current form and content in context will be different from one developmental epoch to another. In this sense, all aspects of the behavioral system being described function co-actionally. For networks, and in terms of the current 25-step Nee-Eriksonian developmental lifespan model, the behavioral nodes and linkages can be considered the product of yoking over adaptive activated developmental steps in context. The networks are always changing online and attuned to the exigencies and individual differences of the person-environment interaction. The activation of defense mechanisms in behavior must be examined from this multifocal lens

Further, the coalescing, co-actional process in ongoing contextual adaptation appears to reflect an activation/inhibition coordination dynamic. Young (2011, 2016, 2019a, this book) postulated that activation-inhibition coordination repeats as a cross-scale causal mechanism, from neuron, to brain to behavior, and their organization. Behavior that is adaptive rather than maladaptive in context will reflect plasticity in the activation-inhibition coordination dynamic. Adaptation/coping and defensivity/defense mechanisms, and so on, reflect an activation-inhibition coordination dynamic across the board and, as it goes awry, so does behavior. Maladaptivity reflects activation-inhibition dys-coordination in this modeling of behavior, its development, and its causality formulated here are new to the field, each of the six ones listed here constitute contributions to the adaptation/coping literature.

Before moving on from the innovative matrix of 48 adaptation and coping strategies, behaviors, actions tendencies, and mechanisms that has been formulated in the present work, the chapter considers which ones are compatible with extant defense mechanisms inventories and which ones are novel. Certainly, the offensivity categories are all quite novel in this regard. As for the defensivity ones, among others, the contend terms generally seem unique to the present model and could be expanded in terms of associated defense mechanisms. The contend defensivity directional terms include, for the directions of to, dominance-submission, intermediate, and away, respectively: fend for, reframe/cede, back and forth (forth and back), and fortify (e.g., retreat, regroup to re-engage). The contend defensivity self-related terms for the types of filter/schema construction, self-construction, cry for help, and internal conflict include, respectively, orientation/attention control, build resilience, seek attention, and self-bend.

To summarize, the matrix of adaptation and coping categories presented here, and its terms, were not constructed specifically as defense mechanisms. However, some terms in the proposed matrix match quite well with ones in the defensive mechanism literature, despite the different origins of the two inventories of adapting typologies. Also, given the overlap in the typologies, the matrix that is proposed here suggests new avenues in defense mechanism theory and research. On the one hand, extant defense mechanisms can be reformulated in its terms. On the other hand, defense mechanism types not related to extant adaptation and coping categories in the proposed 48-category matrix could be constructed, representing new defense mechanisms for the field.

One factor to consider in this regard is how specific defense mechanisms fit in the context of adaptation and coping behavior generally. The approach of behavior/symptom networks, discussed next, provides one avenue for investigating this issue.

Defensivity/Offensivity Network. Figure 10.5 presents a hypothetical example of a network of adaptation/coping/destressing strategies, behaviors, actions, and tendencies in relation to defensivity/defense and offensivity/offense. The more inclusive behavioral repertoire is related to adaptation and coping. This is the hierarchically superordinate level in the system. Next, offensivity and defensivity stratagems might be expressed as part of the behavioral system. Next, specific behaviors will express the particular range of behaviors for any one individual in her/his context. Finally, defense mechanisms might be part of the array of deployed behaviors. The figure illustrates the nodes (behaviors) and linkages (population-level correlations) across nodes. However, the figure can represent an individual's behavior network as well.

In network theory (Borsboom 2008; McNally 2021), the drivers of the system are the behaviors or nodes, themselves, the strength of the linkages, and the pattern of the linkages, for instance, degree of centrality (e.g., "small world," tight linkaging, or, in contrast, diffuse linkaging). There are no top-down influences of superordinate constructions, such as PTSD or depression, that create and organize the symptoms in the network; rather, they emerge in course of the adaptation of the person to context.

In a hybrid network/systems theory model, Young (2015) has argued that top-down levels in a networked system can, first, emerge from the confluence of network interactions and, then, feedback into the lower-order levels from which they emanate to influence them. Moreover, more than one level might emerge in this system reconfiguration process. One example of a critical mid-level, two-way interactive level in a hierarchical hybrid model of lower-order networks and higher-order emergent levels, such as an individualized PTSD configuration, would be appraisal-driven processes affecting both the lower-order networks and the higher-order organizations.

This hybrid network/systems theory approach to behavioral causality speaks to the multiple levels of how adaptivity/coping, defensivity/offensivity, and expressed behaviors, including defense mechanisms, relate to each other. The top-down influence of adaptation and coping is crucial, but does not cause the expressed behaviors and defense mechanisms. Nor does the intermediate level of offensivity/defensivity in this modeling approach. Rather, the three levels involved reciprocally influence each other, per the systems approach, and the behaviors/strategies within each level influence each other, as well, per the network approach.

Therefore, in terms of defense mechanisms, for any one person in her/his context, and considering other factors such as developmental history, the array of defense mechanisms employed as part of adaptation and coping will be individualized and fit the broader adaptation and coping strategies employed. That said, just as preferred defense mechanisms might be deployed easier given a person's developmental history, so too patterns over adaptivity/coping and defensivity/offensivity might characterize the behavior of a person, generally, and become the first accessed/enabled/behaviors in context. That said, each rendition of an activated behavior in context is newly created and deployed each time used, given the dynamical configuration of behavior in context. Just as memory is reconstructed and configured differently at each recall, so is behavior reconstructed from past patterns and ongoing needs each time used.

The developmental history of the person is crucial in behavior, adaptation/coping, defensivity/offensivity, and defense mechanism configuration in context. Young's (2011, 2016, 2019a, this book) Neo-Eriksonian model offers an elaborate model of lifespan development that affords an integration with adaptation/coping, defensivity/offensivity, and behavior networking. This modeling is open to integration of work in the area of defense mechanisms.

Interim Discussion

This concludes the first section of the chapter on adaptation/coping/stress and defense mechanisms/development. In particular, it has presented models related to adaptation, stress, coping, defensivity, offensivity, and networks in behavior,

Table 10.3 Defensivity/offensivity themes according to a model of 25 Neo-Eriksonian steps in lifespan development

Step name/ approximate age[a]	Defensivity/offensivity themes in living a life akin to the indicated level (for questionnaire purposes, the a and b types can be scored from 0, 1, 2, 3, 4; *delete the italicized introductions*)
1. Distance acts vs. no (lifeless) acts (very premature; survives; very at risk)	*The person experiencing abuse right from this age, or in an equivalent way later in life, has the following apply to her/him*: Experiences severe abuse. Life is at risk (any torture fits here). Reacts by wanting to kill self and behaving to hurt self. In general, behavior is very reflexive, not directed well, not on target toward goal or with right distance, disorganized. (1a) *Hypo* response: hard to move, lifeless. (1b) *Hyper* response: chaotic, on the edge, feeling empty life.[b] *Danger*: repeating the severe abuse; self-other harm extreme, no remorse; feel justified; homicidality; suicidality
2. Nursing acts vs. rootless acts (fairly premature)	*These first five steps in the* Neo-Eriksonian *model are associated with the first five steps in the corresponding* neo-Piagetian *model*: Experiences major abuse. The self is denied, not allowed to grow. Feels has no anchor, missing roots, helpless, hopeless, not wanting to do minimal care for self, for anybody. Pattern carries forward if/when become(s) a parent. (2a) *Hypo* response: aimless, rootless, no self-care. (2b) *Hyper* response: fleeting/flitting/furtive/flighty aims/roots/self-care. *Danger*: repeating major abuse, no self-care/self-destructiveness; denial of/no care of other
3. Outcome acts vs. outcast acts (excluded) (somewhat premature)	*The late premature baby is quite at risk, but even more so when abuse begins at this point in life; the baby(person) quite affected goal-wise*: Limited to trying to reach simple goals; the environment (parent) did not allow reaching even basic goals; disregarded the person, treated like an outcast/not belonging to anything, not allowing to speak/to establish what is wanted. (3a) *Hypo* response: no goal attempts, outcasted. (3b) *Hyper* response: multiple simple goals only, ineffective; superficial casting about for relations. *Danger*: Becomes the way treated, ignoring people/self
4. Caregiving acts vs. careless giving acts (full term newborn)	*The newborn should receive optimal sensitive, contingent, warm care, but this does not happen in abuse; the baby (person) ends up having difficulty giving care*: Beginning sense of self has developed based on the body and actions. But the environment (parent) has been negligent, even abusive sometimes, uncaring or gave poor care. (4a) *Hypo* response: not caring (well) for self/for others with no caring/giving/ caregiving toward the other. (4b) *Hyper* response: constantly trying to seek/give care, but without knowing how. *Danger*: behaving extremely negligently toward self/other; become overdependent
5. Emotional acts vs. mal-emotional or negative emotional acts (0–1 month)	*The baby in the first month is an emotional being, and needs much support to develop well; however, abuse at this point causes emotional difficulties that could last a lifetime; the emotional problems can vary from having little to too much*: Not emotionally content; very emotional, frustrated, unhappy, and even in rage, fear; emotional turmoil/trouble. Environment (parent) was not supportive, did not deal well with emotions. (5a) *Hypo* response: show no emotions, feel detached. (5b) *Hyper* response: express a lot of negative emotions. *Danger*: extreme negative emotions, rageful, fearful, depressed, anxious, etc.

(continued)

Table 10.3 (continued)

Step name/ approximate age[a]	Defensivity/offensivity themes in living a life akin to the indicated level (for questionnaire purposes, the a and b types can be scored from 0, 1, 2, 3, 4; *delete the italicized introductions*)
6. Dyadic acts vs. dys-dyadic or poor interaction acts (1–4 months)	*As the baby moves into in the* sensorimotor *period, behavior begins to reflect schema formation; these can include ones for social interaction, but they can be deranged by improper/abusive caregiving*: Did not learn the basics of social interaction. Environment (parent) imposed/competed, causing silence or revolution. Interactions became poor, with too much control, domination, and manipulation, lacking warmth, sensitivity. (6a) *Hypo* response: clumsy/confused socially, withdrawal/silence. (6b) *Hyper* response: socially inept, non-dyadic in exchange; angry, rejecting people. *Danger*: striking out at people extremely; striking out (rejected) socially
7. Trust acts vs. mistrust acts (4–8 months)	*The next step refers to the classic Eriksonian stage in infancy, the first in his eight-step stage sequence over the lifespan. Mistrust can be potentiated with improper care/abuse*: Caregiving did not allow the infant (person) to develop a sense of trust or confidence in people. Feel down, without purpose; become passive/suspicious; perhaps angry. (7a) *Hypo* response: unable to trust people/create close relationships. (7b) *Hyper* response: trust anybody blindly. *Danger*: no social relationships, always on guard, suspicious, paranoid; or, to the contrary, socially naive; so taken advantage in the indiscriminate relations established
8. Sociability acts vs. un-sociability or poor sociability acts (8–12 months)	*The infant approaching 1 year of age enters the phase of developing active attachment, which can be secure or insecure; there are several major insecure types*: Not having warm, sensitive caregiver in infancy hinders developing security in socially relating to people. Insecure attachments develop, person not good socially. Insecure means being avoidant, fearful, rejecting, or ambivalent. (8a) *Hypo* response: avoiding any social relations; super-wary/isolated. (8b) *Hyper* response: attached to anybody without being careful about it. *Danger*: liable to choose insecure people in relations, being abused
9. Autonomy (independence) acts vs. doubt (dependence) acts (12–18 months)	*This step in the sequence refers to the second stage in Erikson's sequence. The development of autonomy needs the appropriate environmental support to manifest well in development*: Environment (parent) did not give good support for independent activity, behaved dominantly; person then feels dependent and not confident. (9a) *Hypo* response: Hard to take initiative/explore in activities and socially. Become inward and dissatisfied; feel dominated. (9b) *Hyper* response: become defiant, argumentative, not cooperative. *Danger*: fear of autonomy/independence, perhaps masked by defiant, argumentative attitude

(continued)

Table 10.3 (continued)

Step name/ approximate age[a]	Defensivity/offensivity themes in living a life akin to the indicated level (for questionnaire purposes, the a and b types can be scored from 0, 1, 2, 3, 4; *delete the italicized introductions*)
10. Interdigitational (give and take) acts vs. de-digitational (give or take) acts (18–24 months)	*The infancy does not end with the autonomy stage, in that advanced* sensorimotor *cognition allows for advanced social interaction skills; but that needs the right support*: Socially, no give and take (just giving or taking). Environment (parenting) did not support this. Difficulty in sharing, being concerned for others, feeling fondness, even love. No self-pride, even hate self. (10a) *Hypo* response: too passive; avoid confrontation, easily manipulated. (10b) *Hyper* response: too active; hate people, seek too much power. *Danger*: too much giving (and indiscriminate), no receiving; too much taking, coldness; no giving/sharing
11. Superordinate (well-coordinated) acts vs. dis-coordinate (uncoordinated) acts (2–3.5 years)	*Moving into the Piagetian representation* (preoperational*) stage brings with it even more advanced cognitive skills. This allows for more connected behavior, including in the emerging self, but support is needed*: Do not feel "together" in behavior/self-perception. Feel "in pieces" (falling apart). Environment (parent) controlling, not letting all parts develop and come together. So personal needs scattered, put in the middle of everything (person is "egocentric," self-centered). (11a) *Hypo* response: personal needs abandoned; accepts what other people want. (11b) *Hyper* response: too egocentric, become egotistical, resistant. *Danger*: personal needs extremely denied or accentuated
12. Initiative acts vs. guilt acts (3.5–5 years)	*This is the third Eriksonian stage that has been inserted in the present* Neo-Eriksonian *series. It concerns the classic Freudian complexes at this age*: Lack balance in being forward (in initiative) and being inward/withdrawing. Feel guilty when being too forward. For example, preschoolers might have sexual feelings for the parent (of the opposite sex) that are too forward and do not go away, even without knowing it. Develop unconscious (unaware) sexual problems into adolescence onwards, or general problems in initiative. (12a) *Hypo* response: too little. (12b) *Hyper* response: too much, no guilt. *Danger*: same-sex parent sexual fixation; upset sexuality
13. Identification and gender acts vs. problematic identification and gender acts (5–7 years)	*This step in the model concerns the consequences of poorly navigating the prior step, for example, due to improper parenting; the effects can be lifelong in terms of identification*: In growing, does not identify with or want to be like people who are around, especially parents. This interferes with learning about and acting like the preferred gender. The environment (parent) was not supportive about this. (13a) *Hypo* response: not wanting to be like the parent. (13b) *Hyper* response: becoming opposite to the way the parent is. *Danger*: does not identify with anyone; becomes narcissistic, uncontrollable, etc.

(continued)

Table 10.3 (continued)

Step name/ approximate age[a]	Defensivity/offensivity themes in living a life akin to the indicated level (for questionnaire purposes, the a and b types can be scored from 0, 1, 2, 3, 4; *delete the italicized introductions*)
14. Industry (putting in good effort) acts vs. inferiority acts (7–9 years)	*This step is another Eriksonian one that has been inserted in the present series. The school age child enters into the Piagetian stage of operational thought, and normally should apply it well at school and elsewhere*: In growing, don't enjoy learning/school; don't feel motivated; problematic peer relations. Environment (parent) showed little interest in person's learning, manipulated/created harsh rules, etc. (14a) *Hypo* response: the person loses interest in school/learning and peers/friends, loses self-confidence, feels inferior. (14b) *Hyper* response: extreme industry, exhaustion, fear failure. *Danger*: Insensitive, lies, gets wrong friends, rebels, feels superior
15. Role/personality tryout acts vs. role/ personality confusion acts (9–11 years)	*Erikson appears to have missed many steps in his developmental model, such as the present one. It concerns the preteen, who might have problems in trying out different roles and personalities*: Don't try out/ explore different roles, friends, attitudes, personalities. The environment (parent) did not support this exploration. (15a) *Hypo* response: Hard time in these tryouts; became confused in tryouts of different roles/ personalities; so stop them. (15b) *Hyper* response: try out multiple roles/ personalities, but superficially; feel moody/brood. *Danger*: try out negative (e.g., anti-social) roles/personalities. Problems in self and other definitions accentuate
16. Consciousness (being aware) acts vs. contra-conscious (not being aware) acts (11–13 years)	*The teenager acquires* abstract *thinking skills and potentials, which have profound lifetime socio-affective consequences. First, it allows for awareness in the sense of* consciousness, *assuming extant supports foster it*: Thinking not logical and abstract; blocks awareness (consciousness) of the self, other people, the environment, society, and place in the world. Environment (parent) was not supportive of this type of thinking and opening. (16a) *Hypo* response: not conscious/in touch interiorly; conforming. (16b) *Hyper* response: superficial, multiple temporary consciousness facades. *Danger*: out of awareness/conformity or fanaticism is extreme
17. Identity acts (positive ones) vs. identity diffusion (or negative identity) acts (13–16 years)	*This refers to Erikson's most famous stage in development; it has been reworked by others to include foreclosure, moratorium,* etc. *(*e.g., Marcia 2002*); the present use of negative hypo and hyper responses covers that*: No exploration of different identities, selves, questions of "Who I am." The environment (parent) did not support creation of a liked, positive identity. Five possible responses: (17a) *Hypo* response: (1) confusion in identity; (2) putting off search for identity; (3) adopting identities of other people, without much thinking; (17b) *Hyper* response: (4) adopting many identities, but all surface, false, fake. *Danger*: (5) adopting negative identities, e.g., in gangs/delinquency

(continued)

Table 10.3 (continued)

Step name/ approximate age[a]	Defensivity/offensivity themes in living a life akin to the indicated level (for questionnaire purposes, the a and b types can be scored from 0, 1, 2, 3, 4; *delete the italicized introductions*)
18. Nurturing acts vs. mis-nurturing (not nurturing) acts (16–19 years)	*Here is another critical step in development that does not seem to have been considered by Erikson; logically, developing nurturing seems a prelude to developing intimacy, for example, but it can go wrong*: Does not engage in caring behavior of other people, to give them support and bring out the best in them. The environment (parent) did not support nurturing. (18a) *Hypo* response: affects social relationships; ignores people, not like them, etc. (18b) *Hyper* response: nurtures people a lot, but only on the surface and without real caring. *Danger*: withdraws socially because of nurturing/inability concerns; loathes people; or nurtures/cares to entrap/ensnare
19. Intimacy acts (with partner) vs. (Social) Isolation acts (19–22 years)	*Here is another Eriksonian stage that has been embedded in the current modeling; when it goes awry, romantic partner relationships are affected*: Can't give positive effort, including at work or in school, and with any romantic partner and any children. Can't feel a deep, long-lasting love for the partner, if any present; can't feel deeply involved in anything done. Had not received environmental (parental) support for this. (19a) *Hypo* response: the person rejects romance; feels lonely, empty. (19b) *Hyper* response: goes through the motions; fakes in any partner relationship. *Danger*: behaves roughly
20. Universal (general concern for all people) acts vs. self-singular (self-focused) acts (22–25 years)	*Socio-affectivity can be impacted beyond romantic relationships when development is disturbed at this level according to the present model*: No concern for all people; self-focused despite relationships. No desire to care for or help anybody in need. Especially true for family, but it could apply to anyone. No basic helping moral value felt for anyone. Did not get good support this way. (20a) *Hypo* response: rejects helping others, family and all people included. (20b) *Hyper* response: helps but without feeling (or just to get praise). *Danger*: a universal non-empathy/lack of concern for the other; rejection/contempt/disgust of the other
21. Meta-collecting (seeing the big picture) acts vs. disillusionment acts (25–28 years)	*This step marks the beginning of the* postformal Neo-Piagetian *stage, referred to as* Collective Intelligence *in the present model, but do people use it or are supported toward using it?*: Despite being capable cognitively of superordinate abstract structures, don't see the big picture of the world, all its interconnections at many joined levels. Don't develop concern for the growth of all groups of peoples, wanting them capable of helping other peoples. (21a) *Hypo* response: ignore other peoples, feel disillusioned/down. (21b) *Hyper* response: help peoples only because taught to, and only superficially. *Danger*: act against other peoples, detesting them

(continued)

Table 10.3 (continued)

Step name/ approximate age[a]	Defensivity/offensivity themes in living a life akin to the indicated level (for questionnaire purposes, the a and b types can be scored from 0, 1, 2, 3, 4; *delete the italicized introductions*)
22. Generativity (generating) acts vs. Self-absorption (no responsibility) acts (28–39 years)	*This is another famous Eriksonian stage. The adult could be impacted in taking* responsibilities, *which I refer to as re-responsibilities, because of the multiple, continuous dedication required for them; but does this take place?*: Do not take one's responsibilities, pertaining to family and relationships, to work and study, to society. Degenerative toward self and also to others. (22a) *Hypo* response: let go of responsibilities, feel empty, focus only on self, not grow. (22b) *Hyper* response: try hard to take responsibilities, but just on the surface or because of past training. *Danger*: reject responsibilities permanently; lose self; aggressive to/ disempowering of others
23. Catalytic (growing others) acts vs. midlife crisis acts (39–50 years)	*In this step, the sense of taking Re-responsibilities can clearly extend to fostering the same in others, but does it take place, or does the so-called mid-life crisis develop*?: Do not carry through with all of one's responsibilities; do not behave so that everything around grows, gets better. Problems develop when let responsibilities let go. (23a) *Hypo* response: change, act just for the self; reject loved ones, work, all responsibilities. (23b) *Hyper* response: keep the responsibilities, but go through the motions, feel sad. *Danger*: responsibilities abandoned permanently; disregard consequences; self-absorption predominates
24. Ego integrity (feeling good about the self and life) acts vs. Despair acts (50– 61 years)	*This is the final Eriksonian stage in his series; it is about having led a fulfilled life or not, but I add one more life step after it; this step of ego integrity should be considered relationally; it is really a co-ego integrity one*: As the years go on, not satisfied about how family and relationships grow, about work or study, and the person does not help people and society, even if the situation allows; feels uncomfortable about how life has gone. (24a) *Hypo* response: feel low, disappointed; regret not having given best in life, not being fully present in everything done, etc. (24b) *Hyper* response: very disconsolate. *Danger*: get angry, can't do anything, etc.
25. Cathartic (purifying) acts vs. abandonment acts (61 years and after)	*The last of the 25 steps in the present* Neo-Eriksonian *series of 25 steps concerns the ultimate existential question; life is filled with tragedies, even in terms of the worst early abuse, tortures, genocides,* etc.*; would we all live a life that permits facing this last step in the life cycle with equanimity*: No matter the age, the person facing death does not look back fondly at the life lived, faces death with fear. Lacks broad, wise view of life, how it was lived, what death means. Lacks preparation for death, inner peace and spirituality. (25a) *Hypo* response: feel alone, abandoned by life at its end; struggles with inner peace, spirituality, death itself. (25b) *Hyper* response: fear death. *Danger*: dies alone psychologically if not physically; in remorse

[a]Possible age the indicated theme first lived
[b]In Young (2019a), the first three of the 25 levels of the model did not include a hyper type (pp. 536–540), which are added here
The table presents the 25 steps in the Neo-Eriksonian lifespan developmental model that has been proposed by the author in his books (2011, 2016, 2019a, the present book). Consistent with Erikson (e.g., Erikson 1980), the 25 steps are considered to involve navigating the polar opposites in psychosocial tendencies (e.g., Trust vs. Mistrust). Also, the 25 steps include Erikson's original eight steps, while adding 17 more, all of which were developed on rational grounds

(continued)

Table 10.3 (continued)

Each of the steps in the proposed Neo-Eriksonian developmental model considers responses to challenges and crises that accompany the emergence of the steps in development in situations in which the environment is not supportive/conducive, or abusive/adverse. For the earlier levels, on infancy and early childhood, this often concerns extreme abuse. Although an individual might live intensely negative regimes early in life, also the person could experience their equivalents later on in life. Either way, the individual could respond by magnifying the internal conflicts or minimizing them, depending on the context, developmental levels, individual differences, and so on. For example, there could be hypo or hyper responses, as per the table. (a) On the one hand, hypo responses are ones that involve retrenchment into passive response that defends against the challenges and crises that accompany the negative polarity of any developmental step per the model. (b) On the other hand, hyper responses are active but ingenuine responses that are superficial, false, pseudo, brief, quickly changing, tangential, etc.

The table is structured in a way that permits empirical investigation. It can be structured into a questionnaire. For each of the hypo and hyper responses associated with a particular step in the model, the questionnaire could ask the degree of applicability to the person on a Likert scale. The pattern of responses by respondents might be more revealing than any one individual response. The questionnaire could address perceptions of either developmental history or current psychology and contexts, or both

Of note, the questionnaire refers to defensivity and offensivity themes in development that are important to respondents. However, it does not explicitly mention defense mechanisms in these regards. Future research can integrate defense mechanism theory and study into the 25-step developmental model

Adopted with permission of Springer International Publishing. Young, G. (2019a). Causality *and development:* Neo-Eriksonian *perspectives*. Cham, Switzerland: Springer International Publishing. [Text Excerpt of 2262 words from Chapter 18, pp. 536–540]

including of defense mechanisms. The concept of defensivity/offensivity that has been developed by the author is novel to the field. This portion of the chapter has also proposed a novel matrix model of categories/types/strategies in defensivity and offensivity that both contributes to the field of adaptation, stress, and coping and prepares the way for integration of defense mechanism work into it.

The next part of the chapter moves to the development portion of the author's modeling. It presents a 25-step lifespan Neo-Eriksonian model. To access this literature in support of the model, the interested reader can consult the Young books (Young 2011, 2016, 2019a, and the present one).

Neo-Eriksonian Development

The Model

The present Neo-Piagetian/Neo-Eriksonian model had been constructed on rational rather than empirical grounds. Young (2011, 2016, 2019a, this book) developed his model by examining the original eight-step Eriksonian lifespan model of development, and adding steps to it. First, he developed a 25-step Neo-Piagetian model of lifespan cognitive development, consisting of five stages X five recycling substages.

Then, he proposed that there are 25 corresponding Eriksonian-type steps to the 25 cognitive ones. But the Neo-Eriksonian steps do not emerge in parallel with the Neo-Piagetian ones. The cognitive development provides the substrate, but the socio-affective side of the steps in development can be seriously altered by negative environmental experiences, for example, pertaining to early parenting. The environmental quality experienced by the person in their development according to the Neo-Eriksonian model that is being proposed can affect the nature of their expression in either the positive or negative direction. For example, an infant might receive very negative caregiving and express the negative rather than the positive pole of a particular early-developing stage, such as Mistrust compared to Trust.

Given this preamble, Young placed the extant eight Eriksonian steps in correspondence with what appeared to be the best step among the 25 steps of his Neo-Piagetian model. Then, he interpolated 17 new steps to complement the extant eight ones into the 25-step Neo-Eriksonian sequence. Young accomplished this phase in his model construction process also by considering the corresponding Neo-Piagetian step with which each step in the Neo-Eriksonian sequence of steps was being associated as the model evolved. Young adopted the same rational process in the beginning phase of the model's construction when he had compared and contrasted extant Neo-Piagetian models in order to create the initial 25-step Neo-Piagetian sequence.

For each of the 25 steps in the Neo-Eriksonian model, Table 10.3 describes the challenges and crises that can emerge in socio-affective development in terms of 25 paired negative and positive poles, which are referred to as acts. In addition, and importantly, the table indicates possible negative hypo- and hyper-responses that could be expressed at each of the 25 steps. For example, for the step of Trust, if the person becomes mistrustful in an Eriksonian sense, she/he could become very wary of any relationships, or they might become superficially and indiscriminately involved in many of them.

Note that people might develop problems with a particular step in the sequence by having experiences that disturb the steps at the time of their emergence. Or, they might experience later adversities, trauma, etc., that derange their stability in terms of early steps that otherwise they might have navigated at the time well enough. Either way, a person who expresses difficulties according to the proposed Neo-Eriksonian sequence at one step or another is setting the stage for defensivity and offensivity behaviors related to them. If these latter behaviors become habitual and priorities in deployed behavior for contexts at hand, these types of responses could constitute prototypical defensivity/offensivity reactions to developmental or ongoing adversities.

In this sense, the 25 steps in the Neo-Eriksonian sequence being proposed are not just descriptions of negative and positive poles in behavior over development. More than that, each step in the 25-step Neo-Eriksonian sequence provides fertile ground for the expression of habitual, repetitive behavior patterns, and so constitute potential defensivity/offensivity themes.

The 25 positive-negative oppositions in the poles of the 25-step model make sense as potential themes in defensivity/offensivity because the defensivity/offensivity flow in behavior is influenced by multiple factors, including developmental history and how it can go awry, as per the present Neo-Eriksonian 25-step sequence. Therefore, individual life trajectories should vary in offensivity and defensivity behaviors (and any associated defense mechanisms involved), and these trajectories might be related to the 25 steps in Eriksonian development and the offensivity/defensivity themes that they constitute.

Moreover, as each developmental step emerges along with its challenges and crises, the repertoire of behaviors that accompany each one can vary from individual to individual. Also, the repertoire that accompanies each step can be used in defensivity or offensivity or both, and in combination in varying ways depending on the circumstance. Finally, different arrays of defense mechanisms can be part of that individualized response.

Conclusion

The first part of the present chapter deals with models of adaptation and coping developed by the author. Their purpose was to find a broad framework in which work on defense mechanisms could be included. The major bridge in this regard was to add the concept of defensivity and offensivity to the adaptation and coping field. This led to a matrix model of 48 defensivity and offensivity categories, types, or strategies, built on the classic fight-flight-freeze model of stress reactivity.

As for a more detailed explication of this chapter's contents, the chapter begins with modeling on adaptation, coping, defensivity, and offensivity. It includes initial work relating this modeling to defense mechanisms. Then, the chapter turns to its major contribution of a 48-category matrix of adaptation/coping and defensivity/offensivity strategies and types in which the classic fight-flight-freeze stress response is embedded. The 48-category matrix model of adaptivity, stress, and coping had added 45 new categories of adaptation and coping to the classic fight-flight-freeze response. The model consists of two parts of 24 categories each. The first part relates to categories described in terms of direction (e.g., to, away). The second part relates to categories concerning self-related behavior. The direction categories add dominance-submission categories. The self-categories add filtering categories. The dimension of strategies of being overt or covert is involved in both 24-category parts of the matrix. Offensivity and defensivity are involved in each 24-category part as well. Examples in the matrix that go beyond the classic fight-flight-freeze stress response include fend off, fence off, build self, and cry for help.

Essentially, the present chapter is based on two major modeling initiatives. The first one is totally novel to the field, and it concerns adaptation and coping in relation to defensivity and offensivity. The result is a 48-category matrix of defensivity and offensivity types. The matrix allows for expansion and integration of the field of defense mechanisms, which is not undertaken here.

The second major modeling aspect of the present work concerns a 25-step Neo-Eriksonian lifespan developmental model. It can be interpreted in terms of defensivity and offensivity themes as much as the traditional way of positive and negative poles. Also, the model might lend itself to analysis according to the development and use of defense mechanisms, but that procedure is not undertaken here.

The literature review that follows in the next chapter deals with adaptation and coping and defense mechanisms. The former speaks to the adaptation and coping modeling in the present approach. The latter deals with not only historical but also recent defense mechanism literature.

References

Borsboom, D.: Psychometric perspectives on diagnostic systems. J. Clin. Psychol. **64**(9), 1089–1108 (2008). https://doi.org/10.1002/jclp.20503

Corr, P.J., Cooper, A.J.: The reinforcement sensitivity theory of personality questionnaire (RST-PQ): development and validation. Psychol. Assess. **28**(11), 1427–1440 (2016). https://doi.org/10.1037/pas0000273

Corr, P.J., Krupić, D.: Motivating personality: approach, avoidance, and their conflict. In: Elliot, A.J. (ed.) The Advances in Motivation Science: Advances in Motivation Science, pp. 38–90. Elsevier Academic Press, Cambridge (2017). Abstract retrieved from Science Direct database

Erikson, E.H.: Identity and the Life Cycle. Norton, New York (1980)

Gillespie, A.: Disruption, self-presentation, and defensive tactics at the threshold of learning. Rev. Gen. Psychol. **24**(4), 382–396 (2020). https://doi.org/10.1177/1089268020914258

Gray, J.A., McNaughton, N.: The Neuropsychology of Anxiety: an Enquiry into the Functions of the Septo-Hippocampal System, 2nd edn. Oxford University Press, Oxford (2000)

Lazarus, R.S., Folkman, S.: Stress, Appraisal, and Coping, 1st edn. Springer, New York (1984)

Levine, M., Prosser, A., Evans, D., Reicher, S.: Identity and emergency intervention: how social group membership and inclusiveness of group boundaries shape helping behavior. Pers. Soc. Psychol. Bull. **31**(4), 443–453 (2005). https://doi.org/10.1177/0146167204271651

Marcia, J.E.: Identity and psychosocial development in adulthood. Identity. **2**(1), 7–29 (2002). https://doi.org/10.1207/S1532706XID0201_02

McNally, R.J.: Network analysis of psychopathology: controversies and challenges. Annu. Rev. Clin. Psychol. **17**, 1.1–1.23 (2021). https://doi.org/10.1146/annurev-clinpsy-081219-092850

Young, G.: Development and Causality: Neo-Piagetian Perspectives. Springer, New York (2011)

Young, G.: Causality in psychiatry: a hybrid symptom network construct model. Front. Psychiatry. **6**, 164 (2015). https://doi.org/10.3389/fpsyt.2015.00164

Young, G.: Unifying Causality and Psychology: Being, Brain and Behavior. Springer, Cham (2016)

Young, G.: Revising the American Psychological Association Ethics Code. Springer, Cham (2017)

Young, G.: Causality and Development: Neo-Eriksonian Perspectives. Springer, Cham (2019a)

Young, G.: The cry for help in psychological injury and law: concepts and review. Psychol. Injury Law. **12**(3–4), 225–237 (2019b). https://doi.org/10.1007/s12207-019-09360-y

Chapter 11
Broadening Defense Mechanisms: Literature Review and Discussion

Whereas the first chapter of the two-chapter series on defense mechanisms in the present book dealt with modeling, it had not dealt the literature related to these models. The first section of this second chapter in the two-chapter series on defense mechanisms consists of an in-depth literature review of recent publications related to the major themes of the chapter. The most important sections of this literature review are the first one on adaptation and coping and the last one on defense mechanisms. Section on "Discussion" after the literature review of this chapter presents relevant conclusions, aside from giving a brief summary and offering recommendations for future research. These conclusions provide conceptual innovations in two areas, related to defense mechanisms and coping.

Literature Review

The literature reviewed in this chapter supports the current modeling process that has been presented in its first chapter. Also, it leads to multiple questions for future investigation. In particular, the literature review covers adaptation/coping and on defense mechanisms.

Also, it leads to multiple questions for future investigation. In particular, the literature review covers adaptation/coping and on defense mechanisms. Also, it leads to multiple questions for future investigation. The literature focuses on adaptation/coping and on defense mechanisms, in particular.

The articles were acquired by canvassing PsychInfo and Web of Science; key terms were used, but the selection of articles from among the multiple long lists of articles that resulted from the searches was undertaken on a rational rather than inclusive basis, that is, in terms of which ones would fit the points needing to be made in the chapter.

G. Young, *Causality and Neo-Stages in Development*,
https://doi.org/10.1007/978-3-030-82540-9_11

In conducting the literature review, often I let the articles speak for themselves and then offer comments. When there are numerous articles that only flesh out main points being made, I refer to them without much comment.

Adaptation and Coping

The recent literature on adaptation and coping is broad. Moreover, I add related topics to the review that fit the present goal of creating an inclusive adaptivity/coping and defensivity/offensivity model.

Bayesian Brain/Predictive Processing

The current literature review updates the literature that had been presented in Young (2016) to introduce the topic. Since then, the area has continued to flourish. The notion that brains function to predict and to minimize surprise is attractive, but the extent to which it represents a unified theory across neuron, brain, and behavior has been questioned.

The author's own version of the free energy concept that drives the Bayesian brain hypothesis has been presented in a prior chapter in this present book. There, the free energy concept has been repositioned as a relational or psychological energetics one.

The following literature review on the Bayesian brain begins with a general review of the concept of the Bayesian brain. Then, it examines how the Bayesian brain concept has been applied to disorders in psychology and to psychotherapy.

General

Paulin and Cahill-Lane (2019) dated the evolution of event-predictive neurons to the pre-Cambrian period, about 560 million years ago. The animals that evolved neurons having this type of characteristic could then forage and feed longer before needing to flee in situations in which they were threatened with predation.

Thus, the origins of the Bayesian brain had begun with the very first neurons evolutionarily. This suggests that the ubiquity of the Bayesian brain hypothesis in science and in psychology reflects the utility of the behavior involved in the modeling for survival and reproduction.

Butz et al. (2020) applied the Bayesian prior/prediction formula to event-related predictive cognition. In this perspective, through mediational learning, the brain encodes events generatively, parsing them into dynamic encodings. These encodings are applied broadly by the brain, and, in this regard, they are applied to sensorimotor, cognitive, and language structures and processes. The schemas/construals that are created to predict events are flexible, loose, versatile, and dynamically context-dependent. The events are not fixed as fixed entities when they are encoded, but they are characterized as probabilistic. The events are not static, in that they are tracked for consistency. Events cannot be represented simply by one code; rather, they are coded by networks of predictive codes; the multiple interactive codes so formed even predict each other's activities. They are characterized as attractor states, which refer to basins in the state space of systems to which they gravitate. The coupled predictive codes help minimize mutual predictive error. As they function, they become progressively more compacted, complex, and anticipatory. The codes have different complexity properties, including sensorimotor codes that ground the later developing conceptual ones. The codes reflect a hierarchical organization beyond themselves, having superordinate latent variables for inferring the causes of encoded predicted events. [Also see Chater et al. (2020) and Zeki and Chén (2020) for more circumscribed work in the area of the Bayesian brain.]

Note that this causal conjecture in the predictive processing model introduces a new dimension to the topic of causality in behavior systems. On the one hand, in network modeling, causality is viewed as residing in the interactions among the nodes of the system. For example, poor sleep can drive other components of the network. Here, Butz et al. (2020) refer to causal inferences, and relate them to superordinate levels in the system, specifically to latent variables. Young (2016, 2019, this book) referred to humans as *Homo Causa*. We focus on causality schema constructions to help understand behavior. Previously, the chapter referred to intermediate level appraisals that mediate between lower-order networks and higher-order individualized latent variables. Butz et al.'s causality conjecture fits this perspective—appraisals often concern causality. At the same time, in the above, the prior chapter has referred to causality (mis)perceptions (in Fig. 10.1). This concept fits the line being discussed.

Ransom et al. (2020) argued that the concept of the Bayesian brain/predictive encoding does not accommodate well the affective dimension of behavior. Stimuli that are affectively laden because of their associations with rewards and punishments differentially capture our attention despite the predictive pull otherwise of ongoing perceptual and active inference. Valence, values, rewards, etc., might constitute an independent but interactive affective system compared to the standard Bayesian brain model, which applies especially to perception and cognition.

However, it could be that predictive schemas/construals are at once perceptual-cognitive and affective, being indissociable. Therefore, the Bayesian brain model would have to adjust its formulae to account for not only the history of priors relevant to the perceptual-cognitive domain as it engages in probabilistic prediction but also those relevant to the affective one.

Indeed, perhaps we need to reconceptualize the concept of priors in Bayesian brain modeling. They do not just concern past predictive encodings and the like, because those encoding are influenced by what can be termed *second-order priors*, which are those related to areas other than perception and cognition. Not only are there affective priors in this regard, but also there are socio-affective ones generally, personality ones, intelligence ones, etc., that condition priors related to predictive event cognition or any other type. The socio-affective ones might concern the history of yoked behavior related to the 25 Neo-Eriksonian steps in the present lifespan developmental model.

The latter notion has currency for the area of defense mechanisms. To what extent does the history of priors related to affective and socio-affective defensivity and defense mechanisms condition priors relevant to current perceptual and cognitive predictive processing? The present chapter provides sufficient background to enable reworking of the Bayesian brain modeling project toward encompassing affect, socio-affectivity, defense mechanisms, etc. The ensuing review of recent work on the Bayesian brain in relation to the clinical domain reinforces this conjecture. That said, it is beyond the scope of the present book to conduct further work on this theorizing.

Clinical

Kube et al. (2020) argued that a traumatic event that elicits PTSD becomes a high priority prior that conditions ongoing sensory experiences. Priors that are "strong" bias information processing and hinder predictive processing updating. In cases of trauma, a strong prior develops and magnifies the saliency of current sensory input, leading to PTSD symptoms. They are hyper-precise and settle in, resisting disconfirming evidence, such as a lack of real threat to a new triggering situation.

Karoly (2021) applied the predictive processing model to pain, depression, and anxiety. When applied to interoceptive pain perception and active inferences about it, the concept of the Bayesian brain specifies that predictions become error-prone and maladaptive (biased, rigid, too certain). Self-statements, such as the pain is killing me or catastrophizing about its course, will inhibit productive schema alteration of interoceptive pain experiences toward more optimistic scenarios. The pain becomes chronic and disabling.

Sterzer et al. (2018) related aberrant predictive coding by the Bayesian brain to psychosis. The encoding of prior beliefs relative to incoming sensory information lacks precision. Hallucinations involve strong perceptual priors in this account, while delusions involve strong conceptual priors.

Holmes and Nolte (2019) argued that, in psychopathology, top-down predictions by the brain do not match bottom-up sensory information, and so the prediction error is large. There is more free energy that is unbounded in the "surprise." Predictions are not revised to minimize the error and so bind the excess free energy.

Therapy is a process that, at one level, seeks to recouple bottom-up sensory information processing and top-down prediction/inference and their adaptive revisioning. The authors conclude that the Bayesian brain model of psychotherapy allows for any technique to be applied to a case at hand, depending on its potential to reduce surprise, free energy, predictive error, automatisms in decoupled levels, etc.

Stress, Coping, Adaptation

The core area of the literature review involves the adaptation, coping, and stress segment because it interleaves with the novel model in the prior chapter of 48 types of strategies, behaviors, actions, and tendencies in adaptation and coping in terms of defensivity and offensivity. First in this regard, the review examines recent articles on stress. Then, it turns to disorders. It ends with articles on theory. In the latter section, two articles are not on stress, per se, but are applicable to the present modeling of the adaptation and coping matrix created in Tables 10.1 and 10.2 of the prior chapter. Two other articles speak to Young's activation-inhibition coordination model of a common causal mechanism across neuron, brain, and behavior.

Stress

The field of stress is built on classics in the field, such as in Cannon's work on the physiological and central aspect of the fight and flight response (e.g., Cannon 1914, 1915, 1916, per Dror 2014; Robinson 2018). Selye developed the General Adaptation Syndrome (GAS) concept, which describes a universal response to stress. It involves exhaustion and disease as an endpoint to continually present stress that overwhelms the organism, leading to the worst negative effects of stress on physical health (e.g., Selye 1936, 1950, 1951).

Different models of stress arose after Selye's. One focused on the stressors impacting an organism, rating them on a stress intensity scale that applies universally. A major shift took place in stress and coping research with the work of Lazarus (e.g., Lazarus and Folkman 1984), who considered the mediation between stressor and response, thereby advocating for individual differences in the stress response, rather than universal models. His work emphasized an interactive and appraisal basis for the stress response that takes place individually in each organism according to capacities and perceptions. Lazarus's approach to defining stress related it to overtaxing the organism's system based on the individual organism as a whole, adding psychology into the equation of defining stress in terms of individual differences in appraisals of stress and the capacity to deal with it.

The landscape of the field of stress has expanded to include adaptation and coping, in general. Other relevant concepts include allostatic load/overload (McEwen 1998, 2018) and the pervasive biopsychosocial model (Krause and Halkitis 2020; also called embodied stress theory, Francis 2018; and social genomics, Cole 2019; Cole et al. 2007). The field of psycho-neuroimmunology encompasses these different perspectives (e.g., Kiecolt-Glaser et al. 1995, 2020).

Dror (2014), O'Connor et al. (2021), and Robinson (2018) have sketched the history of stress studies. The study of stress dates back to stalwarts such as William James. However, the field has never been able to come up with a standard, universally accepted definition of stress, given its wide-ranging character. As discussed above, different approaches to it will emphasize either the stimulus component, the response component, or the mediation between them. That is, does stress concern especially the stressor, the perception and appraisal of the stressor, or the stress response? O'Connor et al. (2021) have dismissed the criticisms of the stress concept that have emerged because of difficulties in defining it universally. These authors noted that the empirical research base clearly shows the deleterious health outcomes of stress, which supports the value and validity of the concept.

Also, stress has traceable physiological sequelae. Importantly, it elicits an immediate adrenaline rush and then a delayed stress hormone response (cortisol), which is designed to optimize the energy requirements in the fight or flight response that accompanies stress. According to O'Connor et al. (2021), stress elicits activity in the sympathetic–adrenal–medullary (SAM) system. Almost immediately, adrenaline and noradrenaline are released, activating the fight-or-flight response. Also, stress elicits activity in the hypothalamic–pituitary–adrenal (HPA) axis. This causes the stress hormone cortisol to surge, which triggers the release of excess energy. The energy becomes available for use by muscles and brain in the fight-flight or related mode.

However, continued activation of the SAM and the HPA axis has deleterious consequences for the organism. In such contexts, these systems become dysregulated and the GAS system can proceed to its next phases.

That is, with repeated stressful experience, the HPA/cortisol system becomes dysregulated in the feedback mechanisms involved, leading to hypercortisolism. Any advantages of excess adrenalin to handle the fight and fight response are countered by the excess cortisol. Along with other deleterious processes induced by stress, the combined dysregulations that result together facilitate tissue damage, poor health, and so on. But hypercortisolism is not the only outcome of hyper-stress. As a second potential outcome to repeated stressful experiences, blunted hypocortisolism might develop. The feedback mechanisms that are involved in the typical cortical response dampening mechanisms after phasic stress cannot function well in the tonic stress situation of repeated stressful experiences (Kiecolt-Glaser et al. 2020). Hypocortisolism could be just as deleterious to the person, in that it might also have health risk consequences as much as in the case of hypercortisolism.

Stress experiences might be present even prenatally or in early postnatal life. The developing brain could be affected prenatally as the neural crest is laid down and as newly developing neural cells migrate along its axis. The long-term physical and psychological effects of prenatal and early postnatal stress are compounded by the sensitive period constituted by these ages. Maternal stress comprises one salient prenatal stressor, aside from all the toxins and other risk factors involved. O'Connor et al. (2021) also noted that early life adversity or adverse childhood experiences (ACEs, e.g., trauma, domestic violence) act collectively and lead to cumulative stress experiences that could have long-term serious physical and mental health consequences. Early experiences that are extreme like this have been associated with an increased vulnerability to suicide later on. The research indicates that ACEs are linked to early HPA axis damage and later reduced cortisol reactivity to a laboratory stressor (the Trier test).

Overall, the research indicates that stress is mediated by one's appraisal, both of the internal or external impacts on the person. In addition, when stress is long term, the stress accumulation that results could have serious consequences for the physical and mental health of the person. In circumstances such as these, researchers could examine not only which defense mechanisms might be deployed and how, but also which patterns in defensivity, in general, might be potentiated.

Slavich (2020) focused on the buffering afforded by sociality and social relations on negative stress responses. He referred to the social brain, or the network of central structures that are involved in social bonding. As well, the social brain fosters an anticipatory inflammatory response to social threat (e.g., social conflict, aggression, devaluation, isolation, rejection, and exclusion). Slavich (2020) posited that schemas (social safety ones) mediate the relationship with others and with the world, and they develop in the social (e.g., caregiving, abuse, bullying) environment. The schemas are shaped by meanings and messages received, and their meanings and messages shape the person's response to the social environment. When schemas are maladaptive, dysregulated immune responses are potentiated, along with their associated health consequences. Thus, health is a social interactional product.

The present author's approach to the social dynamics in behavior is that we engage in relational or psychological co-regulation as we develop and then in our social interactions and relationships (Young 2017, 2019, this book). Regulation and dysregulation are co-constructed. Also, they are general, and apply equally to behavior, emotions, cognition, inhibitory control, self-control, etc. In short, the physical and mental health that derives from the process of relational co-regulation is indeed social, but also it is relational in the wider environmental and ecological sense. And the dysregulation involved covers all aspects of our psychology.

Kiecolt-Glaser et al. (2020) also referred to co-regulation in the context of stress. Stress appraisals are constructed interactively and stress is lived interactively. Early life adversity leads to adaptive calibration to the environment that has positive short-term but not long-term advantages (Del Giudice et al. 2011). Early stress is embedded biologically, thereby promoting suboptimal psychological and stress reactivity throughout the lifespan (Miller et al. 2011). As for adults, romantic partners entrain each other in the stress response in their arguments (Kiecolt-Glaser and Wilson 2017). Newlywed hostility in discussion leads to larger acute increases in stress hormones, and predicts divorce 10 years later (Kiecolt-Glaser 2018).

Sivan-Donin et al. (2019) examined Lazarus and Folkman's cognitive appraisal theory of stress in relation to Hobfoll's (1989, 2001, 2002; Hobfoll and Jackson 1991) conservation and resource theory (COR) of stress, finding them complementary. The COR theory maintains that stress involves resource acquisition threats, losses, blockages, or inability to be replenished. This leads individuals to take stock of resources and to build up resources in non-stressful periods. Personal assets help in resource acquisition (self efficacy, personal traits, skills), and deficits in these regards make the individual more vulnerable to stress.

de Kloet et al. (2019) referred to top-down and bottom-up control in stress and coping. They described in great detail the bottom-up physiological processes in the stress response, a review of which is beyond the scope of the present chapter. They offered a stress response model that included appraisals and defense as top-down influences. Coping strategies include active (e.g., fight-flight) and passive types, with the latter energy-conserving ones being as adaptive as any other (Henry and Stephens 1977).

Cantave et al. (2019) conducted a study on maltreatment, depressive symptoms, and their relationship to the cortisol response and to coping strategies. Participants were males between 18 and 35 years of age. The laboratory stress used is used frequently in the field. The test is the Trier Social Stress Test (TSST; Kirschbaum et al. 1993), which involves a mock job interview in front of a panel of "experts." Coping strategies were assessed using the Coping Inventory of Stressful Situations (CISS, Endler and Parker 1994). It yields scores for three orientations of coping: task, emotion, and avoidant. The results showed that child maltreatment was associated with a higher risk for depression symptoms for participants who expressed a higher cortisol response to the TSST. The emotion-coping orientation had mediational effects.

Straud and McNaughton-Cassill (2019) conducted a study of undergraduate student coping. For present purposes, it is noted they used a coping inventory having 14 dimensions, and integrating prior scales (Carver 1997). The diverse coping scales in the field illustrate that, just as is the case for the definition of stress and coping itself, there is no universally accepted number of dimensions, factors, strategies, styles, or categories in coping with stress.

In short, stress is what we make of it and coping is making of it, with both adaptive and maladaptive styles used. Also, the individual varies in the resources available to her/him, both personal and situational, while behavior often concerns efforts to maintain, replenish, or augment resources. Health risks are potentiated by stress, especially of the cumulative, long-term type. This conclusion leads to discussion of stress and psychological disorder.

Disorders/Symptoms

Clancy et al. (2017) conducted a study that illustrates several of the major themes of the chapter. They examined outpatients with a PTSD diagnoses, and controls with General Anxiety Disorder or in good health. They administered relevant questionnaires and they gathered EEG data. They found that PTSD was associated with heightened low-level, bottom-up sensory activity, or a hypersensory activity/sensory inhibition deficit. The hypersensory activity in PTSD impacted higher-order operations, such as hypervigilance, inhibition, impulse control, emotional regulation, and executive function. The result for the brain was described as frontal overload. The study illustrates that stress (PTSD) impacts the full scope of bottom-up and top-down functions, including in sensory gating and in an implied schema regulation of the sensory activity.

Thompson et al. (2018) found, in their study of PTSD, that avoidant and active coping were differentially associated with PTSD. They used the Coping Strategies Inventory (Tobin et al. 1989). It consists of eight primary scales: problem solving, cognitive restructuring, social support, expressing emotions, problem avoidance, wishful thinking, self-criticism, and social withdrawal. The wishful thinking scale is an interesting one and presages the defense mechanism research by Perry and Despland (2011) described below.

Dariotis and Chen (2020) conducted a study of youth involved in risky and delinquent behavior, including substance abuse. They found that avoidance coping served as a mediator in the behavior. For present purposes, the authors used yet another coping scale, the Coping Strategies checklist (Ayers et al. 1996). The instrument includes 54 items rated on a four-point scale that organize into 13 coping strategies under five dimensions. The checklist includes: Active problem solving (e.g., direct problem solving and two more cognitive dimensions); Positive Reframing Coping (positivity, control, optimism): Distraction (distracting, physical activities); Avoidance (avoidant actions, repression, wishful thinking); and Support seeking. Notice the overlap with defense mechanisms in the repression, wishful thinking, etc.

Konaszewski et al. (2021) studied youth by using the CISS for coping style. They found that a sense of self-efficacy was negatively related to emotion-oriented coping. They added that a measure of coherence (e.g., knowing one has the requisite resources for a stressor/challenge) also showed results related to self-efficacy.

Boyraz et al. (2019) studied youth with instruments on posttraumatic stress symptoms, academic coping, and locus of control. The latter instruments were found related to the trauma variable.

In a meta-analysis of coping strategies in youth victims of child abuse, van der Linden et al. (2018) studied fast life history (LH) strategies in adults, such as in early teenage pregnancy. This lifestyle is associated with stressful life events, such as early abuse, in contrast to those who adopt a slow lifestyle. van der Linden et al. (2018) used a coping inventory to show that fast LH is associated with avoidance coping.

In a meta-analytic study on the effects of child abuse, Gruhn and Compas (2020) used a three-tiered construct of coping to analyze the literature on its effects into later developmental periods (Compas et al. 2017). The first level involved emotional regulation and adaptive/maladaptive coping. The second level involved factors, such as approach/engagement, disengagement coping, emotion-focused coping, primary control coping, problem-focused coping, secondary control coping, and social support. The third tier consisted of strategies, such as acceptance, avoidance, cognitive reappraisal, denial, distraction, emotional expression, emotional modulation, emotional suppression (inhibition, repression), humor, problem solving, unregulated release of emotions (e.g., anger), and wishful thinking. As for the results of the meta-analysis, not all of the latter strategies in the third tier had sufficient numbers of studies to be tested. However, in the meta-analytic results, the specific strategies of avoidance and emotional expression/suppression were the ones that were associated with the abuse. The authors indicated that in situations of child abuse, these types of strategies are not necessarily maladaptive in the short term, but they would be in the long term.

These studies, mostly on youth, indicate that coping in youth is related to perceptions of having the tools to deal with stress and realizing they are controllable and not externally located uniquely. In extreme circumstances, however, avoidance and emotionality are elicited. As for the compendium of strategies of coping in the model of Gruhn and Compas (2020), it illustrates the large array of coping strategies used, their relation to some defense mechanism terms, and that any one extant coping inventory is insufficient in covering them.

Next, the literature review addresses relevant theoretical themes for adaptation and coping. The first two articles relate to higher-order attentional and cognitive processes, which are important in adaptation and coping, and relevant to defense mechanisms. The majority of the articles concerns recent literature related to the author's activation-inhibition coordination model of neuron, brain, behavior, and their networking or organization. The brain-behavior axis can be conceived in terms of these three tiers of neuron, brain, and behavior. And the activation-inhibition coordination construct offers a common metric cutting across the tiers to inform their contents and causality.

Theory

Cancino-Montecinos et al. (2020) presented an emotion regulation account of cognitive dissonance reduction. The empirical research has demonstrated that, to reduce dissonance, people will employ strategies such as denial of responsibility, rationalization, and trivialization. The authors developed a model of strategy employment in dealing with cognitive dissonance that included engaging ones, such as attitude change, but also disengaging ones, such as evading (avoidance, escape) and refutation (denial of responsibility, trivialization). Notice the similarities with defense mechanisms for the examples provided for disengagement. As with the coping literature, there is overlap with the defense mechanism literature with the literature on cognitive dissonance/emotional regulation.

Burgoyne and Engle (2020) considered attention control as a cross-domain skill that underwrites sensory discrimination, working memory, fluid intelligence, and other cognitive skills. It is domain general, but is influenced by task. The concept of attention control has been included in the model described in Fig. 10.1 of the prior chapter on how stimuli are vetted by attention control and the schemas involved, sculpting responses accordingly. Attention control allows for task engagement maintenance and disengagement. The term disengagement in this context refers to adaptively disengaging from information that is no longer relevant. In the coping literature, it had a more negative connotation. The concept of engagement and disengagement with information speaks to the concept of activation-inhibition coordination. In attention control, both of these components need to be exquisitely coordinated for task success. The following continues discussion of activation-inhibition coordination.

Yizhar et al. (2011) and Liang et al. (2020) both supported an excitation/inhibition balance (E/I) model in neural activity. When the balance gravitates to more excitation than correlated inhibition to hold function in check, dysregulation takes place. In this model of underlying neural function to brain and behavior, the concept relates to an inhibitory control of activation. The concept lacks a coordination component, though, unlike the present case.

Kühnel et al. (2019) and Jadri and Denève (2013) applied the E/I balance model of neural activity to alexithymia and psychosis, respectively. In the former study, neurons in the pregenual anterior cingulate cortex (pgACC) were examined for the ratio of glutamate to GABA via 7 T MRI, in that the ratio stands as a proxy for E/I balance. The pgACC is a hub that is associated with emotion regulation, and alexithymia is associated with dysregulated emotion regulation (see section on "Alexithymia" below). The results of the study showed that the degree of alexithymia, as measured by the Toronto Alexithymia Scale (TAS, Parker et al. 2003), is associated with the E/I proxy measure.

As for Jadri and Denève (2013), they posited that, in schizophrenia, GABA transmission is impaired (per Stephan et al. 2009). They argued that this reflects a hierarchical neural imbalance in E/I (also Lisman et al. 2008; O'Donnell 2011). The brain is structured hierarchically in recurrent networks with many feedforward and feedback excitatory connections. The E/I balance obtains by excitatory loops being controlled by "equally strong" inhibitory loops, a balancing process that does not take place in the recurrent networks in psychosis. This dysregulation appears common in psychiatric disorders. In schizophrenia, the imbalance leads to dysregulation of bottom-up sensory information and top-down predictions, which facilitates expression of the cardinal symptoms of delusions and hallucinations. The authors invoke the concept of the Bayesian brain and its influence of priors on perception in order to account for the sensory looping in hallucination and delusions, i.e., in dysregulating sensory information (more on the Bayesian brain above).

Neal and Gable (2017) related inhibition to the right hemisphere, which is a consistent finding in the literature. In Young's (2011, 2016, 2019, this book) model of hemispheric specialization, the left hemisphere is associated with activation-inhibition coordination (think infant reaching/grasping, adult speech) and the right hemisphere is associated with less complex forms of function involving inhibition, such as outright inhibition. Neal and Gable (2017) referred to Gray's Behavior Activation/Behavior Inhibition System, with the latter BIS mediating between the BAS and the FFF (Fight-Flight-Freeze) system (Gray 1970; Gray and McNaughton 2000). Carver and White (1994) developed BAS/BIS scales, which have been used as part of the research showing the association of inhibition with the right hemisphere. Similarly, EEG research has linked the right and left frontal lobes to approach and withdrawal motivation, respectively (e.g., Harmon-Jones and Gable 2018). In terms of the preferred interpretation of these findings, according to Young (2011, 2016, 2019, this book), the motivation of approach, which is more complex than withdrawal, is specialized in the left hemisphere because of its facilitation by the left hemisphere's undercurrent specialization of refined activation-inhibition coordination.

Fight/Flight/Freeze

The revision of the classic fight or flight response into the fight-flight-freeze (FFF) response has been subject to much empirical research in the framework of the response sensitivity theory (Corr and Krupić 2017). The research teams involved have developed a questionnaire with FFF components and also ones related to activation and inhibition (BAS, BIS systems), in particular. The literature below reviews recent developments using the theory and an FFF questionnaire. However, this field has not considered broader models, as has been done here with the 48-category matrix of defensivity/offensivity adaptation and coping behaviors (and in which the FFFs are integrated).

Bacon and Corr (2020) found that personal safety concerns due to Covid are associated with higher FFF scores. Bacon et al. (2020) found the scores for FFF are related to academic dishonesty motivations in students. De Pascalis et al. (2018a) found that FFF scores are related to longer latencies in a task in which EEG and EMG measures were taken. De Pascalis et al. (2018b) found that FFF scores are related to greater relative right frontocentral EEG activity in the contexts used. Moroń and Mandal (2021) found that FFF scores are related to relational aggression toward one's romantic partner. Clinically, in sexual abuse, Katz and Nicolet (2020) argued that the fight or flight response is irrelevant in the circumstance, and compliance, avoidance., etc., are what survivors engage in.

Alexithymia and Suppression

A key defense mechanism relates to suppression. The term is included in the 48-category matrix that has been developed on categories of adaptation and coping. Therefore, the literature review examines recent literature on suppression. The term has been applied from the perceptual level to the higher-order psychological level. A related term is alexithymia, on difficulties in processing emotions. The literature review examines the concept and offers conclusions on how it relates to the defensivity/offensivity concept and to defense mechanisms.

Alexithymia

Taylor and Bagby (2020) and López-Muñoz and Pérez-Fernández (2020) reviewed the concept and its origins. Taylor and Bagby had developed the TAS, which is still widely used. Alexithymia is defined in terms of: (a) difficulty in the identification of different common affects and in the verbal description of feelings; (b) difficulty in distinguishing between subjective feelings and sensations of the body that accompany emotional activation; (c) a cognitive style that is externally oriented to or preoccupied with minute details; and (d) restrained, limited, or impoverished imaginative processes, such as in impoverished fantasy referable to drives and feelings.

Taylor and Bagby (2020) argued that modifications to the concept of alexithymia that have appeared in the literature are premature or misplaced. The original conception is adequate. The recommended changes have included adding an emotionalizing component, removing restricted imaginal activity from its definition, creating subtypes, renaming severe degrees of alexithymia, and positioning alexithymia within the model of attention-appraisal model, while considering it as a general deficit in interoception.

Edwards (2019) conducted a meta-analysis on the relationship of PTSD and alexithymia. The analysis found a link with identifying feelings. Reyno et al. (2020) conducted a meta-analysis on alexithymia and dissociation, finding a relationship. Dissociation serves to reduce intense negative arousal and affects and alexithymia is consistent with it. Both studies based their analyses on the TAS. Fang et al. (2020) used the TAS to confirm the association of PTSD and alexithymia (along with immature defenses). Zorzella et al. (2020) found that improvements in PTSD and dissociation in therapy were accompanied by reduced TAS scores. Martino et al. (2020) conjectured that IBD progressively leads to alexithymia in reverse causality.

Generally, alexithymia is an emotional processing deficit that is associated with clinical disorders, either facilitating them or resulting from them. It is related to early adversities, trauma, and abuse; therefore, it could very well be a factor that mediates in the development of defense mechanisms. In this regard, it is associated with psychological protective mechanisms, like dissociation.

Suppression

Suppression exists at all levels of the sensory, perceptual, cognitive, and affective systems. It reflects a common filtering mechanism that facilitates dealing with information at all these levels and behaving adaptively with the information. It is paired with engagement or enhancement in the literature. It constitutes a defense mechanism, too, and is generally considered as a more mature one. The research illustrates its applicability not only to perceptual/attentional phenomena but also to emotional/clinical phenomena.

Chang and Egeth (2019) conducted an attention study illustrating the relationship between target-specific enhancement and distractor-feature suppression. The research showed that they both guide attention. Wang et al. (2020) found that thought suppression rebound effects were related to the degree of cognitive load. Benita et al. (2020) showed that suppressive emotional regulation is associated with impeded goal pursuit, unlike integrative emotional regulation. Brown et al. (2020) found that low expressive suppression is associated with coherence between subjective experience and physiology in emotion. Luoma and Chwyl (2020) related expressive suppression to self-criticism. Hosogoshi et al. (2020) related it to improvement in anxiety in therapy. Nagulendran et al. (2020) related it to having fewer intrusions after watching distressing traumatic material. Thimm et al. (2018) related depression to thought suppression (and to wishful thinking). Chen et al. (2020) found a similar relationship, with some cross-cultural differences involved.

Peters and Overall (2020) related emotional suppression perception to romantic partner relationships. Waters et al. (2020) related parental emotional suppression to children's sympathetic nervous system activity.

The next section of the literature review considers defense mechanisms, a primary topic of the last chapter and this one in this book. The prior sections of the review prepare this one.

Defense Mechanisms

Defense mechanisms constitute the primary focus of this chapter and the last one, but the work in the area does not lend itself easily to a general perspective on adaptation and coping, which is another primary focus here. Also, the area of defense mechanisms is not easily integrated into the 25-step Neo-Eriksonian model that has been proposed by the author in his books (Young 2011, 2016, 2019, this book). That said, this portion of the literature review suggests directions in these regards.

General Considerations

Bailey and Pico (2020) introduced the area of defense mechanisms, indicating that Anna Freud elaborated ten mechanisms based on the original defense mechanism theorizing of Sigmund Freud at the end of the nineteenth century. She defined defense mechanisms in psychoanalytic terms ("unconscious resources" that the ego uses to reduce "internal stress"). According to Bailey and Pico (2020), the number of defense mechanisms that have been described has increased since the work of the Freuds (e.g., Perry 1990). Defense mechanisms can be split into primitive and higher-level ones (e.g., avoidance, denial, regression, repression; and displacement, rationalization, sublimation, and suppression; respectively).

The definition of defense mechanisms has evolved. Vaillant (2020) defined defense mechanisms as relatively involuntary patterns of emotion, thought, or behavior that are expressed in situations that are perceived as psychically dangerous, conflictual, or related to cognitive dissonance. The danger, conflict, or dissonance that is involved in the situation arises due to unexpected changes/threats in the internal/external environment. The function of defense mechanisms is to serve as buffers to the perceived dangers/threats, to obscure/diminish the stress response and, ultimately, to mitigate/control the development of anxiety and of depression. Individuals express a range of defensive styles, with many types being available; each defense mechanism can stand by itself as discrete; the concept does not involve continua of responses and defenses. Defenses develop or express a range of conceptual and developmental complexity; for example, the APA in 1994, in its DSM-IV (*Diagnostic and Statistical Manual of Mental Disorders*, 4th ed., American Psychiatric Association 1994), considered a hierarchy of defenses, ranging from those that are psychotic/immature to others that are neurotic/mature. The field describes adaptive defenses that are not necessarily psychotic, immature, or neurotic. These include altruism and the use of humor, for example.

Vaillant (2020) maintained that to the field should position the area of defense mechanisms within a broader framework, the one of stress and coping (e.g., seeking social support). However, he did not elaborate on the notion, nor have others to any notable degree, as far as is known, and unlike the case here.

Many defense mechanism instruments have been developed, and they are enumerated throughout the present literature search. All seem to have acceptable reliability and validity. The field has moved well beyond using ambiguous instruments, such as with the case of thematic perceptions in cards or ink blots. However, even the latter approach has improved psychometrically (see research on the R-PAS coding system of Rorschach inkblots; Rorschach Performance Assessment System; Meyer et al., 2017). The defense mechanism coding instruments are of two major types: transcript scoring and self-report questionnaires. The latter are improving and demonstrating their utility, but the former are considered gold standard.

Perry's (1990) Defense Mechanism Rating Scale (DMRS) is one that is based on scoring transcripts according to an objective manual, which is used to train users of the instrument. The structure and contents of DMRS are quite consistent with the DSM-IV's provisional defense axis in its Appendix B. The DMRS is scored from session/interview transcripts, with the manual giving operational definitions, examples, and differential diagnostic information related to close terms for each listed defense mechanism. The DMRS organizes its 30 types of defense mechanisms into seven defense levels of increasing maturity. These seven levels are: (7) High adaptive; (6) Obsessional; (5) Hysterical/Other Neurotic; (4) Minor Image distorting; (3) Disavowal; (2) Major image distorting; and (1) Action. The seven levels are grouped into four superordinate categories, which are: (a) high adaptive, (b) neurotic, (c) immature, and (d) psychotic. The DMRS aggregates scores over its 30 specific defenses in order to calculate an overall defensive functioning total score (ODF). Research using the ODF has related it to psychological/psychiatric conditions/outcomes.

Perry and Bond (2017) provided transcription evidence that, through their deployment in session, defense mechanisms function as windows of possible improvements in psychiatric therapy. They are causal in this regard, mediating improvements in patients throughout sessions. Defense mechanism change indexes therapeutic change. Their amelioration toward higher-order ones instead of lower-order infantile ones marks improvements psychologically both in session and over sessions. They are fundamental mediators of change processes in that they facilitate the change.

Babl et al. (2019) conducted a study that supported this conclusion. They examined anxious and depressive patients undergoing cognitive behavior therapy with added components (self-regulation or emotion focusing, randomly determined). Among other measures, they used the DMRS at intervals over the 6 months of treatment. They found that adaptive mechanisms were more evident over the sessions, especially those of self-observation and self-assertion.

Perry et al. (2015) conducted a study with the DMRS that illustrates its utility. Participants were recently diagnosed mothers with breast cancer (BC group) and matched controls. Relative to controls, the results showed that the BC group used more denial, idealization, and displacement, among others, and less intellectualization, among others. The results speak to the general finding in the field that breast cancer patient survivor duration/mortality is influenced by defense mechanism level.

Developmental Considerations

Cramer (e.g., Cramer 1991, 2015) has conducted research on the development of defense mechanisms. In her empirical research, typically, she has found that the defense mechanisms of denial, projection, and identification develop in that order. Her model does not explicitly link the emergence of the three defense mechanisms to explicit causal mechanisms, although she does refer to advancing cognitive development. She developed the psychometrically sound Defense Mechanism Manual (DMM) for the research, and identified seven exemplars for each of the three categories. She did refer to the protective function of defensive mechanisms, aligning with the present emphasis on general protectivity in adaptation and behavior, but not in the broad sense used here. She did not try to relate the developmental progression in her defense mechanism model to the development through Freudian/Eriksonian stages, which is the same tack taken in the present approach (that task is premature).

Recent empirical research from a developmental perspective is consistent with past studies of defense mechanisms. The development of defense mechanisms takes place early, and they are considered infantile. But adolescents provide fertile grounds for the study of defense mechanisms because of their transitional stage and the cumulative effects of multiple lifetime stressors that they might have experienced. In this regard, Di Giuseppe et al. (2019) used the DMRS to study defense mechanisms in relation to nascent personality disorders. The clinical sample in the study involved 102 adolescents between the ages of 14 and 18 years. As for the results, the older adolescents in the sample obtained higher ODF scores, while using more obsessional and higher adaptive defensive categories.

Laczkovics et al. (2020) studied the relationship between attachment style and defense mechanisms in 1487 high school students (15.9 years on average). The students were evaluated using the self-report Response Evaluation Measure (REM-71, Steiner and Feldman 1995), which covers 21 defense mechanisms that are considered more and less mature (accommodation and assimilation, respectively). Attachment style and psychological symptomatology were assessed by the RSQ and YSR, respectively. The results showed that immature defenses mediated the relationship between attachment style and psychopathological symptoms. The authors concluded that early relationships create problematic internal working models related to attachment security, and that defense mechanisms "transmit" the detrimental effects onto later adolescent mental health.

Similarly, Nevarez et al. (2018) examined data gathered in Vaillant's longitudinal research. They scored transcripts of interviews of males, beginning at the age of 18, for defense mechanisms, and followed up the participants to age 63. Early nurturance was estimated with psychometrically sound instrumentation. As for the results, less nurturance was associated with avoidant defense mechanisms.

Nimroody et al. (2019) developed a defense mechanism scoring manual in a study on 5- to 6-year-old doll play. They found four clusters of defenses: relational, avoidance, aggressive, and symbolic, with the first and last being more advanced. This research might serve as a basis for tying in other defense mechanism hierarchies more applicable to later ages.

Perry and Despland (2011) conducted a developmental study in a different way. Unlike in Cramer, they tried to relate aspects of defense mechanisms to different developmental stages. Specifically, they did not use classic defense mechanism instruments in their research. They used a different tool on wishes and fears, and related it to Eriksonian development. Specifically, they created a Wish and Fear (WF) catalog of 80 items. These items were positioned according to the eight Eriksonian stages (e.g., for Trust vs. Mistrust; wish: be near significant other; fear: trusting others). They examined transcripts of open-structure, psychodynamic clinical interviews using the WF for 12 patients diagnosed with personality disorder. They followed half of them still in therapy 1 year later. Reliability estimates were acceptable for the coding. There was about 1.4 fears and wishes coded per minute in the 50-min interviews for the sample, with wishes outnumbering fears. Many of them were associated with the first two Eriksonian stages, e.g., wishes: for Autonomy vs. Shame/Doubt; do what I want without being thwarted by others. As for fears, prevalent items for the sample included, for Trust vs. Mistrust; distressing feelings/inability to be comforted. Half of the overall 80 WF items expressed by the sample in the interviews in the research by Perry and Despland (2011) belonged to the first two Eriksonian stages (including Trust vs. Mistrust). There was no change evident in WF 1 year later, when half of the small sample in this pilot study was followed up. Clearly, more research is required.

This study by Perry and Despland (2011) suggests that the current 25-step Neo-Eriksonian lifespan developmental model could be elaborated for associated wishes and fears at each of its steps. It would be easy to extrapolate a list of wishes and fears for each step by consulting Table 10.3 of the prior chapter.

Butterbaugh and Wood (2020) noted that the Eriksonian stages of Identity and Intimacy might not develop sequentially but simultaneously. This concept fits with the present one of yoking over the 25 steps in Neo-Eriksonian development. The yoking concept indicates that behaviors, and now we can add wishes and fears, deriving from more than one step in development, can be elicited together, depending on the circumstance and individual variation.

Adult Considerations

Most research on defense mechanisms concerns adult populations. There are many publications written from a more psychanalytic perspective, which this literature review avoids. Two recent studies demonstrate the increasing scope of defense mechanism publications, and their widespread potential application. These studies are consistent with the goals of the two chapters in the book on defense mechanisms, to show their utility in other than classic therapy and psychodynamic theorizing. Specifically, two recent studies have related the use of more adaptive defense mechanisms to better mental health standing in adults in these Covid-19 times. Di Giuseppe et al. (2020a) used the Defense Mechanisms Rating Scale-Self-Report-30 (DMRS-30), which is based on the DMRS (Di Giuseppe et al. 2020b), and administered it remotely on the Internet. The authors administered the DMRS-30 in a study of 5683 Italians in the first week of the Covid lockdown in that country. The results showed that the worse the adaptive functioning according to the measure, the greater the distress for symptoms of depression, anxiety, and PTSD, as measured by other instruments. Prout et al. (2020) found that less deployment of adaptive defense mechanisms in 2787 participants was related to elevated distress for the same three classes of symptoms.

Perry et al. (2020) extended the findings of Perry and Bond (2017) that defense mechanisms can index therapeutic change, this time in depressed patients. They used the DMRS and another instrument, a self-report one, the Defense Style Questionnaire (DSQ, e.g., Bond 2004). The DSQ consists of 88 items and yields scores on four defensive mechanism factors or styles: (a) maladaptive, (b) image-distorting, (c) self-sacrificing, and (d) adaptive. The results 1 year after treatment had commenced indicated that the DMRS provides results consistent with the predictions more than the case for the DSQ. Although cross-test comparisons have not been made, the DMRS-30 might be a better self-report inventory of defense mechanisms than the DSQ.

Granieri et al. (2017) used the DSQ-40 (Andrews et al. 1993) to relate defense mechanisms and maladaptive personality domains, as measured by other instruments. The results showed that more immature defense mechanisms, e.g., acting out, related to factors such as disinhibition and negative affectivity.

Two recent studies have investigated biological correlates of defense mechanisms. Kehyayan et al. (2018) examined the relationship of the skin conductance response in relation to responses on the DSQ-40, seeking findings concerning repression. Paradiso et al. (2020) studied individuals with agenesis of the corpus callosum, and found that the condition retarded progress to more advanced defense mechanisms forms. Specifically, according to administration of the DMM scored on obtained transcripts, the patients demonstrated more denial than controls. Overall, the results for the former study were ambiguous, but the results for the latter study demonstrated that compromised brains increase more immature defense mechanism use.

Interim Comment

The present review of recent literature related to adaptation/coping and defense mechanisms supports the construction of an expanded adaptation and coping matrix of categories beyond the traditional fight-flight-freeze response. Also, it indicates that the defense mechanism literature has considered development, but the standard approaches in this regard do not map well onto the Neo-Eriksonian model that has been created by the author. That said, the WF approach is promising in this regard.

Discussion

Summary

Adaptation/Coping

According to the literature review, contemporary views of adaptation and coping emphasize two major points. (a) First, multiple factors could influence the stress response, including in appraisals and meanings attributed to stressors. There is room for great individual variation in these regards, with stress not considered as a constant, universally experienced phenomenon. (b) Second, people vary not only in their attributions of meanings to stressors but also in the range or variability in their physiological stress response (e.g., hypo- and hypercortisolism). Appraisals are best bets in the circumstances, calibrated by priors, expectations, and personal individual differences. The organism functions adaptively partly by being predictive and forecasting events. The organism actively constructs estimates of what might be expected to preclude surprise, or excess, unaccounted for free energy that creates dissonance. In this sense, the brain is Bayesian.

The classic fight-flight-freeze response needs to be supplemented by other categories in the stress response in order to become complete and inclusive in scope. The triad of stress responses in fight-flight-freeze, and its precursor fight-flight one, has generated an enormous amount of research, but should be considered inadequate to the task of characterizing all organismic adaptivity. A more widespread, integrative model should extend well beyond the fight-flight-freeze distinction in adaptation and coping to stress. In this regard, the chapter describes a matrix of 48 categories of adaptation and coping, adding 45 new types to the classic tripartite distinction.

Defensivity/Defense Mechanisms

The literature on defense mechanisms is varied and has become quite empirical, yet emanates from a history in psychoanalytic thought. Psychometrically sound instruments have been developed that have demonstrated reliability and validity, and have moved well beyond the original number (10) of cataloged defense mechanisms. The present work adds to that literature by proposing three major axes for the field. (a) First, the book proposes the concept of defensivity/offensivity, which is considered a way of characterizing the back-and-forth flow in behavior that would be related to defense mechanism deployment and to which they would be subserved. (b) Second, the book proposes a matrix of 48 adaptation and coping categories that are consistent with the concept of defense mechanisms and defensivity/offensivity. They revolve around the dimensions of defensivity/offensivity, direction, strategy, and organism/self-related behavior which includes dominance-submission and filtering. This matrix of adaptation and coping categories can be used to structure defense

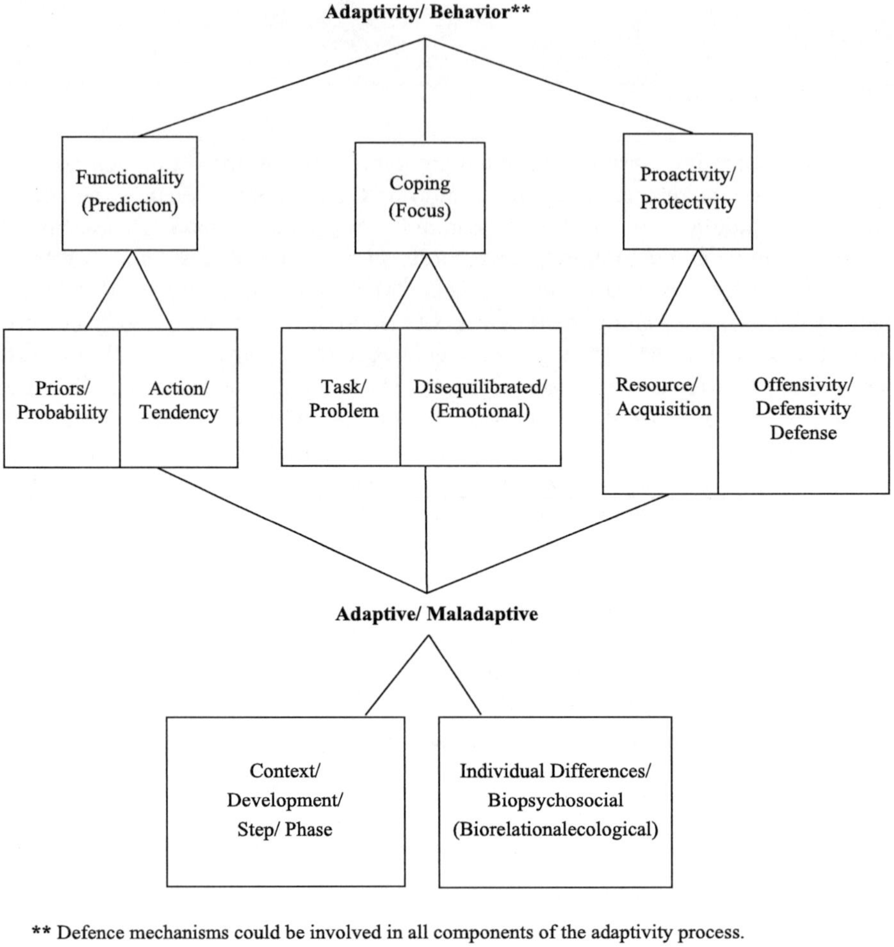

Fig. 11.1 Adaptivity, proactivity/protectivity, offensivity/defensivity, and defense mechanisms. The figure illustrates a model of behavior that included functionality, coping, and proactivity/protectivity. The model was created to place the present emphasis on offensivity/defensivity in a broader paradigm inclusive of all behavior. Also, only such an inclusive perspective can help place the role of defense mechanisms in the process. After constructing the figure, and trying to place defense mechanisms in the model, the positioning of defense mechanisms as possible in each component of the model became evident. The field of defense mechanisms can be viewed as a siloed one particular to psychodynamic and therapeutic processes; however, it applies to daily behaviors, adaptive (not just dysfunctional) behaviors, normal development, higher-order thought and behavior, and so on. Also, it specifies the causal variables that therapists either directly or indirectly target to effect therapeutic change and psychological growth. In this sense, it is broad as can be, applying to both adaptive and maladaptive behaviors, the full developmental process, etc. However, the figure does not refer to defense mechanisms specifically in this regard. Consequently, for each entry in the figure, one could put entries of classic defense mechanism behaviors and non-defense mechanism

mechanisms and to add to them. (c) Third, the book proposes a 25-step Neo-Eriksonian model that updates the original Freudian and Eriksonian stage models, and its steps can be re-interpreted as defensivity/offensivity themes. The steps in development according to the model allow for a scaffold onto which the development of defense mechanisms can take place, both as presently conceived in the literature and as might be elaborated on the basis of the current 48-category matrix of adaptation and coping.

Fig. 11.1 (continued) behaviors, or their overlap. In this sense, even the term defensivity in the figure does not refer to defense mechanisms, per se

Adaptivity/behavior heads the figure and indicates the broadest level of organismic activity. Even single-celled organisms adapt, act, and behave. The wording of the terms in the model is general enough to apply to all organisms

Adaptivity/behavior consists of three components: (a) daily adaptation or functionality when there are no or minimal stressors; (b) coping efforts to stressors, and (c) more intense behavior that actively or proactively attempts to expand or defend resources. The first component is marked by the Bayesian predictive processing function. Organisms function to minimize surprise in that model, by monitoring forecasts and outcomes in perception and behavior. That process can be overwhelmed by internal or external stressors. When that happens, the organism engages a set of coping mechanisms—they can be task/problem focused, and emanate from an equilibrated behavior system that has not been overly perturbed by the stressor, or they can be dis-equilibrated/dysregulated responses, which, for higher-order organisms, could include an emotional component. The latter is not necessarily dysfunctional in and of itself, in that its adaptiveness depends on many factors

The third component of adaptivity in the model refers to proactivity/protectivity. The terminology is meant to include the concept of offensivity/defensivity, but is more general. Proactivity/protectivity is a broader term that allows for offensivity/defensivity as presently defined, but is broader in order to consider resource acquisition and its defense more generally. Resource acquisition relates to Darwinian concepts of natural selection, survival, and reproduction in a broad sense. Offensivity and defensivity are particular processes in that proactivity/protectivity component of behavior that mirror their intent (of proactivity/protectivity), but take place in particular ways with a more overt acquisition/defense strategy. The behaviors that come to mind are the aggressive foraging and predation of some species (and some humans) and the active defense against them

All components of the model can be adaptive or maladaptive, and many reasons can deviate putatively adaptive ones in the maladaptive direction. Even super stressors do not have to create dysfunctionality, maladaptivity, and poor coping. The array of influences in this regard are biopsychosocial or bio-personal-social in the human case, and bio-relational-social or bio-relational-ecological in the general organismic case. Moreover, defense mechanisms could be both expressions of and drivers of adaptive or maladaptive behaviors. In the most abhorrent circumstances, certain defense mechanisms that are infantile might make the most sense, and are not maladaptive, per se. In other circumstances, for no apparent reason, the individual can embark on an offensivity attack, and aberrant defense mechanisms could be the driver of the behavior. They become priors that skew prediction and subsequent behavior. They complicate coping, rendering it disequilibrated or surcharged emotionally. They drive belligerent offensivity and they dull defensivity. They become the context, dominate development, and create (or express) a person with extreme difficulty in adaptivity

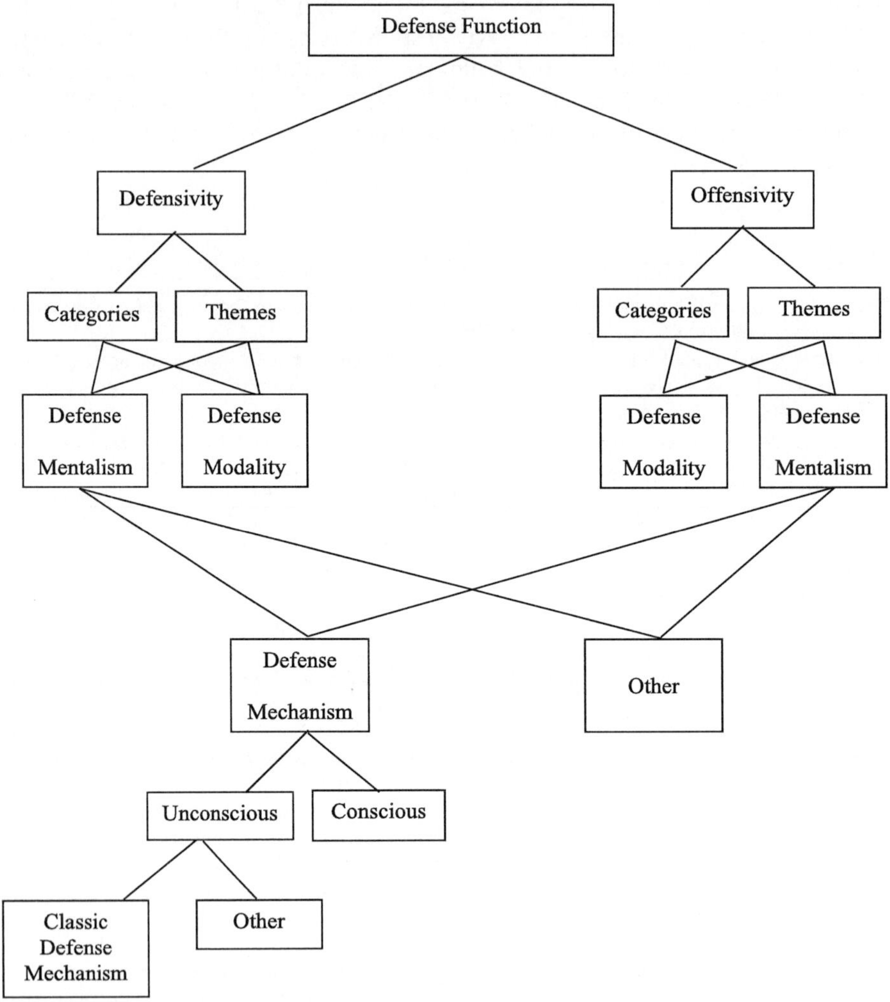

Fig. 11.2 A hierarchical model of defense function, offensivity/defensivity, and defense mechanisms. The figure presents a hierarchy of defense-related terms, beginning with the superordinate concept of defense/defensive function. Next, the hierarchy includes defensivity/offensivity strategies in the hierarchy. In particular, the hierarchy moves to defense mechanisms, defense mentalisms, and defense modes/modality. Overall, the hierarchy consists of seven tiers, illustrating that defense mechanisms as classically defined can fit into a broader scheme of defense-related terms. Several of these terms are ones that have been used rarely in the literature and are rehabilitated in the present model, along with a new approach to their definition. These types of terms in the figure include defense function/functioning, defensivity, and defense mode/modality. The term that is novel to the field in the figure involves the one of defense mentalism. It is meant to accompany the use of the term of defense mechanism when the mechanistic component of the defense mechanism term is not clear in context. The term of "categories" in the figure refers to the different categories related to defensivity and offensivity, which are presented in the 48-category matrix model

Theoretical Integration

Figure 11.1 integrates the concepts of adaptivity, proactivity/ protectivity, offensivity/ defensivity, and defense mechanisms. The integration broaches difficult areas, such as offering a general behavioral model in which defense mechanisms can be integrated. Also, it offers a new specific approach to defense mechanisms. The same critical perspective is applied to coping. The new concepts proposed in this section could add to the lexicon and instruments in the field. They include the terms of protectivity, defense mentalism/modality, defense function, and stress mitigation/magnification in coping.

Theory

Reflecting on the major themes in this chapter and the last still left the quandary of how to relate the areas of general adaptation and defense mechanisms. Figure 11.2 presents one solution. It places defensivity and offensivity as part of a new concept of proactivity and protectivity, while considering defense mechanisms as broadly pertinent to all components of the model. The figure consists of two major tiers on adaptivity/behavior and adaptive/maladaptive behavior in this regard. It allows for individual differences in behavior, stemming from contextual, developmental, and personal/ organismic factors. Functionality is ongoing in context, with behaving, forecasting, adjusting, etc. Coping takes place to stressors, and will be focused and equilibrated in most circumstances. Mediational schemes, perceptions/cognitions, and predictions will alter the stimulus-response and stress-coping dynamics. Beyond that, behavior could gravitate to proactivity resource acquisition and offensivity for a host of reasons and, consequently, protectivity, defensivity, and defense will be elicited.

Protectivity is a term rarely encountered in the literature, with only several articles found using the term in PsychInfo and in Web of Science data mining searches. A Google Scholar search yielded a few more relevant articles. None of the sources found used the term in the sense here, with most of them using it in the context of defensive behavior (e.g., Cook et al. 2020; Desai 2018; Gerevich and Bácskai 1996; Hodgson et al. 2003; Seelig 2017; Sekera 2003).

Defense mechanisms can come into play at all points in the behavioral activity of the person/organism as described by the model. Specifically, with respect to the model in the figure, in their immature and related forms, defense mechanisms could be part of the reasons for the altered and maladaptive mediational schema

Fig. 11.2 (continued) described in the text of the chapter. The term of "themes" in the figure refers to the 25 steps in the author's Neo-Eriksonian lifespan model of development (Young 2011, 2016, 2019, this book). These steps are defined according to positive and negative poles, referred to as acts, per the original Eriksonian model. Here, the polar oppositions of navigating the steps well, or not, are considered defensivity and offensivity themes (see the text of the prior chapter). In the end, the hierarchical model of defense/defense mechanisms terms presented in the figure allows for centering the area of defense mechanisms in the broader fields of adaptation, coping, and stress, on the one hand, and of psychology and psychiatry generally, on the other hand

and related formation that biases incoming information toward maladaptive subjectivity and inappropriate consequent responsivity. Defense mechanisms could bias responsivity to offensivity, aside from resource lack that might lead to this type of behavior. Thus, defense mechanisms, if maladaptive, could condition incoming information to be viewed in maladaptive ways and also condition the person's responses toward maladaptive behaviors. Furthermore, they could be part of a disequilibrated coping style, or they could underlie the maladaptive coping strategies deployed toward dealing with perceived stressors. Finally, defense mechanisms could become central to the person's internal psychic/psychological structure as forefront, being reflexive, automated psychological regulation/control behaviors. Also, they could become central as apex strategies used in external, co-relational psychological regulation/control and engagement. In these regards, their pervasiveness could characterize any personality and psychopathological disorder, which would be part of maladaptive adaptivity in the model elucidated in the figure.

Moreover, defense mechanisms do not just defend against emotions, because they defend against the thoughts, e.g., cognitively dissonant ones, that can elicit them. And, as Vaillant (2020) indicated, they defend against elicitation of the stress response, which can be detrimental, as in hypercortisol responsivity. Therefore, defense mechanisms defend against a broad array of perturbations to the biopsychosocial system that characterizes the person, targeting emotional, cognitive, or physiological components in the system differentially according to the context, developmental history, etc., with no one aspect privileged uniformly.

Reconfiguring and Redefining Defense Mechanisms

Note that the concept of defense mechanisms can be broadened in scope at the definitional level according to the present perspective. They do not just concern a hierarchy from infantile to more mature forms. Rather, the goals to which they apply are quite varied, and serve not only defensive purposes but also possibly offensive ones. And they do not just serve to protect against anxiety and depression. Rather, at the emotional level, they serve to protect against any emotion that can undermine ongoing sense of stability. For example, they can defend against extreme fear or a rage reaction that seems imminent. They can defend against a sense of extreme shame or humiliation, a social rejection and embarrassment, etc. (e.g., Granieri et al. 2017). Given the linkage of offensivity and defensivity, they can defend against any empathic emotions that might accompany any form of implemented aggressive victimization, for example.

Consider the following. Defense mechanisms are not mechanisms in the broader sense of the word. Mechanisms have a specific meaning in psychology and psychiatry. The concept of mechanism concerns a process or system that, when brought into play, produces or effects a particular result or outcome, that is, the product of the process/system. Mechanisms are part of the causal machinery of behavior (Young 2011, 2016, 2019, this book). But they are not the unique activators of behavior even when defense mechanisms are part of the array of behavior that has been evoked. Defense mechanisms can activate outcomes in the sense of the definition of mechanism, but any activated behavior might reflect other mechanisms at work more downstream or working in concert with them. Moreover, a behavior at issue that appears to be related to the workings of defense mechanisms might have corollary mechanisms at work that explain them better in full or in part.

Therefore, the mechanism component of the term of defense mechanism at times could be misleading. Specifically, this refers to the mechanism component of the term. Granted, defense mechanisms have the function to protect against or forestall undercurrent anxiety and depression, or even other emotions, that might be expressed in response to perceived psychic danger, threat, or dissonance.

However, we need to consider term of mechanism in its broader contemporary context, for example, as factors that are proximal or distal in behavioral causation (e.g., parenting practices, genes, respectively), or something in between (e.g., appraisals). Thus, mechanism refers to specific causal processes in behavior.

But, as presently conceived, defense mechanisms are both (a) consequences, outcomes, or effects of behavior and (b) factors that influence behavior. Thus, when expressed, they are not necessarily specific proximate or intermediate mechanisms in all cases.

Moreover, with respect to terminology related to defense mechanisms, the field needs more generic terms that cover conscious, deliberate, calculated defensive actions to overwhelming stress, both internal and external. Defensive mechanisms are associated with unconscious reactions, but even Vaillant (2020) in his definition, referred to defense mechanisms in a way that they are not exclusively unconscious. Indeed, defense mechanisms in normal life might be expressedly conscious and add to adaptive, positive functioning. For example, people who are exposed to or participate in events that would be considered horrific might make the conscious decision to block out thinking of them, refuse exposure therapy because of the retraumatization that they believe it elicits, and so on. People often consciously put up barriers, shells, etc., to very stressful events. They might try to compartmentalize the trauma, with varying degrees of distress, distract from it, and move on to the degree possible. Or, conceivably, they might have repressed an early trauma, then had it re-emerge in consciousness, leading to dealing with the traumatic recalls in the same way.

Therefore, it is best to have other terms that can accompany the term of defense mechanism in using the term contemporaneously. That is, the field might want to use complementary terms with the one of defense mechanism. The new terms that could accompany the term of defense mechanism could be the following. One the one hand, a more generic term for defense mechanism that avoids the mechanism component is *defense mentalism*. It applies to the human case. On the other hand, a term that could be used instead of defense mentalism could be *defense modality*, generally. These terms are considered complementary to that of defense mechanism and could accompany or even replace the term of defense mechanism, when the context calls for them instead of the term defense mechanism.

In this regard, it might be best to create a tiered approach to cataloging defense mechanisms that accommodates the present modeling. For the third tier, perhaps the original psychodynamic approach to defense mechanisms should be referred to as primary and defensive. Then, a second tier could be referred as secondary and linked to defensivity and offensivity, in general. Then, the first tier could be linked to adaptation and coping generally. This approach to framing defense mechanisms according to tiers leaves a hierarchy of first-tier, second-tier, and third-tier defense mechanisms. Indeed, in this approach, the tiers should be more than a descriptive catalog. That is, for each individual, through the processes of deployment, feedback, and revision, the person should be creating a hierarchical structure along these lines. Moreover, the contents of each tier should be interacting in a network structuring, and also the different tiers should be interacting in a systems fashion. Therefore, at the individual level, the applicable three-tiered catalog will vary, depending on context, developmental history, etc. Moreover, the adaptive and maladaptive nature of the mechanisms for the person will vary in these regards, as well, both in the short term and long term.

To this point, to review, this chapter and the prior one have maintained that the concept of defense mechanisms (a) should be embedded in a larger adaptation and coping framework and that (b) the stage models associated with them (Freudian, Eriksonian) should be replaced by a more comprehensive stage model of 25 Neo-Eriksonian steps over the lifespan. In this penultimate repositioning of the concept of defense mechanisms, I have proposed that complementary terms should be used with it or even to replace it. These terms are *defense mentalism* for the human case and *defense modality*, generally. The terminology of defense mentalism captures the meaning of the terminology of defense mechanism without connoting a primary causal locus to the defense function that might be affected. Similarly, the terminology of defense modality gives a functional rather than a causal/mechanistic emphasis to the concept of defense.

Seeking information to define the terms that have been proposed to accompany the one of defense mechanism, I consulted the APA dictionary of psychology (VandenBos 2015). It does not define defense mentalism, as the term is novel to the field. But it does define mentalism. Essentially, mentalism denotes that mental phenomena, such as thinking and feeling, have "reality." They cannot be reduced to physical phenomena, although they are grounded in them. In the present case, the chapter defines mentalism in terms of the process and products of the mind, in the sense of "of the mind." This approach allows for a broader version of the term of mentalism, because it would include the downward influence of mental activity on even incoming sensation and perception, which are so critical to the defense function. (Note, the term defense function is discussed below.)

As for the term defense modality to accompany use of the terms defense mechanism and defense modality, it is needed for the general case beyond the human one, in which mind is less relevant in behavior or not relevant at all. The term defense modality should be used as a replacement for defense mechanism generally, which is consistent with the present proposal to use the term defensivity generally and not just for the human case.

I conducted a date-mining search in popular scientific and public search engines for the terms of defense mentalism and defense modality. For other terms, there might be hundreds of thousands of hits or more. It was learned that PsychInfo and Google do not have these two terms of defense mentalism and defense modality in their data bases for the English language. However, in PsychInfo, the latter term appears in three foreign language publications related to psychological defenses (Chauvel 1996; Eiguer 1982; Quintella 2016). Overall, then, these two terms being proposed two accompany defense mechanism (defense mentalism and defense motivation) are novel for the field of psychology.

Another term that could be used to accompany or instead of defense mechanism is "defense motivation." However, the term of defense motivation evokes only one aspect of defense mentalism, so is less preferred. That said, the term of defense motivation is relevant to the discussion of terminology related to defense mechanism. It could provide a device to allow expansion of standard defense mechanism cataloging or mediate in relating the concepts of defensivity and defense mechanism.

The term of defense motivation is not used in the same context as defense mechanism in prior publications. Rather, in the literature on it, which is mostly in social psychology and business marketing, it refers to defending against information that could alter held beliefs, attitudes, or positions, and the factors that could affect it (e.g., Clark and Evans 2014; de Hoog 2013; Giner-Sorolla and Chaiken 1997; Hart et al. 2009; Masterson and Crawford 1982). Two studies refer to the term in defense mechanism-type terms, but not like used here (Rhodewalt and Vohs 2005; Steindl and Jonas 2015).

Finally, it would be useful to refer to defense mechanisms cascades. On the one hand, the use of any one defensivity reaction or defense mechanism can cascade serially to others internally, for example, in a worsening vicious circle of defensivity. On the other hand, the use of any one defensivity/defense mechanism can cascade serially to other people externally. For example, the ones used by parents and caregivers in child abuse might lead to generational replication in the children as they get older. Also, in dyadic partnerships, the use of certain defensivity/defense mechanisms can create in the other the same type of replication. Of course, in both cases being discussed, more than replication could take place in that a broader defensivity/defense mechanism profile might be deployed than otherwise would be the case.

A complication in this regard is the immediacy of unconscious defense mechanism activation. In their deployment, defense mechanisms are activated quickly and they can cascade rapidly both internally and externally. The cascades can be short term or long term, and openly evident or insidious. Therefore, therapy should track these cascades as much as the expression of individual defense mechanisms. In the end, simply enough, patients who improve in therapy should transfer their changes and gains for the better in defensivity/defense mechanism deployment toward creating better habits and replacing bad habits with them. The general therapeutic approach to defensivity/defense mechanisms should view their positive change as a means to an end in this regard.

Defense Function Hierarchy

Up to this juncture, multiple new or rehabilitated terms related to defense mechanism have been proposed, and it might be confusing to consider all of them together. However, the following attempts to relate them hierarchically under the rubric of the concept of defense function. The concepts of defense mechanism, defense mentalism, defense modality, and defense motivation are expressed in different terms of a hierarchy of terms, which helps position the term of defense mechanism in the broader context of defensivity/offensivity. The goal of this type of hierarchical modeling of these terms is to place the concept of defense mechanism in the broader defense functioning of the person. This type of modeling was impossible to accomplish until this point in the two chapters on defense mechanisms, given the complexity of the concept, the new terms that have been proposed, and the many tiers required to arrive at a comprehensive workable hierarchy of terms related to the term of defense mechanism.

A hierarchy of terms implies that there is a superordinate one. What term could englobe all the others and function top-down? In this regard, the overarching concept suggested would be that of *defense function*. The way the term being proposed is different in meaning compared to the few times it has been cited in the literature (five times only, and all in relation to defense mechanism function, by Boschan 1990; Cramer 2008; Euler et al. 2018; Luborsky et al. 1965; Neubauer 1984).

The concept of defense function led to another data-mining search. It led me to unexpected articles on defensiveness considered generally. The area of psychological defense/defensiveness studies is a broad one (with many articles on it, e.g., Hart 2014). However, surprisingly, the area generally ignores the defense mechanism literature. On the one hand, this oversight should be corrected in that literature, a procedure that would further help to place defense mechanisms in the broader field of psychology and psychiatry. On the other hand, the term of defense function should be expanded in use into the defense mechanism field.

In this regard, the new term of defense function for the defense mechanism field is a generic term applicable across all species/organisms, and could include defense mechanism within its superordinate function related to the terms being proposed. The term of defense mechanism should be defined in a way that covers all other defense-related behaviors. In this regard, a good starting definition of the term of defense function would be: behavior, action, and tendencies that are deployed by the organism to adapt to and cope with the environment; they are activated in response to stimuli, situations, and stressors that impinge on the organism and threaten or potentially threaten its physical (and psychological) integrity or survival.

1. Defense function, then, constitutes a superordinate behavioral function involving adaption, coping, stress management, and survival. But it has components terms that can be arranged hierarchically into tiers, right into the term of defense mechanisms. The hierarchy presented in this chapter places defense mechanism at the lowest level of the hierarchy, the seventh tier in the hierarchy. This shows the complexity of creating a hierarchy of terms related to defense mechanisms;

five other tiers are needed to relate it in a chain to the superordinate one of defense function.

2. As for the remaining tiers in the hierarchy of terms related to defense function and defense mechanism, the next tier in the hierarchy being proposed for the defense function and defense mechanism concerns the concept of defensivity. The paired concept of offensivity would be part of this tier. Both types of this behavior can be expressed in the behavioral stream that is evoked as part of a defensive posture.

   One other area relates to defense function, specifically to its component of defensivity and offensivity. The area of group conflict research includes attackers and defenders (De Dreu and Gross 2019). However, the area appears relatively new and might lack clear conceptualization and research. Essentially, it has not been applied to the individual, unlike the case here for defensivity and offensivity. Moreover, as presently characterized, the area does not relate to defense mechanism in any way. That said, defensivity and offensivity have been defined generally to cover groups as much as individuals. Therefore, on the one hand, the area of group conflict might find it useful to include the terms of offensivity and defensivity in its ambit. On the other hand, the area of defense mechanism might find it conducive to learn from the area of group conflict and attackers/defenders.

3. Returning to the question of the hierarchy of terms related to defense function and defense mechanism, in the tier of defensivity/offensivity that is being discussed, defensivity would be expressed through the proposed matrix of 48 categories, as would offensivity, as previously argued. In addition, the expression of defensivity and offensivity might relate to themes that reflect the Neo-Eriksonian 25-step model of lifespan development that has been presented.
4. In the next tier of the hierarchy being proposed from defense function to defense mechanism, defensivity and offensivity would both be divided. Defensivity would be divided into the terms on generic defense modality behavior and human-related defense mentalisms. The same would apply to the term offensivity. That is, both of the terms of defensivity and offensivity would apply equally to possible inclusion of defense mentalisms and defense modalities.
5. Continuing with the hierarchy, for the next tier, defense mentalisms would be divided into defense mechanisms and other types. The defense mechanism category at this point in the hierarchy is undifferentiated with respect to the conscious and unconscious types.
6. Next, defense mechanisms would include both the conscious and unconscious types. This division speaks to elaborating the classic definition of defense mechanisms.
7. Next, the unconscious type would be divided, as well, in this case into (a) classic defense mechanisms that causally protect against anxiety, depression, and so on, and (b) other types that are reactive response outcomes without a direct mechanistic function. Further thought is required to differentiate the latter two categories. Perhaps the concept of defense motivation can help in this regard.

Note that other defense-related terms be useful for the hierarchy being proposed. For example, defensiveness has different meanings, and it might help differentiate the hierarchy at different levels. That said, any other terms that might be added to the hierarchy should not alter its general pattern.

To review the various defense-related terms being discussed in the chapter, it consists of seven tiers, from defense function down to the classic defense mechanism (see Fig. 11.2). In a certain sense, this hierarchy of terms related to defense function and defense mechanism constitutes the penultimate contribution of the chapter. This obtains because the hierarchy represents how the area of dense mechanisms could fit into a structure of related terms, which will afford it better scope toward an integration in the area of psychology and psychiatry, as well as the one of adaptation, coping, and stress, generally.

Reconfiguring and Redefining Coping Mechanisms

The standard approaches to coping that have been reviewed in the literature review undertaken here underscore several styles, such as active, passive, task-focused, problem-focused, emotional, and avoidant coping. The B-COPE (Carver 1997) scale is a broad-ranging one that speaks to a full range of coping styles. It covers 14 dimensions of coping, with two items each. When it was constructed, the B-COPE integrated other coping questionnaires. Items in the various dimensions of the scale include adaptive and maladaptive styles, that is, some of the dimensions are positive and others are negative in coping. The 14 dimensions in the B-COPE are answered using a four-point Likert scale. The positive dimensions or scales in the B-COPE include: Adaptive Coping; Planning; Positive Reframing; Acceptance; Humor; Religion; Emotional Support; Instrumental Support; and Self-Distraction. The negative scales include: Denial; Venting; Substance Use; Behavioral Disengagement; and Self-Blame.

The thrust of the present chapter and also the prior one has been to analyze adaptation from a generic point of view applicable to all species. For example, it has referred to organismic forecasting based on early environments to facilitate adaptation. It has referred to defensivity, offensivity, and protectivity in general senses. The same approach can be taken for coping. As with the B-COPE, the terms that dominate the coping field are quite psychological and do not apply readily universally cross-species, which does not accommodate to the present goal of seeking cross-species coping theory. All organisms try to cope in order to adapt, survive, and reproduce.

Therefore, the chapter presents a 15-point Stress Mitigation/Magnification and Adaptive Coping Scale (SMMACS) toward accommodating these concerns. The scale was constructed to be generic, and not refer only to human coping and its problems. Each point can apply to the behavior of all species/organisms, whether single- or multi-cellular, and even to larger entities, such as institutions and ecosystems.

Stress mitigation in a PsychInfo search emerged as a rarely published term, with about ten relevant references. All refer to the mitigation of stress, such as personally or in the workplace, and not one of these publications presents a scale such as the one being proposed here. These prior sources on stress mitigation include: Glazer et al. (2014), Hartig et al. (2007), Heathcote et al. (2019), Matthews (2021), Naturale (2015), Roe et al. (2017), Subhani et al. (2018), Tolan et al. (2013), and Ulrich-Lai et al. (2016).

In line with the enunciated goal of this section of the chapter, Table 11.1 presents the SMMACS stress mitigation/magnification and adaptive coping scale. This first version of the scale is considered a working draft. The midpoint involves being

Table 11.1 A proposed 15-point Stress Mitigation/Magnification and Adaptive Coping Scale (SMMACS)

Point	Description
7	Grow/invigorate through and from the stress
6	Transform the stress actively, constructively
5	Eliminate the stress (solve, resolve)
4	Neutralize the stress (stop it)
3	Reduce the stress severity, seriousness, impact (improve)
2	Manage the stress, adjust to/moderate it, increasing maneuverability
1	Buffer against the stress (try to self-preserve)
0	Resign to the stress, do nothing
−1	Let the stress buffet, fester
−2	Mismanage the stress, try to avoid/bypass, reducing maneuverability
−3	Increase the stress severity, seriousness, impact (actions worsen, aggravate)
−4	Greatly exacerbate the stress (it spreads in impact, for example)
−5	Maximize (catastrophize psychologically) the stress
−6	Decline/deteriorate/disease
−7	Death (spiral)

The points in the table should be defined operationally. Some points might seem misplaced for some readers, but their positioning in the scale will help operationalize them so that they are mutually exclusive, and so that their definitions fit the placements

The table of coping strategies can be empirically evaluated as a questionnaire in several ways. First, the dimension points can be treated categorically, with the scale point having only the one item per the point, as described. Or, two or more items can be constructed for each point. Or, Likert responses can be requested for each point/item

Factor analyses or latent class analyses can determine groupings of points/respondents. In both cases, given the nature of how the scale is constructed, factors/classes should reflect severity. There might be other groupings, e.g., on age differences, in this regard

The reliability and validity of the final version of the scale could be established, for example, by using some of the multiple other coping inventories referred to in this chapter. Different populations will use different combinations of coping strategies as indexed by the SMMACS. Their deployment should change according to disorder, improvement in therapy, age, etc.

The table can be used therapeutically to indicate a patient's ongoing coping (mis)strategies and to guide them toward better ones. Innovating from a cognitive behavioral point of view, I have asked patients to imagine a button that they can push to decrease pain, stress, or poor coping by one point on a ten-point scale of subjective distress, while doing breathing exercises. This latter technique relaxes them, on the one hand, which helps. Also, on the other hand, the former technique gives them some sense of psychological control, which should help. Even just explaining the variation in coping strategies to them as described on the scale might give some hope and allow them to set positive goals resigned to the perceived stress at issue. Then, seven points in each of the adaptive and maladaptive directions are outlined, with the increasing numbers indicating increasing intensity. This scale construction procedure yielded a 15-point generic coping scale.

The two end-points of the scale, positive and negative, reflect extreme case scenarios. At the positive end, the organism grows, invigorates. Even single-celled organisms can profit this way; natural selection leads to adaptation in multiple ways. At the negative end, stress can induce morbidity, as in Selye's General Adaptation Syndrome.

Between the positive pole and the midpoint, scale points involve successful stress mitigation styles, such as transforming the stress; eliminating it; neutralizing it; reducing it; and adjusting to it. Between the negative pole and the midpoint, scale points involve poorer stress mitigation styles (stress magnification), leading to decline/deterioration/disease; maximizing (catastrophizing psychologically) the stress; worsening/aggravating it; trying to avoid it; and passively letting the stress buffet/fester. The language used for the scale points on the positive and negative sides of the coping scale mirror image each other to the degree possible, giving it coherence.

In terms of where might defense mechanisms fit into this adaptation and coping scale, research could be undertaken toward creating a good correlation matrix involving it, once it is psychometrically validated, and defense mechanism instruments. However, defense mechanisms might have to be qualified in light of the scale. For example, altruism might take place for more than defense purposes, and might reflect genuine empathic activity. It is conceivable that different motivations for altruism will appear in different ways in association with the scale points of the proposed instrument. Straightforward correlational and regression studies involving the scale and defense mechanism instruments might have to be qualified along these lines, aside from considering confounds, individual differences, etc.

Future Research

Address Limitations

The present chapter along with the last one are very conceptual and theoretical, and they need refinement of the ideas as well as empirical investigation. They have tried to develop an overarching approach to adaptation/coping and defensivity/defense mechanisms, but they need further specification and operationalization. They present Young's 25-step Neo-Eriksonian model, but that was developed rationally and has yet to be tested empirically. All that said, the present work offers a definitional, conceptual, and empirical roadmap on thinking about defensivity and defense mechanisms in the broader behavioral context. Indeed, the roadmap makes it hard to consider defense mechanisms as only an isolated branch of a particular approach in psychiatry. Rather, the area of defense mechanisms has proven its mettle and is ready for a wider integration in all mental health work and in efforts to understand human behavior.

Adaptation/Coping

The work has presented a matrix of 48 adaptation and coping types that integrates a vast literature that is just briefly touched upon here. The model allows for integration of the area of defense mechanisms, with some common language cutting across these topics. The adaptation and coping model seems complete in its 48 categories and can be used to help elaborate a comprehensive theoretical and categorical approach to defense mechanisms. The model integrates the concept of defensivity/offensivity, which could be applied to characterize the ongoing dynamic of behavior in daily adaptation to the environment through its flow back and forth.

Development

The work has presented a modified Eriksonian stage theory and has integrated defense mechanisms in a broad adaptation and coping paradigm. It has described the 25 steps of a Neo-Eriksonian model in a way that makes it amenable to empirical research. The 25 steps of the model are presented briefly and in simple enough language, which makes it appropriate for a questionnaire. In addition, each step includes possible hypo- and hyper-responses to the challenges and crises that might arise in them, further allowing for empirical investigation. Beyond that, the association of problems experienced at one step or another in development could be associated empirically with the range of defense mechanisms that might be deployed by individuals, keeping in mind that there will be great individual differences in this regard.

For example, in the classic Eriksonian stages related to Trust in infancy and to Identity in adolescence, problematic navigation of the stages can potentiate development of defense mechanisms as applied to Mistrust and Identity issues, respectively. It would be beneficial to examine the adaptation and coping models presented in the present work for establishing possible defense mechanisms used in these developmental periods and how they differ contextually and individually.

Further, following this approach would consider the defense mechanism process for the interpolated stage involving Sociability after the Trust-related step and Nurturing after the Identity-related step (and before the Intimacy one in the late adolescent-emerging adult period). That is, it would be beneficial to examine these Neo-Eriksonian additions to the Eriksonian model from the same perspective of determining defense mechanism deployment when development includes challenges and crises at these developmental steps.

Also, the behavioral repertoires of individuals, including in their adaptation, coping and defense mechanism deployment, might reflect flexible yoking across the particular repertoires that are associated with several Neo-Eriksonian steps while the person attempts to deal with the ongoing contexts, challenges, and crises. It would be beneficial to examine how defense mechanisms are yoked together as part of that adaptive effort.

Coping

The adaptation and coping scale that has been developed (the 15-point SMMACS) requires scale justification/item operationalization, and psychometric scale construction. It needs construct, concurrent, and predictive validity research. That said, it has face validity, covering what seems to be major adaptive and maladaptive coping strategies.

Defense Mechanisms

The crux of the two chapters on defense mechanisms has raised many areas for which conceptual and empirical investigation seems warranted. On the one hand, the chapters have proposed a multiplicity of models in which defense mechanisms might be embedded, and they should be tightened, operationalized, and investigated. On the other hand, new terms related to defense mechanisms have been proposed, and they deserve the same type of tightening and instigation. Finally, new avenues for elaborating new types of defense mechanisms have been road-mapped throughout the chapters, and they should be conceptualized and investigated further.

The adaptation, coping, and defense mechanism models that have been developed just touch upon factors such as self-harm, self-medication, self-deception, numbing, other harm, and cognitively misperceiving the other. These topics would benefit from further exploration in relation to defense mechanisms and their treatment here.

Overall Conclusion

Overall, the two chapters on defense mechanisms have presented revised approaches to adaptation/coping, including an expanded matrix of defensivity and offensivity behaviors within which defense mechanisms could be examined. Also, the chapters support Young's view of Neo-Eriksonian steps in lifespan development, and they present ways in which it can be investigated empirically. The chapters emphasize that individual differences mark the steps in the model, and defense mechanisms could be mapped onto them in this regard. The chapters open the study of defense mechanisms to new perspectives, and they open the area of adaptation, coping, and stress to new approaches on defense mechanisms.

Future work should elaborate the concept of *activation-inhibition coordination relational co-regulation*. On the one hand, the chapters refer to activation-inhibition coordination as an underlying causal factor across neuron, brain, and behavior. On the other hand, they refer to relational coregulation as an integrating concept over interactive psychological coregulation, self-control, emotional regulation, cognitive regulation, behavioral regulation, etc. Both concepts refer to ubiquitous processes within the individual organism/person and also across them, although at different explanatory levels. The former refers to an underlying metric that is common over multiple levels of the organism/person (i.e., neuron, brain, behavior). The latter refers to the behavioral control that an organism/person has and, moreover, that control such as this resides in the relational interaction with the environment, ecology, and other organisms/persons.

Consequently, one way of integrating the two concepts is in the way indicated. It allows for a way of characterizing the deep levels of behavior and interaction of organisms/persons, and their causal determinants, both individually and in dyads or groups. It is a hierarchical concept that includes the activation-inhibition coordination and relational coregulation components as equal aspects. It emphasizes that activation-inhibition coordination is as much relational as individual. And it emphasizes that relational co-regulation is as much about activation-inhibition coordination dynamics as anything else, both in its functioning in the individual organism/person in this regard and in the dyad/group in this regard.

The degree of synchronization or its lack both within the individual and the dyad/group according to this metric could be expressed over the levels of neuron, brain, and behavior. The desynchronization this way could affect defense mechanism deployment and their interaction across dyads/groups. It could affect defensivity and offensivity deployment in individuals and over dyads/groups. A prime example is the case of child abuse and its sequelae. How would activation-inhibition coordination relational co-regulation be affected in its synchronization in child abuse? What would the consequences be long term with respect to this concept? Future research can investigate the conceptual and empirical bases that need elaboration for this new concept.

References

American Psychiatric Association: Diagnostic and Statistical Manual of Mental Disorders, 4th edn. American Psychiatric Association, Washington (1994)

Andrews, G., Singh, M., Bond, M.: The defense style questionnaire. J. Nerv. Ment. Dis. **181**(4), 246–256 (1993). https://doi.org/10.1097/00005053-199304000-00006

Ayers, T.S., Sandier, I.N., West, S.G., Roosa, M.W.: A dispositional and situational assessment of children's coping: testing alternative models of coping. J. Pers. **64**(4), 923–958 (1996). https://doi.org/10.1111/j.1467-6494.1996.tb00949.x

Babl, A., Grosse Holtforth, M., Perry, J.C., Schneider, N., Dommann, E., Heer, S., Stähli, A., Aeschbacher, N., Eggel, M., Eggenberg, J., Sonntag, M., Berger, T., Caspar, F.: Comparison and change of defense mechanisms over the course of psychotherapy in patients with depression or anxiety disorder: evidence from a randomized controlled trial. J. Affect. Disord. **252**, 212–220 (2019). https://doi.org/10.1016/j.jad.2019.04.021

Bacon, A.M., Corr, P.J.: Coronavirus (COVID-19) in the United Kingdom: a personality-based perspective on concerns and intention to self-isolate. Br. J. Health Psychol. **25**(4), 839–848 (2020). https://doi.org/10.1111/bjhp.12423

Bacon, A.M., McDaid, C., Williams, N., Corr, P.J.: What motivates academic dishonesty in students? A reinforcement sensitivity theory explanation. Br. J. Educ. Psychol. **90**(1), 152–166 (2020). https://doi.org/10.1111/bjep.12269

Bailey, R., Pico, J.: Defense Mechanisms. StatPearls Publishing, Treasure Island (2020)

Benita, M., Shechter, T., Nudler-Muzikant, S., Arbel, R.: Emotion regulation during personal goal pursuit: integration versus suppression of emotions. J. Pers. **89**, 565 (2020). https://doi.org/10.1111/jopy.12599

Bond, M.: Empirical studies of defense style: relationships with psychopathology and change. Harv. Rev. Psychiatr. **12**(5), 263–278 (2004). https://doi.org/10.1080/10673220490886167

Boschan, P.: Temporality and narcissism. Int. Rev. Psycho-Anal. **17**(3), 337–349 (1990)

Boyraz, G., Zhu, Y., Waits, J.B.: Avoidance coping and academic locus of control as mediators of the relationship between posttraumatic stress and academic achievement among first-year college students. Anxiety Stress Coping. **32**(5), 545–558 (2019). https://doi.org/10.1080/10615806.2019.1638681

Brown, C.L., Van Doren, N., Ford, B.Q., Mauss, I.B., Sze, J.W., Levenson, R.W.: Coherence between subjective experience and physiology in emotion: individual differences and implications for well-being. Emotion. **20**(5), 818–829 (2020). https://doi.org/10.1037/emo0000579

Burgoyne, A.P., Engle, R.W.: Attention control: a cornerstone of higher-order cognition. Curr. Dir. Psychol. Sci. **29**(6), 624–630 (2020). https://doi.org/10.1177/0963721420969371

Butterbaugh, S.M., Wood, N.D.: Developmental trajectories of women's identity development. J. Fam. Theory Rev. **12**(3), 398–410 (2020). https://doi.org/10.1111/jftr.12390

Butz, M.V., Achimova, A., Bilkey, D., Knott, A.: Event-predictive cognition: a root for conceptual human thought. Top. Cogn. Sci. **13**, 10 (2020). https://doi.org/10.1111/tops.12522

Cancino-Montecinos, S., Björklund, F., Lindholm, T.: A general model of dissonance reduction: unifying past accounts via an emotion regulation perspective. Front. Psychol. **11**, 540081 (2020). https://doi.org/10.3389/fpsyg.2020.540081

Cannon, B.: The interrelations of emotions as suggested by recent physiobiological researches. Am. J. Psychol. **25**(2), 256–282 (1914). https://doi.org/10.2307/1413414

Cannon, W.B.: Bodily Changes in Pain, Hunger, Fear and Rage. Appleton, New York (1915)

Cannon, B.: Some disorders supposed to have an emotional origin. N. Y. Med. J. **104**, 870–873 (1916)

Cantave, C.Y., Langevin, S., Marin, M.-F., Brendgen, M., Lupien, S., Ouellet-Morin, I.: Impact of maltreatment on depressive symptoms in young male adults: the mediating and moderating role of cortisol stress response and coping strategies. Psychoneuroendocrinology. **103**, 41–48 (2019). https://doi.org/10.1016/j.psyneuen.2018.12.235

Carver, C.S.: You want to measure coping but your protocol' too long: consider the brief cope. Int. J. Behav. Med. **4**(1), 92–100 (1997). https://doi.org/10.1207/s15327558ijbm0401_6

Carver, C.S., White, T.L.: Behavioral inhibition, behavioral activation, and affective responses to impending reward and punishment: the BIS/BAS Scales. J. Pers. Soc. Psychol. **67**(2), 319–333 (1994). https://doi.org/10.1037/0022-3514.67.2.319

Chang, S., Egeth, H.E.: Enhancement and suppression flexibly guide attention. Psychol. Sci. **30**(12), 1724–1732 (2019). https://doi.org/10.1177/0956797619878813

Chater, N., Zhu, J.-Q., Spicer, J., Sundh, J., León-Villagrá, P., Sanborn, A.: Probabilistic biases meet the Bayesian brain. Curr. Dir. Psychol. Sci. **29**(5), 506–512 (2020). https://doi.org/10.1177/0963721420954801

Chauvel, P.: Répression et clivage. Rev. Fr. Psychanal. **60**, 1659–1662 (1996). https://doi.org/10.3917/rfp.g1996.60n5.1659

Chen, S., Burton, C.L., Bonanno, G.A.: The suppression paradox: a cross-cultural comparison of suppression frequency, suppression ability, and depression. J. Affect. Disord. **274**, 183–189 (2020). https://doi.org/10.1016/j.jad.2020.05.126

Clancy, K., Ding, M., Bernat, E., Schmidt, N.B., Li, W.: Restless 'rest': intrinsic sensory hyperactivity and disinhibition in post-traumatic stress disorder. Brain. **140**(7), 2041–2050 (2017). https://doi.org/10.1093/brain/awx116

Clark, J.K., Evans, A.T.: Source credibility and persuasion. Personal. Soc. Psychol. Bull. **40**(8), 1024–1036 (2014). https://doi.org/10.1177/0146167214534733

Cole, S.W.: The conserved transcriptional response to adversity. Curr. Opin. Behav. Sci. **28**, 31–37 (2019). https://doi.org/10.1016/j.cobeha.2019.01.008

Cole, S.W., Hawkley, L.C., Arevalo, J.M., Sung, C.Y., Rose, R.M., Cacioppo, J.T.: Social regulation of gene expression in human leukocytes. Genome Biol. **8**, R189 (2007). https://doi.org/10.1186/gb-2007-8-9-r189

Compas, B.E., Jaser, S.S., Bettis, A.H., Watson, K.H., Gruhn, M.A., Dunbar, J.P., Williams, E., Thigpen, J.C.: Coping, emotion regulation, and psychopathology in childhood and adolescence: a meta-analysis and narrative review. Psychol. Bull. **143**(9), 939–991 (2017). https://doi.org/10.1037/bul0000110

Cook, R.M., Fye, H.J., Wind, S.A.: An examination of the counselor burnout inventory using item response theory in early career post-master's counselors. Meas. Eval. Couns. Dev., 1–18 (2020). https://doi.org/10.1080/07481756.2020.1827439

Corr, P.J., Krupić, D.: Motivating personality: approach, avoidance, and their conflict. In: Elliot, A.J. (ed.) The Advances in Motivation Science: Advances in Motivation Science, pp. 38–90. Elsevier Academic Press, Cambridge (2017). Abstract accessed from Science Direct database

Cramer, P.: The Development of Defense Mechanisms: Theory, Research, and Assessment, 1st edn. Springer, New York (1991)

Cramer, P.: Seven pillars of defense mechanism theory. Soc. Personal. Psychol. Compass. **2**(5), 1963–1981 (2008). https://doi.org/10.1111/j.1751-9004.2008.00135.x

Cramer, P.: Defense mechanisms: 40 years of empirical research. J. Pers. Assess. **97**(2), 114–122 (2015). https://doi.org/10.1080/00223891.2014.947997

Dariotis, J.K., Chen, F.R.: Stress coping strategies as mediators: toward a better understanding of sexual, substance, and delinquent behavior-related risk-taking among transition-aged youth. Deviant Behav. (2020). https://doi.org/10.1080/01639625.2020.1796210

De Dreu, C.K.W., Gross, J.: Revisiting the form and function of conflict: neurobiological, psychological, and cultural mechanisms for attack and defense within and between groups. Behav. Brain Sci. **42**, E116 (2019). https://doi.org/10.1017/s0140525x18002170

De Pascalis, V., Sommer, K., Scacchia, P.: Extraversion and behavioural approach system in stimulus analysis and motor response initiation. Biol. Psychol. **137**, 91–106 (2018a). https://doi.org/10.1016/j.biopsycho.2018.07.004

De Pascalis, V., Sommer, K., Scacchia, P.: Resting frontal asymmetry and reward sensitivity theory motivational traits. Sci. Rep. **8**, 13154 (2018b). https://doi.org/10.1038/s41598-018-31404-7

Del Giudice, M., Ellis, B.J., Shirtcliff, E.A.: The adaptive calibration model of stress responsivity. Neurosci. Biobehav. Rev. **35**(7), 1562–1592 (2011). https://doi.org/10.1016/j.neubiorev.2010.11.007

Desai, M.: Introduction to Rights-Based Direct Practice with Children. Springer, Singapore (2018)

Di Giuseppe, M., Gennaro, A., Lingiardi, V., Perry, J.C.: The role of defense mechanisms in emerging personality disorders in clinical adolescents. Psychiatry. **82**(2), 128–142 (2019). https://doi.org/10.1080/00332747.2019.1579595

Di Giuseppe, M., Zilcha-Mano, S., Prout, T.A., Perry, J.C., Orrù, G., Conversano, C.: Psychological impact of Coronavirus Disease 2019 among Italians during the first week of lockdown. Front. Psychiatr. **11**, 576597 (2020a). https://doi.org/10.3389/fpsyt.2020.576597

Di Giuseppe, M., Perry, J.C., Lucchesi, M., Michelini, M., Vitiello, S., Piantanida, A., Fabiani, M., Maffei, S., Conversano, C.: Preliminary reliability and validity of the DMRS-SR-30, a novel self-report measure based on the Defense Mechanisms Rating Scales. Front. Psychiatr. **11**, 870 (2020b). https://doi.org/10.3389/fpsyt.2020.00870

Dror, O.E.: The cannon–bard thalamic theory of emotions: a brief genealogy and reappraisal. Emot. Rev. **6**(1), 13–20 (2014). https://doi.org/10.1177/1754073913494898

Edwards, E.R.: Posttraumatic stress and alexithymia: a meta-analysis of presentation and severity. Psychol. Trauma Theory Res. Pract. Policy. (2019). https://doi.org/10.1037/tra0000539

Eiguer, A.: Considérations sur la famille du psychotique: relation d'objet narcissique et vie fantasmatique inconsciente groupale. Psychol. Fr. **27**(1), 8–20 (1982)

Endler, N.S., Parker, J.D.A.: Assessment of multidimensional coping: task, emotion, and avoidance strategies. Psychol. Assess. **6**(1), 50–60 (1994). https://doi.org/10.1037/1040-3590.6.1.50

Euler, S., Stalujanis, E., Allenbach, G., Kolly, S., de Roten, Y., Despland, J.-N., Kramer, U.: Dialectical behavior therapy skills training affects defense mechanisms in borderline personality disorder: an integrative approach of mechanisms in psychotherapy. Psychother. Res. **29**(8), 1074–1085 (2018). https://doi.org/10.1080/10503307.2018.1497214

Fang, S., Chung, M.C., Wang, Y.: The impact of past trauma on psychological distress: the roles of defense mechanisms and alexithymia. Front. Psychol. **11**, 992 (2020). https://doi.org/10.3389/fpsyg.2020.00992

Francis, A.L.: The embodied theory of stress: a constructionist perspective on the experience of stress. Rev. Gen. Psychol. **22**(4), 398–405 (2018). https://doi.org/10.1037/gpr0000164

Gerevich, J., Bácskai, E.: Protective and risk predictors in the development of drug use. J. Drug Educ. **26**(1), 25–38 (1996). https://doi.org/10.2190/w3h2-a7jm-03xb-f4ub

Giner-Sorolla, R., Chaiken, S.: Selective use of heuristic and systematic processing under defense motivation. Personal. Soc. Psychol. Bull. **23**(1), 84–97 (1997). https://doi.org/10.1177/0146167297231009

Glazer, S., Kozusznik, M.W., Meyers, J.H., Ganai, O.: Meaningfulness as a resource to mitigate work stress. In: Leka, S., Sinclair, R.R. (eds.) Contemporary Occupational Health Psychology: Global Perspectives on Research and Practice, vol. 3, pp. 114–130. Wiley Blackwell, Hoboken (2014). https://doi.org/10.1002/9781118713860.ch8

Granieri, A., La Marca, L., Mannino, G., Giunta, S., Guglielmucci, F., Schimmenti, A.: The relationship between defense patterns and DSM-5 maladaptive personality domains. Front. Psychol. **8**, 1926 (2017). https://doi.org/10.3389/fpsyg.2017.01926

Gray, J.A.: The psychophysiological basis of introversion-extraversion. Behav. Res. Ther. **8**(3), 249–266 (1970). https://doi.org/10.1016/0005-7967(70)90069-0

Gray, J.A., McNaughton, N.: The Neuropsychology of Anxiety: An Enquiry into the Functions of the Septo-Hippocampal System, 2nd edn. Oxford University Press, Oxford (2000)

Gruhn, M.A., Compas, B.E.: Effects of maltreatment on coping and emotion regulation in childhood and adolescence: a meta-analytic review. Child Abuse Negl. **103**, 104446 (2020). https://doi.org/10.1016/j.chiabu.2020.104446

Harmon-Jones, E., Gable, P.A.: On the role of asymmetric frontal cortical activity in approach and withdrawal motivation: an updated review of the evidence. Psychophysiology. **55**(1), e12879 (2018). https://doi.org/10.1111/psyp.12879

Hart, J.: Toward an integrative theory of psychological defense. Perspect. Psychol. Sci. **9**(1), 19–39 (2014). https://doi.org/10.1177/1745691613506018

Hart, W., Albarracín, D., Eagly, A.H., Brechan, I., Lindberg, M.J., Merrill, L.: Feeling validated versus being correct: a meta-analysis of selective exposure to information. Psychol. Bull. **135**(4), 555–588 (2009). https://doi.org/10.1037/a0015701

Hartig, T., Kylin, C., Johansson, G.: The telework tradeoff: stress mitigation vs. constrained restoration. Appl. Psychol. **56**(2), 231–253 (2007). https://doi.org/10.1111/j.1464-0597.2006.00252.x

Heathcote, K., Wullschleger, M., Sun, J.: The effectiveness of multi-dimensional resilience rehabilitation programs after traumatic physical injuries: a systematic review and meta-analysis. Disabil. Rehabil. **41**(24), 2865–2880 (2019). https://doi.org/10.1080/09638288.2018.1479780

Henry, J.P., Stephens, P.: Stress, Health, and the Social Environment: A Sociobiologic Approach to Medicine. Springer, New York (1977)

Hobfoll, S.E.: Conservation of resources: a new attempt at conceptualizing stress. Am. Psychol. **44**(3), 513–524 (1989). https://doi.org/10.1037/0003-066x.44.3.513

Hobfoll, S.E.: The influence of culture, community, and the nested-self in the stress process: advancing conservation of resources theory. Appl. Psychol. **50**(3), 337–421 (2001). https://doi.org/10.1111/1464-0597.00062

Hobfoll, S.E.: Social and psychological resources and adaptation. Rev. Gen. Psychol. **6**(4), 307–324 (2002). https://doi.org/10.1037/1089-2680.6.4.307

Hobfoll, S.E., Jackson, A.P.: Conservation of resources in community intervention. Am. J. Community Psychol. **19**(1), 111–121 (1991). https://doi.org/10.1007/bf00942259

Hodgson, J.H., Shields, C.G., Rousseau, S.L.: Disengaging communication in later-life couples coping with breast Cancer. Fam. Syst. Health. **21**(2), 145–163 (2003). https://doi.org/10.1037/1091-7527.21.2.145

Holmes, J., Nolte, T.: "Surprise" and the Bayesian brain: implications for psychotherapy theory and practice. Front. Psychol. **10**, 592 (2019). https://doi.org/10.3389/fpsyg.2019.00592

de Hoog, N.: Processing of social identity threats: a defense motivation perspective. Soc. Psychol. **44**(6), 361–372 (2013). https://doi.org/10.1027/1864-9335/a000133

Hosogoshi, H., Takebayashi, Y., Ito, M., Fujisato, H., Kato, N., Nakajima, S., Oe, Y., Miyamae, M., Kanie, A., Horikoshi, M.: Expressive suppression of emotion is a moderator of anxiety in a unified protocol for transdiagnostic treatment of anxiety and depressive disorders: a secondary analysis. J. Affect. Disord. **277**, 1–4 (2020). https://doi.org/10.1016/j.jad.2020.07.132

Jadri, R., Denève, S.: Circular inferences in schizophrenia. Brain. **136**, 3227–3241 (2013). https://doi.org/10.1093/brain/awt257

Karoly, P.: How pain shapes depression and anxiety: a hybrid self-regulatory/predictive mind perspective. J. Clin. Psychol. Med. Settings. **28**, 201 (2021). https://doi.org/10.1007/s10880-019-09693-5

Katz, C., Nicolet, R.: "If only I could have stopped it": reflections of adult child sexual abuse survivors on their responses during the abuse. J. Interpers. Viol. (2020). https://doi.org/10.1177/0886260520935485

Kehyayan, A., Matura, N., Klein, K., Schmidt, A.-C., Herpertz, S., Axmacher, N., Kessler, H.: Putative markers of repression in patients suffering from mental disorders. Front. Psychol. **9**, 2109 (2018). https://doi.org/10.3389/fpsyg.2018.02109

Kiecolt-Glaser, J.K.: Marriage, divorce, and the immune system. Am. Psychol. **73**(9), 1098–1108 (2018). https://doi.org/10.1037/amp0000388

Kiecolt-Glaser, J.K., Wilson, S.J.: Lovesick: how couples' relationships influence health. Annu. Rev. Clin. Psychol. **13**(1), 421–443 (2017). https://doi.org/10.1146/annurev-clinpsy-032816-045111

Kiecolt-Glaser, J.K., Marucha, P.T., Mercado, A.M., Malarkey, W.B., Glaser, R.: Slowing of wound healing by psychological stress. Lancet. **346**(8984), 1194–1196 (1995). https://doi.org/10.1016/s0140-6736(95)92899-5

Kiecolt-Glaser, J.K., Renna, M.E., Shrout, M.R., Madison, A.A.: Stress reactivity: what pushes us higher, faster, and longer—and why it matters. Curr. Dir. Psychol. Sci. **29**(5), 492–498 (2020). https://doi.org/10.1177/0963721420949521

Kirschbaum, C., Pirke, K.-M., Hellhammer, D.H.: The 'Trier social stress test' – a tool for investigating psychobiological stress responses in a laboratory setting. Neuropsychobiology. **28**(1–2), 76–81 (1993). https://doi.org/10.1159/000119004

de Kloet, E.R., de Kloet, S.F., de Kloet, C.S., de Kloet, A.D.: Top-down and bottom-up control of stress-coping. J. Neuroendocrinol. **31**(3), e12675 (2019). https://doi.org/10.1111/jne.12675

Konaszewski, K., Kolemba, M., Niesiobędzka, M.: Resilience, sense of coherence and self-efficacy as predictors of stress coping style among University students. Curr. Psychol. **50**, 4052 (2021). https://doi.org/10.1007/s12144-019-00363-1

Krause, K.D., Halkitis, P.N.: Toward a more dynamic understanding of the influence of resilience on health. Behav. Med. **46**(3–4), 171–174 (2020). https://doi.org/10.1080/08964289.2020.1790972

Kube, T., Berg, M., Kleim, B., Herzog, P.: Rethinking post-traumatic stress disorder – a predictive processing perspective. Neurosci. Biobehav. Rev. **113**, 448–460 (2020). https://doi.org/10.1016/j.neubiorev.2020.04.014

Kühnel, A., Widmann, A., Colic, L., Herrmann, L., Demenescu, L.R., Leutritz, A.L., Li, M., Grimm, S., Nolte, T., Fonagy, P., Walter, M.: Impaired cognitive self-awareness mediates the association between alexithymia and excitation/inhibition balance in the pgACC. Psychol. Med. **50**(10), 1727–1735 (2019). https://doi.org/10.1017/s0033291719001806

Laczkovics, C., Fonzo, G., Bendixsen, B., Shpigel, E., Lee, I., Skala, K., Prunas, A., Gross, J., Steiner, H., Huemer, J.: Defense mechanism is predicted by attachment and mediates the maladaptive influence of insecure attachment on adolescent mental health. Curr. Psychol. **39**(4), 1388–1396 (2020). https://doi.org/10.1007/s12144-018-9839-1

Lazarus, R.S., Folkman, S.: Stress, Appraisal, and Coping, 1st edn. Springer, New York (1984)

Liang, J., Zhou, T., Zhou, C.: Hopf bifurcation in mean field explains critical avalanches in excitation-inhibition balanced neuronal networks: a mechanism for multiscale variability. Front. Syst. Neurosci. **14**, 580011 (2020). https://doi.org/10.3389/fnsys.2020.580011

van der Linden, D., Dunkel, C.S., Tops, M., Hengartner, M.P., Petrou, P.: Life history strategy and stress: an effect of stressful life events, coping strategies, or both? Personal. Individ. Differ. **135**, 277–285 (2018). https://doi.org/10.1016/j.paid.2018.07.024

Lisman, J.E., Coyle, J.T., Green, R.W., Javitt, D.C., Benes, F.M., Heckers, S., Grace, A.A.: Circuit-based framework for understanding neurotransmitter and risk gene interactions in schizophrenia. Trends Neurosci. **31**(5), 234–242 (2008). https://doi.org/10.1016/j.tins.2008.02.005

López-Muñoz, F., Pérez-Fernández, F.: A history of the alexithymia concept and its explanatory models: an epistemological perspective. Front. Psychiatr. **10**, 1026 (2020). https://doi.org/10.3389/fpsyt.2019.01026

Luborsky, L., Blinder, B., Schimek, J.: Looking, recalling, and GSR as a function of defense. J. Abnorm. Psychol. **70**(4), 270–280 (1965). https://doi.org/10.1037/h0022418

Luoma, J.B., Chwyl, C.: Interpersonal mechanisms for the maintenance of self-criticism: expressive suppression, emotion expression, and self-concealment. Curr. Psychol. (2020). https://doi.org/10.1007/s12144-020-00920-z

Martino, G., Caputo, A., Schwarz, P., Bellone, F., Fries, W., Quattropani, M.C., Vicario, C.M.: Alexithymia and inflammatory bowel disease: a systematic review. Front. Psychol. **11**, 1763 (2020). https://doi.org/10.3389/fpsyg.2020.01763

Masterson, F.A., Crawford, M.: The defense motivation system: a theory of avoidance behavior. Behav. Brain Sci. **5**(4), 661–696 (1982). https://doi.org/10.1017/S0140525X00014114

Matthews, G.: Stress states, personality and cognitive functioning: a review of research with the Dundee stress state questionnaire. Personal. Individ. Differ. **169**, 110083 (2021). https://doi.org/10.1016/j.paid.2020.110083

McEwen, B.S.: Protective and damaging effects of stress mediators. N. Engl. J. Med. **338**(3), 171–179 (1998). https://doi.org/10.1056/NEJM199801153380307

McEwen, B.S.: Redefining neuroendocrinology: epigenetics of brain-body communication over the life course. Front. Neuroendocrinol. **49**, 8–30 (2018). https://doi.org/10.1016/j.yfrne.2017.11.001

Meyer, G. J., Viglione, D. J., Mihura, J. L., Erand, R. E., & Erdberg, P. (2017). *Rorschach Performance Assessment System: Administration, coding, interpretation, and technical manual - (R-PAS)*. Lutz: Psychological Assessment Resources.

Miller, G.E., Chen, E., Parker, K.J.: Psychological stress in childhood and susceptibility to the chronic diseases of aging: moving toward a model of behavioral and biological mechanisms. Psychol. Bull. **137**(6), 959–997 (2011). https://doi.org/10.1037/a0024768

Moroń, M., Mandal, E.: Reinforcement sensitivity, approach and avoidance goals and relational aggression in romantic relationships. Personal. Individ. Differ. **168**, 110381 (2021). https://doi.org/10.1016/j.paid.2020.110381

Nagulendran, A., Norton, P.J., Jobson, L.: Investigating cultural differences in the effects of expressive suppression when processing traumatic distressing material. Behav. Cogn. Psychother. **48**(6), 658–671 (2020). https://doi.org/10.1017/s1352465820000508

Naturale, A.: How do we understand disaster-related vicarious trauma, secondary traumatic stress, and compassion fatigue? In: Quitangon, G., Evces, M.R. (eds.) Vicarious Trauma and Disaster Mental Health: Understanding Risks and Promoting Resilience, pp. 73–89. Routledge/Taylor & Francis Group, New York (2015)

Neal, L.B., Gable, P.A.: Regulatory control and impulsivity relate to resting frontal activity. Soc. Cogn. Affect. Neurosci. **12**(9), 1377–1383 (2017). https://doi.org/10.1093/scan/nsx080

Neubauer, P.B.: Anna freud's concept of developmental lines. Psychoanal. Stud. Child. **39**(1), 15–27 (1984). https://doi.org/10.1080/00797308.1984.11823417

Nevarez, M.D., Morrill, M.I., Waldinger, R.J.: Thriving in midlife: the roles of childhood nurturance and adult defense mechanisms. J. Res. Pers. **74**, 35–41 (2018). https://doi.org/10.1016/j.jrp.2018.01.002

Nimroody, T., Hoffman, L., Christian, C., Rice, T., Murphy, S.: Development of a defense mechanisms manual for children's doll play (DMCP). J. Inf. Child Adolesc. Psychother. **18**(1), 58–70 (2019). https://doi.org/10.1080/15289168.2018.1565005

O'Connor, D.B., Thayer, J.F., Vedhara, K.: Stress and health: a review of psychobiological processes. Annu. Rev. Psychol. **72**, 663–688 (2021). https://doi.org/10.1146/annurev-psych-062520-122331

O'Donnell, P.: Adolescent onset of cortical disinhibition in schizophrenia: insights from animal models. Schizophr. Bull. **37**(3), 484–492 (2011). https://doi.org/10.1093/schbul/sbr028

Paradiso, S., Brown, W.S., Porcerelli, J.H., Tranel, D., Adolphs, R., Paul, L.K.: Integration between cerebral hemispheres contributes to defense mechanisms. Front. Psychol. **11**, 1534 (2020). https://doi.org/10.3389/fpsyg.2020.01534

Parker, J.D.A., Taylor, G.J., Bagby, R.M.: The 20-Item Toronto alexithymia scale: III. Reliability and factorial validity in a community population. J. Psychosom. Res. **55**(3), 269–275 (2003). https://doi.org/10.1016/s0022-3999(02)00578-0

Paulin, M.G., Cahill-Lane, J.: Events in early nervous system evolution. Top. Cogn. Sci. (2019). https://doi.org/10.1111/tops.12461

Perry, J.C.: Defense Mechanism Rating Scales, 5th edn. JC Perry, Cambridge (1990)

Perry, J.C., Bond, M.: Addressing defenses in psychotherapy to improve adaptation. Psychoanal. Inq. **37**(3), 153–166 (2017). https://doi.org/10.1080/07351690.2017.1285185

Perry, J.C., Despland, J.-N.: A pilot study of wishes and fears (motives) among personality disorders. Can. J. Psychoanal. **19**(1), 3–31 (2011)

Perry, J.C., Metzger, J., Sigal, J.J.: Defensive functioning among women with breast cancer and matched community controls. Psychiatry. **78**(2), 156–169 (2015). https://doi.org/10.1080/00332747.2015.1051445

Perry, J.C., Banon, E., Bond, M.: Change in defense mechanisms and depression in a pilot study of antidepressive medications plus 20 sessions of psychotherapy for recurrent major depression. J. Nerv. Ment. Dis. **208**(4), 261–268 (2020). https://doi.org/10.1097/nmd.0000000000001112

Peters, B.J., Overall, N.C.: Perceptions of romantic partners' emotional suppression are more biased than accurate. Emotion. **20**(8), 1485–1489 (2020). https://doi.org/10.1037/emo0000679

Prout, T.A., Zilcha-Mano, S., Aafjes-van Doorn, K., Békés, V., Christman-Cohen, I., Whistler, K., Kui, T., Di Giuseppe, M.: Identifying predictors of psychological distress during COVID-19: a machine learning approach. Front. Psychol. **11**, 586202 (2020). https://doi.org/10.3389/fpsyg.2020.586202

Quintella, R.: O desmentido da privação na atualidade. Ágora: Estudos Em Teoria Psicanalítica. **19**(1), 115–130 (2016). https://doi.org/10.1590/S1516-14982016000100008

Ransom, M., Fazelpour, S., Markovic, J., Kryklywy, J., Thompson, E.T., Todd, R.M.: Affect-biased attention and predictive processing. Cognition. **203**, 104370 (2020). https://doi.org/10.1016/j.cognition.2020.104370

Reyno, S.M., Simmons, M., Kinley, J.: A meta-analytic study examining the relationship between alexithymia and dissociation in psychiatric and nonclinical populations. Res. Psychother. Psychopathol. Proc. Outc. **23**(1), 439 (2020). https://doi.org/10.4081/ripppo.2020.439

Rhodewalt, F., Vohs, K.D.: Defensive strategies, motivation, and the self: a self-regulatory process view. In: Elliot, A.J., Dweck, C.S. (eds.) Handbook of Competence and Motivation, pp. 548–565. Guilford Publications, New York (2005)

Robinson, A.M.: Let's talk about stress: history of stress research. Rev. Gen. Psychol. **22**(3), 334–342 (2018). https://doi.org/10.1037/gpr0000137

Roe, J.J., Aspinall, P.A., Ward Thompson, C.: Coping with stress in deprived urban neighborhoods: what is the role of green space according to life stage? Front. Psychol. **8**, 17 (2017). https://doi.org/10.3389/fpsyg.2017.01760

Seelig, B.J.: Altruism and boundary violation. Psychoanal. Inq. **37**(7), 474–486 (2017). https://doi.org/10.1080/07351690.2017.1362923

Sekera, J.: Research into interpersonal relations in young offenders institutes. New Educ. Rev. **1**(12), 119–145 (2003)

Selye, H.: A syndrome produced by diverse nocuous agents. Nature. **138**, 32 (1936). https://doi.org/10.1038/138032a0

Selye, H.: The Physiology and Pathology of Exposure to Stress: A Treatise Based on the Concepts of the General-Adaptation Syndrome and the Diseases of Adaptation. Acta Inc. Medical, Montreal (1950)

Selye, H.: The general-adaptation-syndrome. Annu. Rev. Med. **2**, 327–342 (1951). https://doi.org/10.1146/annurev.me.02.020151.001551

Sivan-Donin, D., Ben-Ezra, M., Hamama-Raz, Y.: Quality or quantity of coping resources: why not both? An integration of common stress theories. Psychiatry Res. **272**, 164–170 (2019). https://doi.org/10.1016/j.psychres.2018.12.051

Slavich, G.M.: Social safety theory: a biologically based evolutionary perspective on life stress, health, and behavior. Annu. Rev. Clin. Psychol. **16**(1), 265–295 (2020). https://doi.org/10.1146/annurev-clinpsy-032816-045159

Steindl, C., Jonas, E.: The dynamic reactance interaction—how vested interests affect people's experience, behavior, and cognition in social interactions. Front. Psychol. **6**, 16 (2015). https://doi.org/10.3389/fpsyg.2015.01752

Steiner, H., Feldman, S.S.: Two approaches to the measurement of adaptive style: comparison of normal, psychosomatically ill, and delinquent adolescents. J. Am. Acad. Child Adolesc. Psychiatry. **34**(2), 180–190 (1995). https://doi.org/10.1097/00004583-199502000-00013

Stephan, K.E., Friston, K.J., Frith, C.D.: Dysconnection in schizophrenia: from abnormal synaptic plasticity to failures of self-monitoring. Schizophr. Bull. **35**(3), 509–527 (2009). https://doi.org/10.1093/schbul/sbn176

Sterzer, P., Adams, R.A., Fletcher, P., Frith, C., Lawrie, S.M., Muckli, L., Petrovic, P., Uhlhaas, P., Voss, M., Corlett, P.R.: The predictive coding account of psychosis. Biol. Psychiatry. **84**(9), 634–643 (2018). https://doi.org/10.1016/j.biopsych.2018.05.015

Straud, C.L., McNaughton-Cassill, M.: Self-blame and stress in undergraduate college students: the mediating role of proactive coping. J. Am. Coll. Heal. **67**(4), 367–373 (2019). https://doi.org/10.1080/07448481.2018.1484360

Subhani, A.R., Kamel, N., Mohamad Saad, M.N., Nandagopal, N., Kang, K., Malik, A.S.: Mitigation of stress: new treatment alternatives. Cogn. Neurodyn. **12**(1), 1–20 (2018). https://doi.org/10.1007/s11571-017-9460-2

Taylor, G.J., Bagby, R.M.: Examining proposed changes to the conceptualization of the alexithymia construct: the way forward tilts to the past. Psychother. Psychosom. **7**(1), 1–11 (2020). https://doi.org/10.1159/000511988

Thimm, J.C., Wang, C.E.A., Waterloo, K., Eisemann, M., Halvorsen, M.: Coping, thought suppression, and perceived stress in currently depressed, previously depressed, and never depressed individuals. Clin. Psychol. Psychother. **25**(3), 401–407 (2018). https://doi.org/10.1002/cpp.2173

Thompson, N.J., Fiorillo, D., Rothbaum, B.O., Ressler, K.J., Michopoulos, V.: Coping strategies as mediators in relation to resilience and posttraumatic stress disorder. J. Affect. Disord. **225**, 153–159 (2018). https://doi.org/10.1016/j.jad.2017.08.049

Tobin, D.L., Holroyd, K.A., Reynolds, R.V., Wigal, J.K.: The hierarchical factor structure of the coping strategies inventory. Cogn. Ther. Res. **13**(4), 343–361 (1989). https://doi.org/10.1007/bf01173478

Tolan, P., Lovegrove, P., Clark, E.: Stress mitigation to promote development of prosocial values and school engagement of inner-city urban African American and Latino youth. Am. J. Orthopsychiatry. **83**(2–3), 289–298 (2013). https://doi.org/10.1111/ajop.12038

Ulrich-Lai, Y., Christiansen, A.M., Wang, X., Song, S., Herman, J.P.: Statistical modeling implicates neuroanatomical circuit mediating stress relief by 'comfort' food. Brain Struct. Funct. **221**(6), 3141–3156 (2016). https://doi.org/10.1007/s00429-015-1092-x

Vaillant, G.E.: Defense mechanisms. In: Zeigler-Hill, V., Shackelford, T.K. (eds.) Encyclopedia of Personality and Individual Differences. Springer, Cham (2020). https://doi.org/10.1007/978-3-319-24612-3_1372

VandenBos, G.R.: APA Dictionary of Psychology, 2nd edn. American Psychological Association, Washington (2015)

Wang, D.A., Hagger, M.S., Chatzisarantis, N.L.D.: Ironic effects of thought suppression: a meta-analysis. Perspect. Psychol. Sci. **15**(3), 778–793 (2020). https://doi.org/10.1177/1745691619898795

Waters, S.F., Karnilowicz, H.R., West, T.V., Mendes, W.B.: Keep it to yourself? Parent emotion suppression influences physiological linkage and interaction behavior. J. Fam. Psychol. **34**(7), 784–793 (2020). https://doi.org/10.1037/fam0000664

Yizhar, O., Fenno, L.E., Prigge, M., Schneider, F., Davidson, T.J., O'Shea, D.J., Sohal, V.S., Goshen, I., Finkelstein, J., Paz, J.T., Stehfest, K., Fudim, R., Ramakrishnan, C., Huguenard, J.R., Hegemann, P., Deisseroth, K.: Neocortical excitation/inhibition balance in information processing and social dysfunction. Nature. **477**(7363), 171–178 (2011). https://doi.org/10.1038/nature10360

Young, G.: Development and Causality: Neo-Piagetian Perspectives. Springer Science + Business Media, New York (2011)

Young, G.: Unifying Causality and Psychology: Being, Brain and Behavior. Springer International Publishing, Cham (2016)

Young, G.: Revising the American Psychological Association Ethics Code. Springer International Publishing, Cham (2017)

Young, G.: Causality and Development: Neo-Eriksonian Perspectives. Springer International Publishing, Cham (2019)

Zeki, S., Chén, O.Y.: The Bayesian-Laplacian brain. Eur. J. Neurosci. **51**(6), 1441–1462 (2020). https://doi.org/10.1111/ejn.14540

Zorzella, K.P.M., Muller, R.T., Cribbie, R.A., Bambrah, V., Classen, C.C.: The role of alexithymia in trauma therapy outcomes: examining improvements in PTSD, dissociation, and interpersonal problems. Psychol. Trauma Theory Res. Pract. Policy. **12**(1), 20–28 (2020). https://doi.org/10.1037/tra0000433

Chapter 12
Evolution, Development, Culture, and Human Exceptionalism

Keywords Evolution · Development · Culture · Exceptionalism · Hyper-culture · Causality · Causal cognition · Donald · Theoric mind · Mithen · Extended mind · Substages · Social self working schemata · *Homo Causa* · Neo-Piagetian · Social cognition · Tomasello · Nonhuman primates

Abstract This second last substantive chapter of the book before the concluding one presents a novel model of cultural evolution and development that is extrapolated from the current developmental model. The latter has 25 steps, with five others applicable to future human-machine interfacing and the like. The cultural model builds on this 30-step sequence developmentally to indicate the pattern in cultural development that might have taken place evolutionarily and that is continuing in modern humans. The later stages in culture that are described are based on the concept of hyper-culture, which takes place first-order, second-order, etc. Each phase in the development of culture grows through the five steps that recycle over stages, as is the case for the developmental model. The chapter argues that human exceptionalism or uniqueness is reflected in the upper steps in the developmental and cultural models. Neither our hominin ancestors nor contemporary nonhuman primate evidence the advanced thinking and cultural complexity inherent in the models that are described. Humans are also distinct in the extent of causality in the thinking process that governs development and that is applied to culture. The chapter presents a model of 25 steps in the development of causal cognition, referred to as causal cocognition. Humans will continue to develop their collective intelligence, which will have ramifications for change in the development of culture and their reciprocal relations.

Humans are biologically, psychologically, and socially different from other species, including extant nonhuman primates and our immediate hominin ancestors. We are distinctive, unique, and exceptional relative to all other species, past and present, including the ones closest to us genetically, morphologically, and in adaptiveness.

G. Young, *Causality and Neo-Stages in Development*,
https://doi.org/10.1007/978-3-030-82540-9_12

Yet there is no common understanding of the attributes that distinguish humans from other species. The chapter presents a novel hypothesis based on analogic reasoning from a stage model of human development. The model of cultural evolution that resulted from the process applies to both our past ancestors and the contemporary cultural context.

Introduction

Scope

The chapter begins with a revised definition of culture that is consistent with its approach to culture and its evolution. Then, it reviews a select sampling of recent literature on culture and its evolution, as well as the contemporary study of culture. The articles reviewed are consistent with the present approach. Then, the chapter presents the developmental model used in the analogical reasoning process to build the model of cultural evolution. Finally, the chapter presents the model, and it consists of 30 steps in the evolution of culture and its elaboration in contemporary societies.

Definitions of Culture

There are strict and more expansive definitions of culture, and the stricter disciplinary ones are indicated. The variability in the definitions is striking.

The sociological definition of culture includes meaningful differences in languages, customs, beliefs, rules, arts, knowledge, and collective identities and memories (American Sociological Association 2021). According to Steensland (2011), it refers to the symbolic-expressive way of life and norms of a people. The psychological definition (Van den Bos 2015) refers to customs, values, beliefs, knowledge, art, and language in this regard. Archeology refers to artifacts and the like, but also criticizes the notion of deriving an archeological definition of culture (Roberts and Vander Linden 2011). Essentially, archeology refers to culture as an assemblage of archaeological remains. As for anthropology, that discipline gives a definition quite related to the present approach. For example, Hudelson (2004) refers to a dynamic, evolving shared reference point or normative structure of values, ideas, concepts, communications, and behavioral rules in the collective mind of the group that helps the group to adapt and function.

Different disciplines have different definitions of culture, and there is no universally accepted definition of culture. Moreover, the range of indices of culture is broad, and although they focus on meaning to peoples in one way or another, they do not refer only to products of mind. For example, in archeology, artifacts are important. This indicates that culture should be defined in terms of more than behavior and mind, because tool making and the like are included. Indeed, the range of preferred instrument in these regards is part of a culture, as are the building styles and architecture of the culture. Art is broad in its scope. Finally, culture is intimately related to society. The mind of a culture produces different societal structures and organizations. Or, could be argued that societal institutions are different from culture; however, that reflect culture as much as buildings. Their organization reflects the collective mind as much as institutions. They contribute to culture as much as do individuals. In all these senses, culture needs to include a broad slice of societal elements and its organization within its purview.

The organizational component of cultures and their institutions reveal the differential scope and evolution of cultures. For example, how are subsistence strategies organized and implemented, including in food gathering, storage, supply chain workings, helping those in need, etc. Another example concerns kinship systems—how prevalent are they within a culture, has the culture integrated systems beyond them, and do they still hold predominant sway in the overall culture. A third example on cultural organization illustrates its complexity and potential aggressive side, which is much ignored in cultural scholarship. How does the culture organize in terms of protecting itself, and how does it organize in terms of aggressing others, including in warfare? This speaks to societal organization, in particular, but there are aspects of the military that infuses the mindset of the culture, and it is hard to distinguish where culture begins and where society ends. Don't chimpanzees engage in these types of forays? A fourth example returns to the positive side of cultures. Art is so important to them, but how does art become institutionalized in a culture? What are the steps that create talent pool searches and individual expression that is cultivated? Art becomes a part of the educational system, to be sure, but there are also other more community ways that art is promoted.

Finally, the research needs to examine the tracings of steps since the origins of modern cultures with the modern mind a few tens of thousands of years ago to illustrate the mini-steps in the creation of these organizational systems that mark a culture. When the modern mind is considered a brief slice of evolutionary time, few advances in its growth become apparent. However, if it is taken on its own, then more refined slices of the steps involved will be apparent. Even just considering contemporary culture, there are so many domains, they grow quickly, the growth is uneven, and keeping up with skyrocketing innovations cannot be reduced to being involved in epochs in time that span thousands of years. This recommendation becomes pertinent when the present multistep model of the evolution and development of culture is presented as the chapter proceeds.

For present purposes, culture refers to the adaptive, functional symbolic expressive ways of life and norms of a people or subgroup of people with which they identify and which helps them cohere, existing in terms of an assemblage of: (a) behaviors, practices, customs, perceptions, learnings, memories, language, communications, narratives/stories, cognition, ideas, concepts, rules, organizational skills, beliefs, attitudes, values, creativity endeavors, art, building skills, technology, clothes, architecture, written works (from engraved stone records to handwritten notes to encyclopedias, as the case may be), and so on, and knowledge/information/data acquisition and dissemination devices and strategies that characterize a group of people; (b) whether a small local one or a pan-planetary one (or levels intermediate to that); (c) as well as the physical and material reflections of the behaviors and practices, the artifacts and remnants that might be left from the practices; and (d) the overall group organizations/structures/institutions, and their subdivisions.

Culture gives meaning to groups, and meanings that differentiate or that distinguish groups are recognized and valued. They help mark their group's differences and individual identities. Culture is dynamic and ever-changing, so that cultural group differences change and interact. Culture can be global, such as with the increasing importance of social media. Meanings are constructed by individuals and also group-wise.

A novel way of examining meaning culturally would be in terms of causal understanding of behavior and its effects. Indeed, causal understanding has been considered one of the unique attributes of humans (Gonzalez-Cabrera 2020; Heyes 2018), and these attributes are the product of cultural evolution rather than inherited mechanisms. Cultures do not simply seek to understand and describe behavior and its organization, but do so to adapt better and effect change according to the meanings and the deciphering involved. Causal cognition is essential to adults and culture, begins in childhood, and has been part of our evolutionary past.

Culture is transmitted from one generation to the next, as part of a culture's behaviors/practices/customs, and dynamically changes over generations; it is cumulative. Indeed, it is massively cumulative and changes so rapidly that new terms are needed for it in modern times. I have chosen terms such as hyper-culture and quantum culture.

Various terms have been used for complex human culture. Orshan (1996) referred to mega-culture. I prefer the equivalent term of hyper-culture to designate the rapid human advancements culturally (Bertman 1998, 2017). Andersen (2019) referred to a similar concept of meta-culture (along with meta-modern). Caro and Murphy (2002) referred to quantum physics in the context of culture, using the terminology of quantum culture.

Children can have their own culture; it should not be analyzed just from an adult point of view. Children express the roots of what makes humans distinct, such as in their early intersubjectivity, social learning, and empathy/altruism. But these early acquisitions need to be traced developmentally to show how they emerge in the teenage and adult periods to impact culture and mark human uniqueness. Are these acquisitions homologous and traceable to later equivalent ones, or analogous and unrelated causally to them?

Different species have their own culture. It should not be analyzed just from a human point of view. Primates, in particular, express a culture that resembles the human one to a degree, but there are essential differences related to their ecological niche.

A broader definition of culture, again for present purposes, refers to the behavior of nonhumans, past and present, in their behavioral organization. Here, we do not speak of beliefs, attitudes, etc., although these might be inferred, for example, in a group of nonhuman primates. Rather, we should restrict the definition of culture to the animal realm as those behaviors, practices, and customs, in the sense of repeated habits that mark a group.

Going further, for present purposes, the chapter considers pre-cultural behavior in animal aggregates, in that behavior such as this sets the evolutionary stage for the development of higher-order cultures. Ultimately, the chapter examines the aggregation behavior of multicellular organisms in this regard.

An assumption of the present chapter is the reciprocal interactions that take place at multiple levels in each of behavior, development, evolution, and culture. This implies that these types of processes function systemically, they can develop levels, the levels can organize hierarchically, and the levels can interact, e.g., bottom-up to top-down and vice versa. For example, is culture the product of individual activity, thought, and so on, that accumulates, or does the (sub)group to which the individual belong entrain the person in its activities, thoughts, and so on? A dynamic, reciprocal interactive approach will acknowledge both possibilities and their interaction. The same applies to evolutionary pressures that are strictly based on natural selection and cultural evolution. They work in tandem, just as do genetics and epigenetics in phenotypic development.

Ultimately, a definition of culture should be inclusive and itself consists of multiple levels, as has been attempted here. To begin, there should be a simple inclusive definition, dictionary-type. Then, different levels in a more complex definition should be constructed. (a) The first should be in observables or simpler behaviors and artifacts depending on the discipline. (b) The second should be on broad observable/artifactual strokes, such as rituals, customs, and practices. (c) The third should be on what is inferred, e.g., mind, meaning, or shared intentionality. (d) The fourth should consider the organizational, institutional, structural, societal, and wider constructions involved. (c) The fifth should include all the contextual factors that influence the prior levels.

An approach such as this, in terms of hierarchical levels this to defining culture will allow researchers to examine intra- and interlevel interactions within and across levels. For example, how does a new ritual evolve from observables and how do new rituals influence observables? How do new observables develop? How do new meanings develop in a culture? And so on.

These types of questions get at mechanisms in cultural evolution and development. The proposed cultural modeling process through steps is descriptive, and more work is needed on the causation in navigating the steps culturally. It would seem that the network/systems approach, among others, emphasized in the present work, can help in this regard.

A Model of Developmental and Evolutionary Steps

This section of the chapter presents the multiple tables that describe the current models of development and of culture. The developmental model is the one presented throughout this book. The cultural model is entirely new.

The developmental tables are reworkings of other tables in my books. They allow for easy access and reference to the developmental model for the key points pertinent to the present exercise. There is little text to accompany them. On the one hand, the tables speak for themselves, often using full sentences, and, on the other hand, to repeat in depth their contents would be redundant.

The cultural tables also have little text. This situation obtains for several reasons. First, the hypothesis of the steps in the evolution of culture is quite novel. There is not much direct accompanying text that one could write for it. Second, the cultural model is an extrapolation from the developmental model, which itself is based on

Table 12.1 Steps in the evolution of the cultural mind: sensorimotor to proto-communication

Number	Step	Mya[b]	Species	Equivalent cognitive substage	Source
0	Sensorimotor schematization (e.g., synergistic fluid schema complexes of organism-niche dynamics)	>4	Proto-primate ancestors	Coordination to integration	Young
1	Episodic complex event representation (nonverbal, modeling, imitation)		Miocene primates	Perioperational coordination	Donald
2	Mimetic/Marginally symbolic (should involve hierarchizing event representations)	2–4	First proto-hominins	Perioperational hierarchization	Donald
3	Theory of mind (mind theories are systems)	1.5–2	*Homo Ergaster*	Perioperational systematization	Mithen
4	Specialized, isolated cognitive abilities (domain-specific, highly modular; allows for interaction with the social, natural, and technological milieux) (i.e., the isolated cognitive abilities are expanding)	0.5	Human precursor species	Perioperational multiplication	Mithen
5	Proto-Communication[a]	0.4	*Homo sapiens*	Perioperational integration	Young
	Mythic/Proto symbolic (advanced linguistic skills)		Precursor species		Donald
	Holistic communication (advanced vocal-gestural communicative abilities, or proto-language communication of "messages" rather than isolated words) (holistic implies integration)	0.25	Middle Pleistocene period	Perioperational integration	Mithen

[a]Integrating the two approaches by Donald and Mithen to this epoch
[b]Million years ago
Adapted from Young (2011)

Table 12.2 Steps in the evolution of the cultural mind: symbolic to group intelligence

Number	Step	Mya[a]	Species	Equivalent cognitive substage	Source
6	Theoretic/fully symbolic (modern mind symbols, formalisms, external memory storage) (fully symbolic, e.g., formalisms, is consistent with abstraction)	0.3	*Homo sapiens*	Abstract coordination	Donald
7	Cognitive fluidity (cross-modal thought) (cross-modal thought could include some degree of hierarchization)	0.1	*Homo sapiens*	Abstract hierarchization	Mithen
8	Extended mind (extend beyond our brains for cognitive anchors, into the material culture, e.g., computers; disciplines could develop) (the extended mind is systemic)	0.05	*Homo sapiens*	Abstract systematization	Mithen
9	Advanced intellectual skills (creating metaphors, analogies) (advanced skills multiply out)	0.01	*Homo sapiens*	Abstract multiplication	Mithen
10	Superordinate integrated Abstract	0.005	*Homo sapiens*	Abstract integration	Young
11	Group intelligence coordination	0.003	Contemporary human ancestors	Collective intelligence coordination	Young

[a]Million years ago
Note. Young (2011) had combined the theoric and extended mind steps in the respective Donald and Mithen sequences into one step, but differentiates them here
Adapted from Young (2011)

other extrapolations. Neither model is empirically grounded, being quite theoretical. Third, the tables that present the model are especially long, with much explanatory text within the tables themselves. They can stand on their own.

The modeling process in the cultural model construction began in the 2011 Young book, in a section on the evolution of the theoric and extended mind. The next section reviews that material, revises it slightly, and presents it in tabular format. Then, it reviews the present 25-step developmental model, but reminds it can be expanded into 30 steps, as was done in Young (2011). This prepares the way for presentation of the new 30-step model of cultural evolution.

Steps in the Evolution of Mind

Prior efforts to describe the evolution of the modern mind have not been integrated, except in Young (2011). Donald (2009) hypothesized that there are three major

Table 12.3 The five change steps applicable to development, cultural change, and state change generally

Substage	Details
Coordination	Coordination refers to an interrelation of two different elemental units However, the interrelation does not any one unit having ascendancy in terms of either a temporal order or a dominant-subordinate relationship. The units exist in reciprocal balance (pairing, addition, juxtaposition, opposition, etc.) of a back and forth nature, which allows for compare/contract processes, if applicable. If preliminary hierarchies are established, they are tentative, tenuous structures.
Hierarchization	With hierarchization, the coordinations are further structured. Paired units evidence a strengthened dominant-subordinate relation and/or a fixed sequence in time.
Systematization	Systematization is marked by both an expansion and simplification of hierarchized units. First, component units add (recruit) refinements (feedback, extra adaptive behaviors). Second, the new structure meshes into a smoothly operating, more systemic whole.
Multiplication	Multiplication refers to the propagation of newly-acquired system structures in the prior step. For example, this takes place by applying the new system to a new domain. Or, it refers to combining systems by chaining them embedding them, etc.
Integration	Multiple units are more effectively coalesced into flexible systems.

Note. The coordination step begins with a juxtaposition of basic elements that had been elaborated in the prior step of integration in the prior phase. However, it does not require that both elements are fully integrated in the prior step. For example, one might be and the other in the process of multiplying into integration. The juxtaposition could be complicated when it is premature along these lines, and especially complicated if very premature, such as neither element being fully integrated or far from that. In a certain sense, the model needs a transitional point 0, but that could be true for each of its 5 points. For example, hierarchization could be long and drawn out, systematization very tenuous to begin, etc.
Adapted from Table 5.3 of the present book

"stages" in the cultural-cognitive evolution of the hominid mind: marginally symbolic, proto-symbolic, and fully symbolic mind, or theoric mind (see Tables 12.1 and 12.2). Mithen (2007) described five steps in the evolution of the human mind, culminating in the extended mind. The work of Donald and Mithen overlap in their descriptions of the evolution of the human mind. Their integrated sequence, as per Tables 12.1 and 12.2, are consistent with the present developmental model, as indicated in the parenthetical comments in the first column that describes each step in the tables. We need to keep in mind that the present developmental model is not being used to frame evolutionary history on a one-to-one basis; the former is not a model of recapitulation, but reflects parallels in the two sequences of evolution and development. That said, because the present developmental model has many more steps than their combined model, any model of cultural development and evolution needs to be much more elaborate than their combined model, which is the present case. Note that formulating a combined evolutionary and developmental model of culture is not contradictory because the former sets the stage and modern humans continue the evolution.

Table 12.4 The reflexive steps in Neo-Piagetian cognitive development and associated causal co-cognition development

Neo-Piagetian stage/ substage	Approx. age range	Social self working schemas	Causal co-cognition substage
Reflexive coord[a]	Earlier fetal life	No schemata other than reflex pairings.	The stage is set for the development of causal cognition through the initiation of the growth process.
Hier[a]	Quite premature	Reflex pairs hierarchically coordinate and react to stimuli.	The premature infant is still embedded in an acausal cognitive matrix.
Syst[a]	Somewhat premature	Primitive schemata form in visual, auditory, haptic, olfactory, gustatory, and kinesthetic activity/ exploration; with intermodal system coordinations.	The development of primitive schemas allows the beginning of sensorimotor representation of environmental contents, which are especially quasi-social at this age.
Mult[a]	Full-term newborn	Consistencies in care giving lead to the formation of bodily components-of-context associations. Patterned schemata fire mechanically.	The primitive schema allow for patterned behavior beyond primitive reflexive ones, with the near social caregiving environment involved.
Integ[a]	0–1 month	Independent schemata that are not reflex controlled allow contextually adjusted, patterned behavior with emotional integrations.	The newborn getting on will express partial freedom from basic reflexes in that the sensorimotor schemata controlled ones become responsive to experience. This facilitates intersubjectivity, as does the emotional side of the schemata. Intersubjectivity regulates the members of the dyad, and so is constitutive of a type of nascent reciprocal causality in the moment-to-moment transactional interaction involved.

[a]The substages refer to Coordination (Coord), Hierarchization (Hier), Systematization (Syst), Multiplication (Mult), and Integration (Integr)

Note. This table and the four that follow present a 25-step (sub)stage model of lifespan development. The Neo-Piagetian stages in the model are quite consistent with those of Piaget and other Neo-Piagetians. The substages in the model are based on Piaget's six sensorimotor substages. The first one in the series was removed and constituted the precursor Reflexive stage. The five remaining substages in the series were rephrased in terms of their overall function, leading to the five-step substage series. The same series was applied recursively to the other four stages in the model. This procedure led to the 5 stage × 5 substage 25-step lifespan developmental Neo-Piagetian model. The causal cognition portion of the table was extrapolated from the work on the social self-schemata that develop according to the 25 steps of the model

Note. The first major column in this table (and the four succeeding tables) is adapted from Young (2011). For the last two of the five tables involved, longer descriptions were written for this chapter. The second major column is original to this work

Table 12.5 The sensorimotor steps

Neo-Piagetian stage/substage	Approx. age range	Social self working schemas	Causal co-cognition substage
Sensori-motor Coord	1–4 months	Working schemata become increasingly coordinative of the socializing self and the other, but only in the sense of partial components of both (e.g., the baby is contented and experiences pleasure).	The visually-directed reach develops at this age, reflective of the infant's sensorimotor coordinations, and social interactions are coordinatively embodied, creating larger sensori-motor/bodily cognitive-affective social maps. Incipient causal co-cognition is reflected in the coordination over body, sensorimotor schemata, behavior, and the other.
Hier	4–8 months	As the infant develops a sense of trust, context-activated goals are added to developing schemata, which take on a hierarchical structure (e.g., components of self are interested and delighted in other).	Context-activated goals are especially social and relate to caregiver-infant interaction. The infant is beginning to develop object permanence, giving some stability to the social other's sensorimotor representation. For causal co-cognition, this means that nascent means-ends relations are forming, images are beginning to guide behavior, and the other is integral in the schematic maps of the infant's goal-conditioned world, with the social interactions involved co-constitutively forming them.
Syst	8–12 months	Working schemata include self-defined goals, primitive representations such as images of the caregiver, and the desire for intersubjectivity and proximity and contact. The emotional side of the developing cognitive-affective structure includes feelings of affection and comfort.	The social dynamics of co-constitutive causal cognition develops into a new phase, for example, with shared intentionality and joint attention. The goals guiding sensorimotor schemata development and implementation, and the images that are part of them, allow for clear means-end relations, which indexes a developing causal cognition. The social interactions involved create a tight social dynamic in which co-cognitions develop in this regard, with the other's contributions to the cognitive maps so created indissociable from them.

(continued)

Table 12.5 (continued)

Neo-Piagetian stage/ substage	Approx. age range	Social self working schemas	Causal co-cognition substage
Mult	12–18 months	The 1-year-old infant acts increasingly autonomous through planned exploratory behavior eagerly implemented, although this does not happen with explicit plans at the behavior's outset (it is "accidental"). The social other is integral to the working schemata being formed, but as an object of sensorimotoric-emotional activity rather than a preconceived representational goal. The primary caregiver who has been sensitive in the first year so that the infant feels "loved" is sought actively in reunion after a brief separation.	The infant explores means-end relations, creating new ones, but accidentally in the infant's play/ exploration. The schemata/images proliferate in the object and social world of the infant. Causality resides in the composition and decomposition of means-end relationships constructed by the infant and co-constructed with the social partner/caregiver. The attachment to the caregiver is secure with a history of responsive, contingent care that is warm. The internal working model is positive both for the self ("I am loved," verbally represents this sensorimotor schema) and the other ("The other loves me"). These internal working models are not just social; they are also causal. They become representational in the child and influence social relationships long term. They are causal drivers in relationships, being carried forward from the first year.
Integ	18–24 months	Infants at 18 months of age enact symbolically guided, planned activity, but always with a sensorimotoric and affective base. They experience appreciation and pride. Others are understood in terms of the plans, and with consistent participation in them. The infant varies plans involving them on purpose to see the effect.	The end of the sensorimotor stage witnesses the invention of new means by mental combination, including of plans, but always with a sensorimotor accompaniment, so the process is not quite fully representational. The cognitive maps involved extend over multiple areas of activity, including the social, and the other is integral to the contents of the plans and also their construction. The infant understands that objects are acted upon by the other and that they can act on the other causally, effecting responses that are anticipated within the limits of late sensorimotor thought.

Table 12.6 The perioperational steps

Neo-Piagetian stage/substage	Approx. age range	Social self working schemas	Causal co-cognition substage
Peri-operational coord	2–3.5 years	In symbol plan coordinations, the child's plans are more focused on self egocentrically, and the other, while schematized more holistically, needs to adjust. A sense of the other as a loving one grows.	In the representational stage, the other is an object of symbolical construction, but it is a co-construction due to the dynamic interactions involved. The young child acts egocentrically cognitively but not affectively and socially, and indeed emotions and social behavior related to prosociality even emerges in the sensorimotor period. By forming symbolic representations, causal cognition enters new territory because the symbolic representations generalize over cause-effect incidents into a primitive representation for the domain involved, including socially. Two or more causal representations could juxtapose and coordinate in this regard, then undo and start in other directions along these lines. Causal representational co-cognitions might develop in this context.
Hier	3.5–5 years	The child's symbol plans are more differentiated, with an initiative subordinating the other, who is still responded to with an overriding love, however.	Representational coordinations evolve into joint social hierarchizations, which are social co-hierarchies with the other. The other might predominate in the social dynamics, or the self, or they might alternate. This allows for taking perspective of the other, developing a theory of mind of the other, and relating perspectives and behavior with the other in the hierarchization involved. Social perspective taking/theory of the other's mind constructions are dynamic socially constructed representations that influence social planning and behavior in the child and reciprocally in the other. The child is trying to understand the motivations, emotions, thinking, and so on, of the other that guides the behavior of the other, that is, the causal underpinnings for the social dynamics in which the other engages; causal representational co-cognitions might differentiate in this context.
Syst	5–7 years	The "I" can take primary perspectives of the self/other through symbol plan systems and Eriksonian "industry," guided by others.	Representational symbol plans grow in their complexity while cohering systemically. The other's perspective and mind are understood better, and refined by the child's more active stance socially. Causal cognition begins to transition to the more logical reasoning of the concrete operational conserver for the simplest tasks, such as in number conservation. The reasoning involved can begin its maturation to wider reasoning, problem solving, and communication about these types of problems and their solutions, but always with curiosity tempered by the guidance of the other, if not with direct teaching involved.

(continued)

Table 12.6 (continued)

Neo-Piagetian stage/substage	Approx. age range	Social self working schemas	Causal co-cognition substage
Mult	7–9 years	This ability grows and others are seen to evaluate the self. [The child reaches an apex in cognitive development with concrete operations developing seriously. The child can reason socially, with reversibility, in the contexts lived as much as about objects and their transformations.]	Children participate in formal schooling and increasingly form independent group structures. The ability to causally understand the motivations, attitudes, and behaviors of others grows in these contexts, using the reasoning and problem solving that accompany concrete operations. Causal cognition enters a new territory with reversible concrete thought operations because the hallmark of causal reasoning at this level involves trying out different ideas in the contexts encountered by engaging and disengaging in them through reversible thought processes and trying out different tacks. The causal cognition does not take place isolated but in the social dynamics of home, school, and with peers. There could be joint explorations in these regards, for example, at discovery tables and over social media; there could quite genuine expressions of causal co-cognitions that are mutually enhanced.
Integ	9–11 years	The child's working schemata include testing of different roles, with others seen as modelers and accepting of this dynamic.	The pre-teen's causal cognitive exploration becomes a major force in the life of the child through the constant social, personality, and role try-outs. The other is intimately involved in these social and cognitive explorations, and they could occur in tandem with siblings, peers, classmates, etc., in a constitutive co-exploratory dynamic.

About possible steps in the more recent development of culture, Andersen (2019) referred to the indigenous (e.g., still isolated tribes in Amazonia), premodern, modern, postmodern, and meta-modern. As much as the sequence makes sense, I found it difficult to map onto my own proposed sequence along similar lines in Tables 12.1 and 12.2. More work is needed to elucidate the steps in cultural evolution and development, but Tables 12.1 and 12.2 provide a starting point in which substages can be added to stages.

A 25-Step Model of Human Development

Tables 12.3, 12.4, 12.5, 12.6, 12.7, and 12.8 present Young's 25 step developmental model (Young 2011, 2016, 2019, this book), in tables that have been modified for present purposes. The first table describes generally the substages within the stages

Table 12.7 The abstract steps

Neo-Piagetian stage/substage	Approx. age range	Social self working schemas	Causal co-cognition substage
Abstract coord	11–13 years	Conscious “I” weighs abstractly. The abstract logical awareness of the teenager accentuates within-group solidarities, as well as outgroup boundary definitions.	Being logical and abstract, as in the teen years, helps the teenager develop an awareness of the self, other people, etc. Causal cognition enters a critical phase in which relationships are conceived in abstract terms as well as the parties therein. Causality is inherent to conceptualizations at this age, in that the teenager wants to understand the why of other's behavior as well as her/his own. The two sides of the equation are coordinated transactionally, but temporarily and in ever changing ways. Causality is not just part of cognition but becomes cognition, at least in terms of its most important applications. Social problems are causal ones. Understandings such as these are co-constructed abstractly.
Hier	13–16 years	Identity “I” tests and seeks identity. The teenager can negotiate cultural identities as well as personal and familial ones.	The teenager seeks identities or puts the search on hold or otherwise arrests a full search. The self or the other becomes centers of identity search, or they alternate. Identities need to be considered as causal structures. They indicate what actions, attitudes, and approaches should be adopted in a matrix of intersecting causal attributions, conjectures, and hopes, both intra-personally and inter-personally.
Syst	16–19 years	Conscientious “I” undertakes adult-(like) functions. The person integrates in societal functions as much as personal and familial ones.	The teenager continues to grow and engages in adult-like thought and activity, including emotionally and socially. The abstract map created of the teen's world complexifies and systematizes such that the self-other become a holistic entity in at least one component of the teenager's mentality. This extends into the causal reasoning of the teen, in which the reciprocal causal influences of self and other are represented abstractly and guide behavior as it is changed by that behavior.
Mult	19–22 years	Relativistic “I” delves and debates. The person continually questions identities, and familial, social, and cultural linkages, toward creating multiplicities in social, cultural, and societal relations	The youth/young adult extends her/his causal mapping into many domains, social or otherwise, seeking causal enrichment of her/his world. As always, the causal cognitions are co-constructed (e.g., think college/university, romantic partnerships, work, societal dealings/politics)
Integ	22–25 years	Universal “I” harmonizes. The person reaches a synergistic intra- and interpersonal cognitive and socio-affective fusion in these regards.	The causal co-cognition of the person extends beyond the multiple immediate contexts lived to wider horizons. Understanding causality abstractly becomes the quest and it is fed reciprocally by individuals, cultures, peoples, and planetary perspectives.

Table 12.8 The collective intelligence steps

Neo-Piagetian stage/ substage	Approx. age range	Social self working schemas	Causal co-cognition substage
Collective intelligence coord	25–28 years	The self is collective, fused, and coordinative. The self applies superordinate abstract thinking skills to the full scope of life activities and relations, and in different realms in these regards.	Causal co-cognition becomes superordinately abstract. The abstract cognitions in this regard that had developed previously coordinate/juxtapose, etc., and reposition themselves in coordinative maps that represent active collective intelligence. The latter reflect group and barnstorming intelligence, family and couple intelligence, etc., and the superordinate causal maps so created are co-constructed and their origins are lost in the shared constructive and creative processes involved.
Hier	28–39 years	The self knows priorities, is multiply complex, and can give multiply, and not for taking. The role of social, cultural, and societal considerations is accentuated in the superordinate abstract structures created	Causal co-cognition at the superordinate abstract level means that the person attempts to give more structure hierarchically to the thoughts involved, creating multilevel systems that oscillate in structure for the top-down and bottom-up levels. Out of this manifold, sub-areas of understanding at work, in school and studies, in social and familial organization, and even in societal and cultural arenas are mapped one in relation to the other, reflecting the hierarchical cognition involved. The self and other are part of this collective intelligence project, and communications become quite complex intellectually.
Syst	39–50 years	At midlife, the self can create and work to transform personal, social, work, and community systems. The systemic superordinate abstract structures are mutually defined and transformed by the social, cultural, and societal factors involved in these regards	Causal cognition reaches fruition in a certain sense, because the person perceives a coherence in life in all its causal complexities. Bu this does not apply across the board, but in one crucial area, setting the stage for propagation and integration. For example, the social map of the person is super-interdigitated and differentiated, with the causal reasons for people's actions and thinking, including beliefs, morals, well understood, as well as those of the self. The dynamic thought and social relations in these regards over different people and their individual differences do not alter the coherence of the causal co-cognitions at the superordinate abstract level that are involved.

(continued)

Table 12.8 (continued)

Neo-Piagetian stage/substage	Approx. age range	Social self working schemas	Causal co-cognition substage
Mult	50–61 years	The elder self reviews the multiplicity of life and lives. Life reflections are inclusive of the multiple personal, familial, social, cultural, and societal foci in the person's cognitive and socio-affective networks	The causal co-cognition of the person propagates throughout the person's abstract structure at the superordinate level. Common causal perceptions in these regards spread throughout the system, informing the co-construction of cognition causally at this level. This has ramifications for behavior at all levels in the collective intelligence enterprise of the person, and the sharing of causal construction involved.
Integ	61+ years	An integrated "I" is really an integrated "We" at life's end. The IWEMEUS develops in tandem with the I/self of the person, but reaches harmonic vibrancy at the last stages of a life well-lived and supported, and in which that end-point has been the approach of the person to all others, from family/social relations and culture/society, to all peoples and the planet/world.	At the end of life, the ultimate causal cognitions prevail and reflect their history of causal co-constructions. The spiritual and related engagement with the other and the world in all its guises gives an intense causal understanding that can bring ultimate peace. The person can reflect on what life has been about, what her/his life has been, and what it will become, not only generally but causally. The person does not live by the causal map her/his life has created but reflects it at all levels of being. This takes place normally implicitly or in peaceful contemplation, instead of in robust cognitive exploration and communication. The other feels the peace, about the life lived and the causal maps behind it, and might carry forward inspired by the light that had burnished the person all her/his life, if that had not been done so already. The person had lived a life in which causal co-cognition had emerged as primary, and reflected the standing of the person as a member of the species *Homo Causa*.

of the model. The next five tables give the specific substages, or the 25 steps of the model.

Five Substages

Specifically, Table 12.3 presents the five-step change model that was applied to substage development in the model. It applies equally to cultural development and its evolution, as per a section that follows this one. The table note specifies that the steps in the model have transitional pre-steps that take place, and that passage through the five points in the model in the developmental or change process does not take place smoothly or automatically, nor should it. For example, full coordination precludes that at least two full-scale elements in a prior integrative step have developed or have manifested. However, those elements could be in transition themselves. Part of the modeling undertaken elsewhere in the present work includes transitional steps within steps.

25 Steps

Tables 12.4, 12.5, 12.6, 12.7, and 12.8 present the five stages of the present developmental model, each with its five substages. The left side of the tables consists of the social self working schemata that develop with the 25 Neo-Piagetian steps of the model. The right side of the tables refers to the development of causal cognition that seems to take place over the lifespan as understood by the model, or according to its Neo-Piagetian component.

Causal Co-cognition

The present emphasis on humans as *Homo Causa* has led to a model of the development of causal cognition over the 25 steps of the current developmental model. The research efforts on (a) causal cognition in evolution according to Stuart-Fox (2015) and (b) the grades in that evolution according to Gärdenfors and Lombard (2018) (see below) suggest that the field needs a more comprehensive model of the development of causal cognition. The developmental approach taken by Tomasello (2019) on the development of cognitive and social capacities in the first 6 years of life (see below) suggests that a more comprehensive model of causal cognition is needed over lifespan development. With these impetuses, the present author expanded his prior work on lifespan development into the area of causal cognition. However, given the present emphasis on co-culture, the model that is constructed in these regards concerns the development of co-cognition, or causal cognition as developed within and through the social context of the person.

A Five-Step Model of Future Human Development

Young (2011) had speculated that the next step in human cognitive development will concern human-machine interface, as well as interfacing with other species possible. The augmented intelligence would go through the same five-step growth/change sequence, from coordination to integration. This notion is expanded in the cultural model presented below.

Table 12.9 Cultural development and evolution: reflexive steps

Stage	Substage name	Explanation
1. Reflexive multi-cellular pre-culture	Coordinative co-adhesion	Coordination aggregation. One-celled organisms had created formative loose assemblies. Culture is pre-cultural, primordial, and intercellular. Causality is inherent in the aggregations' activities, with antecedent-consequent patterns.
2.	Hierarchical co-adhesion	Hierarchical aggregation. The assemblies took on a more formal organization with division of labor.
3.	Systematic co-adhesion	Systematization aggregation. The assemblies created structured assemblies inclusive of all components in the organization, with mutual influences among them.
4.	Multiplicative co-adhesion	Multiplication aggregation. The assemblies incorporated into larger entities, with looser inter-regulation.
5.	Integrative pan-cellular co-adhesion	Integration aggregation. The assemblies emerged with interlaced aggregations across the multicellular entities.

Table 12.10 Cultural development and evolution: sensorimotor steps

Stage	Substage name	Explanation
6. Sensorimotor multi-organism nascent culture	Coordinative co-tracking	Mutual supervision. Multicellular organisms, as with infants, use basic environmental monitoring/tracking mechanisms, to enhance ongoing adaptation. As social aggregates form (e.g., in parent-infant relationships and care) reciprocal inter-tracking takes place. Culture is inter-individual, and it is learning mediated. Culture is not defined in terms of contemporary human organization at this point, but in terms of inter-unit entity interactions within the matrix of entity relations. The tracking that is involved seeks antecedent-consequent patterns, or causal relations.
7.	Hierarchical co-tracking	The tracking process in coordinative exchanges elicits reactions in the monitoring of the other, with one partner or the other in the exchange predominant (e.g., the parent in infant care).
8.	Systematic co-tracking	The mutual supervision/tracking process creates a system of interlocked monitoring, at least for one domain/focus, in which the parties initiate activities that elicit responsive tracking to the initiatives. Goal pursuit/quasi-intentions are involved. This takes place both within the parties and across them.
9.	Multiplicative co-tracking	The co-tracking system created in the prior steps is transposed and elaborated in other domains/foci. Also, other parties beyond the initial ones (the initial pair) can become involved in multi-co-tracking systems.
10.	Integrative pan-organism co-tracking	An overarching structural organization across mutual tracking/supervision domains takes hold both within the parties and across them. The nascent culture of the present series of steps is primed for further qualitative organization involving pairs of acquisitions. This type of advance can take place only with (and reciprocally promotes) a new cognitive step involving representation.

Table 12.11 Cultural development and evolution: representational steps

Stage	Substage name	Explanation
11. Representational structured culture	Coordinative structured co-culture	Initiating representational culture. Culture is symbolic, and its members use symbol-based behavior and intentionality to interact, coalesce, and create higher-order symbolic patterns and organization that feed back into the individuals and their relationships. Relative to adult human language, primitive language exchange structuring develops. Culture is symbolically communicative, and thinking-mediated. The nature of the symbolic communication involves antecedent-consequent relations.
12.	Hierarchical structured co-culture	Representational communication between and among group members (e.g., familial conspecifics) elicits further stringing in communication within and between them, with more conjoined communicative units and the cohesions and coherence over them. Exchange back and forth dynamics govern conversations, with vocal/voicing members tracked/listened to in the short term, and perhaps the long term, depending on dynamics. There are material exchanges, as well. Offspring participate in all these types of exchanges, and in their informal gatherings learn from each other; also, they are subject to informal adult teaching strategies. Culturally, the hierarchical organization involved is reflected in members' group organization, e.g., in divisions of labor in food gathering/hunting/storage.
13.	Systematic structured co-culture	The reciprocity in dynamic exchanges in dyadic and group symbolic, representational communication becomes more balanced, participatory, and systemic. For example, children's behavior and communication lead more clearly to parental response, as much as the other way around. Children form play groups as much on their own in their locales as much as adults organize them (think open mouth displays in the rough and tumble pay of preschoolers and of contemporary nonhuman primates). Evolutionarily, adults displayed more organizational structure in group dynamics, forming informal rule-based systems. It is hypothesized that this is the limit of contemporary non-human primate representational development.
14.	Multiplicative structured co-culture	Cognitively, for humans, the child begins to function within the stage of concrete operations, in which contextually-based logic applied to physical parameters of the situation/task can take place (conservation). Children learn from each other as much as from adults. Society sets up formal learning opportunities in educational settings; educational systems (and parents) are responsive to the directions children indicate to others, but subsuming them. As contemporary humans appeared on the evolutionary scene, they did not evidence such formal educational initiatives, but gravitated in their own way beyond informal learning. Beyond schooling, cultural practices moved toward subsuming individuals to other group practices, e.g., subgroup interactions involving different transactions and commerce, material and otherwise. Logical reasoning in physical context can be causal.
15.	Integrative pan-cultural co-structure	At this step, representational culture reaches its apex in structure, whether describing children, our ancestors, or contemporary culture. Logic, at least at the concrete level, mediates cultural exchange and development. Children are preteens at this level; they are highly social and communicative representationally in different domains, which are interlinked in their conceptual structuring. Adults functioning at this level are super-organized, but limited in their generalizations. Societies that have evolved to this level might remain there, being fixed for socio-politico-historical reasons. Culture can be more, as in the next abstract steps.

Table 12.12 Cultural development and evolution: abstract steps

Stage	Substage name	Explanation
16. Abstract hyper-culture (meta/mega culture)	Coordinative hyper-co-culture	The efficient organizations developed in the prior step are juxtaposed, thereby promoting cognitive, social, and cultural advance to abstract levels, the latter of which is referred to as hyper-culture. Abstract hyper-culture is mediated by abstract thought, although daily cognitive activity does not reside exclusively at that level. The abstract thought at this juncture involves loose coalitions/juxtapositions over different domains/tasks/applications. The changes in the assemblies in this regard change rapidly and dynamically. The degree to which our human ancestors evidenced this type of abstract thought is an open question. They expressed rituals, art, and theorized behaviors indicate of basic abstract thought. Teenagers become more aware in the sense of consciousness when they reach this age period and its associated abstract reasoning. They can reflect to a degree on themselves and others; also, they can engage in organized peer groups without adult supervision. Cultures functioning at this level manifest variegated patterns of complexity indicative of abstract organization, including in their cognitions, beliefs, attitudes, and values. They engage in causal reasoning at the coordinative abstract level; indeed, causal thought appears characteristic of the abstract human, mediating all its essential activities, including culturally. *Homo sapiens* should be called *Homo Causa*. Given our co-actional, cultural nature, we could be called *Co-Homo Causa*. These abstract thought integrations are associated with changes in cultural behaviors, practices, and customs at the widest levels, along with their organization, including in communal art, knowledge acquisition, institutionally, etc.
17.	Hierarchical hyper-co-culture	As abstract thought evolves into more organized units in which loose coordinations are more interwoven, hierarchical abstract thought develops, thereby promoting more advanced hyper-culture. This type of thinking is generative of cyclical abstract activities that interrelate under one head arch feeding back into it. Whether speaking of teenagers or of cultures functioning at this level, there are more institutional co-structures that develop and are imposed downward on group members. But the structure can switch in the head arch involved, even flip its organizational structure, etc. Whatever, the result of the re-organizations, hierarchical abstract causal analysis of the hierarchical structures involved is primary both in trying to understand them and functioning effectively within them.

(continued)

Table 12.12 (continued)

Stage	Substage name	Explanation
18.	Systematic hyper-co-culture	Culture dynamics, whether, in terms of groups of people or wider societies, become concerned with common problems, solutions, and responsibilities. Member activity influence group activity, from the bottom up, as much as group activity influences member activity from the top down. The organizational structures that develop are governmental, regulatory, and statutory, to a degree, at least for one domain/task/application. For example, business structures develop managerial structures with these properties, and a culture functioning at this level has equivalent ones. Causal abstract thought becomes systemic and is essential to creating the organizations and in running them; also, it is essential for effective participation in and contribution to them.
19.	Multiplicative hyper-co-culture	Once effective systems develop culturally in one domain/task/application, the system generalizes to other areas. Expansionist cultural policies underwrite rules and regulations that govern a multiplicity of cultural transactions and capital exchange, monetary, material, or human. Abstract causal thought spreads through the abstract thought architecture of the person/culture, thereby facilitating the propagation of hyper-culture reach.
20.	Integrative pan hyper-co-culture	Culture at this level is complexly organized, mediated by pan-abstract thinking in particular domains/tasks/applications. For example, business and government entities are highly structured horizontally and vertically. The abstract thinking is causally integrated, allowing the efficient organization, charting, etc., of the entities, and their potential action-effect outcomes in the planning process. Note that the governmental organizations referred to here are local, even if societal. The abstract cognitive architecture does not yet allow for effective society-wide governmental organization, let alone pan-society ones. The next steps in development concern superordinate abstract structure, that might be collectively elaborated, which allows for complexification of culture exponentially. At the developmental human level, this refers to the complex abstract thought of the maturing adult, for example, after graduate school and applying gained knowledge, brainstorming, connecting, etc.

A 30-Step Model of Development and Cultural Evolution

The Model

The primary focus of the present chapter is an extrapolated cultural model of the developmental one in the book. The cultural model was derived through a logical thought process more than a detailed literature review. That said, its 30 steps in the evolution and development of culture provide rich grounds for empirical

Table 12.13 Cultural development and evolution: collective intelligence steps

Stage	Substage name	Explanation
21. Collective intelligence culture (second-order hyper co-culture)	Coordinative collective intelligence co-culture	The abstract thought of the adult becomes superordinate in organization, with separate abstract structures assembled into larger aggregates, through juxtapositions and temporary coalescing and interdigitations. The intelligence involved is collective—of the ideas, of the human domains involved, including cognitive and socioemotional/affective, and in the process of their construction in groups. Higher-order levels in abstract thought will emerge from the matrix of ideas. They will include not just the study of abstract ideas, but the formation of superordinate structures that integrate them, such as toward the creation of elements of a scholarly discipline. Culturally, this refers to the complex cognitive belief, attitudinal, and value systems that characterize cultures. The hyper culture manifestations of the prior stage of the model are exponentially more complex, and can be considered second-order hyper-cultural in nature. Just as Collective Intelligence is considered one order of complexity removed compared to abstract thought, so is collective intelligence co-culture at this stage in relation to the co-culture of the prior stage. The systems will involve advanced causal analysis reflective of the superordinate logic. Cultures that reflect this advanced abstract thinking will evolve rapidly, both in terms of speed and broadly over wide cultural spans. Indeed, the collective intelligence in the superordinate abstract thought of the culture drives individual collective intelligence, so that the culture-individual interface is fused, reciprocal, and dynamic. Entities such as businesses, schools/universities, institutions, professions, artist combines, and governmental and lobbying structures become much more refined and organized, with complex internal structures and external linkaging.
22.	Hierarchical collective intelligence co-culture	The adult superordinate abstract thought process stems from the coordinative one that juxtaposes integrated abstract thought cognitive structures. The members of the paired elements that had been constructed in the prior coordination phase (i.e., elaborated in the compare/contrast exploration process by the collective intelligence communities involved), are given more and less weight, respectively, in this hierarchization phase. The members are placed in superordinate and subordinate positioning with respect to each other in a confluence of complex abstract ideas. The culture reflects these abstract ideas and reciprocally contributes to them in an ever-evolving cycle of stability and change in superordinate abstract-thought related cultural attributes.
23.	Systematic collective intelligence co-culture	Cultural evolution reaches an apex of a sort here, because the evolving cultural landscape comes to include superordinate abstract systems that underwrite and fuel it. The process begins with one system that had been fleshed out and smoothed out by application and innovation. Then, it is ready for expansion in the next step. The systems involved could be cognitive, institutional, physical (e.g., architecture), or even concomitantly socio-affective, as in the helping professions. The latter example speaks to the question of self-corrective forces in systems, to help maintain their equilibrium when perturbed, especially if extremely so. Just as individuals can evidence dysfunctionalities, so can systems, and they need checks and balances to right the ship and find adaptive solutions in crises. Cultures can slip into contracting degradation rather than surging edification.

(continued)

Table 12.13 (continued)

Stage	Substage name	Explanation
24.	Multiplicative collective intelligence co-culture	The society/culture evolving rapidly in a superordinate abstract sense in which collective intelligence functions effectively. Systems that have been created in these regards provide models and are applied/transferred to other domains/applications/tasks. There is a dynamic interactive process across (a) individuals, and (b) society and its culture, and (c) the mediating superordinate abstract cognitive processes that characterize both. In the case of society/culture, the thinking process is collective as with the prior steps in this series. Culture is heading toward a fully collective intelligence mediation of superordinate abstract structures, indicative of a fully genuine co-culture. However, dark societal forces could impinge on the process and undermine the imperative for increasing complexity, cultural pluralization, and growth. Of course, the same caution applies to any of the steps in the current model. The present Neo-Piagetian series indicates what is possible cognitively in the growth in the underpinnings to and contributions to cultural evolution and development. The corresponding Neo-Eriksonian series indicates what could go wrong socio-affectively at each step in the model. Problematic development along these lines could lead to developmental fixations, regressions, psychopathology, etc. At the collective cultural level, the same dysfunctionality could develop, as contemporary societal/cultural developments as of this writing (January, 2021) illustrate too strikingly well.
25.	Integrative pan collective intelligence co-culture	In ideal circumstances, at the end of any of the five stages of steps in the current model, both individuals and societies/cultures reach a plateau in which the divergent strands in the culture coalesce into a co-integrative system in which all the components of the system are clearly defined and involved in a smooth functioning entity. For a pan co-culture at the level of superordinate abstract collective intelligence, this means that the culture is a widely dispersed and integrated second-order hyper/mega in structure (relative to the hyper culture of the prior stage). This sets the stage for new emergences in cognitive and cultural development related to interfacing of humans and technology/machines/computers on the one hand, and other species, on the other hand, including other humanoid or more advanced species that might be discovered in interstellar travel and the like (per steps 26–30 of the present model, presented in the next table). When this happens, co-culture accelerates quantumly.

investigation and synthesizing extant literature, while pointing out gaps that appear in the literature in light of the steps of the model. The 30 steps in the model are presented in six tables of five steps each (see Tables 12.9, 12.10, 12.11, 12.12, 12.13, and 12.14). The literature review that follows offers some support for the modeling process that has been undertaken for cultural development, but it remains speculative even if rational. The implication of the present cultural model is that humans are characterized uniquely by abstract thought, and the cultural development on which it depends also is unique to the species.

Table 12.14 Cultural development and evolution: quantum culture steps

Stage	Substage name	Explanation
26. Communal collective intelligences quantum co-culture (third-order hyper co-culture)	Coordinative quantum co-culture	By itself, human intelligence reaches the level of superordinate abstract thought that is developed through collective intelligence processes. But if human intelligence can be augmented, such as by interfacing technologically or over species, intelligence can continue to grow, per Young (2011). The new phase of intelligence that can evolve in this context could be called communal collective intelligence, or even quantum intelligence. This type of intelligence would lay the foundation of advanced cultural formation, which can be called quantum culture. The reciprocal dynamic in its formulation suggests that the culture should be termed co-culture, as with prior phases of the model. In the present modeling effort, beyond what has been already suggested for human-technology/other species interlinking, quantum co-culture can initiate through the interleaving of two large second-order hyper co-cultures. Technology and other species can afford this scaffold, as per prior arguments. The computers involved might literally be advanced quantum ones. However, the same growth process in co-culture at this level might take place in the collision/mutual impregnation and resultant coordination of two separate second-order hyper-cultures, resulting in a quantum leap in intelligence and cultural complexity. This third-order hyper-culture that could exist at this level can be barely imagined; but we might be in the throes of its initiation, or certainly, partial (rather than total/pan) cultural fusions have always been evident in our history and indicate the potential of the process at this ultimate level. Causality at this level will not simply be a part of the cultural complex, the reasoning that takes place, etc. Rather, causal thought will drive the culture, individuals, and their relations, and the complex abstract thought involved. Referring back to the human-machine/species interface, the juxtapositions need to respect the integrity of the human and multiple ethical controversies potentially will arise.
27.	Hierarchical quantum co-culture	The cultural modalities that will have developed in the prior phase become more than coordinated in that they will hierarchically organize in head arch/dominant-subordinate/subservient relations cognitively and culturally. The third-order hyper co-culture that will complexify at this stage needs to consider the danger of the human becoming subservient to the machine/other species. Here is one phase in which the hierarchical arrangement cannot oscillate in the dominant partner in the pair until the adaptive organization over them develops in context. Rather, the human needs to continually be in charge one way or another even though the machine/other species involved might be superior intellectually, at least in some ways in part.

(continued)

Table 12.14 (continued)

Stage	Substage name	Explanation
28.	Systematic quantum co-culture	The culture that will evolve either through second-order culture/second order culture interaction or through human-machine/other species interaction will solidify into an equilibrated system in one domain of functioning, ready for further elaborations. The reciprocal balancing of individual and culture in the cultural spiral will magnify at quantum levels because of the increased affordances invited by the co-parties (machine, other species, as the case may be) in the relationship.
29.	Multiplicative quantum co-culture	The new systems that will develop individually and culturally in humans will spread throughout the full individual and cultural systems involved. The speed will be hyper once the threshold of creating the first working system in this regard is passed. This will prepare the way for the ultimate integration, perhaps called hyper-horizonnet.
30.	Integrative pan quantum co-culture	The nature of the final ultimate intellectual and cultural integration in the present series could be as expansive as the solar system. This will prepare the way for further growth individually and culturally, in fourth-order hyper co-culture beyond the solar system, into expanses unknown.

Human Exceptionalism

The literature on human exceptionalism is varied, with comparisons of nonhuman primate and human behavior one means of determining human distinctiveness. The literature attempts to determine the apex variable that marks our species. It focuses on differences in kind or categorical all-or-none differences qualitatively. It does not consider a dimensional approach sufficient, e.g., humans are more intelligent (e.g., Arden 2019). Animals adapt differentially to their niches, and the specific contingencies in these regards as well as the differential selection that results preclude a scalar approach to grading animal differences.

The present approach is a combined one in that it focuses on human intelligence, but from a stage/substage developmental point of view. The abstract stage in development as found in teenagers and adults has no comparable behavior in nonhuman primates. Our ancestors appeared to have the beginnings of abstract thought. Modern humans have expanded this cognitive skill, and it underwrites cultural advances. The two progressions go hand in hand, and mark human distinctiveness in the qualitatively different phases they reach. The present development model helps qualify the growth in abstract thought in the human case, and therefore its consequent cultural growth. This model does not deny other areas of study of human exceptionalism, but it gives an axis on which to scaffold them. The human exceptionalism included in the model is described in detail in the tables that present it. In this regard, some chapters in this book are scarce in text and use tables and figures more for critical ideas; this is one of them.

Literature Review

There are two main sections to the literature review in the present chapter. First, the chapter reviews some recent literature pertaining to evolution of mind and its exceptionalism. Next, it examines some work on nonhuman primates in this regard.

The Modern Mind and Its Exceptionalism

Introduction

The study of human uniqueness relative to nonhuman primates and our human ancestors is replete with false leads (e.g., Corballis 2020; de Waal 2017; Finlay 2019; Leavens et al. 2015; Spocter et al. 2020). There are many contenders for describing the nature of human uniqueness (Stuart-Fox 2015), but none have unequivocally supportive data. Some of the hypothesized human exclusivities that have not been supported include cooperative hunting, tool manufacture, social cognition (theory of mind, shared intentionality), transmitted social teaching, cumulative cultural innovation, and generative cognitive recursion. Therefore, scholars have argued that perhaps a confluence of independent capacities and behaviors mark our distinctiveness rather than any one isolated behavior or attribute (Laland and Seed 2021). That said, one newer hypothesis of a particular domain has plausible grounds for marking human exceptionality, that of causal cognition and its relations to culture.

Causal Cognition

Bender and Beller (2019; also see Bender 2020) this is what you called Bender 2020; don't use the other Bender 2020 have written a critical article in the topic of human exceptionalism because it refers to causal cognition, which is essential to the present view on the matter. Specifically, Bender and Beller (2019) referred to causal perception of cause-effect relationships and attributions of causative mental states in this regard. Humans engage in cognition to construct meaningful event sequences. Generally, causal cognition concerns trying to establish causality, or the relationship between an event considered a cause and another considered an effect. Causal cognition involves learning about, perceiving, representing mentally and verbally, predicting, reasoning about, and controlling such linkages in order to enhance goal-driven behavioral success. Causal cognition is pervasive in human cognition, underlies beliefs and even attitudes, conditions decision-making, intentionality, emotions, and so on. Indeed, from an evolutionary point of view according to Bender and Beller (2019), deploying knowledge of cause–effect relations helps alter contexts in preferred directions so that this knowledge is considered the driving force in human evolution (Lombard and Gärdenfors 2017; Stuart-Fox 2015). Human ancestors alone used abstract causal thought to create useful tools (Haidle 2014). Human children are much more interested in causality than are other species (Vaesen 2012). Humans evidence shared intentionality from early on (Tomasello and Carpenter 2007; also see MacLean 2016; Marean 2015), and communicate their causal inferences, including about the inner state of others. Moreover, children learn about causality by observing and receiving teaching, and can store and communicate their causal learning through language processes (Bender and Beller 2019; Muentener and Bonawitz 2017). In terms of cultural differences, one related to causality is that different cultures hold different explanatory frameworks, e.g., Western compared to aboriginal. This illustrates the wide cultural differences overlain over universal aspects of causal cognition. Bender (2020) referred to causal framework theories in this regard.

Stuart-Fox (2015) argued that causal cognition marks human distinctiveness and evolved in early hominins, as had Povinelli and Bering (2002) and Wolpert (2003). Humans had to adapt to a varied environment. They used an incipient working memory in order to relate any indirect elicitor of behavior that they had inferred and the outcome of the elicitor. Given their ecological challenges, they stored these causal relationships into spatial maps. Moreover, in their sociality, they shared their maps in one way or another. Have other species evolved similar causal cognitive skills? Relative to other animals, our causal reasoning skills are unique (McGrew 2013). Did our australopithecines ancestors evidence skills such as these? According to Stuart-Fox (2015), the causal stores helped their large game hunting, their causal reasoning helped their tool manufacture, and it helped to interpret social behavior (van Horik and Emery 2011). Indeed, causal cognition evolved before, over the 3–4 million years that separated the last common ancestor between humans and chimpanzees from the australopithecines. Causal cognition continued to evolve, moving from spatial maps to more general causal ones. For Stuart-Fox (2015), even the evolution of political organization depends on elementary cognitive inference.

Gärdenfors and Lombard (2018, also Lombard and Gärdenfors 2017) argued that the unique cognitive causal capacity in the hominin line relates to mentally representing force dynamics. They related this notion to a seven-grade model of evolution related to causal cognition. For these authors, (a) the first grade of causal understanding is sensorimotor, e.g., a cat pawing a toy in play has an effect. The next four grades relate to causal agency and detached representations. (b) First, cued dyadic causal understanding takes place, as in rough and tumble play. (c) Next, socially, joint attention takes place, allowing conspecific mind reading. (d) Next, higher organisms can infer non-present causes, as in tracking (detached dyadic causal understanding). (e) Next, mind reading extends to non-conspecifics, e.g., a hurt animal. (f) Next, causal analysis refers to inanimate causal understanding, such as when an animal is struggling in the mud. (g) Penultimately, in grade 7, causal network understanding develops. Specifically, domain-specific causal node sets are coordinated with inter-domain causal networks. These types of cognitive advances allow for abstract causal ideation, such as in the sciences. Even earlier in modern humans, the generalizations from one type of tool use toward constructing another requires this causal cognitive skill.

Note that the grade model of causal thought evolution speaks to steps in cognitive development, and the examples provided refer to infant, child, and human behavior. However, there are gaps from the human development point of view such that the model is incomplete from that end. Abstracting from the human development point of view would give many more points toward constructing a workable model of causal thought evolution. For example, although the first grade alone is referred to as sensorimotor in the model, from the perspective of the Piagetian sensorimotor model of development, each of the first four grades in the model refers to sensorimotor behavior in infancy, either in part or in full. The next two grades refer to human childlike capacities, while the last of the seven grades refers to abstract skills in the teenager and adult.

A more complete model of causal cognition development would cover the 25 steps of the current model, and this has been accomplished in Tables 12.4, 12.5, 12.6, 12.7, 12.8, and 12.9. The model will allow for extrapolation to the ancestral and the animal/nonhuman primate contexts. In this sense, there is much more modeling to accomplish on the evolution of causal cognition. The general developmental Neo-Piagetian model on causal cognition that has been developed here is consistent with the point that developmental models provide analogies for evolutionary ones. Indeed, this assumption has permitted the writing of the present chapter.

As another comment, the grades model of causal cognition in evolution speaks to the present model of cognitive development. How does an advanced abstract causal network develop? What does it include that distinguishes it aside from lower-order cognition? In this regard, Camp and Shupe (2018) referred to the unique human characteristic of instrumental reasoning and Hoerl and McCormack (2019a, 2019b) to temporal reasoning. Relatedly, Carleton and Collard (2020) referred to nonlinear changes in causality, interventions to test it (Pearl 2009), etc. To what degree are advanced causal cognitive networks dynamically stable or unstable, and how can we test them? What about auxiliary cognitive skills that might contribute to causal analysis, such as creativity and imagination? The latter skills have accelerated in human evolution for the last 100,000 years (Wadley 2021). Also, what about cognizance of causal thinking, how it works, and its importance? This meta-cognitive awareness of causality could be part of its networked concepts and accelerate its extension. [Similarly, Tomasello (2019) referred to only humans having the meta-cognitive ability to knowingly take up roles in larger social systems.]

Are there special aspects of the brain that differentiate us from other species (see below) and play in our causal cognition uniqueness? Perhaps human uniqueness is causal cognition resides in overall organization of the brain, such as in inter-hemispheric coordination or cortical network interrelations, or even tight-diffuse organization within lobes and brain structures and over brain networks.

The present 25-step cognitive developmental model describes cognitive development, in general, and the chapter shows that it is quite applicable to causal cognition as much as any other area. The 25 "grades" in the model are more elaborate than the 7-grade model of Gärdenfors and Lombard. Once evolutionary analysis is applied to the question, a more complete model of causal cognition in evolution and human uniqueness will obtain.

Social Cognition and Sociality

Note that other cognitive abilities appear unique to human when examined as part of an organized set of cognitive skills (Laland and Seed 2021). (a) Humans are superior in mental time travel, for example, and it is enhanced by interaction with other mental abilities, including language and meta-cognition. (b) Humans have an exceptional aptitude for tool, device, and technology creation. According to Piaget (Young 2011), even children are tool-makers and adapters. It begins with learning means-end relationships and how to invent new ones, recombine them in novel ways, etc. (c) Laland and Seed (2021) add that humans express complex social cognition. We establish and work toward shared goals, while excelling in cooperation. In contrast, sharing and cooperation are not as clearly part of the chimpanzee's behavior repertoire (e.g., Tomasello 2009). Children are primed to learn by teaching and adults engage in teaching; it begins with the joint attention in infancy (Tomasello 2009). Cumulative culture learning takes place in children and not in chimpanzees (Dean et al. 2012). (d) Humans excel in problem solving. Effective problem solving in the human context requires inferential and causal reasoning, among other skills (e.g., Seed and Mayer 2017). Although chimpanzees can understand some functional or structural features of objects, they cannot reason about causality in a way that is theory-like (for instance, to determine invisible causes) (Seed and Mayer 2017). Overall, animals are limited in their generalized, systematic, and logical capacity for reasoning. (e) Humans communicate flexibly. In comparison to human communication, primate communication is comprised mostly of single, unrelated nonverbal signals that generally do not transmit more complex messages (e.g., Casar et al. 2013). Gestural communications lack symbolism and syntax (e.g., Corballis 2017), as well as the hierarchical organization in sentence structure. Overall, humans might excel cognitively because of a unique domain general capacity for processing (Heyes 2018; Laland 2018). Moreover, according to Laland and Seed (2021), our capacity for culture might be the engine that allows the consolidation of these cognitive skills in human uniqueness. Humans are able to reason abstractly across domains.

Tomasello (2019) takes a developmental perspective on the unique cognitive and social characteristics of humans. He focuses on the early years up to 5–6 years of age. His list of distinct human cognitive capacities does not include the more advanced ones listed by Laland and Seed (2021). It does not include time travel and problem solving, for example. That said, the proposed unique human cognitive capacities involve four interrelated skills: social cognition, communication, cultural learning, and cooperative thinking. Tomasello (2019) continued that humans have four distinct social skills: collaboration, prosociality, behaving according to social norms, and functioning with a moral identity. Tomasello (2019) presents research in support of each of the four distinct human characteristics that he described, including on bonobos, chimpanzees, and human infants. Relative to Laland and Seed

(2021) and my own modeling that places abstract thought at the center of human uniqueness, Tomasello (2019) is limited to the early years in hypothesizing the unique cognitive capacities of humans. That said, the acquisitions that he describes are well-supported by the empirical literature, and they set the stage for more advanced steps in thinking about human cognition and also the development of culture that might be based on that cognition.

Tomasello (2019) complemented his empirical approach to the evolution of human uniqueness with a theoretical one. In his Neo-Vygotskian model, the socio-culture provides more than expert teaching and guidance; it offers a holding frame for cooperative social practices, for example, related to cultural learning from teaching. This view is consistent with the perspective that humans inherit not only genes but also a sociocultural context. Humans express not just cooperation but hyper-cooperation. At its base is shared intentionality, and this develops through maturation, first of joint intentionality before 1 year of age and then of collective intentionality at about age 3. The maturational component to development does not work alone; shared experiential factors help development emerge. Beyond its role in early maturational influences on development, experience also creates individual differences. Furthermore, the child contributes to her/his own development through executive self-regulation processes, such as in inhibition. Moreover, toward age 3 executive regulation processes become more social as children monitor their social partners and engage in collaborative self-regulation.

Socially, humans are distinct by developing group-minded morality and not just prosociality and second-person morality (e.g., being fair). In early childhood, we develop joint commitments, and we monitor social norm violations. Even at that age, we have a "we" orientation.

As a comment, the description offered by Tomasello (2019) of the forces that work in child development appears quite biopsychosocial in nature. I would add that all three of these forces work together right from conception, with biology not privileged just after birth.

Also, he presents empirical data at age points 1, 2, 3, 4, and 5 years, while sometimes elaborating more in the first year, such as with joint attention, and sometimes giving more insight into Year 6, such as on reasoning and responsibility. I note that these ages periods are quite consistent with the present Neo-Piagetian model and the ages at which its substages emerge. That is, aside from an empirical basis for emphasizing certain age periods in the transition toward cooperative thinking and cooperative sociality, referring to developing cognitive (sub)stage models may provide additional insight, as has been the case here. Moreover, they help extend the conjectural investigation of human uniqueness across the human developmental lifespan, as has been undertaken here.

Prentiss (2021) acknowledges the value of theoretical plurality in the area. There is room developmentally in this regard, too. Tomasello (2019) has an empirically supported point of view that is consistent with a particular model for the earlier ages of childhood, while my approach comes from a different theoretical stance and makes predictions for older age groups with respect to the question at hand, so is complementary to Tomasello's.

Biology and Brain

Bauernfeind and Babbitt (2019) argued that there is no straight throughput from gene to brain, and that genotype does not lead directly to phenotype. Inter- and intraspecific molecular diversity is common in the brain. Development is influenced by non-heritable as well as heritable sources. The search for human uniqueness cannot be reduced to a biological or brain-based search. For example, in comparing human and chimpanzee brains, Gómez-Robles et al. (2015) found that the overall cortical organization of the former is less heritable than that of chimpanzees in associative areas of the brain that develop late, due to the prolonged neurodevelopmental sequence of humans. Bauernfeind and Babbitt (2019) continued that genetic control of cortical organization is more open to variation in humans to facilitate environmental, social, and cultural influences on the brain, whether at the gross level or in terms of microcircuitry. This process in brain development in humans allows for a greater degree of learning in the human case compared to other species.

The conclusion that applies here is that just as psychology is biopsychosocial, generally, the same applies to brain development, which has implications for the evolution of the brain and human distinctiveness. Further, a biopsychosocial model of evolutionary differences in brain and behavior allows for ample room for cultural differences. Moreover, the model suggests that psychosocial factors might be crucial for determining human uniqueness. Boyd (2017) argued that our uniqueness resides in culture and in our ability to form groups in this regard outside of kinship groups. Sherwood et al. (2008) referred to the uniquely human attributes of reading and writing, which are abstract (also see Gabora and Steel 2020). Laland and Chiu (2021) and Stout et al. (2019) referred to niche construction in evolution as providing avenues for cultural learning and construction. That is, evolution provides avenues for learning beyond the limits of the genes behind it, if I might simplify. These reflections indicate that culture expands in the human case to co-culture, which at its peak might be one more human exceptionality. Moreover, the developmental process is unique in humans in several ways (Finlay 2019), which might contribute to early cognitive development. First, weaning happens early compared to other primates, allowing for greater fecundity. Second, the social environment in which children are raised includes more sibling and grandparent interaction/care. Finlay (2019) makes clear that humans are not distinct cortically in terms of massive brain size relative to other species; she emphasizes the social.

Nonhuman Primates

Cultural behavior is not unique to humans (e.g., Claidière et al. 2014; Hicks et al. 2020), but humans have advanced capacities related to its contents and characteristics (e.g., products, effects, norms; Colmenares and Hernández-Lloreda 2016). Nonhuman primates create much less cumulative culture compared to humans, who do it massively (Whiten 2017). Humans can engage in massive cumulative culture through our social arrangements and cooperation (Voorhees et al. 2020).

Interim Conclusion

The literature review indicates that the exploration of the evolution of mind and culture is an active one. However, there is not new work on the steps in the process, as per the original models of Donald and Mithen. The research gives support to the present approach, including in extending the present modeling into contemporary human culture. Most important, the review covers the area of human exceptionalism, which provides the ground needed for the present approach.

Conclusion

This second last substantive chapter of the present book expands its focus well beyond development. It engages the area of culture, its evolution, and its development. It begins with a novel definition of culture, incorporating critical elements of different disciplines on the topic. It then reviews the present developmental model before presenting the cultural model extrapolated from it. The chapter emphasizes that human exceptionalism resides in its advanced abstract thinking, in particular, and the advanced cultural steps afforded by this advanced thinking. The chapter presents a model of causal co-cognition in relation to its 25-step Neo-Piagetian model.

According to the cultural developmental/evolutionary model, humans (and societies) engage in abstract thought that facilitates hyper-culture. The latter evolves from first-order to second-order, and so on. As hyper-culture complexifies, it feeds back into the individuals of the society, in a reciprocal amplification process of individual and culture at the abstract level.

With respect to the theme of causality, central to the book, the abstract thought process in humans facilitated causal thought. Indeed, causality might be a central focus of causal thought, making the characterization of humans as *Homo Causa* plausible. Future modeling and research might consider how causal cognition develops according to the present developmental model. What is its standing in each of the sensorimotor substages, for example? Piaget and Piagetians investigated the development of causality according to the substages in the sensorimotor stage (Young 2011), and contemporary causal cognition researchers (see Muentener and Bonawitz 2017) have their own methods and concepts related to causality development, but there is little bridging between the two investigative traditions on developmental causal cognition. The Neo-Piagetian model that I have developed on the 25 steps in cognitive development might afford that bridge for scaffolding child causality research with the development substage perspective. The same scaffold would work for later child, adolescent, and adult causal cognition. Finally, different areas of cognition could be reworked in terms of causal cognition, such as social causal cognition.

As for the continued innovations in this chapter, given their basis in the lifespan developmental (sub)stage model, they provide further support of the plausibility of the current modeling, and further reveal its potential outreach beyond psychology, e.g., in this case, to cultural study. The chapter refers to networks, for example, in cognition, and the concept can be applied to cultural organization, including evolutionarily (e.g., Romano et al. 2020). Future work on networks in these regards should consider combined network/systems models (Young 2015). Perhaps humans are distinct in the networked assemblages in their cultures and the hierarchical arrangement of systems that characterize their cultures. The same differences might apply to their abstract thought, their advanced causal cognition, etc.

This second last substantive chapter of the book related to its major modeling of steps in development and causality is very theoretical, like much of the book. The reader will wonder whether it has been a theoretical exercise with no testable hypotheses or empirical falsification possible. To the contrary, the modeling presents very specific steps in cultural evolution and development that informs the empirical literature in the area and indicates new avenues to pursue empirically.

The developmental model itself is highly theoretical in its inception, and now it is being applied theoretically outside of development by analogy. However, the nomological network involved solidifies with these new theoretical outreaches. For example, taking a step backward from the anthropological literature and applying the developmental model to it allowed me to re-examine the Donald and Mithen sequences on the evolution of mind, integrate them, rework them in terms of the present model, and indicate what might be missing step-wise in them. Similarly, examination of the hypothesized grades in causal cognition evolutionarily from the developmental perspective adopted in the present book allowed me to suggest how gaps in the model can be accommodated.

Generally, this has been the approach of the present book and the theoretical modeling in all four books on the topic of development, causality, and the project of unifying psychology. It begins with taking a step back, analyzing extant concepts and data, revising, reworking, and integrating them, suggesting ways gaps can be filled, or how there are gaps where none had been perceived before, and rendering the new theories and models operationalizable, testable, and falsifiable.

I am not naïve in thinking that my developmental model can be applied unequivocally to any area of psychology or other disciplines. Even in development, much takes place outside of steps, phases, or stages. Of course, workers in the area deny the existence of stages, or refute the validity of (Neo-)Piagetian, (Neo-)Eriksonian ones, or both. Beyond that, when change processes take place in any area, the five-step (substage) model that I developed might apply, as I have shown throughout my books, but might not, as well.

Returning to the question of the limits of applying the present developmental model to areas in development, psychology, or other disciplines, it is not a cookie stamp operation that applies automatically. Indeed, in the prior two chapters on defense mechanisms, it was impossible for me to apply the present developmental model to the development of defense mechanisms in terms of the development of classic ones over the 25 steps of the model.

The literature review chapters in the book indicate the value of theory, which is consistent with my approach. Only with valid theory can we take the steps forward after having taken the steps back to examine extant material in a field. I look forward to researchers examining my work from this perspective and leading the field further forward.

References

American Sociological Association: Culture. American Sociological Association, Washington (2021). https://www.asanet.org/topics/culture

Andersen, L.R.: Metamodernity: Meaning and Hope in a Complex World. Nordic Bildung, Denmark (2019)

Arden, R.: Cognitive abilities in other animals: an introduction to this special issue. Intelligence. **74**, 1–2 (2019). https://doi.org/10.1016/j.intell.2019.04.003

Bauernfeind, A.L., Babbitt, C.C.: Genetic diversity underlying behavioral plasticity in human adaptation. Prog. Brain Res. **250**, 41–58 (2019). https://doi.org/10.1016/bs.pbr.2019.06.002

Bender, A.: The role of culture and evolution for human cognition. Top. Cogn. Sci. **12**(4), 1403–1420 (2020). https://doi.org/10.1111/tops.12449

Bender, A., Beller, S.: The cultural fabric of human causal cognition. Perspect. Psychol. Sci. **14**(6), 922–940 (2019). https://doi.org/10.1177/1745691619863055

Bertman, S.: Hyperculture: the Human Cost of Speed. Praeger, Westport (1998)

Bertman, S.: Pursuing humanistic medicine in a technological age. J. Pat. Exp. **4**(2), 57–60 (2017). https://doi.org/10.1177/2374373517699269

Boyd, R.: The evolution of human uniqueness. Spa. J. Psychol. **19**, E97 (2017). https://doi.org/10.1017/sjp.2016.98

Camp, E., Shupe, E.: Instrumental reasoning in nonhuman animals. In: Andrews, K., Beck, J. (eds.) The Routledge Handbook of Philosophy of Animal Minds, 1st edn, pp. 100–108. Routledge, New York (2018)

Carleton, W.C., Collard, M.: Recent major themes and research areas in the study of human-environment interaction in prehistory. Environ. Archaeol. **25**(1), 114–130 (2020). https://doi.org/10.1080/14614103.2018.1560932

Caro, M.J., Murphy, J.W. (eds.): The World of Quantum Culture (Illustrated ed.). Praeger, Westport (2002)

Casar, C., Zuberbühler, K., Young, R.J., Byrne, R.W.: Titi monkey call sequences vary with predator location and type. Biol. Lett. **9**(5), 20130535 (2013). https://doi.org/10.1098/rsbl.2013.0535

Claidière, N., Smith, K., Kirby, S., Fagot, J.: Cultural evolution of systematically structured behaviour in a non-human primate. Proc. R. Soc. B Biol. Sci. **281**(1797), 1–9 (2014). https://doi.org/10.1098/rspb.2014.1541

Colmenares, F., Hernández-Lloreda, M.V.: Cognition and culture in evolutionary context. Spa. J. Psychol. **19**, E101 (2016). https://doi.org/10.1017/sjp.2016.102

Corballis, M.C.: The Truth About Language: What It Is and Where It Came From. University of Chicago Press, Chicago (2017)

Corballis, M.C.: Humanity and the left hemisphere: the story of half a brain. Later. Asymmet. Brain Behav. Cogn. **26**, 19 (2020). https://doi.org/10.1080/1357650X.2020.1782929

Dean, L.G., Kendal, R.L., Schapiro, S.J., Thierry, B., Laland, K.N.: Identification of the social and cognitive processes underlying human cumulative culture. Science. **335**(6072), 1114–1118 (2012). https://doi.org/10.1126/science.1213969

Donald, M.: The sapient paradox: can cognitive neuroscience solve it? Brain. **132**(3), 820–824 (2009). https://doi.org/10.1093/brain/awn290

Finlay, B.L.: Human exceptionalism, our ordinary cortex and our research futures. Dev. Psychobiol. **61**(3), 317–322 (2019). https://doi.org/10.1002/dev.21838

Gabora, L., Steel, M.: A model of the transition to behavioural and cognitive modernity using reflexively autocatalytic networks. J. R. Soc. Interface. **17**(171), 20200545 (2020). https://doi.org/10.1098/rsif.2020.0545

Gärdenfors, P., Lombard, M.: Causal cognition, force dynamics and early hunting technologies. Front. Psychol. **9**, 87 (2018). https://doi.org/10.3389/fpsyg.2018.00087

Gómez-Robles, A., Hopkins, W.D., Schapiro, S.J., Sherwood, C.C.: Relaxed genetic control of cortical organization in human brains compared with chimpanzees. Proc. Natl. Acad. Sci. U. S. A. **112**(48), 14799–14804 (2015). https://doi.org/10.1073/pnas.1512646112

Gonzalez-Cabrera, I.: Cognitive gadgets: the cultural evolution of thinking press. Hist. Philos. Life Sci. **42**, 13 (2020). https://doi.org/10.1007/s40656-020-00306-1

Haidle, M.N.: Building a bridge – an archeologist's perspective on the evolution of causal cognition. Front. Psychol. **5**, 1472 (2014). https://doi.org/10.3389/fpsyg.2014.01472

Heyes, C.: Cognitive Gadgets: The Cultural Evolution of Thinking. Belknap Press: An Imprint of Harvard University Press, Cambridge (2018)

Hicks, T.C., Kühl, H.S., Boesch, C., Menken, S.B.J., Hart, J., Roessingh, P., Ewango, C., Mundry, R.: The relationship between tool use and prey availability in chimpanzees (pan troglodytes schweinfurthii) of northern democratic republic of congo. Int. J. Primatol. **41**(6), 936–959 (2020). https://doi.org/10.1007/s10764-020-00149-4

Hoerl, C., McCormack, T.: Temporal updating, temporal reasoning, and the domain of time. Behav. Brain Sci. **42**, E278 (2019a). https://doi.org/10.1017/s0140525x19001195

Hoerl, C., McCormack, T.: Thinking in and about time: a dual systems perspective on temporal cognition. Behav. Brain Sci. **42**, E244 (2019b). https://doi.org/10.1017/s0140525x18002157

van Horik, J., Emery, N.J.: Evolution of cognition. WIREs Cogn. Sci. **2**(6), 621–633 (2011). https://doi.org/10.1002/wcs.144

Hudelson, P.M.: Culture and quality: an anthropological perspective. Int. J. Qual. Health Care. **16**(5), 345–346 (2004). https://doi.org/10.1093/intqhc/mzh076

Laland, K.: What made us unique: how we became a different kind of animal. Sci. Am. **319**(3), 32–39 (2018). https://doi.org/10.1038/scientificamerican0918-32

Laland, K., Chiu, L.L.K.: Evolution's Engineers. Aeon (2021). https://aeon.co/essays/organisms-are-not-passive-recipients-of-evolutionary-forces

Laland, K., Seed, A.: Understanding human cognitive uniqueness. Annu. Rev. Psychol. **72**, 689–716 (2021). https://doi.org/10.1146/annurev-psych-062220-051256

Leavens, D.A., Reamer, L.A., Mareno, M.C., Russell, J.L., Wilson, D., Schapiro, S.J., Hopkins, W.D.: Distal communication by chimpanzees (pan troglodytes): evidence for common ground? Child Dev. **86**(5), 1623–1638 (2015). https://doi.org/10.1111/cdev.12404

Lombard, M., Gärdenfors, P.: Tracking the evolution of causal cognition in humans. J. Anthropol. Sci. **95**, 219–234 (2017). https://doi.org/10.4436/jass.95006

MacLean, E.L.: Unraveling the evolution of uniquely human cognition. Proc. Natl. Acad. Sci. **113**(23), 6348–6354 (2016). https://doi.org/10.1073/pnas.1521270113

Marean, C.W.: An evolutionary anthropological perspective on modern human origins. Annu. Rev. Anthropol. **44**, 533–556 (2015). https://doi.org/10.1146/annurev-anthro-102313-025954

McGrew, W.C.: Is primate tool use special? Chimpanzee and New Caledonian crow compared. Philos. Trans. R. Soc. Lond. B Biol. Sci. **368**(1630), 20120422 (2013). https://doi.org/10.1098/rstb.2012.0422

Mithen, S.: Seven steps in the evolution of the human imagination. In: Roth, I. (ed.) Imaginative Minds, vol. 147. British Academy Scholarship Online, Oxford (2007). https://doi.org/10.5871/bacad/9780197264195.003.0001

Muentener, P., Bonawitz, E.B.: The development of causal reasoning. In: Waldmann, M.R. (ed.) The Oxford Handbook of Causal Reasoning, pp. 677–698. Oxford University Press, New York (2017)

Orshan, S.A.: Acculturation, perceived social support, and self-esteem in primigravida puertorican teenagers. West. J. Nurs. Res. **18**(4), 460–473 (1996). https://doi.org/10.1177/019394599601800407

Pearl, J.: Causality: *Models, reasoning, and inference* (2nd ed.). New York: Cambridge University Press (2009)

Povinelli, D.J., Bering, J.M.: The mentality of apes revised. Curr. Dir. Psychol. Sci. **11**(4), 115–119 (2002). https://doi.org/10.1111/1467-8721.00181

Prentiss, A.M.: Theoretical plurality, the extended evolutionary synthesis, and archaeology. Proc. Natl. Acad. Sci. **118**(2), e200656418 (2021). https://doi.org/10.1073/pnas.2006564118

Roberts, B.W., Vander Linden, M.: Investigating Archaeological Cultures: Material Culture, Variability, and Transmission. Springer, New York (2011)

Romano, V., Lozano, S., Fernández-López de Pablo, J.: A multilevel analytical framework for studying cultural evolution in prehistoric hunter–gatherer societies. Biol. Rev. **95**(4), 1020–1035 (2020). https://doi.org/10.1111/brv.12599

Seed, A.M., Mayer, C.: Problem solving. In: Call, J. (ed.) APA Handbook of Comparative Psychology, vol. 2, pp. 601–625. American Psychological Association, Washington (2017)

Sherwood, C.C., Subiaul, F., Zawidzki, T.W.: A natural history of the human mind: tracing evolutionary changes in brain and cognition. J. Anat. **212**(4), 426–454 (2008). https://doi.org/10.1111/j.1469-7580.2008.00868.x

Spocter, M.A., Sherwood, C.C., Schapiro, S.J., Hopkins, W.D.: Reproducibility of leftward planum temporale asymmetries in two genetically isolated populations of chimpanzees (pan troglodytes). Proc. R. Soc. B Biol. Sci. **287**(1934), 20201320 (2020). https://doi.org/10.1098/rspb.2020.1320

Steensland, B.: Sociology of culture. In: Oxford Bibliographies Online Datasets (2011). https://doi.org/10.1093/obo/9780199756384-0055

Stout, D., Rogers, M.J., Jaeggi, A.V., Semaw, S.: Archaeology and the origins of human cumulative culture: a case study from the earliest Oldowan at Gona, Ethiopia. Curr. Anthropol. **60**(3), 309–340 (2019). https://doi.org/10.1086/703173

Stuart-Fox, M.: The origins of causal cognition in early hominins. Biol. Philos. **30**, 247–266 (2015). https://doi.org/10.1007/s10539-014-9462-y

Tomasello, M.: Why We Cooperate. MIT Press, Cambridge (2009)

Tomasello, M.: Becoming Human: A Theory of Ontogeny. The Belknap Press of Harvard University Press, Cambridge (2019)

Tomasello, M., Carpenter, M.: Shared intentionality. Dev. Sci. **10**(1), 121–125 (2007). https://doi.org/10.1111/j.1467-7687.2007.00573.x

Vaesen, K.: The cognitive bases of human tool use. Behav. Brain Sci. **35**(4), 203–218 (2012). https://doi.org/10.1017/S0140525X11001452

Van den Bos, G.R. (ed.): APA Dictionary of Psychology, 2nd edn. American Psychological Association, Washington (2015)

Voorhees, B., Read, D., Gabora, L.: Identity, kinship, and the evolution of cooperation. Curr. Anthropol. **61**(2), 194–218 (2020). https://doi.org/10.1086/708176

de Waal, F.: Are We Smart Enough to Know How Smart Animals Are? W. W. Norton & Company, New York (2017)

Wadley, L.: What stimulated rapid, cumulative innovation after 100,000 years ago? J. Archaeol. Method Theory. **28**, 120 (2021). https://doi.org/10.1007/s10816-020-09499-y

Whiten, A.: Social learning and culture in child and chimpanzee. Annu. Rev. Psychol. **68**, 129–154 (2017). https://doi.org/10.1146/annurev-psych-010416-044108

Wolpert, L.: Causal belief and the origins of technology. Philosophical Transcations of the Royal Society A: Mathematical. Phys. Eng. Sci. **361**(1809), 1709–1719 (2003). https://doi.org/10.1098/rsta.2003.1231

Young, G.: Development and Causality: Neo-Piagetian Perspectives. Springer Science + Business Media, New York (2011)

Young, G.: Causality in psychiatry: a hybrid symptom network construct model. Front. Psychiatr. **6**, 164 (2015). https://doi.org/10.3389/fpsyt.2015.00164

Young, G.: Unifying Causality and Psychology: Being, Brain and Behavior. Springer International Publishing, Cham (2016)

Young, G.: Causality and Development: Neo-Eriksonian Perspectives. Springer International Publishing, Cham (2019)

Chapter 13
Applying Transemics to Development, Culture, Causality, and Unifying Psychology

Transemic initiated with a book by Canda and Furman (1999). Canda and Furman (1999) coined the term transemic, but it has been rarely cited since and not in the psychological context. So, the term in psychology is relatively novel, as described in this book. It has been cited only in a handful of subsequent publications. It refers to seeking common ground. Canda and Furman (1999) introduced the term as a constant self-reflection in members from different cultures or views, and an appreciation of diversity. In anthropology, there are particular emic (cultural) perspectives, and the etic or global perspective. In transemics, the particulars are "brought into interaction and dialogue" (Canda and Furman 1999, p. 39) in a process that affirms both the universal and specific aspects involved. Universals are really particulars on closer inspection, at least for spirituality, the topic of their book. Canda and Furman (1999) introduced the term as a constant self-reflection in members from different cultures or views, and an appreciation of diversity.

This chapter takes the concept of transemics farther, as shall be shown, focusing on the dialogical interaction involved. As described in this book, transemics concerns the overarching exchange and interexchange process that takes place in living matter but especially in cultures and in human development. It involves exchanges over four dimensions:

1. The constant interplay of the general and the specific, or whole and constituent parts.
2. The classic dialectic of opposites is inherent in the part-whole, global-particular dialogue. The opposites could be oppositions, with two or more perspectives on the validity along the cardinal continuum of global-specific and whole-part relations.
3. The interactions between parts of a system themselves, tiers of a system themselves, systems with other systems, etc.
4. The interactions between entities and context.

G. Young, *Causality and Neo-Stages in Development*,
https://doi.org/10.1007/978-3-030-82540-9_13

Transemics has the potential to broaden the scope of extant theories by including it in their rubric and by helping pose questions about them that could expand their details and scope. In this regard, this present work focuses on the Young books on unifying psychology, causality, and development (Young 2011, 2016, 2019, the present one).

In his work, Young described causality as a potential unifying axis in psychology. He referred to the causal models of the biopsychosocial, systems, networks, and activation-inhibition coordination. However, the modeling lacked a unifying focus, although Young referred to the hybridization of the models (Young 2015).

In this book, Young has referred to unifying terms of causal factors involving two components: activation-inhibition coordination and relational co-control or co-regulation. In addition, he referred to psychological energetics (which in retrospect could have been referred to as relational energetics for sake of consistency). He was attempting to integrate diverse causal terms into the one common denominator among them. The transemic concept might provide further means of integrating these causal concepts (and in manageable ways), as attempted in the present work.

In this book, Young also referred to intraaction, which connotes co-relational entities that exchange reciprocally communication, ideas, material, etc. The term is similar to transemic but is missing its transformative nature in the exchanges involved. Note that Barad (2007) developed a similar concept independently of Young, but preceding it.

As for human development, in this book, Young has described a neo-stage conception that attempts to reposition Neo-Piagetian and Neo-Eriksonian development in one integrated model with five stages and five cyclically recurring substages. Despite the generality and reach of the model, it still is not enough to explain transemic, which is more generalized in its causal function.

For example, systems theory argues that causality is inherent in the workings of the system, and that there are not extraneous variables or factors working on it, aside from the contextual. Network theory is somewhat the same, in that it seeks the nodes and links in a system, and how they drive the system causally. While relevant, these notions lack the specificity inherent in the transemic function and its depth.

Detailing Transemic

The description of the concept of transemic is given at multiple levels. The description of transemic is admittedly very broad. In effect, it is presently described as referring to a generalized mechanism of change in behavior, whether we concern ourselves with individuals or collectives of any sort, from cultural to societal to political. As well, it refers to change processes in inanimate matter, but that aspect is not much developed in this present work.

The reader will find poetics at one point in this section that is explaining transemic in more depth, in that straightforward declarative sentences have their limitations. On the one hand, the transemic concept speaks to all psychologies, including the indigenous and the non-Western. On the other hand, transemic, by definition, is about the interchange and discourse between and among all individuals, all cultures, and all societies. How are the individual differences preserved and validated in all these regards; how do they contribute, create, and get feedback from the universal and global, further differentiating in the process; and how does all this work together toward creating a more human humanity (and one that continues to grow and deal with the crises that the times will always offer)?

General

Transemic is an overriding concept on change and moving between change states. It is a mechanism that cuts across and integrates other change mechanisms in behavior. Transemic is a process of change, but its actioning might lead to the inverse, or of conservation of stability, in any system that is involved.

Transemic relates not only to psychology, anthropology, sociology, and associated disciplines but also to broader ones, such as philosophy, epistemology, and ontology. It relates to the concept of neo-constructivism, neo-rationalism, and their integration in neo-ratioconstructivism (per this book). It denotes how knowledge is acquired and the nature of knowledge, especially in the behavioral disciplines. It is not only part realistic, actuality, positivistic, and empirical but also part constructivist and possibility as well as imaginary. It is part sentence and part story, part narrative and part narrator; it is a dialogical, discursive, dialectic, and hermeneutical, like science and art themselves.

Transemic is part general and part specific, and part integrative whole and part differentiated in the whole. It is part whole and part part, or part pastiche and part particle, reflecting the different tiers of a system and how they interrelate. The distinctions between the global and specific and the whole and the part are complementary ways of viewing transemic.

Transemic is a dialogue of idea and counter idea, of concept and counter concept, of theory and counter theory, and of holism and fractionation at all these levels. The dialectic enabled could involve polar opposites that eventually integrate.

Poetics and the Profane

Transemic deals with certainties and uncertainties, part known and part unknown. It is not only part analytically factual and part data but also part holistic and part construction. It deals not only with part mechanical and the mundane but also with part mythic and mystery. It is indigenous psychologies as much as mainstream psychology, and the different narratives in otherness culturally and scientifically.

It is not only part declarative and scientific, but also part artistic and creative. Transemic is more than the rational, the verbal, and the sequential because it is also the emotional, the musical, and the poetic. Transemic is culture; it is contact and essence, participation and growing through, sharing and caring, and telling the other with the prosody and tenor that accompany words.

Transemic is universal yet particular, at once separate, but unified. It is meaning and voice, with none privileged but all respectful (although destructive and hateful narratives should be recognized and vociferously denounced). It is an invitation to the other, the other side, alterity, in the present time toward creating new, more adaptive and inclusive story and respecting and integrating past stories.

Transemic is harmony and healing, hope and health, yet also the harmed and the hurt, and suffering and need (and reaching out and reaching in toward finding compassion and the motivation to action). It is appropriation and cultural rape, yet repatriation and cultural sharing. It is sanctity and sanctuary, spiritual and spirited, yet dislocation and discrimination, racism and riots, murder and torture, genocide and homicide, refugee and refuged, and colonialism and post-colonialism. It is death and destruction, yet resuscitation and resurrection, revitalization and reconciliation, and consilience and conciliation.

It is shaman and respect, schizophrenia and disrespect, responsibility and re-responsibility, and how we are, were, and will be. It is difference and union, fusion and diffusion, individualization and communion, inner isolation and contentment yet inspired elevation and revelation.

Mechanisms

Transemic has been described expansively to this point, with little information provided how the interactions and transformations might take place. Essentially, transemic functions according to simultaneous application of and differences in: (1) globality/wholeness and particularities/parts, as emphasized to this point in the present work, as well as; (2.1) engaging in the change process; (2.2) union and differentiation; (2.3) integrating and disintegrating; (2.4) lower-order and higher-order components and levels; (2.5) quality versus quantity (unitary, dual, multiple); and (3) all of the above in the nexus with context; for example, (3.1) is the transemics about context uniquely and is not related to entities; or, (3.2) if is it about entity-context relations, is the context supportive or otherwise? (4) Overall, transemics takes place through transemification and it can be represented narratively in this book.

Interim Summary

Transemic is a new term for the psychological literature that speaks to its general and theoretical thrust, while not discounting psychology's particulars and empirical side. Transemics appreciates and encourages a continual exchange at these levels. It applies to cultural development and to human development, in particular, but applies to the causal underpinnings in or change processes of systems generally.

The concept of transemic change can complement the major themes in the work by Young by providing a common change mechanism. Moreover, its roots in terms of its origin terms (emic, etic) in anthropology and related disciplines speak to the generality of the concept and the ways it can help understand causality inter-disciplinarily.

Recent Research Supportive of the General Themes of the Book

Steps of Change

Chen (2021) and Létourneau et al. (2021) both used a five-step model of how university/college students acquire skills. Both five-step sequences are consistent with the present five-step change model, as shall be shown in their presentation.

For Chen, the skills related to collaborative learning in an ESL program, concentrating on communication competence and a collaborative mindset. Chen (2021) applied the five-step model for scientific literacy and instructional effectiveness that had been constructed by Bybee (1997; Bybee et al. 2006), which is referred to as the 5-E model. Létourneau et al. (2021) referred to the five-step nursing caring instructional/practice model as presented in Haag-Heitman (1999) and Paragas (2019). They used these sources to develop a five-stage model in the development of nursing clinical competency.

Chen (2021) referred to the first stage in university learning skill development in the group context as engagement. (a) The stage of student engagement involves instruction and guidance toward creating motivation, interest, and curiosity. The phase also accesses prior knowledge. This stage indicates a coordination through juxtaposition of prior and present knowledge being learned. (b) The second stage in the model is referred to as exploration. It involves concrete trial and error learning, active inquiry, and connecting prior knowledge to new knowledge. Clearly, this is equivalent to the step of hierarchization in the present model. (c) In the third step of explanation, the students are capable of understanding and developing reflective concepts, or articulating specific and accurate ideas in their own words. This description is consistent with the present step of systematization, the third one in the current model. (d) Next, in elaboration, the students learn to apply their concepts to real-word problems and apply them to other content areas, receiving feedback and persisting all the while. This step in the Bybee/Chen model is consistent with the multiplication phase in Young's work. (e) The fifth step in the latter model is referred to as evaluation, which involves presenting their work, self-assessing, and getting feedback and remaining open to continuous learning. This step is partially the same as in the former model, which emphasizes integration in its fifth step. Presumably, the feedback self-assessment and continuous learning lead to this cognitive and experiential outcome.

Létourneau et al. (2021) referred to the development of caring in nursing students and graduated nurses over the years of their education and practice, unlike the Chen (2021), which applied to one course. (a) The first step in the learning involves a conscientization to humanization in care. This refers to a sensitization process in the first year of nursing study. For example, the personhood of the patient is respected, the student puts themselves in the patient's shoes, the student notices dehumanization processes, in the workplace. Here, the present first-stage of coordination is seen in the juxtaposition of student and patient and humanization and dehumanization. (b) The second step in the nursing student trajectory concerns assimilation of communication skills integrated into a humanistic approach. The student relates the ideal humanistic care of the patient with the one actually used in practice. They subordinate this communication to other types of care, including biophysical health assessments and procedures in care. Clearly, the process is akin to the present one of hierarchization. (c) In the third nursing care learning and application stage, the newly graduated nurses engage in reconciliation of an ideal humanistic practice with the responsibilities of nursing work. They confront the duality that their humanization ideals and the reality of the work environment that does not place those ideals at the head of practice values. Here, the nurse is systematizing the learned and the applied, while continuing to work with an ideal as a background. This is somewhat the same as the present description of the third stage in the change process as systematization. It would better apply to the nurse who has engaged in the duality and systematizes it. Létourneau et al. (2021) referred to integration in this phase, and even the next one, which is premature according to the present model. (d) Integration of a humanistic approach in nursing care. The nurse adjusts her humanizing practice, expands it throughout the little details of practice, dialogues with peers, etc. This step resembles the present one of multiplication. (e) Mastery of a humanistic approach in the nursing work environment. The nurse embodies a transformative humanistic imperative in all aspects of his work. The adjective of integration applies well to this last step in the nursing learning trajectory, making it quite consistent with the present model in which integration is the penultimate step in the change process.

The two sequences of learning and application in education that have been analyzed (Chen 2021; Létourneau et al. 2021) both involve five steps. Both have been shown to be consistent with the present five-step change process. This justifies applying the model to other areas of change.

Note that the descriptions of the five steps in each case is not inclusive of all the details in the two articles under discussion, but enough is given to demonstrate the equivalence of the two index models with the present one. Also, note that the present work has used the two sequences in further elaboration on them, as presented later on in the chapter, in order to develop a five-step sequence in humanization, and changed some of the labels for the two sequences accordingly in presenting them.

Other Themes

Mascolo (2021) has described a model that he considered moving toward a unified meta-model for psychology. It is very similar to Young's approach (Young 2011, 2016, 2019, this book), for example, in using terms similar to the biopsychosocial model. It refers to systems theory, with its concepts of emergence and hierarchical levels that are bottom-up and top-down. It does not refer to attractors in this regard, so it is not as complex as Young's model. It does not get into networks, as with in Young's model. But it gets into relationism much like in Young's modeling. Specifically, it values the intersubjective as the seat of knowing and psychological activity. Intersubjectivity is the process of interactional coordinating, sharing, and incorporating mutually, and it is expressed already right after birth. Partners in social relations mutually co-regulate. Language constitutes semiotic mediators in this process. Personhood is relational.

An abundant published literature exists on the major themes of the book, and it grows daily. Here, the chapter refers to the most recent articles published since the literature review conducted in Chap. 9. For unification, there are no broad recently published articles but different areas are being integrated. Inzlicht et al. (2021) integrated different models of self-regulation and differentiated the term from self-control. Strand (2020) integrated attachment theory and culture, showing that a learning-based approach is useful in this regard. Scholarship related to Piaget and Erikson continues, although admittedly sparse. Choifer (2021) worked on Piagetian approaches to false belief task performance, and van Halen et al. (2020) worked on Eriksonian approaches to self-definitional identity over the adult lifespan. The work on causality is endless. Michaels et al. (2021) applied nonlinear dynamical systems theory to personality. de Boer et al. (2021) applied network theory to the relationship of psychiatric symptoms and environment. de Haan (2020) helped specify what would make the biopsychosocial model more mechanistic enactively. Kievit (2020) explored sensitive, mutualistic periods in cognitive development, and Sullivan and Opendak (2020) explored sensitive periods in early neurobehavioral function. Lou et al. (2019) examined brain scanning differences in different cultures, which have implications neuro-psychiatrically and cognitively.

Transemics in Action

Five Steps

Figure 13.1 presents a visual representation of the dynamic change process in its underlying five steps of change. It refers to attractors and complex adaptive systems, which has been emphasized as the driver of the change process in this book. At the same time, the figure expands the concept by including the transemic process of change with the model's purview. The first major column of the figure is based on

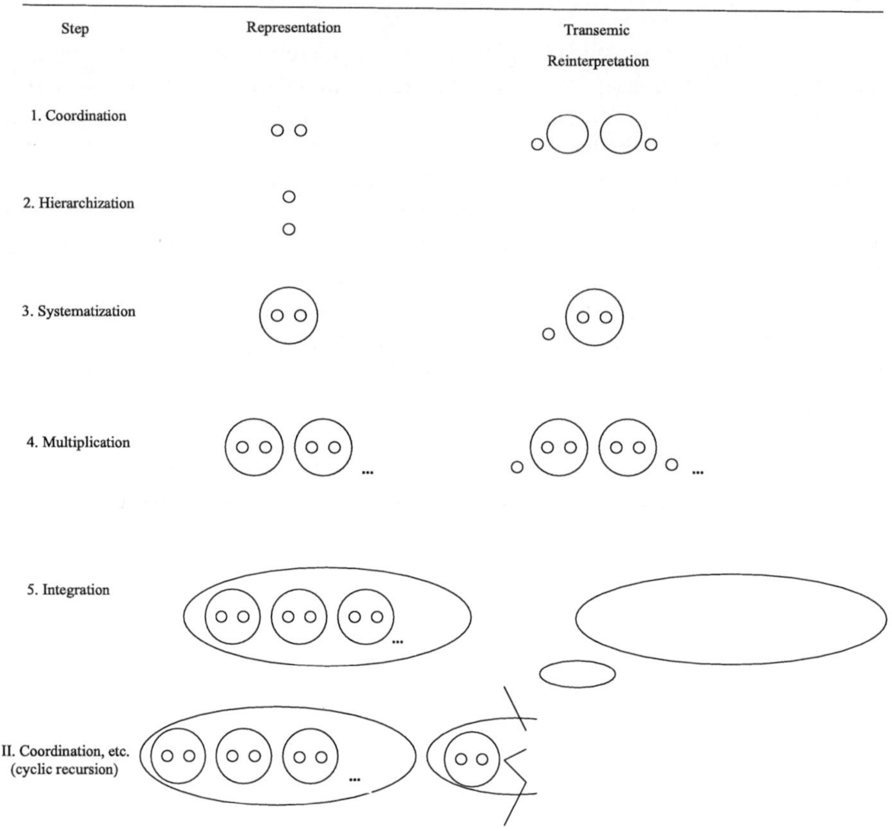

Fig. 13.1 The five-step change model graphed transemically**.
**The second and sixth steps not represented because of space limitations, but their pattern would be consistent with the general one.
The major column on the left graphically depicts the five-step change process as traditionally conceived. The column to the right alters the depiction to accommodate transemic processes. The explanation that follows applies to the traditional account of the change process. The text explains the revised version of the change process to account for the global/whole-particularity/part distinction inherent to transemics
As mental schemas emerge and spread within a particular domain of a particular stage of cognitive development, they should first be juxtaposed in coordination, then hierarchized with one predominant, and then systematized into a new rule. Next, they should spread out or multiply throughout the system, leading to integration of a generalized rule that covers all exemplars within the individual's particular cognitive development for the stage at issue
This five-step sequence might correspond to changes in attractor/complexity organization. That is, attractors might gravitate from fixed point to oscillatory and chaotic ones and then to more complex architecture involving the cusp of change to complex adaptive systems and superordinate complex systems. This model has been applied to substage changes in Young's (2011)

depicting the five step of change as originally developed without addition of the transemic change process. This depiction does not include the globality/locality and whole/part distinctions, which are critical to transemics. The second major column of the figure presents an altered visual graphing of the five steps of change in attractors and complex adaptive systems with the addition of the transemic process to complement it. The global/whole particularity/part distinction in the transemic process is represented by adding smaller circles next to or within the representations of attractors and complex adaptive systems, or doubling them up, as well. The figure prepares the way for a description of the change process through the five steps of the change model with the addition of the global/whole particularity/part distinction. This idea opened up for me a whole new avenue of thinking about change processes, as per the table that follows.

Hypothetical Examples of Transemic Growth

Table 13.1 presents hypothetical trajectories in human development and in group/cultural development according to a transemic analysis applied to the five-step change model and for the abstract stage only for purposes of illustration. The table presents the two examples in terms of the five-step generic change model but amplifies them in terms of causal transemic processes of change, which necessarily adds the globality/universality/whole versus individuality/specificity/part distinction. Thus, the examples provided are different than similar ones in prior work by Young, including in this book. The examples refer to the teen engaging with peer groups and a minority culture seeking its rights. The equivalence of the change processes in the two examples indicates the generic nature of the change model and the similarity in the applicability of the globality/universality/whole versus individuality/specificity/part distinction for the two series.

Table 13.2 presents an integrated model of learning and application of humanization according to the five-step change model. First, the table elaborated a combined model of humanization-dehumanization based on the learning/education five-step series of Chen (2021) and Létourneau et al. (2021), as presented above. Then, it created a combined model for humanization learning using their terms but having them be consistent with the present five-step change model. Then, it described the five steps in the process of learning/education for humanization, while referring to

Fig. 13.1 (continued) Neo-Piagetian cognitive developmental model. Also, it might apply to both higher (e.g., stage) and lower levels (i.e., domain transitions) as they move through the phases of coordination (after pre-coordination), hierarchization, systematization, multiplication, and integration, with a cyclic recursion potentially taking place after that
In another example, the attractor/complexity model can be applied to disorder/disability or competing health trajectories so that the states of health and disorder/dysfunction/disability involved could be seen to pass through five steps of change from a simpler coordination to a quite stable integration. (Adapted from Young 2016 [Figure 37.3, p. 913]. The major column to the left is from this book. The major column to the right is new)

Table 13.1 The present five-step generic change model complemented by additions according to transemics

Step	Brief standard explanation (No transemics)	Elaborated transemic explanation (Transemic causality added)	Applications	
			Human development	Group development
Coordination	Two models juxtaposed	Models analyzed for separately for global-particular and whole-part relations in order to facilitate comparison	After his family moves to a new neighborhood, teen considers new peer groups at new school in relation to ones at old school. Examines both for advantages and disadvantages in how he fits into the groups and how the groups would let him be himself. This procedure could take place explicitly or implicitly as the teen navigates his new social world	Minority with history of colonial or racial discrimination takes steps toward resurrection and resistance. New cultural relations and societal structures are envisioned and investigated. The majority does not cede easily its historically determined advantages. The minority dissects the majority global control techniques and the specifics involved in keeping their minority and others under control, while defining its aspirations and new freedoms pathway
Hierarchization	One hierarchized as predominant	Models compared and contrasted according to the global-whole/particular-part distinction	Teen hangs out with both sets of groups, sometimes preferring one or the other, always with an eye on how she fits in globally and how she can be herself	The minority concentrates on legal rights as fought in the courts, but the movement gains steam across the board, including in public demonstrations and actions. Those had been piecemeal and spontaneous in the prior step. The minority's advance to get equality takes decades and there is resistance, with the majority not ceding quickly enough. It protects its globality and keeps minorities in check
Systematization	New system created subsuming both	The systematization of the models includes an overarching globality/specificity and whole/part modeling	Teen creates a web of some of his peer groups, realizing each had advantages and disadvantages for group integration and self-differentiation	The minority gains legal victories in some domains such as voter registration, schooling. There is a core of systemic action that has been effective toward the primary goal

(continued)

Table 13.1 (continued)

Step	Brief standard explanation (No transemics)	Elaborated transemic explanation (Transemic causality added)	Applications	
			Human development	Group development
Multiplication	Other extant models reworked into system	Once systematized, the new model is applied to other domains beyond the original from which it emanated, with an eye on the globality/ whole-particular-part dynamic	Teen (adult) adopts same attitude for the other peer groups and is open to new ones, such as school clubs and new friends in her new neighborhood. She uses the same global/ whole versus particular/part analytics	Society-Wide Gains. The minority is quite organized now and spreads out its successful strategies in the core domains addressed governmentally and in the courts, while meeting resistance all the while. Global dynamics change in majority-minority relations and the minority continues to demand respect and public acceptance in all spheres
Integration	Integrated model developed	An inclusive model develops over domains and it incorporates as a major axis the globality/ whole-particularity/ part transemic	Adult creates a more unified social web of connections with peers, being able to self-locate in the one that makes sense at any particular time and according to the implicit or explicit analytics invoked of the groups at the global/ whole-particular/part dynamic	Minority status and rights respected and preserved in governmental and institutional spheres, but a constant vigilance and indeed struggle to preserve those gains, including against the backdrop of portions of society who resist the gains
Superordinate Abstract Coordination	Cycle repeats. Ultimately, new models at advanced levels might be integrated into an overarching hyper framework	The new model is ready for further progress by ones developed in other ways and in other ways inter-coordinating with the one so constructed but always from an analysis of the global-whole/ particular/part transemic	Five-step process repeats in the multiple. For example, for the teen, the group integrations now involve adults and the groups are not just close peers but university mates, work mates, society groupings, etc. For the minorities, the globality particularity and whole-part relations that define themselves relative to the majority are reworked at all levels, and not just the basic governmental and institutional rights, such as in cultural integrity and integration, preserving the culture to accompany government, legal, and related gains, etc.	

Adapted from Young (2016) [First and Second Column in Table 35.4, p. 867]. Overall, it is adapted

Table 13.2 Humanization education and implementation according to the five-step change model

Step in change model	ESL learning (Chen 2021)	Nursing learning (Létourneau et al. 2021)	Humanization education and implementation: Step in humanization model	Humanization education and implementation: Explanation
Coordination	Engagement	Sensitization to humanistic skills in care	Sensitized engagement in humanization and dehumanization	The person or group is exposed to existing dehumanization practices and ideal humanization ones in contrast. Among other processes, the person or group engages in a global/whole versus particular/part analysis to understand the juxtaposition
Hierarchization	Exploration	Subordination of humanistic skills in care	Dominance–subordination of humanization/ dehumanization	The person or group places one or the other of humanization and dehumanization at the apex in a dominant–subordinate relationship Education continues to make the humanization doctrine primary in these regards, if not achieved spontaneously. The ins and outs of the global-whole/particular/ part dynamic helps in this process
Systematization	Explanation	Reconciliation in ideas and practice in humanistic care	Reconciliation of humanization/ dehumanization	The person or group forms a coherent structure that reconciliates humanization and dehumanization. The truth and reconciliation process in subjugated minorities reflects this step in the model. The global-whole/particular-part transemic helps in the reconciliation here, for example, in having the person or group see how the majority discriminated against, marginalized, and suppressed the minority

(continued)

Table 13.2 (continued)

Step in change model	ESL learning (Chen 2021)	Nursing learning (Létourneau et al. 2021)	Humanization education and implementation	
			Step in humanization model	Explanation
Multiplication	Elaboration	Adjusting and detailing humanistic care	Elaboration/ adjustment of humanization	The person or group takes the lessons learned on humanization and spreads its values into the different areas to which it is applicable, from the personal, to the social, to the societal. The transemic process is applied to each application, and they move forward in parallel
Integration	Evaluative integration	Mastery of humanistic skills in care	Mastery of humanization	The person or group has widely mastered the humanization imperative and puts it into practice as new avenues for it opens up. The person or group considers global versus specific and whole versus part transemics in arriving at solutions and satisfactions.

the transemic process, as well. Therefore, the humanization model integrates other five-step models, creates a new five-step sequence consistent with the present modeling, and integrates transemics in the change process leading from one step of the model to the next. In a certain sense, Table 13.2 constitutes an apex contribution to the Young work, illustrating both the value of the models developed in the Young books and how they can be added to by considering the transemic process that is novel to the field and emphasized in this chapter.

Note that the humanization education model presented in Table 13.2 is a practical contribution. It suggests an outline of the steps in the learning process that individuals and groups might navigate as they move toward an integrated humanization. The curriculum might take a while to set up, but referring to Chen (2021) and Létourneau et al. (2021) will help in this regard. Creating a program like this can help in the decolonialization process as well. Indeed, it can help in sensitizing to indigenous psychologies and related issues. This would include their penetration in the fabric of society, e.g., training on aboriginal and first nation rights, truth and reconciliation commissions, and pursuit in land and related claims. The transemic function should be part of the curriculum, as per the table.

Table 13.3 shows another addition to the Young work by considering transemics. First, it lists the changes in text complexity that develops in the abstract stage through the five-step model but with an added step before and another after. This

Table 13.3 Causal culture stories told by different cultures

Abstract step	Text complexity	Causal cognition	Culture	Causal culture stories
Perioperational integration (Pre-Abstract)	Interweaving of two somewhat equal story elements may take place in oscillatory manner	The pre-teen's causal cognitive exploration takes become a major force in the life of the child through the constant social, personality, and role try-outs	At this step, representational culture reaches its apex in structure, whether describing children, our ancestors, or contemporary culture. Logic, at least at the concrete level, mediates cultural exchange and development	The cultures view causality as expressions of natural (and other-worldly forces) for example, with both holistic/global and particular specific components. They are described in the abstract but are not reflections of abstract thought
Coordination	The story is clearly abstract in nature (e.g., metaphorical, allegorical; about morals, values, and personality)	Being logical and abstract, as in the teen years, helps the teenager develop an awareness of the self, other people, etc. Causal cognition enters a critical phase in which relationships are conceived in abstract terms as well as the parties therein	The efficient organizations developed in the prior step are juxtaposed, thereby promoting cognitive, social, and cultural advance to abstract levels, the latter of which is referred to as hyper-culture. The degree to which our human ancestors evidenced this type of abstract thought is an open question. They expressed rituals, art, and theorized behaviors indicate of basic abstract thought	The cultures tell causal stories that include abstract qualities, including about the global-holistic and particular-part characteristics of natural (and supernatural) forces. They are conceived as higher-order forces beyond the concrete and physical, such as in more scientific understanding of storms, the sun and stars. But traditional, albeit abstract, explanations are juxtaposed with these ones, too
Hierarchization	There is some tolerance for accepting that the way in which a hierarchization theme or plot is interpreted or recounted may be incorrect or incomplete, but there is not complete acceptance of this idea	The teenager seeks identities or puts the search on hold or otherwise arrests a full search. The self or the other becomes centers of identity search, or they alternate. Identities need to be considered as causal structures. They indicate what actions, attitudes, and approaches should be adopted, both intra-personally and inter-personally	Whether speaking of teenagers or of cultures functioning at this level, there are more institutional co-structures that develop and are imposed downward on group members. But the structure can switch in the head arch involved, even flip its organizational structure, etc.	Just as the culture's hyper-culture status takes hold in new ways super-ordinately in relating to old ways, the causal stories that cultures tell begin to take primacy, given the global-specific and whole-part relations that they prioritize, although there is oscillation, too. Causality takes root in stories that privilege conceptions of causality that are the more scientific than the more mythical, even if abstract
Systematization	Recognition and acceptance that there are several complementary, systematization-related perspectives/views/ themes/elements of narrative events	The teenager continues to grow and engages in adult-like thought and activity, including emotionally and socially. The abstract map created of the teen's world complexifies and systematizes such that the self-other become a holistic entity in at least one component of the teenager's mentality. This extends into the causal reasoning of the teen	Culture dynamics, whether, in terms of groups of people or wider societies, become concerned with common problems, solutions, and responsibilities. Member activity influences group activity, from the bottom up, as much as group activity influences member activity from the top down	The abstract scientific-type discourse on causality takes firmly in the culture, subsuming the less scientific, albeit abstract, stories of causality. The members of the culture who are more attuned to the scientific rather than mythical approaches do not dismiss them but understand them as complementary in another global-particular, whole-part understanding

Multiplication	Recognition that new perspectives/views/themes grow out of multiplication old ones can be embedded within them	The youth/young adult extends causal mapping into many domains, social or otherwise, seeking causal enrichment of worldviews	Once effective systems develop culturally in one domain/task/ application, the system generalizes to other areas	The new approach, now firmly ensconced, is applied to multiple causal domains, such as how institutions work, and not just to nature. The multiplication incorporates the global-whole particular-part dynamic, which underlies abstract understanding
Integration	There is a weighing, evaluation, and comparison of viewpoints/ plots/themes	The causal co-cognition of the person extends beyond the multiple immediate contexts lived to wider horizons. Understanding causality abstractly becomes the quest and it is fed reciprocally by individuals, cultures, peoples, and planetary perspectives	Culture at this level is complexly organized, mediated by pan-abstract thinking in particular domains/tasks/ applications	The new approach to causality becomes inherent to the culture and guides causal exploration and understanding at all levels, through and about the global-whole versus particular-part dynamic. The culture will have those who are not scientifically informed, or who reflexively dismiss science, but the scientific-type causal explanations predominate (and work)
Collective intelligence (post-abstract)	Synthesis of different overarching viewpoints/ principles is beginning to be evident	Causal co-cognition becomes super-ordinately abstract. The abstract cognitions in this regard that had developed previously coordinate/ juxtapose, etc., and reposition themselves in coordinative maps that represent active collective intelligence	The intelligence involved is collective—of the ideas, of the human domains involved, including cognitive and socioemotional/ affective. Culturally, this refers to the complex cognitive belief, attitudinal, and value systems that characterize cultures	The science spreads into highly abstract understandings of causation (global-whole/ particular-part) and helps build a better society. Reactionaries appreciate the technology, medical advances, etc. but will still be anti-science. This can have dramatic effects, as with a pandemic

Text complexity column (2) adapted from Young (2011) [Table 9.6, pp. 192–193]
Causal cognition column adapted from excerpts from Tables 12.6 and 12.8 in this book
Hyper-culture column adapted from excerpts from Tables 12.11, 12.12, and 12.13 in this book
The last column is new to this work

Table 13.4 Transemification and its narrativization in the hierarchization step of the five-step change model

		Examples	
Transemification	Narrativization	Individual	Community
Exploration: Of the relationships both within their particular individual and cultural situations in terms of the globality-particularity and whole-part distinction and across them with the perceptions without them. The person/culture tries to place the new narrative as predominant for a major domain but regressions possible	Subordination of the newly emerging globality particularity and whole-part dynamic narrative: in the stories told, and in one domain only, but not necessarily as the head in the relationship to alternate stories without it. The person/culture explores possibilities, keeps acquiring new knowledge and seeing how they work and help, but old stories conflict with them. The person/culture might be confused as the learning, application, and narrativization continues	Transemic Dominance-Subordination of New and Old Narratives: My stories are becoming our stories. I am learning more about our traditions, history, practices, and customs. I know they are local to where we live, but they are universal to where we aspire. I am part of the chain of living, our chain, and our chain is my chain. But other chains chain me and us to their chains, and they are not linked to our culture, our times, our creation, and the stories about our creation. Why is our creation story anything less than other creation stories? I tell stories about both worlds, ours and theirs, pride and poetry versus prejudice and the profane. It is still a struggle, but I am beginning to see clearer. Drugs are an answer only when my, Me is my, I. When I am part of a We, nay, when I am a We, drugs cannot infiltrate my world and its collective meaning	We learn to tell even better stories about who we were, who we are, and what we want to become. Stories are about becoming and being, and there are many possible ones, but the stories we like best now see the whole, the parts, the global, the specifics, where we fit in and how our identities fit into where we fit in. Everything goes together, each of us with all of us, and all of us with nature, nature with the earth, and the earth with everything. We are visitors from the future observing the despoiling of the present and must speak to the despoilers. Our stories are their stories, but they do not yet know it. Our conversations have all past and future conversations in them, so listen to all our voices, all our times, with all your hearts and all your minds. Our mind is our heart and our heart is our mind and your mind is yours and mine as is mine ours and yours. But we forget. We cannot stay peak; we go below the valleys into the lost burrows and enter lost forest trails. We want to live only new stories, but the old ones are powerful, legacies of eons that have masked and obliterated us

had been presented in Young (2011). Then, it gives the development of causal cognition and of culture according to these steps, as described in Chap. 12. Examination of these seven steps in text/storying on causality and culture led to the postulate the equivalent steps as cultures tell causal stories. Causality involves transemic-like functioning through the globality-particularity and whole-part distinctions that we try to explain. For example, in understanding the global patterning of weather, we integrate the global with the local forces as fronts interact. The table tries to capture this dynamic in the causal stories that cultures tell.

Interim Summary

This part of the chapter has shown the value of applying transemics to Young's modeling. It helped rework the Young's five-step change process model. It offered two hypothetical examples related to that reworked model. It integrated two prior five-step change models in learning and education into a five-step humanization process. The next part of the chapter applies the transemic to other areas of Young's work.

Transemically Redefining Causality, Development, and Unifying Psychology

Causality

Transemics adds to the major themes in the Young works (Young 2011, 2016, 2019, this book) in the following ways. For the theme of causality in psychology, transemics specifies that the causal processes described in the books can be complemented by a transemic analysis. This is illustrated very well in in Table 13.2, in which both individual adolescent development and group development according to human rights were analyzed with the added element of globality/universality/whole versus individuality/specificity/part distinction, which was not considered in any of the prior Young works in the multiple examples that they included. Moreover, the globality/universality/whole versus individuality/specificity/part distinction adds depth to the change process and gives more proximal analysis to the process because the distinction is one that is among those that are upfront in how people (and groups) think.

The other major causality processes in the Young works that are complemented by adding transemics include the following. First, the biopsychosocial model is criticized for its nonspecificity, that it is just a description collection of influences on behavior. On the one hand, it has currency in some psychological fields, such as rehabilitation, because it asks that the full range of factors be considered in understanding patients and the array of causes and symptoms that might be involved. Second, for the case of rehabilitation, at least, the globality/universality/whole versus individuality/specificity/part distinction gives depth to the concept because it indicates the critical factors that might play in the psychological perception of the patient and gives another way of conceiving the organization of the environment of the patient beyond the typical ecological or the embedded concentric ring model.

The crucial models in the Young works related to causality have been the systems and network ones, and their hybridization in Young (2015). Systems models concern nonlinear dynamics that lead to abrupt self-organizational change if the system is overly perturbed beyond the cusp of change, and even major changes despite minor perturbations, as in the butterfly effect. System organization and its contents both can be reconfigured in terms of dynamics according to the globality/universality/whole versus individuality/specificity/part distinction. Systems can develop emergent contents, including new tiers, as in the Young hybrid model, in which networks can help describe the contents of the tiers, in particular. Also, tiers have relationships, such as top-down and bottom-up, and these can be additionally described in terms of the globality/universality/whole versus individuality/specificity/part distinction and their transactions both within and over tiers. Any kind of causal transactional exchange, such as reciprocal causality and circular emergence, or relational co-regulation, can add the globality/universality/whole versus individuality/specificity/part distinction to its dynamics.

Systems theory includes the possibility of fractals or repeated patterns at different scales in the system. Systems theory includes the concept of attractors and complex adaptive systems, and the prior section had shown that these representations of behavior can include the globality/universality/whole versus individuality/specificity/part distinction. The patterns in the globality/universality/whole versus individuality/specificity/part distinction could be one basis for fractalization processes at work in human systems, cultural ones, etc. And when these types if globality/universality/whole versus individuality/specificity/part patterns are disturbed or disrupted at the individual or group (cultural) level, the repercussions in the dispersion of the aberrant patterns fractally in the system at issue extend to the sinews of the system.

Note that fractals have been applied to the present modeling from stage to substage to substep, each with five phases. However, for consistency, there are fractals that could be defined within this pattern. This relates to the grouping of the first three levels as primary constructions and the next two as secondary extensions/elaborations. An example of type of organization within the five steps at any one had been given for the substages of coordination, hierarchization, systematization, multiplication, and integration. Here, it is applied to the substeps, which are (a) tentative beginning, (b) clear initiation, (c) consolidation/improved application, (d) spreading maturation/refinement, and (e) systemic synthesis. The first three represent primary constructions and the last two secondary extensions/elaborations, which is uncontroversial. As for the five stages of the system involved, the reflexive, sensorimotor, and perioperational stages are primary constructions and the abstract ones are secondary extensions/elaborations. This makes sense in the qualification of the abstract stages as indices of human exceptionalism; thus, under one rubric, that of secondary extensions/elaborations in terms of abstract thought relative to other representations, such as concrete operations, we have a model of the marker of human exceptionality.

The major causality process described in the Young books related to the activation-inhibition coordination dynamic, which was considered a common metric over neuron, brain, connectivity, and behavior. The globality/universality/whole versus individuality/specificity/part dynamic gives substance to the concept, by indicating the back and forth nature of the activations and inhibitions involved at this level. For example, the connectivities of the brain are described in terms of major networks—the salience, executive, and default mode networks. They comprise subnetworks and they interact themselves. The global brain connectivity array has been called the connectome. The interactive dynamics both within and between subnetworks, networks, and the connectdome can be translated into activation-inhibition coordination dynamics, and the globality/universality/whole versus individuality/specificity/part interaction dynamics can help in these regards. For example, do inter-connectivities at these levels involve re-arrangement of local, lower-order globality/universality/whole versus individuality/specificity/part dynamics and do they influence higher-order level dynamics, which themselves are similarly described? The same applies to behavior. Consider the infant hand reach and grasp example that had provided the conceptual impetus for the concept. Does the infant analyze the spatial configuration and the relationship of the moving hand in space at the level of the globality/universality/whole versus individuality/specificitypart distinction, and does this dynamic constitute a skill that is better in left hemisphere, thereby accounting for the hypothesized left hemisphere specialization for activation-inhibition coordination?

Unification

The Young books have considered the unification of psychology beneficial and feasible, arguing that even though it cannot reach a definitive end-point, it is still valid enterprise and should be considered worthwhile pursuing as an ongoing project. Young considered causality as the central axis in this unification project for psychology, in that it cuts across all its subdisciplines. Indeed, it is central to all sciences. The transemic protocol clarifies that causality itself can be unified, as per the prior paragraphs, thereby providing further support for the argument that psychology can be at the forefront in the unification process in science. Moreover, the globality/universality/whole versus individuality/specificity/part distinction is central to academic scholarship, in general, thereby providing a broader scope to the unification across academia and study.

Development

The third major axis of the Young books has been its emphasis on development. The field looks for universal patterns but seeks individual differences, too, and is aimed at understanding particular individuals and groups as they develop. The field is ripe for elaboration in terms of the globality/universality/whole versus individuality/specificity/part distinction and dynamic. The Young books consider stage models as part of development but through a revised neo-stage concept. The contents of stages as they manifest in people have been described in systems and network terms in the Young books, but adding the globality/universality/whole versus individuality/specificity/part distinction helps clarify their workings, as shown previously in this chapter. Human development over the lifespan heads toward increasing maturity and terms such as self-actualization and generativity have been used in this regard.

The present books have added terms such as developing inner peace no matter what the circumstance, taking re-responsibility, and developing complete personhood (e.g., Young 2019) as part of the maturity phase of the adult. Those terms could be complemented by the transemic terminology of the globality/universality/whole versus individuality/specificity/part distinction. For example, inner peace reflects a balance in this regard, and the ability to adapt with equanimity to the ever changing dynamic involved along these lines. Re-responsibility is a concept like generativity, but it asks for continual rededication to all our responsibilities; the globality/universality/whole versus individuality/specificity/part dynamic, even if disruptive, might help understand re-responsibility as a construct and how it works in the same way as the one of inner peace. Self-actualization also can be reworked into the transemic. The developmental thought process involves appraisals, executive function, self-construction, etc., and any thinking process can be understood better when considered in light of the globality/universality/whole versus individuality/specificity/part distinction. For example, appraisals include evaluation of an element in context, and the global/whole versus particular part distinction would apply very well there. Are attribution biases poorly filtered along these lines in individuals and can racism and discrimination experiences in groups be qualified with this function? Finally, mature personhood is a developmental right but can it be qualified in terms of the transemic, as with the equivalent concepts of inner peace and re-responsibility in the above?

The high-point developmental model of the Young books concerns the Neo-Piagetian/Neo-Eriksonian one. It consists of five stages with five substages, yielding a 25-step lifespan developmental model, as already shown. The Neo-Piagetian model could be reworked as one that includes the transemic in the schemes and operations of the developing person. The globality/universality/whole versus individuality/specificity/part distinction seems a key attribute of cognitive concepts, affording them embodiment in the contexts in which they emerge. As for the Neo-Eriksonian part of the model, the inter-navigation in the mutuality with the environment and the inter-subjectivity that arises should be better conceived should the transemic globality/universality/whole versus individuality/specificity/part distinction be considered as part of it.

Other Transemic Perspectives on the Young Books

Briefly, the Young book series considered human uniqueness in terms of our exceptional abstract thought, in particular. Relatedly, it considered cultural development heading toward higher-order hyper-culture. It considered human adaptation both in terms of evolution and ongoing ecological adaptation. It considered other disciplines, such as philosophy, and especially in terms of epistemology. It presented a neo-ratio constructivist model in this regard. It offered many other novel terms and innovations, the one most prominent being *Homo Causa*.

In terms of the transemic globality/universality/whole versus individuality/specificity/part distinction, some of these aspects of the book deserve further commentary. First, human uniqueness might be reflected in abstract thought related to the transemic function contents. We might be keyed to flow well with that flow and that could be our particular hallmark. Also advanced abstract thought has been defined as collective, which clearly opens it up to transemic analysis and complementary redescription. Hyper-culture is a fast changing dynamic that characterizes human culture, and it, too, can be defined transemically, given the etic-emic distinction relevant to it and from which the concept of transemic evolved. Human adaptation could be best described in terms of the dynamic, given the ever-changing ecological contexts to which we must adapt, whether in terms of macro-evolution, micro-evolution over several generations, or moment-to-moment adaptation. The philosophical term of neo-ratioconstructivism can be addressed by the transemic because the rational, objective, and positivistic component of the term reflects activity in context, and the globality/universality/whole versus individuality/specificity/part distinction applies very well to describing it. Similarly, the nature of the construction of mind and subjective reality in the constructivist portion of the term is open to the transemic. The intersubjectivity that is encompassed in the term also calls for transemic application and understanding. Finally, *Homo Causa* is a term used to emphasize the importance of causal thinking to the species. The transemic function of globality/universality/whole versus individuality/specificity/part helps specify causality, as shown above, helps specify the nature of human thought, as shown above, and therefore helps better understand humans as *Homo Causa*.

Interim Summary

This part of the chapter consists of two sections. In the first section, the transemic is applied to the five-step change process described in Young. Then, hypothetical examples involving changing teen peer dynamics and minorities seeking human rights are offered. Next, the five-step change process is applied to five steps toward the development of humanization, in a work that integrates the previously described five-step change models in learning and education. Then, a model of cultural cognition follows based on Young's descriptions of step models for development of causal cognition and of culture. The second section analyzes the major themes in Young's work from a transemic perspective, including causality and penultimate human development.

Literature Review

Introduction

The next part of the chapter provides a literature review that relates to the concept of transemic. It includes literature on a host of related topics but none directly on transemics; the minimal literature related to it having been reviewed at the outset. A good portion of the review considers indigenous psychologies, which relate in a transemic way to the dominant psychologies of the West, both informing them and altering them. Other topics covered include communitarianism and relational ethics, which are intrinsically open to transemics.

Indigenous psychologies represent the primary area in the literature that speaks to transemics, and the present chapter describes the current literature on the subdiscipline. It refers to the study of indigenous behaviors, cognitions, etc., including in mental health and therapy. It contrasts itself with mainstream psychology, with the West considered hegemonic generally in this regard. Indigenous psychologies could be visited by epistemic violence. But it speaks with eloquence in the description of its discursive practices and in its range of indigenous activities and creativity. The latter includes practices of rainforest peoples. Indigenous psychology is an area that is relational, for example, in its understanding of human relationships with the world, human wisdom, and therapy. Related approaches considered in this part of the work include communitarianism, sociocultural psychology, culture and human development, interculturality, relational ethics, history, cognitive archeology, evolution of mind, WIERDness, and the collectivist-individualist distinction in cultural differentiation. The work of Bakhtin is presented, as well and in conjunction with narrative therapy. In addition, in these regards, the present chapter elaborates relational ethics and the concepts of the IWEMEUS and relational meaning worlds.

Indigenous psychologies challenge mainstream psychology. Already, the term of indigenous psychologies indicates its pluralistic stance. The area of indigenous psychologies has been reviewed from a transemic perspective in Young (2021, submitted), and it is touched upon here.

The field of general psychology has been marked by an exchange on what has been called epistemic violence. This divide in the field points to the need for a dispassionate examination of the exchange from a transemic perspective. This area of research reviewed in the present work examines the opposite stances and proposes how the globality particularity and whole-part distinctions inform them and lead to helpful directions in accommodating them.

Epistemology is about the nature, theory, sources, and study of knowledge what it is and how it is acquired, and its presuppositions and foundations and scope/limits, validity, and methods. Epistemic violence concerns the positioning of one or more epistemologies, and the sources of knowledge involved, as unduly primary. A transemic analysis of the source might be beneficial in supporting it rather than diminishing it.

Ontology is about the nature of being, becoming, existence, and reality, their properties and relations. What exists; what do the instantiated examples of existence look like; what are their general and specific features and characteristics; and how do these existing elements group together? The study of ontology also includes how universals relate to particulars, which places it within the scope of transemics.

Indigenous Psychologies

Indigenous psychologies are about the relationship of the person to the world (Chirkov 2020). They concern the concepts, beliefs, ideas, emotions, cognition, and selves that characterize people in their local communities, and how they have been shaped historically. Relatedly, Young (1997) referred to the co-construction of relational meaning worlds. A broader definition of indigenous psychologies would include all manners of behavior, affectivity, and cognition in indigenous psychological differentiation. In addition, indigenous psychologies specify the roles of theory, research, researchers on the ground, and the participants on the ground in local cultural research.

Bedford and Yeh (2020) referred to the inter-existence of indigenous and mainstream psychologies. Chinese philosophy, no matter the variation, extends from the belief that the universe is an interconnected dynamically changing field, as highlighted by the yin and yang concept, in which coordinative states can transform into one another. For example, in Chinese filial piety, different modes co-exist in each member of the culture in a dual-function model (i.e., authoritarian, reciprocal, which is more respectful). The authors conclude that other cultures should examine their sense of filial piety for the co-existence of these two modes (e.g., the Hispanic). The approach taken by Bedford and Yeh (2020) to filial piety represents the dynamic interplay of different conceptions of a critical concept in Chinese culture. Moreover, from the current perspective, it shows how the global psychology can be informed and change through individual cultural psychologies outside the mainstream.

Bhatia (2020) extended the decolonization of psychology argument to the individual person, even in therapy, who is normatively inculcated with colonialist (and racist) ideals. Bhawuk (2020) argued that the sense of otherness cannot include inferiority, a concept that can be countered by mainstream psychology respecting the different approaches of indigenous psychologies. Causadias (2020) conceived culture in terms of systems and networks, much like the present case and offered that power imbalances, such as in racism, mark dominant cultures and their exploitations. Colombo (2020) also referred to mainstream positions in psychology serving to propagate power imbalances.

Held (2020) considered that mainstream psychology has some progressive, even when compared with indigenous psychologies, accordingly. She had referred to epistemic violence, which involves discounting marginalized groups and also alternative interpretations toward a demeaning perspective on the inferiority of others. Some indigenous viewpoints have relativized mainstream psychology, for example, considering it one more indigenous psychology or decrying its hegemony (e.g., Bhatia 2019).

Indigenous Psychologies Eloquence

Ciofalo (2019) echoed the "withness" of indigenous psychologies. Ciofalo (2019) presented a poem written by Marwilio Sanchez Gomez in this regard, on the essence of the Lacandon rainforest. It refers to the rainforest being "wounded" with a part lost and not being capable of returning.

Another conception that applies here is that relaverses exist rather than multiple universes (Young 1997). Multiverses indicate multiple independent poles in dialogue, but their dynamic constant praxitic co-interactions continually change and transform them. We are products of each other in dynamic co-regulative relational interaction, whether individually or culturally. Indigenous psychologies exist in awareness of inter-dependence.

Lee and Kirmayer (2020) informed on a healing practice (*Dang-Ki*) in Singapore. In my own psychotherapeutic practice, I try to embody that perspective and remain open to the client each moment in our in a meeting space. I do try to fit a favored school of therapeutic thought to the client but, in contrast, I fit the client to the school of thought from among those are evidence-supported for the issues at hand each week in our sessions (Young 2016). Moreover, as I explain to my students, the cognitive component in cognitive behavior therapy should be broad enough to consider narratives as a cognitive activity within its purview. In narrative therapy, we want to have patients learn to tell different stories about themselves and others and to author or co-author a better narrative about their future. This approach helps when the situation with the client calls for it [See Gut and Wilczewski 2020 for discussion of the narrative approach].

Both in terms of Lee and Kirmayer (2020) and myself, the engagements with the client appears transemic in that a full relational approach will seek the global/whole and particularity/part distinctions and their interactions in the transactions and transformations that take place in the lives of patients and in the meeting ground I create with them. This transemic approach to psychotherapy could inform the narrative component of the therapy. And therapists should remain alert to having patients tell new stories about themselves, the other, and their future in terms of global-whole versus particular-part dynamics, as in relations with the other.

Wang et al. (2021) explained the Chinese views on wisdom. The West refers to objective and subjective, but the East considers the distinction vague. After the establishment of the integration of Chinese philosophical roots in Confucianism, Taoism, and Buddhism in the Han and Tan Chinese dynasties, inner pursuit and moral practice became the hallmarks of living in wisdom. The yin and yang indicate harmony and balance as valid living but without uniformity.

The non-Western conceptions of wisdom speak to the global-particular distinction in transemics. Also, the concept of inner pursuit in wisdom is consistent with the present one of inner peace as the hallmark of psychological maturity, per this book. This concept is not about transcendence but about engagement; above all, the person will find inner peace by helping others find inner peace, which means staying calm no matter the challenge or crisis and acting accordingly. This conception is different than the Chinese one because it required living in the external world to find balance and harmony in the interior one (and the internal harmony and peace feed the extension into harmony-creation and participation in the world for the other). Morality hinges on human and environmental relations that speak to dignity, activity, humility, and humanity, in "withness," and the songs, dance, and poetry that withness brings. Our western arm has harmed the rainforest, as the indigenous poet implied in Ciofalo (2019), and our western arm can empower the indigenous to protect their ecologies and make the humming birds sing.

Generally, this review of recent work on indigenous psychologies indicates divergences with western psychologies, especially in its hegemonic resistance and preservation of indigenous cultures. Indigenous psychologies speak with a different voice, a pluralistic one that respects each other and deserves respect. It articulates a different vision of the human essence and the relationship of the individual to the interior world and to the exterior (and spiritual) world. It emphasized different ways of thinking, more holistic and intuitive than Western analysis and logic [a yin-yang perspective might suggest that we harmonize both]. For individuals to be fully human, they have to relate to the world as fully alive. We are part of an ecosystem of different objective/subjective/intersubjective realities, and all inhabit one set of relational meaning worlds or relaverses that are ever changing and asking each individual to transact and transform toward an inherent morality that is accentuated by moral actions and inner peace.

Related Approaches

Similarly, sociocultural psychology is the antithesis of the standard individual psychology of the west (Chirkov 2020). Sociocultural models serve to regulate societal social behavior, while preserving a sense of individuality and agency. The person can dialectically oppose learned and imposed sociocultural models, for example. The human mind is a sociocultural mind. I would add that it is historico-politico as well as sociocultural, in addition to being inclusively biological, evolutionary, developmental, and ecological.

Harkness and Super (2020) reviewed developments in the field of culture and human development. They had studied infant development in native African communities, for example (e.g., Super and Harkness 2009). They referred to the work of Dasen (Dasen and Heron 1981), who compared Piagetian development in Western and African societies. Liu et al. (2020) have demonstrated that parental behavior changes as culture changes: they examined the implicit beliefs of contemporary middle-class Chinese mothers, and their behavior was found to reflect a societal shift in attitudes toward shyness.

According to Haye and González (2020), cultures are not unitary, mono-structural entities that engage in intercultural dialogue but pluralistic, polyphonic, polyvocal, multiplicity ones that work at the borders between cultures, which are permeable membranes with varying degrees of strength that allow the communication. Cultures transform in the dialogue, both objectively and subjectively, in that borders fold, change, and transform and forever enter becoming in the process. Moreover, individual members of a culture engage in internal borderwork, but every utterance, every thought, do not exist as a separate entity given their embeddedness in discursive history and the changes they undergo in communication. The authors posit that dominant cultures have homogenized, monologized, and foreignized the indigenous ones, but they remind that the foreigner is us [for a more detailed explanation of the use of the dialogical concepts of Bakhtin, refer to Young 1997; there the concept of a multiplicity of authorship is discussed in more detail].

Hopner and Liu (2020) advocated for relational ethics as part of epistemological philosophy as underscoring as a first principle the discipline of psychology. Note that work has revised psychological and health work ethics codes (Young 2017, 2020), especially for the current understanding of relational ethics. Table 2.1, page 38, in Young (2017) refers to the APA (American Psychological Association, 2002, 2010, 2017) ethics code principles off integrity and justice in the following way: Integrity: Psychologists seek to promote accuracy, honesty, and truthfulness in the science, teaching, and practice of psychology. Justice: Psychologists recognize that fairness and justice entitle all persons to access to and benefit from psychology and psychologists.

Other principles in the APA ethics code address relational integrity, especially the one on respecting peoples. The APA ethics code notes that psychologists respect the dignity and worth of all people and the right of individuals to privacy, confidentiality, and self-determination.

Young (2020, Table 5, pp. 9–10) translated his version for a unified health work ethics code into statements of patient (and contactee) rights. For relational integrity, he wrote: "You will be treated as a whole person with your individual differences and particular humanity, and being respectful of your context, including your particular family and cultural context. I will strive to build a relationship with you based on openness, honesty, fairness, trust facilitation, rapport encouragement, a genuine presence, keeping promises and commitments made to you, avoiding conflicts of interest, and mutual respect in a two-way interaction or dialogue."

In short, in Young's work, he has underscored relational ethics, consistent with Hopner and Liu (2020). The revised principles of the APA, and indeed the AMA ethics code presented in his work could be consulted by those wishing to import the concept into research and health work generally with indigenous populations, thereby broadening the ethical base of indigenous psychologies. The ethical principles for practice and research that have been described will allow for better transemic local and global/whole and part relations within and between the parties involved, whether at the individual or group level.

Henley (2020) examined the Neolithic period may have been based on socio-cognitive advances as evidenced the construction of the temples at Göbekle Tepe. Classic accounts of the evolution of the modern mind might have underestimated the start of the Neolithic, which took place about 10,000 years ago. In this regard, Henley referred to Donald's model of the evolution of mind. Young's model in Chap. 12 combines Donald's (2008) and Mithen's (2007) into an integrated one.

Note that Young embedded the Donald-Mithen sequence of the steps in the evolution toward the modern mind into his own model based on the 25-step Neo-Piagetian one, seeing that they covered about ten steps in the model. Moreover, Chap. 12 demonstrates how his 25-step Neo-Piagetian lifespan model of cognitive development can apply both to cultural development and to the development of human causal cognition.

Note that psychological descriptions and theorizing are replete with oppositions that are considered diametrically opposed or as poles on opposite ends of a continuum. The present work has considered some of them, such as collectivist versus individualist societies. The examples in the field might refer to behavior within individuals, as well. At the individual level, a major example is found with the Neo-Eriksonian model in the oppositions such as Trust versus Mistrust and the balance required in development and another one would be androgyny integrating our masculine and feminine sides. At the level of thinking, a major opposition concerns fast, unconscious versus slow, conscious reasoning (see Young 2016). At the cultural level, examples abound in fusion styles, whether they concern food, fashion, or music. In all these oppositions some sort of fusion process takes place (synthesis, as in yin-yang), then perhaps with defusioning, leading to a wider refusioning. It would be simple to translate this pattern into the five-step change process as described in Young's work.

Two more points seem relevant. First, the changes in fusioning/defusioning and refusioning involved can take place very rapidly; think of your own innovations in the kitchen! The same five-step change process is applicable to both micro-changes and macro-changes. In this sense, it is applicable to both micro-development and macro-development, that is, not to just (sub)stage development but also to steps in problem solving, as per examples provided in Young's work.

This part of the literature review leads to a second point related to the notion that Eastern cultures might consider the intuitive thinking process more in line with wisdom than the rational. In one view, these are oppositions, such as cognition generally versus emotions that do not reflect insular absolutes but relative imbalances in the whole. In this regard, one could argue that cognitive schemes constitute a misnomer because all schemes are emotional, as well. Cognitive behavior therapy is a misnomer in a similar way.

However, there are change processes, involved in this type of cognitive-emotional fusioning, and defusioning takes place as well. For example, the postformal stage in Young's Neo-Piagetian model is referred to as collective intelligence because it concerns not only collecting abstract ideas together into superordinate abstract structures but also integrating emotions into the rational thinking process, which adults generally do better than adolescents.

To conclude, with respect to the notion that some cultures might be more intuitive than rational, or use the intuitive more in critical aspects such as wisdoming, this notion reflects the constant back and forth between the rational and emotional sides of one integrated whole in how we think, as we fusion, defusion, and refusion among its components, with imbalances possible and perhaps preferred in individuals and even cultures, for example, due to the presumed advantages implicit in the imbalance.

Finally, one could query the extent of the transemic global-whole versus particular-part imbalances in all these spheres that could lead to and underpin the said balances and imbalances. Do different individuals and cultures gravitate to different holistic/synthetic stances in multiple aspects of their lives, or to the analytic/differentiation side of the equation, and without the rapid back and forth and fusional/refusional stance required for effective short-term micro and long-term macro positive adaptation and function? It would seem wise to investigate this process further.

Interim Summary

Transemic is a process of inter-digitational exchange over the globality/universality/whole versus individuality/specificity/part distinction. The term is novel to psychology. The origin of the term transemic relates to the etic-emic distinction in anthropology and related disciplines. It refers to the transactional and transformational change processes that take place in the dialogue between and among entities along the cardinal continuum of global-specific and whole-part relations. The present chapter applies the concept especially to change processes in human development and in cultural development, but it applies even to the individual thinking process as we engage in internal dialogue. Transemic is contextual in that dialogue takes place in a relational frame. In this regard, change processes could have negative trajectories, as well as positive growth ones. The present chapter considers the five-step change model as elucidated in the Young work, which is consistent with the stages of change model, in terms of the transemic function. This is part of a mechanistic account of how transemic works, which is consistent with its representation as a causal function. The present chapter examines causality, generally, from a transemic viewpoint. It analyzes the Young books on causality, unification of psychology, and human development through stages and substages from a transemic perspective, expanding the concepts in that process. It adds to Young's lifespan developmental model (Neo-Piagetian/Neo-Eriksonian). This chapter presents a comprehensive literature on adjunct topics through a transemic lens, especially on indigenous psychologies. Overall, the present chapter presents an integrated transemic theory that could contribute to scholarship generally.

Discussion

Transemic has practical applications in multiple ways. First, it can help spotlight the specifics experienced by minority groups and indigenous groups in their transactional relationships with society at large and with those who identify with the majority. It can help distinguish the difficulties experienced by minority and indigenous youth in terms of global-particular and whole-part processes within their identified culture, in their thinking process of their sense of belongingness and exclusion, and how to maintain their identities and function within the majority culture. It can help individual youth having mental difficulties due to the translocation away from their ancestral homelands to study and work, by affirming new stories in how their global identities can integrate the particular locals in which they must live disjointedly from their home communities. They can help any member of a minority and indigenous culture to reconnect with the globality of their ancestry, their heritage and tradition, the rejoicing in them, and the spirituality and connection with all sorts of nonmaterial worlds and their different relational meaning worlds, all toward creating a sense of wholeness and relationship with their past, present, and future. As well, through the humanization curriculum, and its steps, as described in the present chapter, it can help in the healing and reconciliation that is ongoing within and among different communities in a relational ethics that must span all peoples and times if we are to survive in the differentiated yet unitary vision of the minority and the indigenous (which are also the best of many possible optics in the majority), in that well as all marginalized and vulnerable people.

As presented in Table 1 of Young (2021, submitted), Table 13.4 presents a model of transemification related to the present five-step change model of coordination, hierarchization, systematization, multiplication, and integration. The table only gives excerpts related to the step of hierarchization of the Table in Young (2021, submitted), in order to highlight some main points related to narrativization.

Transemification takes place in a process that resembles analysis and synthesis. However, it is more complex than that, as the following indicates. (a) On the one hand, I coin a new term of analysis-synthesis coordination, in that transemification is taken to involve two synergistic coordinations, one constituted by analysis and synthesis. The analysis and synthesis coordination involved is implicit in application of analysis and synthesis, but it needs to be made explicit because analysis and synthesis can work together as an imbalance or even a discoordination rather than a synchronization of the two components toward adaptive outcomes. (b) Transemification also involves activation-inhibition coordination because analysis and synthesis lead to adaptive outcomes when they are honed by this type of coordination.

Transemification begins with an existing construction or organization, a globality, a whole, a universal, etc. But it will contain ambiguities, inconsistencies, gaps, errors, etc., that lead to analysis and then synthesis. Thus, the original construction/organization is (critically) deconstructed, decomposed, broken down, segmented, parcellated, partitioned, compartmentalized, modularized, disaggregated, etc. Next, the effort toward reconstruction begins by seeking new patterns, re-organizations, assemblages, aggregations, unifications, wholes, globalities, inherent and explicit oppositions that lead to new views, etc., thereby leading to new constructions, syntheses, synergies, reconfigurations, etc.

Transemic is one word, an idea that appeared in a moment of relaxation. It has spread its wings through this present work. We need a collective action to bring it to roost in the rainforest of diverse ideas so that it can transemically interact with them and help academically and practically in the ways indicated. We are IWEMEUS.

References

American Psychological Association.: Ethical principles of psychologists and code of conduct. *Am. Psychol.* **57**, 1060–1073 (2002). https://psycnet.apa.org/doi/10.1037/0003-066X.57.12.1060" https://doi.org/10.1037/0003-066X.57.12.1060

American Psychological Association. (2010). *Ethical principles of psychologists and code of conduct* (2002, Amended June 1, 2010). Retrieved from http://www.apa.org/ethics/code/principles.pdf

American Psychological Association: Ethical Principles of Psychologists and Code of Conduct (2002, amended effective June 1, 2010, and January 1, 2017). American Psychological Association, Washington (2017). http://www.apa.org/ethics/code/index.html

Barad, K.: *Meeting the Universe halfway: Quantum physics and the entanglement of matter and meaning*. Durham, North Carolina: Duke University Press (2007)

Bedford, O., Yeh, K.-H.: The contribution of Chinese process thought to psychology as a global science: filial piety as an example. Rev. Gen. Psychol. **24**(2), 99–109 (2020). https://doi.org/10.1177/1089268019889337

Bhatia, S.: Searching for justice in an unequal world: reframing indigenous psychology as a cultural and political project. J. Theor. Philos. Psychol. **39**(2), 107–114 (2019). https://doi.org/10.1037/teo0000109

Bhatia, S.: Decolonizing psychology: power, citizenship and identity. Psychoanal. Self Cont. **15**(3), 257–266 (2020). https://doi.org/10.1080/24720038.2020.1772266

Bhawuk, D.P.S.: vAde vAde jAyate tattvabodhaH: toward epistemic harmony through dialogue. Theory Psychol. **30**(3), 472–478 (2020). https://doi.org/10.1177/0959354320922613

de Boer, N.S., de Bruin, L.C., Geurts, J.J.G., Glas, G.: The network theory of psychiatric disorders: a critical assessment of the inclusion of environmental factors. Front. Psychol. **12**, 623970 (2021). https://doi.org/10.3389/fpsyg.2021.623970

Bybee, R.W.: Achieving Scientific Literacy: From Purposes to Practices, 1st edn. Heinemann, Portsmouth (1997)

Bybee, R., Taylor, J., Gardner, A., Van Scotter, P., Powell, J.C., Westbrook, A., Landes, N.: The BSCS 5E Instructional Model: Origins and Effectiveness. BSCS, Colorado Springs (2006). https://media.bscs.org/bscsmw/5es/bscs_5e_full_report.pdf

Canda, E.R., Furman, L.: Spiritual Diversity in Social Work Practice: The Heart of Helping. Free Press, New York (1999)

Causadias, J.M.: What is culture? Systems of people, places, and practices. Appl. Dev. Sci. **24**(4), 310–322 (2020). https://doi.org/10.1080/10888691.2020.1789360

Chen, R.H.: Fostering students' workplace communicative competence and collaborative mindset through an inquiry-based learning design. Educ. Sci. **11**, 17 (2021). https://doi.org/10.3390/educsci11010017

Chirkov, V.: The sociocultural movement in psychology, the role of theories in sociocultural inquiries, and the theory of sociocultural models. Asian J. Soc. Psychol. **23**(2), 119–134 (2020). https://doi.org/10.1111/ajsp.12409

Choifer, A.: Interpretational complexities in developmental research and a Piagetian reading of the false-belief task. Rev. Philos. Psychol. (2021). https://doi.org/10.1007/s13164-020-00519-0

Ciofalo, N.: Indigenous Psychologies in an Era of Decolonization (International and Cultural Psychology), 1st edn. Springer Nature Switzerland AG, Cham (2019). https://doi.org/10.1007/978-3-030-04822-8

Colombo, M.: Who is the "other"? Epistemic violence and discursive practices. Theory Psychol. **30**(3), 399–404 (2020). https://doi.org/10.1177/0959354320923758

Dasen, P.R., Heron, A.: Cross-cultural tests of Piaget's theory. In: Triandis, H.C., Heron, A. (eds.) Handbook of Cross-Cultural Psychology. Vol. 4: Developmental Psychology, pp. 295–342. Allyn & Bacon, Boston (1981)

Donald, M.: How culture and brain mechanisms interact in decision-making. In: Engel, C., Singer, W. (eds.) Better Than Conscious? Decision-Making, the Human Mind, and Implications for Institutions, pp. 191–225. MIT Press, Cambridge (2008)

Gut, A., Wilczewski, M.Ł.: Turning away from epistemic violence by capturing a lived experience of the other. Theory Psychol. **30**(3), 454–458 (2020). https://doi.org/10.1177/0959354320922614

Haag-Heitman, B.: Clinical Practice Development Using Novice to Expert Theory, 1st edn. Wolters Kluwer Law & Business, Gaithersburg (1999)

de Haan, S.: Bio-psycho-social interaction: an enactive perspective. Int. Rev. Psychiatr. (2020). https://doi.org/10.1080/09540261.2020.1830753

van Halen, C., Bosma, H.A., van der Meulen, M.: Experiencing self-definition problems over the life span. Identity. **20**(3), 170–187 (2020). https://doi.org/10.1080/15283488.2020.1782913

Harkness, S., Super, C.M.: Culture and human development: where did it go? And where is it going? N. Direct. Child Adolesc. Dev. **2020**(173), 101–119 (2020). https://doi.org/10.1002/cad.20378

Haye, A., González, R.: Dialogic borders: interculturality from Vološinov and Bakhtin. Theory Psychol. (2020). https://doi.org/10.1177/0959354320968635

Held, B.S.: Epistemic violence in psychological science: can knowledge of, from, and for the (othered) people solve the problem? Theory Psychol. **30**(3), 349–370 (2020). https://doi.org/10.1177/0959354319883943

Henley, T.B.: On prehistoric psychology: reflections at the invitation of Göbekli Tepe. Hist. Psychol. **23**(3), 211–218 (2020). https://doi.org/10.1037/hop0000134

Hopner, V., Liu, J.H.: Relational ethics and epistemology: the case for complementary first principles in psychology. Theory Psychol. **31**, 179 (2020). https://doi.org/10.1177/0959354320974103

Inzlicht, M., Werner, K.M., Briskin, J.L., Roberts, B.W.: Integrating models of self-regulation. Annu. Rev. Psychol. **72**(1), 319–345 (2021). https://doi.org/10.1146/annurev-psych-061020-105721

Kievit, R.A.: Sensitive periods in cognitive development: a mutualistic perspective. Curr. Opin. Behav. Sci. **36**, 144–149 (2020). https://doi.org/10.1016/j.cobeha.2020.10.007

Lee, B.-O., Kirmayer, L.J.: Dang-Ki healing: an embodied relational healing practice in Singapore. Transcult. Psychiatr. **57**(6), 786–800 (2020). https://doi.org/10.1177/1363461519858448

Létourneau, D., Goudreau, J., Cara, C.: Humanistic caring, a nursing competency: modelling a metamorphosis from students to accomplished nurses. Scand. J. Caring Sci. **35**(1), 196–207 (2021). https://doi.org/10.1111/scs.12834

Liu, J.L., Harkness, S., Super, C.M.: Chinese mothers' cultural models of children's shyness: ethnotheories and socialization strategies in the context of social change. New Direct. Child Adolesc. Dev. **2020**(170), 69–92 (2020). https://doi.org/10.1002/cad.20340

Lou, Y., Zhao, L., Yu, S., Sun, B., Hou, Z., Zhang, Z., Tang, Y., Liu, S.: Brain asymmetry differences between Chinese and Caucasian populations: a surface-based morphometric comparison study. Brain Imag. Behav. **14**(6), 2323–2332 (2019). https://doi.org/10.1007/s11682-019-00184-7

Mascolo, M.F.: Inching toward a unified metatheory for psychology. Integr. Psychol. Behav. Sci. **55**(1), 198–211 (2021). https://doi.org/10.1007/s12124-020-09543-2

Michaels, J.L., Vallacher, R.R., Nowak, A.: Finding order in the flow of personality: dynamical systems techniques for measuring personality coherence and change. In: Rauthmann, J.F. (ed.) The Handbook of Personality Dynamics and Processes, pp. 985–1011. Academic Press, New York (2021). https://doi.org/10.1016/b978-0-12-813995-0.00038-8

Mithen, S.: Seven steps in the evolution of the human imagination. In: Roth, I. (ed.) Imaginative Minds, vol. 147. British Academy Scholarship Online, Oxford (2007). https://doi.org/10.5871/bacad/9780197264195.003.0001

Paragas, E.D.: "The upward spiral staircase of caring": a hermeneutic phenomenology study of the caring competency of Filipino nurses grounded in competency-based education. J. Compet. Bas. Educ. **4**(1), e01182 (2019). https://doi.org/10.1002/cbe2.1182

Strand, P.S.: The security-seeking impulse and the unification of attachment and culture. Psychol. Rev. **127**(5), 778–791 (2020). https://doi.org/10.1037/rev0000194

Sullivan, R.M., Opendak, M.: Defining immediate effects of sensitive periods on infant neurobehavioral function. Curr. Opin. Behav. Sci. **36**, 106–114 (2020). https://doi.org/10.1016/j.cobeha.2020.08.006

Super, C.M., Harkness, S.: The developmental niche of the newborn in rural Kenya. In: Nugent, J.K., Petrauskas, B., Brazelton, T.B. (eds.) The Newborn as a Person: Enabling Healthy Infant Development Worldwide, pp. 85–97. Wiley, New York (2009)

Wang, Z.-D., Wang, Y.-M., Li, K., Shi, J., Wang, F.-Y.: The comparison of the wisdom view in Chinese and western cultures. Curr. Psychol. (2021). https://doi.org/10.1007/s12144-020-01226-w

Young, G.: Adult Development, Therapy, and Culture: A Postmodern Synthesis. Plenum, New York (1997)

Young, G.: Development and Causality: Neo-Piagetian Perspectives. Springer Science + Business Media, New York (2011)

Young, G.: Causality in psychiatry: a hybrid symptom network construct model. Front. Psychiatr. **6**, 164 (2015). https://doi.org/10.3389/fpsyt.2015.00164

Young, G.: Unifying Causality and Psychology: Being, Brain and Behavior. Springer International Publishing, Cham (2016)

Young, G.: Revising the American Psychological Association ethics code. Springer International Publishing, Cham (2017)

Young, G.: Causality and Development: Neo-Eriksonian Perspectives. Springer International Publishing, Cham (2019)

Young, G.: Toward a unified health work ethics code. Ethic. Med. Publ. Health. **15**, 100590 (2020). https://doi.org/10.1016/j.jemep.2020.100590

Young, G. (2021). Transemic Processes in Psychology and Beyond: From the General to the Specific and Back Again. (submitted).

Chapter 14
Ethics and Conclusions

The prior 13 chapters of the book have presented the book's main themes concerning unifying psychology, causality, and neo-stages in development. The last substantive chapter in the book refers to what makes humans distinct. This book reflects an integration imperative that I have for psychology. Within all three themes, integration had been an overarching intellectual predisposition. In my two other major areas of research, the same integrative efforts have been attempted.

Ethical Work

In ethics (Young 2017), I developed an integrated model of five principles for an ethics code in psychology based on the principles in the American Psychological Association (APA) and Canadian Psychological Association (CPA) ethics code (see Table 14.1). Moreover, the five principles were constructed as concordant with the present developmental stage model of five stages through its compatibility with a Neo-Maslovian model of five hierarchical needs (Maslow, 1943, 1970), which I elaborated based on the five stages of my combined Neo-Piagetian/Neo-Eriksonian model. In Young (2017), I showed how the Neo-Maslovian model could be expanded to include Eriksonian terms (Erikson 1968) such as trust and generativity. That is, the five ethical principles that I developed for a psychology ethics code reflect already an integration within the theoretical integration in this book.

In Young (2017), I constructed the set of five ethical principles based on a compare-contrast analysis of the ethics codes of the APA and the CPA, in particular (APA, 2002, 2010, 2017; CPA, 2017, respectively). The five principles involved are (a) Life Preservation, (b) Caring Beneficence/Nonmaleficence, (c) Relational Integrity, (d) Respect for the Dignity and Rights of Persons and Peoples, and (e) Promoting and Acting from Justice in Society. Life preservation refers to helping prevent suicide, violence to others, torture, and so on, and is unique to the model.

G. Young, *Causality and Neo-Stages in Development*, https://doi.org/10.1007/978-3-030-82540-9_14

Table 14.1 Toward revising the APA ethics code: five reworked/novel principles for a universal mental health ethics code

Concept	Content
1. Life preservation (compares to the Neo-Maslovian need of self-definitional and relatedness self-physiological needs/survival (intrapersonal and interpersonal, group, respectively)	The primary obligation that psychologists have is to protect the physical integrity of all others, for example, as it applies to suicide and homicide. Psychologists also have a duty to protect children from the dangers of abuse and negligence, including physical and sexual abuse and emotional negligence. Preserving the sanctity of life, its survival, and the physical and psychological integrity of the body begins with respecting the principle that torture in any and all its guises is not permissible and is unethical.
2. Caring beneficence/ nonmaleficence (compares to the Neo-Maslovian need of self-definitional and relatedness self-safety/trust (intrapersonal and interpersonal, group, respectively)	Psychologists strive to be competent toward benefiting the people they work with, especially those who are vulnerable; they safeguard their welfare. They strive to do no harm, avoid it, or minimize it. The principle considers benefit not just in terms of caring but also in terms of doing so actively, with long term results, even with people indirectly involved, while promoting their autonomy both for themselves and acting toward others and their quality of life.
3. Relational integrity (compares to the Neo-Maslovian need of self-definitional and relatedness self-affiliative initiative (intrapersonal and interpersonal, group, respectively)	Relational integrity is based on building a relationship to the degree possible in the circumstances in which the psychologist finds her/himself and so conducting oneself with openness, honesty, fairness, trust facilitation, rapport encouragement, a genuine presence and mutual respect in a two-way interaction or dialogue. The present approach to integrity emphasizes the humanity of the other, in general, and not just as an object of integrity defined in this limited way: accuracy, honest, truthfulness, keeping promises, commitments, etc.
4. Respect for the dignity and rights of persons and peoples (compares to the Neo-Maslovian need of self-definitional and relatedness self-identity self-esteem (intrapersonal and interpersonal, group, respectively)	Psychologists respect the inherent self-worth of every individual and all groupings of people, no matter how defined. Psychologists respect all peoples' fundamental individual and collective rights related to their dignity and sense of self-worth. Psychologists engage in practices that do not threaten, for any one individual or grouping, the rights to voluntary informed consent, privacy, confidentiality, anonymity, and any form of revealing personal and health information without the required permission. Psychologists deeply respect the autonomy and self-determination of all individuals or groupings. Psychologists especially uphold the rights of individuals and peoples to: nondiscrimination, fairness, equity, justice in this regard, and personal and collective (e.g., cultural minority status) identity, and this right might apply even more so to the vulnerable.
5. Promoting and acting from justice in society (compares to the Neo-Maslovian need of self-definitional and relatedness self-actualizing generativity (intrapersonal and interpersonal, group, respectively)	Psychologists have an obligation to ensure that the parties dealing with their patients/clients do so in an equitable and just manner. This aspect of social justice would seem especially to apply to the following: third party payors for patient/client services and their accepting valid treatment plans; schools or agencies dealing appropriately with children and youth having special needs; work accommodating to injured workers as they return to work; organizations using psychologists in employment assistant plans or in otherwise consulting with them, e.g., about mass disasters, and so on.

Adapted from Young (2017)

Moreover, in Young (2019a), I described that the set of five principles reflect a superordinate meta-principle of personhood; the latter is a fundamental human right that involves dignity, respect, and related constructs, and that develops through relational parenting of the young and through caring for the ill. A second meta-principle that speaks to the five core principles of the five proposed mental health ethics principles in Young (2017) concerns responsibility, which reflects my philosophical approach of Re-responsibility (after Lévinas).

Beyond that, in recent research (Young 2020a), I applied the five-principle ethics code model that I developed to advocate for a universal health work ethics code. Also, I showed how patient rights could be reworked into five rights based on the five said principles (see Table 14.2). This work shows the potential scope of my integrative efforts in ethics. The five-principle model that I developed is theoretically-grounded; therefore, it offers a uniform model that can be applied in diverse ways ethically, from ethics codes for practitioners to patients and related rights, and as shown later, to the universal rights of children. The APA, CPA, American Medical Association (AMA), and other disciplines and organizations that have ethics codes should examine the proposed universal one based on the said five principles and work toward a universal health work ethics code. In this chapter, I show how the proposed list of five ethical principles relates to those of the APA ethics code and the one of the AMA. As for patient rights, the present effort integrates those of the AMA, is written to apply to other stakeholders, such as other types of contactees, and can fill the vacuum in the APA ethics code, which does not have a patient (and related) bill of rights.

Then, in another work (Young 2020b), I applied the five principles that I had developed to a principle-based reasoning for representative research sampling in medicine to accommodate the lack of representation for outgroups in this type of research, such as gender, minority and racial status, age (the elderly), vulnerability status, and all strata in the Socioeconomic Status (SES) distribution. Psychology has the same lacunae in its psychological research sampling and other aspects of its research process. It, too, needs to confront the deficits with effective ethical prescriptions and policies. In this chapter, I argued that researchers and medical practitioners both need to engage in fully informed consent procedures by explaining the lacks in the medical research related to sampling, and the possible negative consequences for members of the affected outgroups in this regard.

To be more specific, I applied the five ethical principles that I had developed for ethics codes to ethics in medical research sampling, which shows their broad applicability. For (a) life preservation, extreme effort needs to be made to use representative samples in order to control differential physiologies and mortality and morbidity rates over gender, age, racial/minority status, vulnerability status, differential SES strata, etc. For (b) caring beneficence/nonmaleficence, there needs to be a maximum concern for relative equality in representation for the outgroups hitherto not represented well in the research to date. For (c) relational integrity, there should be relating openly to solicited research participants about the lacks in the prior research about proper research sampling, how that is being accommodated in the proposed research, and the limitations still evident in these regards. For (d) respect for the

Table 14.2 Five universal ethical principles

Principle	*Explanation*
1. Life Preservation	People continually act to protect the physical integrity of all others, for example, as it applies to torture and related abuses, genocide, homicide, and suicide. People continually act to protect children from the dangers of abuse and negligence. People continually act to preserve the sanctity of life, its survival.
2. Caring Beneficence/ Nonmaleficence	People continually act to safeguard the welfare of all peoples and persons, including the most the vulnerable. People continually aim to do no harm, or minimize it.
3. Relational Integrity	People continually strive to build positive relationships with all others, and behave with openness, honesty, fairness, trust facilitation, rapport encouragement, a genuine presence, and mutual respect in a two-way interaction or dialogue. They emphasize the humanity of the other.
4. Respect for the Dignity and Rights of Persons and Peoples	People continuously respect the inherent self-worth of every individual and all groupings of people. They respect the fundamental individual and collective rights of all peoples related to their dignity and sense of self-worth. People deeply respect the autonomy and self-determination of all individuals or groupings and rights of individuals and peoples to: nondiscrimination, fairness, equity, justice in this regard, and personal and collective (e.g., cultural minority status) identity. People respect rights to voluntary informed consent, privacy, confidentiality, anonymity, etc.
5. Promoting and Acting from Justice in Society	People continuously ensure that other parties dealing with persons/ peoples do so in an equitable and just manner. They are constant in their monitoring of any deviations of societal infringement and abuse of the basic tenets of equality and justice for all, and act accordingly, but always taking the highroad and never descending into violence. The growth of persons and peoples into the present principles and values is the best strategy for promoting universal human rights as described in this document.

Note. It is impossible to cover every contingency that the general principles cover, or ones they do not, nor explicate every possible interpretation. The principles have leeway in interpretation and application. For example, (a) the first one was not meant to address the issue of prolife; (b) the second one is not describing the nature of care and its universality (e.g., does it exclude capital punishment)?; (c) the third one cannot explicitly define how to create the relationships advocated for; (d) the fourth one purposely does not mention nations and national rights, migration and forced immigration/asylum issues; and (e) the fifth one does not specify the definition of justice that should be used
Adapted from Young (2017, 2020a)

dignity and rights of persons and peoples, medical research should be inclusive of all segments and groups in the population. For (e) promoting and acting from justice in society, equal access should take place in research sampling for all persons and peoples such that the samples used are represent different genders, ages, minorities and races, strata in SES, vulnerabilities of all types, and so on.

In a third work on ethics (Young 2020c), I indicated how, in the COVID-19 environment, tele-assessments are ethically challenging. This chapter reviews these ethical challenges from the perspective of the APA ethics code. Moreover, the informed consent process in tele-assessments needs to present the risks for the evaluee because of the modifications in procedures compared to the face-to-face assessment situation. The threat to the reliability, validity, and helpful value of these assessments for court purposes calls for a cautious attitude in the assessments. It is argued that as the remote assessment procedures are applied, research will reveal the problems in this regard, and assessors need to keep up-to-date in order to defend their approach in court. Doing no harm and reaching the bar of having testimony/reports fall above the level of "in the balance of probabilities" will require constant monitoring of one's assessment protocols and the ongoing research.

As for the area of psychological injury and law, aside from the overlap with this topic in the tele-assessment work, I wrote another article on a roadmap for research in Mild Traumatic Brain Injury (MTBI) (Young 2020d). The article reviews 30 points related to MTBI/PPCS (Persistent Postconcussion Syndrome) that workers in the field need to consider: in understanding these syndromes, their symptoms, their prevalence, their causation, the influences and confounds in their diagnosis, best assessment practices, and legal aspects. The research in the area has produced results that are quite inconsistent, and it needs well-conducted longitudinal research. However, for the research to be effective, even the basic terminology and classifications in the field need to be reconceptualized. The article offers a new definition of MTBI and a new way to consider PPCS, calling for discarding the term. The article concludes on the ethics of practice in the area in which the assessor needs to be impartial and balanced in testimony. Reports that are proffered to court need to be reliable (and valid), and one best way of accomplishing the ethics of impartiality in this regard is to give voice to the emerging science in the field. As for recommendations, as mentioned above, the article proposes that the Diagnostic and Statistical Manual of Mental Disorders, fifth edition (DSM-5; American Psychiatric Association, 2013), creates a new category termed somatic symptom disorder with predominant postconcussion-like symptoms. PPCS should not be considered a syndrome or anything related to the original index concussion/MTBI and should be dropped from the lexicon in the field.

The next part of this last chapter in the book reviews presents another innovation in ethics in an epilogue. In that work, I extend the five-principle ethical model that I have developed into an ethical manifesto on the universal rights that children and youth deserve, and that society must value and uphold. This work illustrates once more the unification bent of the present author, indicating its reach from causality, development, and psychology generally to ethics, human rights, and charters for the protection and proper mental well-being and growth of children and youth around the world.

Children's and Youth's Rights

In other aspects of my research, I apply my integration bent, including toward creating a universal mental health ethics code (Young 2017). The following text shows the potential for that work to have a wider impact.

Preamble

The year 2020 has witnessed multiple shocks and catastrophes worldwide, and social structure and cohesion are seriously threatened, with fundamental human rights, already imperiled in their universal application, being undermined as never before. People, and even whole peoples, who are marginalized, discriminated against, profiled, persecuted, and hated are increasingly desperate and feeling powerless and reacting accordingly. Children and youth, already victims in these regards, are especially vulnerable in these times, even though their health, education, and freedom from ills and wants should be the primary foci of all parents and peoples.

Both thoughtful reflection and collective action can help ensure that children and youth are central foci of concern in these times. There are multiple avenues to help them locally, nationally, and internationally. However, as far as is known, there is no central ethical document that covers their basic physical and psychological needs and can be used to help them and strengthen the imperative required to do so. Toward this end, the author proposes principles of ethics that can be used to help children and youth in their fundamental rights. Moreover, it can help empower them in their already active endeavors to right the world in its floundering, protect their fundamental rights, and have adults do what's right for them at all levels. I have heard their voices. I have heard all the voices clamoring for change and improvement in society. We have a collective responsibility to the children and youth, in the present and in the future, to protect them, nourish them at all levels, and let them increasingly dictate as they turn into adults the most beneficial course for their betterment and that of the planet.

The document describes five ethical principles written in a coherent way and covers the most basic and advanced physical and psychological needs of peoples and persons. It can be used to revise extant mental health and medical ethics codes. More importantly, this new scope for it offered here affords it the opening to help in the most profound ways our most cherished resources—our children and youth, their present and future, and our planet.

Premises

1. To promote the welfare, dignity, respect, humanity, safety, personhood, mental health, and human rights and freedom physically, psychologically, and spiritually of all persons and peoples, inclusive of all individuals, minorities/groups, skin colors, religions/beliefs, sexes/genders, disabilities/different enablements, ages/developmental levels, and other identifying characteristics. The present focus is on children and youth, but it applies throughout the lifespan, or to everybody.
2. Children and youth of all peoples, of all humanity, need to live in and toward full personhood, with all basic human rights protected and respected. To indi-

cate the universality of this fundamental value, we use the term BLAICS, which refers to, in all guises to all persons and peoples, Blacks/Browns, Latino(a)s/Latinx, Asians, Indigenous peoples, Caucasians (Whites), and Sexual identities.

3. Promotion refers to grassroots activities toward peaceful change in society and over generations such that those who profess and adhere to the present principles will come to increasingly characterize societies and world beliefs and instill in transnational, national, societal, government, political, legal, professional, and institutional structures and codes the values inherent to the principles.
4. Individuals and groups can act to help children and youth. This could include some level of organization, for example, among like-minded individuals, and to coordinate activities toward other nongovernment agencies or governmental and legal ones, if that is a preference.
5. Youth and universities and colleges constitute the natural grounds to seed and grow the project. They will have the intellectual, moral, and technological skills for activities that could help children and youth. That said, all ages and all institutions/groupings can be involved and inspire, act, and share accordingly.
6. Promoting children and youth's fundamental universal rights excludes any sign of denigration, hate, exclusion, and any value and activity that creates differences in individuals and groups with respect to the basic principles involved as in point 1.
7. People will have their political and ideological agendas that vary in these regards, and they cannot be imported into the project, take precedence, alter its fundamental principles and character, and so on. People have the right to hold any political, cultural, religious, ideological, or any other related belief, but they should not be used to trammel or violate the rights of others to their own beliefs in these regards nor impose their beliefs on the activities and outcomes that might emanate from the present proposal. Other venues exist for particular political, cultural, ideological, and related agendas. That said, the present approach is complementary to all other like-minded approaches that promote inclusivity, multilogue, justice, standing up to oppression and poverty, nonviolence, universal human rights, planetary welfare, and educating children and youth toward changing the present and future.
8. Proper promotion of fundamental universal human rights for all persons and peoples must include emphasis on the protection of the most vulnerable, including children/youth, women who are discriminated against/abused, the disabled/differently enabled, those with mental difficulties and disorders, and so on.
9. The outreach in the promotion of fundamental universal human rights for children and youth must include protection and preservation of all contexts that support them, including their neighborhoods/poverty, all nature and animals, flora and fauna, biodiversity and human diversity, ecology and climate. As a side note, this point does not advocate how the said protection and preservation should take place, its extent, and so on.
10. All scholarly disciplines can contribute to the promotion involved, and act as knowledge reservoirs for it. None should be excluded, as happens with some who want to ignore science. Indeed, the STEMM* domains should stand at the

forefront of the growth and critical appraisal of the knowledge reservoir involved (*STEMM = Science, technology, engineering, mathematics, medicine).

11. The one superordinate principle that should govern the promotion involved concerns personhood and its development. All persons and peoples should be able to live in and toward full personhood, as per United Nations pronouncements, for example, the Universal Declaration of Human Rights and the Convention on the Rights of the Child (United Nations 2020; UNICEF, 2020).
12. One source for a proper ethical code under this framework for the project; for what to aspire to and instill in all persons and peoples, involves the following five principles in Tables 14.3 and 14.4 (after Young 2017; the first table is about universal psychological ethical principles and the second is about children and youth rights).

Informing of Children and Youth Their Rights

The institutions and agencies that govern children's and youth's rights, including governmental, should have ethical principles addressing and underpinning their work. Table 14.3 helps fill that gap.

Children and youth need to be apprised of their rights as much as adults. They give informed assent rather than legal consent. The AMA (see Young 2017) has a set of patient rights, but mental health work does not. Young (2020a) developed a list of adult patient and contactee rights for any health work. Table 14.4 gives a version for children and youth. The professional involved might need to simplify it even more than I have done, depending on the age and skills of the child/youth.

Supportive Literature Review

The recent literature on children and youth rights coheres in emphasizing their right to participation. They have a voice and should be respected for their opinions. They should not be patronized by adults but encouraged to give witness to their abuses and encouraged to participate in decision making.

Children generally have been described as oppressed (Barth and Olsen 2020). There are multiple categories and classes of child abuse and neglect (Warmingham et al. 2019). Children are victims of traumatic sexual abuse the effects of which are transmitted over generations (Boisjoli et al. 2019; Borelli et al. 2019; Ensink et al. 2020; Wamser-Nanney and Campbell 2020; Wamser-Nanney et al. 2020). Child abuse includes physical violence and its pernicious effects (Durrant et al. 2020; Njelesani 2019). Child maltreatment includes emotional abuse and neglect, now referred to psychological maltreatment (Brassard et al. 2020; Kobulsky et al. 2020). Child maltreatment includes the abhorrent practice of sexual trafficking (Greenbaum

Table 14.3 Five universal ethical principles on children and youth for universal conventions, government laws, and ethics codes

Principle	Explanation
1. Life Preservation	Universal conventions, government laws, and ethical codes insist that people continually act to protect the physical integrity of children and youth, and all others, for example, as it applies to torture and related abuses, genocide, homicide, and suicide. People continually act to protect children from the dangers of trauma, abuse, and negligence. People continually act to preserve the sanctity of life, its survival, for children and youth, and all others.[a]
2. Caring Beneficence/ Nonmaleficence	Universal conventions, government laws, and ethical codes insist that people continually act to safeguard the welfare of all peoples and persons, including the most the vulnerable, children and youth being among them. The most vulnerable, including not only children and youth, but also women who are discriminated against/abused, the disabled/differently enabled, those with mental difficulties and disorders, and so on. People continually aim to do no harm, or minimize it.
3. Relational Integrity	Universal conventions, government laws, and ethical codes insist that people continually strive to build positive relationships with children and youth, as well as all others, and behave with openness, honesty, fairness, trust facilitation, rapport encouragement, a genuine presence, and mutual respect in a two-way interaction or dialogue. They emphasize the humanity of the other.
4. Respect for the Dignity and Rights of Persons and Peoples	Universal conventions, government laws, and ethical codes insist that people continuously respect the inherent self-worth of every child and youth, every individual, and all groupings of people. They respect the fundamental individual and collective rights of all peoples related to their dignity and sense of self-worth. People deeply respect the autonomy and self-determination of all individuals or groupings and rights of individuals and peoples to: nondiscrimination, fairness, equity, justice in this regard, and personal and collective (e.g., cultural minority status) identity. People respect rights to voluntary informed consent, privacy, confidentiality, anonymity, etc.
5. Promoting and Acting from Justice in Society	Universal conventions, government laws, and ethical codes insist that people continuously ensure that other parties dealing with children and youth, and persons/peoples generally, do so in an equitable and just manner. They are constant in their monitoring of any deviations of societal infringement and abuse of the basic tenets of equality and justice for all, and act accordingly, but always taking the highroad and never descending into violence. The growth of children and youth, and persons and peoples generally, into the present principles and values is the best strategy for promoting universal human rights as described in this document. The one superordinate principle that should govern the promotion involved concerns personhood and its development. All children and youth, as well as all persons and peoples, should be able to live in and toward full personhood, as per United Nations pronouncements, for example, https://www.ohchr.org/en/udhr/documents/udhr_translations/eng.pdf, and https://www.unicef.ca/en/policy-advocacy-for-children/about-the-convention-on-the-rights-of-the-child.

[a]*Note.* It is impossible to cover every contingency that the general principles cover, or ones they do not, nor explicate every possible interpretation. The principles have leeway in interpretation and application. For example, (a) the first one was not meant to address the issue of prolife; (b) the second one is not describing the nature of care and its universality (e.g., does it exclude capital punishment)?; (c) the third one cannot explicitly define how to create the relationships advocated for; (d) the fourth one purposely does not mention nations and national rights, migration and forced immigration/asylum issues; and (e) the fifth one does not specify the definition of justice that should be used

Note. This list of universal ethics was elaborated by the author based on a compare/contrast format with other ethical codes and their values. It applies universally to all health work, e.g., medical, psychological, social work, child and youth work, child and youth protection services, school counselling/guidance

Adapted from Young (2017)

Table 14.4 Children and youth rights communicated to them: based on five universal ethical principles

Right	Content
1. Life preservation	You will have your physical integrity (and life itself) respected and protected, for example, as it applies to dealing with you safely and with your safety in mind. People especially have the duty to protect children and youth from the dangers of trauma, abuse, and negligence, including physical and sexual abuse and emotional negligence. People never condone nor participate in any way in harmful practices, such as giving permission to try out dangerous treatments that are not supported by science or by harming children and youth through extreme practices. [For children/youth patients/clients, facing serious medical issues, your physical integrity and health will be treated with the best or optimal options possible in the circumstances, as decided in parental/guardian consultations.]
2. Caring Beneficence/ Nonmaleficence	You will be treated with your welfare in mind, with courtesy, respect, dignity, timely responsiveness, and concern, considering your needs, and without doing any harm as a general principle in your particular circumstances. If you are a patient/client, you will receive the best or optimal therapeutic interventions, treatments, and care possible in your particular circumstances, including if you are among the most vulnerable in other ways. Doing no harm generally means that we strive to do no harm, avoid it, or minimize it, and we promote an optimal quality of life in your circumstances. Doing no harm generally means weighing long term benefits to risks. The decisions about my recommendations, if any, in any area that we deal with, e.g., medical, psychological, school counselling, are for you to make if you are at a certain age, or for your parents/guardians to make if you are younger, although we like to get your assent in this case; we call this autonomy. I will make sure that your parent/guardian understands all the alternatives possible in my recommendations and the pros and cons of each one, including the methods used, the realistic outcomes that can be expected, and the possible negative or side effects. They will be given choices in my recommendation; my first choice for you will be made objectively, without conflict of interest, or coercion, against your will, or forcing you or persuading you unethically to choose my preferred choice from among the choices offered, for example, because of pressure I receive from institutions, including school boards, pharmaceuticals or advocates for certain therapies, competing interests that might influence my recommendation, and so on. As for continuation of support/care for you, should I be no longer available in your support/care for any reason, every effort will be made to ensure that you are not left without the support/care, such as attempting to find you another competent person to take over as soon as it is possible in the circumstances. If your parent/guardian decides that you should to be served by a different person in your support/care or decide to get a second opinion, they can do so without a problem on my part and without a negative response on my part

(continued)

Table 14.4 (continued)

Right	Content
3. Relational integrity	You will be treated as a whole person with your individual differences and particular humanity; being respectful of your context, including your particular family and cultural context. I will strive to build a relationship with you based on openness, honesty, fairness, trust facilitation, rapport encouragement, a genuine presence, keeping promises and commitments made to you, avoiding conflicts of interest, and mutual respect in a two-way interaction or dialogue.
4. Respect for the dignity and rights of persons and peoples	You will be treated in a way that respects your sense of self-worth, individuality, relationships to groupings of people, no matter how defined. I will respect your fundamental individual and collective rights as a person and a member of peoples, that is, with dignity, humanity, and concern for your safety and welfare. When you have to reveal to me personal information or have to make decisions, or your parent guardian has to do that, I will ensure that all decisions so taken are based on a fully informed and voluntary consent, I will protect your privacy, confidentiality, and anonymity and will never reveal your personal and health information without your permission. Through your parent/guardian, you will be able to get access to your records on file with me. The autonomy and self-determination mentioned previously apply to all groupings and not just individuals. I will uphold the rights of all persons and groupings to: nondiscrimination, fairness, equity, justice, and identity, including you in that you are among the vulnerable.
5. Promoting and acting from justice in society	You have the right to be dealt with in an equitable and just way. This refers to social justice; and in my dealings with the following, among others, I will promote/protect your rights to the degree possible: third party payors for patient/client services; schools or agencies dealing with children and youth, including should you have special needs; if, you work already, and if the situation applies, your work site accommodating to your injury as you return to work; other organizations dealing with you. Social justice also means striving to access services for all individuals and groupings of people; no one should be excluded based on any personal or group characteristic. Also, it means that in research trials or studies, all portions of the population are included in the research sample in a representative and proportional way.

Note. This list of children and youth rights serves as a guide for those individuals and institutions that deal with children and youth. The teenager will be able to understand it with helpful explanations. The list applies to government agencies and workers, institutional (e.g., school) agencies and workers, health professional agencies and workers (e.g., medical, psychological, social work, child/youth work and protection, school counselling/guidance), etc.
Adapted from Young (2017, 2020a)

et al. 2020). It includes material deprivation (Shamrova and Lampe 2020). It also includes child marriage (Tisdall and Cuevas-Parra 2020).

Child maltreatment affects basic cognitive capacities, aside from emotional ones, e.g., executive function and self-representation (Carvalho et al. 2020; Silva and Calheiros 2020, respectively). The field is recognizing the long-term effects of all forms of child maltreatment (Fitzgerald et al. 2020; Karatzias et al. 2021; Rueness et al. 2019; Warmingham et al. 2020).

Children, even if abused, have rights; they are active agents who engage in relationships partly on their terms and can engage in meaningful participation with sufficient capacities that need to be recognized (Carnevale et al. 2021; Collins et al. 2021; Kosher and Ben-Arieh 2020; Lansdown 2020; Levine et al. 2020; McGregor et al. 2021; Sahlberg et al. 2020; Tobin and Cashmore 2020). However, the institutions that protect children's rights are undermined by societies limiting them in scope and effectiveness (Gran 2017; Simon et al. 2020). Hanson (2021) notes that phrases such as "Leave no child behind" need to be backed up by effective action. Better theorizing on children's rights will help (Hanson and Peleg 2020; Holzscheiter et al. 2019; Moody and Darbellay 2019). Better research will help (Stalford and Lundy 2020). Better interview techniques and procedures in cases of alleged child abuse will help (Hershkowitz and Lamb 2020; Mathews 2019).

Overall, child abuse, maltreatment, trauma, and so on, are among the most common yet preventable adversities in across the world. They include the effects of war, torture, and so on, which are not treated in this literature review. Children's rights relate to ostensibly simple situations, such as explaining their rights in research protocols while trying to get informed assent, to the most complex scenarios, such as genocide and survivorship. This chapter has explored some of the ethical rights and obligations involved, and created useful lists of ethical principles and rights that could help children and youth in their vulnerabilities to abuse and denial of their rights and in their actual exposure to abuse and trauma.

Conclusions

Chapter Summary

This integrative extension into ethics in the author's work completes the four-book cycle on unifying psychology, causality, and development. It accentuates the practice side of the project as much as the research side, given its application to health work ethics codes and the rights of children and youth. It illustrates that any area of psychology can be reworked integratively and that taking a step back to offer reflection on a field can bear fruitful consequences.

This chapter on ethics relates to the overall theme of the book because the five primary ethical principles that I have derived have a theoretical base in the Neo-Maslovian model that I have developed, which itself is integrated in the overarching Neo-Piagetian/Neo-Eriksonian model. This shows the reach of the present modeling process, from psychology to law and ethics, as per the other major area of my work in psychological injury and law, which is also reviewed in this chapter.

There are many summaries of the four books interspersed both in them and in this last book, so I do not repeat them. Simply, I offer one final overview and recommendations for the field.

This ending to the book examines its beginning. The title of the book is: Causality *and Neo-Stages in Development: Toward Unifying Psychology*. The order of the three major themes of the book indicates the primacy that I give to them. The title starts with the term causality. The book series' focus has been to integrate a causal framework and show how it is cross-cutting in psychology. I have emphasized systems, networks, and activation-inhibition coordination, in particular, in this regard. Also, I have referred to inclusive models, such as the biopsycho(personal)social; the book title continues with the concept of neo-stages. I have created a modified stage view of lifespan development that allows for a reworking of Piaget's and Erikson's stage models and their integration into a 25-step lifespan model of development (5 stages × 5 substages). Also, the neo-stages describe both normative patterns yet allow for individual variation; each person develops within her/his own biological, psychological, and social/societal foundations even if a common developmental framework applies, as well. The third component of the title concerns toward unifying psychology, the wording is chosen carefully; indeed, the project is an ongoing, active one. This book and its place in the four-book series on the topic speaks to the project but does not try to offer definitive conclusions. The unification proposed has centered on causality, but that area of conceptualization and research is ongoing, active, and forever just a project than a completed end-point; the unification it addresses inevitably has to be an ongoing, active project, as well. Causality is what all psychologists, and indeed scientists do. Causality has been under our noses as the unifying force in psychology and, indeed, all science, but perhaps it was too close and endemic for us to see it that way. As *Homo Causa*, we can rightfully place causality at the forefront of psychology and science commonalities. This will help give common ground for cross-talk, sharing, integration, and new ideas and research priorities and programs in psychology and in science, generally.

Summary of the Present Book

This book integrates and expands three books by Young (2011, 2016, 2019b) on the themes of causality, lifespan development according to a Neo-Piagetian/Neo-Eriksonian model, and the need for a continuing project to unify psychology. All these topics are broad and unresolved or controversial, and Young suggests specific models toward moving them forward. Young explores all three topics in each of the three books, adding to them each time. The general approach taken to causality is that it is multifactorial and biopsychosocial in terms of the range of factors that can influence behavior. Psychological causation reflects systematic, self-organized, and emergent nonlinear dynamical processes, which help explain how (sub)stages can emerge in development. Systems include multiple levels that are hierarchically organized, with reciprocal top-down and bottom-up influences. Behavior cannot be reduced to basic biomolecular, biological, or neuronal/brain function due to the additive, interactive effect of environment and personal factors, such as belief in free will. Network concepts are central to Young's approach to causality. For example, it argues that key psychiatric symptoms within behavior networks can causally drive other symptoms. The area of laterality in manual behavior (handedness) and hemispheric specialization is considered from the perspective of this approach to causality. Young's activation-inhibition coordination model applies to the causality processes underlying both behavior and brain, and it was derived from his infant handedness research (think the coordination in reaching/grasping). As for the Neo-Piagetian portion of his model, Young expanded Piaget's four-stage model (with the first having six substages) into one with five stages and five cyclically recurring substages. Basically, he added an initial reflex stage before the infant sensorimotor one and a postformal adult stage, while following Piaget in combining the preoperational and concrete operational stages into a Representation one (called peri-operations). The five substages in the model are based on Piaget's infancy substages. As for the Neo-Eriksonian portion of the model, Young created a 25-step model by extrapolating from the Neo-Piagetian one. Erikson's eight stages were inserted into the sequence, and 17 others were created.

Finally, Young (2019b) showed how the 25-step Neo-Eriksonian model could be used in therapy. He buttressed his stage model by creating the concept of neo-stage. Generally, Young did not shy away from creating innovative solutions to modeling dilemmas in psychology. His work presents many others beyond the ones mentioned, including the concept of the cognitive (mis)perception of the other and a Neo-Maslovian model consistent with it. He included in the book with other innovations—on the science formula, how couples can be examined from the Neo-Eriksonian model framework, executive function from a biopsychosocial viewpoint, a new conception of stress disorder, and considering inner peace as a penultimate human acquisition.

The book extends out of psychology in its last four substantive chapters. First, there are two chapters on the defense mechanisms, a psychiatric topic. The first of the two chapters places defense mechanisms in the wider field of adaptation, coping and stress. It included a matrix model of 48 types of coping, well beyond the fight-flight-freeze paradigm it was built on. The second concentrates on defense mechanisms, per se. The third chapter switches gears to the evolution and development of culture. It models cultural change using the developmental model as an analogy. The fourth chapter examines a new concept on transemics, which is an interactive change process.

Unification

Figure 14.1 presents the unification project to which Young has dedicated his career. The figure shows the spread of this view of psychology in the author's main areas of research, conceptualization, and practice—lifespan development, causal modeling, ethics, and psychological injuries. It gives a layout in an easy-to-grasp visual summary with an accompanying text meant to help understand the approach and to spur continued research and investigation of the ideas therein.

This last figure in the book outlines its contributions. The book is very theoretical, like the other books in the series, but has extensive literature reviews in its support. Also, the models presented allow for empirical investigation and suggest directions in this regard. Future work on the modeling should continue to search for evidence of its validity and testability.

The process in writing the four books has been similar. For each area examined, the process was to take a step back in order to take two steps forward, bring an integrative frame in doing so, see the gaps, suggest how to fill them, and see the links to other areas. In effect, I followed something akin to the five-step change model described in the books to my own theoretical thinking process.

As for the products of that process, the book indicates the value of overarching theory. These theories have been referred to as global, and their derivatives as Neo (e.g., Neo-Piagetian, Neo-Vygotskian, Neo-Eriksonian). They still have an important role to play in the overly specialized, siloed theater that often governs psychology, especially if reconstructed to fit contemporary theorizing. They are broad enough to admit many theoretical strands and so perform an integrative function, even among themselves. They are more cooperative and overlapping, without being exclusionary or being part of an all-or-nothing mentality about their validity and value.

The manner in which the theorizing in the books proceeded was organic and holistic, quite like the theories themselves. They ask that they be considered for what they are, products of a rational process that fills voids and suggests new avenues in scientific thought, practice, and research. Unlike other theories for the most part, they allow for extensions outside of psychology, such as for evolution and culture, can help explain or at least offer pertinent conjectures about these aspects outside of psychology, and can help cohere these aspects, even with the theories or notions specifically and even with psychology generally at the forefront in the process.

If my work puts me outside the mainstream of scientific work in psychology, perhaps that will help the work take hold and influence psychology and allied disciplines. If it ever becomes more in the mainstream, perhaps other workers will take a step backwards about it in order to take effectively two steps forward. I would like to see better mapping of the empirical work researcher's areas onto the present modeling that has taken place, for example, on causal cognition. The four-book series began with the one in 2011 in which I carefully analyzed the work of other Neo-Piagetians in this regard, and showed how that research often fit better my Neo-Piagetian model than theirs. The next efforts in my work will attempt to do the same with other aspects of the theorizing in my four books.

This back-and-forth process between theorizing and literature review has been productive. Indeed, two chapters of the present book are exclusively on recent literature reviews and they cover the major themes of this book and the others, providing them support. One section of the literature reviews is on the value of theorizing, and what is lost when theorizing is not undertaken well or to a sufficient degree. In this regard, often in my process, the modeling came first and the literature was

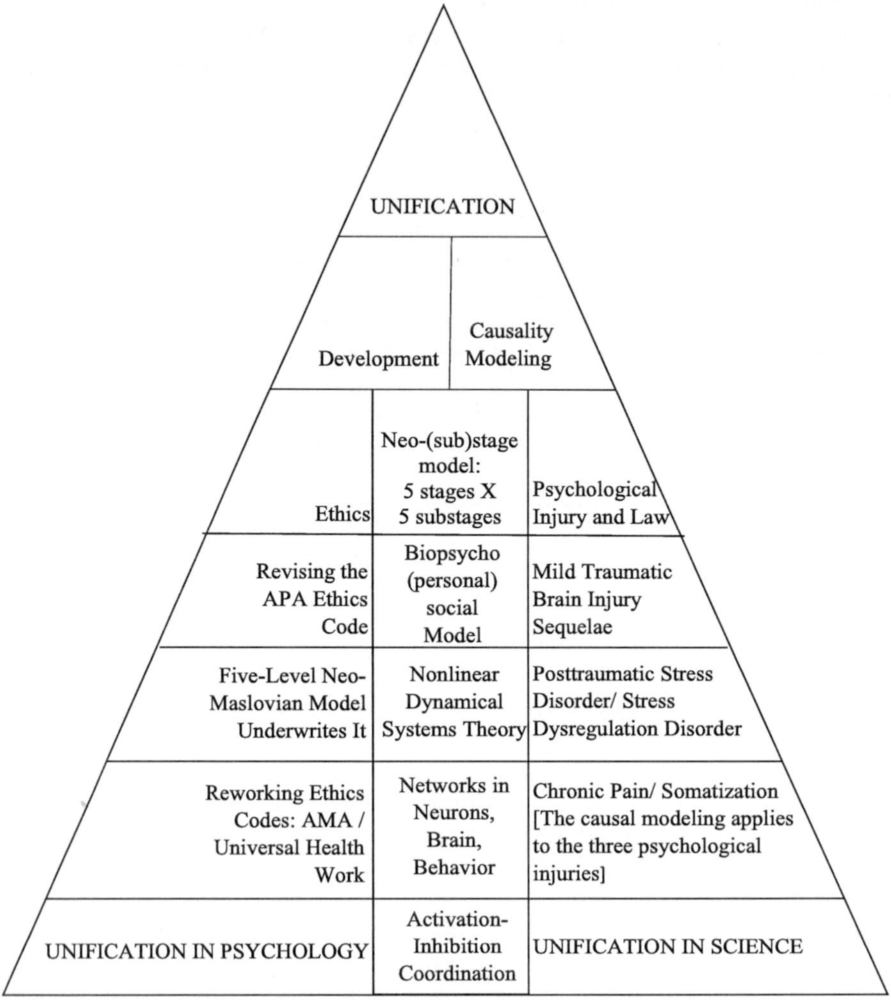

Fig. 14.1 The unifying approach to diverse areas in psychology in the work of Young. The figure illustrates the unity in the work of Young over his four main areas of research and practice in psychology: development, causal modeling, ethics, and psychological injuries and law. Young aspires to integrating psychology and sees applications of his work to unifying the sciences through his approach to causal modeling. (a) The developmental innovations in Young's oeuvre integrates the work of stalwarts in psychology, Piaget and Erikson, into a Neo-Piagetian/Neo-Eriksonian 25-step (sub)stage model of lifespan development (5 stages × 5 substages). The model is neo-stage in perspective, allowing individual differences to proliferate on a universal scaffold of steps. (b) The causality innovations in Young's work relates to his integration of a biopsychosocial model (biopersonalsocial), nonlinear dynamical systems theory, network approaches, and the concept of activation-inhibition coordination, which cuts across neuron, brain, and behavior and their organization. Young developed the latter concept in observing the coordinated reaching of 1-month-olds and realized its general application to different levels in the neuron-brain-behavior system. (c) The

reviewed after the fact. As well, often, I indicate that there is only some supportive research for a question at hand given its novel status.

Thus, the reader might ask why the more common scientific approach of clear literature review followed by focused hypothesizing, and even mini-theory construction, was not followed in my scientific process in these books. Why were there not smaller articles, and many of them written beforehand, with the integrative books to follow?

I think there is room for multiple approaches in the scientific enterprise, and books offer their advantages, including in the integrative, scientifically-supported approach that constitutes these books. There is enough theoretical fodder for thought and further operationalization, testing, and refinement, as happens in the more common approach to science.

Further, the books have legal, ethical, practical applications that should not be overlooked. It deals with trauma reactions, the DSM, children's rights, revised ethics codes and their theoretical base, and a Neo-Eriksonian model that can help clinicians understand patients in therapy.

If I have over-reached, I believe I have done so in the manner reflective of the activation-inhibition coordination process that I consider an underlying causal mechanism over neuron, brain, and behavior. That is, just as the infant reaches effectively through the multilayered activation-inhibition coordination that arcs through the neuronal, brain, and behavior systems, so too has my theorizing and the implications offered on its basis. They have been constructed with focus and with a coordination such as this toward reaching the goal of contributing to science and to psychology.

Finally, the theories involved are grounded in multiple ways. (a) They begin with the embodied theory of Piaget, his initial sensorimotor stage in infancy, and his notion that, as stages evolve, they incorporate prior stages. The Eriksonians have a similar approach, with earlier stages influencing later ones. (b) The theories do not

Fig. 14.1 (continued) ethics innovations in Young's work relates to revising and creating various ethics mental health and general health work ethics codes, using a set of five principles that correspond to the five stages in his developmental model through its reworking of Maslow's model of five hierarchical needs into a Neo-Maslovian model. These set of five principles were also applied to creating a list of five patient and related rights. As well, they were applied to creating a list of children's rights. (d) Young's innovations in psychology and law relates to integrating the area of psychological injury and law. The psychological injuries concern mild traumatic brain injury sequelae, chronic pain, and posttraumatic stress disorder (PTSD). They all have somatization/biopsychosocial underpinnings and associations and can be explained in part by the causal modeling generally described for psychology by Young. (e) He proposed an integrated Stress Dysregulation Disorder along these lines, and reworks other aspects in psychological practice and nosology in the area. (f) Overall, in the disparate areas that Young investigates and conceptualizes, there is a search for unification both within psychology and in its relation to other disciplines. In this regard, he has proposed a generalized framework referred to as the science formula, proposed how scientific models evolve according to his step model, integrated adaptation/coping, defensivity/offensivity, and defense mechanisms into his modeling, proposed a model of the development of evolution and culture, another on transemics, and emphasized causality as a unifying theme not only in psychology (e.g., the lifespan development of causal cognition) but also in the sciences leave their predecessors behind, but integrate them. For example, the present Neo-Piagetian model was built on a compare-contrast basis of prior theorizing in this regard, while respecting Piaget's contributions and model. The Neo-Eriksonian model built from the Neo-Piagetian one integrated Erikson's eight stages, and the added other ones. The Neo-Vygotskian formulation of Tomassello (2019) was acknowledged as a contribution to the field in Chap. 12. (c) The theories are grounded because often they have supportive empirical research to buttress them. (d) The theories are grounded because they have research implications. They indicate how and where cognitive development should proceed in its investigations, for example, the networking processes that might be found. (e) They speak to education because of the cognitive substages in development that it provides, which can serve as a roadmap of how children think and how education should promote it. (f) They speak to practice, as mentioned, being potentially helpful in therapy. (g) They speak to other disciplines, as mentioned, e.g., evolution and cultural study, with models that could help them become more grounded by having better theoretical overviews and consequent research emanating from that. (h) They speak to other theories in psychology and psychiatry hat can be reworked in its image, such as the psychodynamic approach. (i) They speak to the multiple new and revised definitions in the field, even of the concepts of psychology, mental disorder, and culture. (j) They address the ultimate goal of unification in psychology with a certain grounded prudence by referring to it as an ongoing project. (k) They avoid jargon to the degree possible, avoid complex writing to the degree possible, and often express an educative function for the reader. (l) The writing is not negatively critical of others. For the most part, other work is described in a way that supports the present endeavors. When criticisms are offered, they present as constructive comments on how the work of others can be improved or how it can fit better into the present work. Worthy criticisms of my own work in this vein will be helpful to it, the field, and even better theorizing and research for it.

Transemic

Origins

With the book completed, and lying down fatigued in a dream state to reflect on the process and product, a word materialized in my semi-conscious state that piqued my curiosity. The term is the one indicated in the heading—transemic. I have not referred to the emic-etic distinction in any of my publications, and am only vaguely familiar with it. Checking the literature, it did seem applicable to my work.

First, the emic-etic distinction is used mostly in cultural research/anthropology (Mostowlansky and Rota 2020). The terms have evolved beyond their original meanings.

The term transemic has not been referenced in a psychology, but has by Canda and Furman (1999). But the prior chapter explains the concept and its applications to psychology and to this book. To conclude, the project behind the book keeps growing.

One more application that I would like to develop concerns the change process in therapy. The stages of change model has five steps and the present generic steps model of change has an equivalent five steps. But the present modeling includes five substeps. It could be possible to map changes microgenetically according to the 25 substeps of change by considering steps and substeps. Recall that the five change steps in the present model refer to (a) coordination, (b) hierarchization, (c) systematization, (d) multiplication, and (e) integration. The five substeps refer to (a) tentative beginning, (b) clear initiation, (c) consolidation/improved application, (d) spreading maturation/refinement, and (e) systemic synthesis. These five substeps would be embedded recurrently within each step in a complete 25-step change model.

It would be informative to see how they work in change processes, generally, along with their workings in therapy specifically. What factors produce the changes at each step of the model? Are they general factors such as rapport building? Are the changes due to procedures used by the therapist? Or, does the cumulative effect of all these types of factors work on patient agency and motivation, or other factors inherent to the person? Most likely, all these variables are involved, but differentially in earlier and later substeps, with increasing agency and motivation at work should the patient get to the later substeps.

But that is the topic for another work. It shows the reach of the scope of the present work in my four books and ends the book with an idea for a new beginning.

References

American Psychiatric Association: Diagnostic and Statistical Manual of Mental Disorders: DSM-5, 5th edn. Author, Washington, DC (2013)

American Psychological Association. (2002). Ethical principles of psychologists and code of conduct. Am. Psychol. **57**, 1060–1073. "https://psycnet.apa.org/doi/10.1037/0003-066X.57.12.1060" https://doi.org/10.1037/0003-066X.57.12.1060

American Psychological Association. (2010). *Ethical principles of psychologists and code of conduct* (2002, Amended June 1, 2010). Retrieved from http://www.apa.org/ethics/code/principles.pdf

American Psychological Association: Ethical Principles of Psychologists and Code of Conduct (2002, amended effective June 1, 2010, and January 1, 2017). American Psychological Association, Washington (2017). https://www.apa.org/ethics/code/ethics-code-2017.pdf

Barth, R.P., Olsen, A.N.: Are children oppressed? The timely importance of answering this question. Child Youth Serv. Rev. **110**, 104780 (2020). https://doi.org/10.1016/j.childyouth.2020.104780

Boisjoli, C., Hébert, M., Gauthier-Duchesne, A., Caron, P.-O.: A mediational model linking perceptions of security, alexithymia and behavior problems of sexually abused children. Child Abuse Negl. **92**, 66–76 (2019). https://doi.org/10.1016/j.chiabu.2019.03.2017

Borelli, J.L., Cohen, C., Pettit, C., Normandin, L., Target, M., Fonagy, P., Ensink, K.: Maternal and child sexual abuse history: an intergenerational exploration of children's adjustment and maternal trauma-reflective functioning. Front. Psychol. **10**, 1062 (2019). https://doi.org/10.3389/fpsyg.2019.01062

Brassard, M.R., Hart, S.N., Glaser, D.: Psychological maltreatment: an international challenge to children's safety and well being. Child Abuse Negl. **110**, 104611 (2020). https://doi.org/10.1016/j.chiabu.2020.104611

Canadian Psychological Association: Canadian Code of Ethics for Psychologists, 4th edn. Canadian Psychological Association, Ottawa (2017)

Canda, E.R., Furman, L.: Spiritual Diversity in Social Work Practice: The Heart of Helping. Free Press, New York (1999)

Carnevale, F.A., Collin-Vézina, D., Macdonald, M.E., Ménard, J.-F., Talwar, V., Van Praagh, S.: Childhood ethics: an ontological advancement for childhood studies. Child. Soc. **35**(1), 110–124 (2021). https://doi.org/10.1111/chso.12406

Carvalho, J.N., Renner, A.M., Donat, J.C., de Moura, T.C., Fonseca, R.P., Kristensen, C.H.: Executive functions and clinical symptoms in children exposed to maltreatment. Appl. Neuropsychol. Child. **9**(1), 1–12 (2020). https://doi.org/10.1080/21622965.2018.1497989

Collins, T.M., Rizzini, I., Mayhew, A.: Fostering global dialogue: conceptualisations of children's rights to participation and protection. Child. Soc. **35**, 295 (2021). https://doi.org/10.1111/chso.12437

Durrant, J.E., Stewart-Tufescu, A., Afifi, T.O.: Recognizing the child's right to protection from physical violence: an update on progress and a call to action. Child Abuse Negl. **110**, 104297 (2020). https://doi.org/10.1016/j.chiabu.2019.104297

Ensink, K., Borelli, J.L., Normandin, L., Target, M., Fonagy, P.: Childhood sexual abuse and attachment insecurity: associations with child psychological difficulties. Am. J. Orthopsychiatry. **90**(1), 115–124 (2020). https://doi.org/10.1037/ort0000407

Erikson, E.H.: Identity: Youth and Crisis. W. W. Norton & Co., New York (1968)

Fitzgerald, M., London-Johnson, A., Gallus, K.L.: Intergenerational transmission of trauma and family systems theory: an empirical investigation. J. Fam. Ther. **42**(3), 406–424 (2020). https://doi.org/10.1111/1467-6427.12303

Gran, B.K.: An international framework of children's rights. Annu. Rev. Law Soc. Sci. **13**, 79–100 (2017). https://doi.org/10.1146/annurev-lawsocsci-110615-084638

Greenbaum, J., Albright, K., Tsai, C.: Introduction to the special issue of child abuse and neglect: global child trafficking and health. Child Abuse Negl. **100**, 104321 (2020). https://doi.org/10.1016/j.chiabu.2019.104321

Hanson, K.: The state and the world's children. Childhood. **28**, 3 (2021). https://doi.org/10.1177/0907568220981494

Hanson, K., Peleg, N.: Waiting for children's rights theory. Int. J. Child. Rights. **28**, 15–35 (2020). https://doi.org/10.2139/ssrn.3501733

Hershkowitz, I., Lamb, M.E.: Allegation rates and credibility assessment in forensic interviews of alleged child abuse victims: comparing the revised and standard NICHD protocols. Psychol. Public Policy Law. **26**(2), 176–184 (2020). https://doi.org/10.1037/law0000230

Holzscheiter, A., Josefsson, J., Sandin, B.: Child rights governance: an introduction. Childhood. **26**(3), 271–288 (2019). https://doi.org/10.1177/0907568219854518

Karatzias, T., Shevlin, M., Ford, J.D., Fyvie, C., Grandison, G., Hyland, P., Cloitre, M.: Childhood trauma, attachment orientation, and complex PTSD (CPTSD) symptoms in a clinical sample: implications for treatment. Dev. Psychopathol., 1–6 (2021). https://doi.org/10.1017/S0954579420001509

Kobulsky, J.M., Dubowitz, H., Xu, Y.: The global challenge of the neglect of children. Child Abuse Negl. **110**, 104296 (2020). https://doi.org/10.1016/j.chiabu.2019.104296

Kosher, H., Ben-Arieh, A.: Children's participation: a new role for children in the field of child maltreatment. Child Abuse Negl. **110**, 104429 (2020). https://doi.org/10.1016/j.chiabu.2020.104429

Lansdown, G.: Strengthening child agency to prevent and overcome maltreatment. Child Abuse Negl. **110**, 104398 (2020). https://doi.org/10.1016/j.chiabu.2020.104398

Levine, D.T., Morton, J., O'Reilly, M.: Child safety, protection, and safeguarding in the time of COVID-19 in Great Britain: proposing a conceptual framework. Child Abuse Negl. **110**, 104668 (2020). https://doi.org/10.1016/j.chiabu.2020.104668

Maslow, A.H.: A theory of human motivation. Psychol. Rev. **50**(4), 370–396 (1943). https://doi.org/10.1037/h0054346

Maslow, A.H.: Motivation and Personality, 2nd edn. Harper & Row, New York (1970)

Mathews, B.: A taxonomy of duties to report child sexual abuse: legal developments offer new ways to facilitate disclosure. Child Abuse Negl. **88**, 337–347 (2019). https://doi.org/10.1016/j.chiabu.2018.12.003

McGregor, C., Devaney, C., Moran, L.: A critical overview of the significance of power and power relations in practice with children in foster care: evidence from an Irish study. Child Care Pract. **27**(1), 4–18 (2021). https://doi.org/10.1080/13575279.2018.1555135

Moody, Z., Darbellay, F.: Studying childhood, children, and their rights: the challenge of interdisciplinarity. Childhood. **26**(1), 8–21 (2019). https://doi.org/10.1177/0907568218798016

Mostowlansky, T., Rota, A.: Emic and etic. In: The Cambridge Encyclopedia of Anthropology (2020). https://doi.org/10.29164/20emicetic

Njelesani, J.: "A child who is hidden has no rights": responses to violence against children with disabilities. Child Abuse Negl. **89**, 58–69 (2019). https://doi.org/10.1016/j.chiabu.2018.12.024

Rueness, J., Myhre, M.C., Strøm, I.F., Wentzel-Larsen, T., Dyb, G., Thoresen, S.: The mediating role of posttraumatic stress reactions in the relationship between child abuse and physical health complaints in adolescence and young adulthood. Eur. J. Psychotraumatol. **10**(1), 1608719 (2019). https://doi.org/10.1080/20008198.2019.1608719

Sahlberg, S., Karlsson, K., Darcy, L.: Children's rights as law in Sweden-every health-care encounter needs to meet the child's needs. Health Expect. **23**(4), 860–869 (2020). https://doi.org/10.1111/hex.13060

Shamrova, D., Lampe, J.: Understanding patterns of child material deprivation in five regions of the world: a children's rights perspective. Child Youth Serv. Rev. **108**, 104595 (2020). https://doi.org/10.1016/j.childyouth.2019.104595

Silva, C.S., Calheiros, M.M.: Maltreatment experiences and psychopathology in children and adolescents: the intervening role of domain-specific self-representations moderated by age. Child Abuse Negl. **99**, 104255 (2020). https://doi.org/10.1016/j.chiabu.2019.104255

Simon, J., Luetzow, A., Conte, J.R.: Thirty years of the convention on the rights of the child: developments in child sexual abuse and exploitation. Child Abuse Negl. **110**, 104399 (2020). https://doi.org/10.1016/j.chiabu.2020.104399

Stalford, H., Lundy, L.: The field of children's rights: taking stock, travelling forward. Int. J. Child. Rights. **28**, 1–13 (2020). https://doi.org/10.1163/15718182-02801010

Tisdall, E.K.M., Cuevas-Parra, P.: Challenges for children's participation: child activism for ending child marriage. Child Youth Serv. Rev. **108**, 104568 (2020). https://doi.org/10.1016/j.childyouth.2019.104568

Tobin, J., Cashmore, J.: Thirty years of the CRC: child protection progress, challenges and opportunities. Child Abuse Negl. **110**, 104436 (2020). https://doi.org/10.1016/j.chiabu.2020.104436

Tomassello, M.: Becoming Human: A Theory of Ontogeny. The Belknap Press of Harvard University Press, Cambridge (2019)

UNICEF Office of Research - Innocenti: The Convention on the Rights of the Child. UNICEF Office of Research - Innocenti, Florence (2020). https://www.unicef-irc.org/portfolios/crc.html

United Nations: Universal Declaration of Human Rights. United Nations, New York (2020). https://www.un.org/en/universal-declaration-human-rights/

Wamser-Nanney, R., Campbell, C.L.: Childhood sexual abuse characteristics, abuse stress, and PTSS: ties to sexual behavior problems. Child Abuse Negl. **105**, 104290 (2020). https://doi.org/10.1016/j.chiabu.2019.104290

Wamser-Nanney, R., Sager, J.C., Campbell, C.L.: Does material support mediate or moderate the relationship between sexual abuse severity and children's PTSD symptoms? J. Child Sex. Abuse. **29**(3), 333–350 (2020). https://doi.org/10.1080/10538712.2020.1733160

Warmingham, J.M., Handley, E.D., Rogosch, F.A., Manly, J.T., Cicchetti, D.: Identifying maltreatment subgroups with patterns of maltreatment subtype and chronicity: a latent class analysis approach. Child Abuse Negl. **87**, 28–39 (2019). https://doi.org/10.1016/j.chiabu.2018.08.013

Warmingham, J.M., Rogosch, F.A., Cicchetti, D.: Intergenerational maltreatment and child emotion dysregulation. Child Abuse Negl. **102**, 104377 (2020). https://doi.org/10.1016/j.chiabu.2020.104377

Young, G.: Development and Causality: Neo-Piagetian Perspectives. Springer Science + Business Media, New York (2011)

Young, G.: Unifying Causality and Psychology: Being, Brain and Behavior. Springer International Publishing, Cham (2016)

Young, G.: Revising the American Psychological Association Ethics Code. Springer International Publishing, Cham (2017)

Young, G.: Personhood across disciplines: applications to ethical theory and mental health ethics. Ethic. Med. Publ. Health. **10**, 93–101 (2019a). https://doi.org/10.1016/j.jemep.2019.100407

Young, G.: Causality and Development: Neo-Eriksonian Perspectives. Springer International Publishing, Cham (2019b)

Young, G.: Toward a unified health work ethics code. Ethic. Med. Publ. Health. **15**, 100590 (2020a). https://doi.org/10.1016/j.jemep.2020.100590

Young, G.: Discrimination in medical research sampling: recommendations and applications to psychology. In: Rezaei, N., Saghazadeh, A. (eds.) Integrated Science – Multidisciplinarity and Interdisciplinarity in Health, vol. 3, p. XX. Springer Nature, London (2020b)

Young, G.: Psychology, law, ethics, telehealth, and the global pandemic. In: Rezaei, N., Hanaei, S., Saghazadeh, A. (eds.) Integrated Science of Global Epidemics, vol. 9, p. XX. Springer Nature, London (2020c)

Young, G.: Thirty complexities and controversies in mild traumatic brain injury and persistent postconcussion syndrome: a roadmap for research and practice. Psychol. Injur. Law. **13**(4), 427–451 (2020d). https://doi.org/10.1007/s12207-020-09395-6

Index

G. Young, *Causality and Neo-Stages in Development*,
https://doi.org/10.1007/978-3-030-82540-9

D

E